Mineral deposits of Europe

Central Europe

Mineral deposits of Europe

Volume 3: Central Europe

Edited by F. W. Dunning and A. M. Evans

Non-metallic minerals editor A. J. G. Notholt
Production editor M. J. Jones

The Institution of Mining and Metallurgy
The Mineralogical Society

Published by The Institution of Mining and Metallurgy
and The Mineralogical Society, London

© Copyright The Institution of Mining and Metallurgy
and The Mineralogical Society, 1986

ISBN 0 900488 90 5

Computer typeset by SB Datagraphics. Printed in Great Britain by Spottiswoode Ballantyne Printers Ltd

Preface

Anyone who has tried to gather information on the geology of European ore deposits knows the frustrations that such an endeavour entails. No concise, comprehensive description of the ferrous, non-ferrous and non-metallic mineral deposits of Europe is available in English, or for that matter in any other language; in fact, most European countries lack comprehensive descriptions of their own mineral deposits even in their national languages. The need for such a publication is strongly felt by geologists and other specialists in government, the universities and colleges and in industry. Good clear descriptions of the classical and producing mining districts and the larger deposits are required by university lecturers preparing courses in economic geology, by companies interested in prospecting, by organizations requiring mining and mineral statistics, by compilers of atlases and textbooks and by public and private libraries. A worldwide demand exists for an authoritative but compact treatise on the mineral deposits of Europe in the English language.

The *Mineral deposits of Europe* project began in 1970, when a small editorial panel was set up by the Mineralogical Society of Great Britain to examine the proposal. The original concept arose from the work on the *Carte métallogénique de l'Europe 1:2 500 000*. This map, which has created a renewed interest in European ore deposits, is accompanied by an Explanatory Memoir, which, although valuable from the metallogenic point of view, lacks descriptions of the geology and mineralogy of the ore deposits. In this latter respect the *Mineral deposits of Europe* volumes will usefully supplement the map and its Memoir. At its first meeting the panel decided to invite the Institution of Mining and Metallurgy to undertake the project in partnership with the Mineralogical Society. A joint Steering Committee was set up to further the project after it had been approved by the respective Councils of the Society and the Institution. The Steering Committee considered several alternative approaches and made a number of decisions. First, it was decided that the chapters should be written on a national basis, mainly because most users prefer to seek information on that basis and also because potential authors are, with few exceptions, experts on the ore deposits of one particular nation only, generally their own. Then it was decided to arrange the descriptions of ore deposits with a metallogenic framework of epochs and provinces or districts rather than on an alphabetical commodity basis. It was originally intended to present the work in a single volume, but the potential length of the contributions and the size of the capital outlay eventually dictated a multi-volume production. Initially, four volumes were planned: *Northwest Europe, Central Europe, Southeast Europe* and *Southwest Europe*, but the Steering Committee was later persuaded by the National Committee of the German Democratic Republic to embark in principle on a fifth volume, *Eastern Europe*, to include European Russia and Turkey. *Northwest Europe* embraces Denmark with Greenland, Finland, Norway, Sweden, the United Kingdom and Ireland; *Central Europe* includes the Federal Republic of Germany, the German Democratic Republic, Poland, Austria, Switzerland, Czechoslovakia, the Netherlands and Belgium; *Southeast Europe* incudes Albania, Bulgaria, Cyprus, Greece, Hungary, Romania and Yugoslavia; and *Southwest Europe* embraces France, Spain, Portugal and Italy. Each volume has an introductory chapter of the region concerned, and each national chapter also incorporates a short metallogenic-geotectonic introduction.

R. N. Pryor *President of the Institution of Mining and Metallurgy, 1978–79*
R. A. Howie *President of the Mineralogical Society, 1978–79*

Volume 1 (*Northwest Europe*) was published in 1978 and Volume 2 (*Southeast Europe*) in 1982. Volume 3 (*Central Europe*) presents here comprehensive accounts of the ore deposits of The Netherlands, Belgium, the Federal Republic of Germany, the German Democratic Republic, Austria, Switzerland, Czechoslovakia and Poland. For one at least of these countries (West Germany) the chapter in this volume is the first complete account of its ore deposits published in English. As with the previous volumes, the national chapters have been written and submitted over a long period of time, at least eight years separating the first and last drafts to be received.
Where possible, some updating has been done by the authors and/or the editors. Fortunately, there is a timelessness about such works as *Mineral deposits of Europe* that makes these delays less damaging in the long term. The Editors nevertheless apologize to those authors who submitted their chapters expeditiously and punctually and who have been put to the trouble of revising their contributions.

F. W. Dunning
A. M. Evans

Steering Committee

Dr S. H. U. Bowie (Chairman)

Professor G. R. Davis

F. W. Dunning

Dr. R. R. Harding

M. J. Jones

B. R. Young

Contents

Preface v

Steering Committee vii

Introduction by K. Schmidt and B. Kölbel . 1

Fundamental geotectonic division and development of Central Europe . . . 1
Geological-tectonic-minerogenetic characteristics of structural storeys (development stages) in summary 5
   Precambrian structural storeys. . . 5
   Caledonian structural storey . . . 5
   Variscan geosynclinal-orogen structural storey 7
   Post-Variscan platform superstructure . 8
   Alpine geosynclinal-orogen superstructure 9
      Central Alps–Inner Carpathian zone 10
      Northern Kalkalpen (Calcareous Alps) 10
      Flysch zone 11
      Molasse zone (Alpine and Carpathian foredeep) 11
      Superposed Tertiary basins . . . 11

Austria by Herwig F. Holzer 15

Metallogenic theories 15
Main tectonic-metallogenic units . . 17
   Mineral deposits in Bohemian Massif (extra-Alpine basement) and its platform cover 17
      Geology. 17
      Mineral deposits 17
         Iron 17
         Lead 17
         Graphite 17
         Kaolin 17
         Feldspar and quartz . . . 18
         Vermiculite 18
   Mineral deposits in Alpine Foreland (Molasse Zone) and in intramontane basins 18
      Geology. 18
      Mineral deposits 18
         Phosphates. 18
         Diatomite 18
         Bentonite, illite and trass . . 18
   Eastern Alps 18
      Geology. 19
      Mineral deposits 19
         Lead–zinc. 19
         Iron 19
         Iron–manganese ores. . . 20
         Manganese ores. . . . 20
         Bauxite 20
         Uranium 20
         Gypsum–anhydrite . . . 20
         Rock salt 20
         Copper 21
         Cu–Ni–Co ores 22
         Pyrite (with/without Cu, As, Pb) . 22
         Iron deposits 23
         Manganese 23
         Magnesite 23
         Scheelite–magnesite . . . 25
         Cryptocrystalline magnesite . . 25
         Barite. 25
         Talc 25
         Graphite 25
         Gold 25
         Molybdenum 26
         Tungsten (Scheelite) . . . 26
            Geology and petrology . . 26
            Ore mineralogy . . . 27
         Copper 29
         Antimony 29
         Lead–zinc–fluorite . . . 30
         Kyanite 31
         Uranium 31
         Gypsum and anhydrite . . 31
         Barite. 31
         Leucophyllite (mica-kaolin) . . 31
         Talc 31
         Iron 31
         Mercury 32
         Polymetallic deposits (Cu, Ni–Co–Bi, Pb–Zn, Sb) 32
         Silver (Pb, Cu, Fe, barite) . . 32
         Lead–zinc–copper . . . 33
         Pyrrhotite–arsenopyrite–pyrite deposits with precious metals . 33
         Lead (Ag)–zinc deposits . . 33
         Pyrite (with/without Cu, As) . 33
         Lithium 33
   Drauzug, Karawanken Range and Periadriatic Igneous Suite, Southern Alps 33
      Lead-zinc. 33
      Mercury 37

Switzerland by Felice C. Jaffé . . .	41
Geological and metallogenic provinces .	41
Jura	41
Iron	41
Delemont, Jura	41
Herznach-Fricktal, Aargau .	43
Molasse basin	44
Placer gold	44
Allondon, Geneva . . .	44
Napf, Luzern	44
Calcareous Alps	44
Copper	44
Préalpes	44
Mürtschenalp, Glarus . .	44
Gold	44
Calanda, Grisons . . .	44
Iron	44
Chamoson, Wallis . . .	44
Erzegg, Bern	44
Manganese	45
Gonzen, St-Gall . . .	45
Uranium	45
Mürtschenalp, Glarus . .	45
Hercynian massifs	45
Copper	45
Puntaiglas, Grisons . . .	45
Gold	45
Salanfe, Wallis	45
Iron	45
Mont Chemin, Wallis . .	45
Lead–zinc	46
Alp Nadèls, Grisons . . .	46
Bristenstock, Uri . . .	46
Trachsellauenen, Bern . .	46
Goppenstein, Wallis . . .	46
Molybdenum	46
Baltschiedertal, Wallis . .	46
Other occurrences (Wallis) .	46
Uranium	46
Trun, Grisons	46
Naters, Wallis	46
Le Chatelard and Les Marecottes, Wallis	46
Penninic, Austroalpine and southern Alps	47
Copper	47
Alp Ursera, Grisons . . .	47
Grimentz, Wallis . . .	47
Gold	47
Astano, Tessin	47
Gondo, Wallis	48
Iron	48
Val Ferrera, Grisons . . .	48
Lead–zinc	48
S-charl, Grisons . . .	48
Silberberg, Bleiberg and Bärenbühl, Grisons	49
Alp Taspin, Grisons . . .	49
St Luc-Bella Tola, Wallis . .	49
Praz Jean, Wallis . . .	49
Manganese	49
Oberhalbstein, Grisons . .	49
Nickel in ultrabasic rocks . .	49
Poschiavo, Grisons; Totalp, Grisons; and Palagnedra, Tessin . .	49
Nickel–cobalt	49
Kaltenberg, Wallis . . .	49
Uranium	49
Isérables, Wallis . . .	49
Non-metallics	50
Fluorspar	50
Les Trappistes, Wallis	50
Gypsum	50
Bex, Vaud; Granges, Wallis; Leissigen, Bern; Läufelfingen, Basel Land; Kienberg, Solothurn; Felsenau, Aargau; and Ennetmoos, Unterwald .	50
Nephrite	50
Scortaseo, Grisons	50
Phosphates	50
Pizzo Corandoni, Tessin . . .	50
Quartz and other minerals in Alpine fissures	50
Salt	51
Rheinfelden, Aargau-Schweizerhalle, Basel Land	51
Bex, Vaud	51
Conclusions and outlook	51
Acknowledgement	51
Poland by R. Osika	55
Tectonic-metallogenic regions of Poland .	55
Region of Góry Świętokrzyskie (Holy Cross Mountains)	57
Region of Lower Silesia . . .	59
Region of Upper Silesia . . .	59
Region of the Carpathians . .	59
Region of the Carpathian Foredeep .	60
Region of the Precambrian platform .	60
Region of the Palaeozoic platform .	61
Metallic ore deposits	62
Iron ores	62
Endogenous deposits . . .	62
Krzemianka ilmenite–magnetite ore deposit	62
Kowary magnetite–quartzite ore deposit	62
Veins and lenses of hematite, siderite and pyrite	63

Exogenous deposits	65
Sedimentary deposits	65
Ore deposits formed by weathering processes	69
Copper ores	69
Endogenous deposits	69
Vein copper ore deposits in the Sudetes	69
Epigenetic copper ore deposits in the Góry Świętokrzyskie	70
Exogenous deposits	71
Copper ores in Lower Permian terrestrial sediments	71
Copper ores in Upper Permian marine sediments	71
Zinc–lead ores	73
Endogenous deposits	73
Veins of zinc and lead ore in the Sudetes	73
Veins and pockets of lead ore in Góry Świętokrzyskie	74
Exogenous deposits	74
Zinc–lead deposits in Triassic rocks of Silesia–Krakow Upland	74
Chromium, arsenic, tin, nickel and aluminium ores	77
Endogenous deposits	77
Chromium	77
Arsenic	78
Tin	79
Exogenous deposits	79
Nickel	79
Bauxite	80
Important accessory metals in ores and rocks	81
Gold	81
Silver	82
Cadmium and thallium	82
Other metals	82
Deposits of non-metallic minerals for the chemical industry	82
Pyrite and marcasite	82
Endogenous deposits	82
Rudki pyrite deposit	82
Wieściszowice pyrite-bearing schist deposit	83
Exogenous deposits	83
Pyrite deposits in dolomites of Silesia–Krakow Triassic	83
Pyrite deposits in Eocene shales in Carpathians	83
Native sulphur	83
Exogenous deposits	83
Deposits in Carpathian Foredeep	83
Rock salt and magnesium–potassium salts	85

Exogenous deposits	85
Zechstein salt-bearing basin	85
Miocene salt-bearing basin	86
Phosphorites	88
Barite and fluorspar	90
Endogenous deposits	90
Boguszów barite deposit	90
Stanisławów barite deposit	90
Kletno fluorspar deposit	90
Exogenous deposits	90
Strawczynek barite deposit	90
Other non-metallic deposits	91
Endogenous deposits	91
Quartz	91
Feldspar	91
Exogenous deposits	92
Magnesite	92
Gypsum and anhydrite	94
Kaolin	95
Bentonite	96
Belgium by L. Dejonghe	99
Geological framework	99
Lead and zinc deposits	99
Vein-type deposits and associated irregular bodies (so-called 'amas')	100
Other types of deposit	102
Ore deposits of karstic affinities	102
Ore deposits of sedimentary affinities	103
Hypotheses concerning source of metals	103
Barite deposits	104
Fluorite deposits	105
Iron deposits	105
Sedimentary deposits	106
Weathering deposits	107
Ore deposits due to weathering of sediments	107
Palaeozoic	107
Lias	107
Eocene	107
Mio-Pliocene	107
Pliocene	107
Holocene	108
Gossans of sulphide lodes	108
Karstic deposits	108
Manganese deposits	108
Phosphate deposits	109
Copper deposits	109
Gold deposits	109
Kaolin deposits	110
Weathering deposits	110
Sedimentary deposits	110
The Netherlands by H. M. Harsveldt	113

Palaeogeographic setting—Zechstein . . 113
Exploration history 114
Palaeogeographic setting—Upper Bunter . 115
Boekelo concession 115
Exploration history 115
Bitter salts 115
Gypsum 116
Postscript 116

Czechoslovakia by Zdeněk Pouba and Ján Ilavský 117

Mineral deposits of the Bohemian Massif (Zdeněk Pouba) 117
  Mining history 117
  Economic importance of Bohemian ore deposits 118
  Geology of Bohemian Massif . . . 118
  Metallogenic history of Bohemian Massif 121
    Pre-Variscan mineralization . . . 121
    Variscan mineralization . . . 122
    Post-Variscan (Alpine) mineralization 123
  Precambrian ore deposits of Bohemian Massif 124
    Ni–Cu and Zn–Cu deposits in Staré Ransko Precambrian ultrabasic complex 124
    Chvaletice Precambrian FeS$_2$–Mn sedimentary deposit 124
  Palaeozoic sedimentary deposits . . 125
    Sedimentary Fe deposits in Barrandian area 125
  Palaeozoic stratiform deposits . . . 126
    Tisová stratiform Cu deposit . . 126
    Zlaté Hory stratiform Cu–Pb–Zn deposit 126
    Horní Benešov stratiform Pb–Zn deposit 128
  Variscan hydrothermal deposits . . 130
    Jílové Au deposit 130
    Příbram Ag–Pb–Zn vein deposit . 130
    Kutná Hora Ag–Pb–Zn vein deposit . 132
    Jáchymov vein deposit with Ag–Bi–Co–Ni–U ores 134
    Horní Slavkov–Krásno Sn–W deposits 135
    Cínovec (Zinnwald) Sn–W–Li deposit 136
  Regenerated deposits of outer part of Bohemian Massif 137
    Harrachov F–Pb vein deposit . . 137
  Post-Variscan (Mesozoic-Caenozoic) deposits 138
    Křemže lateritic Ni deposit . . . 138
  Non-metallic mineral deposits of Bohemian Massif 138
    Economics of non-metallic mineral deposits 138
    Geological conditions governing formation of the non-metallic raw material deposits 138
    Graphite deposits 139
    Feldspar deposits 140
    Fluorite deposits 141
    Kaolin deposits 142
    Deposits of clays and claystones . . 143
    Deposits of glass sands, quartz and dinas quartzites 144
Mineral deposits of the Czechoslovak Carpathians (Ján Ilávský) 146
  History of mining and geological research 146
  Some economic data on Slovak ore deposits 147
  Geology and structural history . . . 147
  Metallogenic epochs 150
    Caledonian metallogenic epoch . . 151
      Geosynclinal stage 151
    Variscan metallogenic epoch . . . 151
      Geosynclinal stage 151
      Orogenic stage 153
      Early post-orogenic stage . . . 154
      Late post-orogenic stage . . . 154
    Alpine metallogenic epoch . . . 154
      Geosynclinal stage 154
      Early orogenic stage 155
      Late orogenic stage 155
      Early post-orogenic stage . . . 156
      Late post-orogenic stage . . . 156
  Geological description of main types of mineral deposits 156
    Iron ores 156
      Stratiform siderite deposits in Gemeride zone 156
      Hydrothermal veins with siderite and sulphides 157
      Skarn magnetite ores in Central Slovakian Neovolcanic zone . . 158
    Manganese ores 158
    Cupriferous ores 158
      Stratiform cupriferous pyrite deposits in early Palaeozoic . . . 159
      Hydrothermal vein deposits of cupriferous siderite ores in pre-Permian formations 161
      Stratiform volcanosedimentary copper deposits in Permian . . . 161
      Cupriferous and polymetallic deposits in Neovolcanics 162
    Lead–zinc ores 163
      Hydrothermal veins of plutogenic type in crystalline massifs . . 163
      Hydrothermal veins, skarns and metasomatic Pb–Zn ores in Neovolcanics 163

Hydrothermal subvolcanic veins	163
Metasomatic lead–zinc ores	165
Skarn lead–zinc ores	165
Antimony ores	165
Volcanogenic-sedimentary deposits of Sb ores in Palaeozoic rocks	165
Hydrothermal veins of Sb and Au	165
Subvolcanic hydrothermal veins in Miocene Neovolcanics	167
Tetrahedrite type of antimony ores	167
Mercury ores	168
Hydrothermal siderite–sulphide veins	168
Mercury deposits in Miocene Neovolcanic rocks	168
Gold and silver ores	168
Nickel–cobalt ores	168
Pyrite ores	168
Barite	168
Magnesite	169
Deposits of crystalline magnesite in early Palaeozoic of the Gemerides	169
Deposits of crystalline magnesite and talc in Veporide crystalline complex	169
Deposits of crystalline magnesite in Upper Carboniferous of the Gemerides	169
Talc	170
Asbestos	171
Gypsum–anhydrite	171
Halite	171
Kaolinitic clays	172
Bentonites	172
Halloysite	172
Vein quartz	172
Limnoquartzites	172
Quartzites	172
Foundry and glass sands	172
Diatomites	172
Perlites	172
Petrurgical basalt	172
Volcanic tuffs and tuffites	172
Limestones, marls and dolomites	173
Decorative stones	173

Federal Republic of Germany by H. W. Walther 175

Introduction	175
Geological and metallogenic summary	175
Variscan basement	175
Post-Variscan cover	177
Alps and Foreland	179
Mesozoic to Tertiary rift system	179
Weathering deposits	181
History of mining	181
Some data on mine production	182
Mineral deposits in the Variscan orogenic belt	183
Moldanubian and Saxothuringian zones	183
Pre-orogenic endogenic deposits	183
Northeast Bavaria (E. O. Teuscher and W. Weinelt)	183
Black Forest (W. Wimmenauer)	185
Pre-orogenic sedimentary deposits (E. O. Teuscher and W. Weinelt)	185
Variscan epigenetic deposits	186
Northeast Bavaria (E. O. Teuscher and W. Weinelt)	186
Black Forest (W. Wimmenauer)	188
Odenwald (H. Maus)	191
Spessart (W. Weinelt)	191
Saar–Nahe Depression (C. Rée)	192
Late Palaeozoic strata-bound deposits	193
Uranium deposit near Baden-Baden (W. Wimmenauer)	193
Rhenohercynian Zone and sub-Variscan Foredeep	193
Volcanosedimentary deposits of early Variscan age	194
Rammelsberg deposit (G. Gunzert)	194
Meggen deposit (W. Fuchs)	198
Other sulphide barite deposits	205
Red iron deposits in the Lahn–Dill district (H.-J. Lippert)	205
Other red iron and manganese ore deposits	207
Stratiform copper and gold mineralization	208
Lead–zinc deposits in Palaeozoic carbonate rocks (R. Gussone)	208
Aachen–Stolberg district	208
Iserlohn–Schwelm district	209
Brilon district	209
Problems of age and genesis of mineralization in carbonate rocks	209
Nickel and copper mineralization in basic magmatites	209
Vein deposits of Variscan age	209
Iron ore mines of the Siegerland–Wied district (W. Fenchel, M. Lusznat and G. Stadler)	209
Lead–zinc ore veins in the northern and central Rheinische Schiefergebirge	214
Bergisches Land district (J. Hesemann and H. Lehmann)	215
Ramsbeck deposit (P. Podufal)	218
Pb–Zn ore veins in the Southern Rheinische Schiefergebirge (H. W. Walther, K. H. Emmermann and C. Rée)	226

Lead–zinc ore veins in the Western Harz Mountains (H. Sperling)	230
Lead–zinc ore veins in the Sub-Variscan Foredeep (Ruhr district: A. Pilger and F. Stolze)	236
Venn district	240
Marsberg copper stockwork deposit	240
Late Palaeozoic sedimentary iron ore deposits	241
Sedimentary mineral deposits in the epi-Variscan platform cover	241
Evaporites (E. Hofrichter)	241
Summary	241
Chlorides	242
Sulphates	244
Fluorite	245
The Kupferschiefer deposit (H. W. Walther and H.-J. Lippert)	245
Synopsis	245
Kupferschiefer ore seam in Hessian Depression	246
Richelsdorf deposit	248
Other copper orefields and prospects in Hessian Depression	249
Non-ferrous metal mineralization in the Triassic	251
Copper ores in the Bunter	251
Sulphidic ores in the Middle and Upper Triassic	251
Northern Germany (P. Simon)	251
Southern Germany	251
Mineralization in the Oberpfalz (Upper Palatinate) Bight and Freihung lead deposit (H. Gudden)	253
Iron ore deposits (P. Simon)	254
Ores of the Lower Jurassic	256
Ores of the Middle Jurassic (Dogger)	256
Ores of the Upper Jurassic (Malm)	256
Ores of the Lower Cretaceous	257
Ores of the Upper Cretaceous	257
Caenozoic ores	258
Industrial minerals	258
Quartz, quartzite, silica sand and siliceous rocks	258
Vein quartz and quartzites	258
Silica sand and silica sandstone	260
Unconsolidated siliceous rocks	260
Feldspar and feldspar sand	261
Ball clay and mudstone	262
Sulphur and iron sulphides	263
Phosphate rocks	263
Ore deposits in the Alpine orogenic belt	264
Lead–zinc ore deposits (H.-J. Schneider)	264
Geological setting	265
Paragenesis and orebodies	267
Genetic interpretation	267
Mining	268
Manganese ore deposits (H. Gudden)	268
Iron ore deposits (J. H. Ziegler)	269
Mineral deposits bound to the Mesozoic and Tertiary rift system	269
Alpine mineralization in the Sauerland district, northeastern Rheinisches Schiefergebirge (R. Schaeffer)	271
Distribution of mineralization	272
Mineral succession	274
Economic importance	274
Strontianite veins of the Münsterland Bight	275
Mineralization of the Lower Saxony Block	276
Barite–fluorite veins	276
Barite–fluorite veins in the Black Forest, Odenwald and Spessart	276
Barite veins in Hessian Depression and adjacent areas	279
Fluorite–barite veins in westernmost Bohemian Massif	280
Cobalt–nickel–bismuth paragenesis	281
Lead–zinc ore deposits	282
Vein and impregnation deposits in northern Eifel Mountains	282
Lead(–zinc) and copper veins in Devonian rocks	282
Lead–zinc impregnation deposits of Maubach and Mechernich (D. Schachner)	284
Wiesloch deposit	287
Other lead–zinc mineralization	288
Copper and uranium impregnations	289
Niobium mineralization in carbonatites of the Kaiserstuhl	289
Mineral deposits associated with Ries impact	289
Weathering deposits	290
Gossans	290
Iron and manganese	290
Bauxite	291
Phosphorite	291
Kaolin	291
Placer deposits	292
Other mineral concentrations by superficial enrichment	293
German Democratic Republic by L. Baumann, B. Kölbel, M. Kraft, S. Lächelt, J. Rentzsch and K. Schmidt	303
Geotectonic-minerogenetic survey of the German Democratic Republic	303
Geotectonic-minerogenetic subdivision	303

Geotectonic-minerogenetic stages of development	307
Minerogenetic units in the GDR	310
The Fichtelgebirge–Erzgebirge Anticline (sub-zone I)	310
Central Saxony Lineament (sub-zone II)	310
The Granulitgebirge (sub-zone III)	311
East Thuringian–North Saxony Synclinorium (sub-zone IV)	312
Central European Rise (sub-zone V)	312
Elbtal Zone (sub-zone VI)	312
Lausitz Block (sub-zone VII)	312
Harz and Flechtingen–Roßlau Block (sub-zone VIII)	313
Trough in the northern GDR (sub-zone IX)	313
Sub-Hercynian Basin, Thuringian Basin, South Thuringian–Franconian Basin (sub-zones X, XI, XII)	313
Minerogeny (metallogeny) of the GDR territory with regard to typical mineralization	313
Pre-Variscan Stages	314
Variscan geosynclinal-orogen and molasse stage	314
Post-Variscan Platform Stage	318
Sedimentogene mineralization and deposits	318
Magmatogene mineralization and deposits	324
Fe–Mn–Ba association	324
F (–Ba) association	325
Polymetallic F–Ba association	326
Co–Ni–Ag–As association	327
Name index	331
Subject index	337

K. Schmidt and B. Kölbel

Introduction

Fundamental geotectonic division and development of Central Europe

The formation of mineral deposits in a given area is, essentially, the result of geotectonic processes. This relationship, generally recognized and reflected in a variety of standard forms, also applies to the area of Central Europe. Its minerogenetic development, and hence the occurrence of mineralization and ore deposition, as well as the form and location of ore deposits, are directly associated with tectonic-magmatic and petrological-lithological and metamorphogenic processes. The minerogenetic partitioning and assessment of the Central European area are thus largely determined by the geological-tectonic position of its units and the changes that they have undergone in the course of their geological history.

In terms of age and development Central Europe falls under two different geotectonic headings: (1) the West European Platform, formed in the course of Precambrian–Palaeozoic folding and which underwent late Palaeozoic–Mesozoic–Caenozoic development (especially the Central European Depression) and (2) the northern part of the Permian–Caenozoic Alpine–Carpathian tectogene.

The boundary between the two areas is taken as being the Peripenninic Lineament thought to exist beneath the Pre-Alpine flysch–molasse trough.

Central Europe is bounded to the east and north by the late Riphean established Danish–Polish marginal trough (aulacogene) region of the East European Platform (North Sea–Dobruja Lineament, Tornquist–Teisseyre zone); to the northwest and west by the Precambrian London–Brabant Massif with its later superposed formations (southern part of the North Sea Basin, western part of the northern Federal Republic of Germany, northern part of the German Democratic Republic and Poland, East Holland Ridge and Lower Rhine Ems Basin); to the southwest by the graben of the Upper Rhine valley in the Mediterranean–Mjösen zone; and to the south and southeast by the Periadriatic Lineament that separates the northern from the southern Alps.

This chapter is provided by members of the Central Geological Institute, Berlin, German Democratic Republic.

The following major tectonic units may be distinguished in the vertical and lateral composition of these areas: a pre-Variscan basement complex, which comprises the Precambrian Moldanubian–Dalslandian and Assyntic–Cadomian (Brioverian) and the Lower Palaeozoic Caledonian structural storeys; a Variscan geosynclinal-orogen structural storey (including the Molasse or transitional storey); a post-Variscan platform superstructure; and an Alpine geosynclinal-orogen superstructure (including the pre-Permian complexes).

On the basis of the structural outline developed by Kossmat[26] and Stille[44] for the Variscides of Central and Western Europe, and taking account of more recent tectonic theories, the following zonal division may be adopted for the basement (Fig. 1).

(1) The *Moldanubian zone* represents within the Variscan tectogene a median massif—mainly composed of pre-Variscan units—the formation of which was determined by Precambrian orogeneses of Riphean date. Characteristic are strong metamorphic overprinting (up to granulite facies) and anatexis. Typical units of this sort built the Bohemian, Black Forest–Vosges massifs and the French Massif Central. The first two are linked in the south of the FRG by the concealed Vindelician Ridge, which extends eastwards below the Western Carpathians and into the Ukrainian Shield.

(2) The *Saxothuringian zone* stretches in a band some 150 km wide from the Armorican Massif in northern France in an easterly direction across Belgium, the FRG, the southern part of the GDR and into Poland and Czechoslovakia. Its position as a transition zone between the relatively stable Moldanubian and the highly mobile Rhenohercynian zones is the reason for a series of specific features in its geological and minerogenetic development. Particularly important in this connexion is the high proportion of old crystalline complexes and the *Central European Rise*, mainly composed of pre-Variscan structures, with, as its principal element, the Central European crystalline zone (Odenwald, Spessart, Ruhla crystalline, Subsudeten block). This structure, which considerably influences the Variscan development, functioned during the geosyncline stage as an intra-geoanticline (Central German Ridge[13]) between the Rhenish and

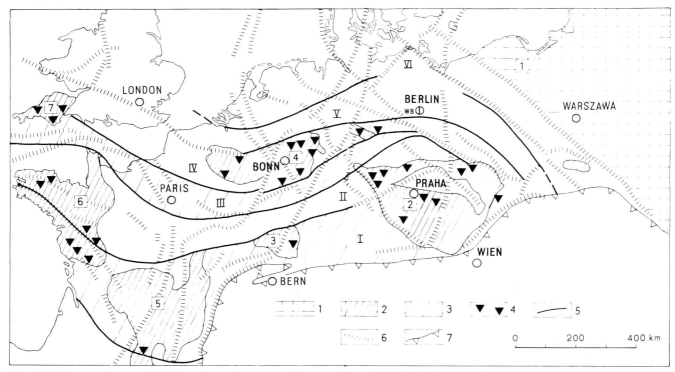

Fig. 1 Geotectonic zonal division of the Central and Western European Variscides. After Kossmat,[26] Stille,[44] Baumann and Tischendorf[6] and Baumann et al.[7] 1, East European Platform; 2, basement complex; 3, anticlinoria (with palingenetic magmatism); 4, centres of initial magmatism; 5, limits of tectonic and metallogenetic zones; 6, important lineaments and deep faults; 7, boundary of the Alpine orogens; I, Moldanubian zone (Variscan median massif); II, Thuringian Trough (synclinorium); III, Central European Rise (anticlinorium) (II and III, Saxothuringian zone); IV, Rhenish Trough (synclinorium); V, sub-Variscan zone (foredeep) (IV and V, Rhenohercynian zone); VI, foreland with Caledonian folded basement and Assyntic (Baikalian) cores (Variscan foreland). Geotectonic units: (1), East European Platform; (2) Bohemian Massif; (3) Vosges–Black Forest Massif; (4) Ardennes–Rheinisches Schiefergebirge; (5) French Massif Central; (6) Armorican Massif; (7) Cornwall Massif

the Thuringian troughs and at the Molasse stage became the carrier of the intermontane basin of the Oos–Saale trough. From the plate tectonic aspect it is ascribed the role of a crest zone or island arc, a subduction or oceanic-continental rift zone probably developing on its northern flank.

(3) The *Rhenohercynian zone* links up in the north with the Central European crystalline zone of the Saxothuringikum. Its structure is characterized by massive Devonian and Carboniferous rock series, which were subjected to intensive Variscan folding with the local formation of gliding nappes and olistostrome structures. Geographically, this zone extends from southwest England through the Ardennes–Rheinisches Schiefergebirge (Cornubian–Rhine Basin) into the Harz Mountains and the Flechtingen–Roßlau block in the territory of the GDR. Further to the east and southeast it shows a connexion with the Palaeozoic of the Subsudeten area up to the Moravosilesikum of Poland and Czechoslovakia that is not yet fully clarified but is probably determined by the Oder lineament. Large parts of the zone are overlain by post-Variscan molasse and platform sediments of the Central European Depression.

(4) The *sub-Variscan zone* (marginal trough) is the outermost folded portion of the Variscan tectogene. It is to be regarded as a foredeep-like flysch–molasse basin with coal-bearing Upper Carboniferous formations that came into being towards the end of the Variscan geosynclinal stage. In the west the zone begins with the synclinorium of Namur south of the Brabant Massif and runs northeast via Liège and Aachen and in a less marked form also to the east over the northern part of the GDR and thence southeast to Gorny Slask in Poland, where it probably appears in the form of a more or less independent basin in a formation similar to that of the Ruhr coal basin.

(5) The *succeeding Variscan External zone* to the north carries, like the sub-Variscan zone, molassoid coal-bearing Namurian and Westphalian displaying only Asturic fault tectonics, with post-tectonically superimposed Stephanian basins. The zone, which is covered, in places, by thick Rotliegende molasse and post-Variscan platform deposits, stretches from the north of the FRG and the GDR into northern and central Poland. In the latter area the Upper Carboniferous portions of the Polish marginal deep/aulacogene (the Polish Furrow) may be viewed as an equivalent of the Variscan External zone.

This zonal division of the basement complex, which is based on the position of the Variscan synclines and anticlines, is both in its arrangement and tectonic overprinting marked out, modified and controlled by deep crustal zones of instability, deep fractures and lineaments. The fundament of the Central European basement is, according to the view that predominates today, formed by the *Moldanubian–Dalslandian assemblage* of the Early Riphean (Early Upper Proterozoic). Its development and formation are assumed to have been caused by a precursory 'Dalslandian tectonomagmatic regeneration' of a crust that had been mostly consolidated during the Gothian folding of the Middle Proterozoic (1750–1500 m.y.)[9,30,51,53] West–east and north–south structures survive the regeneration, which controlled the direction of the formational and folding zones of the Moldanubian–Dalslandian assemblage (main group) by taking in parts of the oceanic crust in continental rift areas and forming island arcs (Moldanubian zone, Central European Rise). The tectogene produced by the Moldanubian–Dalslandian orogenesis was broken up by partly activated northwest–southeast and southwest–northeast-striking lineaments, resulting in a simatic and sialic block structure ('pre-Cadomian structural plan'), which determined the entire future development and was reflected at different times in a variety of posthumous features. The west–east lineamental subcrustal structure is particularly marked, for example, in the late Mesozoic train of positive gravimetric anomalies extending from Bramsche in the FRG into Poland and Czechoslovakia, their Hercynian (northwest–southeast) gradients revealing the influence of the stable East European Platform and its north–south gridding and the effects of the spreading processes in the Atlantic. The Precambrian block structure of Central Europe is shown, first, in the crustal segment of the East European Platform beneath southeast England, the Netherlands and the northwest of the FRG—and also in the basement of the Danish–Polish Furrow—and, second, in the old crystalline complexes of the Saxothuringikum and Moldanubikum.

The block, which was split from or limited by the massifs that had remained stable on the southwest periphery of the East European Platform (Netherlands Platform, Ringköbing–Fyn High, East Elbe Massif, Wielkopolski Block), became the main area of activity of the Caledonian movements, the deposition of the Old Red Sandstone and of sedimentation in the Variscan External zone. It thus plays a mediating role between the cratonic platform and the Variscan tectogene—as is borne out also by results of deep geophysics.

During and just after the Variscan mountain-building that resulted from the Asturic folding in the late Westphalian a general reorganization of the geotectonic regime took place in Central Europe. The chief characteristics of the *Variscan Molasse* or *transitional structural storey* are the emergence of, in part, pre-existing Hercynian (northwest–southeast) and Rhenish (SSW–NNE) directions, the tectonically controlled subsequent volcanism, the marking out of platform structures of the Central European Depression, the disposition of the intermontane molasse basins and the North German–Polish Depression over the Variscan External zone and the inversion of the Central European Crystalline zone.

Crustal kinematics characterized by directional vertical and horizontal (tension) movements is in recent theories linked with intraplate tectonic phenomena related to continental rift processes.[29,34,49,52]

The geotectonic development of the platform superstructure in extra-Alpine Central Europe differed in its timing. In the Precambrian–Caledonian area of consolidation on the southwest edge of the East European Platform it followed on the molassoid Old Red Sandstone in the Lower to Middle Devonian. The succeeding epicontinental clayey limestone and molasse series of the Middle Devonian to the Upper Carboniferous were, in the main, subjected to fault-tectonic stresses only. Above this are the formations of the post-tectogenetic molasse (Stephanian–Saxonian I) of the transitional structural storey.

In the area with Variscan consolidated basement the development of the platform superstructure began with the Saxonian II, intensified by the Zechstein transgression in conjunction with a wide-ranging depression that followed on from the taphrogenic stage (Fig. 2).

The tectonic regime of the platform cover, which determined the arrangement and form of the Central European Depression and its component synclines, took place in several stages (main depression, differentiation, stabilization), which, combined with intensive dyktiogenetic, epeirogenetic and halokinetic movements at different times, resulted in the formation of structural sub-stages (Old Cimmerian, Young Cimmerian, sub-Hercynian–Laramide structural sub-stages). Particularly effective were fault-tectonic processes (Saxonic tectonics), themselves the expression of tectonomagmatic activations that had been triggered by the global processes that affected the mobile and stable areas surrounding the West European Platform (Atlantic spreading, Alpine–Carpathian tectogenesis, East European Platform). This is also shown by the widespread synchronism of the structure-forming and reforming main tectonic processes in the Central European Depression, the Alpine folding phases and the staged spreading processes in the Atlantic.

Two elements, in particular, are especially clear on the general sketch of important fault-tectonic structures (Fig. 3)—taphrogenic (NNE–SSW) structures, mainly represented by the Mediterranean–Mjösen zone, and northwest–southeast structural elements running parallel to the southwest edge of the East European Platform.

The Rhine system, which constitutes the Central European boundary to the west, is closely related to the rift processes in the Atlantic and the North Sea areas

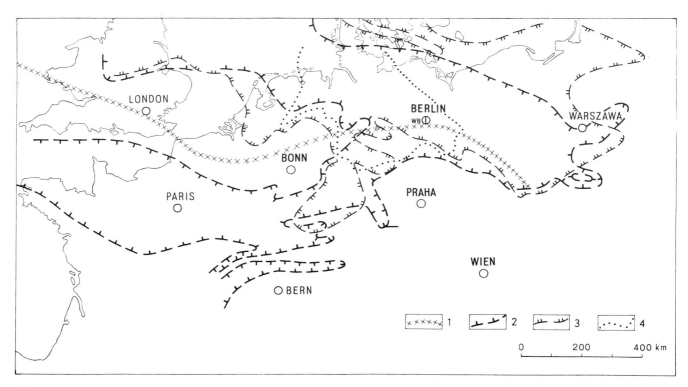

Fig. 2 Position of the basins of sedimentation during Variscan transitional stage and at beginning of platform development. After Kölbel.[25] 1, Limits of area with platform development from Devonian onwards; 2, limits of Rotliegende basins (P_1); 3, limits of Zechstein basins (P_2); 4, limits of Triassic basins (T_1)

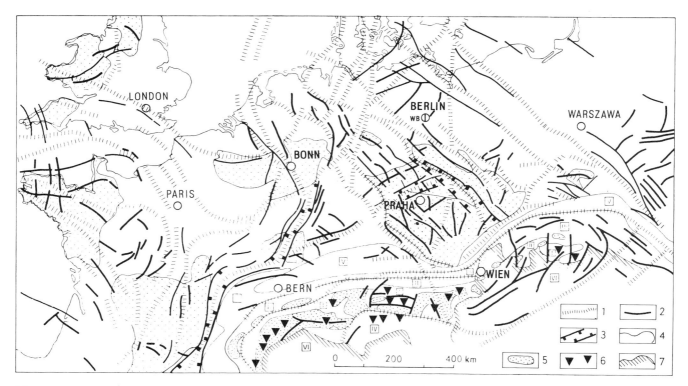

Fig. 3 Fault- and block-tectonic subdivision of post-Variscan Central and Western Europe and zonal division of the Alpine/Carpathian system. After Grumbt and co-workers,[17] Gwinner[18] and Kraus.[27] 1, Lineament, deep fracture; 2, important faults; 3, graben zone, taphrogenic structures; 4, limits of Alpine zones; 5, exposed basement; 6, Alpine initial volcanites; 7, limits of superposed Tertiary basins in Alpine region. Geotectonic structural zones: I, Central Alps–Inner Carpathian zone; II, Northern Limestone Alps; III, Flysch zone and Helvetikum; IV, Southern Alps; V, Molasse zone (Alpine–Carpathian Foredeep); VI, superposed Tertiary basins

and is predominantly marked by tension, but the northwest–southeast system was, in its final phase, determined by compression tectonics that resulted from the northern thrust of the Alpine collision front,[21] leading in the northern part of Central Europe to block tectonics and inversion structures.

At the same time as the block and taphrogenic development of the cratonic post-Variscan platform region was taking place, the development of the Alpine geosynclinal orogen superstructure[18,47] took place in the bordering Alpine region on its southern border, with a marked tectonic zoning—Central Alps–Inner Carpathian zone (= central crystalline zone)–Northern Limestone Alps–Helvetic–Ultra-Helvetic and Flysch zones–Molasse zone (Alpine–Carpathian Foredeep)–Superposed Tertiary basins, and also the Southern Alps zone, which is, of course, outside the Central European area.

Geological-tectonic-minerogenetic characteristics of structural storeys (development stages) in summary

Precambrian structural storeys

In terms of age, the Precambrian structural storeys date from the Riphean (Upper Proterozoic), although Zoubek[53] considered that the older, Moldanubian–Dalslandian Supergroup should be referred to the Middle Proterozoic. Both stages correspond to geosynclinal cycles with more or less marked eugeosynclinal and miogeosynclinal development and orogenic culmination related to the mobile zones of the Dalslandian tectonomagmatic regeneration.

The *Moldanubian–Dalslandian stage* (approximately 1500–1000 m.y.) is today characterized by predominantly leptynitic rock formations associated with magmatic effusive and intrusive formations with some intervening carbonate formations. The polymetamorphic, strongly altered series (granulite, anatexite, migmatite and gneisses) occurs in the core zones of the Bohemian Massif, the Sudeten, the Granulitgebirge, the Münchberg Mass, the older structures of the Central European crystalline zone, and the Black Forest–Vosges Massif within the Central European Variscides. The crystalline complexes in the basement of the southwest peripheral area of the East European Platform (Netherlands Platform, Brabant Massif, Ringkøbing–Fyn High, East Elbe Massif) probably contain substantial Moldanubian–Dalslandian structural components. Minerogenetic activities are not known in connexion with these oldest development stages, although more recent deposits do occur in the rocks.

During the late Riphean Assyntian–Cadomian (Brioverian) stage, which began 900–1000 m.y. ago, geosynclinal development is very marked. The likewise strongly—mainly metamorphically—overprinted, formerly sedimentary-volcanogenic series (including initial spilite–keratophyre volcanism) displays local stratiform mineralization (Cu, Sn, Pb, Zn) and, in particular, pyrite-bearing magnetite skarns and graphite schists (Vychodne Sudeten, Krkonoše and Kaczawskie Mountains in Czechoslovakia and Poland and the Erzgebirge in the GDR and Czechoslovakia). The flysch and molasse stage often reveals itself in low-grade metamorphic, relatively widespread and, in places, thick series of greywackes and shales. The stage finishes with the Assyntian–Cadomian tectogenesis, though the development, in places, continues into the Lower Palaeozoic. The Assyntian–Cadomian movements were followed by an extrusive and intrusive magmatism of apparently subsequent type.

Caledonian structural storey

The Caledonian stage has developed over a basement that has been subjected to varying stress by the Assyntian–Cadomian movements, and which, in turn, still shows marked epi-Karelian (Moldanubian–Dalslandian) framework and components. The beginning and end of the stage are clearly identifiable only in areas of Assyntian–Cadomian and Caledonian consolidation.

The Central European area was, during the Caledonian stage, under the influence of plate margins (East European Platform, Palaeotethys)[42] active to the north and south. From the Anglo–Norwegian Caledonian orthogeosyncline there extended to the southeast a mobile area above the sunken and partly regenerated segment of the East European Platform flanked by stable cratonic areas and zones of depression. On the immediate southwest periphery of the East European Platform was situated an aulacogene type of depression (the Danish–Polish Furrow). In both areas Caledonian movements have had their effect and resulted in Taconic and late Caledonian folding and other tectonic stresses (Ardennes, Brabant Massif, northern Rheinisches Schiefergebirge, Danish–Polish Furrow, including the Góry Świętokryzskie). The Central European area of sedimentation located to the south of this area of Caledonian consolidation was, to judge by its division into rises and depressions, similarly highly mobile, although here the Caledonian folding does not match that of the platform margin. On the other hand, there is widespread intrusive and effusive magmatism (Góry Kaczawskie, Bohemia, northeast Bavaria), combined with strong metamorphism at depth, intracontinental mobilization of material and tectonomagmatic activation processes. One effect of these processes was the anatectic–palingenetic phenomena recognized especially in the core zones of the Moldanubian–Assyntian crystalline complexes, which had earlier formed the rises (Lausitz anatexites and the main metamorphic phase of the Precambrian to Lower Palaeozoic rock sequences). In plate tectonic terms the central part of Central Europe takes the form of a marginal sea

Table 1 Geotectonic structural zones of Central Europe and their minerogenetic characteristics

Epoch	Geotectonic structural storeys	Tectonic and metallogenetic structural zones	Metallogenetically typical mineral concentrations	Typical regional examples
Alpine	Molasse structural storey	Superposed Tertiary basins	Brown coal	Vienna Basin
		Tertiary fault structures	Au–Ag, Pb–Zn, Fe, Cu, Sb	Slovakian Erzgebirge (Banská Štiavnica)
		Alpine and Carpathian Foredeeps	Glass sands, clays, evaporites, S	N. Alpine (Gosau Basin) and Carpathian Molasse basin
	Geosynclinal (orogen) structural storey	Flysch zone	(Fe; Cu, Pb–Zn; Sb, Hg, Sn–W–Mo) Pb–Zn, Cu–Fe, Ba, F	Gemerides (intrusive) Lechtal, Lafatsch
		Northern Limestone Alps	Rock salt, anhydrite–gypsum, limestones	Northern Limestone Alps
	Basement structural storey (e.g. Pre-Alpine)	Central Alps–Inner Carpathian zone	Fe, (Mn), Mg; Cu, Au, Pb–Zn; W, Sb, Hg; U; Ba	Tatroveporides, Gemerides, Hohe Tauern Altkristallin of Eastern Alps
Post-Variscan	Platform superstructure (extra-Alpine)	Mesozoic–Caenozoic fault structures (taphrogenic, germanotype)	F–Ba, Fe–Mn, Cu–Pb–Zn Bi–Co–Ni–Ag–U, As–Hg	Harz, Erzgebirge Thuringian Forest, Black Forest
		Post-Albian depressions	Brown coal, kaolin	Niederlausitz (GDR) Lower Rhine (FRG)
		Old and Young Cimmerian depressions	Fe, (Mn)	Jurassic and Cretaceous semi-basins: Lorraine, Gifhorn, Salzgitter
		Central European Depression	Potassium salts, anhydrite–gypsum limestones Kupferschiefer (Cu, Ag, etc.)	Marginal depressions of the Zechstein basin (Werra, Staßfurt, Mansfeld, Lubin)
Variscan	Transitional structural storey	Sedimentary-volcanogenic depressions and Molasse basins	Coal	Saar–Selke and Oos–Saale basins
	Geosynclinal (orogen) structural storey	External zone	—	At too great depth in Central Europe
		Rhenohercynian and sub-Variscan zone	Fe–Mn, Cu–Pb–Zn–Ba	Lahn–Dill depression, Harz, Rheinisches Schiefergebirge
		Saxothuringian zone	Sn–W, Zn–Pb–Ag, U	Erzgebirge, Northern Brittany
Pre-Variscan	Basement structural storey	Moldanubian zone and median massifs	Au–Sb, Pb–Zn; Fe–Cu (Mo, Sn; U, Ag)	Bohemian Massif (core) French Massif Central

composed of volcanic island arcs and trenches and eugeosynclinal troughs, which extended as far as the Tethys area.[42]

From the minerogenetic point of view the Caledonian stage outside the Alps was not very productive. In addition to oolitic iron ore formations, a number of non-ferrous metal mineralizations in the volcano-sedimentary eugeosynclincal series of the Erzgebirge have been regarded as syngenetic.[50]

Variscan geosynclinal-orogen structural storey

In the areas of Saxothuringian sedimentation in mid-Central Europe the Caledonian stage merges fairly continuously into the Variscan geosynclinal development. In the Precambrian–Caledonian area of consolidation in the East European Platform foreland the Variscan development begins with the markedly discordant Old Red Sandstone (Danish–Polish Furrow) or epicontinental formations (Brabant Massif).

The Variscan geosyncline displays a tendency to develop distinct positive and negative zones, first, in the Silurian and increasing steadily during the Devonian (Moldanubian–Erzgebirge–Lausitz Rise, Thuringian Trough, Central European Rise, Rhenish Trough) and from the Lower Carboniferous onwards, as a result of the northward migration of the main zones of subsidence that overcome and incorporate the pre-Devonian structures, there comes into being the Sub-Variscan marginal trough and the foreland depression of the Variscan external molasse.

This palaeodynamic regime led to the development of a typical geosynclinal series, a eugeosynclinal and ensuing miogeosynclinal stage reaching as far as the Upper Devonian. The internal dynamics of the troughs and rises led, in the Devonian especially, to the manifold differentiations of the Rhenish and Hercynian facies provinces. The Rhenish Trough compared with the Thuringian shows the more typical signs of a gradual process of geosynclinal development. This is also clear in the petrographical sequence, origin and minerogenetic effectiveness of the relatively strong initial magmatism that occurred from England as far as Poland, and which was at its peak during the late Middle to early Upper Devonian. Associated with the volcanosedimentary keratophyre–spilite–diabase series are submarine hydrothermal iron ore deposits—those caused by hydatogenic leaching—of the Lahn-Dill type and the stratiform polymetallic sulphide ore deposits of Rammelsberg and Meggen in the FRG, Zlaté Hory and Horní Benešov in Czechoslovakia and the pyrite ore deposits of the Rio Tinto type at Elbingerode in the GDR. In the Thuringian Trough the Middle to Upper Devonian magmatism is less marked and lacks the petrographic breadth of the Rhenish Trough. The mineralization, which is almost entirely made up of iron ore of the Lahn–Dill type, is not extensive. According to Rösler and Werner,[40] the initial magmatites of the Rhenish Trough should be regarded as mantle derivatives of an island arc nature, whereas those of the Thuringian Trough show signs of a greater crustal-anatectic influence.

The close of the initial magmatism is marked by the 'Deckdiabase', largely emplaced during the Lower Carboniferous, but which are not minerogenetically significant.

In the course of the Variscan tectogenesis that took place from the Upper Devonian to the Upper Carboniferous and reached a maximum in the Sudetic phase at the Lower/Upper Carboniferous boundary, the palaeogeographic configuration of the Variscan geosyncline was transformed into the tectogenetic structures of the Variscides, sometimes with intensive Alpine-type deformation. The main directions of strike of these structures are, to the west of the Elbe line, southwest–northeast (Erzgebirge type) and to the east of the line, northwest–southeast (Hercynian) (Fig. 1). The tectogenesis, which progressed in time from south to north and terminated with the upfolding of the sub-Variscan marginal trough in the Upper Westphalian (Asturic phase), led in earlier-consolidated areas to upthrows, inversions and fault-tectonic deformations. In conjunction with this, synorogenic and post-orogenic, generally acid, plutonites (granodiorites and granites) were intruded into the anticlinal zones. Some of these early Variscan granitoids contain the Au–Sb, As–Au, As–U–Cu (Bohemian Massif, Sudeten) and W mineralization (Erzgebirge).

In recent years mobilistic interpretations derived from global tectonics[14,46] have been used to explain geotectonic and minerogenetic processes during the Variscan geosynclinal-orogen stage and the formation of the Variscan tectogene. This is generally connected with drift movements in the inhomogeneous shelf area of Central Europe flanking the East European Platform to the southwest. The old crystalline zones of the Central European Rise and the Moldanubikum are thus assumed to be island or volcanic arcs.[51] The southward drift results in the folding of the Barrandium of the Prague Basin in the Devonian and continues through the Saxothuringian, Rhenohercynian and sub-Variscan zones into the later Upper Carboniferous.

Various factors point to the involvement of subduction in the overall process, in association with island arcs and smaller crystalline complexes, especially in the Saxothuringian zone. During closure, the Central European crystalline zone functioned as a median crest. Initial magmatism, synorogenic and post-orogenic plutonism and the subsequent magmatism accord with the mobilistic model of the Variscan tectogene taking place under oceanic-continental conditions just as well as do the genesis, types and geographical distribution of the deposits or the degree of minerogenetic activity of the magmatic formations, which differ substantially in character and in time and place.

The *Variscan molasse stage* (transitional structural

storey) covers, according to the course of the tectogenesis, the period late Lower Carboniferous to Saxonian. The post-tectonic molasse formation, which is predominantly composed of continental to shallow marine clastic sediments and subsequent volcanites, developed during the Upper Carboniferous, initially in the inner depressions of the central areas of the Variscan tectogene (Saar–Selke and Oos–Saale basins) and, from the Stephanian onwards, also in the former area of the Variscan foredeep (External Molasse). During the Saxonian post-volcanic molasse then spread over the peneplained surface. The geotectonic development extends from the geosynclinal structure through phases of fault-tectonic restructuring involving the activation of northwest–southeast- and north–south-striking structural elements through to the establishment of the Central European Depression.

The largely subsequent magmatism occurs in both intrusive and effusive form. Especially important minerogenetically in the former case are the geochemically specialized granitoids (Sn, F, Li) of the later Variscan intrusive complex (Erzgebirge tin deposits). The polymetallic vein formations (Fe–Zn–Pb, U, Sb–Ag), too, are probably mainly linked with the subsequent magmatism. The minerogenetic effect of the effusive magmatism, which is predominantly associated with zones of intersection of meridional and Hercynian structure zones, is, by comparison, negligible.

Post-Variscan platform superstructure
With the taphrogenic processes taking place in the Lower Permian, the effects of which were especially marked in the region of the outer Variscides, where they led to the formation of the Oslo Rift and those in the North Sea, the tectonic development of the post-Variscan platform cover was initiated.[31]

Extension of the basin structures during Saxonian II resulted in the formation of the North German–Polish Depression.

The subsequent subsidence over a large area produced the Zechstein transgression) which extends beyond the Variscan morphogene and much further southwards. During this *principal subsidence stage*, which lasted into the Middle Keuper and was brought to a close with the *Old Cimmerian movements* in the Middle and Upper Keuper, there occurs even in the Zechstein, but increasingly from the Lower Triassic onwards, a marked morphogenetic differentiation and hence the emergence of the Meso–Caenozoic structural formation and deformation. Rhenish deep structures show themselves in the palaeotectonic contouring of the areas of sedimentation and these, combined with the further activation of the northwest–southeast system and incipient halokinesis, resulted in the formation of ridges and depressions that extended in a NNE–SSW direction. The establishment of the North Sea graben and the initial rifting in the Tethys and the Atlantic are of approximately the same age.[16,52]

The mainly saline-clayey limestone deposits of the *Zechstein* are associated with important and extensive deposits of Cu, Pb, Zn, Ag (Kupferschiefer), potash and rock salt, anhydrite, gypsum and carbonate rocks.

Similar concentrations of elements took place in the *Triassic*, with Pb–Zn in the Buntsandstein (Maubach and Mechernich in the FRG) and red salts in the Muschelkalk with Pb–Zn (Gorny Slask, Poland).

The Old Cimmerian movements, which express themselves in various forms (fault tectonics, ridge and basin formation, halokinesis and regressions) mark the beginning of a stage of enhanced crustal mobility that results in a differentiation of the palaeotectonic and sedimentological regime. The continuing reactivation, especially of the northwest–southeast fault systems, and also of northeast–southwest structures, is demonstrated by the rapidly sinking troughs at block margins, block-tectonic uplifts and depressions and their resulting alternation of transgressions and regressions. The western part of Central Europe shows in this connexion a more marked influence of meridional extensional tectonics than the eastern part, where Saxonian block tectonics predominates. This development reached its peak with the Young Cimmerian movements in the Upper Jurassic. The transgressions and regressions in the Lower Cretaceous follow, mainly, the palaeotectonic framework, with a noticeable uplifting of old crustal blocks.[52]

The palaeotectonic mobility caused a marked variability in facies both geographically and in terms of time, which is in line with the formation of iron ore that took place over the Jurassic–Lower Cretaceous period. Thus, during the *Jurassic*, oolitic iron ores came into being in some basin areas, such as the Gifhorn Trough in the FRG. In coastal areas of the *Lower Cretaceous* basins isolated deposits of residual iron ore were deposited (Salzgitter, FRG).

The *stabilization* stage, which ensues in the general process of platform development, repeats in a less marked form the tendencies of previous stages. A further wide-ranging process of subsidence that began at the end of the Lower Cretaceous resulted, in consequence of the Albian–Cenomanian transgression, in large areas of Central Europe being included in the sedimentation regime of the Upper Cretaceous. This widespread crustal kinematic activity may be viewed as the effect of the second phase of the tectonomagmatic activation that is linked especially with the Austric collision movements in the Tethys. In palaeotectonic terms the compression tectonics expresses itself as block structure broken up by meridional extension structures and in tectonic inversions associated with intensive fault tectonics, halokinesis and the formation of marginal depressions. The structural changes reached their peak in the *sub-*

Introduction

Hercynian–Laramide movements of the Upper Cretaceous–Palaeogene, which set the basic pattern of the present-day tectonic structure of extra-Alpine Central Europe. In the Caenozoic the sub-Hercynian–Laramide tectonic movements continued to uplift crustal blocks in the central area of the Variscan tectogene.

In minerogenetic terms the period of stabilization is characterized by a plurality of deposit-forming processes, including the phosphorite concretions that occur at the base of the sandy-marly transgressive Albian–Cenomanian (Góry Świętokrzyskie, Poland) and red-bed concentrations and residual iron ores that occur locally in the predominantly carbonate–clay formations of the Upper Cretaceous (northern FRG). In the course of the Tertiary, which is characterized by repeated, regionally extensive transgressions and regressions, the economically important Central European brown coal deposits came into being (Lower Rhenish Bight, Hessen/FRG, Halle–Bitterfeld–Lausitz area of GDR, Ślask/Poland, Bohemia-Czechoslovakia).

The Caenozoic deposits contain, moreover, numerous raw materials used in the construction, glass and ceramic industries, including the kaolins that were formed chiefly during the Upper Cretaceous and Early Tertiary.

A number of different structure-bound endogene deposits in Central Europe can be related to the tectonomagmatic activations that took place during the platform stage.[4] In the formation and geographical distribution of these deposits the kinematics and structures of taphrogenic tectonics and germanotype fault-block tectonics are intensively involved, the areas of intersection of the taphrogenic NNE uplift and fault zones with the NNW and northwest faults being particularly delineated. Although the former by virtue of their considerable vertical range and extension-kinematics are of especial significance for the rise of magma and fluids and their differentiation, the latter structures have the particular function of hydrothermal distribution and emplacement of substances.

This endogene minerogenesis is attributed to a diapiric intrusive platform magmatism (alkali–ultrabasic rock formation). The mineralizations and deposits are characterized, in particular, by the element parageneses Fe–Mn–Ba, F–Ba (–Cu–Zn–Pb), Bi–Co–Ni, Ag(–U), As, Hg. These occur mainly as veins (Sudeten, Bohemian Massif, Erzgebirge, Thuringian Forest, Harz, Rheinisches Schiefergebirge, Black Forest, Vosges, etc.) and, to a lesser degree, as impregnation, replacement and stratiform formations and correspond to the post-Variscan polymetallic mineralization cycle. The often combined occurrence of Variscan (Permo-Carboniferous) and post-Variscan (Mesozoic) mineralization has been shown to exist in various parts of Central Europe.[5,10,11,12,15,37,41]

The chief formational period of the post-Variscan mineralization cycle falls in the timespan of the Young Cimmerian (Upper Jurassic) and especially the sub-Hercynian–Laramide movements of the Upper Cretaceous to Early Tertiary. Then, in the Middle to Late Tertiary the intensity of endogene ore deposition waned. A typical phenomenon of the Tertiary is a similarly tectonically controlled effusive magmatism (basalts, phonolites) in the Central European Variscan tectogene, but which is free of mineralization.

Alpine geosynclinal-orogen superstructure

The structures of the Alpine–Carpathian tectogene are almost exclusively attributable to the Alpine geosynclinal orogeny that took place during the Triassic–Cretaceous–Tertiary period. The course of the Alpine Tethys geosyncline leads one to expect a marked influence of Variscan and even older structural elements.

In the *pre-Upper Carboniferous basement* of the Eastern Alps it is possible to distinguish several rock complexes that differ both lithologically and in terms of age, and which belong to the Lower Palaeozoic-Variscan *Ostalpin* and *Penninikum*. No reliably datable Precambrian and Cambrian are known. The sedimentary-volcanogenic (acid and basic) series of the Ordovician and Silurian have been deposited in an Upper Proterozoic–Lower Palaeozoic geosyncline and subjected to an intensive tectonometamorphic 'Caledonian event'. The formation of the Mittersill scheelite deposit is associated with the basic Ordovician volcanism.[19]

The *Variscan cycle* developed in a trough markedly divided up as regards morphology and facies and probably striking east–west, with carbonate and especially flyschoidal greywacke sedimentation in the Lower Carboniferous. As a result of the Variscan orogeny, which progresses from north to south, the series have been folded and generally strongly metamorphosed. Subsequently, the Variscan tectogene was subjected to denudation with the formation of continental limnic/fluviatile deposits (including Verrucano facies) in the Upper Carboniferous and Permian with acid volcanites ('subsequent' stage). Known mineralizations are the Alpine-overprinted spar deposit of the Styrian Erzberg (? Variscan initial volcanism) and the uranium deposits of the Upper Carboniferous and Permian. The *Frühalpidikum* (Triassic–Neocomian) manifests itself in the formation of the Alpine Tethys, resulting from the subsidence that occurred in the Lower Triassic (exemplified by the Werfen Beds). Where the subsidence continued it led to widespread dolomite–limestone formations during the Middle Triassic. During the Upper Triassic and Liassic the carbonatic area sank and manganese ores were formed there.

During the Dogger the consolidated Variscan basement underwent regeneration,[18] which led to the formation of the Rhine–Danube flysch trough. The possible formation of oceanic crust was maintained until the Lower Cretaceous, with varying minerogenetic effectiveness (ophiolite mineralization).

The *Altalpidikum* (Aptian–Eocene/Oligocene) is characterized by the subduction that begins in the Aptian and reaches its peak in the Campanian (Austric, Vorgosau phase). This was followed by a period relatively free from subduction that is reflected in a continental, limnic, shallow marine sedimentation regime and a southward drift of the ridges.[32] During the Palaeocene and the Eocene another strong subduction phase took place with subduction of the base of the Rhine–Danube flysch zone, the beginning of a plate collision between the southern edge of the Central European Platform and portions of the Alpine tectogene, the formation of the eastern Alpine nappes, piled-up bulges, andesite volcanism, granite intrusions and the formation and reformation of ore deposits. These processes took place during the Laramide, Illyrian and Pyrenean phases of the Alpine orogeny.

The *Jungalpidikum* (Upper Eocene to the present) includes the molasse stage associated with the largely consolidated tectogene that constitutes the Apline–Carpathian mountain belt. The Helvetic molasse trough expanded in the foreland of the tectogene.

Conditions were favourable to the formation of mineral deposits—for example, the gold veins of the Oligocene. The continuous stressing of the crust in the morphogene and the involved Molasse foreland on the Bohemian Massif, in the Western Carpathians, on the sub-Silesikum and in the still-existing flysch basin on the northern perimeter of the Carpathians were the expression of the Helvetic, Savic and Styric dislocation movements.

The individual zones of the Alpine geosynclinal (orogen) structure may be characterized as follows (Fig. 3).

Central Alps–Inner Carpathian zone
The crystalline basement includes large parts of the *Altkristallin* of the Eastern Alps. The most important rocks of the Altkristallin are the old granitic gneisses of the 'coarse gneiss series' with crystalline carbonate intercalations. These are associated with impregnative and lens-shaped mineralizations of magnetite and siderite, as well as pyrite, chalcopyrite, pyrrhotite, sphalerite, galena, native gold, graphite and molybdenite. The 'Zentral Gneissen' of the Hohe Tauern and their Palaeozoic 'Schieferhülle' (schist envelope of serpentinite, amphibolites, greenstone schists, quartzites and limestones) are known to contain pyrite, native gold and Mo–Cu–Pb–Zn-sulphide mineralization.[48] Also dating from the Palaeozoic are the 'Greywacke Zones' found both to the north and south of the Altkristallin. Large areas of the Ordovician–Silurian–Devonian sediments contain stratiform and lens-shaped (partly submarine hydrothermal) as well as metasomatic and discordant ore formations with Cu–Fe and W–Sb–Hg (Mitterberg type, Habach series/Felbertal), with Fahlerz-barite (Schwaz type), with Pb–Zn (Grazer Palaeozoikum) and siderite-ankerite–magnesite (e.g. Erzberg, Radmer). Among others, spathic magnesite deposits and strata-bound Zn–Cu–barite–fluorite and uranium mineralization occur again in the Carboniferous.[43]

The Inner Carpathian zone shows great similarities with the central 'Ostalpin'. In the core rocks (Tatra, Vepor), the pre-Upper Carboniferous basement is highly crystalline. Only in the Gemerides (Zips-Gömörer Mountains) is it less metamorphosed and lithologically can be classified, like the northern Greywacke Zone of the Eastern Alps, partly as Lower Palaeozoic subjected to a considerable Variscan orogeny. The oldest post-Variscan cover formation here is productive Upper Carboniferous, which extends from Gorny Slask in a southward direction. During the Permian continental conditions prevailed and subsiding graben were the sites of a typical Rotliegende sedimentation accompanied by a quartz porphyry volcanism.

Northern Kalkalpen (Calcareous Alps)
The transgression of the Alpine geosyncline began in the Lower Triassic (Scythian stage) over partly metamorphic Variscides. This stage is composed of variegated sandstones and shaley clays (Werfen Beds), sometimes with rock salt. The 1000-m thick Wetterstein limestone belongs to the Middle Triassic (Anisian and Ladinian stages). Following a period of regression (Carnian stage), during the Norian and Rhaetian stages of the Upper Triassic the predominantly carbonate sedimentation continued as the Hauptdolomit or Dachstein limestone. The overall thickness of the Eastern Alpine Triassic is about 2000 m. It is mainly of a shallow marine, miogeosynclinal character with a weak basic magmatism during the Middle Triassic. The carbonate rocks of the Triassic, up to 2000 m thick, form the Northern Limestone Alps. These display marked metallogenetic specialization (FeS_2, Cu, Pb, Zn, F, Ba, etc.), numerous submarine-hydrothermal-sedimentary (Bleiberg type) and metasomatic and structure-bound ore deposits being formed (Lechtal, Lafatsch).

During the Jurassic and Lower Cretaceous marine conditions continued to prevail with a marked division of the geosyncline into basins and ridges with repeatedly varying facies. During the Lower Cretaceous the first coarse detritus indicates the beginning of the Alpine orogeny. The massive Alpine nappe movements caused the sedimentary formations of the Eastern Alpine geosyncline to be pushed as far north as the Pennine area. The result is that today the Eastern Alps are the site of two structural units of different ages lying one on top of the other (Upper Cretaceous Eastern Alpine unit on the Early Tertiary Pennine unit). Toward the east, however, the vertically overlying position found in the Eastern Alps changes in the West Carpathians to lying side by side. Thus the Cretaceous central zone of the Western Carpathians is flanked by the flysch Carpathians on the north. The Eastern Alps continue as the Western Carpathians with the 'Ostalpin', a Penninic–Helvetic flysch and the Molasse zone.

Flysch zone
In the geosynclinal areas the Cretaceous and Early Tertiary periods brought the formation of flysch zones. These, several thousands of metres thick, take the form of rhythmically alternating beds of psammitic rocks (sandstones, greywacke, calcarenites) and pelitic rocks. Sedimentation is thought to have been caused by turbidity currents. Occasionally, 'chaotic' slide masses occur within the marine flysch ('Wildflysch', olistostromes).

These processes are closely connected with the orogeny. Although in the Ostalpin the orogenic movements proper occurred during the Middle Cretaceous, the flysch sedimentation began as early as the Lower Cretaceous. In the Penninikum it took place chiefly in the Upper Cretaceous, and the Helvetic flysch was formed mainly in the Eocene. From the Alps the Flysch zone extends continuously along the northwest perimeter of the interior Vienna Basin into the Western Carpathians.

As early as 1953 Stille,[45] in considering the orogenic Alpine magmatism, surmised that the area of Alpine orogeny was relatively lacking in plutonic intrusions. In the Western Carpathians there are several small occurrences of Cretaceous granite in the Gemerides. These occurrences are thought to be only the uppermost intrusive components of large, deeperlying batholiths. Part of the structure-bound mineralization in this zone (Fe, Cu, Pb, Zn, Ag, Sb, etc.) was attributed to this magmatism.[35,36] Greisen-type Sn–W–Mo mineralization and cassiterite–sulphide mineralization with more or less U, Nb and Ta are associated with minor intrusions.

Molasse zone (Alpine and Carpathian foredeep)
The Alpine orogeny (Cretaceous–Tertiary) was followed in the Alpine foreland by the formation of the Molasse basin. The Molasse sedimentation proper took place chiefly in the Oligocene and Miocene and was, in the main, composed of the material that was removed from the rising Alpine orogen. Fluviatile pebble beds ('Nagelfluh'), delta sediments in the form of sandstones and sandy shales are the main elements of the Molasse formation, which is up to 5000 m thick.

The basement of the Molasse basin of the Northern Alps is formed by the Moldanubikum, which gradually dips to the south with its terrestrial to epicontinental marine Mesozoic and Eocene cover. The axis of subsidence of the basin shifted from south to north.

The Northern Alpine Molasse Foredeep is continuous with the Carpathian Molasse Foredeep under the External Vienna Basin. Whereas in the Northern Alpine Molasse terrestrial-limnic sediments predominate (fresh water molasse, e.g. Gosau Basin), marine influences increasingly predominate in an eastward direction. Thus, to the east of Krakow the Miocene salt formation becomes the characteristic element of the Foredeep. The mainly pelitic series of beds includes, in total, four salt horizons, which form the basis for present-day potash mining. In addition to substantial deposits of raw materials for the construction and ceramic industries (quartz and moulding sands, diatomite and ceramic clays), these foredeeps contain deposits of anhydrite–gypsum and sulphur, as well as substantial quantities of brown coal.

Superposed Tertiary basins
The Alpine geosynclinal (orogen) superstructure is, in part, covered by deposits of more recent basin structures, which came into being after the conclusion of the Alpine orogeny (Oligocene–Miocene). Examples of this are the sedimentary basins that since the Later Miocene have extended from the Vienna Basin via the Pannonian Basin to the Caspian and Aral basins. Here during the latest stages of the Miocene and in the Early Pliocene sediments up to 3500 m in thickness were deposited under brackish or fresh water conditions, and these are associated with deposits of raw materials that are used in the construction and ceramic industries, and also of brown coal and oil and natural gas.

The subsequent magmatism is characterized by rhyolitic and andesitic rocks with late-stage basaltic volcanites. With this fault-tectonic controlled late Tertiary magmatism are associated substantial deposits of non-ferrous metals (e.g. the Slovakian Erzgebirge with the deposits of Banská Štiavnica and Kremnica—Au, Ag, Pb, Zn, Fe, Cu, Sb).[35,36]

References
1 **Andrussov D.** *Geologie der tschechoslowakischen Karpaten* (Berlin: Akademie Verlag; Bratislava: Slovak. Akad. Sci., 1964), 263 p.
2 **Baumann L. and Leeder O.** Paragenetische Zusammenhänge der mitteleuropäischen Fluorit–Baryt Lagerstätten. *Freiberger ForschHft.* C266, 1969, 89–99.
3 **Baumann L. Leeder O. and Rösler H. J.** Die Bedeutung des Fluorits als Rohstoff und seine lagerstättengeologische und minerogenetische Stellung. *Z. geol. Wiss.*, **8**, 1980, 1461–74.
4 **Baumann L. Leeder O. and Weber W.** Beziehungen zwischen regionalen Bruchstrukturen und postmagmatischen Lagerstättenbildungen und ihre Bedeutung für die Suche und Erkundung von Fluorit-Baryt-Lagerstätten. *Z. angew. Geol.*, **21**, 1975, 6–17.
5 **Baumann L. and Rösler H. J.** Zur genetischen Einstufung varistischer und postvaristischer Mineralisationen in Mitteleuropa. *Bergakademie*, **19**, 1967, 660–4.
6 **Baumann L. and Tischendorf G.** *Einführung in die*

Metallogenie–Minerogenie (Leipzig: VEB Deutscher Verlag für Grundstoffindustrie, 1976), 364 p.

7 **Baumann L. Tischendorf G. Schmidt K. and Jubitz K.-B.** Zur minerogenetischen Rayonierung des Territoriums der Deutschen Demokratischen Republik. *Z. geol. Wiss.*, **4**, 1976, 955–73.

8 **Baumann L. and Weber W.** Deep faults, simatic magmatism, and the formation of mineral deposits in Central Europe outside the Alps. In *Metallogeny and plate tectonics in the northeastern Mediterranean* **Janković S.** ed. (Belgrade: Faculty of Mining and Geology, University of Belgrade, 1977), 541–51. (*IGCP-UNESCO Correlation Project* no. 3)

9 **Belyaevskiy N. A. and Borisov A. A.** The role of basic intrusions in magmatically activated platforms and early folded structures. In *Tectonics, magmatism and locations of ore deposits* (Moscow: Nauka, 1969). (Russian text)

10 **Bernard J. H.** Kurze Übersicht der isogenetischen erzlagerbildenden Mineralassoziationen hydrothermalen Ursprungs im tschechoslowakischen Teil der Böhmischen Masse. *Cas. Miner. Geol.*, **12**, 1967, 13–20.

11 **Bernard J. H. and Baumann L.** Variscan paragenetic units of the mineralizations in the Bohemian Massif. *Freiberger ForschHft.* C345 (Topical report of IAGOD vol. VIII), 1977, 29–45.

12 **Borchert H.** Genetische Unterschiede zwischen varistischen und saxonischen Lagerstätten Westdeutschlands und deren Ursachen. *Freiberger ForschHft.* C209, 1967, 47–63.

13 **Brinkmann R.** Die mitteldeutsche Schwelle. *Geol. Rdsch.*, **36**, 1948, 56–66.

14 **Burret C. F.** Plate tectonics and the Hercynian orogeny. *Nature, Lond.*, **239**, 1972, 155–6.

15 **Chrt J. Bolduan H. Bernstein K. H. and Legierski J.** Räumliche und zeitliche Beziehungen der endogenen Mineralisation der Böhmischen Masse zu Magmatismus und Bruchtektonik. *Z. angew. Geol.*, **14**, 1968, 362–76.

16 **Frisch W.** Plate motions in the Alpine region and their correlation to the opening of the Atlantic ocean. *Geol. Rdsch.*, **70**, 1981, 402–11.

17 **Grumbt E. Ludwig A. and Meier R.** Materialien zum tektonischen Bau von Europa—tektonische Bruchstörungen. *Veröff. ZentInst. Physik der Erde* no. 47, 1976, map 7.

18 **Gwinner M. P.** *Geologie der Alpen* (Stuttgart: Schweizerbart'sche Verlagsbuchhandlung, 1971), 477 p.

19 **Höll R. and Maucher A.** The strata-bound ore deposits in the Eastern Alps. In *Handbook of strata-bound and stratiform ore deposits, volume 5: regional studies* **Wolf K. H.** ed. (Amsterdam, etc.: Elsevier, 1976), 1–36.

20 **Illies J. H.** Intraplattentektonik in Mitteleuropa und Rheingraben. *Oberrhein. geol. Abh.*, **23**, 1974, 1–24.

21 **Illies J. H. and Greiner G.** Regionales Stressfeld und Neotektonik in Mitteleuropa. *Oberrhein. geol. Abh.*, **25**, 1976, 1–40.

22 **Illies J. H. and Mueller St.** eds. *Graben problems: proceedings of an international rift symposium, Karlsruhe, 1968* (Stuttgart: Schweizerbart'sche Verlagsbuchhandlung, 1970), 730 p. (*Int. Upper Mantle Project Sci. Rep.* no. 27)

23 **Kölbel B.** Tektonophysikalische Vorgänge im mittleren und unteren Mantel bei der Bildung von Senkungsstrukturen. *Z. angew. Geol.*, **25**, 1979, 403–12.

24 **Kölbel B.** Beitrag zum Studium salinartektonischer Bewegungen. *Z. angew. Geol.*, **27**, 1981, 301–7.

25 **Kölbel H.** Regionalgeologische Stellung der DDR im Rahmen Mitteleuropas. In *Grundriß der Geologie der DDR, Band 1* (Berlin: Akademie Verlag, 1968), 18–66.

26 **Kossmat F.** Gliederung des variszischen Gebirgsbaues. *Abh. Sächs. geol. Landesamt* no. 1, 1927, 40 p.

27 **Kraus E.** *Die Baugeschichte der Alpen, II Teil: Neozoikum* (Berlin: Akademie Verlag, 1951), 489 p.

28 **Laubscher H. P.** Grundsätzliches zur Tektonik des Rheingrabens. In reference 22, 79–87.

29 **Leeder O. Weber W. and Baumann L.** Kontinentale Riftprozesse und ihre minerogenetische Bedeutung im postvariszischen Mitteleuropa. *Z. geol. Wiss.*, **10**, 1982, 501–10.

30 **Magnusson N. H.** Age determinations of the Swedish Precambrian rocks. *Geol. För. Stockh. Förh.*, **82**, 1960, 407–32.

31 **Nöldeke W. and Schwab G.** Zur tektonischen Entwicklung des Tafeldeckgebirges der Norddeutsch–Polnischen Senke unter besonderer Berücksichtigung des Nordteils der DDR. *Z. angew. Geol.*, **23**, 1977, 369–79.

32 **Oberhauser R.** ed. *Der geologische Aufbau Österreichs* (Wien: Springer Verlag, 1980), 699 p.

33 **Oberhauser R.** Das Altalpidikum. In reference 32, 35–48.

34 **Olszak G. and Thierbach H.** Einige geologisch-geophysikalische Strukturelemente der Norddeutsch–Polnischen Senke und ihre möglichen Beziehungen zu Tiefenbau und Entwicklung dieses Krustenabschnitts. *Z. geol. Wiss.*, **1**, 1973, 155–72.

35 **Petrascheck W. E.** Die alpin-mediterrane Metallogenese. *Geol. Rdsch.*, **53**, 1964, 376–89.

36 **Petrascheck W. E.** Die zeitliche Gliederung der ostalpinen Metallogenese. *Sber. öst. Akad. Wiss., m.-n. Kl., Abt. I*, **175**, 1966, 57–74.

37 **Pouba Z.** On some causes of the repetition of mineralization in ore regions and ore deposits of the Czech Massif. In *Symposium: Problems of postmagmatic ore deposition, volume II: lectures, short communications, discussion* **Štemprok M.** ed. (Prague: Geological Survey of Czechoslovakia in the Publishing House of the Czechoslovak Academy of Sciences, 1965), 82–9.

38 **Rösler H. J.** Bemerkungen zur Genese von Geosynklinalmagmatiten. *Rep. 21st Int. geol. Congr., Norden, 1960* (Copenhagen: Berlingske Bogtrykkeri, 1960), pt 8, 96–107.

39 **Rösler H. J. Baumann L. Lange H. Fandrich K. and Scheffler H.** Geosynklinalmagmatismus und submarinhydrothermale Erzlagerstätten. *Rep. 23rd Int. geol. Congr., Prague, 1968* (Prague: Academia, 1969), section 7, 185–96.

40 **Rösler H. J. and Werner C. D.** Zur stofflichen Entwicklung und strukturellen Stellung variszischer Initialmagmatite in Mitteleuropa. *Z. geol. Wiss.*, **6**, 1978, 967–83.

41 **Sattran V. and Cadek J.** Zur räumlichen Verbreitung varistischer, saxonischer und noch jüngerer Mineralisationen im Böhmischen Massiv. *Freiberger ForschHft.* C209, 1967, 65–71.

42 **Schmidt Kl.** Der altpaläozoische Magmatismus. *Z. dt. geol. Ges.*, **128**, pt 1 1977, 121–41.

43 **Schulz O.** Metallogenese im Paläozoikum der Ostalpen. *Geol. Rdsch.*, **63**, 1974, 93–104.

44 **Stille H.** Das mitteleuropäische variszische Grundgebirge im Bilde des gesamteuropäischen. *Geol. Jb., Beihefte*, no. 2, 1951, 138 p.

45 **Stille H.** Der geotektonische Werdegang der Karpaten. *Geol. Jb., Beihefte*, no. 8, 1953, 239 p.

46 **Thierbach H.** Zur Entwicklung globaltektonischer Anschauungen und deren Einfluß auf die Interpretation tektonischer Hauptelemente Mitteleuropas. *Z. geol. Wiss.*, **3**, 1975, 417–29.

47 **Tollmann A.** *Ostalpensynthese* (Wien: Verlag Deuticke, 1963), 256 p.

48 **Tufar W.** Zur Altersgliederung der ostalpinen Vererzung. *Geol. Rdsch.*, **63**, 1974, 105–23.

49 **Weber W. Baumann L. and Leeder O.** Zur minerogenetischen Bedeutung der Krustenbewegungen im Vorfeld der Osteuropäischen Tafel. *Z. geol. Wiss.*, **8**, 1980, 577–91.

50 **Weinhold G.** Zur prävaristischen Vererzung im Erzgebirgkristallin aus der Sicht seiner lithofaziellen und geotektonisch-magmatistischen Entwicklung während der assyntisch-kaledonischen Ära. *Freiberger ForschHft.* C320, 1977, 53 p.

51 **Zeman J.** Die Krustenentwicklung im präkambrisch und paläozoisch mobilen Europa außerhalb der Osteuropäischen Tafel. *Z. geol. Wiss.*, **8**, 1980, 393–404.

52 **Ziegler P. A.** Northwestern Europe: subsidence patterns of Post-Variscan basins. In *Geology of Europe from Precambrian to post-hercynian sedimentary basins* **Cogné J. and Slansky M. eds.** *Mém. BRGM* no. 108, 1980, 249–80. (*26th Int. geol. Congr., colloque* C6)

53 **Zoubek V.** Korrelation des präkambrischen Sockels der mittel- und westeuropäischen Varisziden. *Z. geol. Wiss.*, **7**, 1979, 1057–64.

Herwig F. Holzer

Austria

The Republic of Austria occupies about 84 000 km^2, roughly 70% of which can be attributed to the Alps and 30% to the forelands and the extra-Alpine Basement (Bohemian Massif). A map (Fig. 1) of the metalliferous and non-metallic mineral deposits[18,63] shows many hundreds of localities where such minerals are mined or have previously been worked. At present 65 mines are in operation (excluding coal and hydrocarbons). Six mines exploit metalliferous minerals and 56 produce non-metallics. The vast majority of Austria's mineral deposits lie in the Eastern Alps. The forelands, basins and the Bohemian Massif contain few deposits and these are mainly non-metallic. Production statistics are given in Table 1.

Mining has a long history in Austria. In prehistoric times Celtic–Illyric miners produced considerable quantities of copper. The total output of 'black' copper between 1800 and 100 B.C. is estimated at about 50 000 tonne. Graphite has been used in neolithic ceramics and rock salt has been mined in the Alps since about 900 B.C. (Hallstatt period, 800–400 B.C.). The Celtic people of Noricum were famous for their iron. This led to peaceful annexation by the Romans, who extended the border of their empire to the Danube in A.D. 15. Gold and silver have been mined since Roman times at numerous localities and precious metal mining reached its peak roughly between A.D. 1480 and 1560. The mines in Tyrol and Styria were then the leading producers in Europe. The Holy Ghost shaft at the Tyrolean Röhrerbühel had in A.D. 1600 a depth of 886 m and remained for 300 years the deepest shaft in Europe.

Metallogenic theories

The multitude of mineral deposits in various geologic units has attracted the attention of many researchers for the past hundred years. Consequently, a wealth of articles on this subject has been published. The origin and age of the Alpine deposits have remained a central theme and several convincing theories have been presented. Much, however, is still to be investigated before the Alpine 'enigma'[15] can be solved.

The first and for many years the generally accepted explanation of the origin of the Alpine deposits was elaborated by Petrascheck in 1926.[76] The roughly symmetric and spatially zoned distribution of the deposits (Au in the centre, Fe, Cu and Mg occurring with increasing distance from a hypothetical core and Pb–Zn in the peripheral zones) was assumed to derive from a geologically young (Tertiary) magmatic source

Table 1 *Production statistics**

Year	Commodity and tonnage		
	Iron ore	Lead–zinc ore	Copper ore
1950–54	12 340 000	677 000	463 000
1955–59	16 380 000	896 000	804 000
1960–64	18 290 000	965 000	664 000
1965–69	17 940 000	987 000	772 000
1970–74	20 760 000	1 724 600	984 000
1975–79	17 054 135	2 227 795	252 045
1980–83	13 120 000	3 216 360	—
	Antimony ore	Graphite (raw)	Magnesite (crude)
1950–54	57 000	84 600	3 605 000
1955–59	56 000	138 000	5 669 000
1960–64	83 700	459 900	7 999 000
1965–69	97 700	248 000	8 120 000
1970–74	98 100	114 600	7 462 000
1975–79	111 501	179 951	5 281 399
1980–83	105 998	125 375	4 514 180
	Talc	Kaolin	Feldspar
1950–54	290 500	1 037 300	13 400
1955–59	332 300	1 422 700	14 080
1960–64	380 400	1 720 900	17 300
1965–69	408 600	1 764 200	9 400
1970–74	465 600	1 584 500	8 850
1975–79	514 172	1 429 981	9 480
1980–83	472 353	1 410 443	25 326
	Barite	Gypsum	Anhydrite
1950–54	32 600	1 078 000	43 500
1955–59	46 700	1 898 500	597 700
1960–64	18 200	2 226 500	953 000
1965–69	9 700	2 775 000	732 000
1970–74	2 100	3 011 500	644 700
1975–79	1 099	3 234 380	623 956
1980–83	249	2 559 976	552 397
	Diatomite		
1950–54	17 200		
1955–59	20 100		
1960–64	21 300		
1965–69	15 900		
1970–74	13 900		
1975–79	4 230		
1980–83	—		

* After *Oesterr. Montanhandbuch*, B. Min. f. Handel, Gewerbe & Industrie, Montanverlag Wien, 1955–1983.

underneath the Central Alps. This was seen as indicative of a decrease in the temperatures of the ore-forming fluids towards the marginal zones. This theory of a 'uniform Alpine' origin (in the sense of an epigenetic origin in Late Cretaceous–Tertiary times) was later modified by a number of authors (Clar,[9] Friedrich,[18] W. E. Petrascheck[77,78] and others). They assumed that many ore-bearing solutions originated not from magmatic bodies but from young centres of recrystallization during the Alpine regional metamorphism, the thrust planes of nappes being the preferred loci of emplacement. Schneiderhöhn[90] suggested that the metals of the Alpine deposits were derived from Hercynian granites, so these metal concentrations would have to be considered as rejuvenated Hercynian deposits.

stage, syn-orogenetic type deposits and mineralization related to subsequent magmatic suites.

The new concept of global tectonics and plate movements has only been tentatively applied to the Eastern Alps.[38,79] Evans[15] suggested that the seeming paucity of post-Hercynian mineralization, especially the apparent absence of porphyry copper and Cyprus-type massive sulphide deposits, could best be explained by the assumption that subduction of oceanic crust did not take place on any significant scale during the evolution of the Alpine geosyncline or its subsequent deformation. Tischler and Finlow-Bates[143] concluded that the 'notably limited post-Hercynian mineralization of the eastern Alps is ... a direct function of the particular plate tectonic history of the region'.

There can, by now, be no doubt that plate tectonics

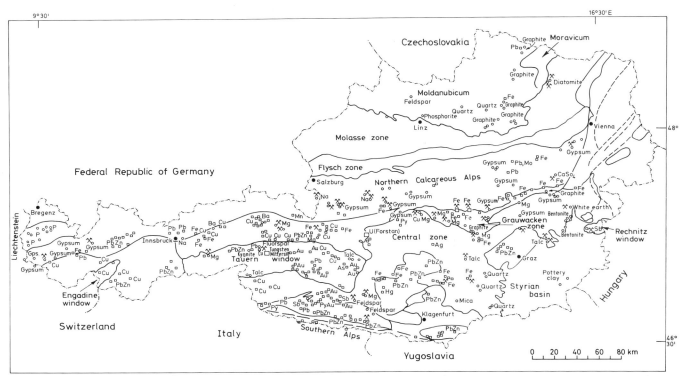

Fig. 1 *General map showing mineral deposits of Austria*

The concept of a uniform, predominantly Alpine metallogenesis was increasingly attacked by researchers who, from detailed studies, concluded that the great majority of the deposits are strata-bound and were formed more or less contemporaneously with their host rocks in Palaeozoic times (Höll, Maucher, Schroll, Schneider, Schulz, Tufar and others).[42,44,46,68,88,94,108,139a] Metamorphic, syn-sedimentary and diagenetic fabrics were described and syngenetic models of deposition were postulated. In 1968 Friedrich[23] reviewed the eastern Alpine deposits again and distinguished between those of pre-Hercynian, Hercynian and Alpine ages. The Alpine deposits he divided into mineralization of the geosynclinal

have played a significant role in the evolution of the Alpine orogeny as in other orogenic systems worldwide. The recent series of earthquakes in the Italian region of Friuli and in adjoining parts of Carinthia, Austria, can be interpreted as a result of the continuing northward movement of the African plate. The recognition of the ophiolite nature of major Palaeozoic ultramafic massifs in the Central Alps of Styria provides evidence for plate tectonic processes connected with the Hercynian orogeny in the Eastern Alps. A considerable amount of research work is still required before a comprehensive model for the plate tectonic evolution of the Alps will be available.

The present author considers the Alpine mineral

deposits as products of a polycyclic development in which the Alpine orogenesis had an important role. They comprise various genetic types and range in age between pre-Hercynian and late Tertiary.

Main tectonic-metallogenic units

Mineral deposits in Bohemian Massif (extra-Alpine basement) and its platform cover

Geology
The Austrian sector of the Bohemian Massif consists of an eastern unit of epi- to mesozonal metamorphics with some pre-Devonian granitic-tonalitic intrusions, the *Moravikum*. The western unit, the *Moldanubikum*, is built of meso- to katazonal metamorphics that were intruded by widespread Hercynian granites, granodiorites and syenites. Most authors agree that the Moldanubikum was thrust eastwards over the Moravikum during the Hercynian orogenesis. The Hercynian structures dip gently southwards under the Alpine chains: a wildcat hole drilled in the Calcareous Alps of Lower Austria, about 30 km south of the present border of the Calcareous Alps, penetrated Bohemian basement rocks at 3015 m. The extra-Alpine basement is cut by major faults that caused considerable horizontal and vertical displacements. Late Hercynian faults were rejuvenated during the Alpine orogenesis. The major faults are of metallogenic importance in the adjacent countries of Germany and Czechoslovakia.

The Austrian sector of the Bohemian Massif is deeply eroded and peneplained and only small relics of the former platform cover (e.g. Permian sandstone) are preserved in places. Beneath the sediments of the Alpine foreland (Molasse Zone), however, the platform cover (intersected by numerous oil wells) consists of sedimentary strata of Upper Carboniferous, Permo-Triassic and Jurassic to Palaeogene age. During the Oligocene and Miocene a marine transgression inundated parts of the Bohemian Massif and marine to brackish sediments were deposited on the basement.

Mineral deposits
The Austrian sector of the Bohemian Massif contains only a few occurrences of metal deposits, none of them as yet of economic interest. Recently, several indications of scheelite mineralization have been found. These, and some geochemical anomalies at the margins of Hercynian granites, are presently being investigated.

Iron Skarn-type magnetite deposits (Fe 20–30%) were worked between 1817 and 1885 at Kottaun near Geras and at some other localities.[49] *Limonitic alteration products* of pyrite-bearing graphite schist and *limonite concretions* in Tertiary sediments were used in small iron works during the last century.

Lead Traces of galena in marble had already been investigated by 1539 near Drosendorf. Some galena in granite at Lauterbach is only of mineralogical importance.

Graphite Metasediments of the Moldanubikum are the host rocks of numerous graphite deposits that can be traced from the Danube valley northwards to the Austrian border. About one hundred occurrences are known, generally bound to a marble–paragneiss sequence. Most of the deposits are of the mesocrystalline type with an average carbon content of 40–60%.

The ore represents a graphite breccia in which graphitic components are embedded in a quartz-feldspar (–tremolite–mica) matrix, pyrite being omnipresent. As accessories, diopside, rutile, sphene, tourmaline, apatite and, in places, corundum were determined. Secondary minerals—clay minerals, limonite, opal, jarosite, etc.—abound near the surface.[50]

Some small *flake-type graphite* (mega-crystalline) deposits occur on both sides of the Danube near Artstetten and around Schärding in Upper Austria. They were mined in small underground workings in the last century and prior to the second world war.[50]

The mesocrystalline graphite deposits, intermittently mined since 1813, reached considerable importance when it was discovered that graphite lump ore could be employed successfully as an additive in the mix of the Donawitz steel works, acting as carbon source in the metallurgical process by partly replacing coke. The SiO_2 content of the graphite also proved useful since quartzite has to be added for the flux of the carbonate iron ore of the Erzberg type. Graphite production started in 1958 from the Zettlitz mine and, after the deposits near Mühldorf were developed, reached its peak between 1962 and 1965 with a yearly production of 60 000–90 000 tonne. In 1967 a sharp decline resulted from increasing production costs and falling prices for coke and graphite mining for metallurgical purposes decreased in 1968. From 1958 to 1968 the total graphite production from the Moldanubikum was approximately 450 000 tonne.

Kaolin There are two groups of kaolin deposits in the Austrian sector of the Bohemian Massif—the Kriechbaum and Weinzierl deposits near Schwertberg, Upper Austria (about 25 km east of the provincial capital of Linz) and the deposits of Mallersbach and Niederfladnitz near the town of Retz in Lower Austria.[52]

Kriechbaum and *Weinzierl* are situated on downthrown blocks that represent *in-situ* formations in Hercynian granite. The maximum depth of kaolinization is about 40 m and the exploitable thickness averages 12–13 m. The overburden consists of marine clay and sand (Oligocene) and some Quaternary gravel. The raw kaolin contains about 34% kaolinite. The deposits are worked in underground mines. The overburden, up to 100 m thick, causes high pressure and heavy timbering is required.

Mallersbach and *Niederfladnitz* open-pit mines are situated in shallow depressions partly delineated by faults. The parent rocks are, respectively, strongly laminated orthogneiss and a pre-Devonian granite. The overburden consists of Quaternary clay and soil. The deposits are interpreted as weathering products, kaolinization being aided by the influence of peat and lignite seams in the overlying strata. The kaolinite content of the Mallersbach–Niederfladnitz deposits averages 44%, quartz and mica making up the rest of the material.

Apart from the above deposits, some occurrences of kaolinized rocks and kaolinitic clays and sands are partly exploited for ceramics and tiles.

The yearly production of raw kaolin during the last ten years (both groups of deposits) amounts to about 200 000 tonne. Reserve figures are not available.

Feldspar and quartz Some pegmatites in Upper and Lower Austria were occasionally worked for feldspar and quartz. The output was small and only of local importance. At present, no production is recorded.

Vermiculite Small occurrences of vermiculite in serpentinites cut by aplitic dykes were recently discovered. Their economic potential is under investigation.

Mineral deposits in Alpine Foreland (Molasse Zone) and in intramontane basins

Geology

The Bohemian Massif and its platform cover are overlain in the south by sediments of the Molasse Zone. These are clastic marine to fresh water deposits of Palaeogene to Middle Miocene age. They are succeeded by fluvial gravels and lacustrine deposits with lignite seams. In northwestern Austria Pleistocene moraines cover large areas. The Molasse sediments in western Austria have a thickness of up to 4000 m. Structurally, the Molasse Zone can be divided into two different units—the flat-lying, little disturbed Molasse beds situated at some distance from the front of the Alps and Carpathians and the Sub-Alpine and Sub-Carpathian Molasse close to the Alpine chains. The Alps and Carpathians were thrust over the Molasse during the Lower and Middle Miocene, which caused complicated imbrication structures. Boreholes in the Alpine Flysch Zone, drilled 7 km south of the Alpine front, penetrated Molasse rocks underneath Flysch strata.

The *Vienna Basin* is limited by deep-reaching faults (its western border is marked by a number of thermal springs) and is filled by dominantly marine deposits of Middle to Upper Miocene age, by lacustrine beds (Lower Pliocene) and fluvial deposits (Upper Pliocene to Quaternary). The total thickness is more than 5500 m. Several small, intramontane ('inner-Alpine') basins were downfaulted along Alpine structures. Some were filled by Upper Eocene to Lower Miocene, partly marine sediments (with coal seams), others consist of marine to fluviolacustrine strata (with lignite) of Miocene to Pliocene age. The Tertiary basins bordering the Hungarian Plains represent former inlets and gulfs in the eastern marginal zone of the Alps in the vicinity of the cities of Eisenstadt and Graz. Dominantly clastic, Middle Miocene to Lower Pliocene sediments (with lignites) reach a thickness of up to 4000 m.

The eastern border of the Alps is affected by important faults and flexures. The *Pannonian (Hungarian) Basin* proper was downfaulted during the Pliocene. Some Miocene andesites and basalts were extruded at the eastern border of the Alps.

Mineral deposits

Phosphates Phosphorite-bearing sands occur in the area of Eferding–Prambachkirchen and Plesching, east of Linz. They overlie Oligocene sand and clay and represent beach deposits. The phosphorite grain content is about 3%. The ore-bearing sands are 2 to 11 m thick. The reserves are estimated to be in the neighbourhood of 400 000–500 000 tonne of phosphorite (grain content) with 23–25% P_2O_5. The deposits were investigated during and after the last war, but were not put into production.

Diatomite Deposits near Eggenburg (Limbach and Oberdürnbach) have been worked for many years. The diatomite is used for the production of insulating materials. The small mines produce about 5000 tonne per annum. Large unexploited deposits of diatomite-bearing clay occur in the basin of Aflenz (Styria), where the diatomite beds reach a thickness of more than 10 m. Other occurrences were discovered recently near the Austrian–Czechoslovakian border (Herrenbaumgarten), but quality and quantity have not been investigated. All the diatomite deposits occur in Oligocene and Miocene strata.

Bentonite, illite and trass For several years after the second world war Austria maintained a small production of *bentonite*. Small deposits are located in Styria (Gleichenberg, Friedberg, etc.) and represent altered tuffaceous layers of late Tertiary volcanics. At present all workings are abandoned. *Illitic clays*, partly explained as former crater lake deposits, are worked at Fehring and Kapfenberg (Styria) and at Andorf (Upper Austria) for the production of Leca (light expanded clay aggregate). The yearly production amounts to 300 000–400 000 tonne. *Trass*, a term applied for altered trachytic-andesitic rocks with hydraulic properties, is mined in the Gleichenberg area of Styria. The yearly production is 25 000–30 000 tonne. Mineralogically, the trass consists mainly of opal and is used for the production of hydraulic lime.

Eastern Alps*

The term 'Alps', *sensu lato*, comprises the French, Italian, Swiss and Austrian Alps. From a geological-

---

* In summarizing the main geological-structural units of Austria, the author has followed Oxburgh's outstanding paper[74] on the geology of the central Eastern Alps, in which the difficult task of translating and defining German terminology into English was solved with great care and understanding.

geomorphological point of view, the Austrian Alps represent the *Eastern Alps*. They extend for about 500 km in an east–west direction and form an elongated zone of mountain ranges. In the region of the upper Rhine they pass westwards into the Western Alps and at Vienna eastwards into the Carpathians. The northern boundary is marked by a distinct topographic contrast with the low hills and plains of the foreland. The southern limit is assumed to run along the Gail valley ('Gailtal' Line), the Judicarian Line and the Insubric Line. The mountains south of this boundary are known as the *Southern Alps* and are regarded geologically as part of the *Dinarides*. Only small parts of the Southern Alps are within the borders of Austria.

The Eastern Alps are built of a pile of allochthonous sheets, often extending laterally for hundreds of kilometres but usually little more than a few kilometres thick. The mountain-building process, the Alpine orogenesis, reached its peak in Cretaceous–Tertiary times and frontal movements of the Calcareous Alps continued into the Miocene.

Geology
The Eastern Alps are divided into a *Northern Zone*, which contains mainly sedimentary rocks of Permo-Triassic to Eocene age and Palaeozoic metasediments and volcanics, and a *Central Zone*, which consists dominantly of igneous and metamorphic basement rocks, overlain by a series of Palaeozoic, Triassic, Jurassic and Lower Cretaceous strata that are generally weakly metamorphosed.

Mineral deposits
The *Northern Zone* is made up of three structural and metallogenic units. These are the Flysch and Helvetic Zones, the northern Calcareous Alps and the Grauwacken Zone.

In the first of these units thrust sheets consisting of alternating beds of marl, shale and sandstone with graded bedding represent original shallow marine deposits that were transported by turbidity currents into deep troughs for final deposition. Their age is Lower Cretaceous to Middle Eocene. The so-called *Helvetic Zone* or Helvetikum is formed of thrust slices of Jurassic to Lower Cretaceous sediments beneath the Flysch Zone and in the form of klippen along the front of the northern Calcareous Alps.

The only *mineral occurrence of the Helvetic Zone* of any significance is that of *phosphorite beds* in quartzitic sandstone of Lower Cretaceous age in western Austria (Vorarlberg Province) in the environs of Bezau, Götzis and Feldkirch. The phosphorite-bearing strata are about 1 m thick and contain approximately 10% P_2O_5. Although large quantities are available, the deposits are considered uneconomic because of the low grade, environmental considerations and the fact that the steeply dipping beds would have to be mined underground.

The Flysch Zone, thrust over Molasse sediments in the north, is itself overthrust in the south by the nappes and thrust sheets of the northern Calcareous Alps. They extend from the Rhine to Vienna and form a belt of conspicuous mountains 20–40 km wide. They consist predominantly of carbonate rocks of Triassic and, locally, of Jurassic and Lower Cretaceous age. Upper Cretaceous to Eocene sedimentary strata ('Gosau Beds', locally coal-bearing) deposited in places on the Mesozoic strata provide an age-indicator for movements in the Calcareous Alps.

Lead–zinc Some 60 occurrences of lead–zinc mineralization are known in the northern Calcareous Alps of Austria. Many small mines existed in the past, but few lasted into the twentieth century. Most of the deposits are concentrated in the western sector between the Arlberg and the area north of Jenbach and appear to be bound to a single tectonic unit, the Inntal Nappe. In the central and eastern sectors Pb–Zn mineralization is scarce and scattered and only the deposits around Annaberg and Türnitz in Lower Austria had some economic significance in the last century. At present none of the deposits is mined. The paragenesis* is galena (cerussite), sphalerite (wurtzite, smithsonite, hemimorphite, etc.), pyrite/marcasite, wulfenite, fluorite, barite, celestite, calcite and dolomite. Some microscopic inclusions of Cu–Sb–As minerals are only of mineralogical interest.

The ores occur mainly in Upper Triassic limestone (Wetterstein-Kalk), but a few are reported to belong to Anisian and Carnian stage carbonates (Middle to Upper Triassic). The orebodies are partly stratabound, partly in the form of veins, lenses, fissure-fillings and pipes. A Triassic age is generally accepted. The genesis is discussed later.

The deposit at Lafatsch[139] (east of Scharnitz) was examined by underground exploration. The potential ore reserves are estimated at about 1 000 000 tonne. Exploitation would, however, cause considerable hydrologic difficulties as a number of communities draw their water supply from this particular mountain range. Further potential reserves of lead–zinc ore are thought to exist in the Heiterwand area (north of Imst), but the deposits have not been investigated underground by modern exploration methods.

Iron A number of supergene iron deposits (e.g. concentrations of limonitic alteration products of sedimentary pyrite, 'sphaerosiderites', formed by chemical processes in coal seams and limonite fillings of karst cavities) were occasionally exploited in small mines for local consumption.

In the Abtenau–Werfen area (Salzburg) limonite-siderite (ankerite–breunnerite) ore in shallow depressions of the Lower Triassic Werfen Beds was mined. The mineralization is bound to a mylonitic horizon at the base of the Calcareous Alps and was of some

---
* Paragenesis is used here with the European meaning of mineral association and *not* for paragenetic sequence.

economic importance. The deposits were explained by Friedrich[23] as being syn- to post-tectonic, whereas Heissel[39] assumed a sedimentary origin. The ore reserves are exhausted and the mines closed. Similar mineralization from the Arlberg area was described by Koch[59] as of post-tectonic, hydrothermal-metasomatic formation.

Iron–manganese ores At some locations in the Calcareous Alps small bodies of manganiferous siderite (with ankerite–dolomite) and their oxidation products were mined in the last century. Although of no economic importance, these occurrences were interpreted as metasomatic replacement deposits in Triassic and Jurassic limestones, indicative of an Alpine age.

Manganese ores These deposits are strata-bound, being concentrated in laminated marls and limestones (Lower Toarcian–Lower Jurassic). The ore minerals are carbonates of the system $CaCO_3$–$MnCO_3$–$FeCO_3$, with minor amounts of braunite and pyrolusite, which are associated with sedimentary iron minerals such as hematite, goethite, chamosite and pyrite. Germann[28] proved a volcanogenic-sedimentary origin, celadonite-bearing tuffaceous layers being found in the manganese carbonates.

Among these deposits, that of Lechtaler Alpen, Tyrol (Eisenspitze, Dawin Alpe), contains several manganiferous beds with a total thickness of 2–10 m. The estimated reserves are 2 500 000–3 000 000 tonne of ore with 13–14% Mn, 7–8% Fe and 20–25% SiO_2 (plus CaO, MgO and CO_2). At Wader Alm, Hammwald, Tyrol (northeast of Innsbruck), there are similar occurrences. Small-scale mining took place in the last century. The Mn content is 10–29%. The Kammerling Alm deposit near Lofer, Salzburg, contains manganiferous beds 10–15 m thick. Probable reserves total about 3 000 000 tonne and possible reserves 20 000 000–30 000 000 tonne of at least 22% Mn. At Lammereck-Strubberg, Tennengebirge, Salzburg, about 3 750 000 tonne of manganiferous marls has Mn contents of 12–15% and at St. Leonhard near Salzburg there are small deposits with about 28% Mn. These have no economic significance.

Processing of the above ores has proved to be difficult. The deposits are small, the metal content is low and the high mining costs prevent development under present economic conditions.

Bauxite Of the few bauxite deposits of Austria (Brandenberg, Tyrol; Großmain, Wagrein, Salzburg; Hieflau, Styria; and Dreistetten, Lower Austria), only the deposits of *Unterlaussa* (Upper Austria) were of economic significance. All the deposits occur at the base of the Upper Cretaceous Gosau Beds on top of Triassic carbonates.

The Unterlaussa deposits consist of separate, lenticular and axially deformed bodies that pass laterally into conglomerates and are generally overlain by a thin veneer of carbonaceous shale and bituminous coal. The mine was opened in 1939. In the 1950s the yearly production reached about 20 000 tonne. Owing to the relatively high SiO_2 content of the ore (7–9%) and high production costs, mining ceased in 1964. The run-of-mine ore had an Al_2O_3 content of about 53%. In the bauxite ore grains of carnotite were found and the overlying carbonaceous shales contain some minor enrichments in uranitite. Separate mining of these minerals is impossible because of their small tonnage.

Uranium In 1970 Schulz and Lukas[92] found several radioactive anomalies in Upper Permian sandstone (Buntsandstein) of the Fieberbrunn–Hochfilzen area (Tyrol). Mineralogical studies revealed enrichments of pitchblende and coffinite with minor pyrite, chalcopyrite, bornite and other copper minerals. The economic potential of these finds is apparently low.

Other anomalies have been detected in Upper Permian–Lower Triassic rocks (Werfen Beds) at the base of the Calcareous Alps in the Werfen area (Salzburg) and at other locations, but no economic deposit has been opened up.

Gypsum–anhydrite The northern Calcareous Alps contain a large number of gypsum–anhydrite deposits. The majority are of Upper Permian age. Others belong to the basal rocks of the Triassic sequence, the Scythian Werfen Beds. In western Austria evaporite horizons also occur in Upper Triassic (Carnian) horizons. In 1973 twelve mines were in operation, total production being 720 000 tonne of gypsum (about 600 000 tonne from opencast operations) and 160 000 tonne of anhydrite (50% from open-pits).

Large deposits remain untapped because of environmental considerations, terrain difficulties or hydrologic reasons. The largest producer in 1973 was Puchberg mine (Lower Austria, 144 544 tonne), followed by Moosegg (Salzburg, about 80 000 tonne) and Hallberg (Salzburg, 76 114 tonne).

Most deposits consist of an anhydrite stock, often of large depth extension, with a mantle of gypsum of variable thickness. Host rocks are red, argillaceous sandstone and grey, gypsiferous clay (Werfen Beds) or grey sandstone and shale of the Upper Triassic (Carnian).

Rock salt Rock-salt mining in Austria is historically a state monopoly. Total salt production in 1981 was 2 500 000 m^3, produced by underground and borehole solution mining. Austria's salt deposits are restricted to the 'Hallstatt facies' of the Calcareous Alps—a deepwater facies of pale-coloured, red and black shales and pelagic limestones. Locally, there are manganiferous horizons. The fauna consists of ammonites, monotids and microfossils. The thickness of this Triassic sequence may reach 1000 m.

The Upper Permian is represented by the thick saliferous (gypsum, anhydrite and halite), argillaceous 'Haselgebirge' Beds, followed by Lower Triassic Werfen Beds and Gutenstein Limestone and Dolomite. In the Middle and Upper Triassic the Halobia Beds and the Zlambach Marls are distinct argillaceous

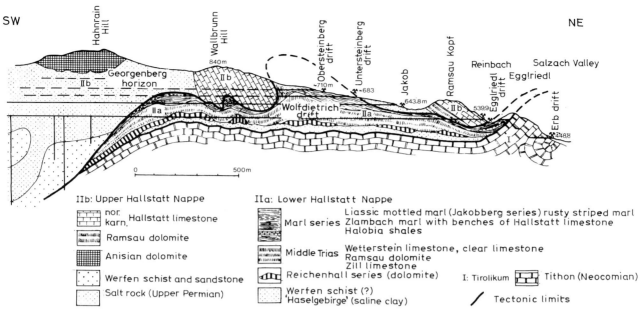

Fig. 2 *Geological cross-section through Hallein salt deposit. After Medwenitsch[147]*

units; the Hallstatt Limestone is the main carbonate rock.

The Haselgebirge is subdivided into various sub-units (grey, green, black Haselgebirge, Rotsalzgebirge, etc.). Some authors interpreted this rock as a sedimentary breccia; others have involved a tectonic origin. Mafic tuffs and isolated diabase were encountered in the saline strata.

The Haselgebirge is an untextured argillaceous sediment of brecciated appearance: rounded fragments of dark and reddish clay and shale, marl and argillaceous sandstone of varying size are embedded in a matrix of haliferous clay. In places, this rock grades into dark, bituminous shale ('Glanzschiefer', 'lustrous shale'). The Haselgebirge encloses halite crystals and irregular masses of dense halite (white, grey, red), often accompanied by anhydrite and minor amounts of polyhalite, glauberite and astrakhanite (bloedite). Loeweite, kainite, langbeinite, vanthoffite, kieserite and sylvine are rare.

In 1981 the following mines were in operation: Altaussee, Hallstatt (underground solution mining), Bad Ischl and Sulzbach (partly borehole mining) and Dürrnberg near Hallein (underground solution mining). The salt mine of Hall in the Tyrol was recently closed for economic reasons. The average NaCl content of the salt brines produced in the various mines is 0·3 tonne/m^3. The proven reserves will permit a steady production for 140 years. Fig. 2 shows the structural setting of the Hallein salt deposit.

The *Grauwacken Zone* consists predominantly of low-grade metamorphics such as phyllites, quartzites and isolated carbonate rocks. Metabasalts and metadolerites as well as metamorphosed quartz porphyries are important in places. They were compared with the geosynclinal spilite–keratophyre association.[109] Stratigraphically, the Grauwacke rocks range from Lower Palaeozoic to Upper Carboniferous. They are divided into an upper (mainly Carboniferous) unit and a lower (Lower Palaeozoic) unit. The Grauwacken Zone dips northwards under the Calcareous Alps and is bordered in the south by steep fault contacts against the rock units of the Central Zone.

Copper Many copper deposits occur throughout the Grauwacken Zone (and in adjacent quartz-phyllite areas) and a number of these were mined in earlier times. The deposits are concentrated in three areas.

In the *Schwaz–Brixlegg district* (Tyrol), apart from some occurrences of siderite, most of the deposits are of vein-type tetrahedrite mineralization in Lower to Middle Devonian dolomite. Minor amounts of stibnite, chalcopyrite, galena, pyrite and orpiment with barite and quartz as gangue have been found. The mineralization was interpreted as Alpine (Upper Cretaceous) because Triassic carbonates of the adjacent Calcareous Alps are mineralized in places. Recently, Schulz[138] described these mineralizations as layered, strata-bound ores in Devonian beds with associated mineralized breccia and vein deposits interpreted as later-remobilized Hercynian and Alpine mineralization.

The many ancient mines of the *Kitzbühel district* (Tyrol) and the above-mentioned district were important copper–silver mining centres during medieval times. Mining activities ceased in the seventeenth and eighteenth centuries. Repeated later efforts at reopening failed and a drilling programme at the formerly famous Röhrerbühel mine had to be abandoned in 1970 because of strong local opposition to mining in this Alpine resort area. Only the former Schwaz copper mine is now working. It produces dolomite in underground operations (80 000–100 000 tonne per annum). The Kitzbühel deposits occur in Lower Palaeozoic phyllites. The bleached wallrock ('Falbenschiefer') proved to be a rutile-rich sericite–chlorite–phyllite. The paragenesis is tetrahedrite and chalcopyrite, with minor amounts of pyrite and traces of linnæite, millerite, pyrargyrite, hematite, etc. Quartz, dolomite and Fe carbonates are the gangue. Vohryzka[111] assumed an Upper Cretaceous age; Schulz[93,94] considered the deposits to be hydrothermal-sedimentary and related to Lower Palaeozoic submarine volcanics.

The *Mitterberg district* (Salzburg) contains probably the largest copper concentration in the Eastern Alps. The total potential of the Mitterberg area is estimated at about 240 000 tonne of copper metal. Up to 1973 about 120 000 tonne had been extracted, including prehistoric production. Modern mining commenced in 1829. The metal content of the ore was about 1·4% Cu. The underground workings had an extent of some 40 km. Three main adits and four shafts gave access to a main ore vein of a total length of 11 km, 0·2–4 m in thickness and 460 to 520 m in minable vertical extent. The vein strikes west–northwest and dips 40–80° south. Six major faults displace the vein down towards the west and, to a lesser degree, towards the north. Three shorter, northwesterly trending ore veins, south of the present mine, were worked in earlier days and similar mineralization occurs east of the Salzach River. All these mines have been abandoned.

The Mitterberg deposit lies at the northern fringe of the Grauwacken Zone near the boundary with the Calcareous Alps. The host rocks are:

Green Series—saline, green shales and mudstones with anhydrite and gypsum, attributed to the Upper Permian–Lower Triassic
Violet Series—? Upper Carboniferous, weakly metamorphosed slates, quartzites and siltstones
Grey Series—Lower Palaeozoic phyllites and sericite-quartzites

The paragenesis is chalcopyrite, some pyrite and minor amounts of tetrahedrite, hematite, arsenopyrite, maucherite and pentlandite with traces of Ni–Co–Sb arsenides. The gangue is quartz and carbonates. Traces of a pitchblende–gold paragenesis were found on an old mine dump, and fine-grained brannerite–uraninite occurrences were detected at several locations[135] in the Violet Series.

The Green Series form an impermeable cap rock in which the ore vein peters out (see Fig. 3). The main ore vein intersects the bedding and the foliation of the host rocks, which are distinctly bleached next to the vein. Radioactive dating of the pitchblende–gold ore (presumably originating from mobilization and reconcentration of the primary uranium content of the Violet Series during emplacement of the ore vein) gave an age of about 90 m.y. All this indicates an Upper Cretaceous emplacement of the Mitterberg main vein, or at least intensive mobilization and reconcentration during the Alpine orogenesis. Bernhard[5] and Weber et al.,[115] however, assumed a late Hercynian age for Mitterberg as well as for most other ore deposits of the Grauwacken Zone. Mitterberg mine closed in 1976 for economic reasons. The reserves include 2 500 000 tonne of probable ore and 3 500 000 tonne of possible ore all running at about 1·4% copper.

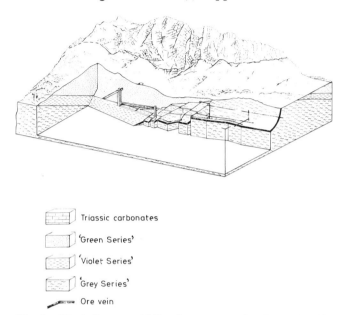

Fig. 3 *Block diagram of Mitterberg copper mine. Reproduced by courtesy of Kupferbergbau Mitterberg GmbH*

Cu–Ni–Co ores In the Leogang area (Salzburg) complex Cu–Ni–Co ores were mined intermittently from A.D. 1550 until the first world war. The mineralization appears to be bound to Lower to Middle Devonian dolomite of the Grauwacken Zone and is concentrated along thrust planes and fracture zones. A late Hercynian age for the deposits has been assumed by some authors; others favour a hydrothermal, Alpine origin. The paragenesis is Hg–tetrahedrite, cinnabar, niccolite, chalcopyrite (malachite, azurite), bornite, chalcocite, galena, pyrite and native silver besides siderite, ankerite and aragonite.[35]

Pyrite (with/without Cu, As, Pb) At many points in the Grauwacken Zone pyrite deposits accompanied by varying amounts of pyrrhotite (Ni), chalcopyrite, arsenopyrite, galena, sphalerite, cubanite, valleriite, etc., and with quartz and siderite as gangue, were mined from the fourteenth to the nineteenth century. Some small mines were worked until the years after the second world war. Most of these deposits are lenticular orebodies in phyllites. Some are apparently linked to Lower Palaeozoic metadolerite; others show no relations to volcanic suites. A submarine, syngenetic origin during the Hercynian geosynclinal phase has been assumed. The ore mineralogy of the deposits can be quite complex.[124,140]

Iron deposits The many iron deposits of the Grauwacken Zone are solely of the siderite type and siderite and its oxidation products have been mined since early medieval times. At present only *Erzberg* mine is in operation.

The Styrian Erzberg, the largest ore mine in Austria, is in the northeastern part of the Grauwacken Zone near its boundary with the Calcareous Alps. The stockwork-like orebody, mainly an intergrowth of siderite and ankerite, occupies a large syncline of mineralized Lower to Upper Devonian limestone and is divided by a barren slate horizon into basal and hanging-wall orebodies (see Fig. 4). The Devonian carbonates are underlain by metakeratophyres and overlain by transgressional formations of the Lower Triassic, which, in places, are also mineralized.

The paragenesis is siderite, ankerite and calcite, accompanied by some pyrite, arsenopyrite, chalcopyrite, tetrahedrite, hematite and cinnabar. In the oxidation zone hematite, limonite, calcite and aragonite, malachite and azurite, gypsum and traces of quicksilver and native copper have been described.

For many years the Erzberg was recognized as a typical metasomatic replacement deposit, formed during Upper Cretaceous times. The evidence cited for this was that the siderite–ankerite mineralization was not affected by any regional Alpine metamorphism, that metasomatic iron replacement can be observed in the mechanically deformed basal conglomerates of the Triassic and that similar, although much smaller, siderite–ankerite bodies also occur in Triassic limestones of the Calcareous Alps. Recently, Hajek[37] considered the Erzberg-type deposits to be primary (Hercynian) diagenetic-volcanic-exhalative deposits widely remobilized and recrystallized in Alpine times.

Detailed geochemical, structural and stratigraphical investigations[118b,119,123,142] showed that the Erzberg-type siderite deposits were formed in several phases. An early sedimentation process was related to Devonian and Lower Carboniferous volcanism. During the subsequent orogenic phases strong recrystallization connected with metasomatic replacement of carbonate rocks took place. Beran[118b] showed that the Fe-rich ankerites were formed at temperatures of about 400°C and pressures of 2–3 kbar.

The run-of-mine ore contains 30–33% Fe, 1·5–2% Mn, 7% CaO, 3–4% SiO_2 and some MgO and Al_2O_3. Present annual production is about 3 800 000 tonne, 80% of which comes from opencast mining on 30 benches that cover an area of 3·5 km^2, the rest coming from underground operations. The reserves consist of 32 700 000 tonne of proven ore and 166 000 000 tonne of probable ore.

The adjacent, geologically and genetically identical (although much smaller) deposit of Buchegg–Radmer has proved reserves of 5 500 000 and 3 400 000 tonne of probable reserves. The production was about 250 000 tonne per annum. This mine was closed in 1979.

Numerous other siderite deposits occur in the northeastern sector of the Grauwacken Zone and in the basal beds of the overlying Triassic, which have been mined in the past. For some of them the same genetic model as for the Erzberg deposit has been suggested. Others were probably formed in a sedimentary environment in Lower Triassic times and were recrystallized during the main phases of the Alpine orogeny.[127]

Manganese In the Veitsch mountains (Styria) two small mines produced in the late nineteenth century some 20 000 tonne of manganese ore with rhodochrosite, rhodonite, psilomelane and pyrolusite. The ore occurs in Devonian limestone and is probably of sedimentary origin.[33]

Magnesite Two types of magnesite deposit are known in Austria—the spathic, coarse-grained type 'Veitsch' and the cryptocrystalline type 'Kraubath', which are genetically linked with ultramafic rocks.

Spathic magnesite bodies occur throughout the Grauwacken Zone from the Semmering in the east to Hochfilzen on the Tyrolean–Salzburg border, in Lower Palaeozoic quartz-phyllites (Innsbruck Quartz-Phyllite Unit) of the Zillertal (Tyrol) and in Palaeozoic metasediments of the Central Zone (Radenthein in Carinthia and Breitenau in Styria). Small deposits of cryptocrystalline magnesite have been worked in previous years in the ultramafic massif of Kraubath (Styria) Central Zone.

Altogether, some 40 magnesite deposits are known, five of which are presently being exploited; the others are either reserve fields or are too small or of low quality. For practical reasons all the deposits are described in this section, though some deposits should be dealt with under *Central Zone*.

The spathic magnesites of the Eastern Alps are genetically linked with dolomites, limestones and associated graphitic slates and sandstones, ranging in age from Upper Gotlandian to Upper Carboniferous. Bedding and cockade textures from some deposits have been described, but the majority represent an undisturbed growth of crystalline aggregates, apparently unaffected by any major metamorphism. Metasomatic replacement phenomena have been widely described and, consequently, the deposits were explained as true metasomatic developments in which the calcium of the carbonate rocks had been replaced by hydrothermal magnesium-rich solutions. The latter were thought to have been derived mainly from ophiolitic complexes. Most researchers have attributed these processes to the Cretaceous–Tertiary Cycle, but others have assumed a Hercynian age.

Siegl,[97] Höll and Maucher[46] and Lesko[64] considered the magnesites as Palaeozoic, syn-sedimentary

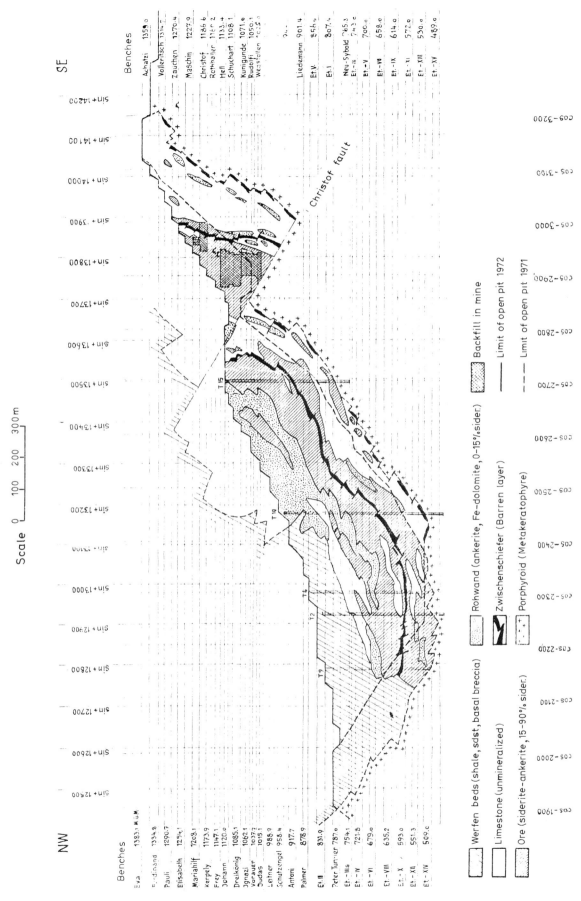

Fig. 4 Vertical section of Styrian Erzberg. After Voest-Alpine AG

deposits, the magnesium being derived from submarine volcanism. Mostler[73] proved the Tyrolean–Salzburg magnesite deposits to be linked to a certain lithofacies with no relations to volcanic suites or a saline facies and assumed a Hercynian age for the metasomatically formed deposits. As a source of the Mg solutions he suggested the adjacent carbonate rocks with chloride solutions being derived from their connate waters. Morteani and co-workers[131] analysed rare-earth elements and their distribution pattern in various magnesite deposits. Their work indicates magnesian metasomatism by hydrothermal solutions during the Alpine and/or Hercynian regional metamorphisms.

Sedimentary magnesite occurs in Permian and Lower Triassic (Scythian) sediments; numerous occurrences of magnesite are known.[97,132] They are of no economic significance, but are of genetic interest. Magnesite was formed during early diagenesis in a hypersaline, intra-supratidal environment (coastal sabkha) by reaction of pre-existing carbonate with magnesia-rich brines.

In 1981 five mines produced 1 400 000 tonne of crude magnesite—one-third from open-pits and two-thirds from underground operations. There are no data available on reserves. The total reserves of Austria are estimated at about 75 000 000 tonne.

Scheelite–magnesite Scheelite mineralization was detected in the magnesite deposit of Tux (Tyrol) in 1957 and the mineral was recovered as a by-product of the magnesite mine until 1971.[116] Total production was about 120 000 tonne of crude ore with a tenor of about 1·22% WO_3. The reserves are exhausted. Minable scheelite enrichments occurred at the contacts between carbonate bodies and the country rock (phyllites) and as rich ore shoots within the magnesite–dolomite. Scheelite stringers in the surrounding phyllites were too poor for exploitation.

Höll and Maucher[46] postulated a sedimentary (Lower Devonian–Upper Gotlandian) origin, linked to basic submarine volcanism, and attributed this deposit to Maucher's Early Palaeozoic 'Sb–W–Hg Formation'.[69]

Cryptocrystalline magnesite This type of magnesite was mined until 1961 in the Kraubath area (Styria, Central Zone), where an ultramafic complex[141] contains an irregular network of magnesite veins, pipes and fissure fillings. The deposit was seen as formed by ascending CO_2-rich thermal solutions.[111] Lesko[64] explained the deposit as weathering products of serpentinite formed under appropriate climatic, oxidizing conditions.

Barite Near Kitzbühel (Tyrol) widespread barite mineralization was mined for some time. The barite, which occurs in Devonian dolomite, is linked to the 'Spielberg Dolomite' (Devonian). Mostler[73] assumed a primary sedimentary deposition with subsequent concentration by lateral secretion in Late Hercynian (Upper Carboniferous Permian) phases.

Talc In the marginal parts of the magnesite deposit of *Oberdorf* (Styria) talc was mined between 1860 and 1962. The fairly pure, metasomatically formed talc is accompanied by dolomite, magnesite, quartz and minor pyrite, chalcopyrite, marcasite, celestite, leuchtenbergite, sepiolite and palygorskite.[31] Similar deposits occur at Lassing, Mautern and Kammern (all in Styria); only Lassing is in operation.

Graphite The second graphite district of Austria is linked to Upper Carboniferous phyllites and conglomerates (Grauwacken Zone), between the Semmering Pass (Lower Austria) and St. Michael (Styria), where numerous deposits were mined in the past. At present the mines of Kaisersberg and Sunk–Hohentauern are in operation. The graphite is of the microcrystalline type with a carbon content in the crude ore of between 40 and 90%. The lenticular, axially deformed orebodies represent metamorphosed coal seams and are exploited by underground mining.[58] The production is 15 000–20 000 tonne per annum and the reserves are (Kaisersberg plus Sunk) 160 000 tonne proven and 1 500 000 tonne probable and possible.

The *Central Zone* also consists of three units. In structurally ascending order these are the Pennine Zone, the Lower East Alpine Unit and the Central Zone, *sensu stricto*.

The *Pennine Zone* (Penninikum) consists of parautochthonous, late Hercynian granitoids ('Central Gneiss') in the form of domes and tongue-shaped bodies with a cover of pre-Hercynian polymetamorphic rocks (amphibolites, feldspathic schists, gneisses) and widespread, low-grade metasediments and metavolcanics ('Schieferhülle') to which a Permo-Triassic to Lower Cretaceous age has been ascribed. The Pennine Zone appears in a major tectonic window ('Tauernfenster') some 40 km wide and 170 km long. To the west the Penninikum is again exposed in the smaller Engadine Window on the Swiss border and in the Rätikon range, from where this unit continues into the Pennine Zone of Switzerland. Pennine rock units are also believed to crop out at the eastern margin of the Alps and near Rechnitz on the Hungarian border.

The Pennine Zone represents the basement over which the East Alpine nappe sheets were thrust from south to north, and all Pennine rock units were affected by epi- to mesothermal metamorphism during the Alpine orogenesis. The ultramafic rocks and the greenschists of the Schieferhülle are considered to be true ophiolites.

Gold Gold mining in the Hohe Tauern dates back to late Neolithic times and a veritable gold rush occurred in Italy in 130 B.C. when Polybius reported rich gold finds in the Alps of Noricum. From the late fifteenth to the early seventeenth centuries gold mines flourished and annual production is estimated at between 200 and 2600 kg of gold. Advancing glaciers and the incipient exhaustion of the deposits led to a decline, though mining continued into the nineteenth and, in places, the twentieth centuries. A rehabilitation of Radhausberg mine between 1938 and 1941 resulted in a production of some 200 kg of gold and 1000 kg of silver, but the mines were finally abandoned. The Pasel adit near Gastein (Salzburg) is presently used for medical purposes because of its high temperature and the significant radon content of the mine air.

The gold ore veins of the Tauern mountains follow conspicuous fault lines ('Fäulen'), which intersected the central gneiss as well as the metamorphics of the Schieferhülle.[57] The young, hydrothermal veins contain quartz, auriferous pyrite, gold, arsenopyrite, chalcopyrite, argentiferous galena, sphalerite, tetrahedrite, pyrrhotite, magnetite and siderite and have quartz, carbonate and chlorite as gangue.

The silver content increases in veins intersecting the Schieferhülle. The primary ore is said to have had a gold tenor of 8–10·6 g/tonne, which was much higher in the surficial zones of enrichment. The centres of gold mining in Salzburg and Carinthia were the Ankogel–Sonnblick Gruppe (Rauris, Gastein) and the Glockner Gruppe around Heiligenblut and Fusch.

Auriferous arsenopyrite was mined in quartz-phyllites of the Ziller Valley (Tyrol) and at Schellgaden–Rotgülden (Salzburg). Placer gold was panned, mainly in the seventeenth and eighteenth centuries, in the Rivers Salzach, Drau, Möll and Mur and even in the Danube.

Recent re-examination of Alpine gold deposits has produced new data. An occurrence in the Ziller Valley (Tyrol) has been described as a stratiform, sedimentary, gold-bearing, sulphide deposit[138] confined to quartzite layers in the Lower Palaeozoic. The abandoned Schellgaden mine (Salzburg) carries tellurides with galena in a gold-bearing sulphide assemblage that occurs in quartzitic layers of a schistose sequence.[134,135] The Waschgang deposit (Carinthia) contains syngenetic and remobilized gold–sulphide mineralization in a Mesozoic ophiolite complex.[134]

Molybdenum Pneumatolytically altered aplite veins in granitic gneiss of the Alpeiner Scharte (south of Mt. Olperer, Tyrol) contain irregular amounts of molybdenite and steeply inclined veinlets. The occurrence was explored between 1938 and 1945, but was found to be of too low a grade for mining in this extreme Alpine elevation.

Tungsten (Scheelite) Scheelite crystals in various rocks of the Pennine Zone and the superimposed Lower East Alpine Unit are known from hydrothermal quartz veins, as fissure fillings and in sulphide deposits. The discovery of the scheelite deposit at Tux triggered systematic prospecting and, based on the concept of Maucher's Sb–W–Hg Formation, Höll[43] and his collaborators explored large sectors of the Central Alps. Numerous scheelite deposits were discovered, the largest and most promising being in the Felbertal near Mittersill (Salzburg).

The distribution of major scheelite occurrences in Austria is shown in Fig. 5; Mittersill is at present the only producing mine. It is situated 9 km south of the town of Mittersill in the Central Hohe Tauern (Eastern Alps). The deposit is topographically divided by the Felbertal into two sections—the Ostfeld and the Westfeld. The deposit was discovered in 1967 in the

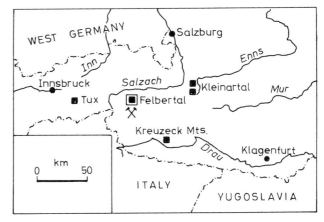

Fig. 5 *Major scheelite occurrences in Austria. From Stumpfl*[140a]

course of a prospecting campaign conducted by Maucher and Höll of the Department of Geology and Mineralogy, Munich University. This discovery was remarkable because it was the first successful demonstration of Maucher's theories[69] on the syngenetic formation of tungsten, antimony and mercury deposits. By 1973 the orebody had been explored by two exploration adits, several exploration shafts and 6400 m of core drilling. Mining activities commenced in 1975 and the ore dressing plant started operations in 1976. Scheelite concentrates are further processed in the Bergla tungsten smelter, Styria. The latter and the mine are operated by Wolfram Bergbau- und Hüttengesellschaft m.b.H., which is owned by Metallgesellschaft Frankfurt, West Germany (47·5%), Voest-Alpine Corporation, Austria (47·5%) and Teledyne Corporation, U.S.A. (5%). Production in 1978 was 291 140 tonne of ore with an average grade of 0·65% WO_3, yielding a WO_3 content of 1954 tonne.

Geology and petrology The Mittersill scheelite deposit is situated in the Pennine Unit of the Lower Schist Cover of the Hohe Tauern (Fig. 6); locally, the term 'Habach Series' has been applied to that unit. The general situation on the northwestern flank of the Granatspitz Dome results, in the 'Ostfeld', in medium to steep northerly dips with east–west strike. The 'Westfeld' is situated lower and shows a 45–95° dip to the northwest, with 070–090° strike. The 'Habach Series' is several 1000 m thick and consists of metamorphosed clastic sediments and submarine lavas and tuffs (termed 'the Eruptive Sequence'), of probable Lower Palaeozoic age. The Eruptive Sequence can be subdivided into Footwall Schist, Lower Hornblendefels Cycle, Intermediate Schist, Upper Hornblendefels Cycle and Hanging-Wall Schist. Its total thickness

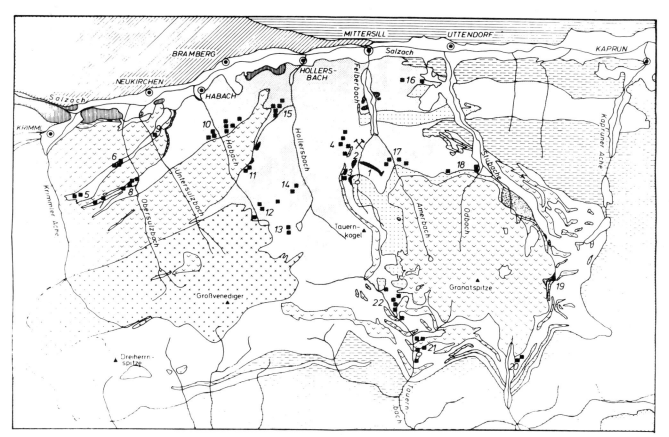

Fig. 6 *Scheelite occurrences in Hohe Tauern area. From Höll[126a]. Finely dotted = Habach Series within Schist Cover; x = granitic and v = tonalitic Central Gneiss; coarsely dotted = basal amphibolites; horizontal stripes = Greywacke Zone; diagonal stripes = Quartz-Phyllite Zone. '1' = Felbertal deposit, Ostfeld; '2' = Felbertal deposit, Westfeld. Other numbered occurrences are at present not of economic significance. Scale: width of map = 47 km*

exceeds 1500 m. Mineralization is strata-bound and confined to the lower part of the Eruptive Sequence. It can be followed along strike over several kilometres and over a thickness of 400 m.

The scheelite-bearing series is characterized by distinct intercalations of volcanic rocks of varying composition. These include ultramafics (now hornblendites and amphibolites), tholeiites (now schists and 'prasinites'), quartz-keratophyres (now albite-gneisses) and rhyodacites (now porphyroid gneisses). A characteristic feature of the Mittersill deposit is the strata-bound intercalation, or crosscutting penetration of all the above main rock types with fine-grained quartzites, which are not encountered anywhere outside the ore zones. There appears to be a distinct spatial and, probably, genetic association of quartz content and mineralization.

The distinct structural and compositional differences between the Ostfeld and the Westfeld are ascribed to the complex interplay of volcanism, sedimentation and mineralization taking place in two adjacent sub-basins. These are separated by a palaeogeographic ridge, which did not, however, prevent the joint evolution of major features, such as the two hornblendefels cycles.

Ore mineralogy Major ore minerals include scheelite, which frequently dominates quantitatively; it may occur as isomorphous intergrowths with powellite. Pyrrhotite may be the most widespread opaque mineral in some ore types; chalcopyrite, molybdenite and bismuth minerals are widespread, but rarely dominant. Pyrite is rare; the prevalence of pyrrhotite can be interpreted as a primary depositional feature and not as a result of metamorphism. In the Ostfeld sulphide ores are rare; in the Westfeld they may contribute up to 5% to the bulk of the ore, thus attaining some economic significance. Molybdenum contents in scheelite do not exceed 1% of total WO_3.

Three generations of scheelite may be distinguished.

About 95% of the scheelite in the Ostfeld occurs in layers with medium grain size of 0·05 mm in a quartzite matrix. These mineralized quartzites occur as concordant horizons with up to 5-m thickness, or as repetitive bands and lenses of centimetre thickness in all the above-mentioned rocks of basic to acid composition. Excellent sedimentary fabrics are revealed by this type of scheelite if viewed in ultraviolet light and have been discussed by Höll and co-workers.[45]

In the Westfeld scheelite of the second generation

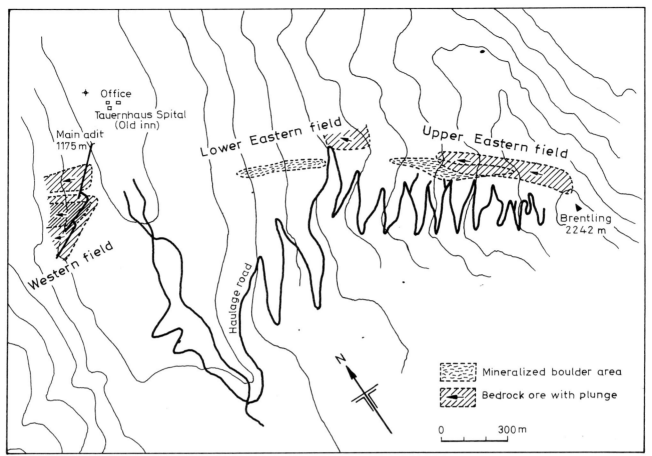

Fig. 7 *Locality map, Mittersill scheelite mine. Difference of altitude is almost 1100 m over horizontal distance of 2000 m. Reproduced by courtesy of Dr. R. Vaché, Wolfram Bergbau GmbH*

prevails; up to centimetre-size scheelite–powellite porphyroblasts occur strata-bound in banded quartz stockworks, together with sulphide ores.

In the Westfeld molybdenum-free scheelite crystals of the third generation, up to several tens of centimetres in size, are found in so-called 'Alpine-type mineral veins' in association with quartz, beryl and carbonates. This scheelite is not of economic significance.

Minor constituents of the ore mineral association include sphalerite, galena, Hg-bearing tetrahedrite, arsenopyrite, galenobismutite ($PbBi_2S_4$), cassiterite and tantalite, as well as Bi, Ag and Au.

The location of the two main areas of mining activity is shown in Fig. 7.

Economic mineralization in the Ostfeld, which extends from 800 to 2200 m above sea-level, is limited to a sequence 50–100 m thick within the 'Lower Hornblendefels-Zyklus'. Within an area 2000 m long and 50–150 m thick there are several elongate lens-shaped orebodies several hundred metres long and of a maximum thickness of 30 m. The 'compositional axis' of the orebodies in the Ostfeld runs parallel to the eastern slope of the Felbertal; up to 90% of the ore in these orebodies can therefore be recovered by opencast methods. Medium WO_3 contents average 0.75%; in pure ore quartzites this may increase to 3.5% WO_3.

A part of the deposit was removed in postglacial times from its original geological position and occurs as a coarse scree below the outcrops. It was in these scree slopes that mining activities commenced in 1975.

In the Westfeld the 'Upper Hornblendefels-Zyklus' and part of the hanging-wall schists are mineralized. The mineralized series has been separated into two parts by the tectonic emplacement of unmineralized 'Basisschiefer'. The Westfeld deposit crops out over 500 m. Within a mineralized thickness of 300 m (Fig. 8) six economic horizons have been established so far. Within these horizons mineralization occurs in orebodies 60–200 m long and 3–20 m thick the compositional axis of which plunges towards the northwest. Economic mineralization (which should be at least 2 m thick at a cutoff grade of 0.3% WO_3) is not sharply differentiated from the country rock either vertically or laterally. Intercalated 'barren' rocks frequently carry 0.15–0.25% WO_3 over thicknesses of tens of metres. Mineralization of the Westfeld with an average content of 0.45% WO_3 is not as rich as the higher concentrations of ore in the Ostfeld (Fig. 9). The total potential reserves of the Westfeld are, however,

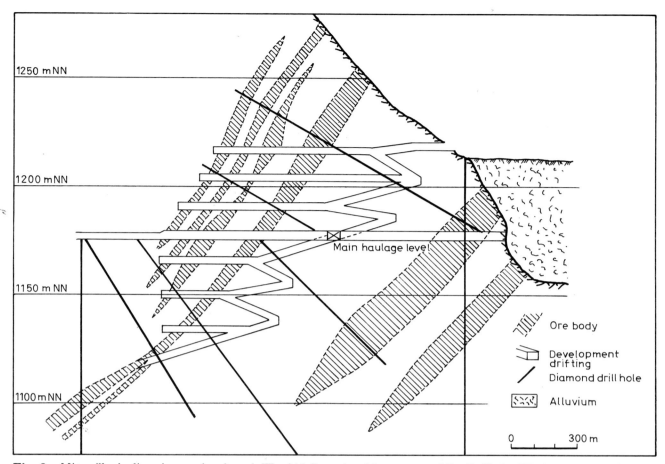

Fig. 8 *Mittersill scheelite mine: section through Westfeld. Reproduced by courtesy of Dr. R. Vaché, Wolfram Bergbau GmbH*

expected to be significantly larger than those of the topographically limited Ostfeld. Underground mining in the Westfeld commenced in October, 1978.

The Mittersill deposit is interpreted as a typical example of time- and strata-bound syngenetic mineralization linked to mafic submarine volcanism. Intense Lower Palaeozoic (? Ordovician–Silurian) magmatic activity culminated in the two Hornblendefels cycles. It was associated with the development of hydrothermal systems that led to the issue of metalliferous solutions through vents on the sea-floor. These were rich in SiO_2 and deposited metal-rich silica gels—the precursors of the present ore quartzites. The extensive distribution of (non-economic, $<0.3\%$ WO_3) scheelite mineralization in all rock types of the series testifies to the continuity of these processes and explains the fact that most orebodies are not sharply delineated but defined by cutoff grade. Crosscutting mineralization may present both remnant 'mini-stockworks' established during the early stages of mineralization and remobilization during the Variscan and Alpine metamorphic events.

Further scheelite occurrences in the Kleinarl valley near Wagrein (Salzburg) are being explored. Scheelite deposits in quartz-phyllite of the Schladming area (Styria) have recently been investigated.

Copper Cupriferous pyrite in Palaeozoic phyllite and in Mesozoic greenschist was previously mined at Brenntal–Untersulzbach and Grossarl (both in Salzburg), at Grossfragant (Carinthia), at Bernstein (Burgenland), in the Engadine Window and at some other locations in the Pennine Zone and the Lower East Alpine Unit. Most deposits were described as layered pyrite impregnations, the ore having about 1% Cu and, in places, traces of Au and Ag. All the mines are abandoned and the remaining ore potential is believed to be of little importance. One of the larger deposits, Grossfragant, was described by Prey[84] as being of syngenetic-sedimentary formation, closely related to Jurassic volcanism and metamorphosed during the Alpine orogenesis.

Antimony A mineralized, east–west-trending fault system in weakly metamorphosed calc-slate has been mined at Schlaining (Burgenland) for many years. The almost monomineralic stibnite ore (with traces of cinnabar, sphalerite and pyrite) occurs generally in the topmost section of the calc-slate, next to the contact with the overlying greenschist.[114] Maucher[69] assigned the Schlaining deposit to the early Palaeozoic W–Hg–Sb Formation and assumed a Palaeozoic age. Recently discovered microfossils, however, proved an upper Jurassic–Cretaceous age of the host rocks. Genetic

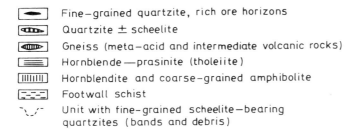
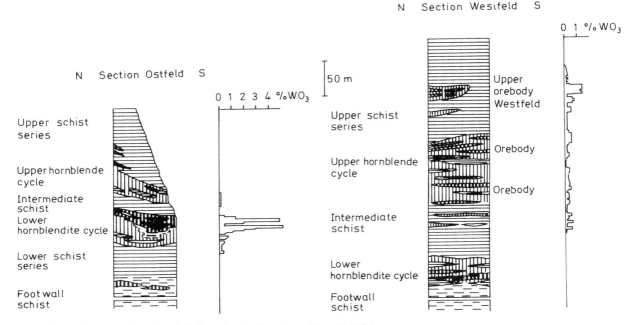

Fig. 9 *Generalized stratigraphy of Felbertal scheelite mine. After Höll[126b]*

relations to adjacent late Tertiary volcanics have been assumed, but the origin of the deposit is still unknown.

In total the mine has produced about 500 000 tonne of ore to date with a grade of 3–5% Sb. The ore of the veins of the south Vincent sector, which is at present being mined, averages 3% Sb. The reserves are about 80 000 tonne of proven and probable ore.

Formerly, other stibnite deposits were mined in phyllites of the Central Zone (Drau valley, Carinthia–East Tyrol). The grade and reserves are believed to be too low for modern mining. Recent exploration in the Kreuzeckgruppe has revealed additional stibnite occurrences. Lahusen,[62] who identified subordinate scheelite and traces of Mo, Pb, Cu and Hg in ore samples of the abandoned mines, explained the deposits as strata-bound, related to early Palaeozoic volcanism, with a subsequent (Hercynian) deformation and metamorphism.

Reimann and Stumpfl[137] have conducted geochemical investigations with the use of X-ray fluorescence and microprobe analysis techniques to clarify the association of strata-bound stibnite and massive sulphide deposits with amphibolite-facies metavolcanics and with metasediments in the Kreuzeck Mountains. The results obtained show that the amphibolites were originally emplaced as ocean-floor basalts, and that mineralization is not exclusively associated with basic rocks but also with intermediate and acid volcanic rocks. This extends Maucher's original concept of a Sb–Hg–W association linked to basaltic rocks.

A conceptual model for the formation of these deposits now includes submarine volcanicity of basic to acid affinity, probably in a shallow back-arc basin, associated with exhalative activity and intermittent clastic sedimentation. Petrological evidence clearly does not favour a spreading situation similar to that of the Red Sea. The ore environment of the Kreuzeck deposits does not differ significantly from that of many strata-bound base-metal deposits within metamorphosed Palaeozoic volcanosedimentary sequences in the Eastern Alps. New exploration concepts for strata-bound stibnite deposits should consider the relevant plate tectonic situation and the significance of acid and intermediate volcanic rocks, in addition to the basic association.

Lead–zinc–fluorite South of Hollersbach (Salzburg) a Pb–Zn deposit in a greenschist–epidote–amphibolite–marble sequence has been intermittently mined since the fifteenth century; it is presently abandoned.

The paragenesis is sphalerite (with Cd), galena, minor chalcopyrite, pyrite, arsenopyrite and greenockite. The gangue of quartz and carbonates carries considerable amounts of fluorite (up to 30% of the total ore). The deposit is unimportant as a metal source, but it probably is the largest fluorite concentration known in Austria.

Kyanite Kyanite-bearing schist in the Wolfendorn area (Brenner Pass, Tyrol) and kyanite–quartzites of the Untersulzbach valley (Salzburg) were thought to be of some economic potential[55] and concentration tests were successfully conducted. The extremely rugged Alpine terrain and transport difficulties proved, however, to be a serious obstacle to mine development.

The *Lower East Alpine Unit* rests upon the Pennine Zone and consists of some pre-Hercynian metamorphics, quartz-phyllites of undefined age (? Palaeozoic) and a weakly metamorphosed sedimentary sequence from Upper Carboniferous to Lower Cretaceous in age.

Uranium Promising anomalies in Lower East Alpine metasediments were recently discovered at Forstau near Schladming (Salzburg–Styrian border). Subsequent drilling, trenching and tunnelling proved a fine-grained uraninite mineralization (with traces of sulphides) linked to carbonaceous matter in sericite schists and quartzites of ?Upper Carboniferous to Permo-Triassic age. The schistosity of the host rock intersects the strike of the ore layers at a high angle. The deposits are interpreted as U enrichments in a marginal marine to deltaic-fluviatile environment. The U content of the ore is about 0·1%. The reserves to date are estimated at 1800 tonne of U metal. Underground exploration and extraction tests were abandoned in 1981 because of the drop in the uranium price.

Other uranium indications have been found in Permo-Triassic quartzites and schists of the Semmering Window (at Rettenegg, Styria) and in similar rocks near Tweng (Salzburg), which were explored unsuccessfully. Uranium occurrences in the Eastern Alps have been described by Erkan.[122]

Gypsum and anhydrite The weakly metamorphosed Mesozoic sequence of the Semmering Window contains in places deposits of high-quality gypsum in Upper Triassic (Keuper) slates and phyllites. The deposits represent dome-shaped anhydrite stocks with a gypsum mantle and were mined at Göstritz and Haidbachgraben (Lower Austria) and east of Kindberg (Styria) in underground mines. Mining ceased in the 1960s because of the exhaustion of reserves.

Barite A small production of barite is derived from barite veins in the Kleinkogel (Lower Austria), which occur in faults between Permo-Scythian Semmering quartzite and Triassic limestone of the Semmering Window.

Leucophyllite (mica-kaolin) Leucophyllites are chlorite–muscovite–quartz schists (with or without kyanite). The Fe-free chlorite is known as leuchtenbergite. Rocks of this type are mined at Aspang (Lower Austria) and at Weisskirchen (Styria). After processing the so-called 'mica-kaolin' is used as a mineral filler and for other industrial purposes, similar to those for true kaolin. The deposits were formed in zones of high stress in orthogneiss by introduction of Mg, Si and OH and by removal of Na, K, Ti and Ca. The Mg solutions were probably derived from the serpentinization of ultramafics during the tectonic movements of the Alpine orogenesis.[72] The leucophyllite production is some 200 000 tonne per annum. No figures for reserves are available.

Talc The major part of Austria's talc production comes from the Rabenwald area (eastern Styria). The deposits are flat layers and cigar-shaped bodies with strong axial deformation, formed by an intensive Mg metasomatism that affected fault planes between a micaschist–orthogneiss series and a quartzite–marble–pegmatite–amphibolite series.[16] The talc ore is accompanied by dolomite, magnesite, breunnerite, leuchtenbergite, kyanite and minor apatite, rutile, fuchsite and sulphides. The mines of the Rabenwald district produce about 70 000 tonne of raw talc per year. No reserve figures are available.

The *Central Zone, sensu stricto*, consists of various metamorphics of different lithologies: ortho- and paragneisses, amphibolite, micaschist, ultrabasics, greenschist, marbles and migmatites. The grade of metamorphism ranges from kata- to epizonal and the rocks often show the effect of local retrograde Alpine metamorphism and multiple folding. The rocks are believed to range in age from Precambrian to Lower Palaeozoic.

In places above the basement series there are Palaeozoic to Mesozoic sequences, locally fossiliferous and generally of low-grade metamorphism. These strata are believed to represent either parts of the original sedimentary cover (though subsequent thrusting and folding has erased much of the primary structures), or part of an allochthonous thrust sheet that rode over the basement complex from the south.

Iron At Hüttenberg, Carinthia, the siderite mine of the Hüttenberger (Carinthian) Erzberg (which closed in 1978) produced about 230 000 tonne of siderite ore (32–35% Fe, 3–4% Mn and 10–12% SiO_2) per annum. The deposit consists of numerous separate orebodies that have been mined since Roman times. The former rich zone of oxidation and its limonite ore is exhausted. About sixty different orebodies are known that contain several thousand to several hundred thousand tonnes of ore each. The siderite bodies were thought to have been formed by epigenetic-hydrothermal replacement of marble within an amphibolite–eclogite–garnet–micaschist–gneiss series.[8] Apart from Fe carbonates, pyrite, quartz and baryte occur in some quantities. Meixner[70] has described a host of other minerals, among them the famous löllingite and Cu, Ag, Ni, Co, Sb and As sulphides, various oxides and carbonates, sulphates, phosphates and silicates. A genetic relationship with the young gold mineralization of the Penninikum and with long abandoned Au–As veins at Kliening (Lavant Valley, Carinthia) has been assumed.

Fuchs,[125] from a detailed petrofabric analysis of Hüttenberg, concluded that a mobilization of already existing iron had taken place during the Hercynian orogeny and that this 'metasomatic' deposit was derived from a concentration of pre-metamorphic sedimentary iron. This opinion was refuted by Clar and Meixner,[118e] who considered the formation of the orebodies to have been by replacement of certain marbles and final precipitation from hydrothermal solutions in open cavities.

A small but valuable production (1974, 10 000 tonne) of specularite (hematite) ore is derived from the Waldenstein (Carinthia) mine, situated north of Hüttenberg. The ore occurs in similar host rocks to those at Hüttenberg and is believed to be of the same origin.

Mercury Some 25 occurrences of cinnabar are known in Austria, but few are of economic significance. The abandoned deposits of the Turrach (Styrian–Carinthian border) occur in phyllitic slates, quartzites and metadolerites of Lower Palaeozoic age. Höll[43] explained the deposits as strata- and time-bound formations; Friedrich[20] as hydrothermal, early Alpine mineralization. At Stockenboi-Buchholzgraben (west of Paternion, Carinthia) there are cinnabar impregnations in a phyllite–sericite–quartzite–metatuffite sequence, which were mined intermittently. Exploration work in 1968 was abandoned because of negative results. The cinnabar deposit at Glatschach near Dellach (Drau Valley, Carinthia) was exploited between the sixteenth century and 1891, with short-lived activities in 1924 and 1941. Quartz, ankerite and cinnabar, besides marcasite, bravoite, linnaeite, neodigenite, etc., were identified.

Polymetallic deposits (Cu, Ni–Co–Bi, Pb–Zn, Sb) In the Schladminger Tauern (Salzburg–Styria) numerous ancient mines produced chalcopyrite–tetrahedrite–ankerite ores, Ni–Co–Bi sulphide and galena–tetrahedrite–stibnite ores with variable Ag content (Giglerbaue, Zinkwand–Vöttern, Obertal, Seekar, Bromriesen, Eiskar). The deposits, of considerable importance in the Middle Ages and, to a much lesser degree, in the eighteenth and nineteenth centuries have been long abandoned. Friedrich,[22] who devoted much of his time to the study of this mineralization, described the deposits as 'Alpine Lagergänge', i.e. formed under the conditions of regional (Alpine) metamorphism whereby the metal solutions were introduced into the foliation planes of the (?pre-Hercynian) host rocks. The lenticular, sub-parallel orebodies are divided into linear oreshoots by Alpine thrusting and folding and are located along thrust planes.

Silver (Pb, Cu, Fe, barite) The abandoned Pb–Ag deposit of Oberzeiring (Styria) was an important silver source in medieval times. Mining began in A.D. 900 and reached its peak in the fourteenth century. During a flooding catastrophe in 1365 all workings below the groundwater-table were flooded and the importance of the mine decreased. Since then, repeated efforts to rehabilitate Oberzeiring have occurred. In the early eighteenth century previously uneconomic iron ore was mined. From 1959 to 1967 some barite was produced, mainly from the backfill of the ancient workings. The host rocks are high-grade metamorphosed marbles in a gneiss–amphibolite series.

The paragenesis is argentiferous galena, argentite, bornite, sphalerite, chalcopyrite, tetrahedrite, tennantite, pyrrhotite, galena, covellite, stibnite, pyrite, marcasite, arsenopyrite, pyrargyrite, bournonite, boulangerite, etc., in a gangue of siderite, calcite, barite

Table 2 *Major ore minerals, host rock, metamorphic grade and age of some strata-bound tungsten deposits. After Stumpfl[140a]*

Deposit	Mineral	Host rock	Metamorphic grade	Age, m.y.
Felbertal, Austria	Scheelite	Volcanosedimentary	Almandite–greenschist	400–500
Kleinarltal, Austria	Scheelite	Carbonate rock in phyllites	Almandite–greenschist	400–500
Kreuzeck Mts., Austria	Scheelite–stibnite	Schists and metavolcanics	Greenschist	400–500
Bindal, Norway	Scheelite	Hornblende–biotite–gneiss and reaction skarns	Amphibolite	500
O'okiep district, South Africa	Ferberite	Quartz veins in gneiss	Granulite	1200
Örsdalen, Norway	Ferberite and scheelite	Cordierite–garnet–schist	Granulite	1480
Bulawayan Formation, Zimbabwe	Scheelite	Carbonate rock	Greenschist–amphibolite	2900

and aragonite. The deposit is structurally controlled. Haditsch[32] recognized several phases of mineralization emplaced during a period of intensive faulting, but after the main thrust movements of the Alpine orogenesis.

Lead–zinc–copper In high-grade metamorphics (gneiss, amphibolites, garnet–micaschist) of the East Alpine Central Zone surrounding the Pennine Engadine Window is some galena–sphalerite–chalcopyrite–(tetrahedrite)–pyrite mineralization that was mined in the past. Mathiass[66] found the deposits to be located in thrust planes and mylonitic fault zones of Alpine age.

Pyrrhotite–arsenopyrite–pyrite deposits with precious metals Numerous sulphide deposits of this type occur in a pre-Hercynian (quartz-phyllite–paragneiss–micaschist–amphibolite–marble–metadiabase) series in Eastern Tyrol and Carinthia (Villgraten Range, Kreuzeckgruppe). The metamorphic series is intersected by numerous dykes of lamprophyric and granodioritic composition. The dyke suite is linked to the Oligocene Periadriatic Intrusions of the Adamello and Rieserferner plutons. The mineral deposits, which in the Middle Ages were an important source of precious metals, were interpreted by Friedrich[23] as genetically related to the subsequent magmatism of the Periadriatic Lineament. The now closed mines of Panzendorf, Tessenberg and Villgraten (Eastern Tyrol), which were worked into the 1950s, are said to contain ore reserves of about 400 000 tonne of pyrite-arsenopyrite ore with a tenor of 0·5–2·3% Cu. For the majority of these deposits a Hercynian sedimentary or volcanogenic origin is generally postulated.

Lead(Ag)–zinc deposits In Lower Palaeozoic carbonate-phyllites, greenschist–metatuffites and limestones of the 'Palaeozoics of Graz' a number of mines were worked between the fifteenth and nineteenth centuries. Some activity occurred at places during the first world war and lasted until around 1927. Exploration work in 1940 and 1950 was again abandoned. At present the area is being investigated in detail by geochemical, geophysical and geological methods as the ore seems to be linked to certain horizons, thus offering a larger ore potential.

The paragenesis is galena (with variable Ag content), sphalerite, minor pyrite, chalcopyrite, pyrrhotite, arsenopyrite, tetrahedrite, proustite, etc., in a gangue of carbonates, quartz and considerable quantities of barite. The mineralization is described as subparallel to stratiform and has been affected by subsequent folding and faulting. Hegemann[40] suggested an extrusive-sedimentary origin; Friedrich[23] attributed the deposits to the 'Alpine Kieslager' and assumed an early Alpine age. Recent investigators[101] explain the deposits as being syngenetic and deposited under reducing conditions, possibly related to submarine volcanism. Work by Weber[145] reinforces this conclusion. Similar deposits were mined in the Gurktal area (Carinthia) in the long abandoned mines of Meiselding, Zweinitz and others.

Pyrite (with/without Cu, As) At several localities pyrite deposits with As, Cu and traces of Ag occur in metasediments and greenschist. The ores show the effect of epizonal metamorphism and are probably pre-Mesozoic in age. Examples are the abandoned mines of Walchen near Oeblarn, Teuchen near Kallwang and Grosstübing near Graz (Styria).

Lithium Spodumene-bearing pegmatitic dykes of economically significant extent and grade were recently discovered by Minerex Co. of Austria. The pegmatites, believed to be of magmatic origin and of late Hercynian age, intersect an amphibolite-gneiss sequence in the Koralpe region, Carinthia, near the border to Styria. The deposit is being investigated by trenching and core drilling.

Drauzug, Karawanken Range and Periadriatic Igneous Suite, Southern Alps

To review the above units under a common heading is incorrect from a structural point of view, but as only parts of these units are within Austria's border and only the Drauzug is of economic interest, the author craves the indulgence of those readers who are familiar with the intricacies of Alpine tectonics.

The Drauzug strata lie in an elongate depression in a metamorphic series of the Central Zone and have been intensely folded and faulted. The rocks are almost identical with those of the Northern Calcareous Alps and are composed mainly of Triassic carbonates. The same applies to the Northern Branch of the Karawanken Range.

South of the Gailtal Line Palaeozoic and Triassic sedimentary sequences form the Southern Alps (in Austria these include parts of the Carnic Alps and the Southern Branch of the Karawanken Range). Their facies is somewhat different from that of the Calcareous Alps and the tectonic movements during late Mesozoic to Tertiary times are thought to have been in a southerly direction (in the Eastern Alps the main movements were directed to the north). Granitic to tonalitic intrusions, accompanied by numerous dykes, were emplaced along the fault lines between the Eastern and Southern Alps. Some—for example, the Eisenkappel intrusive suite—are of late Hercynian age; others—for example, the Rieserferner Tonalite—are of Oligocene age.

Lead–zinc The Drauzug unit and, to a lesser extent, the Austrian sector of the northern branch of the Karawanken carry numerous Pb–Zn deposits in Triassic carbonates. The deposit of Bleiberg-Kreuth (Carinthia), together with the Italian deposit of Raibl-Cave del Predil and the Yugoslavian Miess–Mežica deposits, represent an important ore district.

Bleiberg is at present the only lead–zinc-producing mine in Austria; the total metal content (comprising past production and present reserves) amounts to

2 500 000 tonne combined lead + zinc. Mineralization is linked to lagoonal carbonate sediments of Triassic age ('Wettersteinkalk' and *Cardita* Carbonates'). Crosscutting and strata-bound orebodies are associated with a graben structure and can be followed over an east–west distance of 10 km. Average annual output presently is in the order of 400 000 tonne of ore grading 6–7% combined metal.

Mining activities at Bleiberg date back to the twelfth century. The present underground workings have been opened up in the period since 1880, during which a continuous expansion of production has taken place. The managing company, Bleiberger Bergwerks-Union, was formed in 1867 when the resources and the assets of previous small operators were combined to facilitate large-scale development and the introduction of modern mining methods.

Apart from its position as Austria's leading base-metal producer (providing 50% of the country's lead and 90% of zinc consumption), Bleiberg has a longstanding tradition as one of the testing grounds of the 'hydrothermal' versus 'sedimentary' hypotheses, providing, as it does, features to support either genetic model unless a comprehensive view is taken. Schneiderhöhn[137a] discussed Bleiberg under the heading 'metasomatic lead–zinc ores of the Eastern Alps' and concluded that 'the mineralization reveals most clearly its origin by metasomatic replacement'; Friedrich[18] catalogued it under the heading 'ore deposits of magmatic derivation'; in 1964, however,[19] he suggested that metal-bearing solutions, originating from a deep source, may partially have reached the sea-floor, resulting in a syn-sedimentary component. On the other hand, Bechstädt[146] in 1975 suggested that 'the first metal enrichment in the separated lagoonal basins was derived from denudation of emerged areas'.

The total thickness of Triassic sediments in the Bleiberg area exceeds 3000 m; they overlie the Permian 'Gröden Sandstone'. Deposition of calcareous sediments commenced during the Anisian stage with 'Alpine Muschelkalk'. The latter changes gradually into the 'Wetterstein-Dolomite' of Ladinian age, which grades into the partly dolomitized 'Wetterstein Limestone' of Upper Ladinian and Lower Carnian age.

Bleiberg is not the only major lead–zinc deposit in this area as similar carbonate sequences extend into the adjoining territories of Yugoslavia and Italy. Evaluation of various genetic aspects of the Bleiberg deposit is facilitated if its mid-Triassic limestone-hosted counterparts in Yugoslavia (Mežica) and Italy (Raibl–Cave di Predil and Salafossa) are also considered. These four deposits account for more than 75% of total lead–zinc production in the Eastern Alps. Fig. 10 shows them to be situated in the vicinity of one of the Alps' most impressive tectonic lineaments, the 'Periadriatic suture'. The association of major strata-bound base-metal concentrations with major tectonic lineaments has been documented on a worldwide scale (Tynagh, Ireland; Mt. Isa, Queensland; Sullivan, British Columbia) and is considered significant in this context.

Mineralization at Bleiberg is confined to four distinct stratigraphic levels (Fig. 11) within the upper 250 m of the Wetterstein sequence and the overlying Raibl beds. The occurrence of stromatolites, rhythmites, black resedimented breccias, calc-arenites and green marls of possible volcanic derivation indicates deposition in a shallow lagoon. Cyclic sequences are characteristic; they consist of littoral sediments (sub-, inter-, and supratidal) and include evaporite layers with barite, anhydrite and fluorite.

Local geology is dominated by Wettersteinkalk, *Cardita* Shale with intermediate dolomite layers ('Zwischendolomit') and main dolomite ('Hauptdolomit'), all of which strike WNW and have been intensely fractured by the graben-type Bleiberg fracture zone ('Bleiberger Bruch'). This resulted in, among others, stratigraphic repetitions and considerable changes in dip, which varies from 20°S to 70°S (Fig. 12).

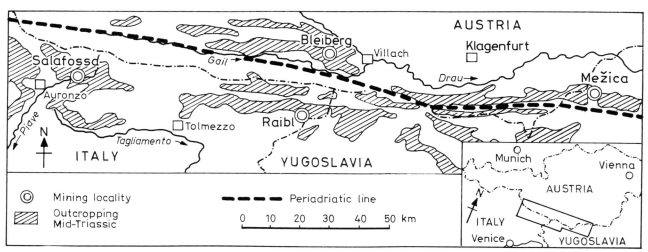

Fig. 10 *Location map of lead–zinc mines of Bleiberg, Mežica, Salafossa and Raibl. From Brigo et al.*[118c]

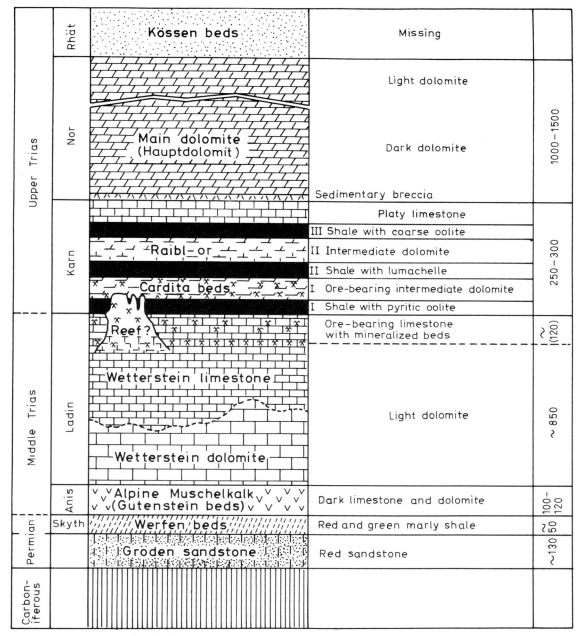

Fig. 11 *Stratigraphy of Triassic in Bleiberg area. From Bouvier et al.*[118d] *Crossed hammers indicate mineralized zones*

Mineralization is limited to a stratigraphic thickness not exceeding 300–400 m. There are four mineralized stratigraphic levels:

(1) Below the '*Megalodus* Bank', about 200 m below the first *Cardita* marker, there are stratiform orebodies of limited size (100-m diameter, 1 m thick)

(2) The uppermost Wetterstein Limestone, between the '*Megalodus* Bank' and first *Cardita* marker: both conformable ore 'runs' (Brigo *et al.*[118c]) and veins can be traced over several hundred metres, with thicknesses of several metres ('runs') and up to 20 m (veins)

(3) The first *Cardita* 'Zwischendolomit' carries orebodies, more than 5 m thick, and of several hundred metres in diameter

(4) The calcareous and dolomitic sediments in the hanging-wall of the third *Cardita* Shale

Most of the present production is derived from stratiform and breccia orebodies within the uppermost Wetterstein Limestone and the 'Zwischendolomit'. As indicated above, mineralization occurs as strata-bound lenses with distinct synsedimentary features, and also as crosscutting vein and pipe-shaped zones and breccia orebodies. The irregular distribution of payable orebodies and considerable variations in grade have posed

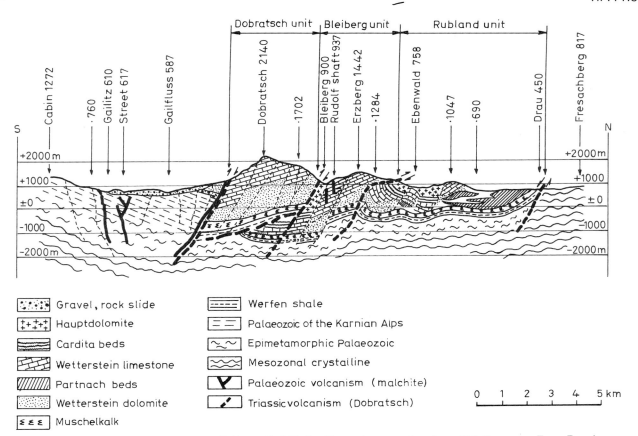

Fig. 12 *North–south section from Drau Valley to Gail Valley illustrating general geology of Bleiberg area. From Bouvier et al.*[118d]

a major problem since the early days of mining in the area. At Bleiberg ore is certainly not 'where you find it'; this has led to an early recognition of the necessity of comprehensive geoscientific investigations. Exploration costs have been halved by the acceptance, about twenty years ago, of the concept of stratabound ore distribution. By 1964 two new orebodies had been discovered in the Western Bleiberg–Kreuth section.

The main ore minerals are galena, sphalerite with minor amounts of pyrite (partly framboidal), marcasite, barite and siderite. Only galena and sphalerite are of economic significance. Silver contents in galena are in the 1–30 ppm range and, thus, considered negligible. Gangue minerals include calcite, fluorite and barite.

Average run of mine ores carry 1·7–4·5% Pb and 4–8% Zn. In recent years some of the old dumps, which still contain 2·4–4·0% Zn, have also been worked. Annual output in 1978 was 476 340 tonne of ore. The average grade was 1·2% Pb and 5·37% Zn, and output totalled 5971 tonne lead concentrates and 39 471 tonne zinc concentrates.

Within the general framework of syngenetic stratabound ore genesis, which has replaced earlier magmatic or metasomatic concepts, various modes of metal supply are presently being considered. As at Mt. Isa or Tynagh, no direct connexion between thin tuff horizons[139a] and mineralization can be established. New geochemical data[139a] that have recently become available are considered significant in this context. Sphalerite carries average values of 100 ppm Tl, 200 ppm Ge and 2000 ppm Cd; As varies from 10 to 5000 ppm, concentrations of Mn, Fe, Co, Cu, Hg, In and Ga are low. In galena only As and Tl are characteristic trace elements. Sulphur isotope data from grey anhydrite from Bleiberg ($\delta^{34}S = +16·1‰$) correspond to those from Upper Triassic sea water; values of sulphides are negative and indicate a derivation by bacterial reduction from sea-water sulphate. These results suggest low-temperature mineralization ($<150°C$) and are supported by temperature estimates on the basis of Sr contents of calcite, fluorite, barite and anhydrite, which indicate a similar maximum value.

Lead isotope data do not reveal any differences between galena from strata-bound or crosscutting orebodies. Lead within the Bleiberg deposit is thus isotopically homogeneous; it is characteristic (Bleiberg)-type lead, giving a model age of 300 m.y. The localization of orebodies in the vicinity of a major, and very old, fracture zone, the presence of both stratabound and crosscutting mineralization, and indications of volcanic activity, are features that Bleiberg has in common with other major base-metal deposits. A concept of introduction of metals into the Triassic Sea by weathering solutions from adjacent continental terrains accords well with presently available geochemical data, though a possible contribution by metalliferous brines, related to volcanic activity, should not be excluded. Precipitation of metals took place as sulphides on the sea-floor and was followed by complex diagenetic processes. Crosscutting ore is not necessarily related to tectonic features and is interpreted as being due to later remobilization, which may also have played a significant role in the formation of breccia orebodies.

Apart from Bleiberg-Kreuth, the other Pb-Zn deposits of the Drauzug and the Karawanken (Mitterberg-Kreuzen, Windisch-Bleiberg, Hochobir-Eisenkappel and in the area south of Bleiberg) have all been abandoned.

A recent study[86] showed that geochemical Zn anomalies in the sector west of Bleiberg-Kreuth are clearly linked to faults. The syn- to post-tectonic metal enrichments are thought to have been derived from a mobilization and redeposition of pre-existing (infra-Triassic?) metal concentrations.

Mercury Except for some siderite and manganese occurrences in Palaeozoic rocks of the Carnian range, the only deposit of the Southern Alps of some importance is the cinnabar deposit of Vellacher Kotschna in Carinthia, south of Eisenkappel and almost at the Austrian-Yugoslav border. In strongly imbricated Permian and Triassic carbonates a cinnabar impregnation in brecciated dolomite was once mined. About 67 tonne of Hg (metal) was produced in this mine—the ore was said to contain between 0·5 and 1·5%. Polegeg[83] explained the deposit as epigenetic-hydrothermal and of infra-Triassic age. As a result of geochemical exploration he considered further investigations to be justified in the search for more ore.

References
1 **Angel F. and Trojer F.** Der Ablauf der Spatmagnesit-Metasomatose. *Radex Rdsch.*, 1953, 315–34.
2 **Angel F. and Trojer F.** Zur Frage des Alters und der Genesis alpiner Spatmagnesite. *Radex Rdsch.*, 1955, 374–92.
3 **Bauer F. K. and Schermann O.** Über eine Pechblende-Gold-Paragenese im Bergbau Mitterberg (Salzburg). *Verh. geol. Bundesanst., Wien*, 1971, A97–9.
4 **Beck-Mannagetta P. Grill R. Holzer H. and Prey S.** *Erläuterungen zur geologischen und zur Lagerstättenkarte 1:1 000 000 von Österreich*, mit einen Beitrag von Ch. Exner (Wien: Geologische Bundesanstalt, 1966), 99 p.
5 **Bernhard J.** Die Mitterberger Kupferkieslagerstätte. *Jb. geol. Bundesanst., Wien*, **109**, 1965, 3–90.
6 **Borchert H.** Zusammenhänge zwischen Lagerstättenbildung, Magmatismus und Geotektonik. *Geol. Rdsch.*, **50**, 1961, 131–65.

7a **Bosselini A. and Hsu K. J.** Mediterranean plate tectonics and Triassic palaeogeography. *Nature, Lond.*, **224**, July 20 1973, 144–6.
7b **Briegleb D.** Geologie der Magnesitlagerstätte am Sattlerkogel in der Veitsch (Steiermark). *Berg- u. hüttenm. Mh.*, **116**, 1971, 359–75.
8 **Clar E. and Meixner H.** Die Eisenspatlagerstätte von Hüttenberg und ihre Umgebung. *Carinthia II*, no. 143, 1953, 67–92.
9 **Clar E.** Über die Herkunft der alpinen Vererzung. *Geol. Rdsch.*, **42**, 1954, 107–27.
10 **Clar E.** Bemerkungen zur Entstehungsfrage der kalkalpinen Pb–Zn-Erzlagerstätten. *Klebelsberg-Festschrift geol. Ges., Wien*, **48**, 1957, 17–29.
11 **Chrt J. Bolduan H. Bernstein K. H. and Legierski J.** Räumliche und zeitliche Beziehungen der endogenen Mineralisation der Böhmischen Masse zu Magmatismus und Bruchtektonik. *Z. angew. Geol.*, **14**, 1968, 362–76.
12 **Cornelius H.-P. and Plöchinger B.** Der Tennengebirgs-Nordrand mit seinen Manganerzen und die Berge im Bereich des Lammertales. *Jb. geol. Bundesanst., Wien*, **95**, 1952.
13 **Dewey J. F. Pittman W. C. Ryan W. B. F. and Bonnin J.** Plate tectonics and the evolution of the Alpine system. *Bull. geol. Soc. Am.*, **84**, 1973, 3137–80.
14 **Emmanuilidis G. and Mostler H.** Zur Geologie des Kitzbüheler Horns und seiner Umgebung. *Festb. geol. Inst. Univ. Innsbruck*, 1970, 547–69.
15 **Evans A. M.** Mineralization in geosynclines—the Alpine enigma. *Mineral. Deposita*, **10**, 1975, 254–60.
16 **Friedrich O. M.** Die Talklagerstätten des Rabenwaldes, Oststeiermark. *Berg- u. hüttenm. Mh.*, **92**, 1947, 66–85.
17 **Friedrich O. M.** Die Goldlagerstätte Schellgaden. *Carinthia II*, no. 143, 1953, 129–31.
18 **Friedrich O. M.** Zur Erzlagerstättenkarte der Ostalpen. *Radex Rdsch.*, no. 7/8 1953, 371–407 (with mineral map 1:500 000).
19 **Friedrich O. M.** Zur Genesis der Blei- und Zinklagerstätten in den Ostalpen. *Neues Jb. Miner. Mh.*, **2**, 1964, 33–49.
20 **Friedrich O. M.** Monographie Kärtner Lagerstätten: II. Die Quecksilberlagerstätten Kärntens. *Arch. Lagerstättenf. Ostalpen*, **3**, 1965, 71–124.
21 **Friedrich O. M.** Bemerkungen zu einigen Arbeiten über die Kupferlagerstätte Mitterberg und Gedanken über ihre Genese. *Arch. Lagerstättenf. Ostalpen*, **5**, 1967, 146–69.
22 **Friedrich O. M.** Monographie der Erzlagerstätten bei Schladming: I. *Arch. Lagerstättenf. Ostalpen*, **5**, 1967, 80–130.
23 **Friedrich O. M.** Die Vererzung der Ostalpen, gesehen als Glied des Gebirgsbaues. *Arch. Lagerstättenf. Ostalpen*, **8**, 1968, 1–136.
24 **Friedrich O. M. et al.** Beiträge über das Gefüge von Spatlagerstätten. *Radex Rdsch.*, no. 2 1968, 113–26.
25 **Friedrich O. M.** Monographie der Erzlagerstätten bei Schladming: II. *Arch. Lagerstättenf. Ostalpen*, **9**, 1969, 107–30.
26 **Fritsch W.** Eine tektonische Analyse des steirischen Erzberges. *Berg- u. hüttenm. Mh.*, **105**, 1960, 225–31.
27 **Gabl G.** Geologische Untersuchungen in der westlichen Fortsetzung der Mitterberger Kupfererzlagerstätte. *Arch. Lagerstättenf. Ostalpen*, **2**, 1964, 2–32.
28 **Germann K.** Verbreitung und Entstehung manganreicher Gesteine im Jura der nördlichen Kalkalpen. *Tschermaks miner. petrogr. Mitt.*, **17**, 1972, 123–50.
29 **Gudden H.** Über Manganerzvorkommen in den Berchtesgadener und Salzburger Alpen. *Erzmetall*, **22**, 1969, 482–8.

30 **Haditsch J.-G.** Die Cu–Ag-Lagerstätte Seekar (Salzburg). *Arch. Lagerstättenf. Ostalpen*, **2**, 1964, 76–120.

31 **Haditsch J.-G.** Die Talklagerstätte Oberdorf an der Laming. *Arch. Lagerstättenf. Olstalpen*, **4**, 1966, 36–83.

32 **Haditsch J.-G.** Monographie der Zeiringer Lagerstätten. *Arch. Lagerstättenf. Ostalpen*, **6**, 1967, 1–218.

33 **Haditsch J.-G.** Die Manganerzlagerstätten der Veitsch. *Arch. Lagerstättenf. Ostalpen*, **7**, 1968, 112–69.

34 **Haditsch J.-G. and Mostler H.** Die Fahlerzlagerstätte auf der Gratl-Spitze (Thienberg bei Brixlegg). *Arch. Lagerstättenf. Ostalpen*, **9**, 1969, 168–94.

35 **Haditsch J.-G. and Mostler H.** Die Kupfer–Nickel–Kobaltvererzung im Bereich Leogang. *Arch. Lagerstättenf. Ostalpen*, **11**, 1970, 161–209.

36 **Haditsch J.-G. and Mostler H.** Mineralisationen im Perm der Ostalpen. *Carinthia II*, 1974, 63–71.

37 **Hajek H.** Über das Auftreten von roteisensteinführenden Porphyroidhorizonten im steirischen Erzberg. *Arch. Lagerstättenf. Ostalpen*, **4**, 1966, 3–35.

38 **Hawkesworth C. J. Waters D. J. and Bickle M. J.** Plate tectonics in the Eastern Alps. *Earth Planet. Sci. Lett.*, **24**, 1975, 405–13.

39 **Heissel W.** Die Hochalpenüberschiebung und die Brauneisensteinlagerstätten von Werfen–Bischofshofen (Salzburg). *Jb. geol. Bundesanst., Wien*, **98**, 1955, 183–201.

40 **Hegemann F.** Über extrusiv-sedimentäre Erzlagerstätten der Ostalpen: II. Blei- Zinkerzlagerstätten. *Erzmetall*, **13**, 1960, 79–84; 122–7.

41 **Hiessleitner G.** Die geologischen Grundlagen des Antimonbergbaues in Österreich. *Jb. geol. Bundesanst., Wien*, **92**, 1949, 1–92.

42 **Höll R.** Scheelitprospektion und Scheelitvorkommen im Bundesland Salzburg/Österreich. *Chemie Erde*, **28**, 1969, 185–203.

43 **Höll R.** Die Zinnober-Vorkommen im Gebiet der Turracher Höhe. *Neues Jb. Geol. Paläont. Mh.*, 1970, 201–24.

44 **Höll R.** Scheelitvorkommen in Österreich. *Erzmetall*, **24**, 1971, 273–82.

45 **Höll R. Maucher A. and Westenberger H.** Synsedimentary-diagenetic ore fabrics in the strata- and time-bound scheelite deposits of Kleinarltal and Felbertal in the Eastern Alps. *Mineral. Deposita*, **7**, 1972, 217–26.

46 **Höll R. and Maucher A.** Genese und Alter der Scheelit-Magnesit-Lagerstätte Tux. *Sber. bayer. Akad. Wiss., m.-n. kl. 1967*, no. 1, 1967, 11 p.

47 **Holler H.** Eine Monographie des Bleiberger Bruches. *Carinthia II*, Sonderheft 32, 1974, 92 p.

48 **Holzer H.** Photogeologische Karte eines Teiles der Goldberggruppe (Hohe Tauern). *Jb. geol. Bundesanst., Wien*, 1958, 25–34.

49 **Holzer H. and Neuwirth K.** Über den ehemaligen Eisensteinbergbau Kottaun bei Geras (Niederösterreich). *Montan Rdsch.*, **10**, 1962, 191–3.

50 **Holzer H.** Geologische Beobachtungen an niederösterreichischen Graphitvorkommen. *Verh. geol. Bundesanst., Wien*, 1961, no. 1, 1961, 90–8.

51 **Holzer H.** Die Flinzgraphitvorkommen im ausseralpinen Grundgebirge Ober- und Niederösterreichs. *Verh. geol. Bundesanst., Wien*, **1964**, 1964, 360–72.

52 **Holzer H. F. and Wieden P.** Kaolin deposits of Austria. *Rep. 23rd Int. geol. Congr., Czechoslovakia, 1968* (Prague: Academia, 1969), pt 15, 25–32.

53 **Ilavský J.** Conclusions concernant la metallogénie de système plissé Alpin de l'Europe Centrale et Sud-Orientale en 2 500 000. *Proc. 10th Congr. Carpato-Balk. geol. Ass.*, 1973, 45–108.

54 **Kanaki F.** Die Minerale Bleibergs (Kärnten). *Carinthia II*, **82**, 1972, 7–84.

55 **Karl F.** Ein abbauwürdiges Disthenvorkommen in den Hohen Tauern (Österreich). *Erzmetall*, **9**, 1956, 599.

56 **Kern A.** Eisenerzlagerstätten in Österreich. In *Symposium sur les gisements de fer du monde* **Blondel F. and Marvier L. eds** (Alger: XIX Congr. Geol. Int., 1952), vol. II, 39–73.

57 **Kieslinger A.** Die geologischen Grundlagen des Goldbergbaues in den Hohen Tauern. *Berg- u. hüttenm. Jb.*, **85**, 1937, 286.

58 **Klar G.** *Steirische Graphite* (Graz: Styria Verlag, 1964), 149 p.

59 **Koch K. E.** Die Vererzung der Krabachjochmasse östlich Zürs am Arlberg. *Notizb. hess. Landesamt. Bodenforsch., Wiesbaden*, **87**, 1958, 202–7.

60 **Kostelka L. and Petrascheck W. E.** Genesis and classification of Triassic Alpine lead–zinc deposits in the Austrian region. In *Genesis of stratiform lead–zinc–barite-fluorite deposits in carbonate rocks (the so-called Mississippi Valley type deposits)* **Brown J. S. ed.** (Lancaster, Pa.: Economic Geology Publishing House, 1967), 138–46. (*Econ. Geol. Monogr.* 3)

61 **Kostelka L. and Siegl W.** Der triadische Geosynklinalvulkanismus und die Blei-Zinkvererzung in den Drau-Kalkalpen. *Symp. Int. Giacimenti Minerali delle Alpi*, 1966, 127–34.

62 **Lahusen L.** Die schicht- und zeitgebundene Antimonit-Scheelit-Vorkommen und Zinnobervererzungen der Kreuzeck- und Goldeckgruppe in Kärnten und Osttirol, Österreich. Dissertation, Naturwissenschaftliche Fakultät, Universität München, 1969, 139 p.

63 **Lechner K. Holzer H. Ruttner A. and Grill R.** *Karte der Lagerstätten mineralischer Rohstoffe der Republik Österreich, 1:1 000 000* (Wien: Geologische Bundesanstalt, 1964).

64 **Lesko I.** Über die Bildung von Magnesitlagerstätten. *Mineral. Deposita*, **7**, 1972, 61–72.

65 **Lukas W.** Tektonisch-genetische Untersuchungen der Fahlerzlagerstätte am Falkenstein by Schwaz/Tirol. *Neues Jb. Geol. Palaeont. Mh.*, 1971, 47–63.

66 **Mathiass E. P.** Die metallogenetische Stellung der Erzlagerstätten im Bereich Engadin und Arlberg. *Berg- u. hüttenm. Mh.*, **106**, 1961, 1–13; 45–55.

67 **Maucher A.** Zur alpinen Metallogenese in den bayerischen Kalkalpen zwischen Loisach und Salzach. *Tschermaks miner. petrogr. Mitt.*, **4**, 1954, 454–63.

68 **Maucher A.** Die Deutung des primären Stoffbestandes der kalkalpinen Pb–Zn-Lagerstätten als syngenetische-sedimentäre Bildung. *Berg- u. hüttenm. Mh.*, **102**, 1957, 226–9.

69 **Maucher A.** Die Antimon–Wolfram–Quecksilber-Formation und ihre Beziehungen zu Magmatismus und Geotektonik. *Freiberger ForschHft.* C186, 1965, 173–88.

70 **Meixner H.** Die Metasomatose in der Eisenspat-Lagerstätte Hüttenberg, Kärnten. *Tschermaks miner. petrogr. Mitt.*, **8**, 1963, 640–6.

71 **Meixner H.** Mineralogisches zur Lagerstättenkarte der Ostalpen. *Radex Rdsch.*, 1953, 434–44.

72 **Modjtahedi M. and Wieseneder H.** Entstehung und Zusammensetzung der Leucophyllite (Weissschiefer) in den Ostalpen. *Arch. Lagerstättenf. Ostalpen, Friedrich Festband*, 1974, 189–213.

73 **Mostler H.** Alter und Genese ostalpiner Spatmagnesite unter besonderer Berücksichtigung der Magnesitlagerstätten

im Westabschnitt der nördlichen Grauwackenzone (Tirol, Salzburg). *Veröff. Univ. Innsbruck*, **86,** 1973, 237–66.
74 **Oxburgh E. R.** An outline of the geology of the central eastern Alps. *Proc. Geol. Ass.*, **79,** 1968, 1–46.
75 **Oxburgh E. R.** Plate tectonics and continental collision. *Nature, Lond.*, **239,** Sept. 22 1972, 202–4.
76 **Petrascheck W.** Metallogenetische Zonen in den Ostalpen. *Proc. 14th Int. geol. Congr., Madrid, 1926,* **3,** 1926, 1243–53.
77 **Petrascheck W. E.** Die alpin-mediterrane Metallogenese. *Geol. Rdsch.*, **53,** 1963, 376–89.
78 **Petrascheck W. E.** Die zeitliche Gliederung der ostalpinen Metallogenese. *Sber. öst. Akad. Wiss., m.-n. Kl., Abt. I,* **175,** 1966, 57–74.
79 **Petrascheck W. E.** Orogene und kratogene Metallogenese. *Geol. Rdsch.*, **62,** 1973, 617–26.
80 **Petrascheck W. E.** Plate tectonics and mineral zoning in the Alpine–Mediterranean area. In *Metallogeny and plate tectonics* **Strong D. F. ed.** *Spec. Pap. geol. Ass. Canada* no. 14, 1976, 353–9.
81 **Petrascheck W. E.** Uranerz in Österreich. *Berg- u. hüttenm. Mh.*, **120,** 1975, 353–5.
82 **Pirkl H.** Geologie des Trias-Streifens und des Schwazer Dolomits südlich des Inn zwischen Schwaz und Wörgl, Tirol. *Jb. geol. Bundesanst., Wien*, **104,** 1961, 1–150.
83 **Polegeg S.** Untersuchung und Bewertung von Quecksilbervorkommen in Kärnten. *Arch. Lagerstättenf. Ostalpen*, **12,** 1971, 69–118.
84 **Prey S.** Der ehemalige Grossfraganter Kupfer- und Schwefelkiesbergbau. *Mitt. geol. Ges., Wien*, **54,** 1961, 163.
85 **Reinold P.** Beitrag zur Geochemie der ostalpinen Salzlagerstätten. *Tschermaks miner. petrogr. Mitt.*, **10,** 1965, 505–27.
86 **Scheriau-Niedermayr E.** Mitterberg–Schekelnock: Beispiel einer störungsgebundenen Blei–Zink-Vererzung im Drauzug. *Mitt. geol. Ges., Wien*, **66/67,** 1975, 159–63.
87 **Schmidegg O.** Die Erzlagerstätten des Schwazer Bergbaugebietes, besonders des Falkenstein: Schwazer Bergbuch. *Schlern-Schr., Innsbruck*, no. 85, 1951, 36–85.
88 **Schneider H.-J.** Facies differentiation and controlling factors for the depositional lead–zinc concentration in the Ladinian geosyncline of the eastern Alps. In *Developments in sedimentology, volume 2* (Amsterdam, etc.: Elsevier, 1964), 29–45.
89 **Schneider H.-J. Möller P. and Parekh P. P.** Rare earth elements distribution in fluorites and carbonate sediments of the East-Alpine Mid-Triassic sequences in the Nördliche Kalkalpen. *Mineral. Deposita*, **10,** 1975, 330–44.
90 **Schneiderhöhn H.** Genetische Lagerstättengliederung auf geotektonischer Grundlage. *Neues Jb. Miner. Mh.*, 1952, 47–89.
91 **Schulz O.** Lead–zinc deposits in the Calcareous Alps as an example of submarine-hydrothermal formation of mineral deposits. In *Developments of sedimentology, volume 2* (Amsterdam, etc.: Elsevier, 1964), 47–52.
92 **Schulz O. and Lukas W.** Eine Uranlagerstätte in permotriassischen Sedimenten Tirols. *Tschermaks miner. petrogr. Mitt.*, **14,** 1970, 213–31.
93 **Schulz O.** Horizontgebundene altpaläozoische Kupferkiesvererzungen in der Nordtiroler Grauwackenzone, Österreich. *Tschermaks miner. petrogr. Mitt.*, **17,** 1972, 1–18.
94 **Schulz O.** Metallogenese im Paläozoikum der Ostalpen. *Geol. Rdsch.*, **63,** 1974, 93–104.
95 **Schulz O.** Resedimentbreccien und ihre möglichen Zusammenhänge mit Pb–Zn-Konzentrationen in mitteltriadischen Sedimenten der Gailtaler Alpen (Kärnten). *Tschermaks miner. petrogr. Mitt.*, **22,** 1975, 130–57.
96 **Schroll E. and Azer J. N.** Beitrag zur Kenntnis ostalpiner Fahlerze. *Tschermaks miner. petrogr. Mitt.*, **7,** 1959, 70–105.
97 **Siegl W.** Zur Entstehung schichtiger und strahliger Spatmagnesite. *Berg- u. hüttenw. Mh.*, **100,** 1955, 79–84.
98 **Siegl W.** Entwurf einer salinarsedimentären Entstehung der Magnesite vom Typ Entachen (Salzburg). *Mineral. Deposita*, **4,** 1969, 225–33.
99 **Siegl W.** Die Uranparagenese von Mitterberg (Salzburg, Österreich). *Tschermaks miner. petrogr. Mitt.*, **17,** 1972, 263–75.
100 **Siegl W. and Felser K. O.** Der Kokardendolomit und seine Stellung im Magnesit von Hohentauern (Sunk bei Trieben). *Berg- u. hüttenm. Mh.*, **118,** 1973, 251–6.
101 **Siegl W.** Ein Beitrag zur Genese der Vererzung des Grazer Paläozoikums. *Mineral. Deposita*, **9,** 1974, 289–95.
102 **Siegl W.** Die Oberkarnische Blei-Zinkvererzung im Rublandverbindungsstollen nördlich von Kreuth. *Berg- u. hüttenm. Mh.*, **120,** 1975, 471–4.
103 **Spross W.** Die Entwicklung des Wolframbergbaues Mittersill. *Berg- u. hüttenm. Mh.*, **120,** 1975, 355–62.
104 **Sterk G.** Zur Kenntnis der Goldlagerstätte Kliening im Lavanttal. *Carinthia II*, 1955, 39–59.
105 **Teuscher E. O. and Weinelt W.** Die Metallogenese im Raum Spessart–Fichtelgebirge–Oberpfälzer Wald–Bayerischer Wald. *Geol. Bavarica*, **65,** 1972, 5–73.
106 **Thalmann F.** Probleme der Abbauplanung und Qualitätssteuerung am Steirischen Erzberg in Abhängigkeit von den geologisch-mineralogischen Verhältnissen. *Mitt. geol. Ges. Wien*, **66/67,** 1974, 245–63.
107 **Tollmann A.** *Ostalpensynthese* (Wien: Deuticke, 1963), 256 p.
108 **Tufar W.** Zur Altersgliederung der ostalpinen Vererzung. *Geol. Rdsch.*, **63,** 1973, 105–23.
109 **Turner F. J. and Verhoogen J.** *Igneous and metamorphic geology*, 2nd edn (New York, etc.: McGraw Hill, 1960), 672 p.
110 **Unger H. J.** Der Lagerstättenraum Zell am See. *Arch. Lagerstättenf. Ostalpen*, **11,** 1970, 33–83; **13,** 1972, 75–98.
111 **Vohryzka K.** Zur Genese des dichten Magnesits von Kraubath. *Berg- u. hüttenm. Mh.*, **105,** 1960, 12–16.
112 **Vohryzka K.** Zur Scheelitprospektion in Österreich. *Mitt. Ges. Geol. Bergbaustud.*, **18,** 1968, 447–58.
113 **Vohryzka K.** Die Erzlagerstätten von Nordtirol und ihr Verhältnis zur alpinen Tektonik. *Jb. geol. Bundesanst., Wien*, **111,** 1968, 1–88.
114 **Weber F. and Kostelka L.** Geophysikalische Prospektion von Antimonit bei Schlaining im Burgenland. *GDMB Schriftenreihe* no. 24, 1972.
115 **Weber L. Pausweg F. and Medwenitsch W.** Zur Mitterberger Kupfervererzung. *Mitt. geol. Ges., Wien*, **65,** 1972, 137–58.
116 **Wenger H.** Die Scheelitlagerstätte Tux. *Radex Rdsch.*, 1964, 109–32.
117 **Werneck W. L.** Faciesdifferenzierung und Erzvorkommen im oberen Wettersteinkalk der nördlichen Kalkalpen zwischen Traun und Enns (Oberösterreich). *Berg- u. hüttenm. Mh.*, **119,** 1974, 211–21.
118 **Wieseneder H.** Über die Bezeichnung Grauwacke. *Tschermaks miner. petrogr. Mitt.*, **7,** 1961, 451–4.
118*a* **Beran A. and Thalmann F.** Der Bergbau Radmer–Buchegg—ein Beitrag zur Genese alpiner Sideritlagerstätten. *Tschermaks miner. petrogr. Mitt.*, **25,** 1978, 287–303.
118*b* **Beran A.** Die Stellung der Ankeritgesteine im Rahmen

der Genese von Sideritlagerstätten der östlichen Grauwackenzone. *Tschermaks miner. petrogr. Mitt.*, **26**, 1979, 217–33.

118c **Brigo L. Kostelka L. Omenetto P. Schneider H.-J. Schroll E. Schulz O. and Strucl I.** Comparative reflections on four Alpine Pb–Zn deposits. In *Time- and stratabound ore deposits* **Klemm D. D. and Schneider H.-J.** eds (Berlin, etc.: Springer, 1977), 273–93.

118d **Bouvier M. et al.** *Blei und Zink in Österreich: der Bergbau Bleiberg-Kreuth in Kärnten* (Wien: Verlag Naturhistorisches Museum Wien, 1972), 35 p.

118e **Clar E. and Meixner H.** Die grundlegenden Beobachtungen zur Entstehung der Eisenspatlagerstätten von Hüttenberg. *Carinthia II*, 1981, 55–92.

119 **Dolezel P. and Schroll E.** Beitrag zur Geochemie der Siderite in den Ostalpen. *Verh. geol. Bundesanst., Wien, 1978*, no. 3 1979, 293–9.

120 **El Ageed A. Saager R. and Stumpfl E. F.** Pre-alpine ultramafic rocks in the eastern central Alps, Styria, Austria. In *Ophiolites: proceedings international symposium, Cyprus, 1979* **Panayiotou A.** ed. (Nicosia: Geological Survey Department, 1980), 601–6.

121 **Erkan E.** Die permischen Uranvorkommen der Steiermark. *Mitt. Abt. Geol. Paläont. Bergb. Landesmuseum Joanneum* no. 38, 1977, 31–40.

122 **Erkan E.** Uran- und gipsführendes Permoskyth der östlichen Ostalpen. *Jb. geol. Bundesanst., Wien,* **120**, no. 2 1977, 343–400.

123 **Flajs G. and Schönlaub H. P.** Bemerkungen zur Geologie um Radmer. *Verh. geol. Bundesanst., Wien, 1978*, 1979, 245–54.

124 **Friedrich O. M.** *Erzminerale der Steiermark* (Graz: Joanneum, 1959), 58 p.

125 **Fuchs H. W.** Korngefügeanalytische Untersuchungen der Sideritlagerstätte Hüttenberg (Kärnten). *Tschermaks miner. petrogr. Mitt.*, **27**, 1980, 233–60.

126 **Haditsch J.-G. and Mostler H.** Late Variscan and Early Alpine mineralization in the Eastern Alps. In *Ore genesis: the state of art* **Amstutz G. C.** ed. (Berlin, etc.: Springer, 1982), 582–9.

126a **Höll R.** Die Scheelitlagerstätte Felbertal und der Vergleich mit anderen Scheelitvorkommen in the Ostalpen. *Abh. Bayer. Akad. Wiss., math. nat. Kl.* no. 157A, 1975, 114 p.

126b **Höll R.** Die Scheelitlagerstätte Felbertal bei Mittersill. *Lapis, München,* **3**, 1978, 54–8.

127 **Horkel A.** Zum Alter einiger Sideritvorkommen im oberostalpinen Permoskyth im Gebiet der Hohen Veitsch (Steiermark). *Berg- u. hüttenm. Mh.*, **122**, no. 2a 1977, 35–41.

128 **Holzer H. and Stumpfl E. F.** Proceedings of the Third international symposium on mineral deposits of the Alps (ISMIDA), Leoben, Oct. 7–10, 1977. *Verh. geol. Bundesanst., Wien, 1978*, no. 3 1979, 175–536.

129 **Holzer H. F. and Stumpfl E. F.** Mineral deposits of the Eastern Alps: Excursion 080C, 26th Int. geol. Congr. *Abh. geol. Bundesanst., Wien,* **34**, 1980, 171–96.

130 **Moreau P.** Le Massif du Rabenwald (Autriche) et ses minéralisations. Thèse, Université de Franche-Comté, Besançon, no. 357, 1981.

131 **Morteani G. Schley F. and Möller P.** The formation of the magnesite deposits in the Northern Grauwackenzone and of the Innsbrucker Quarzphyllit (Austria) as deduced from the rare earth elements (REE) fractionation. *Erzmetall*, **34**, 1981, 559–62.

132 **Niedermayr G. et al.** Magnesit im Perm und Skyth der Ostalpen und seine petrogenetische Bedeutung. *Verh. geol. Bundesanst., Wien, 1981*, no. 2 1981, 109–31.

133 **Oberhauser R.** Die postvariszische Entwicklung des Ostalpenraumes unter Berücksichtigung einiger für die Metallogenese wichtiger Umstände. *Verh. geol. Bundesanst., Wien, 1978*, no. 2 1978, 43–53.

134 **Paar W. H. and Chen T. T.** Ore mineralogy of the Waschgang Au/Cu deposit, Upper Carinthia, Austria. *Tschermaks miner. petrogr. Mitt.*, **30**, no. 3 1982, 157–76.

135 **Paar W. H.** The pitchblende nodule assemblage of Mitterberg (Austria). *Neues Jb. Miner. Abh.*, **131**, 1978, 254–71.

136 **Pak E. and Schauberger O.** Die geologische Datierung der ostalpinen Salzlagerstätten mittels Schwefelisotopenuntersuchungen. *Verh. geol. Bundesanst., Wien, 1981*, no. 2 1981, 185–92.

137 **Reimann C. and Stumpfl E. F.** Geochemical setting of strata-bound stibnite mineralization in the Kreuzeck Mountains, Austria. *Trans. Instn Min. Metall. (Sect. B: Appl. earth sci.)*, **90**, 1981, B126–32.

137a **Schneiderhöhn H.** *Lehrbuch der Erzlagerstättenkunde* (Jena: Gustav Fischer, 1941), vol. 1, 858 p.

138 **Schulz O.** Metallogenese in den österreichischen Ostalpen. *Verh. geol. Bundesanst., Wien, 1978*, no. 3 1979, 471–8.

139 **Schulz O.** Die Pb–Zn-Erzlagerstätte Lafatsch–Vomperloch (Karwendelgebirge, Tirol). *Veröff. Museum Ferdinandeum* no. 61, 1981, 55–103.

139a **Schroll E.** Zur Korrelation geologischer Karbonatgesteine. *Schr. Reihe Erdw. Komm., österr. Akad. Wiss.*, **3**, 1978, 131–58.

140 **Steiner H.-J.** Aufbereitungstechnische Untersuchung von Roherzproben aus der Sulfidlagerstätte Walchen bei Öblarn. *Mitt. Abt. Geol. Paläont. Bergb. Landesmuseum Joanneum* no. 38, 1977, 109–22.

140a **Stumpfl E. F.** Sediments, ores and metamorphism. *Phil. Trans. R. Soc. Lond.*, **A286**, 1977, 507–25.

141 **Stumpfl E. F. and El Ageed A.** Hochgrössen und Kraubath: Teile eines paläozoischen Ophiolit-Komplexes. *Mitt. Abt. Geol. Paläont. Bergb. Landesmuseum Joanneum* no. 42, 1981, 161–9.

142 **Thalmann F.** Zur Eisenspatvererzung in der nördlichen Grauwackenzone am Beispiel des Erzberges bei Eisenerz und Radmer Bucheck. *Verh. geol. Bundesanst., Wien, 1978*, no. 3 1979, 479–89.

143 **Tischler S. E. and Finlow-Bates T.** Plate tectonic processes that governed the mineralization of the Eastern Alps. *Mineral. Deposita*, **15**, 1980, 19–34.

144 **Tufar W.** The Eastern Alps and their ore deposits. *Erzmetall*, **33**, 1980, 153–62.

145 **Weber L.** Die Stellung der stratiformen Blei–Zinkvererzungen im Grazer Paläozoikum. *Mitt. Abt. Geol. Paläont. Bergb. Landesmuseum Joanneum* no. 38, 1977, 123–41.

146 **Bechstädt T.** Lead–zinc ores dependent on cyclic sedimentation (Wetterstein Limestone of Bleiberg-Kreuth, Carinthia, Austria). *Mineral. Deposita*, **10**, 1975, 234–48.

147 **Medwenitsch W.** Zur Geologie des Halleiner Salzberges. *Mitt. geol. Ges., Wien,* **51**, 1969, 197–218.

Felice C. Jaffé

Switzerland

Switzerland is an industrial country with few significant mineral resources, but it should be stressed that the drastic change from an agricultural and pastoral economy would not have been possible without the existence of many small and diversified mineral deposits. The small size and the low grade of these deposits led to their closure in the first half of this century. Thus, mining activities have come to a virtual standstill—in particular, in the field of metallic ores. A reminder of ancient mining activity exists in the many names of mines, mills, smelters and forges in different parts of Switzerland.[1]

Swiss mineral deposits have been studied in detail by generations of geologists—in particular, by university students for their doctoral dissertations. The available literature contains a great wealth of detailed and interesting mineralogical, petrological and geological data, but references to economic geology and to ore controls, grades and reserves are not always adequate. This is probably due, in part, to the absence of a specialized governmental agency, such as a geological survey. To some extent the Swiss Geotechnical Commission* has replaced such a survey, and its contribution to the understanding of domestic mineral deposits should be emphasized.[57,74,78] The Commission has sponsored and financed more than a hundred different raw materials investigations, but the results have been published solely under the authors' personal responsibility, since the lack of financial means and adequate staff has precluded guidance and supervision in the field.

A recent and comprehensive description of Swiss mineral deposits is not available, except for iron ores.[83] The last publication on this subject dates from the period before the second world war.[50] The metallogenic map of France extends into parts of western Switzerland, but without explanatory notes.[12]

Summaries of wider regional interest mainly encompass Switzerland's neighbouring countries—in particular, the Italian Alps.[70,111] Hence, this review is based principally on many different publications and on the excellent geotechnical map of the country.[79-82] To improve the clarity of presentation only the main mineral deposits are described. Although many small and abandoned workings are present in Switzerland, their inclusion would not represent a significant contribution to the understanding of the basic facts and problems of a metallogenic and economic nature.*

Geological and metallogenic provinces

Despite the fact that Switzerland is a small country, its geographical position within the Alpine arc accounts for its highly diversified geological structure.[16,19,42,91,92,110] The country can be subdivided into five major geological provinces, which will be described from north to south (Fig. 1). A good correlation can be established between the geological nature of these provinces and the corresponding mineral deposits. The subdivision into well-defined metallogenic provinces is, however, somewhat hazardous, as deposits of the same kind are rather rare.

Jura

The Jura is a low mountain range approximately 240 km long on Swiss territory. It is composed of Mesozoic rocks—mainly limestones, dolomitic limestones, dolomites and Triassic evaporites. It is characterized by a succession of broad faulted anticlines and synclines, arranged in the so-called Jurassian or Appalachian structural style.

Iron[26,28,29,83]
Delemont, Jura[9] (9)† During the Eocene terrestrial conditions with a hot and humid climate prevailed in the Jura region and numerous residual pisolitic limonite accumulations were formed by the erosion and redeposition of older, ferruginous sedimentary horizons—mainly those which were formed in the Dogger period. Residual iron deposits, *sidérolitique* in French and *Bohnerz* ('bean ore') in German, are irregular in shape and size, ranging from small pod-like fillings of karstic cavities to extended but irregular layers several metres and even up to 30–40 m thick. These deposits were folded with the underlying rocks, generally of

---

* Swiss Geotechnical Commission, Sonneggstrasse 5, 8006 Zurich, Switzerland; sale of publications: Kümmerly und Frey, Hallerstrasse 6, 3012 Bern, Switzerland.

* The geology of the neighbouring Principality of Lichtenstein, which occupies 160 km² between the eastern border of Switzerland and Austria, is well known.[17] No ore deposits are reported from this country.

†(9), etc., indicates locality number in Fig. 1.

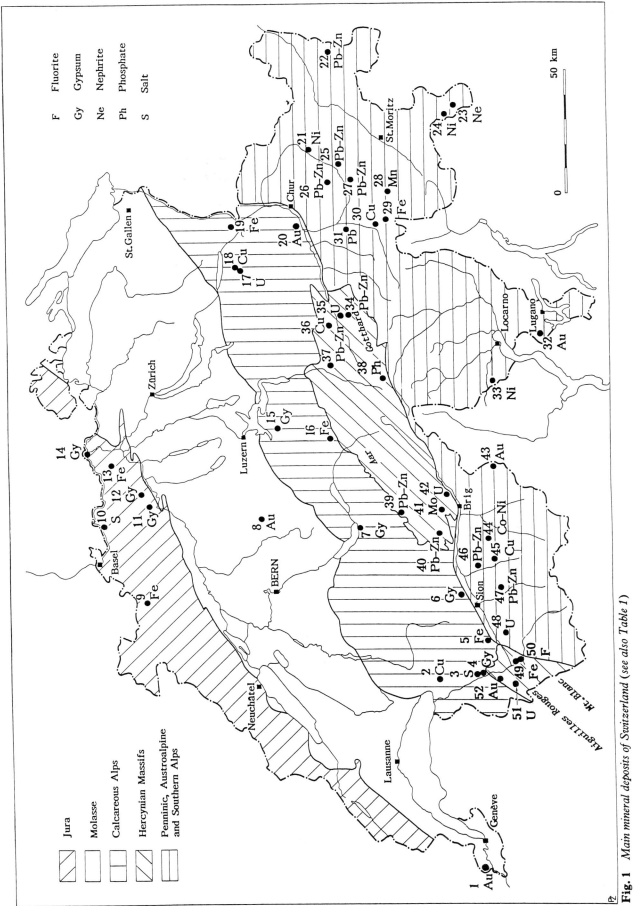

Fig. 1 *Main mineral deposits of Switzerland (see also Table 1)*

Table 1 *Main mineral deposits of Switzerland**

No. on Fig. 1	Locality	Canton	Commodity	Geological province	References
1	Allondon	Genève	Gold	Molasse	73
2	Leysin	Vaud	Copper	Calcareous Alps	65
3	Bex	Vaud	Salt	Calcareous Alps	7, 105
4	Bex	Vaud	Gypsum	Calcareous Alps	81
5	Chamoson	Wallis	Iron	Calcareous Alps	21, 102
6	Granges	Wallis	Gypsum	Calcareous Alps	81
7	Leissigen	Bern	Gypsum	Calcareous Alps	80
8	Napf	Luzern	Gold	Molasse	90
9	Delemont	Jura	Iron	Jura	9
10	Schweizerhalle	Basel Land	Salt	Jura	45
11	Läufelfingen	Basel Land	Gypsum	Jura	79
12	Kienberg	Solothurn	Gypsum	Jura	80
13	Herznach	Aargau	Iron	Jura	30, 32
14	Felsenau	Aargau	Gypsum	Jura	79
15	Ennetmoos	Unterwald	Gypsum	Calcareous Alps	79
16	Erzegg	Bern	Iron	Calcareous Alps	22, 102
17	Mürtschenalp	Glarus	Uranium	Calcareous Alps	4
18	Mürtschenalp	Glarus	Copper	Calcareous Alps	4
19	Gonzen	St-Gall	Iron	Calcareous Alps	25
20	Calanda	Grisons	Gold	Calcareous Alps	5, 6, 15
21	Totalp	Grisons	Nickel	Penninic Alps	72
22	S-charl	Grisons	Lead–zinc	Austroalpine Alps	27, 53
23	Scortaseo	Grisons	Nephrite	Penninic Alps	24
24	Poschiavo	Grisons	Nickel	Penninic Alps	75
25	Silberberg	Grisons	Lead–zinc	Penninic Alps	27
26	Bleiberg	Grisons	Lead–zinc	Penninic Alps	27
27	Bärenbühl	Grisons	Lead–zinc	Penninic Alps	27
28	Oberhalbstein	Grisons	Manganese	Penninic Alps	37, 114
29	Val Ferrera	Grisons	Iron	Penninic Alps	40, 101
30	Alp Ursera	Grisons	Copper	Penninic Alps	27
31	Alp Taspin	Grisons	Lead–zinc	Penninic Alps	27
32	Astano	Tessin	Gold	Southern Alps	39, 55
33	Palagnedra	Tessin	Nickel	Penninic Alps	76, 106
34	Alp Nadèls	Grisons	Lead–zinc	Gotthard	35
35	Trun	Grisons	Uranium	Gotthard	56
36	Puntaiglas	Grisons	Copper	Gotthard	35
37	Bristenstock	Uri	Lead–zinc	Aar	52
38	Pizzo Corandoni	Tessin	Phosphate	Gotthard	104
39	Trachsellauenen	Bern	Lead–zinc	Aar	87
40	Goppenstein	Wallis	Lead–zinc	Aar	49, 109
41	Baltschiedertal	Wallis	Molybdenum	Aar	61, 89, 100
42	Naters	Wallis	Uranium	Aar	58
43	Gondo	Wallis	Gold	Penninic Alps	41, 43
44	Kaltenberg	Wallis	Nickel–cobalt	Penninic Alps	38
45	Grimentz	Wallis	Copper	Penninic Alps	44
46	St. Luc	Wallis	Lead–zinc	Penninic Alps	96
47	Praz Jean	Wallis	Lead–zinc	Penninic Alps	18
48	Isérables	Wallis	Uranium	Penninic Alps	48
49	Mont Chemin	Wallis	Iron	Mt Blanc	46
50	Les Trappistes	Wallis	Fluorspar	Mt Blanc	60, 112
51	Le Chatelard	Wallis	Uranium	Aiguilles Rouges	59
52	Salanfe	Wallis	Gold	Aiguilles Rouges	54, 85, 103

* See also Fig. 1.

Cretaceous age, and covered by horizontal or subhorizontal Oligocene and Miocene molasse sediments.

Small surface workings have been exploited since antiquity in many parts of the Jura. Underground mines were active in the nineteenth and the beginning of the twentieth centuries, the Delemont mining district being the largest and the most important. Residual iron ore has the average chemical composition (%) 44·5 Fe, 0·3 Mn, 11·0 SiO_2, 0·1 Al_2O_3, 0·1 CaO, 0·06 MgO, 0·03 P and 0·1 S. Probable reserves are in the order of 2 500 000 tonne.

Herznach–Fricktal, Aargau[30,32,51,83] (13) Sedimentary Middle Jurassic (or Brown Jura) iron ores are well known throughout Central Europe. They exist in

Switzerland in the Jura mountain range as well as in the Calcareous Alps and are of Callovian (Upper Dogger) age. The ore horizon has a varying thickness of 2·0–7·5 m. The bulk of the iron (80%) is contained in ferruginous ooliths, and the cement is of a marly nature. The ooliths/cement ratio is generally 1:1.

The average chemical composition (%) is 30 Fe, 0·3 Mn, 15 SiO_2, 6·5 Al_2O_3, 15 CaO, 1 MgO, 0·3 P and 0·2 S. Underground reserves with an iron content of 28% and greater are of approximately 30 000 000 tonne.

Molasse basin

The Tertiary sedimentary basin, which consists mainly of sandstones, shales and conglomerates, was formed by the erosion of Alpine rocks and their subsequent sedimentation under marine, lacustrine and fluvio-terrestrial conditions during and mainly after the main phase of the Alpine orogeny.

Placer gold
Allondon, Geneva[73] (1) Small and uneconomic gold placers have been described in the Allondon river gravels near Geneva. The presence of gold in this region is due to the concentration of very small gold particles contained in moraine material composed of gold-bearing Alpine rocks.

Napf, Luzern[57,90] (8) In the Napf region a gold-bearing conglomerate of Miocene age was formed by erosion of Alpine formations situated to the southwest. Small secondary gold-bearing placers exist in the gravels of the streams and rivers that intersect the conglomeratic formations. These placers have an average gold content of 0·45 g/tonne.

Past production for the Canton Luzern has been estimated from historical records at 31·4 kg gold (1523–1800). Larger quantities were produced in the nearby cantons of Aargau and Bern. Figures on reserves in river gravels are not available, but they are believed to be small and uneconomic.

Calcareous Alps

Autochthonous rocks of Upper Palaeozoic and predominantly Mesozoic age were strongly deformed during the Alpine orogeny and emplaced in their present form of classic overthrusts (Helvetic, Ultra-Helvetic and Préalpes nappes). Sediments encountered in the Helvetic overthrusts have a certain similarity to those which exist in the Jura.

*Copper**
Préalpes[65] (2) Interesting copper mineralization of 'red bed' type was recently discovered in a pelagic series of Palaeocene age (*couches rouges*) in the Préalpes Médianes nappe in the Préalpes Romandes (Switzerland) and the Chablais (France). The copper minerals are sparsely disseminated in marls and can be followed along the same stratigraphic horizon for more than 60 km along the strike. In Fig. 1 only the copper showings near Leysin in the canton of Vaud are indicated. The most frequent mineral assemblage comprises bornite, chalcocite, covellite, chalcopyrite and barite. A less frequent association is formed of native copper, cuprite and barite. Minute malachite specks are often visible on weathered surfaces. The genesis of this mineralization is comparable with that of the White Pine, Michigan, copper deposit. The copper mineralization appears to be of no economic significance, but further detailed investigations are warranted.

Mürtschenalp, Glarus[4] (18) Here concordant small mineralized lenses are confined to so-called 'red bed type' Permian breccias, sandstones and dolomite of the Helvetic Glarner nappe. This sequence is also known locally under the name 'sernifite' for the coarser varieties. Bornite and chalcopyrite are the main copper-bearing minerals, often accompanied by tetrahedrite and small amounts of other sulphides. In one of the 18 showings pitchblende has been noted in association with copper-bearing minerals. The genesis of this deposit is somewhat controversial. Grade and reserve figures are not available.

Gold
Calanda, Grisons[5,6,15] (20) The Taminser crystalline series, composed of slightly metamorphosed spilites, keratophyres and their associated volcaniclastics, belongs to the Permian root zone of the Helvetic nappes. These veins occur in the shales of the Lower Dogger, overlying the Taminser crystalline basement. Native gold is found in calcite veins in association with pyrite and arsenopyrite. Faint traces of scheelite and fluorite have been reported from areas adjacent to the abandoned gold mines. The mineralization is considered to be of late Alpine age. Grade and reserves are unknown, but are considered to be small.

Iron
Chamoson, Wallis[21,22,30,83] (5) The sedimentary oolitic iron deposit near Chamoson lies in the Callovian (Upper Dogger) of the Helvetic Morcles nappe. The main oolitic layer horizon has a thickness of approximately 1 m. Such a small iron deposit merits mention because it is the type locality of the mineral chamosite, $(Fe^{+2}, Mg, Fe^{+3})_5 Al(Si_3Al)O_{10}(OH,O)_8$[28]—an iron chlorite well known in many parts of the world. Total reserves of iron ore (at 30% Fe) are approximately 1 000 000 tonne.

Erzegg, Bern[22,30,83,102] (16) This deposit of sedimentary oolitic iron ore is similar to that of Chamoson. Total reserves (with a content of 30% Fe) are estimated at approximately 1 200 000–2 000 000 tonne.

---
* Pure copper ore deposits are not common in Switzerland. More frequently, copper-bearing minerals are associated with galena and sphalerite: hence, they are mentioned in conjunction with the lead-zinc deposits.

Manganese

Gonzen, St-Gall[25,83] (19) A manganiferous iron ore horizon, 1·5–3 m thick, occurs between underlying Sequanian (Upper Jurassic) limestones locally called 'Unterer Quintenkalk' and overlying Kimmeridgian limestones ('Plattenkalk'). All these formations belong to the Malm (Upper Jurassic) of the Helvetic nappes.

A lower ore layer is entirely composed of hematite, with over it an upper layer also of hematite but with local concentrations of manganese ore in the form of elongated lenses. The transition from hematite to manganese ore takes place through a mixed zone of iron–manganese carbonate ore, which is followed by pure rhodochrosite and a core of small hausmannite lenses (1–20 m long and 1 m thick). The transition is very abrupt and the zones in which iron and manganese occur together never exceed 10 cm in thickness. The presence of an iron- and manganese-rich horizon in a calcareous sedimentary sequence is somewhat surprising. It is believed that the coexisting iron and manganese minerals may have been derived from the nearby Lower Penninic ophiolites and that their formation could be the result of precipitation from exhalative-sedimentary solutions.

Figures of average grade are not available, the Fe and Mn contents varying greatly within the deposit, which was not mined selectively. They are of the order of 34% Fe and 12% Mn. Possible reserves are of some 2 000 000 tonne.

Uranium*

Mürtschenalp, Glarus[4] (17) More than 50 concordant mineralized lenses are present in the so-called 'red bed type' Permian breccias, sandstones and dolomite of the Helvetic Glarner nappe to which they are confined. Small concordant copper-bearing lenses are also known in the same region in the same geological environment. Pitchblende is associated with them only in one showing. The uranium-bearing radioactive zones are generally small. They occupy a surface area of 2–100 m² each.

The main uranium-bearing mineral is pitchblende, accompanied by small amounts of different sulphides. The presence of pitchblende in gel-like structures, melnikovite–pyrite and bravoite is of interest since these minerals form at low temperatures. The genesis of these deposits is somewhat controversial. Grade and reserve figures are not available.

Hercynian massifs

The Mt Blanc–Aiguilles Rouges Massif in western Switzerland and the Aar–Gotthard Massif in the central and eastern part of the country consist of granite and granitoid rocks. These intrusive cores are surrounded by a suite of schists formed during the Hercynian and to some extent probably during the Caledonian orogenies. The granitic cores and their metamorphic envelopes were deformed again to some extent during the Alpine orogeny, in which they acted mainly as the stable 'basement' mass of the Alps, against and over which the rocks of the Alpine 'geosyncline' were thrust, generally from the southeast to the northwest.

Copper

Puntaiglas, Grisons[35,113] (36) Four km northwest of Trun a small orebody is present in the metamorphic formations of the Hercynian Gotthard Massif. It contains chalcopyrite in association with magnetite and pyrite.

Gold

Salanfe, Wallis[54,85,103] (52) This deposit is in the metamorphic border zone of the Aiguilles Rouges Hercynian Massif. The bedrock consists of gneisses, micaschists and granite with intercalated marmorized limestones, partly transformed into skarns. The mineralization consists of concordant, irregular, massive lenses and disseminations of arsenopyrite, löllingite and pyrite. Gold is rarely visible under the microscope, but it is always associated with arsenic-bearing minerals. The presence of scheelite associated with gold has been reported recently. Reserves amount to 10 000 tonne at 35 g/tonne gold.

Iron

Mont Chemin, Wallis[46,83] (49) Several small magnetite lenses occur approximately 4 km southeast of the town of Martigny. The host rock is a tightly folded sequence of sericitic gneisses and micaschists with intercalated marble lenses that belong to the metamorphic envelope of the Hercynian Mont Blanc Massif. The main ore mineral is slightly martitized magnetite associated with pyrite (rare) and safflorite (very rare). Hornblende, biotite, garnet and stilpnomelane are the main gangue minerals. The metamorphic nature of the ore and the host rock has completely obliterated all primary features, but it is assumed that the formation of the ore is probably related to Hercynian or pre-Hercynian granitic intrusions.

The average grade is 25–30% Fe. Proven reserves do not exceed 7000 tonne, but the presence of additional reserves in the lower levels of the deposit should not be completely ruled out.

---

* Uranium-bearing minerals as accessory constituents of pegmatites have been repeatedly reported,[67,71] but the systematic search for uranium deposits was initiated only in 1956 with funds provided by the Federal Government and to a lesser extent by Swiss and foreign private industry. The first radioactive anomalies were located in 1957, in the Fionnay–Nendaz tunnel (Valais) during the course of the survey of the tunnels driven to harness the water of the Grande Dixence hydroelectric power scheme.[47] Above this tunnel an interesting ore zone was subsequently discovered in the Isérables region. Radioactive anomalies were also discovered in other tunnels and surface channels, but projections to the surface could not be located or are merely of secondary interest.[23,77] This initial stage of general uranium exploration, with a particular accent on the Alpine part of the country, has been completed and a general report with detailed location maps is in preparation.

Lead–zinc
Alp Nadèls, Grisons[35] (34) Small and narrow galena–sphalerite veins occur in a gangue of quartz and carbonates 4 km south of Trun.

Bristenstock, Uri[52] (37) Small sulphide lenses occur in the metamorphic envelope of the eastern Aar Massif. The main ore minerals are arsenopyrite, galena, sphalerite and chalcopyrite in a quartz–sericite–chlorite gangue. They have been compared with the classic Freiberg 'kiesige Bleiformationen'.

Geochemical orientation surveys with the application of different field methods were carried out in the vicinity of known orebodies. Satisfactory results were obtained by biogeochemical sampling of grasses (*Calamagrostis villosa* (Chaix), *Calamagrostis arundinacea* L., *Astrantia minor* L., *Juncus trifidus* L. and *Astrantia minor* L.).

Trachsellauenen, Bern[87] (39) Several veins, weakly mineralized with galena and sphalerite in a barite gangue, occur in the pre-Triassic migmatitic basement of the western Hercynian Aar Massif. The veins, which are believed to be Hercynian or Alpine in age, have been affected by Alpine metamorphism.

A detailed geochemical survey in this region was successful inasmuch as anomalies in stream sediments and soils can be correlated quite satisfactorily with the known veins. In several instances their extension under the Quaternary cover in a very mountainous area could be located.

Goppenstein, Wallis[8,49,109] (40) This deposit is in the pre-Hercynian metamorphic envelope of the Aar Massif. Granite porphyries, biotite-gneisses and amphibolites are the prevailing rocks of the region. The ore zone is a concordant 'vein' in this metamorphic environment. It can be followed over a total length of 6 km with an average width of 0·50–2 m. The main ore minerals are sphalerite, galena, pyrite, pyrrhotite accompanied by smaller amounts of arsenopyrite, tetrahedrite and chalcopyrite. Quartz, calcite, barite and fluorite form the gangue. The deposit was mined intermittently until the end of the second world war. Grades and remaining reserves are unknown.

Molybdenum
Baltschiedertal, Wallis[61,89] (41) Molybdenite-bearing granite occurs north of Visp in the Bietschhorn region. This granite is a border facies of the Aar granite, the intrusive core of the Hercynian Aar Massif. Ten mineralized quartz veins have been reported in thin shear zones on a rather steep cliff composed of a granite body approximately 300 m long. The lower part of the vein system probably continues under a thick scree cover.

The entire mineralized zone—not just the single veins—has to be considered for the calculation of average grade and reserves and for possible mining operations. The deposit is at a high elevation (2700–3000 m) in difficult terrain and partly hidden under a heavy scree cover. Lichen growth on the rocks makes it difficult to observe the molybdenite in the field. It has been reported recently that molybdenite is associated with scheelite. Results of recent prospecting and drilling activities undertaken by a private mining company are not available.

Other occurrences (Wallis)[100] Other small molybdenite showings have been described from several localities in the western Aar granite.

Uranium
Trun, Grisons[56,113] (35) Radioactive anomalies are present 1·5 km south of Trun in mica-schists and gneisses of the Tavetscher Zwischenmassif, a small elongated body composed of metamorphic rocks, between the Hercynian Aar Massif to the north and the Hercynian Gotthard Massif to the south.

Uraninite is associated with pyrite, magnetite and hematite as well as small amounts of polymetallic sulphides (Co, Ni, Cu, Pb, Mo) and native gold. Quartz, sericite and chlorite are the main gangue minerals. A hydrothermal genesis of Hercynian age with a subsequent Alpine remobilization has been proposed.

Naters, Wallis[58] (42) A narrow zone with weak and apparently irregular uranium mineralization occurs in the southern metamorphic (gneissic) envelope of the Hercynian Aar Massif in the region of Brig. This zone is concordant with the gneisses in which it is situated. Pitchblende occurs frequently as minute accessory granules (1–10 μm in diameter) in mica-rich gneisses and schists, augen gneisses, and on shear planes in intercalated granite–aplite layers. If coarser pitchblende occurs in the same rocks, it is associated with pyrite, galena or molybdenite. The presence of pyrite is evidenced by a faintly gossanous zone on the roadcut near Naters. The mineralization is considered as pre-Alpine (Permian, Hercynian or older). A surface rock sample of approximately 5 tonne yielded an average uranium content of 0·26–0·3 kg U/tonne.

Le Chatelard and Les Marecottes, Wallis[59] (51) Many radioactive anomalies exist in the Vallorcine biotite-granite, an elongate and thin body (15 km × 0·5–1·5 km) that stretches northeastwards from the French border to the Rhône Valley near Miéville. This granite is part of the Hercynian Aiguilles Rouges Massif. The mineralized zones are generally confined to shear zones, mylonites and fissures within the granite, but extensions into neighbouring rocks have also been observed. Pitchblende occurs in quartz or calcite gangue without accompanying ore minerals and, less frequently, with minor amounts of sphalerite and galena. It can be assumed that the uranium ore is of a Hercynian age but underwent a considerable remobilization during the Alpine orogeny.

Heavy vegetation and scree cover in rugged mountain terrain are hindering factors in a detailed exploration of this promising area, in which field work is still in progress. Selected hand specimens yield grades of 0·2–20 kg U/tonne.

Penninic, Austroalpine and southern Alps

This unit, in which the highest mountains of Switzerland are found, consists of a complicated sequence of sedimentary, volcanic and mainly metamorphic rocks of Precambrian (?), Palaeozoic and Mesozoic age. Their deformation, which occurred during the Alpine orogeny, gave rise to large and complicated overthrusts, such as the St. Bernard–Monte Rosa nappe and the Dent Blanche nappe in the western and central part of the country and the numerous Penninic and Austroalpine nappes in the eastern part. Towards the south these overthrusts are separated from the metamorphic southern Alps by what is termed a 'root-zone' in classic Alpine terminology. A new interpretation of this root-zone in the light of plate tectonic concepts is currently emerging, but the original position of the nappes of the whole region before they were thrust into their present position remains conjectural.

Many fundamental and classic studies on Alpine metamorphism have been carried out in this part of the Alps as well as in the Hercynian massifs and the Calcareous Alps. Several interesting reviews on this subject and maps of metamorphic facies are available in the recent literature.[3,33,66,68]

In detail, the polyphase metamorphism prevalent in these geological provinces is rather complicated.

After a more or less well-preserved pre-Alpine metamorphism the first Alpine phase of Upper Cretaceous age was characterized by low-temperature–high-pressure conditions that gave rise to a limited development of blue-schist and eclogite facies rocks. Subsequently, the main phase, of Eocene–Oligocene age, produced rocks of typical Barrovian greenschist–amphibolite facies grade (gneisses, amphibolites, calcareous and pelitic schists, locally called *schistes lustrés* or *Bündner Schiefer*).

The chemical, mineralogical and structural transformations that most ore deposits underwent during Alpine and even earlier phases of metamorphism did not attract the attention of many geologists until recently.[69] There is little doubt that the careful evaluation of the impact of metamorphism on Alpine ore deposits will yield results of great interest for the establishment of modern and more accurate genetic models.

The Casanna schists, which form the crystalline core of the large St. Bernard nappe in Wallis, deserve particular mention, as several generally concordant polymetallic veins occur in them. Originally they were a sedimentary sequence with intercalated acid and basic lavas as well as primary and reworked tuffs. In their present epimetamorphic state they consist of amphibole–chlorite–sericite schists and gneisses, grading into biotite gneisses, massive ophiolites in the greenschist facies, which are locally called 'prasinites', quartz porphyries and thin graphitic layers. The Casanna schists are sheared and tightly folded. A Permo-Carboniferous age is generally put forward although the presence of older rocks cannot be ruled out completely.[11,88]

Most of the polymetallic, strata-bound and metamorphic ore deposits in the Casanna schists are part of the same metallogenic province. In the past they were thought to be of hydrothermal origin, owing to Swiss geologists' almost exclusive exposure to classic magmatic theories, but they may represent the result of a primary syngenetic deposition in a volcano-sedimentary environment with subsequent reconcentration during the Alpine orogeny. If this new working hypothesis is confirmed, they could well be compared with similar deposits in other metamorphic belts. Although such a debate may seem of purely academic nature, it might have a significant bearing on future exploration programmes.

Copper

Alp Ursera, Grisons[27] (30) Near the village of Andeer a small copper deposit occurs between gneisses and Triassic quartzites of the metamorphic core of the Penninic Suretta nappe. The principal minerals of the narrow ore zone are silver-bearing tetrahedrite, chalcopyrite and pyrite with accessory bornite and galena in a barite gangue.

Grimentz, Wallis[44] (45) Cu–Bi–Ag mineralization occurs northeast of the village of Grimentz in the Upper Anniviers valley. It is in sericite–chlorite schists that belong to the Casanna schists of the Penninic St. Bernard nappe. The Casanna schists have been described in this region as a laminated and strongly folded sequence of sericite–chlorite schists and gneisses, with interbedded amphibolites and muscovite–tourmaline-bearing pegmatitic rocks. Mineralized veins, generally concordant with the bedrock, occur mainly in sericite–chlorite schists. In the richest zone, in which the abandoned Baicolliou mine is situated, the average thickness of the ore does not exceed 10–15 cm, but extends for 350 m along the strike and 100 m downdip. The principal ore minerals are chalcopyrite, tetrahedrite, pyrite and bismuthinite. They are embedded in a gangue composed of ankerite, quartz, barite and albite. The average ore grade has been assayed as 1·54% Cu, 0·4% Bi and 69 g/tonne Ag.

The Val d'Anniviers ores have been considered to be of typical hydrothermal origin, but their concordant position in a metamorphic sequence of volcano-sedimentary origin and their constant relationship to the same host rock along the strike raise genetic questions that warrant a modern structural and metallogenic appraisal of the whole district.

Gold

Astano, Tessin[39,55] (32) The Astano region, in the so-called 'Seengebirge', one of the main units of the

Southern Alps, is composed of rocks of sedimentary and volcanic origin with clear evidence of a polyphase metamorphism and a complicated history of major successive structural deformations. Tightly folded meso- to kata-metamorphic K-feldspar, two-mica and plagioclase gneisses were formed in the Astano region (Malcantone). Narrow barren and mineralized veins occur in this region. The veins have a well-defined zonal distribution.

In the veins of the central or Miglieglia zone, occupying a surface area of approximately 4 km², arsenopyrite, galena, sphalerite and chalcopyrite are the most abundant ore minerals. In addition, this zone is characterized by the presence of such antimony-bearing minerals as native antimony and antimonite, as well as of antimony sulphides in variable quantities (tetrahedrite, jamesonite, gudmundite, bournonite, miargyrite, pyrargyrite, etc.). Native gold is frequent, at times in discrete macroscopic grains 1–2 mm in diameter. These grains cannot be seen with a hand lens on weathered or broken hand specimens, but they are clearly visible as soon as a specimen is sawn. Although grades of 226 g/tonne Au and 13·750 g/tonne Ag have been indicated, practically no mining activity has been reported from this area owing to the limited extension of the veins, at least on or near the surface. Quartz and ankerite are the most important gangue minerals. Typical wallrock alteration consists of chloritization, sericitization and ankeritization.

The outer or Astano zone surrounds the central zone. It is completely devoid of antimony-bearing minerals. The typical mineral association of its veins consists of pyrite, arsenopyrite, sphalerite and galena. Pyrrhotite, chalcopyrite and marcasite occur in minor amounts. Gold occurs principally when the four main sulphides are present, and is less abundant when only galena and sphalerite or arsenopyrite and pyrite are predominant. Native gold occurs in the form of inclusions in pyrite and arsenopyrite and also as discrete grains between other sulphide grains. The inclusions have a diameter of 5–15 μm, whereas the discrete grains tend to be somewhat larger (5 μm × 20 μm). Finally, gold also occurs in solid solution in arsenopyrite.

The main gangue mineral is quartz, but the presence of tourmaline is worthy of mention. Sericitization, ankeritization and silicification are the typical wallrock alteration types in this zone. Past production figures of Costa mine are not available. It is thought that remaining reserves are of the order of 10 000 tonne at an average grade of 20 g/tonne gold.

A further interesting and somewhat puzzling feature of the Astano region is the presence of two rather well-delimited areas in which ore boulders of unknown origin occur in Quaternary formations over a surface of approximately 0·8 km² and 2·5 km². Two distinct boulder types have been defined: the first consists of pyrite, magnetite, arsenopyrite, marcasite, chalcopyrite and sphalerite with minor amounts of galena and molybdenite in an ankerite–quartz gangue; in the second only pyrite, sphalerite, galena and some cassiterite are present in a quartz gangue. It would certainly be interesting to establish the origin of these boulders, but the almost sub-tropical density of vegetation renders direct exploration methods difficult. Hence, modern geochemistry and geophysics have to be applied.

Gondo, Wallis[41,43] (43) This deposit is the only known occurrence on Swiss territory of the Italian Monte Rosa metallogenic gold province. More than 20 small gold- and silver-bearing veins cross the two-mica gneiss of the Lower Penninic Antigorio nappe. The thickness of the quartz veins varies greatly, but at times reaches 30 cm. Pyrite is irregularly distributed in the quartz veins and appears to be the main gold-bearing mineral. Small native gold inclusions, exceptionally up to 0·1 mm in diameter, can occasionally be observed in pyrite crystals. Galena, probably silver-bearing, chalcocite and covellite have also been observed. A rare interesting silver mineral is schapbachite (mixed crystals of matildite ($AgBiS_2$) and galena in widely varying proportions).[84]

The average grade of the veins is not well known, but has been tentatively estimated at 5·7 g/tonne from mining records that date from the end of the last century. The gold content of hand-picked specimens can vary between 1 and 84 g/tonne, and the silver content is between 20 and 520 g/tonne. A more accurate re-evaluation of the Gondo gold deposit, though certainly desirable, is made arduous by its location at an elevation of 1000–2000 m in a relatively inaccessible mountainous region.

Iron

Val Ferrera, Grisons[40,82,83,101] (29) Small iron–manganese ore deposits occur in folded epimetamorphic Jurassic quartzites, dolomites and marbles of the Penninic Suretta and Schams nappes. These small orebodies, older than the Alpine movements, are concordant with the folded sediments. The main ore minerals are hematite and braunite in a quartz–sericite–calcite gangue. The iron ore is finely stratified, whereas the manganese ore is concentrated in small lenses and nodules. The ore deposits are considered to be of marine-sedimentary origin, syngenetic with the Triassic sediments. The average grade is not available and reserves are very small. In the same region small veins and lenses of siderite and hematite have also been described in Triassic rocks. They are considered to be genetically related to the nearby iron–manganese ores.

Lead–zinc

S-charl, Grisons[27,53] (22) South of the village of Scuol narrow concordant veins occur in dolomites of Anisian, Ladinian and Carnian (Triassic) age that belong to the Austroalpine Campo nappe. They consist of galena and sphalerite, with accessory jamesonite, tetrahedrite and pyrite in a fluorite–baryte–quartz gangue.

Silberberg, Bleiberg and Bärenbühl, Grisons[27] (25–27) Three small strata-bound deposits occur near Filisur in the Anisian and Ladinian ('Arlberg Dolomit') dolomites of the Penninic Sivretta nappe. The thickness of the mineralized zone is 1·5 m, but the main ore zone is only 0·70–0·80 m thick. The typical mineral association consists of sphalerite (and/or galena) with minor amounts of jamesonite and pyrite. The name of Silberberg is somewhat misleading, no significant silver production ever having been reported.

Alp Taspin, Grisons[27] (31) Near the village of Zillis small and narrow mineralized veins occur in gneiss of the Penninic Margna nappe. The thickness of the veins is 0·20–0·30 m (exceptionally, 1 m). Galena is accompanied by accessory pyrite, tetrahedrite, sphalerite, chalcopyrite and bornite in a quartz–barite gangue.

St. Luc–Bella Tola, Wallis[96] (46) In the lower Anniviers valley there are numerous small concordant veins in the Casanna schists of the Penninic St. Bernard nappe. The usual mineral association comprises galena, sphalerite, tetrahedrite, chalcopyrite and in some instances also bornite. The gangue is composed of quartz, less frequently of quartz and ankerite, and occasionally of baryte.

Praz Jean, Wallis[18] (47) The bedrock of the mineralized zone is composed of sericite schists and gneisses of the Casanna schists of the Penninic St. Bernard nappe. The thickness of the mineralized zone, which is generally concordant with the bedrock, is approximately 20–35 cm. The most common mineral assemblage is a mixture of galena and sphalerite with some tetrahedrite, jamesonite, pyrite, pyrrhotite and chalcopyrite in a quartz–ankerite gangue. Tourmaline inclusions have been noted in the quartz and sphalerite grains.

The silver content of the galena is very high. Some samples have yielded 1·5–2·0 kg/tonne silver in the lead and in one instance even 4 kg. Reserves are unknown, but are thought to be small.

Manganese

Oberhalbstein, Grisons[37,114] (28) Manganese ore deposits are associated in the region south of Bivio with the ophiolites of the Penninic Platta nappe. The manganese-bearing zones are confined to folded red radiolarian cherts. Braunite is the prevailing ore mineral. It may partially or completely replace the quartz test of radiolarian micro-organisms in the cherts. Late fissures contain small amounts of the following secondary manganese minerals, which have been discovered and determined for the first time in this region: tinzenite[31] $((Ca, Mn, Fe)Al_2BSi_4O_{15}(OH))$, sursassite[31] $(Mn_5Al_4Si_5O_{21}\cdot 3H_2O(?))$ and parsettensite[31] $(Mn_5^{+2}Si_6O_{13}(OH)_8(?))$.

Approximately 7000 tonne at an average grade of 30–36% Mn has been mined, reserves being estimated at some 13 000 tonne.

Nickel in ultrabasic rocks

Poschiavo, Grisons;[75] (24) *Totalp, Grisons*;[72] (21) *and Palagnedra, Tessin*[34,76,106] (33) Pentlandite, awaruite and heazlewoodite are normal accessory nickel-bearing minerals in Alpine ultrabasic intrusions. They have been reported from the Malenco serpentinites near Poschiavo, the Totalp serpentinites near Davos and the Finero peridotites in the Centovalli region (Locarno). In the latter intrusion, which belongs to the Ivrea zone, layered chromite concentrations have also been observed. Although the nickel content of these ultrabasic intrusions appears to be normal (0·2–0·3% Ni), higher than average nickel concentrations (up to 1–2% Ni) in the Finero peridotite near the village of Palagnedra are presently being investigated, but results are not available.

Nickel–cobalt

Kaltenberg, Wallis[38] (44) A narrow mineralized and generally concordant zone is present in a chlorite–sericite schist sequence. One layer of hornblende–epidote schist has been observed in this sequence, which is part of the Casanna schists of the Penninic St. Bernard nappe.

The mineral assemblage is composed of a great variety of Ni–Co minerals, and particularly of smaltite, chloanthite, safflorite, rammelsbergite, arsenopyrite, cobaltite, niccolite, maucherite and some magnetite and bismuth. The gangue is essentially composed of carbonates (ankerite, siderite and dolomite) and quartz. A grade of 1·0–1·8% Co, 1–2% Ni and 0·1–2% Bi is indicated. Reserves are unknown, but are considered to be small.

Uranium

Isérables, Wallis[48] (48) A discontinuous uraniferous zone more than 5 km long is present in the Casanna schists of the Penninic St. Bernard nappe. This zone stretches from the Isérables region to the Col des Mines near Verbier. The main host rock is a chlorite–sericite–albite paragneiss. The main ore mineral is pitchblende, which is generally associated with pyrite and minor amounts of chalcopyrite and tetrahedrite.

It has been suggested that the uraniferous minerals were deposited within clastic sediments of Permian age, and subsequently underwent a considerable remobilization during the Alpine orogeny. Preliminary sampling results indicate a rather low average uranium grade of 0·3 kg/tonne. In acid leaching tests the soluble rate of uranium is of 71–93% by weight. Reserves are unknown, and further exploration work in this region is planned.

Non-metallics

Fluorspar

Les Trappistes, Wallis[60,112] (50)

Several fluorite veins exist in the Sembrancher region, among which the Trappistes vein is the best known and possibly the most important. The veins are concordant in laminated two-mica gneisses and quartz porphyries that belong to the metamorphic envelope of the northern termination of the Mont Blanc Hercynian granite massif.

The Trappistes vein is composed of calcite, whitish fluorite, quartz and lenses of country rock, some silver-bearing galena, sphalerite and small amounts of pyrite and chalcopyrite. The fluorite vein is 1250 m long, 800 m deep and 0·5–1·5 m wide. It is lenticular and often ramified. It is believed that the vein is of Permo-Carboniferous age. A rather conservative estimate of reserves of 44 000 tonne at an average grade of 14% CaF_2 has been given.

The fluorite veins in the Tête des Econduits area, in the nearby Col des Planches region, are currently under investigation by a private mining company. The results of this investigation are not available, but renewed fluorspar mining activity in this region should not be completely ruled out.[112]

Gypsum

Bex, Vaud;[81] (4) *Granges, Wallis;*[81] (6) *Leissigen, Bern;*[80] (7) *Läufelfingen, Basel Land;*[79] (11) *Kienberg, Solothurn;*[79] (12) *Felsenau, Aargau*[79] (14) *and Ennetmoos, Unterwald*[79] (15)

Gypsum occurs in considerable quantities in the Triassic evaporites in the Jura and the Calcareous Alps. It is currently exploited in seven localities, mainly for the production of cement additives and plaster. The annual production of 350 000 tonne covers the total needs of the country. Reserves are considerable.

Nephrite

Scortaseo, Grisons[24] (23)

The interesting nephrite–talc deposit of Scortaseo is near the village of Poschiavo. It occurs in a 'Schuppenzone' assigned partly to the Upper Penninic Margna nappe and partly to the reduced continuation of the Schams nappes. The deposit occurs as two lenses, 100 m long, 3–5 m wide and at least 30 m deep. One lens is embedded in dolomitic marbles and the other is at the contact of these rocks and muscovite–chlorite gneisses. The actual nephrite rocks consist principally of very pale green nephrite masses in bundles and tufts that exhibit a finely felted texture. Especially characteristic are aggregations of nephrite in lens-shaped grains (1–10 mm in diameter) surrounded by talc margins and a calcite cement. This fine amphibole felt is an almost pure (Fe- and Al-free) grammatite nephrite.

The nephrite–talc lenses are believed to have been formed through the metasomatism of dolomitic marbles by the introduction of silicic acid solutions. These solutions are genetically related to the nearby Malenco serpentine.

The annual production of the small operating mine reached 1500 tonne of nephrite-bearing rock. The material was used for the manufacture of different types of 'Swiss jade' jewellery, and particularly of necklaces. Talc-rich material was shipped to nearby Italian paper factories. Production ceased because of the danger of rockfalls.

Phosphates

Pizzo Corandoni, Tessin[104] (38)

Two apatite–biotite schist layers are present in two-mica and garnet-bearing gneisses of the metamorphic envelope of the Gotthard Hercynian Massif. The width of the apatite schists varies between 0·3 and 7·9 m, but a width of 1–3·5 m has been used for tonnage calculations.

Quartz and other minerals in Alpine fissures[67,71,98,99]

For many centuries the Swiss Alps have been famous for the magnificent quartz crystals and various other minerals that can be admired in many private and public collections worldwide. In a broad sense Alpine fissures can be considered as ore deposits since the minerals extracted from them have, at times, proved to be of a certain commercial value. They continue to be actively traded, even though, as in the case of quartz, they are no longer used for the production of crystal glass or vases, as in the last century. Accurate production figures of crystal are not available, but, according to rather conservative estimates, they are of the order of value of several hundred thousand Swiss francs per year.

From a consideration of the above facts it becomes evident that the traditional interest in Alpine crystals has led to the special development of Swiss crystallography and mineralogy and this, in turn, has stimulated many young Swiss to devote themselves to the study and practice of earth sciences.

Apart from quartz, classic minerals in Alpine vugs are adularia, a transparent variety of orthoclase (the name originates from Pizzo Adula, Tessin), albite, hematite ('iron rose'), pink fluorite, titanite, epidote, actinolite, anatase, brookite, rutile and many others of interest.

Exploration for and exploitation of Alpine cavities are traditionally the privilege of prospectors who live in Alpine valleys, better known under their German name *Strahlers*. Tales and legends about the discovery and the secret location of famous vugs are numerous and often romantic. Although 'Strahlers' continue to exercise their trade in line with ancestral methods, often passed from father to son and remaining in the same families for centuries, less responsible groups, by the use of mechanized means, have recently changed exploitation methods dramatically. Reports of the utilization of helicopters, jackhammers and dynamite are unfortunately common. This somewhat ruthless search for crystals may rapidly deplete Alpine cavities if appropriate legislation in this field is not enacted and enforced rapidly.

Alpine quartz crystals have also been studied with positive results for their piezoelectric properties and applications, but low reserves of suitable raw materials preclude their use in the electronic industry.[36] It may be mentioned in this regard that the Swiss production and export of synthetic gemstones (rubies, sapphires, etc.) is well developed.

Salt

Rheinfelden, Aargau–Schweizerhalle, Basel Land[45] (10)
This salt layer, which is part of a Triassic evaporite sequence, is intercalated in anhydrite of the so-called sulphate zone. It has been intersected by drilling to a depth of 150–400 m and varies in thickness from 29 to 59 m. The salt is exploited by solution mining in Rheinfelden. Annual production varies between 250 000 and 300 000 tonne. The brine is also used locally for curative purposes in the Rheinfelden spa.

Salt is also extracted by solution mining from the same layer near Zurzach, Aargau, 30 km east of Rheinfelden. It is employed exclusively for industrial purposes, mainly for the production of soda, by the Schweizerische Soda Fabrik, a member of the Belgian Solvay group. Annual production is put at more than 100 000 tonne. The production of the salt deposits immediately south of the Rhine river (and that exploited near Bex, Wallis), meets Swiss domestic and industrial requirements.

Bex, Vaud[7,105] (3)
This salt is contained in an irregular brecciated layer (*brèche salifère*) within a Triassic evaporite sequence that consists mainly of anhydrites and gypsum. Owing to its strong tectonic deformation, the thickness of the entire sequence cannot be measured accurately, but it is estimated to be of the order of 400–500 m. Underground mining took place as early as the fourteenth century. At present salt is extracted by solution mining from underground workings through drill-holes. Annual production is of the order of 15 000–20 000 tonne.

Conclusions and outlook

The purpose of this review is to emphasize the great variety of Swiss mineral deposits. Notwithstanding the wealth of available information, there is ample scope for further pure and applied research in this field. Geochronological dating and detailed structural analysis are required to solve the old controversy of Hercynian versus Alpine emplacement of many vein-type deposits. Ore microscopy studies should be complemented by microprobe trace mineral investigations. Geochemical and geophysical exploration methods, which have been tested in the past in some rare instances, should be applied more frequently and systematically.[52,54,62,63,87,107] Detailed grade and tonnage figures are necessary, but in many instances they cannot be obtained without preliminary clearing and reopening of old workings.

Future investigations could be hindered by various adverse factors, such as the existence of a thick glacial and soil cover in many parts of the country, particularly below the timber line, rising concern for environment and landscape protection in those parts of the country that rely heavily on the tourist industry and the traditional lack of domestic risk capital. These limiting factors are certainly compensated for by a renewed interest in scientific circles in a better understanding of metallogenic and economic problems and by the growing concern in government and industry about the almost total reliance on imported mineral raw materials.

In this respect it may be worthwhile mentioning that from 1980 to 1984 the Swiss National Science Foundation sponsored for the first time a mineral exploration project. This project was carried out in the Hercynian and Penninic formations of the Canton of Wallis by the Universities of Fribourg, Geneva and Lausanne. Modern geochemical and geophysical exploration methods applied to a mountainous alpine environment were utilized to establish an up-to-date metallogenetic model for the known ore deposits, and on a regional base, and to evaluate the potential of the area under study in regard to base metals, gold, scheelite, etc. A comprehensive final report on this project was submitted to the Swiss National Science Foundation in 1985.

Acknowledgement

The author wishes to thank Professor F. de Quervain, Past-President of the Swiss Geotechnical Commission, for his critical reading of this manuscript and his pertinent comments on many Swiss ore deposits.

References

1 **Amsler A.** Die alten Eisenindustrien des Fricktales, bei Erlinsbach und in benachbarten Gebieten des östlichen Juras im Licht der Flurnamen. *Beitr. Geol. Schweiz, geotech. Ser., kleinere Mitt.* no. 6, 1937, 56 p.
2 **Aubert D. and Badoux H.** *Carte géologique générale de la Suisse, 1:200.000, feuille 1, Neuchâtel* (Berne: Kümmerly & Frey, 1956).
3 **Ayrton S. N. and Ramsay J. G.** Tectonic and metamorphic events in the Alps. *Schweiz. miner. petrogr. Mitt.,* **54,** 1974, 609–39.

4 **Bächtiger K.** Die Kupfer- und Uranmineralisationen der Mürtschenalp (Kt. Glarus, Schweiz). *Beitr. Geol. Schweiz, geotech. Ser.* no. 38, 1963, 113 p.

5 **Bächtiger K.** Die neuen Goldfunde aus dem alten Goldbergwerk "Goldene Sonne" am Calanda (Kt. Graubünden). *Schweiz. miner. petrogr. Mitt.*, **47**, 1967, 643–57.

6 **Bächtiger K. Rüdlinger G. and Cabalzar W.** Scheelit in Quartz- und Fluorit-Gängen am Calanda (Kt. Graubünden). *Schweiz. miner. petrogr. Mitt.*, **52**, 1972, 561–3.

7 **Badoux H.** Description géologique des mines et salines de Bex et de leurs environs. *Beitr. Geol. Schweiz, geotech. Ser.* no. 41, 1966, 56 p.

8 **Barbey O.** Le gisement plombifère de Goppenstein. Université de Genève thèse no. 933, 1933, 48 p.

9 **Baumberger E. Schardt H. and Chaix A.** Bohnerz. *Beitr. Geol. Schweiz, geotech. Ser.* no. 13, pt 1, 1923, 1–150.

10 **Bearth P.** Contribution à la subdivision tectonique et stratigraphique du cristallin de la nappe du Grand-St-Bernard dans le Valais (Suisse). In *Livre à la mémoire du professeur P. Fallot* (Paris: Société Géologique de France, 1960–63), vol. II, 407–18.

11 **Bearth P. and Lombard A.** *Carte géologique générale de la Suisse, 1:200.000, feuille 6, Sion* (Berne: Kümmerly & Frey, 1964).

12 **Bureau de Recherches Géologiques et Minières.** *Carte des gîtes minéraux de la France, 1:320.000, feuille Lyon* (Paris: BRGM, 1963).

13 **Buxtorf A.** *Geologische Generalkarte der Schweiz, 1:200.000, Blatt 2, Basel-Bern* (Bern: Kümmerly & Frey, 1951).

14 **Buxtorf A. and Nabholz W.** *Geologische Generalkarte der Schweiz, 1:200.000, Blatt 3, Zürich-Glarus* (Bern: Kümmerly & Frey, 1957).

15 **Cadisch J.** Die Erzvorkommen am Calanda. *Beitr. Geol. Schweiz, geotech. Ser., kleinere Mitt.* no. 7, 1939, 20 p.

16 **Cadisch J.** *Die Geologie der Schweizer Alpen* (Basel: Wepf, 1953), 480 p.

17 **Cadisch J. Allemann F. Blaser R. and Schaetti H.** *Carte géologique 1:25.000 Fürstentum Lichtenstein* (Zürich: Orell Füssli, 1953).

18 **Cheneval R.-E.** Le gisement de galène argentifère de Praz-Jean (Val d'Hérens). *Journal de Genève*, 1947, 7–62.

19 **Collet L. W.** *Structure of the Alps* (Huntington, N.Y.: Krieger Publishing Co., 1935), 304 p.

20 **Collet L. W.** *Carte géologique générale de la Suisse, 1:200.000, feuille 5, Genève-Lausanne* (Berne: Kümmerly & Frey, 1955).

21 **Delaloye M. F.** Contribution à l'étude des silicates de fer sédimentaires. Le gisement de Chamoson (Valais). *Beitr. Geol. Schweiz, geotech. Ser.* no. 13, pt 9, 1966, 71 p.

22 **Déverin L.** Etude pétrographique des minerais de fer oolithiques du Dogger des Alpes suisses. *Beitr. Geol. Schweiz, geotech. Ser.* no. 13, pt 2, 1945, 115 p.

23 **Dietrich V. Huonder N. and Rybach L.** Uranvererzungen im Druckstollen Ferrera – Val Niemet. *Beitr. Geol. Schweiz, geotech. Ser.* no. 44, 1967, 27 p.

24 **Dietrich V. and de Quervain F.** Die Nephrit-Talklagerstätte von Scortaseo (Puschlav, Kt. Graubünden). *Beitr. Geol. Schweiz, geotech. Ser.* no. 46, 1968, 78 p.

25 **Epprecht W.** Die Eisen- und Manganerze des Gonzen. *Beitr. Geol. Schweiz, geotech. Ser.* no. 24, 1946, 128 p.

26 **Epprecht W.** Unbekannte schweizerische Eisenerzgruben sowie Inventar und Karte aller Eisen- und Manganerzvorkommen der Schweiz. *Beitr. Geol. Schweiz, geotech. Ser., kleinere Mitt.* no. 19; *Schweiz. miner. petrogr. Mitt.*, **37**, 1957, 217–46.

27 **Escher E.** Erzlagerstätten und Bergbau im Schams, in Mittelbünden und im Engadin. *Beitr. Geol. Schweiz, geotech. Ser.* no. 18, 1935, 120 p.

28 **Fehlmann H.** Die schweizerische Eisenerzeugung: ihre Geschichte und wirtschaftliche Bedeutung. *Beitr. Geol. Schweiz, geotech. Ser.* no. 13, pt 3, 1932, 255 p.

29 **Fehlmann H. and de Quervain F.** Eisenerze und Eisenerzeugung der Schweiz. *Beitr. Geol. Schweiz, geotech. Ser.* no. 13, pt 8, 1952, 31 p.

30 **Fehlmann H. and Rickenbach E.** Die eisenhaltigen Doggererze der Schweiz. *Beitr. Geol. Schweiz, geotech. Ser.* no. 13, pt 7, 1962, 121 p.

31 **Fleischer M.** *Glossary of mineral species*, 2nd edn (Bowie, Maryland: Mineralogical Record, Inc., 1975), 145 p.

32 **Frei A.** Die Mineralien des Eisenbergwerks Herznach im Lichte morphogenetischer Untersuchungen. *Beitr. Geol. Schweiz, geotech. Ser.* no. 13, pt 6, 1952, 162 p.

33 **Frey M. Hunziker J. C. Frank W. Bocquet J. Dal Piaz G. V. Jäger E. and Niggli E.** Alpine metamorphism of the Alps: a review. *Schweiz. miner. petrogr. Mitt.*, **54**, 1974, 247–90.

34 **Friedenreich O.** Die Chrom–Nickelvererzungen des Peridotitstockes von Finero–Centovalli. *Beitr. Geol. Schweiz, geotech. Ser., kleinere Mitt.* no. 17; *Schweiz. miner. petrogr. Mitt.*, **36**, 1956, 227–43.

35 **Friedlaender C.** Erzvorkommnisse des Bündner Oberlandes und ihre Begleitgesteine. *Beitr. Geol. Schweiz, geotech. Ser.* no. 16, pt 1, 1930, 1–70.

36 **Friedlaender C.** Untersuchung über die Eignung alpiner Quarze für piezoelektrische Zwecke. *Beitr. Geol. Schweiz, geotech. Ser.* no. 29, 1951, 98 p.

37 **Geiger Th.** Manganerze in den Radiolariten Graubündens. *Beitr. Geol. Schweiz, geotech. Ser.* no. 27, 1948, 88 p.

38 **Gilliéron F.** Geologisch-petrographische Untersuchungen an der Ni–Co-Lagerstätte Kaltenberg (Turtmanntal, Wallis). *Beitr. Geol. Schweiz, geotech. Ser.* no. 25, 1946, 51 p.

39 **Graeter P.** Geologie und Petrographie des Malcantone (südliches Tessin). *Schweiz. miner. petrogr. Mitt.*, **31**, 1951, 361–483.

40 **Grünenfelder M.** Petrographie des Roffnakristallins in Mittelbünden und seine Eisenvererzung. *Beitr. Geol. Schweiz, geotech. Ser.* no. 35, 1956, 57 p.

41 **Grünenfelder M.** Erzmikroskopische Beobachtungen an den Goldquarzgängen von Gondo (Simplon, Wallis) und Alpe Formazzolo (Val Calneggia, Tessin). *Beitr. Geol. Schweiz, geotech. Ser., kleinere Mitt.* no. 18; *Schweiz. miner. petrogr. Mitt.*, **37**, 1957, 1–8.

42 **Gwinner M. P.** *Geologie der Alpen* (Stuttgart: Schweizerbart'sche Verlagsbuchhandlung, 1971), 477 p.

43 **Gysin M.** Les mines d'or de Gondo. *Beitr. Geol. Schweiz, geotech. Ser.* no. 15, 1930, 123 p.

44 **Halm E.** Die Kupfer–Wismut-Lagerstätten im obern Val d'Anniviers (Wallis). *Beitr. Geol. Schweiz, geotech. Ser.* no. 22, 1945, 89 p.

45 **Hauber L.** Zur Geologie des Salzfeldes Schweizerhalle-Zinggibrunn (Kt. Baselland). *Eclogae geol. Helv.*, **64**, 1971, 163–83.

46 **Hugi E. Huttenlocher H. F. Gassmann F. and Fehlmann H.** Die Magnetitlagerstätten. *Beitr. Geol. Schweiz, geotech. Ser.* no. 13, pt 4, 1948, 116 p.

47 **Hügi Th.** Uranvererzungen in Gesteinen des Wallis (Schweiz). *Schweiz. miner. petrogr. Mitt.,* **38,** 1958, 393–400.

48 **Hügi Th. Köppel V. de Quervain F. and Rickenbach E.** Die Uranvererzungen bei Isérables (Wallis). *Beitr. Geol. Schweiz, geotech. Ser.* no. 42, 1967, 88 p.

49 **Huttenlocher H. F.** Die Blei–Zinklagerstätten von Goppenstein (Wallis). *Beitr. Geol. Schweiz, geotech. Ser.* no. 16, pt 2, 1931, 1–45.

50 **Huttenlocher H. F.** Die Erzlagerstättenzonen der Westalpen. *Beitr. Geol. Schweiz, geotech. Ser., kleinere Mitt.* no. 4; *Schweiz. miner. petrogr. Mitt.,* **14,** 1934, 21–149.

51 **Jeannet A.** Stratigraphie und Palaeontologie des oolithischen Eisenerzlagers von Herznach und seiner Umgebung. *Beitr. Geol. Schweiz, geotech. Ser.* no. 13, pt 5, 1951, 240 p.

52 **Jenni J.-P.** Die Vorkommen von Bleiglanz, Kupferkies und Zinkblende des Bristenstocks (Kt. Uri). *Beitr. Geol. Schweiz. geotech. Ser.* no. 53, 1973, 145 p.

53 **Kellerhals P.** Neue Beobachtungen in den aufgelassenen Pb–Zn-Bergwerken von S-charl (Unterengadin). *Eclogae geol. Helv.,* **55,** 1962, 468–75.

54 **Koehn Ph.** Contribution géochimique à l'étude du gîte d'or et d'arsenic de Salanfe (Valais). *Matér. Géol. Suisse, Bull. (Beitr. Geol. Schweiz, geotech. Ser., kleinere Mitt.)* no. 38, 1966, 12 p.

55 **Köppel V.** Die Vererzungen im insubrischen Kristallin des Malcantone (Tessin). *Beitr. Geol. Schweiz, geotech. Ser.* no. 40, 1966, 123 p.

56 **Kramers J. D.** Zur Mineralogie, Enstehung und alpinen Metamorphose der Uranvorkommen bei Trun, Graubünden. *Beitr. Geol. Schweiz, geotech. Ser.* no. 52, 1973, 75 p.

57 **Kündig E. and de Quervain F.** *Fundstellen mineralischer Rohstoffe in der Schweiz, mit Übersichtskarte,* 1 : 600.000 (Bern: Kümmerly & Frey, für Schweizerische Geotechnische Kommission, 1953), 214 p.

58 **Labhart T. P.** Die Uranvererzungen am Südrand des Aarmassivs bei Naters (Kt. Wallis, Schweiz). *Beitr. Geol. Schweiz, geotech. Ser.* no. 43, 1967, 30 p.

59 **Labhart T. P. and Rybach L.** Granite and Uranvererzungen in den Schweizer Alpen. *Beitr. Geol. Schweiz, geotech. Ser., kleinere Mitt.* no. 60; *Geol. Rdsch.,* **63,** 1974, 135–47.

60 **Ladame G.** Le gisement de galène et de spatfluor des Trappistes (Valais). *Beitr. Geol. Schweiz, geotech. Ser.* no. 19, 1935, 34 p.

61 **Ledermann H.** Zur Kenntnis der Molybdänglanzlagerstätte im Baltschiedertal (Wallis). *Beitr. Geol. Schweiz, geotech. Ser.* no. 33, 1955, 41 p.

62 **Loup G. and Woodtli R.** Une prospection géochimique stratégique dans la région d'Alesses (Valais). *Bull. Lab. Géol. Mus. géol. Univ. Lausanne,* **157,** 1965, 1–6.

63 **Loup G. and Woodtli R.** Deux exemples de prospection géochimique en Valais: sur l'indice de Cocorier et sur la mine de Bruson. *Bull. Lab. Géol. Mus. géol. Univ. Lausanne,* **157,** 1965, 7–15.

64 **Loup G. and Woodtli R.** Quatre profils géochimiques à travers le Jura vaudois. *Schweiz. miner. petrogr. Mitt.,* **46,** 1966, 353–5.

65 **Martini J.** Un horizon à minéralisations cuprifères dans les Préalpes médianes romandes et chablaisiennes (Alpes occidentales). *C.r. Séanc. Soc. Phys. Sci. nat., Genève,* **6,** 1971, 33–46.

66 **Martini J.** Le métamorphisme dans les chaînes alpines externes et ses implications dans l'orogenèse. *Schweiz. miner. petrogr. Mitt.,* **52,** 1972, 257–75.

67 **Niggli P. Koenigsberger J. and Parker R. L.** *Die Mineralien der Schweizeralpen* (Basel: Wepf & Co., 1940), 2 vols, 661 p.

68 **Niggli E. coordinator.** *Metamorphic map of the Alps,* 1 : 1 000 000, metamorphic map of Europe, sheet 17 (Paris: Unesco, 1973).

69 **Niggli E.** Alpine Metamorphose von Erzvorkommen der Schweizer Alpen. *Schweiz. miner. petrogr. Mitt.,* **54,** 1974, 595–608.

70 **Omenetto P. and Brigo L.** Metallogenesi nel quadro dell'orogene delle Alpi (con particolare riguardo al versante italiano). *Mem. Soc. géol. Italiana,* **XIII,** 1974, supplem., 24 p.

71 **Parker R. L.** *Die Mineralienfunde der Schweizer Alpen* (Basel: Wepf & Co., 1973), 431 p.

72 **Peters Tj.** Mineralogie und Petrographie des Totalpserpentins bei Davos. *Schweiz. miner. petrogr. Mitt.,* **43,** 1963, 529–684.

73 **Pittard J.-J.** La recherche de l'or dans la région de Genève. *Mém. du Globe,* **LXXV,** 1936, 93 p.

74 **de Quervain F.** 50 Jahre Geotechnische Kommission der Schweizerischen Naturforschenden Gesellschaft 1899–1949. *Beitr. Geol. Schweiz, geotech. Ser., kleinere Mitt.* no. 15, 1949, 27 p.

75 **de Quervain F.** Die Erzmineralien des Serpentins von Selva–Quadrada (Puschlav). *Beitr. Geol. Schweiz, geotech. Ser., kleinere Mitt.* no. 30; *Schweiz. miner. petrogr. Mitt.,* **43,** 1963, 295–312.

76 **de Quervain F.** Das Nickelerzvorkommen Val Boschetto im Centovalli (Tessin). *Beitr. Geol. Schweiz, geotech. Ser., kleinere Mitt.* no. 44; *Schweiz. miner. petrogr. Mitt.,* **47,** 1967, 633–41.

77 **de Quervain F.** Die Uranvererzung Valsorey südlich Bourg St. Pierre (Wallis). *Beitr. Geol. Schweiz, geotech. Ser., kleinere Mitt.* no. 59; *Schweiz. miner. petrogr. Mitt.,* **53,** 1973, 203–15.

78 **de Quervain F.** Schweizerische Geotechnische Kommission, Bericht über die Tätigkeit 1949–1974. *Beitr. Geol. Schweiz, geotech. Ser., kleinere Mitt.* no. 62, 1974, 22 p.

79 **de Quervain F. and Frey D.** *Geotechnische Karte der Schweiz,* 1 : 200.000, Blatt 2, Luzern–Zürich–St. Gallen–Chur, mit *Erläuterungen* (Bern: Kümmerly & Frey, 1963), 64 p.

80 **de Quervain F. and Hofmänner F.** *Geotechnische Karte der Schweiz,* 1 : 200.000, Blatt 1, Neuchâtel–Bern–Basel, mit *Erläuterungen* (Bern: Kümmerly & Frey, 1964), 100 p.

81 **de Quervain F. and Frey D.** *Carte géotechnique de la Suisse,* 1 : 200.000, feuille 3, Genève–Lausanne–Sion, avec texte explicatif (Bern: Kümmerly & Frey, 1965), 104 p.

82 **de Quervain F. and Frey D.** *Carta geotecnica della Svizzera,* 1 : 200.000, foglio 4, Bellinzona–St. Moritz, con note esplicative (Bern: Kümmerly & Frey, 1967), 122 p.

83 **de Quervain F. and Zitzmann A.** The iron ores of Switzerland. In *The iron ore deposits of Europe and adjacent areas* **Zitzmann A.** ed. (Hannover: Bundesanstalt für Geowissenschaften und Rohstoffe, 1977), vol. 1, 295–7.

84 **Ramdohr P.** *The ore minerals and their intergrowths* (Oxford, etc.: Pergamon Press, 1969), 1174 p.

85 **Rickenbach E. and von Känel F.** Die Arsen–Gold-Lagerstätte von Salanfe (Wallis). *Beitr. Geol. Schweiz, geotech. Ser.* no. 31, 1953, 52 p.

86 **Rybach L.** Uranprospektion in der Schweiz. *Mitt. Institut Geophysik, ETH, Zürich* 142, 1976.

87 **Saheurs J. P.** Geochemische Prospektion im Gebiet der Blei–Zink–Baryt-Lagerstätten bei Trachsellauenen (Berner

Oberland/Schweiz). *Beitr. Geol. Schweiz, geotech. Ser.* no. 55, 1975, 91 p.

88 **Schaer J. P.** Géologie de la partie septentrionale de l'éventail de Bagnes (entre le Val d'Hérémence et le Val de Bagnes, Valais, Suisse). *Arch. Sci. Genève,* **12**, 1959, 473–620.

89 **Schenker M.** Neuere Beobachtungen über das Auftreten und die Ausdehnung der Molybdänglanzvorkommen in Baltschiedertal (Wallis). *Eclogae geol. Helv.,* **58**, 1965, 423–41.

90 **Schmid K.** Über den Goldgehalt der Flüsse und Sedimente der miozänen Molasse des NE-Napfgebietes (Kt. Luzern). *Beitr. Geol. Schweiz, geotech. Ser., kleinere Mitt.* no. 58; *Schweiz. miner. petrogr. Mitt.,* **53**, 1973, 125–56.

91 **Schweizerische Geologische Gesellschaft.** *Geologischer Führer der Schweiz,* 1–9 (Basel: Wepf, 1967), 915 p.

92 **Schweizerische Geologische Kommission.** *Tektonische Karte der Schweiz, 1:500.000* (Wabern-Bern: Eidg. Landestopographie, 1972).

93 **Schweizerische Geologische Kommission.** *Geologische Generalkarte der Schweiz, 1:200.000, Blatt 4, St. Gallen-Chur* (Bern: Kümmerly & Frey, 1975).

94 **Schweizerische Geologische Kommission.** *Geologische Generalkarte der Schweiz, 1:200.000, Blatt 7, Ticino* (Bern: Kümmerly & Frey, 1975).

95 **Schweizerische Geologische Kommission.** *Geologische Generalkarte der Schweiz, 1:200.000, Blatt 8, Engadin* (Bern: Kümmerly & Frey, 1976).

96 **Sigg J.** Contribution à l'étude pétrographique et minière de la partie inférieure du Val d'Anniviers et plus particulièrement de la région de Saint-Luc–Bella-Tola. *Beitr. Geol. Schweiz, geotech. Ser.* no. 21, 1944, 58 p.

97 **Sommerauer J.** Radiometrische und erzpetrographische Untersuchungen im Muskovit-Alkalifeldspat-Augengneis von Alp Taspegn, Kanton Graubünden. *Beitr. Geol. Schweiz, geotech. Ser.* no. 48, 1972, 46 p.

98 **Stalder H. and Hoverkamp F.** *Minéraux, trésors de nos Alpes* (Lausanne: Mondo, 1973), 175 p.

99 **Stalder H. and Hoverkamp F.** *Mineralien, verborgene Schätze unserer Alpen* (Lausanne: Mondo, 1973), 175 p.

100 **Steck A. and Hügi Th.** Das Auftreten des Molybdänglanz im westlichen Aarmassif und Molybdängehalte von Gesteinen der gleichen Region. *Beitr. Geol. Schweiz, geotech. Ser., kleinere Mitt.* no. 51; *Schweiz. miner. petrogr. Mitt.,* **50**, 1970, 257–76.

101 **Stucky K.** Die Eisen- und Manganerze in der Trias des Val Ferrera. *Beitr. Geol. Schweiz, geotech. Ser.* no. 37, 1960, 67 p.

102 **Tröhler B.** Geologie der Glockhaus-Gruppe. Mit besonderer Berücksichtigung des Eisenoolithes der Erzegg-Planplatte. *Beitr. Geol. Schweiz, geotech. Ser.* no. 13, pt 10, 1966, 137 p.

103 **Wagner J.-J. and Wellhauser F.** Etude des courants électriques naturels liés à la Mine de Salanfe (Valais). *Matér. Géol. Suisse, Bull. (Beitr. Geol. Schweiz, geotech. Ser., kleinere Mitt.)* no. 34, 1965, 7 p.

104 **Zweifel H. and de Quervain F.** Der Biotit-Apatitschiefer des P. Corandoni (Val Cadlimo, Tessin). *Beitr. Geol. Schweiz, geotech. Ser.* no. 32, 1954, 44 p.

105 **Badoux H.** Géologie des mines de Bex, données 1966–1980. *Beitr. Geol. Schweiz, geotech. Ser.* no. 60, 1981, 32 p.

106 **Bianconi F. Haldemann E. G. and Muir J. E.** Geology and nickel mineralization of the eastern end of the Finero Ultramafic–Mafic Complex (Ct. Ticino, Switzerland). *Beitr. Geol. Schweiz, geotech. Ser., kleinere Mitt.* no. 70; *Schweiz. miner. petrogr. Mitt.,* **58**, 1978, 223–36.

107 **Bodmer Ph.** Geophysikalische Untersuchung der Eisenoolithlagerstätte von Herznach–Wölflinswil. *Beitr. Geol. Schweiz, geotech. Ser.* no. 13, pt 11, 1978, 63 p.

108 **Gidon M.** *Carte géologique simplifiée des Alpes occidentales du Léman à Dignes, 1:250.000* (Orléans: Bureau de Recherches Géologiques et Minières, 1978).

109 **Morel F.** L'extension du filon Pb–Zn de Goppenstein (Valais–Suisse), contribution à son étude géophysique et géochimique. *Beitr. Geol. Schweiz, geotech. Ser.* no. 57, 1978, 92 p.

110 **Trümpy R.** *Geology of Switzerland, a guide book. Part A: an outline of the geology of Switzerland; Part B: geological excursions* (Basel, New York: Wepf & Co., 1980), 334 p.

111 **Mastrangelo F. Natale P. and Zucchetti S.** Quadro giacimentologico e metallogenico delle Alpi occidentali italiane. *Ass.. Mineraria subalpina,* **XX**, 1–2 1983, 203–48.

112 **Hubacher W.** L'exploration, de 1971 à 1976, de fluorine à la Tête des Econduits. *Minaria Helvetica, Schweiz. Ges. historische Bergbauforschung,* 1983, 9–20.

113 **Staub T.** Die Fahlerz- und Uranvorkommen bei Affeier (Vorderrheintal, Graubünden). *Beitr. Geol. Schweiz, geotech. Ser.* no. 62, 1982, 67 p.

114 **Suana M.** Die Manganerzlagerstätten von Tinizong (Oberhalbstein, Graubünden). *Beitr. Geol. Schweiz, geotech. Ser.* no. 64, 1984, 92 p.

R. Osika

Poland

In this chapter the metallic ore deposits and the more important non-metallic deposits of Poland are described.

The exploitation of mineral deposits in Poland dates back to prehistoric times. Mining of Cretaceous and Jurassic flint was already in operation in the Mesolithic, but the major development took place in the Neolithic in the region of Krzemionki Opatowskie. During the Halstadt and Lathen periods, about 750–400 years before our era, an iron mining and foundry centre, which was the largest in Europe, was in operation on the slopes of the Góry Świętokrzyskie (Holy Cross Mountains). In the eleventh century, during the reign of King Bolesław Chrobry, gold was extracted from alluvial deposits in the region of Złotoryja and other localities of Lower Silesia. At that time the development of salt mining in Wieliczka was also started. In the fourteenth century silver and lead mines were already in existence in the Góry Świętokrzyskie and in the region of Tarnowskie Góry. In the fifteenth century extraction of native sulphur began in Szwoszowice near Krakow, and its exploitation continued uninterrupted until 1884. In the period between the wars the Rudki pyrite deposit was discovered in the Góry Świętokrzyskie. The main, intensification of prospecting work took place after the second world war.

As the geological structure of Poland became more clearly understood, numerous discoveries of mineral ore deposits were made. Particularly worthy of mention is the discovery of large deposits of native sulphur in the Tarnobrzeg region (1954), of copper ores in the Fore-Sudetic monocline (1957), ilmenite–magnetite ores in the Suwałki region (1962), new deposits of zinc and lead ores in the Zawiercie region (1969), of rock salt and potash in the region of the Bay of Puck (1968), and of numerous deposits of non-metallic minerals. The majority of these deposits are either already being exploited or are being prepared for exploitation.

Considerable quantities of minerals are at present produced in Poland. Apart from hard coal, of which 193 000 000 tonne per annum is produced, approximately 37 000 000 tonne of brown coal is extracted annually. Of the metallic ores that are exploited in Poland, mention should first be made of copper ores

The English translation of this chapter was prepared by Mrs. J. Susskind.

from the Lignica–Głogów mining region and the Bolesławice region in Lower Silesia. In 1980 about 23 500 000 tonne of copper ore was brought to the surface, and this amount increases each year. In second position come the zinc–lead ores mined in the Silesia–Krakow Triassic formations in quantities in excess of 5 400 000 tonne per annum. In third place are iron ores exploited in the Częstochowa–Kłobuck region and in the Łęczyca mining area. Approximately 1 500 000 tonne per annum of iron ore is being produced (100 000 tonne in 1980).

Among the crude minerals used in the chemical industry the most important is native sulphur, produced in the Tarnobrzeg mining region at the rate of about 5 300 000 tonne per annum of pure sulphur. In second place is rock salt mined in the Kujawy area and in the Carpathian Foredeep (approximately 4 000 000 tonne per annum). In addition, many kinds of crude industrial and building minerals are being mined in Poland. Mining of these minerals is concentrated in southern Poland—in particular, in Lower Silesia, Upper Silesia and in the Góry Świętokrzyskie.

The geological and mineral problems of Poland and of the world are the subject of many publications of the Geological Institute, the most important comprehensive works being the multi-volume work by K. Bohdanowicz *The minerals of the world* (*Surowce mineralne świata*), published in 1952; *The mineral deposits of the world* (*Surowce mineralne świata*), edited by A. Bolewski and H. Gruszczyk, 1973–83; *The geology and mineral deposits of Poland* (*Geologia i surowce mineralne Polski*), *The mineralogenic atlas of Poland* on the scale of 1 : 2 000 000 published in 1970 under the scientific editorship of R. Osika and *The map of mineral ore deposits of Poland* (*Mapa złóż surowców mineralnych Polski*) by R. Osika on the scale of 1 : 500 000 published in 1971 and, in 1984, a more complete map.[49] A more complete bibliography of publications relating to Polish mineral exploration can be found in the above works. In the list of references to this chapter the author gives only works quoted in the text.

Tectonic-metallogenic regions of Poland

Examination of the tectonics of Poland against the background of the tectonics of Europe enables three basic areas to be distinguished—the area of the

Precambrian platform of Eastern Europe, the area of the Palaeozoic platform of Western and Central Europe and the area of the Alpides of Southern Europe. The boundary between the platforms is marked by a deep tectonic fracture called the Teisseyre–Tornquist line. This line runs through the centre of Poland in a northwest–southeast direction.

Taking into consideration the diastrophic development as well as the actual structural picture[1] and the mineral ores aspect,[2] the territory of Poland can be divided into seven tectonic-metallogenic regions: (1) the region of the Góry Świętokrzyskie, (2) the region of Lower Silesia, (3) the region of Upper Silesia, (4) the region of the Carpathians, (5) the region of the

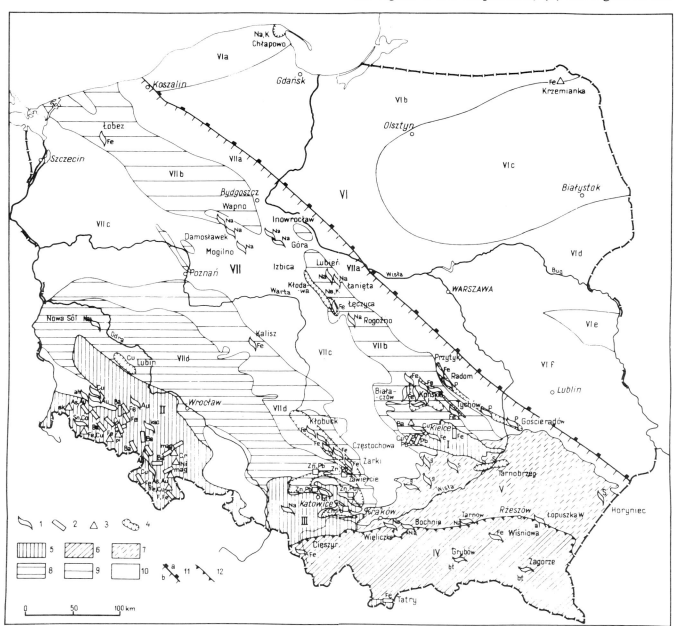

Fig. 1 *Metallogenic map of Poland. After Osika.[2] 1, Bedded deposits; 2, vein deposits; 3, irregular deposits; 4, ore-bearing areas. Fe, iron; Cu, copper; Au, gold; As, arsenic; Cr, chromium; Ni, nickel; Zn, zinc; Pb, lead; Sn, tin; Co, cobalt; Al, aluminium; S, sulphur; pi, pyrite; Na, rock salt; K, potash salts; P, phosphorites; Ba, barite; F, fluorite (fluorspar); Kw, quartz; sk, feldspar; ah, anhydrite; g, gypsum; al, alabaster; mag, magnesite; kao, kaolin; bt, bentonite; 5, Palaeozoides; 6, Alpides–Mesozoic–Caenozoic rocks of Carpathian Flysch; 7, Alpides–Miocene rocks of Carpathian Foredeep; 8, Permo-Triassic horizon; 9, Jurassic horizon; 10, Cretaceous horizon. I, Caledonian region of Góry Świętokrzyskie; II, Variscan region of Lower Silesia; III, Variscan region of Upper Silesia; IV, Alpine region of Carpathian Flysch; V, Alpine region of Miocene of Carpathian Foredeep; VI, region of Precambrian platform: VIa, Łeba uplift; VIb, Peribaltic syncline; VIc, Mazury–Suwałki uplift; VId, Podlasie depression; VIe, Sławatycze uplift; VIf, River Bug depression; VII, region of Palaeozoic platform: VIIa, marginal basin; VIIb, Central Polish Anticlinorium; VIIc, Szczecin–Łódź–Miechów synclines; VIId, Fore-Sudetic and Silesia–Krakow monocline; 11, Teisseyre–Tornquist line—boundary between Precambrian platform (a) and Palaeozoic platform (b); 12, outcrop of Main Carpathian Overthrust*

Carpathian Foredeep, (6) the region of the Precambrian platform and (7) the region of the Palaeozoic platform. The locations of these regions and deposits are set out in the metallogenic map of Poland (Fig. 1).

The first three regions are represented by the Palaeozoides, the next two belong to the Alpides and the last two constitute the platform area. The rocks in these regions were formed under different palaeogeographical conditions and were subject to different tectonic activities. Thus, there existed different conditions for the development of the processes that brought about the mineral concentrations.

Region of Góry Świętokrzyskie (Holy Cross Mountains)

The Caledonian tectonic[1] and metallogenic[2] region is represented in Poland by the Palaeozoic Massif of the Góry Świętokrzyskie together with its extension to the southeast under the Tertiary formations (Małopolska Massif[48]). The following tectonic-metallogenic cycles can be distinguished in this region: the Cadomian (Baikalian), the Caledonian, the Late Palaeozoic and the Alpine. The Cadomian cycle is represented by miogeosynclinal sediments, conglomerates and greywacke intercalations, and the sediments of the Caledonian cycle by shales with limestone intercalations,

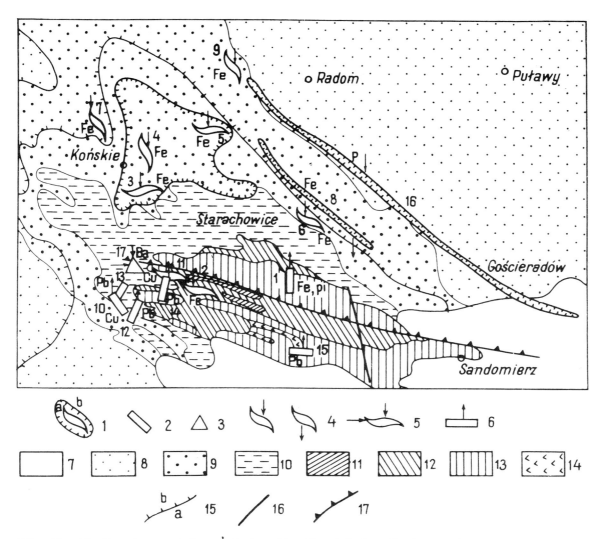

Fig. 1A *Metallogenic map of Góry Świętokrzyskie. After Osika.[2] 1, Bedded deposits: a, deposits; b, area of occurrence; 2, vein deposits; 3, irregular deposits; 4, exogenous deposits: a, sedimentary; b, weathered; 5, sedimentary-metasomatic deposits; 6, hydrothermal deposits; Fe, iron ores; Pb, lead ores; Cu, copper ores; pi, pyrite; P, phosphorites. Iron ores: 1, Rudki; 2, Dąbrowa near Kielce; 3, Stąporków district; 4, Niekłań district; 5, Chlewiska district; 6, Starachowice; 7, Białaczów district; 8, Tychów district; 9, Przytyk; copper ores: 10, Miedzianka; 11, Miedziana Góra; lead ores: 12, Chęciny district; 13, Ołowianka deposit; 14, Kielce district; 15, Łagów district; 16, Radom-Gościeradów phosphorite-bearing belt; 17, barite deposit: Strawczynek. 7, Miocene; 8, Cretaceous; 9, Jurassic; 10, Triassic; 11, Carboniferous; 12, Devonian; 13, Lower Palaeozoic (Cambrian, Ordovician, Silurian); 14, magmatic diabase rocks of Lower Palaeozoic; 15, boundary between Lower (a) and Middle (b) Jurassic; 16, faults; 17, dislocations of overthrust character*

sandstones and greywackes. The Late Palaeozoic cycle is represented by the sediments of the Devonian and the Carboniferous lying discordantly on the Eocambrian and Cambrian–Silurian sediments. As a result of the Variscan fault tectonics, numerous transverse and longitudinal dislocations were formed in which developed a pyrite and hematite mineralization. To the transverse Łysogóry dislocation, with a north–south course, is connected the Rudki hematite, siderite and pyrite deposit.[8] In the longitudinal dislocations occur copper ore deposits (Miedzianka, Miedziana Góra) and concentrations of pyrite and hematite.

In the Alpine cycle, following the tectonic activation, the Variscan displacements of the Palaeozoides of the Góry Świętokrzyskie were deepened and new faults and cracks and fissures also appeared, with which mineralization is associated. In the fissures of the Devonian dolomites and, in particular, in the western part of the Góry Świętokrzyskie, near Kielce, occur deposits of lead ores (mainly galena) and barite

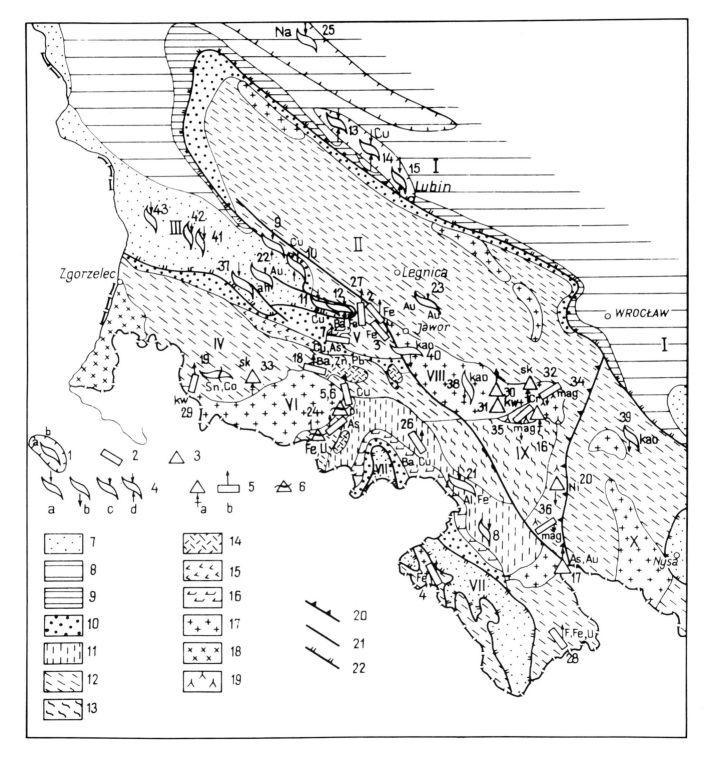

deposits.[3] Iron ore deposits (Lias and Dogger) and phosphorites (Cretaceous) were formed in sediments of Mesozoic cover (Fig. 1A).

In the Tertiary, weathered deposits of gossan type and allochthonous alluvial deposits were formed in the karstic potholes of the Devonian dolomites (Fig. 1B).

Region of Lower Silesia

The following tectonic-metallogenic cycles can be distinguished in this region: the Moldanubian, the Cadomian, the early Palaeozoic, the Variscan and the Alpine.[4] The Moldanubian cycle is represented by Precambrian gneiss and granite-gneiss with amphibolite lenses (Sowie Góry). There are no major ore concentrations in these formations. Occurrences of barite, lithium and niobium appear in the pegmatites.

The Cadomian cycle is represented by argillaceous-arenaceous geosynclinal rocks with alkaline and acid volcanites, which were metamorphosed into amphibolites, gneiss and migmatites, granite-gneiss, leucogranites and greisen. The initial volcanism gave rise to the spilite–keratophyre formation with which are connected pyrite-bearing shales and magnetites. In the chlorite schists (Góry Izerskie) occur cassiterite deposits. Towards the end of the Precambrian, ultrabasic rock intrusions formed round the Sowie Góry block (peridotites and serpentinites) with which chromites are connected.

The early Palaeozoic cycle is represented by metamorphic rocks. Initial volcanism in the Cambrian resulted in polymetallic mineralization in the Góry Kaczawskie.

With the Variscan cycle are connected endogenic and exogenic deposits. Following the Lower Devonian initial volcanism in the Góry Kaczawskie, quartz–siderite and quartz–hematite veins were formed. At the base of the Upper Carboniferous sediments overlying the gabbro-diabase massif deposits of bauxite and fireclay were formed. Towards the end of the Westphalian, geotectonic factors led to the formation of many granitic and plutonic intrusions. Hydrothermal metasomatism resulted in the formation of deposits of arsenic with gold (Złoty Stok). In the mantle of the Karkonosze granite were formed arsenopyrite deposits, including deposits of skarn type. Towards the end of the Carboniferous and in the Lower Permian, during a long period of intensive land sedimentation, molasse deposits were formed. In the intermontane depression of the Inner Sudetes basin concentrations of copper sulphides were formed. In the Lower Permian a period of tectonic activation and subsequent volcanism caused the formation of barite, sphalerite and chalcopyrite veins. Copper and salt deposits were formed in sediments of Zechstein cover. Recent geochronological research indicates an Alpine age for these veins. In the Alpine cycle magnesite deposits formed on the serpentinite massifs and, as a result of the lateritic weathering of the serpentinites, siliceous nickel ore deposits were formed. Weathering of the Variscan granite massifs gave rise to kaolin deposits. In the Quaternary there followed intensive erosion in belts of weathering leading to the concentration of heavy minerals, including gold and chromite (Fig. 1B).

Region of Upper Silesia

This region is characterized by thick clay and sandstone rocks formed in the Variscan Foredeep. Besides coal deposits, blackband ironstone, other types of ironstone (spherosideritic and sideritic iron ores) and bentonites occur in these sediments. Zinc and lead ore deposits (Middle Triassic dolomites) were formed in sediments of Mesozoic cover, as were iron ore deposits (Dogger). Salt deposits occur in Miocene sediments (Fig. 1C).

Region of the Carpathians

This region is divided into two sub-regions—the Tatra and the Flysch. In the Tatra sub-region occur rocks

Fig. 1B *Metallogenic map of Lower Silesia. After Osika.[2] 1, Bedded deposits: (a) deposits; (b) area of occurrence; 2, vein deposits; 3, irregular deposits (nests and stockworks); 4, exogenous (supergene) deposits: a, sedimentary; b, weathered; c, alluvial; d, exhalative sedimentary; 5 and 6, endogenous deposits (hypogene): 5a, magmatic deposits; 5b, hydrothermal deposits; 6, sedimentary-metamorphic deposits. Fe, iron ores; Al, aluminium ores; Cu, copper ores; Zn, Pb, zinc and lead ores; Ni, nickel ores; Sn, Co, tin and cobalt ores; As, arsenic ores; Cr, chrome ores; U, uranium; pi, pyrite; ah,g, anhydrite and gypsum; sk, feldspar; mag, magnesite; kao, kaolin; Na, rock salt; Ba, barite; F, fluorite (fluorspar); Kw, quartz; Au, gold; 1–4, Iron ores: 1, Kowary; 2, Stanisławów; 3, Męcinka; 4, Kudowa; 5–15, copper ores: 5, Miedzianka; 6, Stara Góra; 7, Chełmiec; 8, Okrzeszyn; 9, Lubichów; 10, Konrad; 11, Lena; 12, Noway Kościół; 13, Polkowice; 14, Sieroszowice; 15, Rudna; 16, Chrome ores: Tąpadła; 17 and 18, arsenic ore deposits: 17, Złoty Stok; 18, Czarnów; 19, tin and cobalt ore deposits: Gierczyn; 20, nickel ore deposit: Szklary; 21, bauxite deposit: Nowa Ruda; 22 and 23, occurrences of gold: 22, Złotoryja region; 23, Legnica region; 24, pyrite-bearing shales: Wieściszowice; 25, salt deposit: Nowa Sól; 26 and 27, barite deposits: 26, Boguszów; 27, Stanisławów; 28, fluorspar deposit: Kletno; 29–31, vein-quartz deposits: 29, Rozdroże Izerskie; 30, Krasków; 31, Sady; 32 and 33, feldspar deposits: 32, Strzeblów; 33, Kopaniec; 34–36, magnesite deposits: 34, Sobótka; 35, Wiry; 36, Ząbkowice Śl.; 37, anhydrite deposit: Niwice; 38–43, kaolinitic mineral deposits: 38, Żarów, Kalno, Śmiałowice, Bolesławice; 39, Wyszonowice; 40, Dzierzków; 41, Czerna; 42, Zebrzydowa; 43, Czerwona Woda. 7, Cretaceous; 8, Triassic; 9, Upper Permian (Zechstein); 10, Lower Permian; 11, Carboniferous and Permo-Triassic; 12, Precambrian and Palaeozoic; 13, migmatite and Precambrian gneisses; 14, acidic Post-Variscan rocks; 15, basic Post-Variscan rocks; 16, acid and basic Variscan rocks; 17, post-orogenic Variscan granites; 18, Precambrian granites; 19, ultrabasic Precambrian rocks; 20, overthrusts; 21, faults; 22, Zechstein outcrops under Tertiary sediments (southern extent of sediments of platform cover); I, Fore-Sudetic monocline; II, Fore-Sudetic Block; III, North Sudetic (Bolesławiec) depression; IV, Góry Izerskie; V, Góry Kaczawskie; VI, granite massif of Karkonosze; VII, Intra-Sudetic depression; VIII, Strzegom–Sobótka granite massif; IX, Sowie Góry massif; X, Strzelin granite massif*

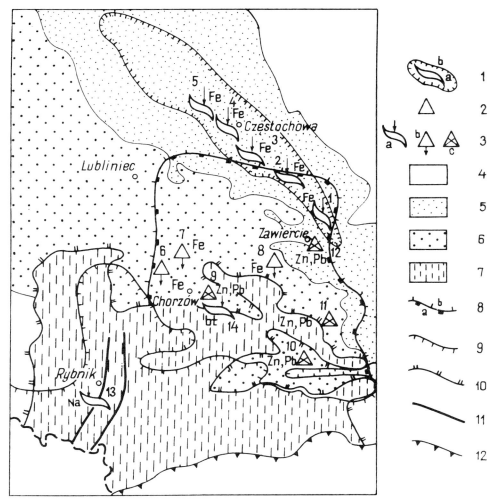

Fig. 1C *Metallogenic map of Upper Silesia. 1, Bedded deposits: a, deposits; b, area of occurrence of deposits; 2, irregular deposits; 3, exogenous deposits: a, sedimentary; b, weathered; c, origin controversial. Fe, iron ore deposits; Zn, Pb, zinc–lead ore deposits; Na, rock-salt deposits; bt, bentonite deposits; Iron ores: 1, Zarki area; 2, Poraj area; 3, Kamienica Polska area; 4, Częstochowa area; 5, Kłobuck area; 6, Tarnowskie Góry; 7, Miasteczko; 8, Mierzęcice; zinc and lead ores: 9, Bytom area; 10, Chrzanów area; 11, Olkusz area; 12, Zawiercie area; 13, rock-salt: Rybnik deposit; 14, bentonite deposit: Radzionków. 4, Cretaceous; 5, Jurassic; 6, Permian and Triassic; 7, Carboniferous; 8, presumed boundary between dolomitic facies (a) and calcareous facies (b) of Middle Triassic; 9, extent of marine Miocene; 10, limit of platform cover rocks; 11, faults; 12, outcrop of overthrust of Carpathian Flysch*

formed in the Mediterranean geosyncline and also intrusions of Variscan granite. Manganese ores occur in Jurassic sediments of the geosyncline, and with the Variscan hydrothermal processes are connected occurrences of hematite. The Flysch sub-region originated in the Alpine miogeosyncline and was marked by a weak alkaline magmatism. In the clayey sediments of the Cretaceous and Eocene occur sideritic clay ironstones, and in the Eocene bentonites and diatomites.

Region of the Carpathian Foredeep

The Carpathian Foredeep originated in the Neogene and is filled with Miocene sediments in the form of molasse. The floor on which the Miocene sediments were deposited in the larger part of this area consists of Mesozoic rocks of platform type, and in the eastern part directly under the Miocene rocks are Precambrian and Palaeozoic formations (Małopolska Massif[48]). From the metallogenic aspect the Tortonian sediments are of interest—in particular, their lower part, characterized by chemical sediments. These sediments can be divided into three facies zones—the chloride zone (the Carpathian borderland), with which are associated rock-salt deposits; the central sulphur zone, with which are associated native sulphur deposits; and the peripheral carbonate zone[31,34] (Fig. 1D).

Region of the Precambrian platform

The Precambrian platform consists of two structural levels—the Precambrian crystalline floor and the Palaeozoic–Mesozoic–Caenozoic platform cover.

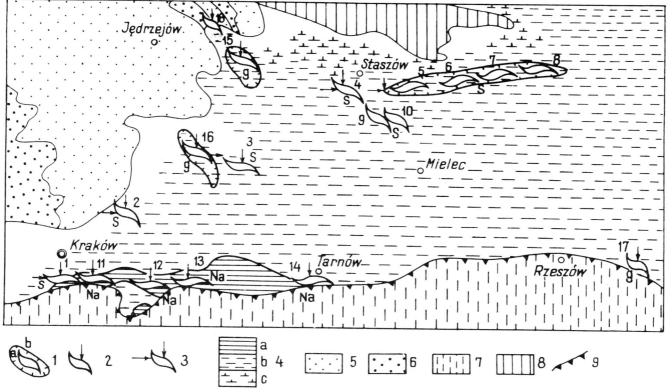

Fig. 1D *Metallogenic map of Carpathian Foredeep. After Osika.[2] 1, Bedded deposits: a, deposits; b, area of occurrence; 2, sedimentary deposits; 3, sedimentary-metasomatic deposits; S, sulphur deposits; Na, rock-salt deposits; g, gypsum deposits; bt, bentonite deposits. Sulphur: 1, Swoszowice; 2, Posądza; 3, Czarkowy; 4, Grzybów; 5, Piaseczno; 6, Machów; 7, Jeziórko; 8, Jamnica; 9, Rudniki; 10, Osiek; salt: 11, Wieliczka–Barycz; 12, Łężkowice–Siedlce; 13, Bochnia; 14, Tarnów; gypsum: 15, Pińczów district; 16, Wiślica district; 17, Łopuszka Wielka; bentonite: 18, Chmielnik. 4, Miocene (Tortonian): a, chloride facies; b, sulphate facies; c, carbonate facies; 5, Cretaceous; 6, Jurassic; 7, rocks of Carpathian Flysch (Cretaceous–Eocene); 8, Palaeozoic; 9, outcrops of Carpathian overthrust*

Within the platform one can separate the Łeba uplift, the Peribaltic depression, the Mazury–Suwałki uplift, the Podlasie depression, the Slawatycze uplift and the Nadbużańska (River Bug) depression.[1,48]

From the metallogenic point of view mention should be made of the Precambrian rocks of the crystalline basement in which occur ilmenite–magnetite deposits and where there are some signs of metalliferous ores.[5] In the Ordovician shales molybdenum–vanadium mineralization has been found; in the rocks of the Lower Carboniferous bauxite mineralization; and in the Zechstein formations rock salt and potash[33] (Fig. 1).

Region of the Palaeozoic platform

The Palaeozoic platform consists of three basic structural levels—the Precambrian crystalline basement, determined by geophysical research, the folded (Caledonian–Variscan) Palaeozoic rocks and the Zechstein–Mesozoic–Caenozoic platform cover, which in the central zones of the region reaches 7000 m. In this region smaller structural units can be distinguished, such as the Fore-Sudetic and Śląsk-Kraków monocline, the Szczecin–Łódź–Miechow downfolds, the Central Polish ridge (palaeo-anticlinorium) and the northwest part of the coastal marginal downfolds.[1,48]

From the metallogenic aspect the Caledonian–Variscan folded Palaeozoic rocks under thin platform cover in the northeast border of the Variscan depression of Upper Silesia are important. In these rocks metalliferous mineralization was detected in the Ordovician–Silurian formations, which are characterized by the presence of tuffaceous formations. Devonian formations are also mineralized in places.

Of major importance are the Zechstein formations, with which are associated copper ore deposits in the Fore-Sudetic monocline, and deposits of rock salt and potash in Kujawy (in salt diapirs) and in the Łeba uplift (Fig. 1).

The dolomites of the Middle Triassic contain important deposits of lead–zinc ores in the Śląsk-Kraków monocline. In the same region in the area of Częstochowa also occur deposits of iron ores in the Dogger. Ores of this era are also known in the region of Łęczyca and on the fringe of the Góry Świętokrzyskie. In the terrestrial sediments of the Lias occur deposits of iron ore and of refractory clays on the fringe of the

Góry Świętokrzyskie. The Cretaceous sediments contain iron ores (Valanginian, Hauterivian) and phosphorites (Albian).

Metallic ore deposits

There are in Poland iron, copper, zinc and lead, and arsenic ores, and also, in smaller quantities, ores of tin, nickel, aluminium, chrome and other metals. Most important are the magmatic-type iron ores that occur in the Suwałki region and the Dogger sedimentary iron ore deposits in the Żarki–Częstochowa–Kłobuck region. Of considerable economic importance are the Zechstein deposits of copper ores in the Fore-Sudetic monocline and zinc–lead ores in the sediments of the Silesian Triassic.

Iron ores

From the genetic point of view iron ore deposits can be divided into endogenous and exogenous deposits.

To the group of endogenous deposits belong (1) the ilmenite–magnetite ore deposit of Krzemianka (Fig. 1), (2) the magnetite–quartzite ore deposit of Kowary (Fig. 1B) and (3) veins and lenses of hematite, siderite and pyrite—veins of hematite and siderite in the Sudetes (Fig. 1B), veins of hematite and siderite in the Tatras and veins and lenses of iron ore and pyrite in the Góry Świętokrzyskie–Rudki (Fig. 1A).

To the group of exogenous deposits belong a wide variety of sedimentary deposits (see Figs. 1, 1A and 1C) and deposits formed by weathering (see Figs. 1A and 1C). Most important are the Dogger iron ore deposits in the Częstochowa–Kłobuck and the Łęczyca regions. Iron ores of Liassic age in the Końskie–Starachowice region were exploited for a long time, but for economic reasons they are no longer worked.

Table 1 *Production of iron ores in Poland*

Year	Ore production, tonne	Average Fe content, %	Metal production, tonne
1955	1 699 000	29·9	508 000
1960	2 182 000	30·6	667 000
1965	2 861 000	27·5	788 000
1970	2 553 000	27·7	706 000
1973	1 439 000	28·4	408 000

The Kowary and Rudki deposits are now exhausted and vein deposits of hydrothermal origin are of purely historical interest. The newly discovered Krzemianka deposit of ilmenite–magnetite ores is only now being evaluated. Until 1976 90% of domestic iron ore production took place in the Częstochowa–Kłobuck area and 10% in the Łęczyca region.

Endogenous deposits
Krzemianka ilmenite–magnetite ore deposit This deposit in the Precambrian crystalline basement, comprised here of Svecofenno-Karelian magmatic rocks, is situated in the northern part of the Mazury uplift, which is formed of Precambrian crystalline basement on which are sediments of the Mesozoic–Caenozoic platform cover with a thickness of between 300 and 850 m.

The Precambrian crystalline basement consists of gneiss, granite-gneiss and granitoids. In the Suwałki region occur Lower Proterozoic alkaline intrusions that consist of anorthosite and norite with which are associated commercial concentrations of titaniferous magnetite and ilmenite. These concentrations occur mainly in the peripheral zones of the Suwałki alkaline massif (Fig. 2).

The ilmenite–magnetite ores occur in the form of lenses from tens of metres to 1 km long, the thickness of the lenses varying from a few to 100 m. The ore lenses and the surrounding rocks are in parallel layers and show a pseudo-stratification at an angle of 45° (Fig. 3). From this it follows that the alkaline massifs have the characteristics of layered intrusions. Besides the ore lenses of the pseudo-stratification there occur in smaller quantities irregular veins or schlieren. Titaniferous magnetite and ilmenite are the main ore minerals with accessory pyrite, pyrrhotite, portlandite, chalcopyrite and cubanite. As was demonstrated by Kubicki,[5] the genesis of this deposit is closely connected with the differentiation of the alkaline magma.

Three stages of mineralization, in which the gradual enrichment of the residual magma into ore components took place, can be distinguished. The first stage is marked by disseminated mineralization of segregation type. In the second stage the pseudo-stratification orebodies were formed (accumulative type of mineralization): these constitute the basic deposit. The third stage is represented by irregular but rich orebodies.

The Krzemianka deposit in its structure and origin shows many similarities with deposits of this type in the Baltic Shield and, in particular, with the Otanmäki deposit in Finland. The Krzemianka deposit was discovered several years ago and is at present under investigation. General reserves are estimated at several hundred million tonne of ore with from 27 to 30% Fe. The ore contains admixtures of TiO_2 and V_2O_5.

Kowary magnetite–quartzite ore deposit The deposit lies in the Sudetes in the complex of metamorphic rocks in the east side of the metamorphic aureole of the Variscan granite of Karkonosze. The magnetite ores form lenses, mainly in the area of contact of crystalline limestones with garnet-epidote gneiss or hornblende schist, skarns or hornfels (Fig. 4). The ore series, together with the surrounding rocks, is steeply layered (Fig. 5). The thickness of the lenses varies from a few centimetres to 12 m and the length from several metres to 200 m. The ore contains 28–35% Fe, the remainder being mainly silicates. Concentration of the iron compounds took place in a Precambrian geosyncline. The geosynclinal sediments were subsequently metamorphosed in later orogenies. The streaky texture and

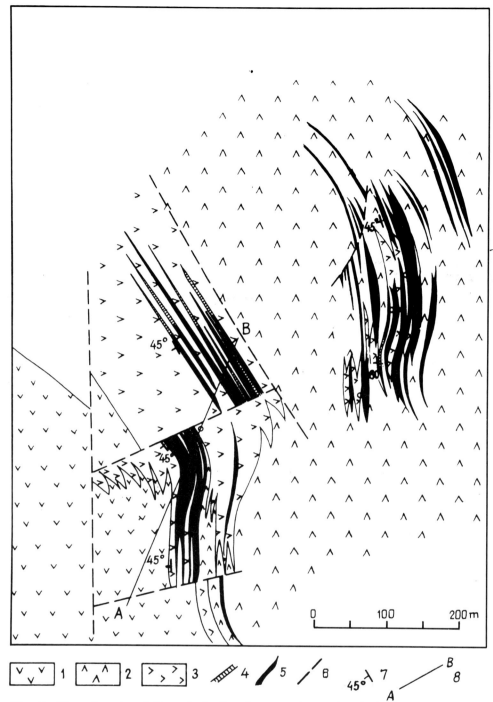

Fig. 2 *Plan of portion of Krzemianka ilmenite–magnetite ore deposit (without overburden of Mesozoic–Caenozoic formations). After M. Subieta. 1, Leucogabbro norites–diorites; 2, anorthosites; 3, norites; 4, magnetite–norites; 5, ilmenite–magnetite ore; 6, dislocation zones; 7, strike and dip of deposit; 8, line of geological section (see Fig. 3)*

remnants of oolitic structure found by Zimnoch[6] indicate that the deposit should be classified as sedimentary-metamorphic.

The Kowary[6] deposit was transformed in the Caledonian orogeny—and, in particular, in the Variscan. The activity of periplutonic solutions of the Variscan granite of Karkonosze gave rise to sulphide and uranium mineralization. Exploitation took place until 1958, when the deposit was exhausted.

Veins and lenses of hematite, siderite and pyrite In the Sudetes, in the region of Chełmiec, veins of hematite and siderite occur in Lower Palaeozoic formations, having been exploited in the Stanisławów and Męcinka mines (see Fig. 1B). The Stanisławów deposit comprises two hematite veins of variable thickness (from 0·5 to 3 m), dipping at an angle of 70°; the ores

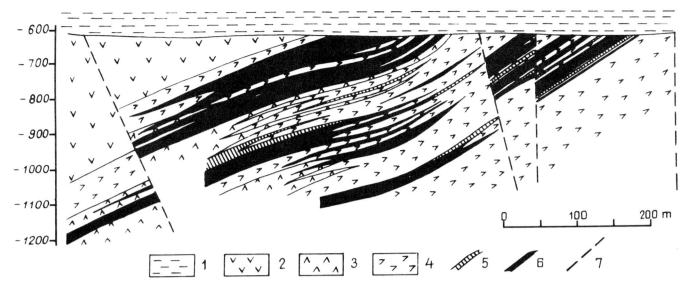

Fig. 3 *Geological section through Krzemianka ilmenite–magnetite ore deposit. After M. Subieta. 1, Cover of Mesozoic–Caenozoic rocks; 2, leucogabbro norites–diorites; 3, anorthosites; 4, norites; 5, magnetite–norites; 6, ilmenite–magnetite ore; 7, presumed dislocation zones (for location of section see Fig. 2)*

contain 41·0–50·7% Fe, 9–13% SiO_2, 2·7% Al_2O_3 and 6·7% $BaSO_4$. The presence of considerable quantities of antimony and arsenic is also noteworthy. Altogether about 170 000 tonne of ore was produced from the mine. Recently, large veins of barite were discovered in the peripheral part of the deposit, which are now under exploitation.

The Męcinka deposit consists of several veins of quartz with siderite of variable thickness from between 10 and 20 cm to 3 m. The ore contains 35–44·5% Fe, 2·3–3·0% Mn and 24–33% SiO_2. Genetically the Stanisławów and Męcinka deposits belong to hydrothermal deposits of medium and low temperatures, akin to the vein deposits of Siegerland in the Federal Republic of Germany and Spisz in Czechoslovakia.

In the vicinity of Kudowa several veins of hematite

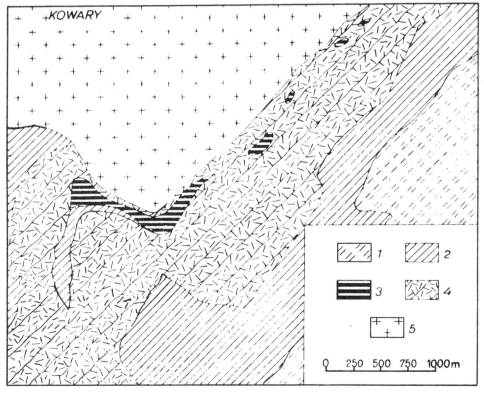

Fig. 4 *Geological sketch of Wolność mine in Kowary. After G. Berg. 1, Amphibolites; 2, sericitic shales; 3, ore-bearing series: hornblende and epidote shales, crystalline limestones and ore; 4, granite gneiss and micaceous schist; 5, granites*

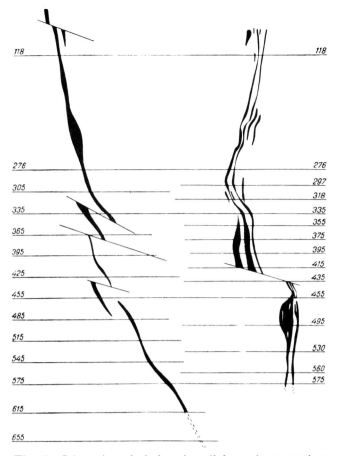

Fig. 5 *Schematic geological sections (left, southwest–northeast through western part; right, south–north through eastern part) through magnetite deposit, Wolność mine, Kowary. After R. Krajewski*

occur in the surroundings of the Variscan granite intrusion. Veins 0·25–0·60 m thick fill tectonic fissures in Precambrian crystalline shales. The content of iron in the ore ranges from 23·7 to 39·0%. The deposit is of hydrothermal origin connected with the post-Variscan magmatism.

In the Tatras ore veins (hematite and siderite) occur in the metamorphic rocks that form the shell of the Variscan granite (Fig. 1). The thickness of the hematite veins is between 10 and 20 cm and that of the siderite veins varies from 0·3 to 1 m. These ores were exploited in the eighteenth century.

In the Góry Świętokrzyskie–Rudki hematite, siderite and pyrite deposits are connected with the large dislocation zone that cuts transversely through the series of Palaeozoic rocks (mainly Silurian and Devonian). The main dislocation zone runs in a north–south direction and dips towards the east at 40–60°. The eastern side of the dislocation is shifted 3 km to the south in relation to the western. The position of the deposit is shown in Fig. 1A and a geological section through the deposit in Fig. 6.

On the western side occur Upper Silurian rocks and on the eastern dolomites of the Eifelian and Lower Givetian. In the dislocation zone appears a large lens of hematite–siderite–pyrite ores. Its thickness ranges from a few to 26·5 m and the length is approximately 600 m. The content of Fe in hematites is 38% and of SiO_2 about 5%. The siderite ores contain 38% Fe, 6·5% S and 1·5% Mn. The main ore of the Rudki deposit is pyrite. The iron cap on the Rudki deposit was first exploited in the second century of our era; then, in the eighteenth century, hematite was mined in the upper part of the deposit. The discovery of pyrite and the deep-seated portion of the deposit took place in 1932. In the years 1931–71 the iron ores were worked out. Poborski[7] considered the deposit to belong to the epigenetic-metasomatic type, but most workers consider the genesis of the Rudki deposit to be metasomatic-hydrothermal.

Exogenous deposits

Sedimentary deposits On the boundary of the Lower and Middle Devonian, and in particular in the dislocation zone between Miedziana Góra and Dąbrowa, near Kielce, numerous occurrences are known of siderite, pyrite and limonite. Larger concentrations occur at Dąbrowa. This deposit has been exploited periodically. Oxide ores occur near the surface, and siderites at depth. By reason of the spiriferid fauna established in the siderites by Czarnocki[8] this deposit has been classified as of sedimentary type. The thickness of the ore bed reaches 3 m, but varies along the strike as a result of tectonic disturbance. The limonite ore contains 42·9% Fe and 18·4% SiO_2, and the siderite ore 38·6% Fe, 10·6% SiO_2 and 2·2% Mn. The ore reserves are not large.

In the Upper Carboniferous sequence in Upper and Lower Silesia there occur siderite and clayey sphaerosiderite intercalations of a thickness between 10 and 20 cm to 1 m. These ores were of economic importance in the past, but at present they are not exploited.

Mesozoic iron ores are known in Poland in the sediments of the Rhaetic, Lias, Dogger and Lower Cretaceous.

In the Rhaetic rocks siderites and limonites, which occur in marly shales near Starachowice, have been exploited. The ore occurs in two layers spaced 1–4 m apart. The thickness of each layer ranges from 0·3 to 0·7 m. The ore contains 27–38·3% Fe. The ores were exploited in the nineteenth century.

Iron ores occur in the sediments of the marine Lias (Łobez deposit) and also in the sediments of the terrestrial Lias (Końskie–Starachowice deposit). In the Łobez deposit clayey siderite and chamosite ores occur in marly shales or in the sandy chlorite mudstones of the Pliensbachian with a marine fauna.[9] In the ore bed there are three (sometimes two) layers of clayey siderite with a combined thickness of 0·58–0·88 m. The principal ore minerals are clayey siderite, siderite and chlorite. Occasionally, siderite and chamosite oolites occur in the ore. Iron content varies from

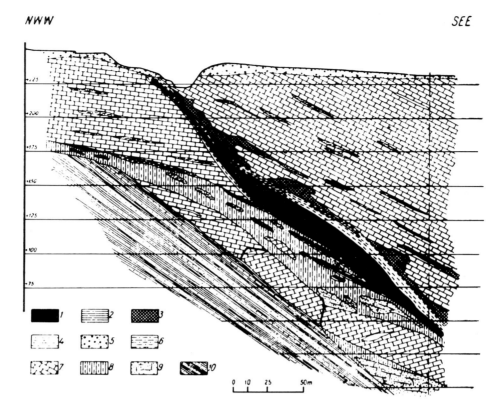

Fig. 6 *Geological section through central part of deposit, Staszic mine, Rudki. After C. Poborski. 1, Pyrite; 2, hematite; 3, siderite; 4, black clays: Pleistocene; 5, altered rock: Middle Devonian; 6, clayey minerals; 7, dolomites: Lower Devonian; 8, clayey shales and clays; 9, quartzite sandstone: Silurian; 10, cherry red and olive green sandstones and shales*

28.7 to 32.7%, with 9–17% SiO_2 and 6–12% CaO + MgO. Total reserves are estimated at about 30 000 000–80 000 000 tonne.

The ore-bearing zone of the Końskie–Starachowice deposit lies at the margin of the Palaeozoic core of the Góry Świętokrzyskie between the localities Końskie, Starachowice and Przysucha (over an area of approximately 200 km²). In the ore-bearing series three ore beds can be separated vertically, occurring 17–25 m apart. Each ore bed consists of two or more layers of clayey siderite ranging in thickness from 5 to 22 cm. These layers are separated by clayey shales (Fig. 7).

The combined thickness of the ore layers in a bed varies from 0.25 to 0.94 m. The ore-bearing series dips gently at an angle of a few degrees. The whole area is intersected by faults of young Cimmerian age, giving the area of the deposit a block form.

The first historical evidence for the exploitation of the ores originates from the sixteenth century; later mining in this area developed at the end of the nineteenth century, and on a larger scale after 1937. General ore reserves in the Końskie–Starachowice area are considerable—more than 120 000 000 tonne. An unfavourable chemical composition, however (Fe 29.5%, SiO_2 19% and CaO + MgO 2%), does not at present permit the mining of this type of ore. Krajewski[10] has shown that the ores were formed in large lake basins and that the concentration of iron is

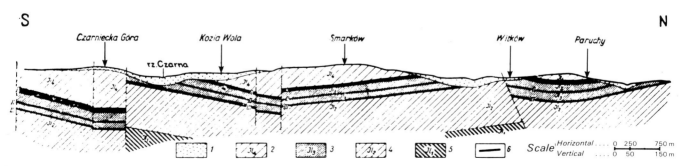

Fig. 7 *Geological section through Końskie–Starachowice deposit. After R. Krajewski. 1, Valley sands; 2–5, Rhaetic–Liassic: 2, Piekło series (Ostrów); 3, Zarzecze ore series; 4, Skłobsk (Gromadziecka) series; 5, (Zagajsk) carbonate series; 6, ore beds*

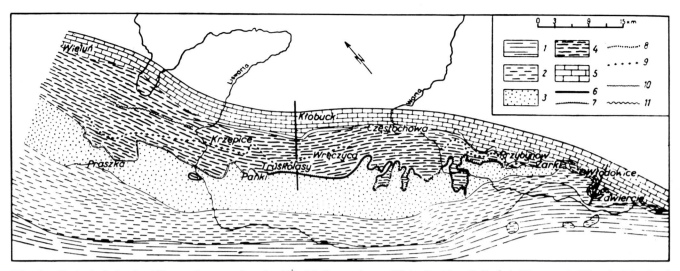

Fig. 8 *Geological sketch of Dogger iron ore deposit of Żarki–Częstochowa–Kłobuck. After Osika.[2] 1, Keuper; 2, Rhaetic–Liassic; 3, Kościeliskie strata; 4, ore-bearing clays; 5, Malm and Callovian; 6, line of section (see Fig. 9); 7, line of exposures of lower ore horizon; 8, line of exposures of sphaerosiderite complex; 9, line of exposures of middle ore horizon; 10 and 11, line of exposures of top ore horizon (10, upper layer; 11, lower layer)*

connected with the periodic precipitation of iron compounds under the influence of climatic factors.

Iron ores occur in the Dogger beds in the Silesia–Krakow area and in the Fore-Sudetic monocline (Żarki–Częstochowa–Kłobuck deposit, Kalisz deposit), in the Central Polish Arch (Łęczyca deposit) and in the northwest periphery of the Góry Świętokrzyskie (Białaczów and Parczów deposits).

In the Żarki–Częstochowa–Kłobuck deposit the iron ores occur in the lower part of the Dogger (Upper Bajocian = Kuiavian). The outcrops of the ore-bearing series run in a belt in a northwest-southeast direction, from Żarki in the south through Częstochowa to Kłobuck. The length of this belt is about 70 km (Fig. 8). The deposit dips gently towards the northeast at an angle of 1–2°. It has been examined to a depth of 300 m downdip—in places to 400 m. The width of the zone of the deposit ranges from 3 to 10 km and the surface of the ore-bearing area is about 400 km².

The thickness of the ore-bearing clays in the northern part of the Kłobuck region is about 220 m; there is gradual thinning towards the south and in the Zawiercie region the thickness is between 10 and 20 m. Studies by Osika and Znosko[11] demonstrated that there are three ore beds in the ore-bearing series. The lower bed is in the basal part of the Kuiavian (Zone of *Garantiana garantiana*), the middle bed in the upper part of the Kuiavian (Zone of *Parkinsonia compressa*) and the upper bed in the upper part of the Bathonian (Fig. 9). The lower bed is of greatest industrial value, followed by the middle bed. The upper bed is very irregular with regard to both thickness and Fe content.

The lower bed consists of several layers of clayey siderite from 0·5 to 20 cm thick (Fig. 10). The combined thickness of the ores in the bed reaches 0·55 m. The middle bed has a similar thickness but is less consistent.

The ore-bearing series, together with the surrounding rocks, is cut by a network of small faults mainly

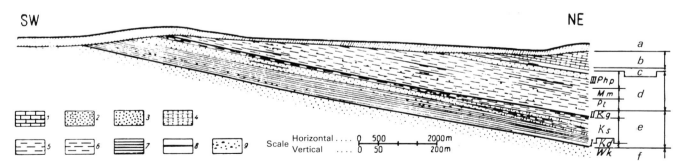

Fig. 9 *Geological section through iron ore deposit in Kłobuck area. After Osika.[2] 1, Limestones; 2, arenaceous limestones; 3, sands; 4, sandstones; 5, mudstones; 6, silts; 7, clayey shales; 8, ore bed; 9, sphaerosiderites; Php, Paroecotraustes heterocostatus and P. paradoxus; Mm, Morrisiceras morrisi; Pt, Perisphinctes tenuiplicatus; Kg, Upper Kuiavian; Ks, Middle Kuiavian; Kd, Lower Kuiavian; Wk, Kościeliskie strata; I, lower ore bed; II, middle ore bed; III, upper ore beds. (For locality section see Fig. 8). a, Pleistocene; b, Oxfordian; c, Callovian; d, Bathonian; e, Upper Bajocian (Kuiavian); f, Middle and Lower Bajocian and Aalenian (Kościeliskie strata)*

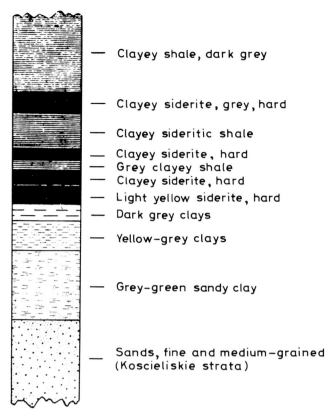

Fig. 10 *Profile of lower iron ore bed, Kłobuck area (scale, 1 : 20). After Osika[2]*

transverse to the strike of the deposit. The ore is made up of siderite and chamosite with an admixture of clay, with numerous fossils and oolites. The deposit has been exploited since the fourteenth century, but mining on a large scale developed only in the nineteenth century. The ore contains 31% Fe, 8% SiO_2 and 8% (CaO + MgO). The ore reserves are estimated at 360 000 000 tonne.

The Kalisz deposit (Fig. 1) is similar to those in the Częstochowa ore-bearing area, except that the ores occur in the upper part of the Kuiavian (Zone of *Parkinsonia compressa*) and that the lower bed wedges out. The ore bed consists of two strata of layered sphaerosiderites of total thickness 0·4–0·5 m. The ore contains 36·9% Fe, 7·5% SiO_2 and 6·1% CaO + MgO. Ore reserves in the explored area of approximately 36 km² are estimated at about 15 000 000 tonne. The deposits were formed in a marine environment.

The Łęczyca deposit occurs in Dogger sediments in the upper part of the Kuiavian (Zone of *Parkinsonia ferruginea*). It is situated in the southeast wing of the salt structure of Kłodawa (Fig. 1). The ore-bearing series of the 5- to 9-m thick *Parkinsonia ferruginea* horizon contains three ore beds. The lower bed occurs in the base of the series, and consists of several layers of shelly sideritic rocks, which attain a joint thickness of 1·14 m. The ores contain 26·5–29·7% Fe, 3·1–8·7% SiO_2 and 11·0–23·5% CaO + MgO. The middle bed has a similar structure. On the other hand, the upper

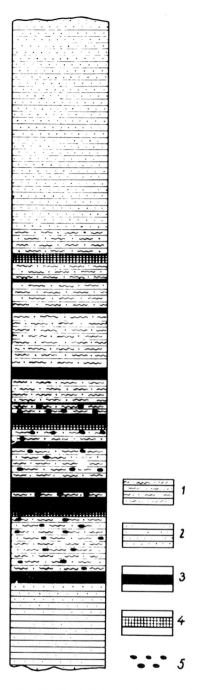

Fig. 11 *Profile of Aalenian iron ore bed, Białaczów deposit (Scale, approximately 1 : 60). After Osika.[2] 1, Sandy mudstones; 2, sandstone; 3, siderite with > 26% Fe content; 4, siderite with Fe content < 26%; 5, siderite pebbles*

bed, represented by clayey siderite, reaches a thickness of up to 0·32 m and contains up to 38% Fe. Clayey shales or siltstones separate the ore beds. The ore series in the eastern wing, which is at present under exploitation, dips gently at an angle of 2–8°. Ore reserves are estimated at several tens of millions of tonnes.

According to Znosko,[12] the deposit is sedimentary, having been formed under conditions of a constantly rising floor consequent on halokinesis. As a result of the weathering process and of secondary accumulation of fauna hard-parts and iron compounds the shelly sideritic rocks were formed.

The deposits at Białaczów occur in sediments of the Lower Dogger, i.e. the Aalenian and the Kuiavian, near the western boundary of the Góry Świętokrzyskie (Fig. 11). The ore-bearing series dips to the west at an angle of 5–7°. The lower ore bed in the Aalenian consists of several layers of conglomeratic siderite with a combined thickness of 1·55 m. The diameter of the sharp-edged fragments of oolitic siderite, which are cemented in an argillaceous-arenaceous or sideritic groundmass, ranges from 1 to 5 cm.

As the dip decreases the conglomeratic character of the ores gradually disappears. The content of iron in the ore varies from 28 to 30·5%. The ore reserves in an area of several tens of square kilometres are estimated at several tens of millions of tonnes. The deposit was formed in marine sediments near a coastline.

The Parczów deposit, which is situated near the Białaczów deposit, consists of a lens of oolitic ores, with a rich fauna, and has a surface of 0·5 km². It occurs in the Middle Kuiavian and the thickness of the ore lens is 2 m. The ore contains 36·8% Fe. The deposit is now exhausted.

At the northern boundary of the Góry Świętokrzyskie, in the sediments of the Neocomian (Lower Cretaceous), occurs an ore bed (the Przytyk deposit) consisting of three layers of clayey siderites intercalated with marly arenaceous shales with glauconite and interbedded with glauconitic siltstones of Hauterivian age. The thickness of the layers reaches 0·35 m. The iron content in the ore is 39·5% and estimates of reserves range from a few million to >12 000 000 tonne.

In the clayey sediments of the Lower Cretaceous and Eocene of the Carpathian flysch there are many occurrences of sideritic iron ores. The ores occur in the form of thin strata of clayey siderites, marly arenaceous sphaerosiderites or manganic sphaerosiderites. These formations are as a rule tectonically crushed and in many places form accumulations, sometimes leached and enriched into orebodies. The Carpathian ores were exploited in the eighteenth and nineteenth centuries in various parts of the Carpathians. The largest concentrations were at Wiśniowa west of Strzyżów, and also in the area of Cieszyn (Fig. 1). The ores were formed in a marine environment on the shelf of the Carpathian miogeosyncline connected with movements of the sea-bed.

Ore deposits formed by weathering processes The limonite ore deposits of the weathering type are associated with the occurrences of Muschelkalk in Upper Silesia in the area of Tarnowskie Góry, Miasteczko and Mierzęcice (Fig. 1C). Iron caps are known over the pyrite deposit in Rudki. The largest deposits of the weathering-residual type occur in the belt of outcrops of Bathonian and Callovian sediments along the northeastern boundary of the Góry Świętokrzyskie, in the so-called Tychowski Range (Fig. 1A). The weathering ores were exploited in the nineteenth century and at the beginning of the twentieth.

Copper ores

From the genetic point of view the copper ores, like the iron ores, can be divided into two principal groups—endogenous and exogenous deposits. Of greatest significance are the deposits of the Upper Permian that

Table 2 *Production of copper ores in Poland*

Years	Ore production, tonne
1956–60	7 131 000
1961–65	10 871 000
1966–70	18 088 000
1971–73	30 536 000

occur in the Fore-Sudetic monocline and in the North Sudetic depression. The remaining types of ores were exploited in the seventeenth and nineteenth centuries, and are now of metallogenic interest only.

Endogenous deposits

Vein copper ore deposits in the Sudetes Vein (polymetallic) deposits connected with the Variscan magmatism occur in the Sudetes in the vicinity of Miedzianka, Stara Góra and Chełmiec. The ore veins are associated with the Variscan granite intrusion of Karkonosze in the western Sudetes.[13] The veins intersect a complex of crystalline schists, which form the envelope of this intrusion. Around this intrusion also occur crystalline schists of an older age, composed of micaceous and chloritic–sericitic schists with intercalations of dolomite, gneiss and amphibolite. These rocks are cut by numerous faults. In the eastern and southern parts of the envelope of this granite occur hydrothermal copper veins and polymetallic veins—in particular, of iron, zinc, lead and arsenic (Fig. 1B). Among the many veins, the Miedzianka and Stara Góra deposits are noteworthy.

The Miedzianka deposit is situated in a dislocation zone that runs in a southeast and SSW direction; it is made up of 24 ore veins located mainly in amphibolites. The thickness of the veins ranges from 1 cm to 3 m. The main ore mineral is chalcopyrite, with lesser quantities of chalcocite, bornite, covellite, arsenopyrite, sphalerite, galena, pyrrhotite and magnetite. The tenor of the ore is very variable: 0–35% Cu, 0·3–2·5% Zn and 16–28% Fe. Quartz, hornblende, epidote and calcite form the gangue.

The Stara Góra deposit consists of six veins that strike west–east, dipping at an angle of 60–87°. The ore veins are associated with Permo-Carboniferous porphyry veins that have undergone propylitization near the ore zones. The ore veins are polymetallic. They contain, among other minerals, arsenopyrite, galena, sphalerite, bournonite, pyrite and cobaltite. These sulphides contain gold and silver. The Cu content of the veins varies from 0·7 to 1·6%. The ores contain 1–18 g/t Au and 75–200 g/t Ag. East of Stara Góra is an occurrence of quartz shale 1 m thick impregnated with chalcocite and arsenopyrite; the Cu content reaches 2%.

The Chełmiec deposit consists of seven sideritic–hematitic veins with barite intersecting Ordovician schists. In one vein chalcopyrite occurs in the siderite in the form of inclusions. The Cu content is 5·7%.

The origin of the deposit is closely connected with the Variscan Karkonosze granite intrusion. On the basis of the distribution of deposits, three hydrothermal mineralization zones can be distinguished—an inner arsenic, a middle copper and an outer sideritic. According to Petrascheck,[27] arsenopyrite associated with quartz and pyrite is the earliest stage of mineralization, whereas chalcopyrite and carbonates formed later.

Epigenetic copper ore deposits in the Góry Świętokrzyskie In the western part of the Palaeozoic core of the Góry Świętokrzyskie are two copper deposits that were exploited formerly—the Miedzianka deposit near Chęciny and the Miedziana Góra deposit near Kielce. The mineralization is connected with considerable overthrusting and faulting, as well as with outcrops of Devonian (Givetian and Frasnian) dolomites and limestones.

In the Miedzianka deposit the ores occur near a zone of dislocation that intersects Givetian and Frasnian limestones. In these limestones ore veins occur between 10 and 20 cm thick and up to 100 m long. A series of Lower Triassic sandstones and conglomerates adjoins tectonically the dislocation on the southwest. At the contact of the Devonian and Lower Triassic sediments the limestones have been subjected to considerable karstification. The karstic basins are filled with clays, in which occur blocks of skeletal vein ore that are secondary deposits. Another type, exploited earlier, comprises ores that occur at the limestone–sandstone contact in the form of clays with copper carbonates. The main ore mineral in the veins is chalcopyrite, which is present in calcite or in calcite breccia. A second mineral, less frequently present, is miedziankite (a zinc-rich tennantite: $2Cu_3AgS_3ZnS$), which occurs in paragenesis with chalcopyrite and galena. The oxidized zones contain malachite and limonite.

The copper content in the blocks in the secondary deposit ranges from 30 to 60%, and in the clayey ore from 10 to 15%. In addition, the ore contains 0·8–13% Ag; 0·2–1·0% Pb, 0·2–3·5% Zn and 100 g/t Ag. The deposit was exploited in the eleventh century and again in the middle of the seventeenth and at the beginning of the twentieth centuries.

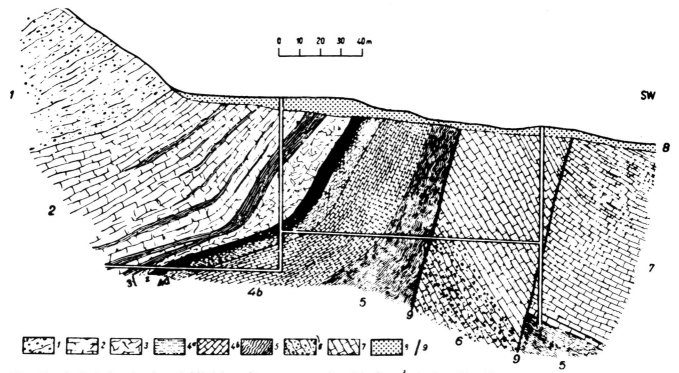

Fig. 12 *Geological section through Miedziana Góra copper ore deposit in Góry Świętokrzyskie. After J. Czarnocki. Lower Devonian: 1, Miedziana Góra conglomerate (Gedinnian); 2, quartzite and shales (Barcza Series); Middle and Upper Devonian: 3, dolomites: 4a, black claystones; 4b, marly shales and black limestones; 5, pinkish limestones; Permian: 6, conglomerate (Zechstein); Trias: 7, variegated sandstone; Pleistocene: 8, sands and local detritus; 9, dislocations; z, copper deposit; cupriferous shales)*

The Miedziana Góra deposit lies within the zone of a large overthrust (Fig. 12). It consists of a bed of cupriferous clay dipping at 30–45° concordantly with the dip of the overthrust series. The thickness of the ore bed ranges from 4 to 6·5 m and the copper content is 8·5%. The deposit was worked in the sixteenth and again at the beginning of the nineteenth centuries.

The Miedzianka and Miedziana Góra deposits are of hydrothermal origin, as indicated by the paragenesis of the primary minerals and their close connexion with the dislocation zones. These deposits, and particularly that of Miedziana Góra, have subsequently undergone weathering.[14]

Exogenous deposits
Copper ores in Lower Permian terrestrial sediments In the lower part of the Lower Permian, among the continental sandstones, occur so-called anthracitic shales mineralized by copper compounds. In the vicinity of Okrzeszyn and Nowa Ruda the thickness of these shales ranges from 0·18 to 1 m, and the Cu content from 0·1 to 2·25%. Ores in the shales take the form of concretions or incrustations, and the shales are often bituminous. The main ore minerals are chalcopyrite and chalcocite. Malachite and azurite occur on the surfaces of cracks in the shale.

Because of considerable variability in ore thickness and Cu content, these concentrations are of no economic significance. The ores were formed in an interior sedimentary basin, and Permian eruptions could have been the source of the copper.

Copper ores in Upper Permian marine sediments In the lower part of the Upper Permian (Zechstein) occur marls and cupriferous shales that in the North Sudetic depression and the Fore-Sudetic monocline contain copper mineralization.[14] In some zones the degree of mineralization is such that these shales are copper ore deposits of economic importance. The Upper Permian formations, together with the younger rocks, constitute the sedimentary cover of the Palaeozoic platform. In the area of the Fore-Sudetic monocline, the Żar pericline and the North Sudetic depression the sediments of the Upper Permian form outcrops beneath the Tertiary rocks. Between the North Sudetic depression and the Fore-Sudetic monocline is the Fore-Sudetic block, which comprises ancient Palaeozoic and Precambrian formations (Fig. 13).

In the North Sudetic depression a layer of marly limestone, with which are associated copper deposits, occurs in the lower part of the Upper Permian. The general profile of these rocks[15] comprises, above the sandstones of the Lower Permian, a thin basal conglomerate (0·6–0·9 m) on which, in turn, rest the basal limestone (0·3–1·9 m) and mottled marl (1·7–2·9 m), mottled limestone overlain by copper-bearing marl (2·2–3·1 m) and, above that, lead-bearing marl (3–12 m). Over this series occur grey limestones (5–29 m) of the Middle Zechstein, followed by sandstones and clays of the Upper Zechstein.

Tectonically, the North Sudetic depression is a component of the so-called Kaczawski Block. This tectonic element is separated from the area to the northeast by a peripheral fault. The axis of the depression runs northwest–southeast concordantly with the direction of the peripheral fault. The depression is filled with Permian, Triassic and Upper Cretaceous rocks; surrounding the depression are Tertiary basalts. Lower Palaeozoic rocks, mainly Silurian, form the basement of these formations.

The depression is divided by longitudinal faults into three local depressions—the Grodziec, Złotoryja and Lwówek.

Two depositional areas are distinguished in the Grodziec depression—Lubichów and Konrad. The

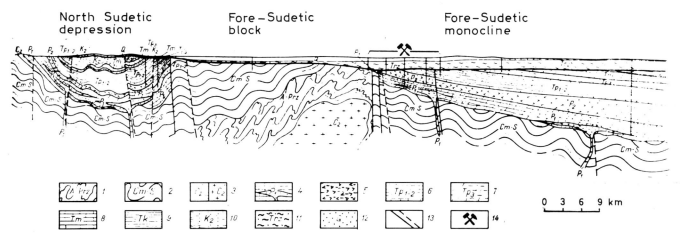

Fig. 13 *Transverse geological section through North Sudetic depression, Fore-Sudetic Block and Fore-Sudetic monocline. After J. Wyżykowski. 1, Archaean–Proterozoic; 2, Older Palaeozoic; 3, Upper Carboniferous (sedimentary rocks, granite); 4, Rotliegende (sedimentary rocks, effusive rocks); 5, Zechstein; 6, variegated lower and middle sandstone; 7, upper variegated sandstone; 8, Muschelkalk; 9, Keuper; 10, Upper Cretaceous; 11, Tertiary; 12, Quaternary; 13, proved and hypothetical faults; 14, Lubin–Głogów copper basin (vertical scale exaggerated five times)*

copper-bearing layer is marl 0·3–0·4 m thick in which can be identified several limestone–marl layers 2–4 cm thick, one of which is conspicuous throughout the deposit. As a rule, the layers of marl directly overlying the red mottled marl are mineralized. The ore-bearing minerals are chalcocite, bornite and pyrite with chalcopyrite. The mineral grains are of the order of 50 μm. The content of copper in the ore ranges from 0·56 to 0·94%. Besides the cupriferous minerals, sphalerite, galena, arsenopyrite and native silver are also present in the ore.

The deposits of the Złotoryja depression (Lena and Nowy Kościół) differ slightly in their structure from those of the Grodziec depression. The cupriferous bed consists of alternating marl and limestone laminae with a combined thickness of about 3 m. The ore-bearing minerals, as in the Grodziec depression, are chalcocite (51%), bornite (10%) and cupriferous pyrite (39%). The average copper content of the ore is 0·55%.[15]

In the region of Głogów in the Fore-Sudetic monocline occur very large deposits of copper that rank among the largest in the world. These deposits were discovered in 1957. At present three deep copper mines are in operation—Polkowice, Sieroszowice, Lubin and Rudna.[4,14,50]

The deposits are located in the basal Zechstein formations of the Werra cyclothem (Z_1). Beneath lie terrestrial sediments of the Lower Permian (Rotliegendes). Overlying the deposit is a thick complex of salt-bearing Zechstein formations. The whole area is overlain discordantly by continental Tertiary rocks.

The Permian formations, together with the overlying Mesozoic and Caenozoic rocks, constitute platform cover. They are a part of a great tectonic unit termed the Fore-Sudetic monocline. The basement beneath the platform formations is composed of Lower Palaeozoic folded rocks. In the southwest the Permian formations are in tectonic contact with Precambrian formations. The whole platform cover series dips towards the northeast at an angle of several degrees. Transverse faults run perpendicular to its strike.

The general geological structure of the area is illustrated by the geological section through the copper deposits in the North Sudetic depression, the Fore-Sudetic block and the Fore-Sudetic monocline (Fig. 13).

The structure of the deposits is simple. The basal cupriferous shales and sandstones constitute the copper-bearing bed. Dolomitic limestones in the cupriferous shales are also mineralized (Fig. 14). The above-named formations are mineralized by copper sulphides and form, respectively, three kinds of copper ore: sandstone, shale and dolomitic. The thickness of the ore bed ranges from one to several metres and the Cu content in the ore from 0·5 to a few per cent (predominantly 2–3%). Along strike as well as downdip certain changes in the thickness of the bed

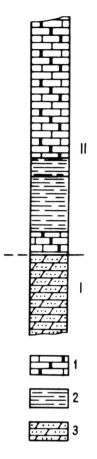

Fig. 14 *Lithologic profile (scale, 1:20) of cupriferous shales in Fore-Sudetic monocline. After J. Wyżykowski. I, Rotliegendes; II, Zechstein–Werra cyclothem (Z_1); 1, dolomitic limestone, mineralized in places by copper sulphides; 2, cupriferous marly dolomitic shale with copper sulphides; 3, sandstone*

and in the copper content of the ore can be noted.

The principal copper ore minerals are chalcocite, bornite and chalcopyrite. In considerably lesser quantities are covellite, malachite, azurite, cuprite, tetrahedrite, native copper, and galena, sphalerite, cobaltite, niccolite, pyrite and native silver. Chromium, rhenium, cadmium, tin, selenium, titanium, manganese, gold, thallium, strontium, mercury, boron and other elements have also been detected in the ore. In the vertical profile a certain regularity in the distribution of the copper minerals has been observed. In the basal parts of the bed chalcocite predominates, with bornite in the middle and chalcopyrite at the top.

The Zechstein copper ore deposits are of the sedimentary-exhalative type. Copper compounds originated from submarine emanations fed directly into the Zechstein basin during the sedimentation of the marly-clayey formations, which are now the cupriferous shale. The existence of submarine emanations, as was stressed by Wyżykowski,[50] is evidenced

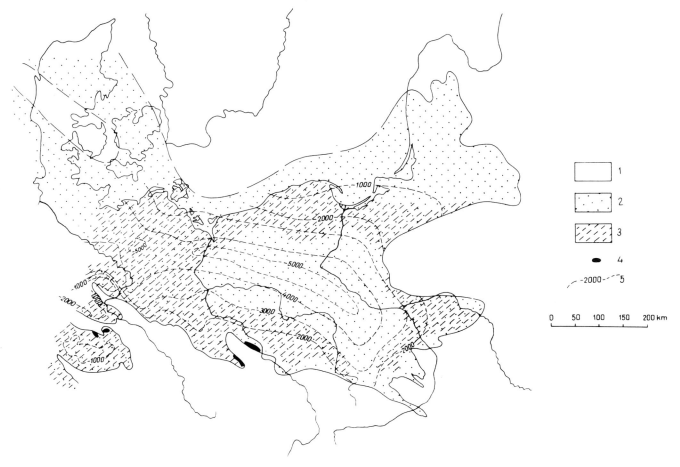

Fig. 15 Sketch of occurrences of shales of Werra cyclothem (Z_1) in Central and Western Europe, passing in places into cupriferous shales. After J. Wyżykowski. 1, Terrestrial areas of Upper Permian; 2, area of actual extent of Upper Permian rocks; 3, area of occurrence of shales forming stratigraphic counterparts of cupriferous shales; 4, cupriferous deposits and areas; 5, depth of basement of Upper Permian rocks, m

by the effusive rocks that, within the extent of the deposits, occur in the formations of the Lower Permian. In the areas that lack these effusive rocks the shales of the Werra cyclothem are not mineralized. These associations are illustrated in the sketch of the occurrences of shales of the Werra cyclothem in Central and Western Europe shown in Fig. 15. The mineralization, as established to date, is marked in the depressions situated in the peripheral zones of the Variscan massifs, i.e. in the Saxothuringian zone and the Rhenohercynian zone in Germany (the Mansfeld deposits) and in the vicinity of the Fore-Sudetic block in the Sudetes in Poland.

Zinc–lead ores

Of economic importance are the deposits of the Silesia–Krakow Triassic, from which comes the current output of zinc–lead ores. Lead ores were exploited in the twelfth century in the Bytom basin. The mining boom in the Tarnowskie Góry and Olkusz areas took place in the sixteenth and seventeenth centuries. To the middle of the present century approximately 16 000 000 tonne of zinc and 4 000 000 tonne of lead was produced. After the second world war exploitation was conducted in three mining areas—Bytom, Chrzanów and Zawiercie. In recent years new deposits have been discovered in the Zawiercie area. Reserves of zinc–lead ore in the Triassic of the Silesia–Krakow region are estimated at several hundred million tonne.

Table 3 Production of zinc–lead ores in Poland

Years	Ore production, tonne
1956–60	10 826 000
1961–65	12 703 000
1966–70	15 436 000
1971–73	12 430 000

Endogenous deposits

Veins of zinc and lead ore in the Sudetes The zinc–lead ores occur in many polymetallic vein deposits—for example, in cupriferous veins in Miedzianka and Stara Góra, in arsenopyrite veins in Czarnów, in sideritic veins in Chełmiec and in barite veins in Stanisławów, Boguszów and Srebrna Góra. These veins have a thickness of several tens of centimetres, less often reaching a thickness of 2 m. The principal ore minerals are galena and sphalerite. The ores contain silver to the extent of about 600 g/tonne of ore.

Veins and pockets of lead ore in Góry Świętokrzyskie In the western part of the Góry Świętokrzyskie is an epigenetic mineralization that embraces formations of the Palaeozoic and Triassic. The most substantial concentrations of lead are associated with Devonian carbonate rocks. Galena forms veins connected with a fracture zone or fills karst caverns developed in zones of tectonic dislocation.

In the Chęciny area galena–calcite veins that occur in dislocation fissures intersecting Devonian dolomite–limestone rocks of the Chęciny anticline were exploited.

Rich veins of galena were exploited in Karczówka near Kielce. The Devonian limestones are strongly karstified, especially at the intersection of a longitudinal dislocation with numerous transverse dip-faults. Sinkholes and caves are filled with Lower Triassic clays and sands, which testify to the Permo-Triassic age of the karstic processes. Galena and calcite form veins that fill fissures and also form pockets in the karstic clays. The veins have a thickness of 1–2 m and extend over a length of up to 400 m. The ore minerals occur on the walls of the fissures and in the calcite, reaching a thickness of 5 cm. In the pockets galena takes the form of lumps enveloped in the residual clays. The galena contains approximately 4800 g Ag per tonne of ore.

The deposits in the Łagów area occur in the central part of the Góry Świętokrzyskie as calcite–galena veins in the Middle Devonian limestones. Galena is also found in the karst sinkholes. The galena veins belong to the youngest phase of the hydrothermal mineralization. According to Rubinowski,[3] they are younger than the copper mineralization. The youngest fissures are connected with the Laramide phase of the Alpine orogeny in the Lower Tertiary. The secondary deposits of karst type are of Miocene age.

Lead ores in the Góry Świętokrzyskie were worked in the thirteenth, sixteenth and mid-nineteenth centuries. The last production of ore took place during the years 1914–18.

Exogenous deposits
Zinc–lead deposits in Triassic rocks of Silesia–Krakow Upland The zinc–lead mineralization encompasses rocks of the Middle Triassic, which are normally limestones but in the area of the ore basin are dolomites. The Triassic formations form part of the Permo-Mesozoic platform cover. These sediments lie discordantly on the Palaeozoic basement, which is made up of folded Palaeozoic (Caledonian) rocks and Devonian–Carboniferous rocks disturbed tectonically in the Variscan orogeny. The Silurian is represented by shales, the Devonian by limestones and dolomites.[14] The Lower Carboniferous is developed in the calcareous facies, whereas the Upper Carboniferous consists of shales and sandstones with bituminous coal.

The rocks of the Permo-Mesozoic cover were deposited on a morphologically highly differentiated basement. Larger hollows and troughs were filled with Permian conglomerates and variegated sandstone. In the Middle Triassic (Muschelkalk) came a marine transgression. In the Lower Muschelkalk mainly limestones were deposited and adjacent to them, dolomites (the Gogolin, Gorażdże, Terebratula and Karchowice layers).

Above the sediments of the Middle Muschelkalk are dolomitic limestones and above them marly clays representing the Upper Muschelkalk. The Upper Triassic (Keuper and Rhaetic) is represented by argillaceous-arenaceous sediments. In the central parts of the basins and in the northeastern part of the area, above the Triassic sediments there occur Jurassic sediments; in the remaining parts of the basins the Triassic rocks occur on the surface or are covered by formations of the Marine Tertiary and Quaternary.

The mineralized area is about 1000 km^2, the deposits occurring in four areas: the western comprises the Bytom and Tarnowskie Góry depressions; the southern the area of the Chrzanów depression; the eastern the vicinity of Olkusz and the northern the vicinity of Zawiercie.

The deposits occur in the upper variegated sandstone, in the dolomitic strata of the Rhaetian and in the Lower Muschelkalk in the dolomitic counterparts of the Gogolin, Gorażdże, Terebratula and Karchowice limestone members, and, secondarily, in the Diplopore Dolomites that form the lower part of the Middle Muschelkalk (Fig. 16). The Rhaetian strata in the area of the basin are mainly dolomites amounting in thickness to about 40 m. In the eastern area of the basin they are weakly mineralized.[16–21]

The Gogolin beds consist of wavy and marly limestones or of dolomites, with intraformational conglomerates. The thickness of the Gogolin beds ranges from 30 to 60 m. Zinc and lead ores occur in the Gogolin beds only when dolomites are present. The Gorażdże beds are oolitic limestones. In the area of the ore basin the equivalents of the oolitic limestones are dolomites the thickness of which varies from 20 to 25 m. In the Bytom and Tarnowskie Góry depressions, the main ore-bearing horizon occurs in these dolomites.

The Terebratula and Karchowice beds are normally limestones and marls, but in the area of the ore-bearing basin they are dolomites from 15 to 30 m thick. The dolomites, especially in the eastern area, are mineralized to various degrees—in places very intensely.

The Diplopora Dolomites, which are only locally mineralized, have a thickness of about 40 m. The

Poland

	Horizon	Name of beds and thickness, m	Lithological formation	
Upper Triassic (Keuper and Rhaetic)		(20–200)	Terrestrial rocks: marls with intercalations of dolomite and gypsum	
Middle Triassic	Upper Muschelkalk	Diplopora (15–50)	Formations of a drying-out basin Dolomitic limestones marly dolomites	
Middle Triassic	Lower Muschelkalk	Karchowickie (10–20)	Ore-bearing limestones or dolomites	Shelf-sea rocks
Middle Triassic	Lower Muschelkalk	Terebratula (5–10)	Limestones with intercalations of wavy limestones or ore-bearing dolomites	Shelf-sea rocks
Middle Triassic	Lower Muschelkalk	Goraźdźe (20–25)	Marly limestones or ore-bearing dolomites	Shelf-sea rocks
Middle Triassic	Lower Muschelkalk	Gogolińskie (30–55)	Wavy limestones or ore-bearing dolomites; in central part conglomeratic limestones or ore-bearing dolomites	Shelf-sea rocks
Lower Triassic	Upper variegated sandstone	Upper Roethian (10–25)	Marly limestones or ore-bearing dolomites	Shelf-sea rocks
Lower Triassic	Upper variegated sandstone	Lower Roethian (20–50)	Marine sediments in drying-out basin: marly dolomites and siltstones with intercalations of dolomites	
Lower Triassic	Middle and lower variegated sandstone	(10–40)	Terrestrial rocks: sands and clayey sandstones, conglomerates	

Fig. 16 *Stratigraphic-lithological profile of Triassic in area of Silesia–Krakow deposits of zinc and lead ores. After F. Ekiert and T. Gałkiewicz (simplified)*

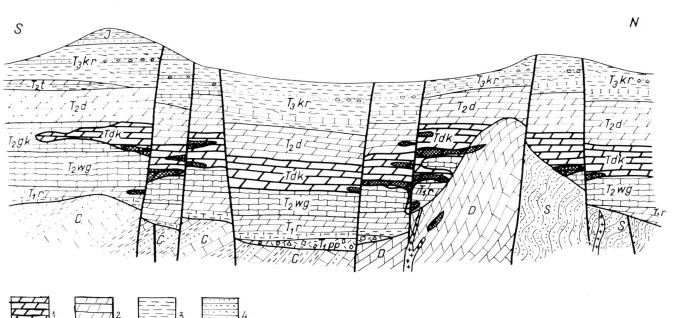

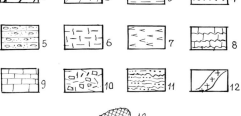

Fig. 17 *Schematic geological section through portion of deposit in northeastern part of Silesia–Krakow area. After S. Przenioslo. 1, Ore-bearing dolomites; 2, dolomites; 3, clays, claystones and mudstones; 4, sandstones; 5, conglomerates; 6, marls; 7, gypsum; 8, wavy limestones; 9, limestones; 10, breccia; 11, argillaceous-arenaceous shales; 12, magmatic rocks; 13, orebodies. J, Jurassic; T_3kr, Keuper-Rhaetian; T_2t, Tarnowickie beds; T_2d, Diplopora beds; Tdk, ore-bearing dolomites; T_2gk, Goraźdźe, Terebratula and Karchowickie beds; T_2wg, Gogolińskie beds; T_1r, upper variegated sandstone (Roethian); T_1pp, lower variegated sandstone; C, Carboniferous; D, Devonian; S, Silurian*

dolomitic equivalents of the Gogolin calcareous beds are ore-bearing. In all four above-mentioned areas the deposits of zinc and lead ores are associated with dolomites. Outside these areas, i.e. in the periphery of the ore-bearing area where these layers are in the calcareous facies, ore deposits do not occur. The base of the ore-bearing dolomites is uneven and does not correspond to the stratigraphic boundary; their thickness is variable and ranges from several to 100 m. The extent of the dolomites is also irregular and they often interfinger with limestones.

The area of the ore-bearing basin is made up of a series of flat-bottomed local troughs. It is cut by dislocations and faults that divide the area into elevated and subsided parts. The disjunctive tectonics is younger than the orebodies. The geological structure is illustrated by the schematic geological section through part of a deposit in the northeast part of the Silesia–Krakow area (Fig. 17).

In the weakly disturbed areas, where there are gentle synclines, the deposits consist of one or several horizons by dolomitic interbedding. In areas that are tectonically more disturbed the orebodies take the form of lenses and pockets that often follow the direction of the tectonic lines. In general, the structure of the deposits is relatively simple. The structure and form of one such deposit (Trzebionka near Chrzanów) are shown in Figs. 18 and 19.

The principal ore minerals are sphalerite and galena, and, less frequently, wurzite and brunckite (cryptocrystalline zinc sulphide). In the ore are also present pyrite, marcasite and melnikovite. In the sphalerite occur Cd, Pb, As, Tl, Ge, Ag, Mn and Cu. In the galena the presence of Ag, As, Sb, Cu, Zn, Fe, Ni and Mn has been noted. The iron sulphides contain As, Ni, Mo, Cu and Mn. In addition to the main metals Zn

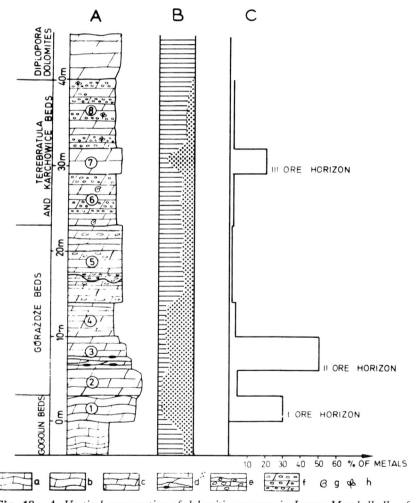

Fig. 18 A, Vertical cross-section of dolomitic sequence in Lower Muschelkalk, of Trzebionka deposit: a, limestone; b, dolomitized wavy limestone; c, dolomite; d, laminated dolomite with cherts; e, intraformational conglomerate in dolomite; f, oolitic dolomite; g, fauna; h, algae. After P. Sobczyński and M. Szuwarzyński. B, Relationship between ore-bearing dolomite (black area), primary dolomites (lined area) and limestone (white area) in section shown in A. C, Distribution of ore mineralization in section shown in A (total amount of metals in dolomites equal to 100%)

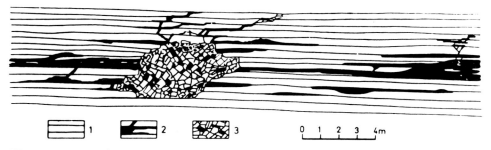

Fig. 19 *Example of structure of ore horizon of Trzebionka deposit. After P. Sobczyński and M. Szuwarzyński. 1, Ore-bearing dolomite; 2, vein and strata-bound deposits; 3, mineralized breccias*

and Pb, cadmium from sphalerite, silver from galena and thallium from iron sulphides are of economic value. In the oxidized zones smithsonite, cerussite and goethite predominate.

In the deposits are compact ores that form concentrations in the dolomite, brecciated ores in which the ore cements fragments of dolomite, and ore impregnations in the dolomite. The metal content of the ore is variable both vertically and horizontally. The rich zones, with 40% Zn + Pb, occur next to ores with 2·5% Zn and 2% Pb and ores of even lower grade. The output contains an average of 4–5% Zn and 1–2% Pb. The Zn content in the deposits is higher than that of Pb. The ratio of Zn to Pb is four or five to one and in some zones eight to one.

The origin of the deposit has long been debated. Four current views explain the formation of the deposit as sedimentary, sedimentary-hydrothermal, hydrothermal and hydrothermal-karstic.

The sedimentary concept is due to Gruszczyk[16] and Smolarska.[17] They presume that in the first phase precipitation of zinc and lead sulphides took place from sea water under reducing conditions. In the second phase, which was considerably longer and more complex, further ore concentration took place. The deposits therefore have a sedimentary-polygenetic character. The pseudo-stratified form restricted to specific stratigraphic levels and lithological formations points to a sedimentary origin, as do the banded textures concordant with the stratification. According to these authors, the veins and breccia formed as a result of later processes—among others, karstic phenomena, to which may be ascribed their polygenetic character.

Ekiert[18] expressed himself for the sedimentary-hydrothermal concept. According to this view, compounds of zinc and lead were fed into the sedimentary basin from hydrothermal solutions associated with deep-seated magma, whereas actual ore deposition was connected with the dolomitization of calcareous sediments by deep infiltration of saline waters during the Middle and Upper Muschelkalk.

Many authors have advocated the hydrothermal concept.[19,20,21] The hydrothermal solutions are held to originate from a deep-lying magma of unknown type, the mineralization thus having an epigenetic character.

The hydrothermal-karstic concept and its geological basis have been summarized by Sass-Gustkiewicz, Dżułyński and Ridge.[22] Intense karstification took place in the early Jurassic and in the early Tertiary prior to the Middle Miocene transgression. The mineralized karst structures are interpreted as products of the flow of hydrothermal ore fluids through the Triassic carbonate aquifers. The localized dolomitization that produced the ore-bearing dolomite is also held to be epigenetic and hydrothermal, part and parcel of the ore-forming process. It appears to be post-Muschelkalk and pre-Middle Jurassic in age. It is important to note, however, that only the disseminated Zn and Fe sulphides are associated with the dolomitization; galena and other massive sulphides are either later replacements of dolomite (in which galena preferentially replaces sphalerite) or cavity fillings of karstic voids and brecciated collapse structures in the dolomite. Some growths within sanded (disaggregated) dolomite give a false impression of syngenetic ore formation.

Chromium, arsenic, tin, nickel and aluminium ores

Endogenous deposits

Chromium Chromite occurs in the area of the Precambrian serpentinite–peridotite–dunite massifs of Lower Silesia, which occupy about 100 km² in the region of Sobótka, Jordanów and Ząbkowice Śląskie (Fig. 20). In the vicinity of these massifs occur younger intrusions of gabbro, granite and syenite. These rocks are set in a framework of Precambrian gneisses and crystalline schists. From many occurrences of chromite the best investigated are the ore concentrations at Tąpadła. Chromite occurs in dunites in the form of nests or lenticular bodies from 8 to 24 m long, from 4 to 8 m wide and 2–4 m thick. In the immediate proximity pegmatite and aplite veins are present. The ores occur in association with dunite or diallage peridotite, carbonated serpentinite and listvenitic antigorite. The vein rocks are sodic aplite, pegmatites or lamprophyres. The chromite ore occurs

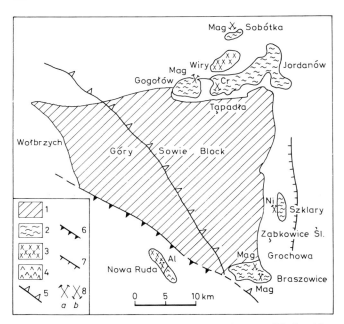

Fig. 20 *Serpentinite massifs and deposits of Lower Silesia. After J. Oberc and R. Osika. 1, Gneisses; 2, serpentinites and peridotites; 3, gabbros; 4, diabases; 5, marginal Sudetic fault; 6, main Sudetic fault; 7, Niemcza Overthrust; 8, deposits and mines: Cr, chromium ores; Ni, nickel ores; Al, aluminium ores; Mag, magnesite; a, working mines; b, non-working mines*

in compact, botryoidal or spotted form. The compact ore consists of chromite grains with a diameter of 1–3 mm interbedded in massive chlorite. The Cr_2O_3 content in the ore ranges from 39·5 to 41·2%. The botryoidal ore contains rounded concentrations of chromite with a diameter up to 5 mm set in a chlorite or carbonate mass. This variety of ore contains about 22% Cr_2O_3. The spotted ore is composed of dark crystals of chromite with a diameter of 1 mm scattered in a chlorite or carbonate groundmass. This variety of ore is of the lowest grade as it contains about 20% Cr_2O_3. In addition to Cr_2O_3, the ores contain from 20 to 25·8% Al_2O_3, 13–19% FeO, 6–14·7% MgO and 14–20% SiO_2. The nickel content in the ores ranges from 0·09 to 0·16%. The formation of the concentrations of chromite is the result of processes of crystallization differentiation.[23] The ore was exploited towards the end of the nineteenth and at the beginning of this century, a total of about 4000 tonne of ore with an average Cr_2O_3 content of 26% being produced.

Arsenic Endogenous arsenic ores occur in several places in the Sudetes, and larger concentrations are known in Złoty Stok and Czarnów.

At Złoty Stok the arsenic ores occur in Precambrian carbonate rocks that were tectonically disturbed during the Variscan orogeny. As a result of metasomatism they were transformed into siliceous limestones or dolomitic limestones. Among the calc-silicate rocks occur diopside and tremolite. Carbonate rocks occur in Precambrian crystalline schists in the form of large irregular bodies. The formation of the deposit is connected with Variscan syenites and granites. Four large orebodies make up the deposit—Góra Hanig and Góra Krzyżowa in the east and Góra Łysa and Góra Biała in the west. In the latter field the ore zone has a length of more than 300 m, a width of 20–30 m and a height of about 100 m. The orebody dips to the southeast at an angle of about 60°. In the eastern field the ores occur in the form of numerous flakes and veins of a thickness from 1 to 20 m. They dip at an angle of 50–70°. The whole deposit is cut by numerous subparallel latitudinal faults.

The orebodies are composed of calcareous-dolomitic rocks or of dolomites impregnated with arsenic sulphides. Adjoining the carbonate rocks are serpentinites, arsenic ores with associated magnetite and pyrrhotite occurring at the contact zones. The ore minerals are arsenopyrite and löllingite, with insignificant magnetite, chalcopyrite and pyrite. Locally, there are small quantities of galena, sphalerite, hematite and stibnite. The arsenic ores contain an admixture of gold.

Three types of occurrence, i.e. massive, stockwork and disseminated ores have been distinguished.[24] The massive ores contain 35–40% As in the form of coarse-grained löllingite. This type of ore occurs in serpentinites and diopside rocks.

Stockwork ores occur in diopside rocks and in serpentinites. They contain 7–20% As. The disseminated ores occur in the form of small concentrations in diopside–tremolite rocks. They contain up to 7% As.

The gold content in the massive ore amounts to about 40 g/t. These ores were worked out in the sixteenth to eighteenth centuries. In the other forms of ore the gold content amounts to 1–8 g/t.

The arsenic ores are associated with Variscan syenite in the northwestern part of the deposit. The mineralized hydrothermal solutions caused metasomatism of the limestones where they are cut by faults, thereby promoting the concentration of the arsenic ores.

Table 4 *Production of arsenic ores at Złoty Stok*

Years	Ore production, tonne
1481–1738	2 168 000
1739–1800	84 000
1801–1900	372 000
1901–44	1 194 000
1945–55	—
1956–60	200 000
1961–65	20 000

The arsenopyrite vein at Czarnów occurs in the midst of Precambrian and Lower Palaeozoic micaceous and chloritic shales with amphibolite and limestone lenses. It dips to the southeast at an angle of 80° (Fig. 21). The thickness of the vein ranges from 0·2

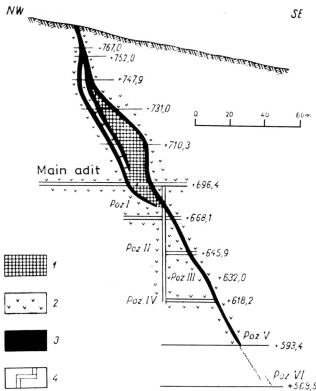

Fig. 21 *Geological section through arsenopyrite vein in Czarnów deposit, Lower Silesia. After E. Konstantynowicz. 1, Limestone; 2, micaschists; 3, arsenopyrite vein; 4, mine workings*

to 3 m, its strike length is 550 m and downdip 200 m. The vein is cut by faults. The principal ore mineral is arsenopyrite. It occurs in the ore in the form of elongated lenses. Galena, chalcopyrite, pyrrhotite, stibnite and cassiterite are accessories.

The average arsenic content in the ore is 14%. In the lower parts of the vein sections were found with 0·31% Sn and 0·49% Bi. The ore was worked from the eighteenth century until 1925, annual ore production being about 300 tonne. The deposit was formed as a result of Variscan hydrothermal action.

Tin Cassiterite occurs in the Góry Izerskie and is associated with chloritic shales at the base of which are granite gneisses. Chloritic shales several metres thick occur on the surface in the form of three parallel bands that mark truncated folded structures. Most studied is the southern belt in the sector Gierczyn-Krobica. In the chloritic shales, which have a phyllitic texture, occur granites, inclusions of amphibolite, cherts and sericitic talc shales. The cassiterite mineralization is marked only in garnetiferous chloritic shales. The ore-bearing belt dips to the north at an angle of 60–70°, but at a depth of 200 m the dips decrease to 20°. The ore-bearing series is cut by a number of transverse faults. The mineralization involves quartz–sericite–chlorite schist with 30% quartz, 50% sericite, about 15% chlorite and approximately 5% garnet. In some parts the garnet content increases to 80%. The tin ore consists of chloritic schist with veins of quartz. In the peripheries of the quartz grains occur small crystals of cassiterite with a diameter of 50–150 μm. Within chlorite and sericite, cassiterite occurs in the form of larger and better developed crystals. Apart from cassiterite, the ores contain sphalerite and cobalt-bearing compounds and also accessory galena, pyrrhotite, pyrite, chalcopyrite and arsenopyrite. The tin content in the ore ranges from 0·1 to 0·7%.

The origin of the Gierczyn deposit has not been explained conclusively: two theories—the sedimentary-metamorphic[25,26] and the hydrothermal[27,28]—exist. According to Szałamacha,[26] cassiterite occurs mainly in the laminae of ferruginous chlorite and micas in paragenesis with aluminosilicates (ferruginous chlorite–almandine–chloritoid–muscovite–biotite). From these facts it follows that the cassiterite is associated with ferruginous chlorites that in the original marine basin could have been chamosite. The supporters of the hydrothermal theory connect the origin of the deposit with Baikalian (Cadomian) or Variscan granite intrusion and pneumatolytic action comparable with the tin deposits in Saxony and Czechoslovakia.

The ores in Gierczyn were exploited in historic times from the sixteenth to the nineteenth centuries. It has now been established that the ore-bearing belts have a wider range and in this field exploratory work is being carried out.

Exogenous deposits
Nickel The deposit of nickel ores at Szklary was formed by exogenous decomposition of Precambrian ultrabasic peridotite-serpentinite rocks. The ores occur in the surficial part of the serpentinite massif, which is exposed as three hills to the north of Ząbkowice Śląskie (Sudetes). The serpentinites occur in Precambrian gneisses and crystalline schists. In the northern part of the massif occur small Variscan intrusions of syenite and diorite. The serpentinite rocks are intersected by quartz-feldspar veins.

As was shown by Daniec,[29] lateritic weathering of the serpentinites developed in tectonically crushed zones. The weathered belts that make up the deposit occur irregularly. Their thickness ranges from 10 to 15 m, and only in deep sinkholes reaches 80 m (Figs. 20 and 22).

The ore is a weathering crust on serpentinite that in the upper part has a rusty colour and is characterized by an increased content of iron compounds. Lower down is a grey-green weathering crust with nickel enrichment. The base of the deposit is formed of serpentinite, in places with veins of magnesite. In the weathering crust and in the serpentinite fissures occur small veins of opal and chalcedony, which is often coloured green by nickel compounds that form the semi-precious stone called chrysoprase.

The ore minerals are pimelite, garnierite and

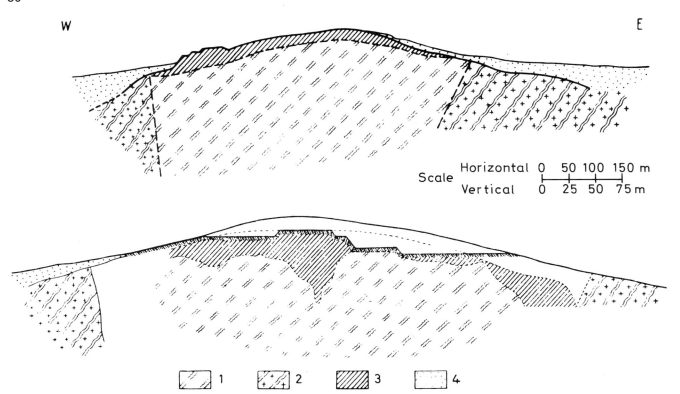

Fig. 22 *Schematic geological sections through Szklary nickel ore deposit. After A. Graniczny. 1, Serpentinites; 2, enveloping gneiss; 3, weathering crust with Ni ores; 4, overburden (Pleistocene and Tertiary sediments)*

suchardite. Pimelite forms green scaly aggregates and encrustations in the weathering crust. Garnierite of a blue-green colour forms kidney-shaped stalagmitic crusts. Suchardite occurs in the form of scaly aggregates of a yellow-green colour. It is a nickel-bearing chlorite, which often passes into chlorites.

The ores contain 0·5–2·5% Ni and 10–12% Fe. The source of the nickel is the ultrabasic rocks in the basement. The olivine in the ultrabasics contains isomorphic admixtures of nickel. In the Miocene, during the period of dry and hot climate, these rocks were subjected to lateritic weathering, which led to the release of nickel in the olivine and its concentration in the weathering crust.

The deposit has, with interruptions, been exploited

Table 5 *Production of nickel ores in Poland*

Years	Ore production, tonne
1956–60	1 066 000
1961–65	1 015 000
1966–70	982 000
1971–73	472 000

since 1891 to the present time, but the richer parts with 1·0–2·5% content have been worked out. Ores exploited at present contain an average of 0·7% Ni. As a result of a multiphase thermal process in rotary kilns ferronickel with 8–10% Ni and about 90% Fe is obtained.

Bauxite In the lower part of the Upper Carboniferous in Nowa Ruda in Lower Silesia occurs a clayey series composed of bauxites, argillites and refractory shales. These rocks occur on a gabbro massif to which the deposits are genetically related. Directly above the massif occurs the gabbroic weathering zone of a thickness that ranges from a few to 60 m. Above the weathering zone occurs a layer of red-brown argillite about 12 m thick, and above that lies an irregular layer of bauxite. On the argillite and bauxite occurs a series of dark clayey shales of the Westphalian *A* (Figs. 20 and 23), which are exploited as refractory shales. On the shale series occurs unconformably a complex of sandstone–clay formations with seams of bituminous coal.

Tectonically, the area of Nowa Ruda belongs to the intermontane Variscan depression. The Nowa Ruda deposit is situated within the boundaries of a monoclinal fold, of which the core is the gabbro massif. The strata are inclined at angles of 10–30°.

The bauxite forms irregular bodies at the boundary of the argillites and dark clayey shales. The average thickness of the bodies is 2·4 m. The bauxites consist of grains of diaspore cemented with clayey material, mainly kaolinite, with small quantities of siderite. Diaspore and siderite form pisolites ranging in diameter from 0·2 mm to 3 cm. The Al_2O_3 content in the bauxites ranges from 38 to 65·6%, SiO_2 from 0·5 to 32% and Fe_2O_3 from 9·7 to 30·1%. The calcination zone fluctuates within limits of 9·5 to 22·8%.

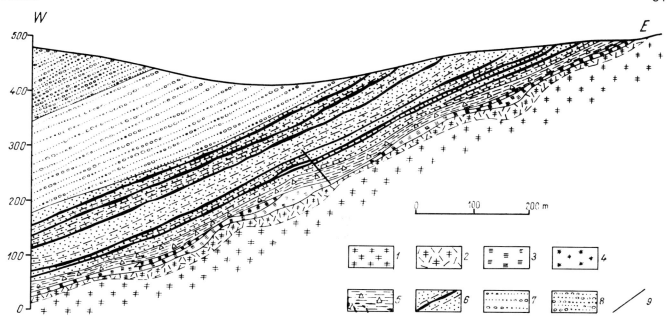

Fig. 23 *Schematic geological section through Nowa Ruda Bauxite deposit. After A. Morawiecki and Z. Górzyński. 1, Pre-Upper Devonian gabbro; Carboniferous: 2, weathered gabbro; 3, argillites; 4, bauxites; 5, clayey shales—ferrous and fire-resisting; 6, sandstone-shale series with coal beds—Zacler beds—Westphalian; 7, conglomerates and arkosic sandstones—Stephanian beds; Permian: 8, Rotliegende sandstones; 9, fault*

Argillites form the gabbroic weathered zone beneath the bauxites. Apart from various clayey minerals, the argillites contain siderite, chamosite and a small quantity of diaspore pisolites. Some varieties of argillite contain considerable quantities of kaolinite, which form pseudomorphs after feldspars. Argillites contain 25–46% Al_2O_3, 24–47% SiO_2 and 2–30% Fe_2O_3. The calcination losses range from 10 to 25%. Overlying the argillites and bauxites are dark refractory shales.

According to Gil,[30] the bauxites and argillites were formed as a result of chemical weathering of the gabbro massif. The weathering products were washed away and deposited in the surrounding lake plains.

Important accessory metals in ores and rocks

Gold

Gold occurs in several places in Lower Silesia, especially in Złoty Stok, where it constitutes an admixture in the arsenic ores. Traces of gold are also known in the quartz veins in the Tatras and in Pieniny. A second form of occurrence of gold is in association with alluvial sands in the region of Złotoryja in Lower Silesia.

Admixtures of gold are known from numerous veins of arsenic ores in Lower Silesia. Gold has been exploited in Złoty Stok from the fifteenth century. The gold content in high-grade arsenic ores was about 40 g/t of ore. Ores with 6% As content contained 3–8 g/t.

In the seventeenth century came a decline in gold mining and production. From the middle of the nineteenth century gold was obtained by the chlorine method during the production of arsenic compounds in quantities of about 30–70 kg of gold per annum. In 1963 production was stopped.

Table 6 *Production of gold in Złoty Stok*

Years	Production, kg
1481–92	600
1493–1516	1920
1517–41	3500
1542–56	1650
1557–1600	800
1601–1700	300
1701–38	35

In the vicinity of Złotoryja in the valley of the River Kaczawa and Bóbr, at the foot of Góry Kaczawskie, occur gold-bearing sands that were exploited in historical times. Gold was also exploited in the Legnica region. The first information dates from the twelfth century, but it is presumed that exploitation was carried out from the sixth century onwards. Exploitation was terminated towards the end of the fourteenth century when the richer deposits were exhausted. Prospecting from the sixteenth to the nineteenth centuries failed to discover deposits of economic value.

Native gold occurs in the sands in the form of small scales that range from tenths of a millimetre to a few mm in diameter. Gold also forms veinlets in quartz grains. In the sands also occur ilmenite, magnetite, rutile, zircon, ruby and epidote.

The primary source of the gold and of the minerals mentioned above are granites and quartz veins in the Sudetes. The gold content varies from 0·2 to 4·6 g/tonne of sand. At present in this region and in other streams panning studies are being conducted. In many places the presence of gold and cassiterite has been confirmed by panning. Panning and geochemical work are aimed at discovering primary vein concentrations of gold and cassiterite.

Silver

Silver occurs in zinc–lead ores of the Silesia–Krakow Triassic, in the lead ores in the Góry Świętokrzyskie, in polymetallic veins in the Sudetes, and also in the Zechstein copper ores in Lower Silesia.

In the zinc–lead ores of the Silesia–Krakow Triassic silver is disseminated in galena and sphalerite. Less frequently, one finds argentite, which usually occurs in the cementation belt as a secondary mineral. In oxidized ores, in the so-called calamines, the Ag content averages 0·015% of the total quantity of zinc and lead, whereas in sulphide ores the silver content averages 0·005%. The galena veins in the Góry Świętokrzyskie in the cementation belt contained up to 0·6% silver.

In the polymetallic veins in Stara Góra the silver content was about 0·02%, and in Czarnów 60–80 g Ag per tonne of arsenopyrite. Certain barite–galena veins contained nearly 600 g of silver per tonne of galena. In the cupriferous shales of the Zechstein the silver content is proportional to the copper content in the ore. On average, from 0·3 to 0·4% Ag is obtained per tonne of metallic copper.

Cadmium and thallium

Cadmium and thallium constitute admixtures in zinc–lead ores of the Silesia–Krakow Triassic.

Cadmium occurs in zinc sulphides and in higher concentrations in calamine ores as the mineral greenockite (CdS). The average content of cadmium in relation to zinc is 0·15% and in calamine ores it ranges from 0·1 to 0·5% in relation to zinc. It has been established that higher contents of cadmium occur in the light-coloured varieties of sphalerite. Cadmium is obtained as a by-product of smelting of zinc ore, produced as a valuable commodity from the middle of the nineteenth century.

Thallium is a trace element in marcasite and in dark varieties of sphalerite. The thallium content in these minerals averages 0·01% in relation to pure marcasite or sphalerite.

Other metals

Other metals, such as indium, gallium, germanium, bismuth, antimony, mercury, molybdenum, tungsten, beryllium, niobium, tantalum and zirconium, occur as trace elements in the zinc–lead ores of Upper Silesia and in copper ores, in arsenic ores or granites and pegmatites in Lower Silesia. To date, these admixtures are of mineralogical interest only.

Deposits of non-metallic minerals for the chemical industry

Minerals in this category in Poland are pyrite, marcasite, native sulphur, rock salt and magnesium–potassium salts, phosphorites and also barite and fluorite. The most important of these are native sulphur in the Tortonian formations in the Carpathian Foredeep, Zechstein rock salt in the Kujawy and magnesium–potassium salts located on the Łeba uplift in the region of the Puck Bay.

Pyrite and marcasite

Endogenous deposits

Rudki pyrite deposit The general structure of the Rudki deposit was described earlier. A pyrite vein 26·5 m thick occurs in a dislocation zone that dips to the east at an angle of 40°. It has been proved to a depth of 160 m from the surface; at greater depth, however, the deposit wedges out.

Table 7 *Production of pyrite in Poland*

Years	Production, tonne
1956–60	1 159 000
1961–65	1 018 000
1966–70	717 000
1971–73	—

The main pyrite vein is at the hanging-wall and footwall enveloped in a thin layer of dark clayey material. In the upper part the hanging-wall and the footwall are made up of Middle Devonian dolomites, whereas in the lower part grey shales occur at the footwall. As well as a vein, pyrite also occurs as impregnations in the Middle Devonian dolomites.

The mineralization takes two forms—earthy pyrite and rock pyrite. The former is a loose-textured rock that formed as a result of tectonic disturbance. The average sulphur content in the earthy pyrite is 48·8%. The rock pyrite is either a compact rock or a breccia. The average sulphur content in rock pyrite is 35%. Belts impregnated with pyrite contain from 10 to 20% of sulphur. The Zn content in pyrite ranges from 0·11 to 1%, with 0·13% Pb, 0·04–0·1% Cu and 0·01–0·046% As.

The form of the deposit and the character of the mineralization point to a hydrothermal origin for the pyrite. Jaskólski distinguished two stages of mineralization, i.e. an older stage of sideritization and a younger stage of pyrite mineralization.[7,14,24]

The pyrite deposit was worked from 1925 to 1969. Exploitation ceased when reserves were exhausted.

Wieściszowice pyrite-bearing schist deposit The pyrite-bearing schists occur in the Precambrian zone of crystalline schists that form the eastern border of the Variscan granite of Karkonosze. The pyrite-bearing series consists of chloritic and sericitic schists adjoining amphibolites. In these schists are disseminated small crystals of pyrite with diameters that range from 0·5 to 5 mm. The thickness of the pyrite-bearing series is about 200 m. The series dips at an angle of 50–70° and extends along strike for about 4 km. The chloritic schists consist of grains of chlorite, sericite and quartz. The grains of pyrite in the chloritic mass are laminated, and those in the sericitic mass are broken. The content of pyrite in the schists ranges from 2 to 35%, more rarely reaching 70%; on average it is 15·5%.[4,24]

In some parts there occur pseudo-strata some 5–10 cm thick, in which chalcopyrite occurs. In these parts the copper content reaches 3%. The remaining parts contain from 0·02 to 0·08% Cu.

The deposit of pyrite-bearing schists formed as a result of metamorphism. Taking into account the absence of epigenetic pyrite filling fissures, it would appear that the primary concentration of iron sulphides took place in a marine basin, syngenetic with the schists in which they occur. The deposit was worked from 1852 to 1925. During that time more than 200 000 tonne of pyrite concentrate was extracted.

Exogenous deposits
Pyrite deposits in dolomites of Silesia–Krakow Triassic
Iron sulphides associated with the zinc–lead ores of the Triassic occur predominantly as marcasite; pyrite and greigite occur in lesser quantities. From the genetic point of view epigenetic and syngenetic sulphides may be distinguished. Epigenetic marcasite occurs in paragenesis with encrusted sphalerite with which it forms colloidal (colloform) structures. The largest concentrations of marcasite occur in the peripheral zones of the zinc–lead ores and also in their hanging-wall. These concentrations have the form of pseudo-bedding or lenses and pockets. The size of the concentrations reaches several tens of thousands of cubic metres. Within the marcasite pockets can be distinguished rock marcasite, in the shape of reniform concentrations, and loose marcasite.

The epigenetic pyrite occurs in paragenesis with crystalline sphalerite, filling the fissures of the dislocation zones. Syngenetic iron sulphides in the dolomites and limestones were formed at the time of the sedimentation of these deposits. They are dispersed throughout the rock mass. The content of iron sulphides in the deposit ranges from 1 to 50% of the volume of the rock.

The origin of the deposit was discussed in regard to the zinc–lead deposits of the Silesia–Krakow Triassic. The epigenetic iron sulphides crystallized in the last stage of the formation of the deposit after the main mass of sphalerite had settled.[24]

Pyrite deposits in Eocene shales in Carpathians Among the very numerous occurrences of pyrite in the Carpathians, some richer concentrations were recorded in Eocene sediments at Bezmichowa near Sanok and also in Eocene shales and in the Lower Cretaceous in Domaradz near Brzozów. In Domaradz pyrite occurs in greenish-blue Eocene shales and in dark shales of the Lower Cretaceous. Pyrite occurs in the form of concretions with a diameter of 0·09–50 mm. The richer parts contain from 115 to 300 kg pyrite to 1 m^3 shales. By reason of their irregular occurrence they are of no economic importance. The Carpathian pyrites are syngenetic rocks formed during the diagenesis of fetid muds.[24]

Native sulphur

Deposits of native sulphur are typically exogenous and occur in Poland only in the Carpathian Foredeep. Mining of sulphur in this area lasted about 500 years. Sulphur was produced from the beginning of the fifteenth century in several localities—Czarkowy, Posądza, Pszów, Czajków. The last mine, Swoszowice near Krakow, was closed in 1884.

Table 8 *Production of native sulphur in Poland*

Years	Production, tonne
1956–60	140 000
1961–65	2 100 000
1966–70	8 200 000
1971–73	9 720 000

A renewal of the intensive development of sulphur mining followed the discovery in 1952 of large sulphur deposits in the northern part of the Carpathian Foredeep in the region of Tarnobrzeg and Staszów and, more recently, in the region of Lubaczów. Initially, sulphur was produced by opencast methods, but in the last decade almost the entire output has been obtained by underground melting of sulphur by means of steam-fed boreholes.

Exogenous deposits
Deposits in Carpathian Foredeep The sulphur-bearing series is associated with gypsum and anhydrite horizons in the Tortonian (Miocene). The sediments of the marine Miocene form a molasse that fills the marginal trough of the Carpathian Foredeep. The basement below the Miocene sediments consists of Eocambrian, Palaeozoic and Mesozoic formations. These rocks are cut by dislocations of meridional direction that divide the area into blocks displaced relative to one another. The Miocene molasse comprises Tortonian and Sarmatian sediments. These rocks are transgressive to the basement formations.

The basal Tortonian sediments, the Baranowskie

strata, consist of sands and sandstones about 100 m thick. In the border areas of the basin and on hummocks, limestones formed at this time. Above the Baranowskie strata occurs a distinct horizon of gypsum and anhydrite; in the peripheral zones of the foredeep gypsum and post-gypsum limestones occur, whereas in the central zones of the foredeep anhydrite and local rock salt prevail.

Above the gypsum–anhydrite sediments is a complex of clayey-marly rocks, the so-called *Pecten* beds, with a thickness of 30 m.

Overlying the Tortonian sediments are the Sarmatian sediments, the lower part of which is composed of clayey rocks that in the central part of the foredeep attain a thickness of 2500 m. The upper part of the Sarmatian is composed of detrital rocks that are preserved only in the border areas. The thickness of these sediments is about 50 m.

The thickness of the Tortonian sediments does not change significantly in the area of the foredeep, whereas the Sarmatian sediments thin considerably towards the peripheries. In the northern part of the foredeep the thickness of the Miocene sediments diminishes to several hundred metres, whereas in the central part they reach 3000 m. In the area of the foredeep, Pawłowski[31] distinguished minor elevations on the gypsum series that extend from the periphery in the direction of the axis of the foredeep. These structures are narrow (around 1 km across) and tens of km long. They played an important role in the formation of the sulphur deposits, and also have a fundamental significance in exploration planning.

Deposits of native sulphur occur in association with Tortonian gypsum and anhydrite. At the top of these formations are impermeable marly-clayey layers, whereas arenaceous rocks occur at the base. The thickness of the gypsum–anhydrite series ranges from 20 to 45 m. In the lower part the gypsum contains large selenite crystals, usually twinned and up to 4 m long. The upper part is composed of compact gypsum with overgrowths of gypsum breccia. Karst forms occur throughout the gypsum series.

According to Pawłowski,[31] the occurrence of native sulphur in the gypsum horizon is restricted to the elongate elevations on the sub-Miocene basement. Structural factors of this type have a fundamental influence on the formation of deposits of native sulphur. All deposits of native sulphur discovered to date occur in similar structural conditions.

The geological structure of the deposits is shown in the geological section (Fig. 24) through the marginal zone of the foredeep. The sulphur-bearing series occurs in the shallower gypsum–anhydrite zone and deposits are more numerous near the boundary of the carbonate littoral facies. The sulphur-bearing series stretches from Krakow through the vicinity of Pinczów to Tarnobrzeg and Stalowa Wola, and next occurs in the district of Horyniec near Lubaczów. The largest deposits occur between Tarnobrzeg and Stalowa Wola, where there is intensive exploitation by the method of underground melting. In this region the deposit is a layer 10–13 m thick. The sulphur-bearing Tortonian limestone formation dips at an angle of a few degrees.

The main components of the sulphur ore are calcium carbonate and sulphur, which together account for 94% of the rock mass. Among the admixtures are gypsum, quartz, aluminium oxides, strontium sulphate and traces of bismuth. The sulphur content ranges from 16 to 35% and averages 24%.

Native sulphur occurs in hollows, caverns and fissures in the post-gypsum limestones. According to

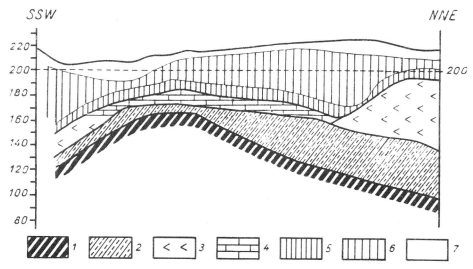

Fig. 24 *Geological section through Miocene sediments in border zone of Carpathian Foredeep. After S. Pawłowski. 1, Mesozoic basement of Miocene sediments; Tortonian: 2, Baranowskie layers; 3, chemical sediments—gypsum; 4, chemical sediments—post-gypsum limestone; 5, Pecten beds; 6, Sarmatian sediments; 7, Pleistocene sediments*

Pawłowski,[31] the process of transformation in crystalline gypsum always begins at the edges of the crystals, and in crevices and cracks, where surface corrosion sets in and precipitation of sulphur and formation of carbonates takes place. The sulphur accumulations take various ball-shaped, vein-shaped and streaked forms with a thickness from several tens of centimetres to several metres. The sulphur is predominantly powdery, but it also occurs in lesser quantities in compact, microcrystalline or crystalline form.

The deposits of native sulphur were formed as a result of metasomatism of gypsum within definite geological structures. These processes took place with the participation of bacteria, mineral waters and bitumens. Mineral waters occur in sands and sandstones under the gypsum–anhydrite series and also fill the fissures and cracks in gypsum. They are protected from above by impermeable sediments of the Tortonian and the Sarmatian. The large proportion of hydrogen sulphide in the waters and their salinity created favourable conditions for the process of transformation with the assistance of certain types of reducing bacteria.

Traces of bitumen occur in the sulphur deposits and their vicinity, and in some zones accumulations of natural gas and crude oil have been observed. As was demonstrated by Pawłowski,[31] the formation of enormous deposits of native sulphur required huge quantities of natural gas, which were derived from deposits in the south-central parts of the foredeep.

The date of sulphur formation is not precisely known. Many data indicate that the sulphur-producing processes developed after the period of sedimentation and consolidation of gypsum and anhydrite and continue to the present.

Rock salt and magnesium–potassium salts

Deposits of rock salt and magnesium–potassium salts belong to the exogenous type of deposits. Polish production figures for the former are given in Table 9.

Table 9 *Production of rock salt in Poland*

Years	Production, tonne
1956–60	7 721 000
1961–65	10 600 000
1966–70	13 600 000
1971–73	8 860 000

Exogenous deposits
Zechstein salt-bearing basin The southeastern boundary of the great European saliferous basin runs through Polish territory. In the area underlain by Precambrian basement the Zechstein sediments, together with the arenaceous series of the Lower Permian, overlie undisturbed Carboniferous–Devonian and older rocks. In the area underlain by Palaeozoic basement the latter consists of folded and consolidated Caledonian–Variscan rocks. In this region the Zechstein sediments fill the Variscan depression—the so-called Danish–Polish Furrow. The Zechstein salt formation was deposited in four cycles. Poborski[32] divided this salt formation into four horizons, correlating them with the Zechstein stratigraphic profile in the territory of Germany: the oldest salts (Werra), the older salts (Stassfurt), the younger salts (Leine) and the youngest salts (Aller).

In the peripheral parts of the basin the thickness of the Zechstein formation amounts to several hundred metres. Towards the central part of the basin it thickens and reaches 1500 m.

The Zechstein sediments are made up predominantly of evaporites, to which belong rock salt and potash salts, anhydrite, gypsum and limestone. The thickness of the salt layers ranges from several tens to several hundred metres. Layers of magnesium–potassium salts occur within the rock-salt formations on two stratigraphic horizons in the highest part of the Stassfurt and in the middle part of the Leine. In the Zechstein basin three facial zones can be distinguished: (1) a central zone of chloride facies with magnesium–potassium salts; (2) a zone of chloride facies devoid of magnesium–potassium salts encircling the central zone; and (3) a zone of sulphate-carbonate–littoral facies taking up the peripheral area of the basin (Figs. 25 and 26). Over the greater part of the basin the salt series occurs under an overburden of Mesozoic–Caenozoic sediments from 2000 to 5000 m thick. In three areas only do they occur at shallower depths—in the Kujawy and the Łeba regions and in the Fore-Sudetic monocline.

In Kujawy the salts form salt diapirs that rise to depths of 100–300 m. Ten salt diapirs are known here and four (Kłodawa, Inowrocław, Wapno and Góra) are being exploited.

The Kłodawa diapir was discovered in 1938 during gravimetric studies, and the negative anomaly was subsequently examined by test drilling. It extends for 25 km and has a width of 2 km. A geological section through the Kłodawa salt diapir is shown in Fig. 27. Adjoining the diapir are Jurassic and Triassic rocks. On the salt rests a clayey gypsum cap. The deposit is worked by underground mining. Under exploitation is the older rock salt (Z_2) with a layer of carnallite-kieserite, the younger rock salt with a carnallite layer (Z_3), and pink rock salt in the lower portion of youngest rock salt (Z_4).

The Wapno rock salt is also exploited underground. The deposit extends horizontally for 750 m and is approximately 400 m wide. It narrows downwards and is club-shaped in vertical section.

The Inowrocław deposit has been worked since 1878. The length of the deposit is 2500 m and the width ranges from several hundred metres to 1 km. The salt

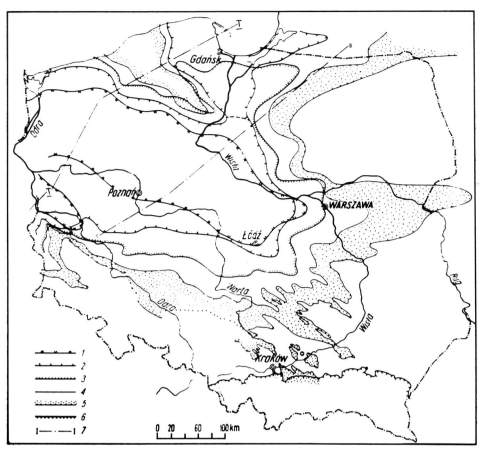

Fig. 25 *Lithofacies map of Zechstein basin in Poland. After J. Poborski. 1, Extent of chloride facies with Mg–K salts in upper section of Zechstein ($Z_3 + Z_4$); 2, extent of chloride facies with Mg–K salts in lower section of Zechstein ($Z_1 + Z_2$); 3, extent of chloride facies (without Mg–K salts) in upper section of Zechstein; 4, extent of chloride facies (without Mg–K salts) in lower section of Zechstein ($Z_1 + Z_2$); 5, extent of peripheral facies (sulphate–carbonate littoral); 6, Carpathian overthrust, 7, lines of lithofacies sections (see Fig. 26)*

surface is between 120 and 190 m below surface. The thickness of the salt series is about 550 m. In the deposit one can distinguish older salts (Z_2), younger salts (Z_3) and youngest salts (Z_4). The series is exploited by leaching with water to meet the requirements of the soda industry. Apart from the above, the following diapirs have been established by boreholes: Damasławek, Mogilno, Góra, Rogoźno, Izbica, Lubień and Łanięta (Fig. 1).

The salt diapirs were formed as a result of halokinesis. The smaller salt diapirs (Wapno, Inowrocław, Góra), which are made up of more plastic, pure rock salt, are more strongly uplifted and their salt therefore lies nearer to the surface.

The rock salt and magnesium–potassium salts on the Łeba uplift were discovered in 1968. The prospect area for the occurrence of salts to a depth of 1000 m is estimated at around several hundred km². Beds of rock salt and magnesium–potassium salts have been established in the region of Puck Bay in the localities Chłapowo, Mieroszyno, Swarzewo and Zdrada.

The magnesium–potassium salts are predominantly polyhalite. The polyhalite occurs in the form of a horizontal lens, at the contact of the rock salt and anhydrite horizons of the cyclothem Z_1. The geological structure of the deposit is illustrated in Fig. 28. The thickness of the lens ranges from a few to 30 m. The K_2O content fluctuates from 7 to 12%. As was demonstrated by Werner,[33] polyhalite was formed as a result of the action of alkaline solutions present in the basin immediately after the deposition of anhydrite. Anhydrite, by the metasomatic activity of alkaline solutions enriched in magnesium–potassium salts, was transformed into polyhalite. These processes took place in the topmost layers of the anhydrite. Reserves of polyhalite salts are estimated at > 500 000 000 tonne and those of rock salt at several billion tonnes.

In the region of Nowa Sól in the Fore-Sudetic Monocline* a rock salt and potassic salts deposit has been discovered in the horizon of older salts (Z_2) by drilling. Further prospecting is in progress.

Miocene salt-bearing basin In the southern part of the Carpathian Foredeep, in the belt adjoining the

---

* 'Monocline' is used here in the continental sense of a uniformly dipping sequence rather than the British sense of a step-fold with horizontal upper and lower limbs and inclined middle limb.

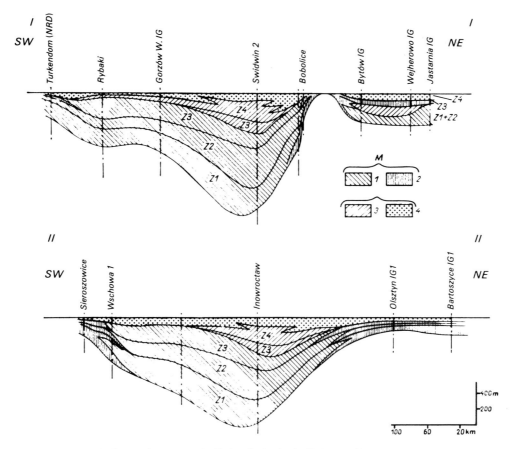

Fig. 26 *Lithofacies sections through Zechstein basin in Poland. After J. Poborski. M, marine macrofacies: 1, chloride facies; 2, peripheral facies (sulphate–carbonate littoral); 3, chloride facies; 4, facies of sub-saline lutites (pelites and aleurites) (for location of sections see Fig. 25)*

overthrust Flysch Carpathians, is a zone of Tortonian rock salt (Fig. 1). In the area of Upper Silesia the salt-bearing series rests on Carboniferous sediments; between Krakow and Dębicą on Jurassic and Cretaceous; and in the vicinity of Rzeszów on the Precambrian. In the area of the Carpathian Foredeep the Tortonian series is composed of sand and clay formations with a thickness of approximately 1000 m; the lower part, about 100 m thick, consists of clay–gypsum or clay–anhydrite sediments. In the belt between Krakow and Tarnów a salt series reposes in the Tortonian. It is developed in the form of beds of rock salt with interbedded anhydrite claystones.[14]

From studies by Poborski and Skoczylas-Ciszewska[34] it appears that in the last orogenic phase of the Carpathians the sediments of the salt-bearing Tortonian were folded. In many places these formations were overthrust by the Carpathian Flysch nappes. A little further north of the Carpathian overthrust the Tortonian sediments are nearly horizontal. At the northern boundary of the Carpathians the salt-bearing formation was strongly folded. As a result, primary salt beds of a thickness of a few metres were buckled and uplifted. In this way were formed large deposits of rock salt in Wieliczka, Barycz, Bochnia and in the regions of Łężkowice–Siedlec and Moszczenica–Łapczyca.

Wieliczka mine is among the oldest in Poland. Salt has been exploited here for about 1000 years. The deposit stretches in an east–west belt for a distance of 6 km, with a width of about 1 km and a depth of 300 m. In its internal structure a lower and an upper part can be distinguished. In the lower part the salt masses occur in the form of folds. In places they pass into *schuppen*. The upper part consists of a mass of clays with blocks of green salt. A geological section through the rock salt deposit in Wieliczka is shown in Fig. 29. The deposit is at present worked by underground leaching. West of Wieliczka occurs the Barycz deposit, which is worked in a similar fashion.

Salt has been exploited in Bochnia for more than 700 years. The main tectonic element is the Bochnia fold, adjoined to the south by the Uzbornia fold. The Uzbornia fold is overthrust by the Carpathian Flysch. To a depth of 300 m the salt deposit is vertical, and at greater depth it dips uniformly at an angle of 15–45°. The length of the deposit along strike is 4 km, and it reaches 200 m in width. The salts are exploited by underground leaching.

The Łężkowice–Siedlec deposit is situated approxi-

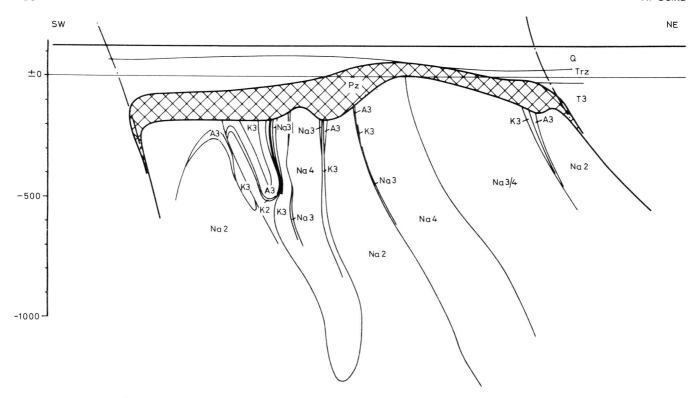

Fig. 27 *Geological section through Kłodawa salt diapir. After J. Poborski. Q, Quaternary; Trz, Tertiary; T_3, Triassic; Keuper, Pz, clay-gypsum cap; Aller Cyclothem (Z_4): Na 4, youngest salts of upper section; Leine Cyclothem (Z_3): Na 3, younger salts of upper section; K3, younger salts of middle section with potash-bearing series; A3, main anhydrite: Stassfurt Cyclothem (Z_2); K2, older potassium salts; Na 2, older rock salt*

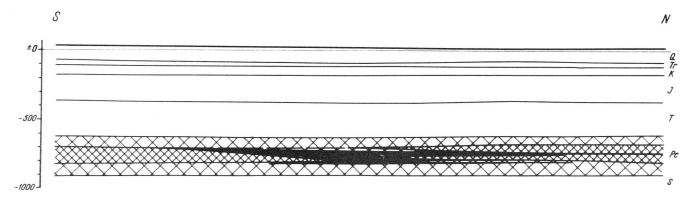

Fig. 28 *Geological section through bedded polyhalite deposit in the region of Puck Bay. After Z. Werner. Q, Quaternary; Tr, Tertiary; K, Cretaceous; J, Jurassic; T, Triassic; Pc, Permian, Zechstein; S, Silurian. 1, Rocks overlying salt; 2, rock salt; 3, polyhalite bed; 4, rock salt; 5, rocks underlying salt*

mately 10 km west of Bochnia. Its length is 3 km and its width ranges from 500 to 700 m. The deposit lies at a depth of between 50 and 500 m. It is leached from the surface through boreholes.[14]

East of Bochnia towards Tarnów the occurrence of autochthonous Tortonian has been confirmed. The rock salt occurs at depths ranging from 700 to 1200 m.

The Rybnik deposit is situated in the area of Upper Silesia in the Rybnik region. Because it is a considerable distance from the boundary of the Carpathians, it has not been folded. The salt series occurs at a depth of 200–300 m. One of the rock-salt beds has a thickness of more than 20 m. To date, the deposit has only been explored through boreholes.

Phosphorites

The phosphorite deposits are of the exogenous type. Production commenced in 1938, but all exploitation

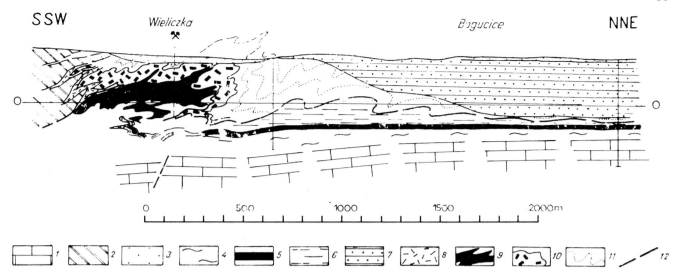

Fig. 29 *Geological section through Wieliczka rock-salt deposit. After A. Garlicki. 1, Jurassic; 2, Flysch rocks of Carpathian overthrust; 3, Quaternary: Tortonian, autochthonous unit; 4, sub-saline sediments; 5, salt series; 6, Chodenickie beds; 7, Grabowieckie beds; Tortonian, overthrust unit: 8, sub-saline sediments; 9, salt series: stratified part of deposit; 10, salt series: clays with lumps of green salt; 11, Chodenickie beds; 12, dislocations*

ceased in 1965, except for the deposits at Annopol-on-the-Vistula, which were worked until 1970.

Table 10 *Production of phosphorites in Poland*

Years	Production, tonne
1956–60	238 000
1961–65	352 000

Deposits of Cretaceous phosphorites occur where Cenomanian–Albian sediments are exposed along the northern boundaries of the Góry Świętokrzyskie. They extend over a distance of more than 100 km from Radom to Gościeradów na Wisła. Cretaceous phosphorites also occur in the region of Burzenin near Sieradz and in the Łeba uplift.[35]

The phosphorite-bearing bed in the Radom-Gościeradów area occurs in Albian sediments. Its thickness

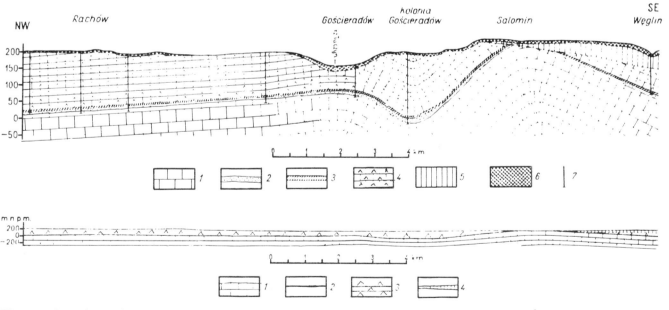

Fig. 30 *Geological section through phosphorite-bearing Cretaceous sediments east of the Vistula in region of Gościeradów. After J. Uberna. Upper section (vertical section exaggerated): 1, oolitic limestones, dolomitic limestones, marls and shelly accumulations of Kimmeridgian; 2, sands of Middle Albian; 3, phosphorite-bearing series of Middle and Upper Albian; 4, rocks and clayey limestones (more rarely marls) of Tortonian with Cenomanian arenaceous limestones and sandy marls with phosphorites at base; 5, carbonate sands and sandy sediments of Tertiary; 6, main arenaceous rocks of Quaternary; 7, drill-holes. Lower section (not exaggerated); 1, carbonate sediments of Kimmeridgian; 2, sandy sediments of Middle Albian and phosphorite-bearing series (highest part of Middle Albian and Upper Albian); 3, carbonate sediments of Turonian and Cenomanian; 4, Tertiary sediments*

varies from 0·5 to 1·5 m, and in places reaches 2·1 m. The bed consists of glauconitic sands, often marly, with numerous concretions of phosphorite. The diameter of the concretions ranges from a few millimetres to between 10 and 20 cm. The yield of phosphate in the deposit varies from 72 to 135 kg/m². The P_2O_5 content in concretions >2 mm averages 17·6%. The geological structure of the deposit is illustrated in Fig. 30.

The phosphorite-bearing series in the Albian sediments in the Burzenin area is located at the boundaries of the Łódź basin. It is best developed in the region of Burzenin near Sieradz. The phosphate yield in the various excavations ranged from 50 to 70 kg/m².

Phosphorites occur in greensands near the base and top of the Cenomanian sediments in the Łeba uplift. The thickness of the phosphorite-bearing layer in the basal Cenomanian ranges from 0·5 to 0·6 m and in the topmost Cenomanian from 0·07 to 0·3 m. The average P_2O_5 content in the +2-mm concentrate is about 14%. The yield of concretions >2 mm across ranges from 51 to 156 kg/m².

Phosphorites occur in Tertiary sediments in several regions of Poland, but nowhere do they form deposits of economic importance. They occur in the region of Kazimierz and Mielnik in sediments of the Upper Palaeogene. They are also known in the Upper Palaeogene in the Łeba uplift and in the Lublin area. The phosphorite-bearing layers are composed of sands with phosphorite concretions. The yield of phosphorites per square metre of the surface of the deposit is low, ranging from a dozen or so to several tens of kilogrammes.

Barite and fluorspar

Endogenous and exogenous types of deposit exist. Barite production figures are given in Table 11. Fluorspar was exploited at Kletno during the years 1956–60, about 8000 tonne having been extracted.

Table 11 *Production of barite in Poland*

Years	Production, tonne
1956–60	133 000
1961–65	215 000
1966–70	252 000
1971–73	179 000

Endogenous deposits

In the area of the Sudetes occur numerous barite–fluorite–sulphide veins. Barite veins are exploited in the region of Wałbrzych in the Boguszów mine and at Stanisławów in the Góry Kaczawskie. Barite was previously also exploited in the Sowie Góry in the Srebrna Góra locality.

Boguszów barite deposit Barite occurs along a northwest–southeast dislocation zone. In this zone occur several steeply inclined veins that intersect the Chełmno rhyolitic massif and Carboniferous rocks. The thickness of these veins varies from 10 cm to several metres.

On the basis of studies by Gruszczyk, three generations of barite have been distinguished: the oldest is represented by white barite with sulphides; to the second belong barite with fluorite; and to the third coarsely crystalline barite with quartz. Barite is accompanied by galena and sphalerite mineralization; chalcopyrite, pyrite and tetrahedrite are accessory minerals. In the northern part, in the deeper levels of the deposit, a gradual increase of fluorite has been observed. In places the fluorite content was 60% of the vein.

Stanisławów barite deposit This deposit also occurs in a northwest–southeast dislocation zone. The zone intersects the early Palaeozoic formations of the Góry Kaczawskie. In the dislocation zone a barite vein dips steeply southwest. Its presence has been proved to a depth of 500 m. This vein shows downdip local swells that take the form of elongated lenses. The thickness of the barite veins ranges from between a dozen or so cm to several metres. The principal mineral is barite, associated with quartz and fluorite, the amount of fluorite increasing markedly downwards. Galena, sphalerite and chalcopyrite occur as accessory minerals.

On the basis of research by Jerzmański,[36] three groups have been distinguished: barite–quartz, barite–fluorite and barite–fluorite with ankerite.

Kletno fluorspar deposit Fluorite occurs in a dislocation zone of overthrust character. The fluorite mineralization is concentrated at the contact of Precambrian crystalline limestones and a schist–gneiss series. The fluorite bodies take the form of nests, short veins or stockworks. Older fluorite with sulphides, barite and quartz, and younger fluorite with calcite and quartz are distinguished. The fluorite mineralization was a cumulative process connected with regional contact metamorphism and hydrothermal activity.[37]

The formation of the barite–fluorite deposits is associated with the last post-Variscan hydrothermal mineralization. The age of this mineralization, according to recent work by J. Pawłowska, is Triassic–Jurassic.

Exogenous deposits

Strawczynek barite deposit Representing the exogenous barite deposits is the Strawczynek deposit in the Góry Świętokrzyskie. The barite mineralization affects Devonian limestone and Triassic dolomites, but the most intensive baritization is developed in the Muschelkalk. In the Devonian Limestone and in the Muschelkalk the mineralization is of a nest–impregnation character. Pawłowska distinguished two generations of barite—the older with pink barite, and the younger with white.

In the Roethian barite occurs in lumps and laminae that were formed during the sedimentation–diagenesis processes. The nest–impregnation barite is epigenetic. Its origin is controversial. Czarnocki and Rubinowski[3] considered this type of mineralization to be hydrothermal, developed in the Laramide phase of the Alpine orogeny. Gruszczyk and Smolarska, however, postulate a sedimentary origin for the mineralization.

By reason of the low barite content in the ore (12–15%), the deposit has not been exploited.

Other non-metallic deposits

In addition to the raw materials for the chemical industry described earlier, more than fifty kinds of mineral raw materials for use in various industries are regarded in Poland as belonging to the group of non-metallic minerals. These include quartz, feldspar, magnesite, gypsum and anhydrite, kaolin and bentonite, various kinds of refractory materials, such as quartzites, shales, clays, fire-resistant dolomites, limestones and cement marls, glass and moulding sands, certain varieties of marbles and many other types of building materials.[38] Only the more important raw materials are considered here.

Endogenous deposits

Quartz

Small veins of quartz occur in several regions of Poland, the largest concentrations being in the area of Lower Silesia, where they are exploited at present.

Table 12 *Production of quartz in Poland*

Years	Production, tonne
1956–60	177 000
1961–65	250 000
1966–70	270 000
1971–73	287 000

Two types of quartz deposit occur in Lower Silesia—concentrations associated with metamorphic rocks and quartz veins cutting through granitic intrusions.

To the former type belong the quartz concentrations that occur in the area of the Rozdroże Izerskie and in Barcinek. In the area of Rozdroże Izerskie quartz occurs in a belt 100–300 m wide that stretches for several kilometres. The concentrations are in the form of nests and overgrowths in mylonite gneisses rich in quartz. This belt dips at an angle of 70° to the southeast. In the central part of the area concentrations with coarse-grained quartz predominate. The diameter of the grains of quartz ranges from 200 to 2000 μm, the SiO_2 content varying from 98 to 99%. White non-schistose quartz for use in the ceramic industry and light rust-coloured schistose quartz for metallurgical use are exploited. According to Morawiecki,[39] the quartz veins that occur in the gneisses were formed as a result of metamorphic processes, during which various substances—silica, among others—were introduced.

Quartz veins occur in the Strzegom–Sobótka granitic massif. They are worked in the Sady and Krasków localities.

In the Sady deposit the veins intersect kaolinized granite. The veins often pass into lenses, on the peripheries of which occur thin veinlets of quartz separated from the main lens by altered granite. Two varieties of quartz are present, coarse-grained forming the main substance of the vein and fine-grained occurring mainly in the lenses. The SiO_2 content of the quartz ranges from 95 to 97%.

In the Krasków[40] deposit, as in the Sady deposit, the veins intersect granite. On the basis of microscopic studies[40] two generations of quartz, coarse-grained and fine-grained, have been recorded. The first-generation quartz contains numerous inclusions of liquid and gas and shows undulating extinction, which is explained as the result of tectonic pressures. The second generation, to which belongs the fine-grained quartz, occurs in the form of thin veinlets within the coarse-grained variety. These veinlets run perpendicular to the elongation of the grains. The Krasków quartz contains 98–99% SiO_2. The vein quartz within the granites was formed by hydrothermal processes. Quartz from the Sady and Krasków deposits is utilized in ceramics, in the production of porcelain glazes, and metallurgically for refractory products and in ferrosilicon.

Feldspar

Various types of feldspathic rock occur in Poland, including leucogranites, weathered granites, trachytes, phonolites and arkosic rocks. To date, only leucogranites in the area of Lower Silesia are of practical importance. The two regions of occurrence of leucogranites in Lower Silesia are Strzeblów near Sobótka and the Pogórze Izerskie.

Table 13 *Production of feldspar in Poland*

Years	Production, tonne
1956–60	123 000
1961–65	220 000
1966–70	290 000
1971–73	202 000

In Strzeblów feldspathic rocks have been exploited for 200 years. These are white Variscan granites that contain potassium–sodium feldspars (leucogranites). The mineral takes the form of a light coloured non-micaceous rock made up of quartz, plagioclase and perthitic microcline. The Strzeblów deposit is situated in the border zone of the Strzegom–Sobótka granite intrusion. The white varieties of granite are the product of post-cataclastic autometamorphism. Near the surface they have undergone kaolinization.

The chemical composition of the feldspathic rock from Strzeblów is: 64·2–79·29% SiO_2, 0–0·09% TiO_2, 10·61–23·48% Al_2O_3, 0·06–0·03% Fe_2O_3, 0·10–0·27% MgO, 0·43–1·26% CaO, 4·2–8·0% Na_2O, 2·00–4·62% K_2O and 0·60–1·45% H_2O. The rock is utilized in the glass, ceramic and electrotechnical industries. A processing plant that produces ground feldspar is located on the site.[38]

In recent times a dozen or so new leucogranite deposits have been located in the Pogórze Izerskie area. They occur along the northern boundary of the Izera gneisses with a series of crystalline schists, between Czerniawa Zdrój and Wojcieszów. Among the largest deposits is Kopaniec, which is being prepared for exploitation. The mineral consists of sodium–potassium leucogranites. As was indicated by Pawłowska,[41] the leucogranite deposits formed as a result of metasomatism of gneissic rocks under the influence of solutions that contain sodium, boron and fluorine.

Exogenous deposits

Magnesite

The magnesite deposits occur in serpentinite rocks. The peridotite–serpentinite massifs are situated in Lower Silesia in the region of Sobótka, Gogołów and Ząbkowice Śląskie (Figs. 20 and 31); their total area amounts to several tens of square kilometres. The peridotite–serpentinite massifs are located in the peripheral region of the Sowie Góry and are regarded as the oldest tectonic element of the Sudetes. They are connected with alkalic initial magmatism, and resulted from the emplacement of the Sowie Góry block and the formation of deep fractures along which the peridotites were intruded. Somewhat later occurred intrusions of gabbroic rocks. The age of the peridotite–serpentinite rocks is Proterozoic, though some authors connect it with the Caledonian magmatic cycle.

The exploitation of magnesite commenced in 1912 in the region of Ząbkowice Śląskie and in 1920 in the region of Sobótka. A new magnesite deposit was

Table 14 *Production of magnesite in Poland*

Years	Production, tonne
1956–60	104 000
1961–65	159 000
1966–70	142 000
1971–73	107 000

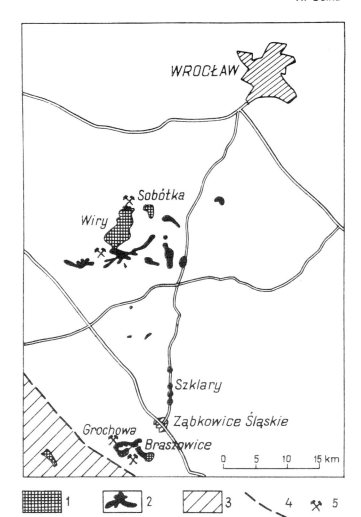

Fig. 31 *Sketch of occurrences of serpentinites and magnesite deposits in Lower Silesia. 1, Gabbro and amphibolite; 2, serpentinite; 3, Palaeozoic massif of Sudetes; 4, main Sudetic fault; 5, magnesite deposit*

discovered in 1965 in Wiry. The reserves of magnesite are put at >1 000 000 tonne. The annual tonnage of magnesite produced in the period 1930–44 ranged from 9000 to 16 000.

At the Sobótka magnesite deposit the serpentinite massif is in contact on the south and east with amphibolites, and on the west with kaolinized granites. The deposit has been mined to a depth of approximately 150 m. In the serpentinites are magnesite veins (Fig. 32) that, according to their thickness and form, can be divided into three kinds—thick veins (0·5–4·8 m), thin veins (0·5–0·1 m) and magnesite in the form of irregular net-veining (thickness of the veinlets from a few millimetres to 0·1 m).

The thick veins run southwest–northeast and generally dip to the southeast, predominantly at an angle of 40–70°, though a few have a northwest–southeast direction and dip towards the southwest. The length of the veins ranges from a dozen or so to 300 m; their thickness is variable and they also show breaks in continuity. In the vertical direction the thick

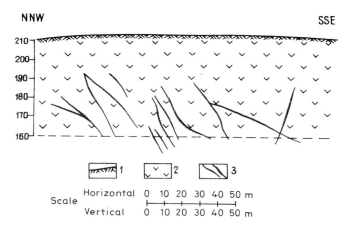

Fig. 32 *Geological section through Sobótka magnesite deposit. After Osika. 1, Soil; 2, serpentinite; 3, thick magnesite veins*

veins show continuity on several horizons to a depth of 10–20 m, but at greater depth they often pinch or wedge out. The contact of the magnesite veins with the serpentinites is in places a planar surface with a decidedly rectilinear course; more often, however, it forms 'rugged' planes with numerous forkings of diminutive veins. The thin veins are very numerous, but their length ranges from several to not more than a dozen or so metres, and in the vertical direction they exceed no more than a few metres.

Reticulate net-veining occurs throughout the massif, but the largest accumulations are observed in a few specific zones in the serpentinite. The content of reticulate magnesite in these zones ranges from a few to a dozen or so per cent, and these magnesites are workable.

The Wiry magnesite deposit occurs in the Gogołów serpentinite massif. This massif follows a parallel of latitude and is 25 km long. In the surroundings of this massif occur Precambrian gneisses and crystalline schists and in the northern part gabbro and granites. The mineralized zone has an area of a few square kilometres. As in Sobótka, there are veins up to 4 m thick and up to 200 m long. A second form of occurrence of magnesite is as thin veinlets that run in various directions and form a reticulate mesh. The amount of magnesite in the reticulate parts ranges from a few to 16% of the total mass. The depth of the mineralized zone ranges from 30 to 90 m, but in the dislocation zones it reaches in places 250 m.

To the west of Ząbkowice Śląskie are several magnesite occurrences, the largest of which are the Szczęść Boże and Konstanty deposits. Magnesite also occurs in Szklary to the east of Ząbkowice Śląskie.

The serpentinite massif of the Szczęść Boże deposit is surrounded by crystalline schists, and on the east occurs gneissic quartz syenite with syenite apophyses that intersect the serpentinites. The geological structure of the deposit is similar to that of Sobótka. Magnesite occurs here as thick veins, thin veins and in the form of vein-networks. In the mine a dozen or so thick veins with near east–west directions have been established that dip south at an angle 30–70°. The length of the veins ranges from 50 to 200 m, but they are often disconnected; their thickness ranges from 0·5 to 1·2 m, more rarely reaching 2·2 m. Thin veins, as in Sobótka mine, are very numerous. Apart from the magnesite veins, there often occur here talc–chlorite veins that mostly run transversely to the magnesite veins and dip towards the north. Talc–chlorite is often associated with and mantles the syenite apophyses.

The Konstanty deposit is basically located in serpentinite, and only in the southeast do gabbroic rocks occur. The geological structure of the deposit differs considerably from that of the deposits described above. In the previously described mines there occurs only white magnesite, but in Konstanty mine three varieties may be distinguished—white magnesite, white magnesite with a yellow ferruginous coat, and yellow and brown ferruginous magnesite. The particular varieties of magnesite are closely connected with the degree of weathering of the serpentinites. In the fresh serpentinite occurs white magnesite, in the weathered serpentinite white magnesite with a yellow envelope, and in the disintegrated serpentinite yellow and brown magnesite. The whole serpentinite mass is cut by a fine net of fissures with WSW–ENE direction, which may reach considerable depths and are filled with magnesite, more rarely with talc–chlorite. The length of the veins reaches 100 m, and their thickness varies between 0·2 and 0·5 m. Some serpentinite zones have very dense magnesite veining, the thickness of the veins ranging from a few millimetres to 0·2 m. The western and northern parts of the mine are located in weathered and disintegrated serpentinite, in which occurs predominantly yellow ferruginous magnesite in the form of a fine net of veins making up from several to 20% of the mass of the serpentinite rock. These parts are at present exploited entirely by opencast methods (Fig. 33).

In Szklary the magnesite occurs beneath the nickel deposit in the form of several veins up to 15 cm thick or, more often, in the form of net-veins. The veins run southwest–northeast and dip to the south at an angle of 80°. Generally, the course of the veins at Szklary

Table 15 *Composition of yellow (ferruginous) magnesite from Konstanty mine*

Composition	Crude magnesite, %	Calcined magnesite, %
MgO	45·44	86·92
CaO	0·99	1·89
SiO_2	2·01	2·82
Fe_2O_3	2·19	4·18
Al_2O_3	1·67	3·19
Calcination loss	47·70	—

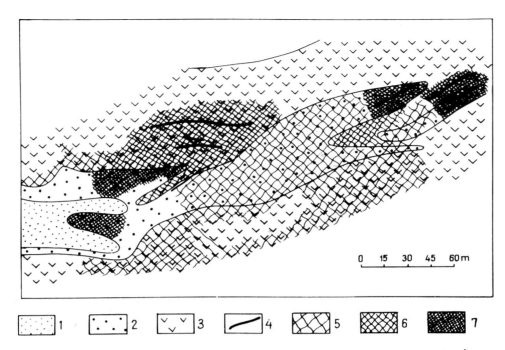

Fig. 33 *Plan of part of magnesite deposit at Konstanty mine in Braszowice near Ząbkowice Śląskie. After Osika. 1, Decomposed serpentinite; 2, weathered serpentinite; 3, fresh serpentinite; 4, thick veins of magnesite; 5, concentration of magnesite net-veining, 1–3%; 6, concentration of magnesite net-veining, 3–7%; 7, concentration of magnesite net-veining, >7%*

conforms with the course of the veins in the deposits in the Braszowice region.

In the main, the magnesite contains 43·6–47·7% MgO, 2·52–9·83% SiO_2 and 1·27–2·44% CaO. From the technological point of view one may distinguish magnesite with a low silica content and increased iron content, which is utilized in the production of metallurgical refractories, and magnesite with a high content of SiO_2 for the building industry for the production of Sorel cement.

For refractory purposes magnesites with up to 2% SiO_2 and 1% CaO are utilized.

The primary serpentinite–peridotite rocks were the source of the magnesite constituents. The nature of the process that led to the formation of the deposits is controversial: some workers connect the formation of the deposits with the action of hydrothermal waters,[42] whereas others[43] attribute it to weathering processes brought about by descending surface waters.

Gypsum and anhydrite
Gypsum and anhydrite occur in Poland in the area of Lower Silesia in Upper Permian (Zechstein) sediments and in Miocene sediments in the area on the Carpathian Foredeep.

Gypsum and anhydrite in the Upper Permian are present over large areas of Poland; however, they occur predominantly at considerable depths. They occur at shallow depths in Lower Silesia in the southern part of the North Sudetic Depression. In this region they crop out in the localities of Niwice, Gierałtów and Żarska Wieś. The gypsum series is 30 m thick and dips at an angle of 20–30°. Stratigraphically, it represents the Stassfurt cyclothem (Z_2). Near the surface there occurs pure gypsum with 96% $CaSO_4 . 2H_2O$, but at the lower levels of exploitation this content decreases.

Table 16 *Production of gypsum and anhydrite in Poland*

Years	Production, tonne
1956–60	3 400 000
1961–65	5 130 000
1966–70	7 600 000
1971–73	5 800 000

In the Niwice processing plant calcined stucco, moulding and alabastrine gypsum are produced. In the Nowy Ląd mine in Niwice anhydrite for the production of sulphuric acid is also exploited.

Gypsum occurs in the sediments of the marine Miocene in three areas of the Carpathian Foredeep— Nida, Rzeszów and Silesia–Krakow.

The deposits of the Nida River area are among the largest in the world. Stratigraphically, they correspond to the Middle Tortonian. Gypsum is widely distributed along the southern side of the Góry Świętokrzyskie. According to Gaweł,[44] in this region there can be distinguished coarsely crystalline, skeletal, granular and compact gypsum. Coarsely crystalline gypsum is composed of very large crystals (from 0·5 to 3·5 m in length) twinned in the shape of 'dovetails'; it occurs in the region of Pińczów and Wiślica. The thickness of the gypsum bed ranges from 3 to 4 m. Coarse crystalline gypsum contains from 94 to 99% $CaSO_4.2H_2O$. Skeletal gypsum was formed as a result of recrystallization of the primary gypsum sediment. It consists of crystals from several to a dozen or so centimetres long. The thickness of the bed ranges from several to 12 m. Granular gypsum consists of grains of gypsum a few millimetres in diameter embedded in a gypsum matrix. The most widely developed gypsum is the compact gypsum, which is very finely crystalline gypsum with from 65 to 85% $CaSO_4.2H_2O$.

In the Rzeszów area gypsum occurs in Tortonian sediments in the vicinity of Strzyżów and Przemyśl. Alabaster exploited in Łopuszka Wielka near Przemyśl is noteworthy. The exploitation of the deposit has continued since the nineteenth century.

From work by Garlicki[45] it is known that the gypsum deposit has the form of a lens 10 m thick. Within the gypsum occur nodules of alabaster several tens of centimetres in diameter. Alabaster is a dense variety of white coloured gypsum; it is utilized for ornamental and sculpture purposes. The chemical composition of alabaster is 99·15% $CaSO_4.2H_2O$, 0·19% MgO and 0·26% SiO_2.

Gypsum occurs in Upper Silesia in the area of Rybnik, where, together with the salt-bearing series, it fills a basin. The gypsum is produced at Czernica. Gypsum also occurs near Krakow and in Dzierżysław near Kietrze, where it is exploited by underground mining. The thickness of the gypsum lenses reaches 60 m and the average thickness is 36 m. The $CaSO_4.2H_2O$ content in gypsum ranges from 48 to 92%.

The Miocene gypsum is widely utilized—as rock gypsum, gypsum constructional binders, stucco work gypsum, moulding gypsum, high durability gypsum, anhydrite cement, fast-setting gypsum and other gypsum products.

Kaolin
Kaolin deposits occur in Lower Silesia within the Variscan granite massifs and, in particular, within the Strzegom–Sobótka massif and the Strzelin massif. The kaolin deposits were formed in the Tertiary as a result of the weathering of the above-named granite massifs, gneissic rocks and other formations.

One-third of domestic requirements is provided by these deposits. Three types of kaolin deposit are distinguished—residual (primary) deposits, transported (secondary) deposits, and sedimentary deposits.[46]

Kaolinization developed on a regional scale. It encompassed granitic intrusions and metamorphic rocks that occupy considerable areas of the Fore-Sudetic block. These massifs are, in the main, covered by Tertiary sediments. Kaolins occur under these formations in topographic depressions in granites or gneisses. This situation is illustrated in the schematic geological section through a kaolin deposit (Fig. 34). The thickness of the kaolinized zone generally ranges from several to 40 m and only in places reaches 80 m. In most cases the original kaolinitic alterations have been washed away: only the deposits in the tectonic troughs or under the cover of younger Tertiary sediments have been preserved. To these belong the Żarów, Kalno, Śmiałowice, Bolesławice, Wyszonowice and other deposits.

The Żarów deposit is an example of a primary deposit formed on granite. The kaolinized zone has a thickness of 50 m. At the base of the decayed granite occurs a two-mica granite. Above the kaolinitic alteration zone are Upper Miocene clays with brown coal. The connexion between the occurrence of brown coal and of kaolins should be stressed. As the distance from the brown coal deposits increases in the horizontal and vertical directions, the degree of the kaolinization of the granite decreases. Thus, the process of kaolinization was influenced by CO_2-containing waters that existed in the brown coal environment. These waters migrated downwards to the granite basement, so accelerating its decomposition. Kaolin from Żarów is utilized in the production of refractory articles. The refractoriness of this material exceeds 1710°. Kaolins upgraded in hydrocyclones are utilized in the production of refractory materials with superior heat resistance.

The Wyszonowice deposit is an example of a primary deposit formed on gneisses. The kaolinized zone is 24 m thick and yields white-grey and cherry-red kaolins. The white-grey kaolins meet the requirements of kaolins for the production of fine china and, in lesser quantity, for porcelain.

The mechanism of kaolin weathering is connected with the warm and humid climate that prevailed in the Palaeogene and Neogene. The activity of acid waters associated with brown coal played an important role in removing iron and bleaching the kaolin.

The secondary kaolins were formed in the Oligocene and Miocene as a result of the washing out of the primary weathering kaolin. Deposits of this type occur in the marginal zone of the western part of the Strzegom–Sobótka granite massif. Representing this

Table 17 *Production of kaolin minerals in Poland*

Years	Production, tonne
1956–60	86 000
1961–65	260 000
1966–70	990 000
1971–73	775 000

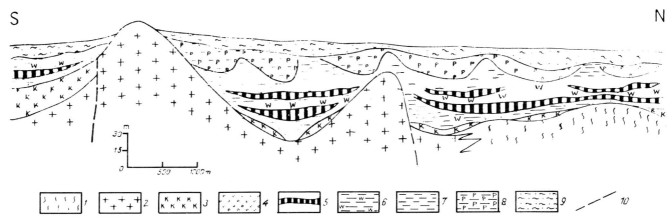

Fig. 34 *Schematic geological section through deposits of kaolin and fire-resistant clays in the region of Strzegom. After Z. Kozydra. Pre-Tertiary basement: 1, metamorphic schists; 2, granite; Tertiary: 3, kaolin; 4, sand and gravel; 5, brown coal; 6, clays with brown coal; 7, fireclays; 8, variegated clays; Quaternary: 9, aqueoglacial sand and gravel and drift clays; 10, faults*

type of secondary accumulation is the Dzierżków deposit, which occurs in Tertiary sediments near the outcrops of granites. Kaolins occur in the form of layers and lenses up to 76 m thick. A lens is composed of various kinds of kaolin, suitable for the production of porcelain and making up between 10 and 20% of the mass of the deposit. Kaolins of the porcelain type show a high resistance to deformation (up to 20 kg/cm^2).

The kaolinitic sandstones exploited in the Bolesławiec basin represent the sedimentary type of kaolin deposit. The kaolinitic sandstones are of Senonian age. They are delta-shaped sedimentary accumulations formed at the foot of weathering granite and gneiss massifs. These sandstones are made up of grains of quartz bound by kaolinitic material. The thickness of the layer of the kaolinitic sandstones ranges from 10 to 70 m.

The Czerna deposit is a bed of sands and friable kaolinitic sandstones 24 m thick. After mechanical enrichment of the fraction below 0·025 mm, concentrations are obtained that contain 37–39% Al_2O_3 with a low content of Fe_2O_3 (0·6–0·8%).

The Zebrzydowa deposit has been exploited since 1965. The thickness of the kaolinitic sandstone layer is 32 m. After upgrading, kaolin with 80–83% of clayey substances is obtained. These kaolins find application in the ceramics, paper and food industries. In the production of kaolin, glass sand is also obtained as a by-product.[4]

The kaolinitic sandstones in the Czerwona Woda deposit have a thickness of 18 m. After crushing and screening through graders of 0·06-mm diameter, a kaolinitic fraction amounting to 34% is obtained.

Bentonite
Bentonites and montmorillonite clays of economic importance occur in Poland in Upper Carboniferous sediments, in sediments of the Carpathian Flysch and in Miocene sediments.

Table 18 *Production of bentonites in Poland*

Years	Production, tonne
1956–60	11 000
1961–65	22 000
1966–70	349 000
1971–73	230 000

The Upper Carboniferous (Namurian A) bentonites occur in the lower part of the montmorillonite clay formation in Upper Silesia. The thickness of the clay formation ranges from 6 to 8 m, but the thickness of the bentonite layer does not exceed 1 m. In the upper part of the montmorillonite formation are bentonitic clays between 2 and 5 m thick.

Bentonites are strongly altered volcanic ashes. These are sodic bentonites and they show great lithological variability. They are exploited in Radzionków mine and used in the foundry industry.

In the rocks of the Carpathian Flysch bentonites occur mainly in the Eocene sediments. Here are distinguished bentonites proper, consisting of sodic montmorillonite, from Zagórze near Sanok, and bentonites composed of calcic montmorillonite (fuller's earth), which occur near Grybów. These minerals may be utilized in the production of moulding bodies.[4,38]

In the Miocene beds of the Carpathian Foredeep bentonites of industrial importance occur in the localities of Jawor, Górki and Chmielnik. The bentonites are associated with a Tortonian pyroclastic horizon.[47]

The Jawor deposit comprises three layers of bentonite with a joint thickness of 2 m. The bentonite consists of 60% montmorillonite and 30% illite. Bentonites from Jawor and Górki, after beneficiation with sulphuric acid, make good-quality bleaching earths. In the Chmielnik deposit two layers of bentonite are worked for foundry and petroleum industry needs.

References

1 **Znosko J. ed.** *Geological atlas of Poland, scale 1 : 2 000 000* (Warsaw: Institute of Geology, 1968).
2 **Osika R. ed.** *Mineralogenic atlas of Poland, scale 1 : 2 000 000* (Warsaw: Institute of Geology, 1970).
3 **Rubinowski Z.** Strefowość okruszcowania ołowiowo-cynkowo–barowego w Górach Świętokrzyskich. *Biul. Inst. Geol.* no. 241, 1971, 91–9. (English abstract, 102–3).
4 *Surowce mineralne Dolnego Śląska* **Dziedzic K. Kozlowski S. Majerowicz A. and Sawicki L. eds.** (Wrocław: Ossolineum, 1979).
5 **Kubicki S.** Persypektywy poszukiwań złóż rud metali w podłożu krystalicznym platformy prekambryjskiej na obszarze Białostoczyzny. *Przew. XLV Zjazdu Pol. Tow. Geol. Inst. Geol., Warszawa*, 1973.
6 **Zimnoch E.** Zmetamorfizowane złoża rud żelaza w Sudetach na tle innych złóż tego typu. *Geol. Sudetica*, **3**, 1967, 251–96.
7 **Poborski C.** Złoże i kopalnia rud "Staszic" w Rudkach, w Górach Świętokrzyskich. *Przegl. górn.*, **4**, 1947.
8 **Czarnocki J.** Złoże rud żelaza w Dąbrowie pod Kielcami w związku z zagadnieniem rud dewońskich w Świętokrzyskim. *Trav. Sérv. géol. Pol.*, **7**, 1951, 95–114.
9 **Osika R.** Osady pliensbachu na Pomorzu Zachodnim (w związku z zagadnieniem poszukiwania złóż rud żelaza). *Kwart. geol.*, **3**, 1959, 914–38. (English abstract, 936–8).
10 **Krajewski R.** Złoża żelaziaków ilastych we wschodniej części powiatu koneckiego. *Biul. Państw. Inst. Geol.* no. 26, 1947, 134 p. (English summary, 122–34).
11 **Osika R. and Znosko J.** *Badania geologiczne iłów rudonośnych jury krakowsko–wieluńskiej, t.I i II* (Warszawa: Inst. Geol., 1954).
12 **Znosko J.** Wznoszenie się wysadu kłodawskiego w jurze i jego wpływ na genezę muszlowców syderytowych. *Kwart. geol.*, **1**, no. 1 1957, 90–105. (English abstract, 104–5).
13 **Konstantynowicz E.** Sudeckie złoża polimetaliczne. In *Geologia złóż surowców mineralnych Polski: Surowce metaliczne* (Warszawa: Inst. Geol., 1960).
14 *La géologie et les gîtes mineraux en Pologne* **Osika R. ed.** (Warsaw: Wydawnictwa Geologiczne, 1979), 703 p. (French edition of *Biul. Inst. geol.* no. 251, 1970)
15 **Konstantynowicz E.** Mineral distribution in the Permian Formations of western Poland. In *Mineral deposits* **Campbell F. A. and Wilson H. D. B. eds** (Ottawa: I. G. C., 1972), 373–80. (*24th Int. geol. Congr., Canada, 1972*, sect. 4)
16 **Gruszczyk H.** The genesis of the Silesian–Cracow deposits of lead-zinc ores. In *Genesis of stratiform lead-zinc-barite–fluorite deposits in carbonate rocks (the so-called Mississippi Valley type deposits)* **Brown J. S. ed.** (Lancaster, Pa.: Economic Geology Publishing House, 1967), 169–77. (*Econ. Geol. Monogr. 3*)
17 **Smolarska I.** Comparative study of the mineralization of Triassic rocks in Poland. Reference 15, 381–9.
18 **Ekiert F.** Les minerais de zinc et de plomb. Reference 14, 384–92.
19 **Gałkiewicz T.** Genesis of Silesian–Cracovian zinc–lead deposits. Reference 16, 156–68.
20 **Harańczyk C.** Złoża Zn–Pb typu śląsko–krakowskiego i ich związek komagmowy ze skałami alkalicznymi. *Rudy Metale Nieżel.*, **10**, 1965, 132–39; 187–93.
21 **Krajewski R.** Uwagi na temat genezy górnośląskich złóż cynkowo-ołowiowych. *Przegl. geol.*, no. 7 1957, 311–4.
22 **Sass-Gustkiewicz M. Dżułyński S. and Ridge J. D.** The emplacement of zinc–lead sulfide ores in the Upper Silesian district—a contribution to the understanding of Mississippi Valley-type deposits. *Econ. Geol.*, **77**, 1982, 392–412.
23 **Spangenberg K.** Die Chromerzlagerstätte von Tampadel am Zobten. *Z. prakt. Geol.*, **51**, 1943.
24 *Geologia złóż surowców mineralnych Polski: Surowce metaliczne* **Krajewski R. ed.** (Warszawa: Inst. Geol., 1960).
25 **Jaskólski S.** Złoża cyny w Gierczynie. *Przegl. geol.*, no. 5 1967, 238.
26 **Szałamacha M.** O mineralizacji cynowej we wschodniej części Pasma Kamienieckiego w Górach Izerskich. *Przegl. geol.*, no. 6 1967, 281–4.
27 **Petrascheck W. E.** Die Erzlagerstätten des Schlesischen Gebirges. *Arch. LagerstättForsch.* no. 59, 1933, 53 p.
28 **Chilińska H.** Perspektywy poszukiwawcze złóż rud cyny na tle metalogenezy Sudetów. *Przegl. geol.*, no. 1 1965, 21–5.
29 **Daniec L.** Rudy niklu. In reference 24.
30 **Gil Z.** Rudy glinu. In reference 24.
31 **Pawłowski S.** Geologia złóż siarki w Polsce. In reference 14.
32 **Poborski J.** Cechsztyńskie zagłębie solne Europy środkowej na ziemiach Polski. *Pr. Inst. Geol.*, **30**, no. 2 1960, 355–75.
33 **Werner Z.** Les sels gemme, de potassium et de magnesium. In reference 14, 350–5.
34 **Poborski J. and Skoczylas-Ciszewska K.** O miocenie w strefie nasunigcia karpackiego w okolicy Wieliczki i Bochni. *Roczn. pol. Tow. geol.*, **33**, no. 3 1963.
35 **Uberna J.** Les phosphorites. In reference 14, 470–3.
36 **Jerzmański J.** Wstępne wiadomości o złożu barytu w Stanisławowie na Dolnym Śląsku. *Przegl. geol.*, no. 3, 1957.
37 **Banaś M.** Przejawy mineralizacji w metamorfiku Śnieżnika Kłodzkiego. *Prace Geol., Polska Akad. Nauk* no. 27, 1965, 1–84.
38 **Kozłowski S.** *Surowce skalne Polski* (Warszawa: Wyd. Geol., 1975).
39 **Morawiecki A.** Uwagi o żyle kwarcowej w Białej Górze na Rozdrożu Izerskim. *Przegl. geol.*, no. 9 1954, 369–75.
40 **Heflik W. and Smolarska I.** Badania petrograficzne skały kwarcowej z Kraskowa koło Świdnicy na Dolnym Śląsku. *Zesz. nauk. Akad. górn.-hutn., Krakow* no. 123, *Geologia* no. 7, 1966.
41 **Pawłowska J.** Leukogranity Pogórza Izerskiego jako źródło surowca skaleniowego. *Biul. Inst. geol.* no. 223, 1968, 5–90. (English summary, 87–90).
42 **Spangenberg K.** Zur Genesis der Magnesitlagerstätte vom Galgenberg bei Zobten (Schlesien). *Neues Jb. Miner. Geol. Paläont. Mh. A*, no. 8 1949, 177–90.
43 **Osika R and Gajewski Z.** Magnezyty. In reference 4.
44 **Gaweł A.** Złoża gipsu w Polsce południowej. *Cement, Kraków*, no. 6 1955, 11–20.
45 **Garlicki A.** Budowa geologiczna rejonu złoża alabastrowego w Łopuszce Wielkiej. *Kwart. geol.*, **6**, no. 4 1962.
46 **Budkiewicz M.** Złoża kaolinu w Polsce. *Przegl. geol.*, no. 5 1964, 207–8.
47 **Fijałkowska E. and Fijałkowski J.** Bentonity w utworach miocenu południowego obrzeżenia Gór Świętokrzyskich. *Biul. Inst. geol.* no. 194, 1966, 95–129. (English summary, 126–9).
48 **Książkiewicz M. Oberc J. and Pożaryski W.** *Geology of Poland, volume IV: tectonics* (Warsaw: Wydawnictwa Geologiczne, 1977).
49 **Osika R. ed.** *Map of mineral raw materials deposits of Poland, scale 1 : 500 000* (Warsaw: Institute of Geology, 1984).
50 **Wyżykowski J.** Rudy miedzi. In reference 4.

L. Dejonghe

Belgium

The bedrock of Belgium has been exploited for various metals—for example, Fe, Zn, Pb, Mn, Cu and Au—as well as for several minerals—barite, fluorite, phosphates and kaolin.

Mining activities in Belgium date back to prehistoric times, as is attested by the Neolithic underground flint workings of Spiennes. Metallic mineral exploitation was also a very early activity. Iron ore deposits were being worked by the Gallic people before the Roman invasion and it is also believed that gold panning was taking place at that time in the rivers of northeastern Belgium. Lead and zinc mines were operated during the Middle Ages, La Calamine (Moresnet), the largest zinc ore deposit in Belgium, being one of the very few in the world to be actively mined for zinc during that period. In 1802 one of the later operators of this orebody (J. J. Dony) invented the first process for the industrial recovery of zinc, the process being patented by Napoléon I in 1810.

The metallic mining industry reached its apogee between 1850 and 1870, after which activity steadily declined, though a few mines survived into the early part of the twentieth century. The last sulphide mine (Vedrin) was closed in 1945; the last iron oxide mine in the Meuse Valley (Couthuin) was closed in 1946; the Toarcian 'Minette' iron ore deposit of the Belgian Lorraine was mined at Musson and Halanzy up to October, 1978.

Table 1 *Total Belgian ore production (tonne)*

Fe	40 000 000 hematite plus limonite; 1 000 000 pyrite
Zn	2 900 000 oxidized zinciferous ore plus sphalerite
Pb	450 000 galena plus lead oxides
Barite	700 000
Phosphate	18 000 000 phosphatic crude ore
Mn	180 000 manganiferous ore
Fluorite, kaolin and Cu	Very small
Au	Not known

The major need for barite for oil drilling has, however, given rise to new operations on the old barite orebody of Fleurus. Production was restarted in 1979. Kaolin is also exploited on a very small scale.

Total production of Belgian ore is estimated in Table 1.

Geological framework

The bedrock of Belgium is chiefly made up of sedimentary rocks; igneous rock occurrences are very limited both in number and extent.

Three major groups may be distinguished (Fig. 1):
(1) A basement, made up of Cambrian, Ordovician and Silurian rocks (mainly slaty schists and quartzites) belonging to the Caledonides
(2) An old cover, made up of Devonian and Carboniferous rocks (alternations of sandstones, shales and limestones) belonging to the Variscides
(3) A young cover, made up of rocks of Permian and younger age (Mesozoic and Caenozoic)

Groups 1 and 2 are folded, whereas the young cover is flat-lying and sub-horizontal. The three groups are separated by angular unconformities. The Variscan orogeny is characterized by a major overthrust nappe, the Dinant synclinorium overlapping the Namur synclinorium along the Midi–Eifel thrust.

Regional metamorphism (epizone–mesozone) affects several regions of the Ardenne area and always rocks of Lower Devonian age or older.

Manganese deposits belong to the basement. Iron, zinc, lead, copper, barite, fluorite and kaolin deposits are located in the old cover, this formation supporting the major ore deposits in Belgium. The young cover contains only phosphate and some small iron and kaolin deposits. Gold has been exploited in alluvial deposits.

In this review, deposits are dealt with element by element or mineral by mineral. A selection of relevant publications is noted.

Lead and zinc deposits[4, 26, 31, 35, 36, 38, 44, 46, 55, 70]

Lead and zinc exploitation has been recorded from more than 200 localities. The main ore deposits are indicated in Fig. 2. The largest deposit was that of La Calamine* with around 600 000 tonne of zinc metal. Six other high-grade deposits have produced more than 50 000 tonne of combined metals—Schmalgraf, Bleiberg (in French, Plombières), Fossey, Eschbroich, Engis and Haies-Monet.

* This ore deposit is also known under several other names: 'Altenberg', 'La Vieille Montagne', 'La Grande-Montagne' and 'Moresnet'. It is situated in the territory of La Calamine, but before 1919 it belonged to the 'Territoire neutre de Moresnet'.

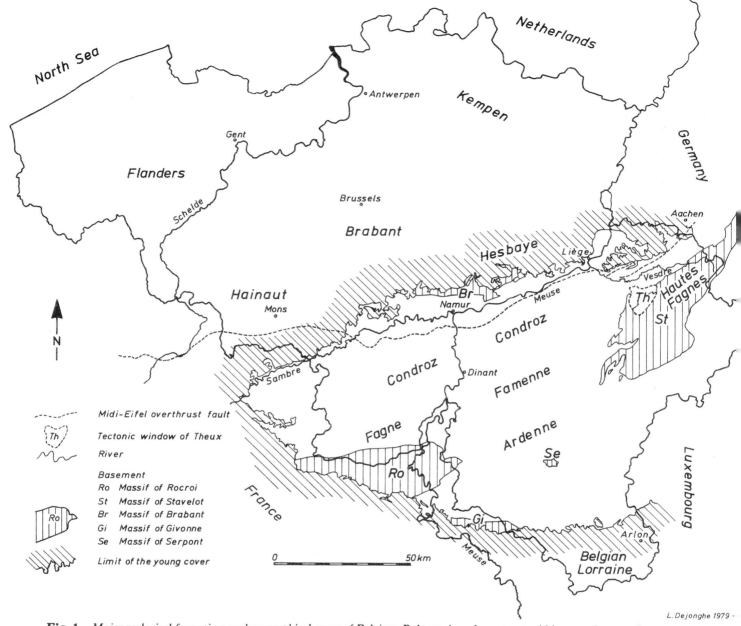

Fig. 1 Major geological formations and geographical areas of Belgium. Palaeozoic rocks crop out within central parts of young cover

Pyrite and marcasite were subordinate by-products of lead and zinc ores in most mines, but at Vedrin and Rocheux-Oneux pyrite and marcasite were the dominant sulphides. Gossans capped most of these ore deposits.

Production is given in Table 2 (figures taken from Dejonghe and Jans[26]). The production of the district of the Herve–Vesdre–Theux Massifs (the main metallogenic district and the only one for which a study of all lead–zinc deposits has been done[26]) is compared with that of Belgium as a whole. These ore deposits belong to the category of 'Mississippi Valley type deposits'. They may be divided into two classes.

Table 2 Production (tonne) of ore of Belgian lead–zinc deposits for 1837–1936[26]

	Herve–Vesdre–Theux Massifs	Belgium	Grade, %
Calamine	1 872 693	1 979 962	29–37
Sphalerite	674 780	813 960	45–57
Lead ore (including oxides)	197 742	265 499	55–75
Pyrite	324 534	961 240	35

Vein-type deposits and associated irregular bodies (so-called 'amas')

Economic mineralization of this type is mainly

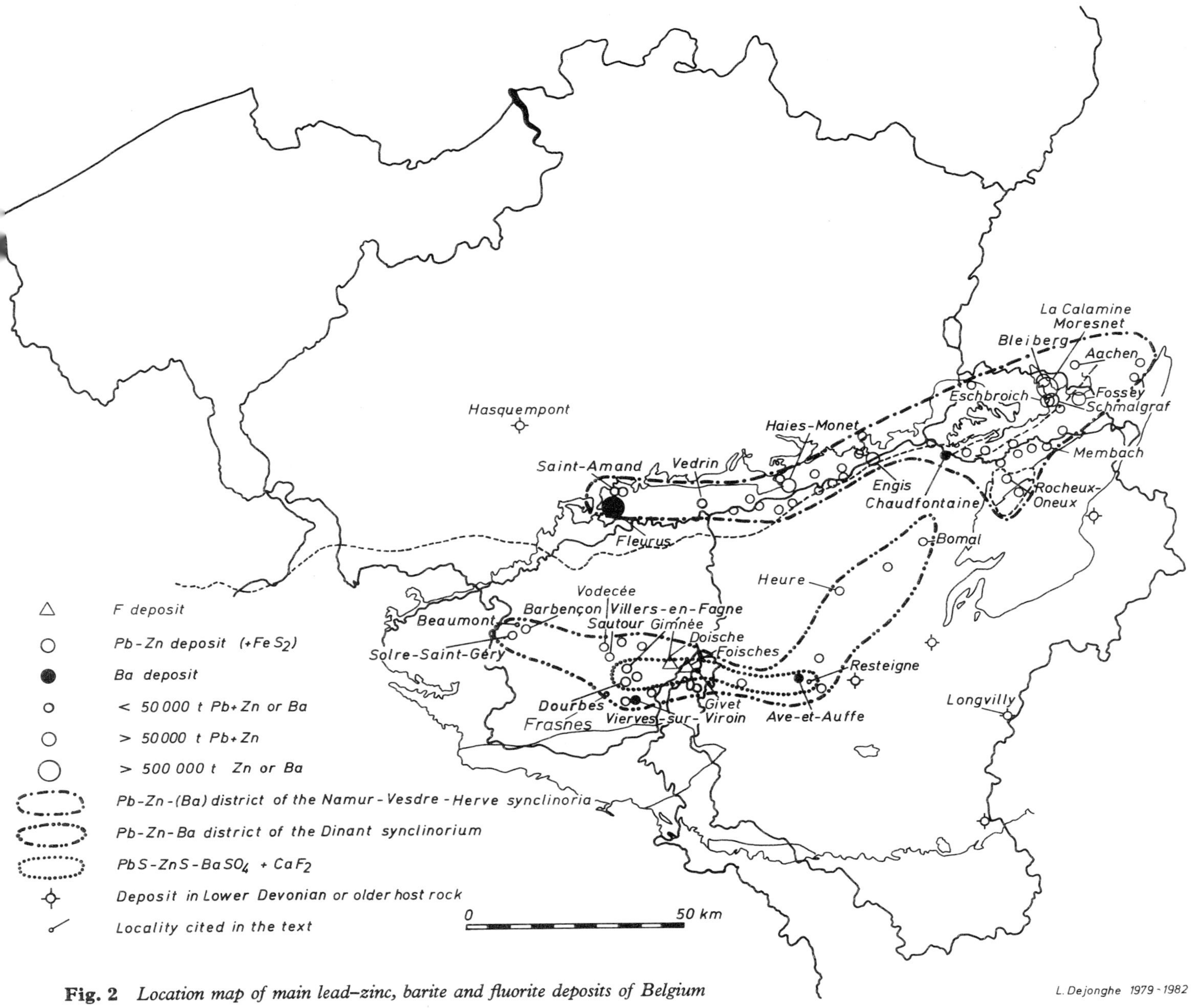

Fig. 2 Location map of main lead–zinc, barite and fluorite deposits of Belgium

L. Dejonghe 1979-1982

Legend:
- △ F deposit
- ○ Pb–Zn deposit (+FeS$_2$)
- ● Ba deposit
- ∘ < 50 000 t Pb+Zn or Ba
- ○ > 50 000 t Pb+Zn
- ○ > 500 000 t Zn or Ba
- –·– Pb–Zn–(Ba) district of the Namur–Vesdre–Herve synclinoria
- – – Pb–Zn–Ba district of the Dinant synclinorium
- ···· PbS–ZnS–BaSO$_4$ + CaF$_2$
- ✧ Deposit in Lower Devonian or older host rock
- ⌐ Locality cited in the text

restricted to the intersections of faults with limestones and dolomites of the Devonian (mainly Givetian and Frasnian) and of the Dinantian. Ore deposits hosted in the detrital rocks of the Lower Devonian and the basement are very rare.

Most of these deposits, and especially those with the largest tonnages, are hosted in the Dinantian carbonate formations of the Namur synclinorium (to the west) and the Herve–Vesdre–Theux Massifs (to the east). They lie along a belt 10–25 km wide, extending for 120 km from Saint-Amand to east of Aachen (first lead–zinc district, Fig. 2). These Dinantian limestones bear lead and zinc mineralization only where their lower part is dolomitized. The deposits consist of irregular lens-like masses (in French, *amas*) connected to fissure-filling veins. These 'amas' concordantly rest at the very top of the Dinantian limestones immediately below the base of the pyritic Namurian shales (the so-called *ampélites*). Ore from the 'amas' as well as from the veins often exhibits a brecciated fabric. In comparison with the veins, the overlying 'amas' have yielded by far the largest tonnages.

Another lead–zinc district is located in the Dinant synclinorium along a knee-like belt 10–15 km wide that extends for 125 km from Beaumont to Bomal via Givet (second lead–zinc district, Fig. 2). There some small fissure-filling veins, never capped by any 'amas', were mined, yielding only a small production (usually only a few thousand tonne of metal and seldom more than 10 000 tonne). These veins are hosted in the carbonate formations of the Devonian—mainly in the axial zone of anticlines and often with trends transverse to the axial plane.

Lastly, some rare small veins (without 'amas') also

exist in the detrital formations of the Lower Devonian. The largest deposit is that of Longvilly, near the Belgian–Luxembourg border (production, < 10 000 tonne of ore). Veins that cut the pre-Devonian basement are even rarer and smaller. The latter are only known in the Brabant Massif—for example, at Hasquempont (Ittre).

Water problems, combined with the fact that the lodes were thinning out in depth, were the two main factors that were responsible for the closure of the mines.

According to de Magnée,[31] the genesis of these ore deposits is linked with the deep circulation of connate and/or meteoric waters dissolving metals contained within the sediments. The precipitation of the sulphides occurred in the ascending parts of deep channelways under reducing conditions and by liberation of CO_2. It is related to the near-surface portions of the sub-vertical faults transverse to the axial planes of the folds. These faults are post-Variscan in age. This hydrothermal theory was confirmed by Bartholomé and Gérard[5] on the basis of a detailed study of the Engis ore deposit. In general, the northeast longitudinal thrust faults, linked with the Variscan orogeny, are not mineralized. Only the post-Variscan faults, which trend northwest transversely to the folds, are mineralized. These tectonic traps seem to have various origins.

In the Herve–Vesdre–Theux Massifs most of the mineralized fractures belong to the fault network of the Rhine Graben. These faults seem to have started in the Permian and to have been reactivated at various periods of the Caenozoic and the Mesozoic. This tectonic pattern is more and more pronounced in the northeast direction. Such faults may sometimes be traced for several kilometres. Mineralization is present where carbonate formations are intersected (mainly the Dinantian, and to a lesser extent the Frasnian and Givetian). Lodes usually disappear in the shale and sandstone country rocks. Some small lodes are, however, known within the detrital Famennian (for example, at Fossey). But no lode is hosted within the Silesian, the basal shales of which have acted as an impervious screen (this circumstance also explains the setting of the 'amas'). Bleiberg, the third largest lead–zinc deposit in Belgium, is a unique and major exception. There, a lode cuts the Silesian over a distance of more than 1000 m. Bleiberg is also the most northeasterly of the Belgian deposits, in which direction the block-faulting tectonics is assumed to be at its most intense.

In the Namur and Dinant synclinoria metals have been trapped mainly by a set of transverse fractures and to a lesser degree by a conjugate set of longitudinal fractures. Displacements of the walls are negligible.

In every case, lodes seem to occur where the country rocks have been slightly domed—a circumstance leading to the opening of tectonic traps.

Most of the lodes are characterized by the following features: (1) the main fracture is accompanied by minor parallel satellite fractures; (2) in the vicinity of the pre-Triassic palaeo-surface the main trap fracture is well formed and the mineralization is concentrated in one or several planes, the mineralized thickness of which may sometimes reach several metres; (3) the lode pinches out at depth; and (4) at still greater depths, the main fracture grades into a complex network of small fractures, the mineralization becoming a true stockwork.

The mechanical behaviour of the rocks is that of a flexed beam with, on each side of the neutral core, a body in tension (single open fracture) and a body in compression (crushed rock material without important voids).

The brecciated structure of the lodes is related to the reactivation of the faults. The cement is dominantly carbonate (mainly calcite) with subordinate quartz. It seems that the period of hydrothermal sulphide activity has been relatively short in comparison with the subsequent period of hydrothermal carbonate and quartz activity (mineralized veins are intersected by barren veins, as, for example, at Heure;[23] the lode metals would have been deposited between the end of the Variscan orogeny and the beginning of the Cretaceous[31]).

Other types of deposit

Into this category fall all those ore deposits to which the perascendent hydrothermal model described by de Magnée[31] and Bartholomé and Gérard[5] does not apply. This section refers to the strata-bound (peneconcordant) and stratiform (concordant) deposits. It includes those of karstic affinities (insofar as the karst is not linked with hydrothermal activity) and those of sedimentary affinities (syn- and/or early diagenetic), the latter very often in a shale and carbonate reef environment.

Ore deposits of karstic affinities

This category of ore deposit is poorly recognized in Belgium and also controversial. The metallogenic interest of the palaeo-karst has been underlined by Pirlet[62] in relation to the Viséan and by Dejonghe[20] in a broader sense, but Balcon[4] has made the most substantial contribution to this topic. According to Balcon,[4] the Dinantian should be particularly rich in mineralizations as a result of the circulation of meteoric groundwaters. He distinguished three levels of emersions to which metalliferous concentrations are linked: the system of intra-Viséan emersions, the system of infra-Namurian emersions and that of post-Variscan to present-day emersions. In fact, it is likely that the largest Belgian deposit, La Calamine, is genetically related to the Palaeozoic–Mesozoic unconformity through karstic processes.[26]

La Calamine, already cited by Lindgren[56] as an ore deposit without any relationship with magmatic activity, was exploited for centuries by the 'Vieille Montagne' company. The German name of this society appears for the first time in a letter, written in German, dated 4 January, 1421, in which ten nobles of the 'Duché de Limbourg' recognized that the city of Aachen had, from the earliest times, exploited in association with them and their ancestors the mine of Calamine ('Kailmijnberg') situated at La Calamine ('Kelmijs').

For the period prior to 1825 no production statistics are available, but it is estimated that at least 100 000 tonne of zinc metal had already been extracted by then; 473 800 further tonne of zinc metal was produced prior to the exhaustion of the orebody and the closure of the mine in 1884.

La Calamine orebody extends over a length of 500 m and a width of 100 m, at its deepest part reaching 110 m. It is located in the nose of a plunging syncline. The orebody forms part of an enormous pocket that rests on Famennian detrital rocks. This pocket is filled with silicified dolomite, predominant at the bottom, and enormous irregular bodies made up of red clay and 'calaminar'* ore (Zn grade, 30–37%).

The reasons for distinguishing the ore deposit of La Calamine from vein-type deposits have been set out by Dejonghe and Jans.[26]

Ore deposits of sedimentary affinities
In the Dinant synclinorium numerous occurrences of low-grade disseminated mineralization occur in the reefal Frasnian dolomitized limestones. In some localities (Barbençon, Solre-Saint-Géry, Sautour, Vodecée) concentrations at the junction of the dolomitic and calcareous facies have been of economic interest, though these deposits never yielded large tonnages. Pel and Monseur[61] described in the peripheral part of a bioherm of Frasnian age ($F2h$) and its enveloping sediments, at Frasnes, mineralization of galena and pyrite. The tendency of lead to concentrate in the outer zone of reefs was underlined.

In the other districts ore deposits of sedimentary affinities are very rare. Although some (for example, Membach) are clearly controlled by the stratification, their sedimentary origin has not been demonstrated.

Nevertheless, a sedimentary barite orebody, with accessory pyrite, sphalerite and galena, was discovered at Chaudfontaine by boreholes drilled between 1964 and 1973. This ore deposit is described under *Barite*, but we can say that it is situated in a back-reef environment. The fact that sulphides, mainly sphalerite, are relatively abundant suggests that a sulphide-dominant zone is probably adjacent to the barite zone.[25] Furthermore, this discovery underlines the metallogenic importance of the Upper Frasnian (Aisemont Formation, *sensu* Coen-Aubert and Lacroix[18]) for the prospecting of concealed stratiform deposits situated at the margin of the Brabant Massif. As several Devono-Dinantian anhydrite formations have been discovered during the last thirty years by drilling, and because of the link that many geologists see between evaporites and lead–zinc mineralization, in Belgium[6,9,22,31,38,65] as elsewhere, new hopes for the discovery of sedimentary deposits arise.

Lastly, it should be pointed out that, in the Dinant synclinorium, disseminated-type mineralization and concentrated vein-type mineralization often occur very close together. As Dejonghe and de Walque[23] have indicated for the Heure ore deposit, the veins were probably derived by leaching of the sedimentary country rocks. This hypothesis is supported by lead isotope studies.[15]

Hypotheses concerning source of metals
The source of the metals remains conjectural. Following Fourmarier,[46] all later authors have classified the lead–zinc deposits of Belgium in the category of hydrothermal ore deposits, genetically connected with hypothetical magmatic intrusion (telethermal ore deposits). That connexion was questioned by Van Wambeke,[72] but it was de Magnée[31] who radically broke with tradition by searching for the source of the metals elsewhere than in a hypothetical pluton. de Magnée[31] has said: 'la minéralisation apparaît comme une conséquence de l'érosion post-orogénique. Son intensité dépend de la vitesse de cette érosion et de la teneur géochimique en Pb, Zn, Ba des sédiments érodés'.*

On the basis of detailed studies of individual ore deposits or of metalliferous districts other authors[4,22,23,24,38,61] have come to the conclusion that the metals were embodied in carbonate–shale sediments during the Devono-Dinantian sedimentation, with eventual early remobilization during diagenesis. Studies on the lead isotopic geochemistry of Belgian galenas and pyrites have, however, led Cauet and co-workers[14] to exclude the Dinantian as the main source of the metals.

Lithogeochemical studies[68,71] do not confirm or refute the sedimentary capture of the metals. They are unable to conclude whether the Pb–Zn strata-bound anomalies eventually encountered are contemporaneous with the sedimentation or if they are due to epigenetic metasomatism of particular stratigraphical horizons.

Finally, the model that actually fits best with the available data is that outlined below.

---

* In the ancient literature oxidized zinciferous ore is called 'calamine': it is a mixture of hemimorphite, smithsonite and willemite (the latter mineral was discovered at La Calamine).

* The mineralization appears to be a consequence of post-orogenic erosion. Its intensity depends on the speed of the erosion and on the geochemical tenor of Pb, Zn and Ba in the eroded sediments.

During the Middle Devonian, the Frasnian and the Dinantian the sea is considered to be the vector of transportation of the metals, the initial source of which remains hypothetical. Under the appropriate palaeogeographical, sedimentological and physico-chemical conditions (e.g. within confined environments) enrichment of the environment in metals takes place and, locally, sedimentary ore deposition. Diagenetic mobilizations take place as a result, *inter alia*, of the early dolomitization of the limestones.

During the Permo-Trias, after folding and overthrusting during the Variscan orogeny, development of transverse faults (in most cases linked with the block-faulting tectonics of the Rhine graben) occurs. Opening of these fractures in their superficial parts owing to local upwarping (induced, for example, by the movement or by the solution of underlying evaporites) takes place. Filling of the tectonic traps by leaching of the surrounding rocks (mainly the dolomites) follows, the metals being transported by groundwaters, the chemistry of which has probably been conditioned by the leaching of evaporites. Precipitation occurs in the fissures and in associated solution cavities by modification of the hydrodynamic conditions (necking-down effects) as well as the physico-chemical conditions (liberation of CO_2 and H_2S).

During the various periods of emersion there is superficial reworking of the ore deposits and karstic reconcentration.

In this model the metals in all types of deposit have not only a common source (consanguinity) but also a complex history: the same metalliferous stock has been remobilized and reconcentrated several times.

Barite deposits[30,32]

The only barite ore deposits that have been mined are those of Fleurus, Vierves-sur-Viroin and Ave-et-Auffe. They differ from one another in shape, geological habit, associated minerals and tonnage. In other deposits barite was an accessory mineral—generally not recovered. For example, at Villers-en-Fagne nine lodes (two of them important) that cut Frasnian carbonate rocks have yielded galena, pyrite and barite, but the latter was discarded, not having found any industrial use at the time of exploitation.

On the basis of tonnage the Fleurus ore deposit is certainly the most important of the Belgian barite deposits. It is mainly made up of unconsolidated barite, varying from a very fine powder to debris a few centimetres in length and, exceptionally, of decimetre length. In a very few places are found irregular barite bodies, relatively coherent, though easily breakable with the hammer. The fine-grained barite is dusted with iron oxides, clay minerals and siliceous material. At the bottom of the mineralized body black shale preponderates. It forms, at the contact with the underlying limestone, a relatively continuous though irregular layer, which may reach several metres in thickness. This layer contains quartz pebbles and, locally, sandstone cobbles and boulders. In some places black shales also rest on barite bodies. Galena is extremely rare and only known as small disseminated spots in the eastern part of the orebody. The ore fills a karstic depression in Viséan limestones (*V2b*). This pocket extends for 450 m in length and 125 m in width. At the centre the base is located 40 m below the palaeosurface of the Palaeozoic formations. The overlying Caenozoic formations have a thickness of 10–25 m and are made up of glauconitic sands, argillaceous at the base. Above the baritic body is a conglomerate with quartz and chert (phtanite) pebbles. de Magnée and Doyen[32] assumed that the barite was precipitated in a karstic depression under lacustrine or palustrine conditions. The Fleurus deposit has been exploited sporadically from 1890 to 1928. Total production reached 694 500 tonne of commercial barite. Reserves under the water-table have been assessed by drilling and have been estimated at 833 000 tonne of pure barite, which has justified new exploitation by Baroid Mineral, Inc.; open-pit mining operations (Fig. 3) commenced in 1979.

Fig. 3 *View of Fleurus barite open-pit exploitation (June, 1980). Numerous timbers that emerge from ground are pit props of ancient underground works*

At Vierves-sur-Viroin the orebody is a lode located in a north–south fault cutting limestone and shale of the Middle and Upper Devonian for a distance of more than 2 km perpendicular to the folding. Barite and calcite with disseminated sulphides are typical of the infilling of the southern part of the lode (extending for 460 m), whereas the adjacent northern prolongation is richer in marcasite, sphalerite and galena. The lode is lenticular in shape with a maximum thickness of 14 m, which is exceptional in Belgium: at that place the lode is built up of three layers of barite, with a useful thickness of 4·5 m, and calcite intercalations. Exploitation has been episodic and was abandoned finally in 1962. Total production reached about 19 000 tonne.

The Ave-et-Auffe ore deposit, which extends into the communes of Villers-sur-Lesse and Lavaux-Ste-Anne, is also a vein-type deposit, but with a pattern different from that of Vierves-sur-Viroin. Here the limestones of the Fromelennes Formation (Upper Givetian) form a large anticline cut by two sets of lodes, longitudinal and transverse. Their thicknesses vary from 0·20 to 1·50 m. Barite constitutes the main infilling of the veins. Calcite, fluorite (mainly disposed near the walls) and galena (very scarce spots located at the eastern and western extremities of the orebody) are accessory minerals. The walls are slightly silicified. The first mine working dates back to the nineteenth century and the latest to 1949. Statistics for the period 1864–1948 mention a total production of 8191 tonne.

This section would be incomplete without further information on the Chaudfontaine deposit, which has already been mentioned. It is a new type of deposit in Belgium. It was discovered by three boreholes drilled between 1964 and 1973. The mineralization lies on the two flanks of a faulted anticline at depths between 80 and 210 m. In one of the drill-holes the stratigraphical thickness of the mineralized zone reaches 10·75 m. The ore is mainly made up of barite, with accessory pyrite, sphalerite and galena (chalcopyrite and bravoite are very scarce and only visible under the microscope). The rhythmic pattern of layering of barite and sphalerite ore is sometimes well marked. Alternations of massive barite layers, more or less mineralized layers, and barren beds are of centimetre, decimetre and metre amplitudes. Also present are sedimentary fabrics involving barite crystals such as slumpings, load-casts, intraformational breccias and small sedimentary faults. According to Dejonghe,[22] this deposit is of sedimentary origin and was deposited in a back-reef shaly and carbonate environment of Upper Frasnian age (Aisemont Formation *sensu* Coen-Aubert and Lacroix[18]). This conclusion has been confirmed by the study of sulphur isotopes of barite[24] and fluid inclusions of barite.[25] It may be noted that 1 km farther east of the drill-hole area, at a place called La Rochette, a small lead–zinc lode has been exploited in the past. Barite and quartz were abundant as gangue minerals, which is very unusual in this district. Furthermore, bravoite has been found in both deposits. This indication of similar mineral assemblage supports the idea of derivation of the veins from the leaching of the surrounding rocks or, eventually, from pre-existing sedimentary concentration.

Fluorite deposits[12]

Fluorite has been noted in many localities, but the major occurrences occupy a narrow band (around 50 km in length and 5 km wide) that extends from Dourbes to Resteigne, which coincides with the central part of the lead–zinc district of the Dinant synclinorium (Fig. 2). There temporary small exploitations are recorded—principally those of Gimnée, Doische and Foisches (France).

Givetian and Frasnian carbonate rocks are the host rocks of most occurrences.

The usual habit of the fluorite is isolated cubes or readily cleavable aggregates. Crystals, generally purple, may also be colourless, yellow or greenish. Fluorite appears as dispersed spots and infillings of fractures in carbonate rocks and as isolated crystals in calcite veins. The richer concentrations are hosted by the Fromelennes Formation (Upper Givetian) within a silicified level described as *à rogneux* by the local miners. Fluorite is sometimes concentrated in residual clay filling solution cavities. Lastly, fluorite is also associated with pyrite, galena and barite in some crosscutting veins (at Villers-en-Fagne, Ave-et-Auffe and Resteigne).

Fluid inclusion and trace-element data[65] confirm that Belgian fluorite and, by implication, the associated Pb–Zn–Ba–Fe mineralization, may be classed with deposits of the Mississippi Valley type. Homogenization temperatures fall in a range below 150°C. The salinity varies from 10·2 up to 18·2% equivalent NaCl (in weight). Na/K ratios are, however, unusually low with high K concentration in the inclusion brines. These mineral deposits could result from movement of connate brines from thick sedimentary sequences in sedimentary basins adjacent to the mineralized areas. The brines would possibly have been modified by contact with evaporites at some stage of their evolution.

Iron deposits[1,3,16,20,21,27,28,63]

The Belgian iron ore deposits, already worked by the Gallic people before the Roman invasion, have contributed greatly to the industrial development of the country. Until about 1860 the iron industry was wholly fed by production from Belgian orebodies, part of which was exported. The mining industry had its most prosperous period between 1850 and 1870, but after the discovery of the Thomas dephosphoration process in 1878 activity declined quickly with the consequent access to the ore deposits of Lorraine and Luxembourg.

The parcelling of the exploitations as a result of the mining regulations applicable to iron deposits and the shape of the orebodies (often followed for long distances at outcrop) did not allow large mines to develop. A vast number of small workings is recorded; in the Vezin area, however, iron ore exploitation was very intense, some mines employing several hundred men.

Belgian iron ore deposits may be divided into two genetic groups—those of sedimentary origin and those formed by weathering.

Sedimentary deposits

The marine sedimentary iron ore deposits are distributed throughout the Palaeozoic (mineralized horizons are encountered within the Gedinnian, the Couvinian, the Givetian, the Frasnian, the Famennian, the Tournaisian and the Silesian) and in the Mesozoic (the Toarcian) (Fig. 4).

The sedimentary ore consists of hematite, sometimes with chamosite and/or siderite. Oolitic fabric is a constant feature. The iron orebodies occur as lenticular layers (average thickness, approximately 1 m; maximum thickness 5 m) that outcrop over long distances. Average analyses of the most important orebodies are shown in Table 3.

In the Couthuin area intensively pyritized parts are linked with the existence of crosscutting mineralized veins with marcasite and galena. Pyrite decreases and disappears away from the veins.

The origin of the pre-Silesian sedimentary iron ore deposits is to be found in the denudation of the Caledonian belt, on the remnants of which the Devono-Dinantian seas successively transgressed from south to north. Indeed, these iron ore deposits are of a more recent age the farther north they lie. Their coastal marine genesis, shown by their oolitic and fossiliferous features, accords with the direction of transgression.

A relationship between the Frasnian and Famennian ironstones and the volcanic activity of the Rhenish Massif has been proposed by Dreesen,[41] who has also indicated their allochthonous character within subtidal offshore sediments, probably associated with

Fig. 4 *Location map of main iron, phosphate, manganese, copper and kaolin deposits*

Table 3 Average analyses (%) of iron ore deposits of Belgium[21]

Formation	Fe	P	S	SiO$_2$	CaO	MgO	Al$_2$O$_3$	Mn
Gedinnian	43	1·03–1·17		17·25–21				
Couvinian	34·86–42·02	Up to 0·42		18·24–18·50	0·49–7·59	Up to 0·85	2·15–18·70	
Famennian	25–52 (exceptionally 56)	Up to 0·48	Up to 0·68	Up to 17·1	2·65–10·61	0·3–5·71	6·13–13·63	Up to 0·63
Tournaisian	30–35	Up to 0·22	Up to 0·644	4·10–5·15	13·00–13·62	4·32–5·71		
Silesian	25–30	Up to 0·128						
Toarcian	35–39	0·5–0·6	0·070–0·074	14–23	2–11	0·45–0·80	5·70–5·80	0·32–0·35
Diestian	18·0–28·0 (exceptionally 38)	0·077–0·247	0·082–0·116	51·03–60·67	Up to 13	0·36–0·82	0·77–4·90	Up to 0·16
Holocene	35–48	0·4–3·0		7·45–11·40	1·15–1·50	Tr.	0·91–1·03	
Gossans	25–35 (exceptionally 50)							

small-scale epeirogenic movements at the border of the sedimentary basin.[40] These ironstones would have been transported by storm wave events (turbid surficial clouds) to the open shelf.[42]

The Silesian iron ore deposits also have a sedimentary origin, but they belong to a continental subaqueous facies. Lastly, the Toarcian iron ore deposit was formed by leaching, under wet and hot climatic conditions, of the emergent Lower Liassic rocks, followed by transport to the sea in temporary regression and then sedimentation in the Gulf of Luxembourg.

Weathering deposits

Weathering deposits may be, in individual cases, qualified by the terms 'secondary', 'substitution', 'replacement' or 'impregnation' in conformity with the terminology of Routhier.[64] Indeed, they may be divided into various types—for example, ore deposits formed by the weathering of sediments, gossans of the sulphide lodes and karstic deposits.

Ore deposits due to weathering of sediments
All these deposits reflect oxidation processes accompanied by either residual concentration or leaching, transport and deposition of iron under the predominant control of climatic conditions.

In general, during the Caenozoic, and particularly during the Miocene and the Pliocene, climatic variations were responsible for the creation of iron duricrusts. The latter have been well studied in the Belgian Lorraine.

Deposits due to the weathering of sediments are reviewed according to the age of the host rock.

Palaeozoic A number of iron ore deposits are controlled by the lithostratigraphy, as in the case of numerous limonitic orebodies of the northern limb of the Dinant synclinorium (Condroz area, Figs. 1 and 4). They follow the contact between carbonate and detrital formations, and preferentially follow the base of the carbonate unit rather than the top. In depth, limonite grades to siderite, which itself grades to pyrite. A comparable strata-bound iron ore deposit of hematite and goethite has been described by Dimanche and Toussaint[37] at Esneux in a bed of sandstone that separates calcareous rocks of the lowest Givetian from conglomerates and red rocks of the uppermost Couvinian. According to these authors, the precipitation of iron is due to contact between a reducing aqueous medium and an oxidizing medium that was responsible for the reddening of the underlying rocks.

Lias The so-called *minerai de fer des prés*, also named *Wascherz* or *minerai de fer tendre* (Fe, maximum 57%; P$_2$O$_5$, 0·55–3·32%) covers vast areas in Luxembourg and also extends into the Belgian Lorraine. It takes the form of concretions (crusts or nodules) included within lenses made up of yellow or greyish clay that are spread over the irregular erosional surface of the Middle and Upper Lias. This ore contains oolitic debris reworked from the Toarcio-Aalenian 'minette' ore.[49] The weathering processes, the mobilization and the concentration of iron have occurred under temperate humid climatic conditions during the Upper Oligocene[50] or the Lower Miocene.[57]

Eocene Lenses of limonitic sandstones enclosed within Lutetian (Bruxellian) sands have been the subject of ancient exploitation in the area of Groenendael in the Soignes Forest (Fig. 4).

Mio-Pliocene Within the sands of the Diest Formation (Upper Miocene or Lower Pliocene) lenses of ferruginous sandstone are encountered (Fe, average 18–28%, exceptionally 38%; P, ~0·07%). They have been exploited in various localities of the Hageland area, especially in the vicinity of Rotselaar, Wesemaal and Gelrode (Fig. 4).

Pliocene Ferruginous sands grading to limonitic sandstones of Pliocene age (Scaldisian–Poederlian) have been exploited in the past on the hills of Poederlee and Lichtaart.

Holocene The main ore deposits take the form of lenticular lenses (maximum thickness, 1·5 m) and are located in the swampy valleys of the Limburg and Antwerp Kempen in the regions where the glauconitic sands of the Diest Formation crop out (Fig. 4). This so-called *limonite des prairies* (Fe, 35–48%; P, 0·4–3%) was actively exploited between 1845 and 1914. The richer parts are now exhausted. Their genesis was explained by de Magnée[29] as follows: during the oxidizing leaching of the glauconitic sands by recent meteoric waters the iron derived from the glauconite is dissolved and carried away by the phreatic groundwaters. These solutions feed the peat of low-lying bogs, which are spongy and continuously drained. Ferric hydrates precipitate near the surface by the action of micro-organisms, replacing almost completely (90%) the vegetable matter. de Magnée[29] estimated that such a deposit could be reformed within a period of 50 years.

It may also be noted that bog ore in Holocene alluvia has been worked in the Belgian Lorraine. It would have been reworked from the underlying Liassic iron ore (*minerai de fer métis*).

Gossans of sulphide lodes
The lead and zinc lodes were very often accompanied by pyrite and/or marcasite. In some deposits the sulphides of iron were even predominant (e.g. Vedrin, Rocheux-Oneux, Heure (Fig. 2)). At Rocheux-Oneux, for example, the following production figures (tonne) may be noted for the period 1859–80, after which the mine was closed: calamine, 70 000; lead ore (including oxides), 32 000; pyrites, 220 000; and limonite, 132 500.

Iron oxide and sulphide productions are, however, very often mixed in the statistics. The oxidation of these sulphides has yielded many gossans with limonite (goethite, hydrohematite, lepidocrocite), calamine (hemimorphite, smithsonite, willemite) and cerussite. Even in the very weakly mineralized Tournai area (northern limb of the Namur synclinorium on the western side of the lead–zinc district) it has been shown that the small limonitic bodies (the so-called 'amas') that occur there were inherited from small pyritic veins.[13,19] But it is on the basis of petrological and geochemical studies on drill-hole cores from the pyritic vein of Heure that the relationships between the hypogene and supergene assemblages have been most clearly described. There a model for the oxidation and hydrolysis of the primary ore mineral has been presented and an attempt has been made to establish a geochemical balance sheet.[23]

In Belgium these gossans, which have been exploited from olden times, were intensively worked in the nineteenth century. Until 1870 they supplied the main part of the Belgian iron ore production. The average annual extraction exceeded 500 000 tonne between 1850 and 1865. Then it decreased quickly, yielding first place to the Famennian and Tournaisian oolitic hematites, and ceased altogether around 1890.

Karstic deposits
Karstic iron ore deposits are well known in the Grand Duchy of Luxembourg. They are made up of brown to black iron concretions, mixed with a kind of laterite (the so-called *bolus*), which fill up karstic cavities in the Bajocian limestone. Such deposits also exist in Belgium in the limestone of Longwy southwest of Ruette (Fig. 4). As the ore was of excellent quality and the orebody easy to exploit, the deposit was quickly exhausted. These ore deposits would have been emplaced in the Oligocene in two stages: first, solution of the limestones and marls of the Upper Jurassic and, eventually, of the Lower Cretaceous, giving a residual argillaceous material that would have undergone lateritization under dry and hot climatic conditions, followed by mobilization of the iron-bearing laterites and deposition in a concretionary form.[49,57]

On the other hand, some ferriferous bodies seem to have been trapped in palaeo-karstic structures (the so-called *abannets*) in the area of Nismes and Couvin[97] (Fig. 4). Limonite and Caenozoic sands fill up these karstic cavities, sometimes of large size (cavities 100 m in length and 50 m in width and depth are reported). They have been worked in Devonian limestones. Delmer[28] mentioned that a lode is very often found at the very bottom of these 'abannets'.

Manganese deposits[2,8,11,53]

Belgian manganiferous occurrences are all located on the southern and southwestern limbs of the Cambro-Silurian Massif of Stavelot (Fig. 4). They are of small size, the only manganese ore deposit of any extent being located in the Lienne Valley, at Bierleux (Chevron) and Meuville (Rahier). This is a sedimentary ore deposit interbedded in Tremadocian (Salmian, *Sm2*) slaty schists and quartzites forming a syncline complicated by transverse folds and minor faults. Kramm[51] interpreted the high manganiferous content of the Salmian 2 as a consequence of volcanic activity.

The orebody consists of two mineralized layers separated from each other by 30–55 m of barren sediments. In fact, each layer is made up of several interbedded mineralized and barren thin layers. The useful thickness of the lower layer reaches 0·70 m. The upper layer is lenticular and limited in extent (useful thickness, up to 1·1 m).

	Mn	Fe	P
Upper layer	7–16	17–26	0·23
Lower layer	9–12	24–25	0·27

The ore is a ferromanganiferous arenite with quartz, hematite, rhodochrosite, kutnahorite, spessartine, siderite, pyrolusite, chlorite and muscovite. The grades (%) are distributed as shown above.

The orebody was discovered in 1845 and exploited periodically between 1856 and 1934. Total production amounted to 180 000 tonne of ore, underground workings reaching a depth of 116 m.

In the same area there are similar orebodies of lesser extent (not worked at Werbomont, but worked at Lierneux and Arbrefontaine). Also present are secondary enrichments (nodules, lenses, crustifications, etc.) in altered schists, which have been worked at Bihain and Malempré.

Finally, mention should also be made of the famous *coticule* beds in the area of Bihain, Salmchâteau (Vielsalm) and Recht. Coticule is chiefly made up of microscopic garnets (spessartine) and contains 28% MnO and 4·5% FeO. Exploited for centuries, not for its manganese content but as stone to sharpen razors (whetstone), it has been exported throughout the world. Bastin[7] reported that the coticule from Vielsalm was known in Rome from very early times. Coticule is a metamorphic rock for which Kramm[51] considered a volcanoclastic sediment the primary source material.

Phosphate deposits[10,58]

Belgian phosphatic deposits are chiefly linked to Cretaceous formations. They are distributed in two areas—the Hainaut to the west and the Hesbaye to the east (Figs. 1 and 4).

In the Hainaut area the richest phosphatic formation is the Ciply chalk—a lenticular formation of Maastrichtian age that contains numerous disseminated phosphatic granules, pebbles and remanié fossils. The thickness of this phosphatic chalk increases with the subsidence of the Cretaceous basin of Mons. Its maximum thickness is 58 m, where the base of the Ciply chalk is at a depth of 150 m. Grades vary greatly (average P_2O_5 content, 8–10%, between extremes of 5 and 16%). Close to the outcrop of the Ciply chalk phosphate with P_2O_5 grades as high as 65% was naturally concentrated in solution pockets. The Ciply chalk was exploited in the Ciply and Baudour areas from 1874 until the second world war, after which mining activities declined continuously. Total production of crude ore amounted to about 14 000 000 tonne.

In the Hesbaye area the phosphatic deposits are residual accumulations formed by solution of the Maastrichtian chalk. The phosphatic formation is made up of two to five layers, each around 10 cm in thickness, alternating with barren layers. The ore consists of granules, nodules and fossil remains crowded together in an earthy sandy-clayey groundmass. The deposits were chiefly exploited around 1900. Total production of crude ore amounted to about 4 000 000 tonne.

Copper deposits

The main copper occurrences are indicated in Fig. 4. Copper has been exploited on a very small scale (preliminary exploration) at Rouveroy. There malachite and azurite fill fissures and sedimentary partings of the Burnot Formation (Lower Devonian) made up of shaly sandstones and conglomerates with predominant red colours. Production dates back to the nineteenth century and is estimated at about 5000 tonne of copper. Oxidized copper minerals are also encountered in the Burnot Formation throughout Belgian territory, but only in very low amounts.

At Salmchâteau (Vielsalm) and Lierneux exploratory work was undertaken on small mineral occurrences with chalcopyrite, bornite and oxidized copper minerals that fill quartz-bearing fissures cutting Tremadocian schists.

Except for occurrences of academic interest, no economic copper mineralization is associated with the lead, zinc, barite and fluorite ore deposits hosted in the Devono-Dinantian limestones. Dolembreux is an exception: this very small occurrence is hosted in Givetian limestones. Its production has been negligible.

No magmatic rock has ever been mined in Belgium for its mineral content, but special interest has been aroused by an igneous intrusion (the composition of which varies from monzodiorite to tonalite) located in the Hautes Fagnes area (Fig. 1) along the La Helle River at a place named Herzogenhügel. This sill-like intrusion and the associated stockwork of quartz veins carry chalcopyrite and molybdenite. According to Van Wambeke[72] and Weis and co-workers[74] the mineralization is of the porphyry copper type. A drilling programme in 1976–77 by Union Minière indicated 20 000 000 tonne of proven reserves. Cu and Mo grades vary from place to place, but a general trend is to higher grades close to the contacts of the sill where quartz veins are much more abundant.

Analysis of this intrusion has given an average of 0·17% Cu (extremes 0·01–0·45%) and 0·02% Mo (extremes 0·001–0·097%).

The other copper mineral occurrences, though abundant (see Melon and co-workers[59]), have only a mineralogical interest.

Gold deposits[7,33,34,43,47,48,73]

According to Bastin,[7] alluvial gold exploitation in Belgium dates back to Celtic or Gallo-Roman times. He put forward the hypothesis that the gold that Caesar brought back to Rome came partly from Gaul. Some workings were still operating during the nineteenth century in the high Amblève River area.

Gold has been found around the Massifs of Stavelot and Serpont and north of the Rocroi Massif, where Cambrian, Silurian and Ordovician formations outcrop (Fig. 1). In general, it was found in ancient colluvia and alluvia that fill the bottom of the valleys and, occasionally, in recent alluvia. In most cases these gold occurrences are spread over underlying Gedinnian rocks. This observation led de Rauw[33] to put two questions on the source of the gold: Does the gold come from sedimentary formations or from crosscutting veins?—If the gold is sedimentary, are the host rocks of pre-Devonian or of Gedinnian age?

The discovery by Lepersonne[54] of gold lamellae in a quartz vein at Bovigny partly answers the first question. But Hanssen and Viaene,[48] after a study of the morphology of the alluvial gold grains of the southern and southeastern margins of the Stavelot Massif, as well as their silver content, concluded that even if the gold originated initially from veins, it was incorporated in the Gedinnian and Siegenian sediments as a detrital mineral. Indeed, the high roundness index of some gold particles and their low silver content indicate, on the one hand, a transportation of several tens of kilometres and, on the other, a leaching compatible with a long transport.

Again, in the case of gold, the notions of inheritance and permanency from Cambrian to Holocene periods are well illustrated around the Caledonian Massifs.

Kaolin deposits[17,39,45,69]

Kaolin (china clay) deposits are classified into two categories on the basis of their geological features and their geographical location (Fig. 4). Both types of deposit provide very modest supplies of ore.

Weathering deposits

These have arisen from the weathering of arkoses, feldspathic sandstones and slaty schists of Palaeozoic age during the peneplenation of the Ardenne Massif at the end of the Caenozoic. At Malvoisin drilling has shown that weathering effects extended down to at least 35 m. All kaolin deposits of industrial interest are located in the Ardenne, in a location of wet plateaux, within an elongated band 20 km long from Haut-Fays to Libin. All the deposits of this type are inherited from Gedinnian rocks. Water problems usually limit the depth of exploitation to around 20 m. Small occurrences are also located along a more southerly band 40 km long from Louette-St-Pierre to Bras and Libramont, and including the Cambrian of the Serpont Massif.

Sedimentary deposits

These are associated with argillaceous sands or fine-grained sands that fill karstic holes in Dinantian limestones of the Condroz area. They are hosted in a local marine formation, of Upper Oligocene or Lower Miocene age, preserved from further erosion in karstic cavities. The kaolinite content decreases from the bottom to the top of the deposits, whereas illite, smectite and various interstratified clay minerals increase. The argillaceous-sandy sediments that overlie these kaolin deposits are sometimes intercalated with lignite layers that testify to the lacustrine conditions prevalent at the end of infilling of the karstic depressions. The most representative kaolin deposit of this type is the Oret deposit.

References

1 **Ancion Ch.** Les minerais de fer de la Belgique. In *XIX Int. geol. Congr., Algiers, 1952: Symposium sur les gisements de fer du monde*, volume II, 1952, 75–91.

2 **Ancion Ch. Calembert L. and Macar P.** Les ressources en minerai de manganèse du sous-sol de la Belgique. In *XX Int. geol. Congr., Mexico, 1956: symposium sobre yacimientos de manganeso*, volume V, Europe, 1956, 9–17.

3 **Ancion Ch. and Van Leckwijck W.** Les minerais de fer du sol belge. In *Congrès 1947, Centenaire de l'Association des Ingénieurs sortis de l'École de Liège (A.I.Lg): section géologie* (Liège: A.I.Lg, 1947), 96–104.

4 **Balcon J.** Quelques idées sur les minéralisations plombo-zincifères dans les formations carbonatées en Belgique. *Bull. Soc. belge Géol.*, **90**, 1981, 9–61.

5 **Bartholomé P. and Gérard E.** Les gisements plombifères de la région d'Engis, province de Liège, Belgique. *Annls Mines Belg.*, 1976, 901–17.

6 **Bartholomé P. et al.** Métallogénie de la Belgique, des Pays-Bas et du Luxembourg. In *Mémoire explicatif de la carte métallogénique Europe* (Paris: Unesco, 1984), 165–80. (*Sciences de la Terre/Earth Sciences* no. 17).

7 **Bastin J.** Anciennes mines d'or dans l'Ardenne septentrionale. *Annls XXIIe Congr. Féd. archéol. hist. Belg., Malines*, vol. 2, 1911, 1–19.

8 **Berger P.** Les dépôts sédimentaires de manganèse de la Lienne inférieure. *Annls Soc. géol. Belg.*, **88**, 1965, 245–68.

9 **Bless M. J. M. et al.** Evaporites anté-silésiennes sur la bordure orientale du Massif de Brabant et dans le fossé rhénan: une hypothèse. In *Hommage à Léon Calembert* (Liège: Georges Thone, 1980), 24–32.

10 **Calembert L.** Phosphates de la Hesbaye. In *Congrès 1947, Centenaire de l'Association des Ingénieurs sortis de l'École de Liège (A.I.Lg): section géologie* (Liège: A.I.Lg, 1947), 341–4.

11 **Calembert L. and Macar P.** Les minerais de manganèse de Belgique. In *Congrès 1947, Centenaire de l'Association des Ingénieurs sortis de l'École de Liège (A.I.Lg): section géologie* (Liège: A.I. Lg, 1947), 104–10.

12 **Calembert L. and Van Leckwijck W.** Les gisements belges de fluorine et leur intérêt industriel. In *Congrès 1947, Centenaire de l'Association des Ingenieurs sortis de l'École de Liège (A.I.Lg): section géologie* (Liège: A.I.Lg, 1947), 110–3.

13 **Camerman C. and Baudet J.** Sur un amas important de pyrite rencontré dans le calcaire dinantien à Gaurain-Ramecroix. *Bull. Soc. belge Géol. Paléont. Hydrol.*, **48**, 1939, 589–93.

14 **Cauet S. Weis D. and Herbosch A.** Genetic study of Belgian lead–zinc mineralizations in carbonate environments through lead isotopic geochemistry. *Bull. BRGM II*, no. 4 1982, 329–41.

15 **Cauet S. and Weis D.** Lead isotope study of a lead–zinc vein mineralization and its host sediments, Heure, Belgium: basis for a genetic model. *Econ. Geol.*, **78**, 1983, 1011–6.

16 **Cayeux L.** Minerais famenniens de Belgique. In *Étude des gîtes minéraux de France*, Paris, **1**, 1909, 227–42.

17 **Claude L.** Les gisements de kaolin en Ardennes. *Prof. Pap. Serv. géol. Belg.* no. 10, 1968, 19 p.

18 **Coen-Aubert M. and Lacroix D.** Le Frasnien dans la partie orientale du bord sud du synclinorium de Namur. *Annls Soc. géol. Belg.*, **101**, 1979, 269–79.

19 **Corin F.** Filons de pyrite de Tournai et d'Ath. *Bull. Soc. belge Géol. Paléont. Hydrol.*, **48**, 1938, 435–7.

20 **Dejonghe L.** The iron ore deposits in Belgium. In *The iron ore deposits of Europe and adjacent areas: volume I, text* (Hannover: Bundesanstalt für Geowissenschaften und Rohstoffe, 1977), 97–100.

21 **Dejonghe L.** The iron ore deposits in Belgium. In *The iron ore deposits of Europe and adjacent areas: volume II, lists and tables* (Hannover: Bundesanstalt für Geowissenschaften und Rohstoffe, 1978), 27–32; 310–1.

22 **Dejonghe L.** Discovery of a sedimentary Ba (Fe, Zn, Pb) ore body of Frasnian age at Chaudfontaine, Province of Liège, Belgium. *Mineral. Deposita*, **14**, 1979, 15–20.

23 **Dejonghe L. and de Walque L.** Pétrologie et géochimie du filon sulfuré de Heure (Belgique), du chapeau de fer associé et de l'encaissant carbonaté. *Bull. BRGM II*, no. 3 1980–81, 165–91.

24 **Dejonghe L. Rye R. O. and Cauet S.** Sulfur isotopes of barite and lead isotopes of galena from the stratiform deposit in Frasnian carbonate and shale host-rocks of Chaudfontaine (Province of Liège, Belgium). *Annls Soc. géol. Belg.*, **105**, 1982, 97–103.

25 **Dejonghe L. Guilhaumou N. and Touray J. C.** Les inclusions fluides du gisement sédimentaire de Chaudfontaine (Province de Liège, Belgique). *Bull. Soc. belge Géol.*, **91**, 1982, 79–89.

26 **Dejonghe L. and Jans D.** Les gisements plombo-zincifères de l'Est de la Belgique. *Chron. Rech. min.* no. 470, March 1983, 3–23.

27 **Delmer A.** La question du minerai de fer en Belgique. *Annls Mines Belg.*, **17**, 1912, 854–940.

28 **Delmer A.** La question du minerai de fer en Belgique (suite). *Annls Mines Belg.*, **18**, 1913, 325–448.

29 **de Magnée I.** Note sur les minerais de fer des prairies de la Campine. *Annls Soc. géol. Belg.*, **55**, 1932, B71–83.

30 **de Magnée I.** Les gisements de barytine belges. In *Congrès 1947, Centenaire de l'Association des Ingénieurs sortis de l'Ecole de Liège (A.I.Lg): section géologie* (Liège: A.I.Lg, 1947), 113–5.

31 **de Magnée I.** Contribution à l'étude génétique des gisements belges de plomb, zinc et barytine. In *Genesis of stratiform lead–zinc–barite–fluorite deposits in carbonate rocks (the so-called Mississippi Valley type deposits)* **Brown J. S. ed.** *Econ. Geol. Monogr.* 3, 1967, 255–66.

32 **de Magnée I. and Doyen L.** Le gisement de barytine de Fleurus. Symposium gîtes filoniens Pb–Zn–F–Ba basse température, Orléans: abstract, 1982.

33 **de Rauw H.** L'or en Ardenne. *Annls Soc. géol. Belg.*, **40**, 1913, 104–14.

34 **de Rauw H.** Les alluvions aurifères de la Haute Belgique. *Annls Soc. géol. Belg.*, **43**, 1920, B270–8.

35 **Dewez L.** Les gisements filoniens de plomb, zinc, cuivre, pyrites. In *Congrès 1947, Centenaire de l'Association des Ingénieurs sortis de l'Ecole de Liège (A.I.Lg): section géologie* (Liège: A.I.Lg, 1947), 75–96.

36 **de Wijkerslooth P.** Sur la région métallifère de Moresnet–Bleyberg–Stolberg–Limbourg néerlandais. *Proc. K. Akad. Wet.*, **40**, 1937, 292–4.

37 **Dimanche F. and Toussaint G.** Gisement de fer au contact Givétien–Couvinien (Esneux, province de Liège). *Annls Mines Belg.*, 1977, 533–40.

38 **Dimanche F. Ek C. and Frenay J.** Minéralisations plombo-zincifères belges—minéralogie, gîtologie, minéralurgie. *Annls Soc. géol. Belg.*, **102**, 1980, 417–29.

39 **Dosogne Ch.** Les gisements de kaolin du Bruly, de Haut-Fays et de Malvoisin. *Bull. Soc. belge Géol.*, **59**, 1950, 213–25.

40 **Dreesen R.** Importance paléogéographique des niveaux d'oolithes ferrugineuses dans le Famennien (Dévonien supérieur) du Massif de la Vesdre (Belgique orientale). *C.R. Acad. Sci. Paris*, **292**, 1981, 615–7.

41 **Dreesen R.** A propos des niveaux d'oolithes ferrugineuses de l'Ardenne et du volcanisme synsédimentaire dans le Massif Ardenno-Rhénan au Dévonien supérieur: essai de corrélation stratigraphique. *Neues Jb. Geol. Paläont. Mh.*, 1982, 1–11.

42 **Dreesen R.** Storm-generated oolitic ironstones of the Famennian (Falb-Fa2a) in the Vesdre and Dinant synclinoria (upper Devonian, Belgium). *Annls Soc. géol. Belg.*, **105**, 1982, 105–29.

43 **Dumont J. M.** Haldes d'orpaillage et réserves naturelles en Ardenne. *Glain et Salm, Haute-Ardenne*, **4**, 1976, 64–71.

44 **Evrard P.** Minor elements in sphalerites from Belgium. *Econ. Geol.*, **40**, 1945, 568–74.

45 **Fabry J.** Recherches sur les kaolins de l'Ardenne. *Annls Soc. géol. Belg.*, **66**, 1943, 150–60.

46 **Fourmarier P.** Le problème des gisements filoniens de la Belgique. *Revue univlle Mines*, **10**, 1934, 202–8.

47 **Gillet J. C.** *Les chercheurs d'or en Ardenne* (Gembloux: Duclot, 1976), 72 p.

48 **Hanssen E. and Viaene W.** Données minéralogiques sur les paillettes d'or de la bordure S. et S.E. du massif de Stavelot. *Bull. Soc. belge Géol.*, **88**, 1979, 225–35.

49 **Kaboth D.** Zur Genese der Bohnerze und Rasenerz Luxemburgs. Thesis, University of Münster, 1969.

50 **Kienzle M. V.** Morphogenese des westlichen Luxemburger Gutlandes. *Tübinger geogr. Studien*, **27**, 1968.

51 **Kramm V.** The coticule rocks (spessartine quartzite) of the Venn–Stavelot Massif, Ardennes: a volcanoclastic metasediment? *Contr. Miner. Petrol.*, **56**, 1976, 135–55.

52 **Kramm V.** Herkunft und Ablagerungsmilieu der manganreichen ordovischen Gesteine des Venn–Stavelot Massivs, Ardennen. *Z. dt. geol. Ges.*, **131**, 1980, 867–88.

53 **Krusch P.** Manganerzlagerstätten Belgisch-Luxemburgs in ihrer Beziehung zur Verwitterung der alten Oberfläche. *Z. dt. geol. Ges.*, **67**, 1916, 204–17.

54 **Lepersonne J.** Contribution à l'étude des filons de l'Ardenne (or, quartz, albite, biotite, grenat). *Annls Soc. géol. Belg.*, **57**, 1934, 74–9.

55 **Lespineux G.** Étude génétique des gisements miniers des bords de la Meuse et de l'Est de la province de Liège. In *Congrès international des mines, de la métallurgie, de la mécanique et de la géologie appliquées, Liège, 1905: section de géologie appliquée* (Liège: Vaillant-Carmanne, 1905), 55–79.

56 **Lindgren W.** *Mineral deposits* (New York, London: McGraw-Hill, 1933), 930 p.

57 **Lucius M.** Étude sur les gisements de fer du Grand-Duché de Luxembourg. In *XIX Int. geol. Congr., Algiers, 1952: Symposium sur les gisements de fer du monde, volume II*, 1952, 349–87.

58 **Marlière R.** Phosphates du Hainaut. In *Congrès 1947, Centenaire de l'Association des Ingénieurs sortis de l'École de Liège (A.I.Lg): section géologie* (Liège: A.I.Lg, 1947), 330–4.

59 **Melon J. Bourguignon P. and Fransolet A. M.** *Les minéraux de Belgique* (Dison: G. Lelotte, 1976), 280 p.

60 **Pasteels P. Netels V. Dejonghe L. and Deutsch S.** La composition isotopique du plomb des gisements belges: implication sur les plans génétique et économique (note préliminaire). *Bull. Soc. belge Géol.*, **89**, 1980, 123–36.

61 **Pel J. and Monseur G.** Minéralisations de galène et pyrite dans le récif F_2h du Frasnien de Frasnes (Belgique). *Annls Soc. géol. Belg.*, **101**, 1979, 389–97.

62 **Pirlet H.** L'influence d'un karst sous-jacent sur la sédimentation calcaire et l'intérêt de l'étude des paléokarsts. *Annls Soc. géol. Belg.*, **93**, 1970, 247–54.

63 **Rey M. and Legraye M.** Les ressources de la Belgique en minerais métalliques. In *La valorisation des matières premières* (Bruxelles: Comité central industriel Belgique, 1940), vol. 1, 10–27.

64 **Routhier P.** *Les gisements métallifères* (Paris: Masson, 1963), 1282 p.

65 **Smith F. W. and Hirst D. M.** Analysis of trace elements and fluid inclusions in fluorite from the Ardennes massif. *Annls Soc. géol. Belg.*, **97**, 1974, 281–5.

66 **Souchez-Lemmens M.** Les indurations ferrugineuses et l'évolution géomorphologique de la Lorraine belge nord-orientale. *Revue belge Géogr.*, **95**, 1971, 1–143.

67 **Swysen L.** Les lapiès du "Fondry des chiens" à Nismes (Belgique). *Annls Soc. géol. Belg.*, **94**, 1971, 165–71.

68 **Swennen R. and Viaene W.** Lithogeochemistry of some carbonate sections of the Dinantian in the Vesder region (Belgium). *Bull. Soc. belge Géol.*, **90**, 1981, 65–80.

69 **Thorez J. and Bourguignon P.** Kaolin survey and characterisation in Belgium. In *Kaolin symposium, international clay conference, Madrid*, 1982, 71–80.

70 **Timmerhans Ch.** Les gîtes métallifères de la région de Moresnet. In *Congrès international des mines, de la métallurgie, de la mécanique et de la géologie appliquées, Liège, 1905: section de géologie appliquée* (Liège: Vaillant-Carmanne, 1905), 297–324.

71 **Van Orsmael J. Viaene W. and Bouckaert J.** Lithogeochemistry of Upper Tournaisian and Lower Visean carbonate rocks in the Dinant basin, Belgium. *Meded. Rijks geol. Dienst*, **32**, 1980, 96–100.

72 **Van Wambeke L.** La minéralisation des tonalites de La Helle et de Lammersdorf et leurs relations avec les autres minéralisations. *Bull. Soc. belge Géol.*, **64**, 1956, 534–81.

73 **Wery A.** Résultats de récentes recherches pour or primaire dans le Paléozoïque du Sud de la Belgique. *Bull. Soc. belge Géol.*, **57**, 1948, 280–97.

74 **Weis D. Dejonghe L. and Herbosch A.** Les associations des minéraux opaques et semi-opaques de la roche ignée de La Helle. *Annls Soc. géol. Belg.*, **103**, 1980, 15–23.

H. M. Harsveldt

The Netherlands

In The Netherlands rock salt is exploited from the Zechstein and Upper Bunter formations.

Palaeogeographic setting—Zechstein

Tectonic movements that were associated with the Asturian phase of the Variscan orogenesis resulted in the development of an orogenic belt that was uplifted further at the end of the Carboniferous (Saalian phase). It was followed by a prolonged period of denudation of the land surface and by infilling of the lower ground with Rotliegende sediments, largely under continental conditions, including evaporites in localized basins. In the late Permian a basin was initiated that continued its subsidence until the end of the Triassic. This basin, of which The Netherlands formed a part, extended between the London–Brabant and Rhenish Massifs in the south to the Fennoscandian Shield in the north. The northwestern entrance of this inland sea was situated somewhere between Scotland and Norway. The succeeding marine transgressions resulted in the deposition of the Zechstein. The hot and dry climate caused heavy evaporation, leading to the fourfold cyclic depositon of thick Zechstein layers.

The four well-known cyclothems (oldest to youngest Werra Series—Stassfurt Series—Leine Series—Aller Series) are well developed in the eastern Netherlands, where thick rock salt layers that locally contain potassium salts alternate with anhydrite, limestones and dolomitic limestones.

Rock salt is exploited by the Royal Dutch Saltworks from the salt domes of Winschoten and Zuidwending[1] (Fig. 1). In the *Winschoten* salt dome the top of the rock salt has been found at approximately 400-m depth, the base, according to seismic information, lying between 2500 and 3000 m. Directly above the rock salt there is a cap rock, 6–40 m thick, of rather pure anhydrite. The rock salt is clear to locally dull translucent, and contains salt crystals up to about 15 cm long. The salt is rather coarse and contains a few impurities in the form of stringers, lenses and nodules of anhydrite and gypsum.

Because of the lack of continuous clay–anhydrite or dolomite layers it is difficult to identify exactly the cycle to which the salt belongs, though it is very probable, based on lithological criteria, that it is the Stassfurt.

The potassium content is negligible, varying between 1 and 2%. Extraction is by solution mining,[2] which is carried out between 1400 and 800 m over a solution height of 600 m. Current production is from nine boreholes.

Reserves at the Winschoten salt dome are estimated at 19.4×10^9 tonne of rock salt within the 1600-m contour.

In the *Zuidwending* salt dome the top of the rock salt has been found to lie between 170 and 185 m below ground and is covered by a cap rock that consists mainly of anhydrite with minor admixtures of gypsum. The cap rock is 40–50 m thick. The composition of the rock salt is the same as that in the Winschoten salt dome and, again, the salt probably belongs to the second cycle (Stassfurt). So far seven boreholes have been drilled.

Extraction is also by solution mining, use being made of three concentric tubes. Current production takes place over a height of some 600 m between 900 and 1500 m. Only the northern culmination of the Zuidwending dome is exploited, reserves here being put at about 18.6×10^9 tonne, within the 1600-m contour.

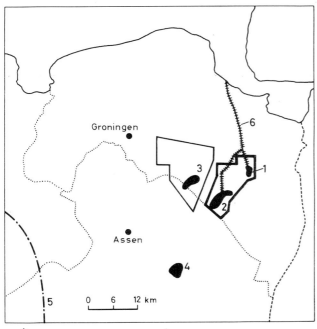

Fig. 1 *Concessions: 1, Winschoten salt dome; 2, Zuidwending salt dome; 3, Veendam salt pillow; 4, Schoonlo salt dome; 5, salt boundary; 6 pipeline for brine*

Exploration history

From the gravimetric map of the province of Groningen it became clear that the minima that showed up were caused by salt plugs. The minimum at Winschoten was explored in detail by Nederlandse Aardolie Maatschappij at the request of Royal Dutch Saltworks and refraction seismic investigations were carried out in consultation with the State Geological Survey. Subsequently three exploration holes were drilled to a depth of 1000 m, these boreholes meeting the top of the rock salt at about 400-m depth. In none of the boreholes was the base of the rock salt reached. The Adolph van Nassau concession for the exploitation of the Winschoten dome has been in existence since 1954.

The Zuidwending salt dome was discovered in the same way, the concession—actually, an extension of the former—being granted in 1967.

Table 1 *Rock-salt production (tonne) in Adolph van Nassau concession**

1958	14 895	1973	2 221 783
1963	767 946	1978	2 171 548
1968	1 433 856	1983	2 059 481

* From Winschoten salt dome in 1958 and 1963; from Winschoten and Zuidwending domes thereafter.

A concession has also been granted, but exploitation has not yet been started, for the Weerselo salt pillar, which is situated a few kilometres northeast of the town of Hengelo (Fig. 2) (the concession was obtained by Royal Dutch Saltworks in 1967). Five boreholes have been drilled in the salt section, the top of the rock salt being encountered in Weerselo 1 at 476-m depth. At the final depth of 889·50 m the base of the salt had not been reached, seismic information indicating the base to occur at approximately 1700 m. The salt belongs to the Zechstein formation.

Above the salt a cap rock of 28-m thickness, consisting of crystalline white anhydrite, has been found. The salt is colourless to yellowish, translucent, coarse and crystalline with locally thin veins and stringers of anhydrite. The bulk of the salt belongs to the Stassfurt cycle, the Main dolomite occurring in one of the boreholes. Below the Stassfurt salt some Werra salt occurs, cores taken from the latter showing translucent fine-grained rock salt with local anhydrite. From geological and seismic data a rather disturbed salt pillar, pressed upwards along an upthrust (the Gronauer upthrust) may be inferred. Throughout the pillar the salt thickness, according to seismic data, lies between 200 and 1200 m, reserves being roughly estimated at about 80×10^9 tonne.

Other as yet unexploited salt areas are situated around the village of Winterswijk (Fig. 2). Within these areas

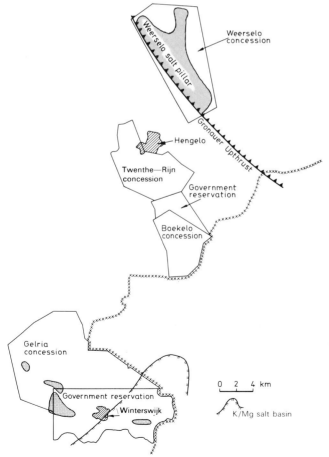

Fig. 2 *Rock-salt concessions*

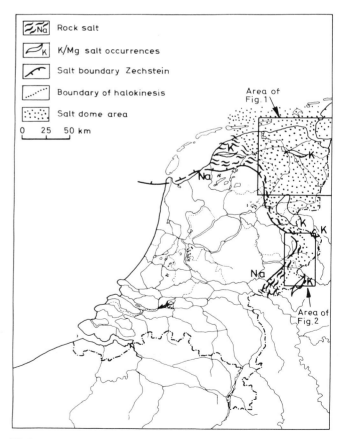

Fig. 3

(the Gelria concession of Nederlandse Maatschappij tot het verrichten van Mijnbouwkundige Werken, granted in 1930, and the Dutch Government Reservation) Zechstein salt pillows occur.[3] Within the Gelria concession five boreholes have been drilled, rock salt of the Zechstein formation being found in four holes. The rock salt is grey to brownish-grey to sometimes reddish, locally translucent, with scarce impurities in the form of anhydrite. No bitter salts have been encountered. The salt belongs to the Werra cycle. The thickness of the salt found in the pillows lies between 100 m and 400 m, the pillows occurring at a depth of 500–700 m. The salt is covered by a dolomite cap rock. The size of the pillows differs, the smallest measuring 1 km × 1½ km and the largest 3 km × 2 km. Reserves are put at 18×10^9 tonne of rock salt.

Palaeogeographic setting—Upper Bunter

During Zechstein IV and Bunter the connexion with the open sea in the northwest between Scotland and Norway closed. By this time the former Zechstein basin had gradually deepened to the east, which, towards the end of the Bunter, resulted in a connexion with the Mediterranean. Through this connexion a sea ingression of short duration in a northwesterly direction started. A salt basin developed in the Upper Bunter in western Germany and the eastern Netherlands, with up to 150 m of salt in the centre, that was situated in the neighbourhood of Braunschweig. Rock salt from this basin is exploited by Royal Dutch Saltworks in the Twenthe–Rijn concession (obtained in 1933) south of the town of Hengelo (Fig. 2). To date, more than 250 boreholes have been drilled through the salt section. The salt layer has a thickness that varies between 30 m in the north and 70 m in the south. Locally, a thickness of 100 m has been drilled. The salt occurs between 285 and 500 m below ground and dips in a southwesterly direction. Solution mining is again employed.[1]

A closer examination of the Upper Bunter salt layer shows that it is not continuous but can be subdivided into four separate layers, designated A–D (oldest to youngest). Salt layer A is the thickest layer. The salt is colourless to brown grey, sometimes milky white, dull, medium to coarsely crystalline and interbedded with stringers and lenses of anhydrite and clay. Layer B is thinner than A, medium to coarsely crystalline, dull and strongly impregnated with inclusions of anhydrite and clay. Layer C is thicker than B, but thinner than A. The salt is grey white to milky white to colourless, medium to coarsely crystalline and contains anhydrite stringers, clay stringers and lenses. Towards the base red colours are predominant in the salt, these colours being specific for layer C. Layer D, the thinnest layer, is characterized by orange red to yellowish-orange colours and is interbedded with anhydrite and clay layers. The separation between the salt layers *sensu stricto* is formed by sandy clay layers with anhydrite lenses and nodules.

Only the separating layer between salt B and A is formed by an anhydrite–dolomite layer locally entirely dolomitic. Directly below layer A is a massive anhydrite layer that forms the base of the Upper Bunter formation.

Lithological studies of the salt show that higher up in the section the salt becomes less pure. This is caused by recessive sedimentation and is directly contrary to what is seen in the Zechstein salt series, which becomes purer upwards.

Boekelo concession

The Boekelo concession was granted in 1918 and was exploited to 1952. During the period 1918–32 Royal Dutch Saltworks sank eight production wells. All these wells encountered the Upper Bunter salt at depths from 270 to 300 m. The Upper Bunter salt dips in a westerly direction and the strike of the salt layer is approximately north–south (thickness, 68–93 m). Here again the salt series is subdivided by shale and anhydrite layers into four halite layers of the same composition as indicated above.

Exploration history

The discovery of the Upper Bunter salt in The Netherlands was fortuitous. In 1886 a borehole, drilled for the purpose of obtaining fresh water, hit salt water at a depth of about 516 m. This stimulated exploration for salt, which was carried out successfully by the Government Institute for the Geological Exploration of the Netherlands, leading in 1918 to the granting of the Boekelo concession to Royal Dutch Saltworks. Production figures are given in Table 2.

Table 2 *Rock-salt production (tonne), Boekelo and Hengelo areas*

Boekelo		Hengelo	
1919	6 107	1936	2 000
1924	31 347	1941	121 000
1929	46 594	1946	170 000
1934	77 895	1951	446 000
1939	79 100	1956	610 000
1944	24 340	1961	696 000
1949	42 820	1966	1 212 000
1952	9 228	1971	1 800 000
		1976	1 490 200
		1981	1 734 100

Bitter salts

In The Netherlands plans exist to exploit the bitter salts from the third cycle of the Zechstein formation. Exploration was started in 1969 in the provinces of Groningen, Friesland and Drenthe. Exploration and production will be by Billiton Delfstoffen B.V. The potassium salts (carnallite–sylvite–bischofite and kieserite) occur as heavily folded layers within the Zechstein salt. Exploitation will take place in salt cushions, where the K/Mg salts are relatively thick. This is the result of a process called 'preferential salt flow'.[4] The bedding is still more or less horizontal. To date, five boreholes have been drilled on the edge of salt cushions. Special permission for exploitation was granted for borehole Veendam N.E.1 in 1972 and a request for a concession in the Veendam area has been sought of the Government. The purpose of the future exploitation is to produce a brine rich in $MgCl_2$ and KCl, which will be reworked to pure MgO, pure $MgCl_2$ and KCl. The MgO will be used for the manufacture of fireproof bricks for lining furnaces in the steel industry, the $MgCl_2$ for magnesium production and the KCl for agricultural purposes. In the Veendam area the salts occur at a depth of 1400–1600 m. Annual production capacity is set at 100 000 tonne MgO.

Gypsum

An unexploited deposit of gypsum is to be found in the cap rock of the Schoonlo salt dome[5] (Fig. 1). In Schoonlo 1 a cap rock of gypsum was encountered between 142 and 226 m. Reserves of gypsum amount to some 1 600 000 tonne.

Postscript

After the text of this chapter had been written the Veendam K/Mg salt concession was granted (in 1980). Six wells have been drilled to date (1985), four of which are producing. Production is linked to the capacity of the nearby magnesia plant. At present some 140 000 tonne of $MgCl_2$ is produced annually.

References

1 **Harsveldt H. M.** Salt resources in the Netherlands as surveyed mainly by AKZO. In *Fifth symposium on salt, 1978* **Coogan A. H. and Hauber L. eds** (Cleveland, Ohio: Northern Ohio Geological Society, 1980), 65–81.

2 **Cox R.** The production of salt in The Netherlands. *Verh. ned. geol.-mijnb. Genoot., Geol. Ser.*, **21**, pt 1 1963, 97–115.

3 **Harsveldt H. M.** De diepere ondergrond van Winterswijk. *Grondboor Hamer*, no. 2 1966, 58–65.

4 **Coelewij P. A. J. Haug G. M. W. and van Kuijk H.** Magnesium-salt exploration in the northeastern Netherlands. *Geologie Mijnb.*, **57**, 1978, 487–502.

5 **Mulder A. J.** De zoutpijler van Schoonlo (the Schoonlo salt dome). *Geologie Mijnb.*, **12**, 1950, 169–76.

Zdeněk Pouba and Ján Ilavský

Czechoslovakia

Mineral deposits of the Bohemian Massif

Mining history

The Bohemian Massif of Central Europe is an area with a long tradition of mining. Famous deposits, such as Cínovec (Zinnwald), Jáchymov (Joachimsthal), Příbram and Kutná Hora, all of which played a major role in the mining industry from the Middle Ages onwards, lie mainly in Bohemia. Other deposits, such as Freiberg and Altenberg, are situated in neighbouring Saxony (German Democratic Republic). These are dominantly deposits of tin (Cínovec, Altenberg) and silver ores (Jáchymov, Příbram, Kutná Hora, Freiberg, etc.).

The Bohemian Massif, however, was originally an area of gold mining. The most extensive gold production came from placers. According to Pošepný,[1] the Celts exploited placer gold from this area. Thus, tin, silver and gold were the chief metals mined in the early history of Bohemia. It was not until the Middle Ages that the mining of primary deposits was started, though the Celts are assumed to have partly exploited primary gold-bearing veins.

It is known that mining continued throughout the Bohemian Massif area in the Middle Ages; its centre was the region of the Central Bohemian pluton—a complex granitoid body of Variscan age surrounded by the largest gold veins. It was not until recently that mining came to an end at the last of these gold deposits—Jílové near Prague—and it is by no means certain that all the ore there has been exhausted.

In historic times the Jílové deposit supplied gold for the Royal court, but it was the Kutná Hora silver mines that for a long time were the main source of income for the Czech kings. The exploitation of these deposits acquired extraordinary proportions, leading to technical developments without parallel elsewhere in the Middle Ages. At Osel mine, for example, depths in excess of 500 m were reached as early as the fourteenth century.

Discovered in 1516 in a sparsely inhabited area of the Krušné Hory Mountains (Erzgebirge) on the Bohemian–Saxonian frontier, the Jáchymov deposit was another mining centre that helped to create the wealth of the medieval Czech state and, at the same time, to promote the development of mining and geological sciences. In the course of twenty years the deposit had led to the creation of a mining town that ranked among the largest in Europe at the beginning of the sixteenth century. In addition to miners, numerous outstanding men were attracted to this centre, including a notable physician of Saxon descent (from Chemnitz, now Karl-Marx-Stadt), Georgius Bauer, who wrote under the Latin name of Agricola. His works, especially *De re metallica*, became the foundation of modern mining science and of the geology of ore deposits. The book was an account of the experience of miners working in the Jáchymov deposit. (Similarly, a summary of the data obtained during the mining of the Freiberg deposits in Saxony formed the basis of the papers by Abraham Gottlob Werner.)

In 1716 the earliest known mining school was founded in Jáchymov, playing the role of a lower professional school. The high level of Czech mining techniques, mining law—outstanding in its time (the mining code originated in the 1360s in Jihlava)—and, later, mineralogy led to the establishment in Prague of the earliest university course in mining. In 1762 a department that specialized in mining and geology was set up at Charles University.

The teaching of mining geology was later transferred to Mining Academies (first to the Mining Academy in Banská Štiavnica in Slovakia, later to Příbram). The study of this subject culminated in the second half of the nineteenth century, thanks to Pošepný.[2] His important papers, like those of other Czech geologists, have their roots in the Czech ore mines. Bohemian ores were also the subject of very important physical studies. Uranium ore from the Jáchymov mines used by H. A. Becquerel and M. Curie led to the discovery of radioactivity. In this way the deposits of the Bohemian Massif contributed to the development of mining as well as to scientific discoveries that have influenced the present-day development of human civilization.

The publishers regret the delay in the publication of this chapter. A limited amount of the more recent data has been included.

Economic importance of Bohemian ore deposits

The present role of Bohemia's ore deposits in the national economy bears no comparison with that which they played in the past. Their importance is overshadowed by the exploitation of coal and of non-metallic raw materials, the economic value of which is much higher than that of the ores, except those of uranium.

The exploitation of iron ore in Bohemia ceased after 1960 when the import of ores from the Ukrainian Krivoi Rog deposit increased and when the exploitation of siderite from the Slovak deposits became more intensive. At about the same time the exploitation of poor pyrite–manganese ores from the large Precambrian Chvaletice deposit came to an end with supplies of pure sulphur from the Polish Tarnobrzeg deposit and of increased amounts of manganese ore from the U.S.S.R.

With regard to polymetallic deposits, the deposits of Cu–Pb–Zn ores of the Variscan tectogenetic zone are becoming more important. This zone surrounds the core of the Bohemian Massif on its northwest and northeast margins, where the Zlaté Hory (Cu and Cu–Pb–Zn) deposits and Horní Benešov (Pb–Zn) deposits are being mined with success. In the well-known vein deposits of Příbram and Kutná Hora polymetallic ores are being exploited against the background of the considerable economic difficulties that are common in classical vein-type deposits. These difficulties led to the cessation of exploitation of some of the smaller vein deposits (e.g. the Stříbro deposit), but deposits that contain a higher amount of Ag (the Vrančice polymetallic deposits) or that accompany industrial minerals (e.g. the Harrachov fluorite deposit) continue to be worked. The deposits of tin and tungsten ores located in two classical ore districts (Cínovec and Horní Slavkov) in the Bohemian Massif are of increasing economic value.

The exploitation of the Bohemian gold deposits came to an end after the second world war. In the Jílové deposit gold was mined until 1960. The Krásná Hora deposit, where antimony occurs in addition to gold, has attracted attention because of the increase in the prices of these two metals. Economic interest is being focused on the newly discovered Čelina–Mokrsko deposit and on polymetallic ores that contain gold as an admixture—an example is the gold that accompanies stratiform types of ores in the region of the Zlaté Hory deposit, where gold was intensively mined in historic times.

Increased prices for some metals are arousing renewed interest in some deposits that hitherto have been regarded as uneconomic. These are primarily Ni deposits of lateritic type that occur in the ultrabasic rocks of the granulite zone in the southern part of the Bohemian Massif near Křemže, as well as in Western Moravia. The second type involves the Staré Ransko sulphide deposits (Sudbury type) from the southern margin of the Železné Hory Mountains. To date, only sulphide ores of Zn have been mined in the Staré Ransko deposit, and these do not seem to be genetically related to the Ni sulphide ores. Nevertheless, the Ni ores of the Staré Ransko deposit might play a role in the future.

Data on production in Bohemia are given in Table 1.

Table 1 *Production (t) of ores, metals, minerals and mineral products in Bohemia (Czech Socialist Republic)*

	1981	1982	1983	1984
Iron ore	1 935 000	1 861 000	1 902 000	1 869 000
Steel	15 270 000	14 992 000	15 024 000	14 831 000
Lead (metal)	21 000	21 000	21 000	21 000
Zinc (metal)	2 000	2 000	2 000	1 200
Copper (metal)	30 000	30 000	33 000	33 000
Cement	10 645 000	10 325 000	10 498 000	10 530 000
Kaolin (washed)	652 000	648 000	662 000	668 000
Limestone	24 156 000	23 818 000	23 519 000	23 684 000
Lime	3 234 000	3 088 000	3 100 000	3 117 000
Gypsum	767 000	794 000	848 000	842 000
Calcined magnesite				
For brickmaking	331 000	331 000	330 000	336 000
For steelmaking	330 000	341 000	332 000	324 000
Brown coal (gross output)	93 096 000	95 504 000	98 878 000	101 084 000
Lignite	3 269 000	3 440 000	3 538 000	3 659 000
Black coal (net output)	27 512 000	27 463 000	26 915 000	26 421 000
Coke	10 323 000	10 566 000	10 340 000	10 302 000

Geology of Bohemian Massif

The Bohemian Massif (Fig. 1) is a tectonic block that consists of Central European Precambrian and Palaeo-

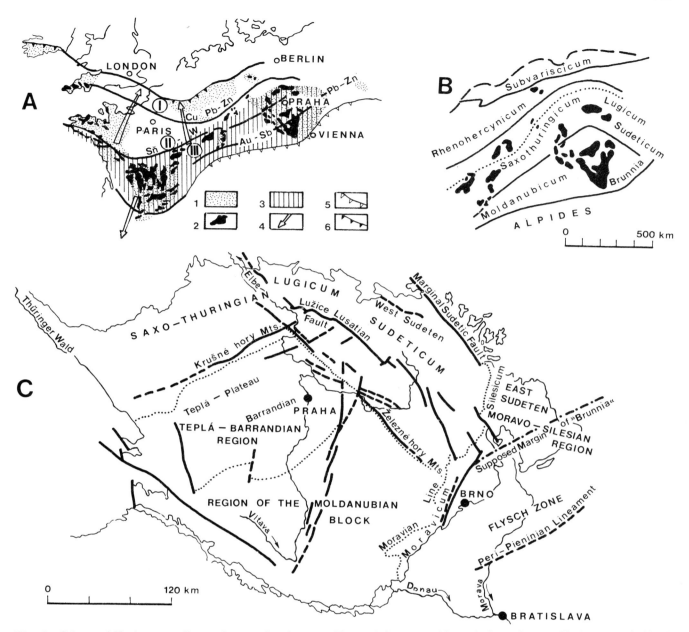

Fig. 1 Scheme of Variscan metallogeny in central and western Europe (A) (1, pre-Mesozoic formations; 2, Variscan granitoids; 3, region of Variscan metamorphism; 4, polarity of orogen; 5, Alpine overthrust; 6, Variscan overthrust.) Modified from Aubouin.[79] B, chief geological units of Bohemian Massif and boundaries of Alpides. Modified from Hösel.[80] C, structural-geological units of Bohemian Massif. After Máška and Zoubek in Svoboda et al[4]

zoic complexes surrounded and partly covered by Mesozoic and Cenozoic sediments. According to Stille,[3] it represents a significant unit of Meso-Europe, i.e. a geological unit associated with the culmination of tectogenetic history in the Variscan orogeny and includes Bohemia, the greater part of Moravia and adjacent parts of Poland, Saxony, Thuringia, Bavaria and Austria.

Following the period of post-Variscan consolidation, the Bohemian Massif appeared as a rising block, forming a continent in the Central European epicontinental seas. As early as in the late Palaeozoic the Bohemian Massif was surrounded by an epicontinental Permian sea. At the beginning of the Mesozoic period, when the Alpine geosyncline was developing, the Bohemian Massif was uplifted as a continental ridge between the Alpine-Carpathian geosyncline and the German epicontinental Jurassic and Triassic sea. The sediments of the latter form the bulk of the foreland of the Massif. In the Cretaceous the epicontinental sedimentation extended as far as the northern part of Bohemia and, accordingly, nearly half of the Bohemian Massif is covered by the Cretaceous series. The Tertiary sedimentation was restricted to the fresh-water lakes, which arose mainly in tectonic depressions in the southern and northwestern part of the Bohemian peneplain.[4] Brown coal seams are characteristic of these depressions. The coal-bearing measures and the Cretaceous sediments are penetrated by Tertiary alkaline volcanic rocks of continental type that form the České Středohoří Mountains. These volcanics occur in the main in the deep northeasterly bearing fault zone that forms a young rift system developed between the Saxonian and Bohemian parts of the Bohemian Massif. No significant ore deposits are connected with the Tertiary volcanism.

extensive granite massifs, belong in part to the Caledonian orogenic cycle, but predominantly to the Variscan orogenic cycle (Fig. 2). K–Ar dating[7,8,9] shows the majority of the Variscan granitic rocks to be 270–300 m.y. old. The distribution of granitoids of different ages shows that the Variscan granite development moved from the core towards the periphery of the Bohemian Massif. The youngest granitic intrusions penetrated to shallow crustal depths in the Carboniferous and Permian. The final stage of the

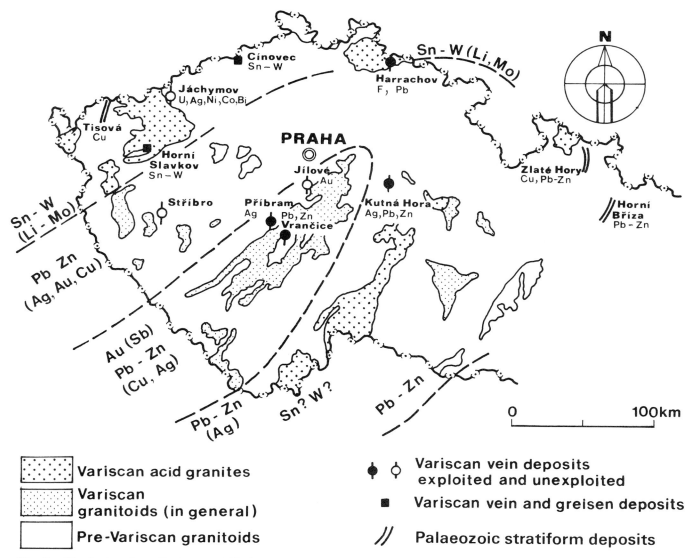

Fig. 2 *Distribution of pre-Variscan and Variscan granitoids and of related hydrothermal ore deposits in Bohemian Massif*

The majority of magmatic rocks responsible for the ore mineralization in the Bohemian Massif are Precambrian and Palaeozoic in age. They are distributed in the Moldanubian orogen (supposedly early Proterozoic or Archaean), and the Baikalian (Cadomian?), Caledonian and Variscan tectonic complexes.[4,5,6] All these orogenic events were accompanied by basic submarine magmatism in their geosynclinal stages. The bulk of acid plutonic rocks, particularly

Variscan magmatic activity is represented by the Permian palaeobasalts (melaphyres).

With the exception of the continental Carboniferous and Permian coal-bearing basins, the Palaeozoic sedimentation is of marine origin. The non-metamorphosed Cambrian, Ordovician, Silurian and Devonian sediments occur in the Barrandian area (Central Bohemia). The Devonian is mainly built up of carbonate rocks that conformably overlie the Silurian limestones. The Ordovician and Silurian sequences are accompanied by basic volcanic rocks.

The northwest and northeast peripheries of the Bohemian Massif are built up of different Palaeozoic rocks of geosynclinal type. These geosynclinal series form a continuation of the West European Variscan belt (Fig. 1) in which the Devonian and Lower Carboniferous rocks exhibit a specific facies evolution. The Lower Devonian transgressive clastic rocks overlie the earlier Caledonian or Precambrian units. The Middle Devonian clastic and carbonate sediments and spilite–keratophyre submarine volcanics belong to the eugeosynclinal evolutional type. The Lower Carboniferous rocks have a typical diastrophic character (Culm facies). Thus, the Palaeozoic of Central Bohemia that pertains to the Mediterranean facies evolution is clearly distinct from the Palaeozoic in the northern periphery of the Bohemian Massif (the Sudeten Mountains and Western Moravia), which is closer to the Rhine–Harz facies.[10]

The Caledonian units, which consist mostly of metamorphic rocks and granites, are known from the West Sudeten Mountains on Czechoslovakia's northern frontier (Fig. 1). The presence of Caledonian rocks in other areas has not yet been established with sufficient certainty.

The pre-Caledonian basement of the Bohemian Massif consists of Precambrian complexes of different age and origin. Several structural levels of the Proterozoic can be distinguished, yet their stratigraphy is still largely debatable. In central and western Bohemia the unmetamorphosed Proterozoic (supposedly late Proterozoic) rocks underlie the Cambrian conglomerates. There is an angular discordance between them. The Proterozoic of the Barrandian area (Fig. 1) consists of shales, greywackes, basic volcanics (spilites), cherts with siliceous stromatolites and conglomerates. A rock complex devoid of cherts, but otherwise similar, is also known from the adjacent area—the Železné Hory Mountains. The complexes can be divided into a lower series with eugeosynclinal clastic rocks and submarine volcanics, and an upper series with conglomerates and monotonous flysch-like facies. Both series were folded during the Baikalian (Cadomian) orogeny.

There are many metamorphic complexes of Precambrian age in the outer part of the Bohemian Massif, mainly in Saxony and the Sudetic regions.[6] Many of them were strongly migmatized or granitized during the Variscan orogeny, which also affected their potassium–argon ratio. Only in the 'Brno granite' has a Precambrian age been determined with certainty by the K–Ar method. The 'Brno granite' is considered to be part of a very old geological unit—the 'Brunnia' (Fig. 1)—situated in central and eastern Moravia.[4]

In spite of the above, many geologists hold the Moldanubicum to be the oldest part of the Bohemian Massif.[5] Made up of gneisses and micaschists with abundant interlayers of metamorphosed marls, dolomites, calc-silicate rocks, quartzites, leptynites, ultrabasic and granulitic rocks, this unit forms the core of the Massif in central and southern Bohemia. Thus, the history of the oldest geological units of the Bohemian Massif is still largely undetermined.

Metallogenic history of Bohemian Massif
In the Bohemian Massif pre- and post-Variscan (i.e. Alpine) mineralization can be distinguished. The pre-Variscan metallogeny includes a theoretical Caledonian mineralization, traces of which were obliterated by later events. The Precambrian mineralization is much more evident—in particular, in the unmetamorphosed Proterozoic complexes and in the crystalline complexes that underlie the early Palaeozoic series. The metamorphic regeneration of many magmatic rocks and sedimentary series makes the determination of the age of several deposits difficult. Owing to the strong influence of Variscan heating[7,8,9] the K–Ar method has very often given Variscan ages for the Precambrian complexes.

The majority of metallogenic events are of Variscan age, but it is sometimes uncertain whether the primary concentration of metals was Variscan or originally pre-Variscan in age. On the other hand, zones of combined mineralization and repetition of metallogenic activity have been determined in several areas.[11,12] The metal concentration is strikingly persistent, chiefly in the zones of younger (Alpine) reactivation, being represented by the occurrences of regenerated fluorite, baryte and lead–zinc ores throughout the belt encircling the core of the Bohemian Massif (Fig. 3).[12,13] Age determinations of pitchblendes by the common lead method have revealed similar regenerations in some deposits of marginal areas (e.g. Jáchymov, Abertamy, Harrachov, etc.).[14]

The concentration of different types of ores is influenced by the geochemical composition and history of magmatites, and predominantly by their petrometallogenic type. This problem was studied in detail by Sattran and Klomínský.[15] The relation of metallogeny to volcanism was investigated by Pouba[16] and general trends in the metallogeny of the Bohemian Massif by a number of workers.[17–21] The general features of the metallogeny can be found in the metallogenic map of Czechoslovakia.[22]

Pre-Variscan mineralization
There are many iron, pyrite–pyrrhotite and pyrite–manganese deposits in the Precambrian series of the Bohemian Massif (Fig. 4), but none is of economic value. They are mostly stratiform deposits of FeS_2, or FeS_2 and Mn ores in the Proterozoic series of Central Bohemia (the Barrandian area) and the Železné Hory Mountains—Hromnice and Chvaletice.[23] Oxide iron ores are known from the metamorphosed Precambrian complexes in the Silesikum (East Sudeten (Fig. 1)).

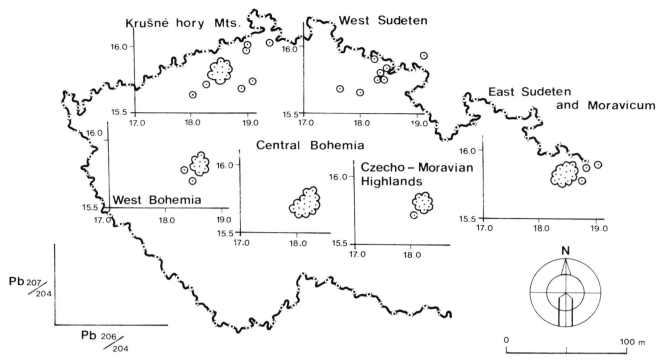

Fig. 3 *Isotopic composition of lead in galena ($^{207}Pb/^{204}Pb : ^{206}Pb/^{204}Pb$) in deposits of main metallogenic areas of Bohemian Massif. Compiled by Pertold after Legierski and Vaněček.[14,60] Diagrams show Alpine mineralization or remobilization in marginal areas of Bohemian Massif (see also Fig. 1)*

Some of them form horizons of banded magnetite-quartzites[24] or banded magnetite–limestone ores.[25] All these deposits are situated in a sigmoidal zone that crosses the boundary between the Silesikum and the Železné Hory–Barrandian area, where they have a sulphidic character. The change of chemical composition can be explained by the depositional conditions in the Proterozoic sea. The oxide Fe formation seems to be indicative of shallow-water conditions. The sulphidic Fe and Fe–S–Mn formation represents a euxinic facies (graphitic pyrite shales) around submarine volcanoes. Stromatolites have recently been found in the siliceous rocks on the margins of both facies (volcanic island arc?).

There are many small skarn deposits in the crystalline complexes of the Moldanubicum (Fig. 4). They also form more or less distinct zones, but their origin is still debatable (Vlastějovice, Budeč, Županovice, etc.).

In the continuation of the Železné Hory Mountains, where the Chvaletice FeS_2 deposit is emplaced, the Staré Ransko ultrabasic body occurs with uneconomic Sudbury-type pentlandite–chalcopyrite mineralization.[26] A separate sphalerite deposit in the ultrabasic rocks—Obrázek—is being exploited at present: it is the only Precambrian deposit of economic value in the Bohemian Massif.

Variscan mineralization
The Variscan mineralization involves (*a*) the pretectonic sedimentary deposits of late Palaeozoic age in the Barrandian (Central Bohemia) and Sudetic areas (NNE Bohemia and Moravia), and (*b*) the posttectonic metalliferous manifestation of Variscan magmatism and its postmagmatic hydrothermal activity distributed all over the Bohemian Massif.

The late Palaeozoic deposits are mainly oolitic iron ores of Ordovician, Silurian and Devonian age. The Devonian deposits are associated in a more or less perceptible way with basic submarine volcanism. During the Ordovician metallogenic processes in the Barrandian area between Praha (Prague) and Plzeň gave rise to the well-known sedimentary chamosite and hematite oolitic ores that were mined until 1965. In the Silurian the metallogenic processes moved northward into the Železný Brod area (West Sudeten). In the Devonian the centres of submarine metallogenesis became active in the 'Rhenish facies' of the East Sudeten Variscan geosyncline. The iron ores of the 'Lahn–Dill' type occur in the Middle Devonian of the Vrbno Group (Vysoký Jeseník Mountains—Altvatergebirge) and in the Šternberk–Benešov zone (Nízký Jeseník Mountains). In both cases economic concentrations of non-ferrous metals have also been found in stratiform deposits (the Zlaté Hory Cu–Pb–Zn deposit and the Horní Benešov Pb–Zn deposit).

The Palaeozoic migration of magmatic centres and magmatic mineralization towards the periphery seems to be connected with the consolidation of the core of the Bohemian Massif. This trend can also be traced later during the period of granitization and doming of central parts of the Bohemian Massif—and also during

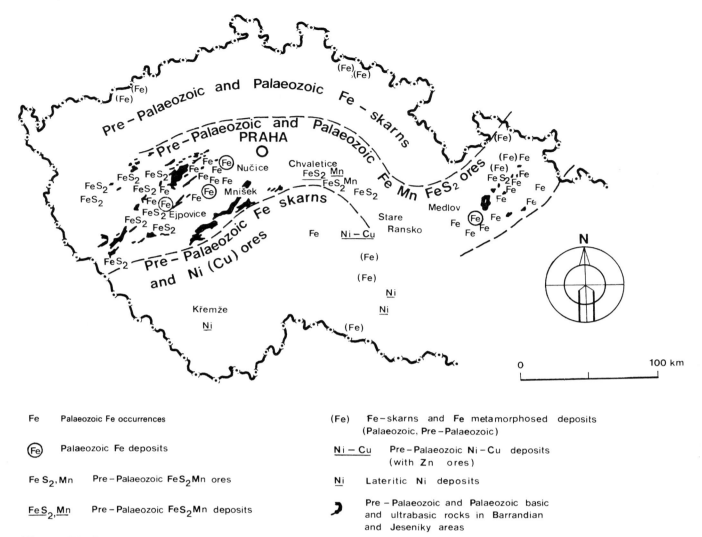

Fig. 4 *Distribution of pre-Palaeozoic and Palaeozoic ores of Fe, FeS$_2$, Mn and Ni–Cu in Bohemian Massif*

the subsequent Permian volcanism and even during the Alpine orogeny, when the processes of mineralization moved to the margins of Bohemia.[19]

The Variscan hydrothermal deposits are associated with different types of granites. Two types of granites have recently been distinguished—the older, to which the bulk of the granites belong, lies in the core of the Bohemian Massif and the younger in its periphery (Fig. 2).

The geochemical differences between the older granites of the core (260–350 m.y.) and the younger granites of the periphery of the Bohemian Massif (250–270 m.y.) were studied by Sattran and Klomínský.[15] The older granites are mineralized mainly with Au, Au–Mo and Pb–Zn ores related to tonalitic and granodioritic magmatic sources. The younger granites are characterized by Sn–W–Mo mineralization connected with magmatic sources of the 'normal' granites and adamellites. The younger granites are very often slightly autometamorphosed. The strongly autometamorphosed granites (with greisens) are accompanied by Sn–Li mineralization.

The origin of uranium concentrations in granites and their surroundings is still debatable all over the Bohemian Massif and especially in the Central Bohemian and Českomoravská vrchovina Highlands. According to Bernard and co-workers,[27] the distribution of Variscan plutons, characterized by specific mineral associations, coincides with the distribution of the positive and negative gravity fields (total Bouguer anomalies) and residual gravity anomalies. This supports the opinion[15] that two principal groups of Variscan granites and mineral associations may be recognized by different methods. The paragenetic conditions of all the hydrothermal deposits of the Bohemian Massif were studied in detail by Bernard.[28]

Post-Variscan (Alpine) mineralization
The young mineralization processes associated with the Alpine orogeny are confined to the border of the Bohemian Massif. In its central parts the Massif remained unaffected by magmatism, whereas volcanic belts developed at its margins. The mineralization associated with these belts has a specific chemical

composition represented by fluorine and barium, and partly by lead, zinc and uranium, which could have been regenerated from earlier granites and Cretaceous sediments. The distribution of F and Ba may be traced in some recent mineral waters. Even nowadays barite continues to precipitate from mineral springs in the Teplice Spa. Some metallogenic features of a rift system have also been discovered in the Bohemian volcanic range. Volcanic rocks of kimberlite type were found that bear typical 'Czech garnets' (pyropes).

Precambrian ore deposits of Bohemian Massif

Ni–Cu and Zn–Cu deposits in Staré Ransko Precambrian ultrabasic complex

The ultrabasic complex of Staré Ransko (Fig. 4) and its mineralization were described by Mísař et al.[26] According to their detailed petrological studies, the ultrabasic complex represents a strongly differentiated intrusive body of peridotites, troctolites and gabbro with a liquid segregation of Ni–Cu ores and high-temperature Zn–Cu sulphide ores. In the second half of the nineteenth century the oxidized parts of the orebodies were mined as nickel-bearing iron ores. In 1957 low-grade primary copper–nickel ores were found by drilling and in 1961 high-grade zinc ores with copper were discovered. The deposits of Cu–Ni sulphides consist of pyrrhotite, chalcopyrite and pentlandite (together with minor amounts of cubanite, pyrite, mackinawite and magnetite). The ore minerals are disseminated in gabbro and troctolite. The average Ni/Cu ratio is 0·97 in troctolite and 0·77 in gabbro. In general, the Cu content is 6 to 24 times lower than that of Ni. The ore is uneconomic at present, but this may be changed by increased prices of nickel in the future.

The high-grade zinc ores with copper are being intensively exploited in the Obrázek deposit. They form a massive aggregate that consists mainly of sphalerite. The massive ores are very often banded, sometimes rich in barite and connected with metasomatic (?) quartzites. The origin of the ore is debatable. The Precambrian to Cambrian age of the ultrabasic complex was determined by a palaeomagnetic method.[29] A Variscan magmatic event is also postulated.

Chvaletice Precambrian FeS_2–Mn sedimentary deposit

The Chvaletice FeS_2–Mn deposit (Fig. 5), mined for a long time, was the largest of the sedimentary pyrite deposits of Proterozoic age. The deposit of pyrite shales and manganese silicate and carbonate ores was exploited in a huge open-pit at Chvaletice at the time when Czechoslovakia was under embargo. In this post-

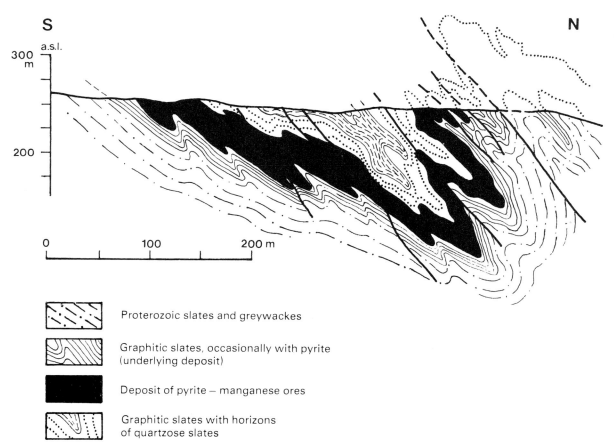

Fig. 5 *Schematic section across Chvaletice FeS_2–Mn deposit in Železné Hory Mountains. After Svoboda et al.*[4]

second world war period pyrite was needed in the Czech chemical industry.

In spite of the extremely low content of sulphur (about 8% S) in the Chvaletice deposit, the pyrite ore was treated by flotation and a concentrate of adequate quality was produced. When a new large sedimentary deposit of native sulphur was discovered in Poland the mining in Chvaletice ceased. Because of its complicated and variable composition the manganese ore was never utilized in industry.

The pyrite–manganese orebody occurs in a large syncline in the Proterozoic (Fig. 5). Overturned to the southwest, with a plunge of 15° SE, the syncline is cut by longitudinal faults and by numerous transverse faults. The ore-bearing complex has been subdivided[23] into three formations—Pre-ore, Ore and Post-ore.

The Pre-ore formation comprises grey graphitic shales or slates with intercalations of calcareous, arkosic and tuffaceous greywackes. In the middle part of this formation spilites and spilitic pillow lavas occur. The uppermost part of the Pre-ore formation consists of conglomerates.

The Ore formation contains a Mn horizon (predominantly made up of $MnCO_3$ + $FeCO_3$ with smaller amounts of $MgCO_3$ + Mn silicates). The Mn horizon is gradually superposed on graphitic shales. Upwards, the Mn horizon makes an abrupt contact with the pyrite body, represented by graphite shales with pyrite bands or impregnations.

The Post-ore formation is represented by a succession made up of sandy shales, tuffaceous shales, greywackes, black cherts (lydites) and conglomerates. Effusive porphyrites and dykes of gabbro diabase are common in both the Ore and Post-ore formations.

The ore comprises various mineral assemblages. The primary mineral assemblage consists of Fe sulphides, Mn carbonates and silicates. The members of the primary mineral paragenesis were affected by a slight regional metamorphism and an intense contact metamorphism produced by a granite intruded during the Cadomian tectogenesis. The Mn carbonate horizon was altered into silicate hornfelses with spessartite, rhodonite, tephroite, Mn cummingtonite and other minerals. In addition to pyrrhotite, pyrite, F–OH–Cl apatite and pink kutnahorite also occur. Rare accumulations of galena, sphalerite, chalcopyrite and marcasite have also been found. Specific mineralogical studies were published by Žák.[30,31] A geochemical study of the ore was published by Hoffman[32] and some data concerning sulphur isotopes by Šmejkal et al.[33]

The ore concentration in the Proterozoic sea is currently thought to have been associated with submarine hydrothermal activity introducing a large amount of iron and sulphur into the sea water. This process accompanied the spilitic volcanism and gave rise to the euxinic facies of the Proterozoic basin.

Palaeozoic sedimentary deposits

Sedimentary Fe deposits in Barrandian area

The sedimentary oolitic iron ore deposits are of marine origin and of Ordovician age; they occur between Prague and Plzeň. Two—the Nučice and Zdice deposits (Fig. 4)—comprise chamosite–siderite ore; the Ejpovice, Krušná Hora, Mníšek and many other deposits consist of hematite–siderite ore. Although poor in iron (25–35% Fe) and enriched in phosphorus, both the ore types were used as crude ore or, after treatment, as concentrates in the local iron and steel industry for more than a hundred years. Following a

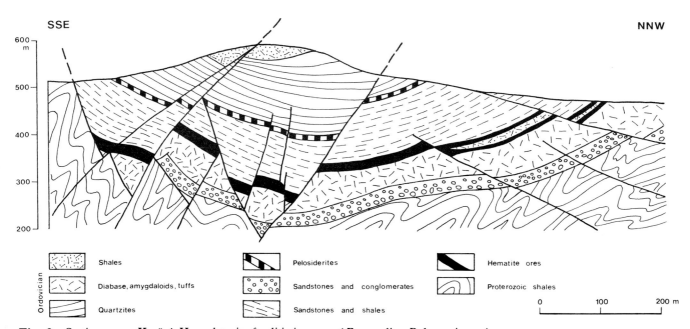

Fig. 6 *Section across Krušná Hora deposit of oolitic iron ores (Barrandian Palaeozoic ores)*

period of increased mining activity during and after the second world war, mining ceased in 1960–65 because of the growing imports of iron ore from the U.S.S.R. (Krivoi Rog ore).

The last mines to be operated were the Ejpovice open-pit near Plzeň and the underground mines in Chrustenice–Nučice and Krušná Hora. The hematite ores of Ejpovice were very poor in iron and rich in SiO_2. In the Chrustenice–Nučice deposit the ore was represented by siderite and chamosite with some magnetite and pyrite. An increased content of pyrite is usually observed in the marginal parts of the orebodies, especially in the transitional zone into the adjacent shale, which represents a deeper-water facies. In addition to the exploited hematite ore, the Krušná Hora deposit (Fig. 6) also contains low-grade pelosiderites, which were explored for several years, but with a negative result.

The stratigraphic position of the deposits is well known from the detailed studies of Svoboda and Prantl.[34] Only uneconomic iron concentrations exist in the Tremadoc and Arenig. The Ejpovice deposit belongs to the important Klabava ore horizon (Llanvirn) and the Krušná Hora deposit is also Llanvirnian in age. Other ore layers occur in the Llandeilo, Caradoc and Ashgill stages, but only the Caradoc ore horizon with the Nučice–Chrustenice deposits has proved to be of economic value.

Metallogenic conditions were studied by Petránek.[35] His papers present many paragenetic and geochemical data concerning the distribution of ore minerals and ore types in relation to the lithofacies conditions and the palaeogeography. The ores are of sedimentary origin and their iron was brought into the marine basin predominantly from the nearby land. Locally, submarine volcanic activity may also have been a source of iron (especially in the Komárov area), possibly as a result of sea water–basalt interaction at increased temperatures.[36] Thus, some of the Ordovician iron ores of the Barrandian area may be genetically associated with the Devonian iron ores in the Jeseníky Mountains (East Sudeten), where a relationship of the orebodies to submarine basalts has been proved.[37] Exploitation of the Devonian iron ores in the East Sudeten ceased at the beginning of this century with the exception of the Medlov and Krákořice deposits, which were abandoned after the second world war.

Palaeozoic stratiform deposits

Tisová stratiform Cu deposit

The Tisová Cu deposit (Fig. 2) is one of the genetically most problematical deposits in the Saxothuringian border zone of the Bohemian Massif. It is made up of several conformable layers of sulphidic ore in the Palaeozoic phyllite complex (Ordovician?), forming the mantle of the Eibenstock–Karlovy Vary granite body. It is not known whether the magma was the primary source of metals or whether the mineral concentration of the deposit is a result of a syngenetic sedimentary accumulation of sulphides, later influenced by metamorphism and granite intrusion.

Like many other deposits in the Krušné Hory Mountains the Tisová deposit has been mined since the thirteenth century. This mine produces pyrite-chalcopyrite–pyrrhotite ore with accessory arsenopyrite, sphalerite, galena and magnetite, the latter forming irregular isolated accumulations. The deposit is situated in the vicinity of the town of Kraslice in a monotonous phyllite complex that contains rare quartzites and metabasites.

The sulphide ore, forming several layers in the phyllite complex, consists of massive ore and impregnations, the two being separated by a very sharp boundary. The massive ore consists of pyrite, pyrrhotite and chalcopyrite. The ore locally displays layered texture. The layering is often due to rhythmic changes of coarse-grained and fine-grained pyrite. Two generations of pyrite are visible under the microscope. The second generation is represented by very fine-grained pyrite, which originated from pyrrhotite and cements the brecciated grains of older pyrite. These are also sometimes cemented by other members of the first mineral generation, such as chalcopyrite, arsenopyrite, sphalerite and galena. This seems to be a result of synmetamorphic or synkinematic recrystallization of the ore. The ore layers strike north–south, dip at 20–30°W and are slightly folded.

In spite of many indications of a syngenetic origin for the ore (predominantly the conformable position of the ore layers within the phyllite complex), Škvor[38] assumed that the mineralization is of hydrothermal epigenetic origin and occurred during the last phase of the metamorphic process. Burdová and co-workers[39] have recently discovered that the ore is concentrated in the horizons with relatively high contents of organic compounds. This fact may throw new light on the genesis of this deposit.

Zlaté Hory stratiform Cu–Pb–Zn deposit

The Zlaté Hory (Zukmantel) Cu–Pb–Zn deposit (Figs. 2, 7 and 8) belongs to the metamorphosed stratiform deposits of the Variscan eugeosyncline. It occurs in a complicated folded structure in the Devonian rocks of the East Sudeten, representing the Sudetic equivalent of the ore-bearing Rhenohercynian belt, which contains the famous Rammelsberg Cu deposit in West Germany.

The ores in the Zlaté Hory ore district have been the subject of interest since the thirteenth century. Underground mining started in the second half of the fourteenth century, peak prosperity being reached in the sixteenth century. At that time two large gold nuggets (1·386 and 1·780 kg in weight) were found. The main object of exploitation, however, was copper

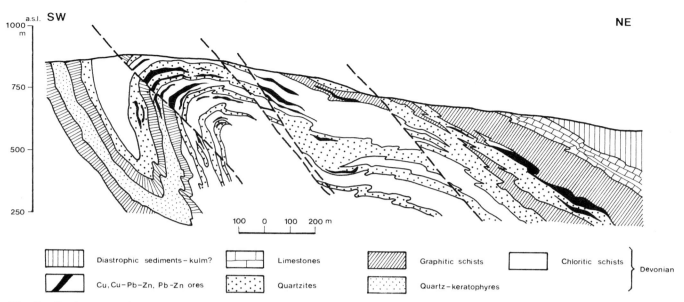

Fig. 7 *Section across Zlaté Hory stratiform deposit of Cu–Pb–Zn ores*

and, later, lead, zinc and iron. After a long gap in the mining history and after a relatively short period of exploration, larger commercial reserves of Cu, Pb–Zn and Au ores were found, mainly by drilling. This encouraged new mining activity and the construction of a flotation plant.

The Zlaté Hory ore district belongs to the weakly metamorphosed Devonian formation of the Vrbno Group, partly overlain by the Upper Devonian–Lower Carboniferous (?) Andělská Hora Group. The Lower Devonian quartzites (their Siegenian age was proved by fossils) and conglomerates lie on the crystalline complexes of the core of the Desná dome (pre-Devonian/Precambrian (?) in age). The quartzites exhibit frequent intercalations of graphitic phyllites, chloritic phyllites and chloritic quartzites, their number increasing towards the top of the Vrbno Group. The phyllite series includes various types of metadiabase, greenschist, meta-keratophyre and quartz-keratophyre. There is no megascopic difference between the ore-bearing quartz-keratophyres and the quartzites in some places. Thus, it is not clear if the ore is in sedimentary or volcanic rocks or in both.

The youngest members of the Vrbno Group are calcite–phyllites and limestones. Microtectonic analysis has revealed that the epizonal metamorphic rocks of the Vrbno Group are B-tectonites with a distinct planar and linear syntectonically formed fabric. The ore has a similar fabric and seems to be partly premetamorphic or synmetamorphic in origin.

In the Zlaté Hory South deposit Pertold and Constantinides[40] showed that there are several types of mineralization within one deposit. These types have different relations to the structural and metamorphic history of the host rocks. The economically important Cu ores are of metamorphic and post-metamorphic types (emplaced between B_2 and B_3 folds and after B_3 folds, respectively). In the Zlaté Hory South deposit they form separate orebodies.

The orebodies are predominantly developed in chloritic quartzites or quartz-keratophyres beneath a phyllite roof and have the form of (1) monometallic chalcopyrite in stratiform deposits, (2) more or less massive chalcopyrite ore in quartz veins, (3) complex strata-bound galena–sphalerite–pyrite–chalcopyrite ores partly in chloritic quartzites (keratophyres?) and partly in limestones and (4) similar ores in quartzites with gold. The first and second types of ore are mined in the Zlaté Hory South ore field and the third and fourth in the Zlaté Hory East (Fig. 8) and Zlaté Hory West ore fields. The mineralized series occurs in an arch-like structure about 10 km long that conforms with the northern closure of the Desná (Orlík) dome. The deposits consist of a system of layers or long lenses, which are very often associated with the local anticlinal structure and form a complicated part of the anticlinorium.

The metals are concentrated mainly along the boundary of two mechanically different rock types, i.e. quartzites and graphitic phyllites, particularly when the graphitic phyllites are underlain by the quartzites. The ore is mostly medium-grained and often banded. In crystalline limestones the signs of metasomatic replacement by ore components or by scarce barite are visible mainly in the Zlaté Hory East ore field (Modrá štola = 'Blue gallery'). In addition to the main ore minerals, pyrrhotite, arsenopyrite, tennantite and other minerals occur in the complex ore. In the Modrá štola the Fe hydroxides, glockerite (described for the first time from the Zlaté Hory mines) and alumina minerals (alumogel and allophane) are the secondary weathering products of the sulphide ores and wallrocks.

Study of the minor elements in the ores has revealed

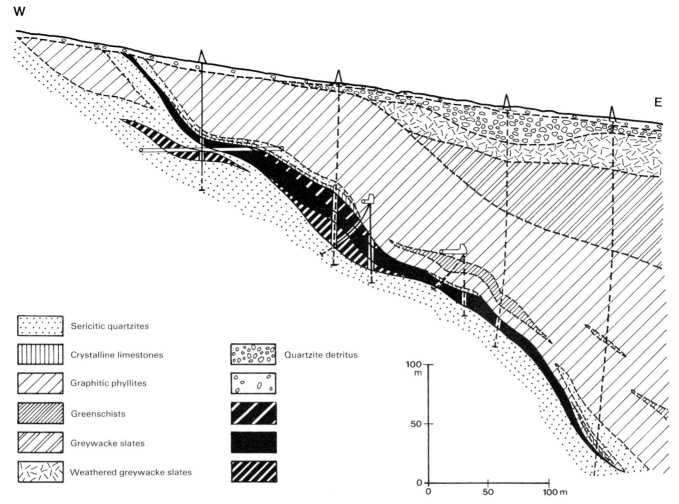

Fig. 8 *Section across Zlaté Hory East deposit of Cu–Pb–Zn ores*

two types—copper ores (Zlaté Hory South and Hornické skály) with sulphides relatively rich in Se and poor in Ag and polymetallic ores (Zlaté Hory East and Zlaté Hory West) with sulphides poor in Se and rich in Ag or Au (Zlaté Hory West). The geochemical study of individual deposits did not show any significant differences: thus, earlier and later types of mineralization[41] are assumed to have been derived from the same source.

Economic interest is currently focused on the monometallic Cu ore in the Zlaté Hory South deposit, where the stratiform chalcopyrite mineralization in chloritic quartzites and chloritic schists and the quartz–chalcopyrite ore veins are being explored. The complex types of ores in the Zlaté Hory East and Zlaté Hory West deposit are being prepared for mining. Present exploration is being concentrated on seeking blind orebodies beneath the Upper Devonian–Lower Carboniferous series developed in the 'Culm facies' of the Nízký Jeseník Mountains.

Several hypotheses exist in regard to the origin of the ores. An epigenetic hypothesis was emphasized by Janečka and Skácel[42] and syngenetic hypotheses have repeatedly been advocated by Havelka.[43] A polygenetic concept was put forward by Pouba.[11]

Horní Benešov stratiform Pb–Zn deposit
Genetically, the Horní Benešov deposit (Fig. 9) of lead, zinc and barite in Silesia (East Sudeten) is one of the most interesting of Variscan stratiform deposits. It is emplaced in the Devonian rocks that crop out from beneath the Carboniferous sediments in the Nízký Jeseník Mountains. As with many other small lead and zinc deposits in Silesia, the exploitation of the Horní Benešov deposit started no later than the second half of the thirteenth century. Since 1949 the deposit has been explored by drilling and underground working and low-grade Pb–Zn ores and sometimes barite have been selectively mined. New ore reserves justified the construction of a new modern shaft and dressing plant.

The deposit is situated in a very sharp fingerlike anticline of Devonian rocks that penetrate the Lower Carboniferous (Culm). A stratigraphic and also tectonic disharmony exists between the two systems. The Devonian rocks consist of shales and the products of

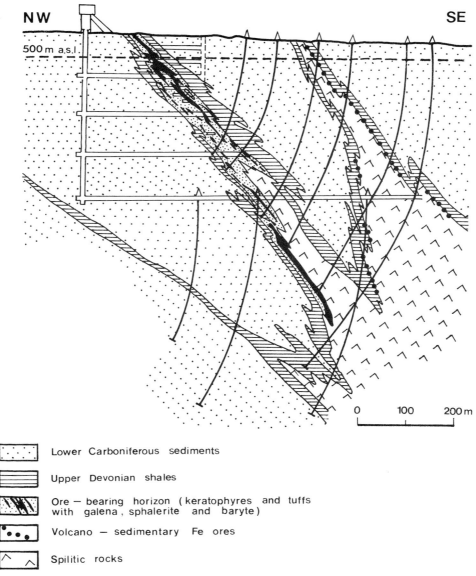

Fig. 9 *Section across Horní Benešov stratiform deposit of Pb–Zn ores*

spilite-keratophyre submarine volcanism of Eifelian–Givetian age. Faunal evidence (trilobites, etc.) of Eifelian age was found in shales and limestones that form intercalations in volcanic rocks. The volcanic complex consists of different varieties of diabases, diabase porphyrites and spilite porphyrites. Different spilites and pyroclastics were described by Barth,[44] Fojt[45] and others. Acid volcanic rocks are represented by quartz-keratophyres and their tuffs. Some of the keratophyres rich in feldspars have been considered to be metasomatic rocks.[46] Spilite-keratophyres can be classified as weilburgites in some places. The whole volcanic complex is partly overlain by organo-detrital limestones of Givetian and Lower Frasnian age. The Famennian is represented by tuffaceous shales with black cherts and graphitic shales with thin limestone intercalations.

The contact between the Devonian and Lower Carboniferous (Culm) strata is discordant owing to complicated disharmonic folding and to longitudinal faults that accompany the narrow anticlines (Šternberk–Horní Benešov zone). The Culm beds are represented by grey shales and greywackes or conglomerates. Near Nové Těchanovice and other places the Culm slates are exploited as roofing slates.

The mineralization in the Horní Benešov ore district is known from two main Devonian anticlines: the underlying (western) anticline is the carrier of stratiform Pb–Zn mineralization; the eastern contains syngenetic submarine hydrothermal iron ores of the Lahn–Dill type. Other accompanying mineralized structures have the form of feather or of *en-échelon* systems.

The Pb–Zn ores take the form of fine-grained impregnations in sericitic keratophyric tuffs, in quartz-keratophyres, calcareous shales and limestones. The economic parts of the deposit consist of numerous strata-bound lenses. The main orebody extends over a

1500-m length in a NNW–SSE direction with a dip of about 45°ESE.

The mineral assemblage is composed of pyrite, galena and sphalerite. Galena forms medium-grained aggregates associated locally with barite and massive layers of pyrite. Very fine-grained grey barite from the Horni Benešov deposit is similar to that from the Meggen deposit in West Germany, which is situated in a similar geological unit. The origin of the barite is considered to be metasomatic. Galena, rich in silver, very often occurs near the boundaries of massive barite with sericitic shales. Because of tectonic deformation the grains of galena in the massive layers form parallel bands that bend round the sphalerite grains.

Sphalerite occurs as fine-grained impregnations in sericitic shales, where it has a brown-yellow colour. Other minerals include tetrahedrite, chalcopyrite, arsenopyrite, bornite, chalcocite, covellite and supergene minerals. Quartz is widespread in much of the ore and becomes more abundant with depth, and barite decreases in the same direction. The absence of iron-rich sphalerites indicates a low-temperature origin, as does the high content of mercury in the ore. Several types of sphalerite ore are also rich in cadmium.

In the lower part of the deposit cockade ore occurs in which potassium feldspars are interbanded with sulphides. Thus, it is suggested that the ore components were deposited from hydrothermal solutions related to the last stages of submarine volcanic activity. This is in agreement with the recognition of the pre-kinematic and pre-metamorphic origin of the ore and the spatial relationship to acid submarine volcanics (quartz-keratophyres) of Devonian age.[47–50]

Variscan hydrothermal deposits

Jílové Au deposit

The gold-bearing quartz veins of the Jílové deposit (Fig. 2) have been known for almost 800 years and during this period the ore veins have been mined and abandoned many times. The last stoppage was in 1969, shortly before the increase in the gold price.

The gold-bearing quartz veins are situated in the Central Bohemian Proterozoic complex of effusive and intrusive rocks (termed the Jílové zone) near the boundary with the Central Bohemian pluton. The ore veins, bearing predominantly NNE, are very simple in composition. The main mass of quartz originated after the deposition of carbonates connected with the pyritization of the country rocks. Gold appeared mainly towards the end of the next phase of mineral deposition, which contains chalcopyrite, arsenopyrite, meneghinite, bournonite, galena and small quantities of tellurides of Bi and other metals. The last phase gave rise to calcite with sporadic pyrite and marcasite. The trace elements show a zonal distribution. W, Mo, Te and Bi occur predominantly in the southern part and Ag, As, Cu, Pb and Sb increase towards the north.[51]

From their structural nature and gold contents three types of deposit may be distinguished: (1) the ore veins (Šlojíř, Tobola, Kocour), which represent mineralized thrust zones, have a medium dip to the SSE: these ore veins are up to 1 m thick with a gold content up to 10 g t^{-1}; (2) stockworks (near Bohuliby) of quartz–pyrite veinlets with a diameter of up to 8 m and 3–4 g t^{-1} of gold in the ore, which are situated in the lamprophyres and diorite porphyrites; and (3) impregnations and smaller stockworks situated in the Klobásy ore zone near the margin of an intrusive rock complex, which form a large but low-grade ore reserve (2 g t^{-1}).

The country rocks of spilite-keratophyre form an anticlinal structure that plunges NNE. The volcanic formation plunges gently under the Proterozoic shales. The ore veins do not cross the boundary between the volcanic and sedimentary complexes and are mainly emplaced in the central part of the volcanics. The Proterozoic rocks are slightly metamorphosed and partly affected by the Variscan granodiorite and quartz-diorite intrusions that crop out in the eastern part of the Jílové zone. Variscan dykes commonly fill the WNW transverse faults. It may be assumed that the Variscan granitoids are responsible for the mineralization in the Jílové ore district. On the other hand, sporadic stratiform polymetallic ores were also found in the Proterozoic volcanics and these seem to be syngenetic. Thus, both Proterozoic and Variscan mineralization may have occurred.

Příbram Ag–Pb–Zn vein deposit

Several hydrothermal vein deposits around the Central Bohemian pluton belong to the Variscan post-orogenic magmatism (Fig. 2). The quartz veins at Jílové, Krásná Hora, Libčice, Kašperské Hory and Roudný are gold-bearing, but none is exploited at present. The rocks of the Central Bohemian pluton, represented by biotite–granodiorite, contain the Vrančice polymetallic vein deposit. Because of the higher silver content and the presence of copper (chalcocite, bornite) in the zinc ore (red sphalerite and very rare willemite), the deposit is being exploited in spite of its small dimensions. In some respects the ore of this deposit is similar to that of the Příbram district, which is situated about 10 km to the northwest. The lead–zinc mineralization in Příbram that was mined until 1978 represents the deeper part of the veins; at higher levels the veins were silver-rich. The upper part of the deposit was exploited in the Middle Ages, but successful mining reached high points at the end of the nineteenth century and after the second world war. Five shafts in the Příbram district are more than 1500 m deep and exploitation faced economic problems. The depth of 1000 m was attained in the Vojtěch shaft in 1875 for the first time in European mining history. At present the deepest shaft is the Prokop (1579 m with 41 levels).

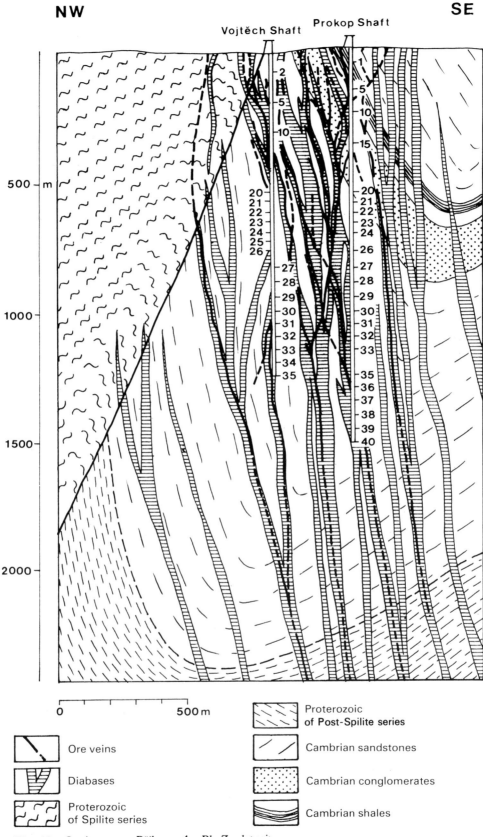

Fig. 10 *Section across Příbram Ag–Pb–Zn deposit*

The Příbram ore district (Fig. 10) is situated along a marked fault that separates the Cambrian clastic formation from the Proterozoic series. This fault, called the 'Clay Fault', is a reverse fault that brings the

Proterozoic over a syncline in the Cambrian. The ore veins are feather structures associated with the Clay Fault. They accompany diabase dykes and form a similar structural pattern. The Clay Fault trends northeast and has a steep northwest dip, the ore veins striking north and having a variable, dominantly easterly dip. There are two other northeast faults in the vicinity of Příbram, i.e. the Dědov Fault and the Dubenec–Druhlice Fault (which control the uranium mineralization). The Příbram ore district consists of the historic Březové Hory ore field and the newly opened Bohutín ore field. The uranium deposits to the east of Příbram have been described by Mirovský and co-workers,[52] Petroš[53] and others. Deep mining in the Bohutín deposit revealed an intrusion that consists predominantly of quartz-diorite, which contains some ore veins. This magmatic body is considered to be one of the differentiates of the Central Bohemian pluton.

The historic part of the Příbram district has been mined since the thirteenth century and there is a very complicated system of workings beneath the town of Příbram. The main mines at present in operation are the Vojtěch, the Anna and the Prokop. The main concentration of ore veins is in the Cambrian syncline—very few veins cross the Clay Fault and penetrate the Proterozoic block. The ore veins in the Cambrian have many branches, the vein system becoming simpler with increasing depth. Simple veins having a northerly trend include the Hlavní, Vojtěch, Matka Boží, Ševčín, Václav and Ležatá veins.

The vein filling is very complicated both from a mineralogical and structural point of view. There are many mineral generations and, thus, the mineralization is classified as polyascendent.[54] The tectonic movements that occurred during the mineralization processes influenced the distribution of minerals and gave rise to the ore shoots. The typical 'Dürrerz' (Krušek in Czech), representing a complex intergrowth of quartz, siderite, pyrite, sphalerite of the first generation, galena, boulangerite, etc., forms the main ore type at greater depth. The next stage carries siderite with sphalerite of the second generation and chalcopyrite. The third and fourth stages are characterized by carbonates.

Vertical zoning is apparent in the rich development of silver minerals in the upper level (pyrargyrite, stephanite, diaphorite, and many others) and an increase of galena and sphalerite downwards. Sphalerites of both generations contain Cd, Mn, Ge and a variable amount of In. Galena is almost always silver-bearing. Today on the deepest levels (38–41) the ore is often diluted by barren quartz.

The Bohutín deposit is in the southern part of the Příbram district and is in many respects similar to that of the Březové Hory ore field, which is situated to the north. The most significant veins are the Klement vein (north–south, vertical) and the Řimbaba vein (strike, northwest; dip, southeast). The polymetallic veins are spatially connected with diabase dykes that cross the Cambrian sediments, but the Klement vein penetrates the quartz-diorite.

According to Píša,[55] the polymetallic mineralization originated during four stages: (1) galena–sphalerite, (2) galena–sphalerite–sulphoantimonides, (3) stibnite and (4) carbonates. There were more than ten pulses of mineralization and the zonal distribution of the individual monoascendent generations is tectonically controlled. The ascent of ore-bearing hydrothermal solutions may have been along the Clay Fault zone. The Clay Fault zone itself is, however, always barren.

Judging from the geological position of the Příbram ore deposit and its paragenesis we can postulate the dependence of the hydrothermal solutions on granitic magmatism. High contents of siderite have, however, encouraged some workers to suggest other sources for the carbonates. The carbonate rocks in the Proterozoic series could be the source of this material.[56]

Kutná Hora Ag–Pb–Zn vein deposit
The Kutná Hora ore district (Fig. 11) belongs to the typical Variscan polymetallic mineralization in the Bohemian Massif, characterized by supergene silver enrichment in the uppermost part of the veins. The primary mineral assemblage and the vertical distribution of some ore minerals in the Kutná Hora ore veins exhibit a striking similarity to the famous Freiberg deposit in Saxony, where pyrrhotite and arsenopyrite increase with depth at the expense of pyrite and Pb–Zn minerals.[57]

According to historical data, the exploitation of silver-rich ores started during the thirteenth century, but some indications suggest still earlier mining activity. This opinion is supported mainly by the earlier existence of a silver coinage in the vicinity of this mining centre and also by the nature of the workings. The historic importance of mining in Kutná Hora is also evident in the Kutná Hora code of mining law, which is one of the oldest in Europe.

The Kutná Hora ore district consists of a system of parallel ore veins and ore zones associated with faults in gneisses and migmatites of the Kutná Hora crystalline complex. This complex belongs to the northern periphery of the Moldanubian core, which is strongly folded. It consists of biotite–muscovite gneisses, kyanite–garnet–mica schists and various migmatites with a distinct alkaline metasomatism. Intercalations of amphibolites, eclogites and serpentinites connected with leptynites are common.

The north–south ore veins dip steeply (60–80°) and show a characteristic mineral zoning. The depositional temperature of the ores increased considerably from south to north. Sb, Pb and Zn minerals (sulphides and sulphosalts) occur in the southern part,[58] Pb, Ag and Zn sulphides in the middle part and Cu, As, Fe and Zn minerals (sulphides) in the northern part of the ore district. A certain amount of Sn is found in the north.

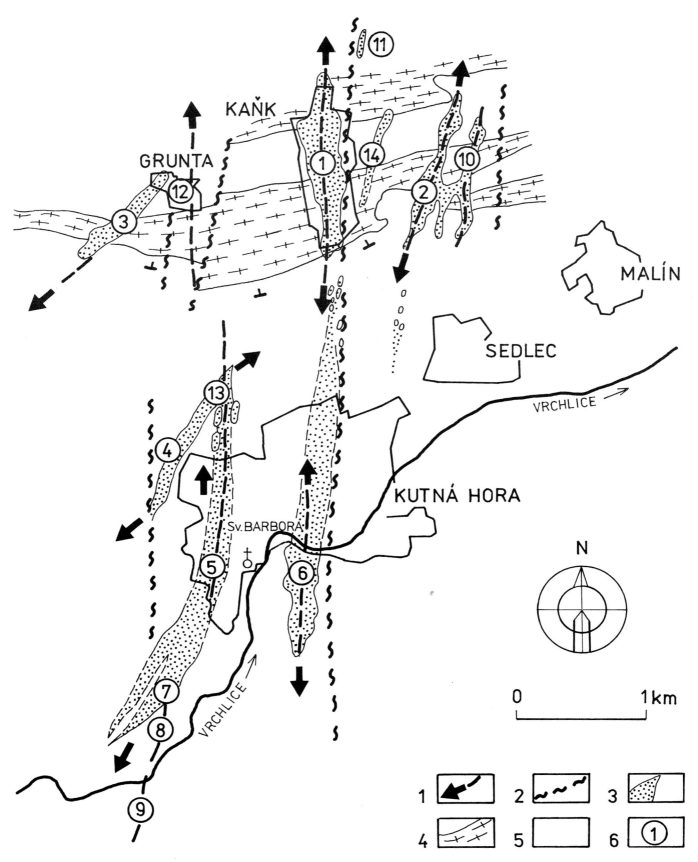

Fig. 11 Schematic map of distribution of ore veins and zoning of vein minerals of Kutná Hora Ag–Pb–Zn deposit. (1, direction of zoning; 2, deep faults; 3, old dumps; 4, migmatite; 5, gneiss; 6, ore shoots, 1–15)

The amount of In and Fe in sphalerites increases to the north and downwards. The ore is very irregularly distributed in the veins and it is usually brecciated. The ore often forms lenses and massive shoots up to 15 m thick.

Intensively mined in the Middle Ages, the central part of the ore district consists mainly of the Osel and Grejf zones. These zones were very rich in silver to a depth of several hundred metres and have been interpreted as epithermal mineralization. Besides native silver and silver sulphosalts, the main source of silver was silver-bearing galena and freibergite.

The Rejská vein is mesothermal with some hypothermal parageneses. The sphalerite–pyrrhotite assemblage of the Turkaň and Staročeská zones, which are currently being mined, originated at relatively high temperatures. Dark sphalerites in this ore have 11–15% Fe, 0·26–0·57% Cd, 0·22–1·05% Mn and 0·02–0·11% In. In addition to sphalerite, pyrrhotite, galena and subordinate stannite and chalcopyrite are present in the commercial ores. These ore veins have strong wallrock alteration, mainly sericitization, silicification and pyritization.

Owing to the physical and chemical character of the altered rocks and of the ore itself, several geochemical and geophysical methods can be used in ore prospecting. Prospecting is currently being directed to the areas where the northern part of the ore district is covered by Cretaceous and Quaternary sediments.

Jáchymov vein deposit with Ag–Bi–Co–Ni–U ores

The Jáchymov ore district (Figs. 2 and 12), discovered in 1516, was during the Middle Ages one of the most significant silver-producing centres in Bohemia. After the discovery of radium in Jáchymov pitchblende at the end of the nineteenth century, this deposit was for a long time the only world producer of radium. After the second world war the Jáchymov uranium ores were intensively exploited. At present the Jáchymov mines are closed and the underground radioactive waters are used for medical purposes in the Jáchymov Spa.

The silver- and uranium-bearing veins are situated in the mantle of the Karlovy Vary (Carlsbad) granite massif. The mantle rocks consist of different varieties of phyllites and micaschists. The Karlovy Vary granite is composed of older standard granite (normal granite) and younger autometamorphic granite. The autometamorphic granite forms a blind body at a depth of 500–800 m beneath the surface in the mineralized area. Numerous dykes of granite por-

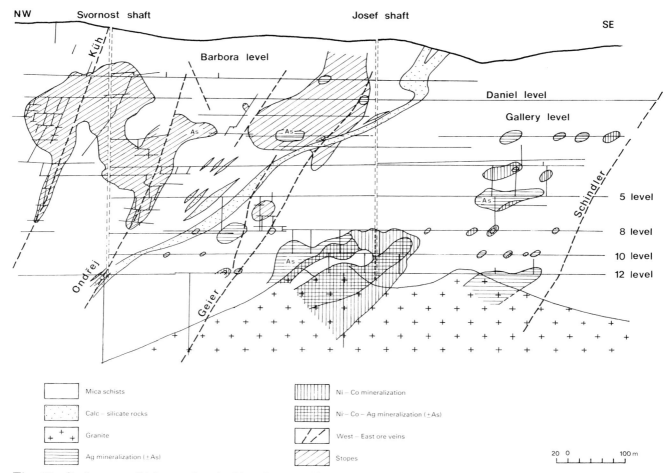

Fig. 12 *Section across Jáchymov deposit. After Chrt et al.*[18]

phyry, lamprophyre and aplite that pre-date the ore veins penetrated the mantle rocks. There are also pre-ore basalt dykes, which are members of the Tertiary basic volcanism, the centre of which lies in the Doupovské Hory Mountains (several kilometres east of Jáchymov).

The ore district contains about 180 ore veins of varying significance. The majority of ore veins strike north or east. At their intersections more important ore shoots were formed. Commonly, the veins were as much as 1 km long and very thin—usually 30–40 cm. The thickness of the ore veins increased occasionally to 5 m. High-grade ore was concentrated where the veins crossed porphyry dykes or other favourable rocks. At the boundary with granite the ore veins became barren and only some of the thicker veins continued into the granite body.

In the ores several phases of mineralization can be distinguished. According to Mrňa and Pavlů,[59] the following succession of phases can be discerned: (1) pre-ore phase with ferruginous quartz, (2) earlier sulphide phase with pyrite, galena, sphalerite, arsenopyrite and chalcopyrite, (3) uranium phase with pitchblende and carbonates, (4) arsenide phase with Co–Ni arsenides, native silver and native bismuth, (5) sulphoarsenide phase with proustite, stephanite, pyrargyrite, argentite, stibnite and realgar and (6) younger sulphide phase with calcite, tennantite and realgar in some places.

With each succeeding phase the volume of minerals deposited decreased, as did the number of veins reached by solutions depositing the younger phases. It is difficult to determine whether the hydrothermal solutions that deposited the younger phases were of primary or secondary origin, i.e. whether they originated from magmas or by mobilization and regeneration of older mineral associations. Several remobilizations seem to have occurred, judging from the age determinations on uraninites.[14,60]

Horní Slavkov–Krásno Sn–W deposits

The tin–tungsten deposits of Horní Slavkov (Schlaggenwald) and Krásno (Schönfeld) (Figs. 2 and 13) are typical greisen deposits situated in the apical part of a granite batholith. They belong to the Karlovy Vary (Carlsbad) granite massif, the continuation of which is the Eibenstock granite body (GDR). The uppermost part of the batholith seems to be deeply denuded, with the exception of lateral cupolas that are situated near the town of Horní Slavkov.

Mining activity was started in the thirteenth century in this area and since that time tin, and later tungsten, have been mined intermittently to the present day. The upper parts of the deposits were very rich, and one of them, the Huber stock, supplied more than 10 000 tonne of metallic tin. Cassiterite crystals from its ore shoots (which also contain topaz) are well known in numerous mineralogical collections.

The Schnöd stock is a similar greisen body that represents a massive greisen accumulation with the same mineral assemblage—cassiterite and topaz. Both deposits are situated between Horní Slavkov and Krásno, where several hidden cupolas occur on the same northeast-trending granite ridge. Some of them have been partly eroded.

The greisen mineralization originated from the replacement of lithium albite–granite. The following vertical ore distribution was found in underground

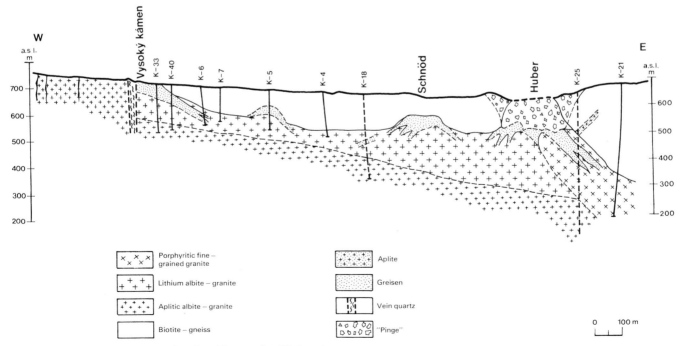

Fig. 13 *Section across Horní Slavkov–Krásno Sn–W deposit*

workings. The upper part of the orebody consists of topaz greisens with quartz, topaz and ore minerals—cassiterite, wolframite and sulphides (chalcopyrite, pyrite, etc.). In the lower part of the greisenized granite protolithionite and zinnwaldite are very common, in addition to quartz and topaz. The vertical extent of the greisen zone is about 150 m.

Between the greisen bodies and barren granite there are several transitional zones, formed of albite–granite, lithium albite–granite with K-feldspar, topaz and Li biotite. Feldspars, topaz and some Li-mica were replaced by kaolinite, sericite, quartz, fluorite and other minerals in the altered zones.

Aplitic albite–granite is known to attain a vertical extent of up to 200 m in the Vysoký Kámen deposit. This leucocratic granite is suitable for the ceramic and glass industry and is quarried. (Albite prevails slightly over K-feldspar, the total sum of feldspars being about 65%.) The lithium albite–granite is topped by the aplitic albite–granite. These rocks show a close genetic relationship of alkali metasomatism to greisenization.

Besides the greisens the mineralization is also present in ore veins in the southern part of the Horní Slavkov–Krásno ore district. The 'Gelnavská' and 'Marie' are the main ore veins and they are nearly 1 km long and 1 m thick. The mineral assemblage comprises more than fifty minerals, such as topaz, wolframite, cassiterite, chalcopyrite, molybdenite, sphalerite, bismuthite and fluorite. The earliest members of the mineral assemblage include topaz, zinnwaldite, cassiterite, beryl and apatite. In the second stage sulphides with fluorite and apatite appear, the third stage being represented by feldspars.

Current interest is focused on the greisen ores, the cassiterite and wolframite content of which is economic, though the very fine-grained nature of the cassiterite ore poses technological problems.

Cínovec (Zinnwald) Sn–W–Li deposit

The tin–tungsten ore deposits in the Krušné Hory Mountains (Figs. 2 and 14) are closely associated spatially with small granite cupolas of lithium albite–granite, which intruded the metamorphic or magmatic rocks of the Saxonian–Thuringian zone of the Variscan orogen. The Cínovec deposit is situated in a granite body, which, in turn, intruded a body of Permian quartz porphyry. Accordingly, this deposit belongs to the younger Variscan granite of the Bohemian Massif.

Historical accounts of tin mining come from the fourteenth century and since that time tin and later tungsten (since 1879) have been mined. The ore is extracted underground and treated by gravity to yield a mixed Sn–W concentrate. The old classic mine will be replaced by a new mine in the 'Southern deposit', which was discovered recently by surface drilling and underground exploration.

The granite massif of Cínovec consists of four main granite types.[61] The top of the granite cupola is built up of albitized medium-grained zinnwaldite granite underlain by porphyritic zinnwaldite microgranite, coarse-grained porphyritic granite and porphyritic biotite microgranite. All the granite varieties belong to the complex of younger tin-bearing granites. The granite rocks and part of their mantle rocks were affected by secondary alteration, the most significant being the greisenization, which was ore-bearing in some places. The granite rocks form the apical part of the Krušné Hory granite batholith, which is mostly hidden and was found by geophysical investigations. In the western part of the Krušné Hory Mountains, the barren granite ('Berggranite') is exposed through erosion to a deeper level.

The Cínovec Sn–W–Li deposit is situated on the Czechoslovak frontier about 12 km NNE of Teplice

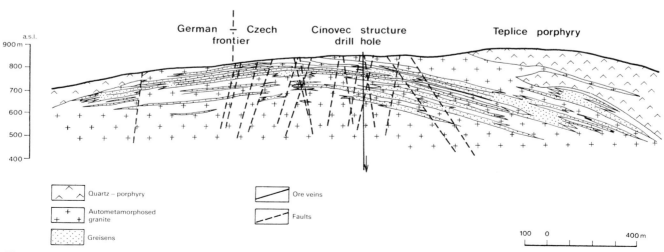

Fig. 14 *Section across Cínovec Sn–W deposit*

Spa. Its western part extends into the territory of the German Democratic Republic (Zinnwald). The ore is associated with a small granite cupola that intruded the Teplice quartz porphyry of Permian age. The granite contact descends from an elliptically shaped outcrop at a moderate angle under the quartz porphyry mantle. The size of the outcrop is approximately 1·5 km × 0·5 km. There is a very regular vein system in the granite body. Flat veins form regular dome structures that are very typical of the Cínovec deposit. They simulate the surface of the granite body, which also controls the pegmatite-like rim called 'Stockscheider'. The flat (sub-horizontal) veins vary in their thickness from 10 to 150 cm. The ore consists mainly of quartz, zinnwaldite, topaz (pycnite), K-feldspar, fluorite, wolframite, scheelite and cassiterite. The wallrocks of the flat veins are strongly greisenized. The main zone of discrete greisen bodies is about 60 m beneath the vein zone. The greisen lenses vary from several cm to about 15–25 m and are made up of quartz, zinnwaldite, topaz and clay minerals.

The distribution of minerals in the flat veins locally shows a distinctive zoning. Quartz is the oldest member of the minerals in the flat veins and in the steep fissures, which mainly penetrate the quartz porphyry near its boundary with the western granite. Greisenization took place in the second mineralization stage along with the replacement of quartz in the veins. It was followed by the crystallization of hydrothermal feldspar of the adularia type and, subsequently, by sulphide mineralization, which principally affected the steep veins. Feldspar metasomatism gave rise to vein textures closely resembling pegmatites.[62]

As a result of extensive exploration in recent years a new deposit (the 'Southern deposit') was found. It consists of greisen lenses the composition of which is identical with those of the central district (cassiterite, wolframite and scheelite and greisen minerals). The ore grade is low (Sn:W ratio, 5:1). Mineralization started with a period of alkalization, followed by greisenization, and was terminated by final alkalization. Two greisenization cycles have been determined in some places. The first—tungsten-bearing—is characterized by zinnwaldite and the second—tin-bearing—by muscovite. These new ore reserves will ensure the continuation of mining activity in the Cínovec ore district.

Regenerated deposits of outer part of Bohemian Massif

Harrachov F–Pb vein deposit

The Harrachov deposit (Figs. 2 and 15) lies in the Krkonoše granite, which itself occurs in the northern part of the Bohemian Massif near the Czechoslovak–Polish frontier. The deposit consists of fluorite–barite veins with galena in their deeper levels. Metallogeni-

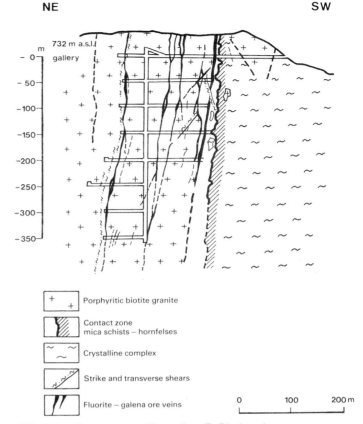

Fig. 15 *Section across Harrachov F–Pb deposit*

cally the deposit belongs to the West Sudetic sub-province.[63,64,72] The veins, which occupy a shear zone and its offsets, dip almost vertically. They form a system of faults along the tectonic boundary of the Krkonoše granite massif and its mantle. The granite, Variscan in age, caused the contact metamorphism of the early Palaeozoic and Proterozoic crystalline schists.[65] The vein system occurs in the biotite–granite (the Oldřich, Čendova, Nová, U skoku veins) and at its contact (the Křemenný val vein). The vein system is about 1 km long and is known to a depth of 400 m. The thickness of veins varies from 1 to 8 m. The ore consists of a banded fluorite–quartz–barite assemblage, the galena content increasing downwards. Chalcopyrite, pyrite, sphalerite and opals form accessories. There are several generations of fluorite and two generations of barite in the upper part of the deposit. At greater depth galena occurs as the main member of the sulphide mineral association.

With the exception of small veinlets of second-generation barite, the ore veins are accompanied by distinctive zones of hydrothermal alteration. The alteration particularly affects the pinkish K-feldspar and yellowish plagioclase. The chemical and mineralogical changes due to this alteration were studied by Deb.[66] In the altered feldspars the concentrations of illite, dickite and montmorillonite were determined and their temperature of origin (around 350°C) was established. A much lower temperature was determined by the study of fluid inclusions in fluorite (180–210°C, according to Benešová and Čadek[67]). The vein mineral association shows indications of regeneration. Young opal occurs sporadically and the age determination of galena[60] (190 and 200 m.y.) has revealed that the sulphide mineralization was much later than the Variscan granitization. Thus, a combination of Variscan and Alpine metallogeny may be supposed. The combination of the Variscan and Alpine geological activity is typical of the external metallogenic units of the Bohemian Massif.[12]

The present exploitation of the Harrachov deposit is concentrated chiefly on fluorite-rich veins, but the deeper blocks of ore reserves show the possibility of economic exploitation of the fluorite–galena ore in the future.

Post-Variscan (Mesozoic–Caenozoic) deposits

Křemže lateritic Ni deposit

The ultrabasic massifs in the Moldanubicum, especially those in its southern and eastern areas (southern Bohemia, western Moravia), were often subjected to intensive lateritization during the Cretaceous and Tertiary periods. The serpentinites, in particular, were altered into different types of laterites and other types of strongly weathered rocks. Many of them were originally mined for iron ores in the Middle Ages, but only a few have been mined as nickel ores (New Caledonia type). They contain 0·5–1% Ni as Mg–Ni hydrosilicates (garnierite, népouite, schuchardtite, etc.).[68] Owing to the low grade of the ore and the low ore reserves the deposits are considered at present as uneconomic.

One of the best known Ni deposits of this type is the Křemže deposit near Český Krumlov in southern Bohemia. This deposit was explored by drill-holes and opened up experimentally as an open-pit at the close of the second world war and just afterwards. According to Čech and Koutek,[69] the garnierite nickel ore forms an irregular body in the weathered serpentinite. Ores with Ni content >1% are concentrated in a lens about 6 m thick beneath a red laterite cover. The ore consists of greenish soil surrounded by grey-greenish weathered serpentine with about 0·5% Ni. The altered serpentinite lies at a depth of about 20 m. There are many lumps and blocks of silicophytes, opals and chalcedony in the ore, which lower its quality. A similar situation can be observed in the Moravian Ni deposits in the eastern part of the Moldanubicum.

Non-metallic mineral deposits of Bohemian Massif

Glassmaking raw materials and kaolin have always been the traditional non-metallics produced in the Bohemian Massif (Fig. 16). These materials are the basis of an important industry that produces porcelain and the world-famous glass that are important Bohemian exports. Also exported are different types of refractory clays and claystones for the production of refractory ware and these are therefore mined in an amount that exceeds domestic requirements.

Historically, the earliest worked non-metallic raw material of Bohemia is graphite, which was exploited by the ancient Celts and used in the production of loam pottery. The output of graphite is currently being increased to cover foreign as well as domestic demands. Other non-metallic raw materials, such as fluorite, diatomite, bentonite, gypsum, etc., are being mined in relatively large amounts; their output has been greatly increased in recent times. Naturally, the greatest attention has been focused on deposits of building materials, which have a growth in output higher than that of any other raw materials.

Economics of non-metallic mineral deposits

Apart from coal production, the extraction of non-metallic raw materials is undoubtedly the most important sector of the Czechoslovak mining industry. Non-metallic raw materials production is about 125 000 000 t per year. In Bohemia metal ores are extracted from about fifteen mines, whereas non-metallic raw materials are being exploited in about 500 open-pits and mines and their number is growing steadily. The output of building, glass and ceramic raw materials is increasing significantly. Since 1948 the output of building materials has risen approximately tenfold and that of glass and ceramic materials about six times. The production of the Czech Socialist Republic constitutes about 65% of the output of the Czechoslovak Socialist Republic as a whole. A considerable part of this production is exported, both to socialist and capitalist countries. The output of building materials per capita population is comparable with that of other developed states of continental Europe (France, Belgium, Austria, etc.). Czechoslovakia's output of glass and refractory materials far exceeds the average output of other European states. About 50% of glass production goes to art and ordinary glassware. Refractory materials make up about 66% and building ceramics about 26% of the output of the ceramic industry.

The production of Bohemian glass—a traditional export—is rising steadily. In contrast, the output of the classical Karlovy Vary (Carlsbad) porcelain has dropped compared with the production of building ceramics—in particular, of wall and floor tiles.

Geological conditions governing formation of the non-metallic raw material deposits

The origin of the bulk of the non-metallic deposits of the Bohemian Massif, i.e. mainly the deposits of ceramic, glass and building materials, was governed by the denudation and weathering of the old basement.

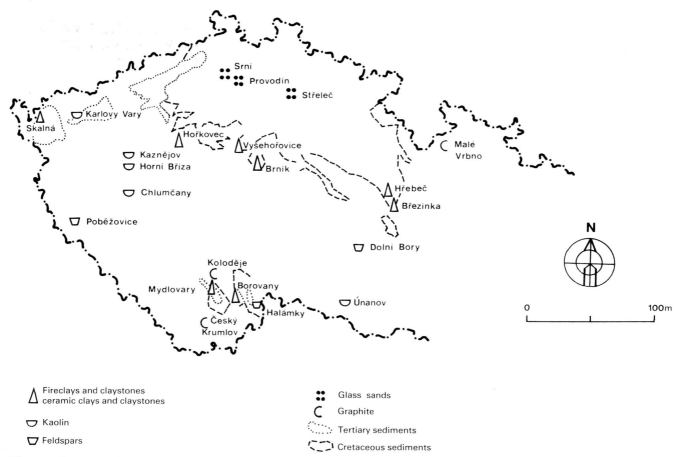

Fig. 16 *Non-metallic deposits in Bohemian Massif (fluorite deposits shown in Fig. 18 omitted)*

Granites and crystalline schists succumbed to the effects of erosion and intensive weathering of kaolinic type at the end of the Variscan orogeny, at the beginning of the Mesozoic, prior to the deposition of Cretaceous sediments, and during the Tertiary.

The effects of surface processes of different ages are often combined and it is difficult to decide which period was most important in the formation of many deposits. During all three periods of extreme tropical climate transportation and grading of weathered rocks took place and sedimentary deposits of kaolinite and deposits of refractory diagenetic quartzites originated. In the Cretaceous the separation of clay fractions from quartz attained such a degree of perfection that important deposits of very pure glass sands were formed in addition to high-grade deposits of kaolinitic clays. The volcanic Tertiary tuffs and tuffites gave rise to montmorillonite sediments and bentonite deposits.

The deposits of primary non-metallic raw materials within the crystalline basement were formed by metamorphic and magmatic processes. Of greatest importance among the metamorphic deposits are those of graphite in the Moldanubicum of the core of the Bohemian Massif and in the Moravo-Silesian unit that adjoins the latter in the east. Believed to be Precambrian in age, these deposits are mostly associated with crystalline limestones, which occur in a series with a great variety of rock types.

The vein deposits of non-metallic materials are grouped around Variscan and Tertiary intrusions. The fluorite and barite deposits are associated with Variscan granites and Tertiary alkaline volcanics. Variscan pegmatites, feldspar granitoids and feldspar sands of Quaternary age yield feldspars for Bohemia's ceramic and glass industry. Petrurgical* raw materials are concentrated in Tertiary volcanic zones.

Graphite deposits
There are three regions with graphite deposits in the Bohemian Massif. Two of them lie in the Moldanubicum of southern Bohemia and one in northern Moravia (Fig. 16). The deposits of southern Bohemia are emplaced in a series of biotite paragneisses with sillimanite, which enclose intercalations of quartzites, amphibolites, marbles and graphite.[70] The graphite beds are strongly folded or segmented into lenses. The cores of the lenses contain macrocrystalline graphite ('flinc') and form the most valuable part of the deposits.

* Basaltic rocks that are melted and cast into acid-resistant pipes and tiles.

The deposits of northern Moravia, situated in the Staré Město series, are made up of micaschists with intercalations of marbles and of graphite-rich schists that locally contain pyrite.

Until recently, the Domoradice graphite deposit has been the main deposit of 'flinc' graphite in *southern Bohemia*. This formed a layer between marbles and calc-silicate rocks ('erlan') accompanied by amphibolites; its thickness was up to 6 m and the C content is more than 23%. The Český Krumlov graphite deposit forms a complex of lenses with a thickness of 5–7 m and a length of 200–300 m. Macrocrystalline floccose graphite is present in the deposit.

The Koloděje deposit has a lower C content, is made up of three lenses formed tectonically from a single layer and occurs in biotite and biotite–sillimanite gneisses. The lenses are, on average, 60 m thick and contain several layers of minable graphite of a thickness of 0·5–16·0 m. The graphite layers locally enclose crystalline limestones.

Dressed by flotation and chemically, the refined graphites of southern Bohemia attain a purity of 99·5%.

Consisting only of microcrystalline graphite with C contents up to 39%, the graphite deposits of *northern Moravia* lie in graphite schists or in graphitic limestones that belong to the Staré Město micaschist series. The graphite schists contain an admixture of pyrite. The two types occur in a formation with a dome-like structure. This graphite can only be used in the iron and steel industry for foundry facing.

The Malé Vrbno graphite deposit (thickness, 0·5–4 m) is emplaced in crystalline graphitic limestones that are locally dolomitic in character. The Velké Vrbo graphite deposit (Fig. 17) forms a tectonically complicated synclinal structure. The deposit is 26 m thick and is being quarried. A continuation of the deposit and reserves for the future have been found in a recent survey.[71]

All the Bohemian and Moravian graphite deposits are metamorphosed deposits of sedimentary origin. This is evidenced by their position in paragneisses and marbles and also by their high phosphorus and vanadium content.

Feldspar deposits

Feldspars for glass and ceramic industries come from three types of deposits in the Bohemian Massif—pegmatites, feldspar-rich granitoids and feldspathic arkoses and sands.

Pegmatites are mined in southwest Bohemia near Poběžovice and Domažlice, in western Bohemia near Přílezy and in the Českomoravská vrchovina Highland near Dolní Bory. Near Poběžovice and Domažlice the basic massif is pierced by pegmatite veins with a thickness of up to 10 m and a length of up to 1 km. Veins with a predominant potassium component are mined. In Přílezy similar pegmatites with low Fe_2O_3 content are mined and used in the production of porcelain. The pegmatite deposits of Dolní Bory, which show a great variability, have been exploited since the end of the last century. These deposits are now mined underground.

Leucocratic granitoids are currently mined as a

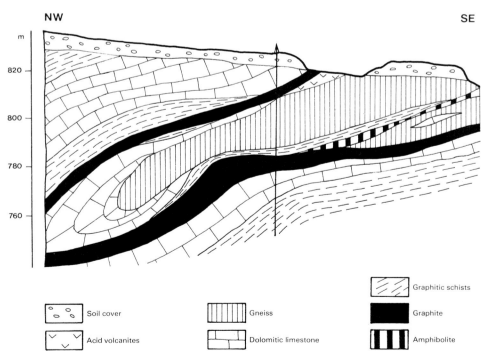

Fig. 17 *Section across Konstantin graphite deposit in northern Moravia. After Harazim*[71]

feldspathic raw material in the region of the Karlovy Vary pluton near Krásno–Vysoký Kámen. Exploitation of this material is concentrated in the feldspar-rich portions of aplitic granite.

Kaolinized arkoses are mined for kaolin near Chlumčany. Quartz sand with feldspars is washed out from the raw material. This raw material is used in the production of floor tiles.

Feldspathic sands occur mainly in the region of Tertiary and Quaternary sedimentary basins in southern Bohemia. Pleistocene feldspathic sands are found, in particular, in the valley of the Lužnice river (Halámky).

Fluorite deposits
With the exception of the Javorka deposit, situated near the tectonic line that delimits the Železné Hory Mountains in central Bohemia, all the important vein deposits of fluorite lie in the area of the Krušné Hory Mountains and the West Sudeten Mountains (Fig. 18). Also in this group is the Harrachov fluorite deposit with galena (see earlier).

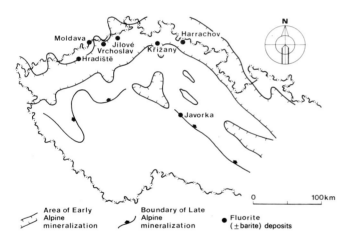

Fig. 18 *Regions of Alpine mineralization with fluorite and barite deposits in Bohemian Massif. Modified from Chrt and Reichmann.*[63,64] (*It is evident from distribution of deposits that their origin or remobilization was controlled by Alpine tectogenesis (see also Fig. 16)*)

The Moldava, Hradiště and Jílové deposits are mined in the Krušné Hory Mountains. These deposits were described in detail by Reichmann and Sattran.[72] The Vrchoslav deposit (now closed) near Teplice lies close to the contact of the biotite orthogneisses with the Teplice quartz porphyry. The deposit consists of eight thin veins (thickness about 50 cm), which have a relatively simple composition—fluorite and quartz, locally containing finely dispersed hematite and Cu sulphides. Opal is scarce. The fluorite forms a banded structure with quartz. The deposit is believed to be post-Variscan in age. The Moldava deposit is situated close to the frontier with the GDR. Consisting of the Josef fluorite–barite vein, the thinner Papoušek veins and the less important New vein of barite, this deposit ranks among the most important fluorite deposits in the Krušné Hory Mountains. The Josef vein is up to 5 m thick and >700 m long, and its barite–fluorite mineralization is very complex. Quartz is the earliest mineral, followed by fluorite with barite, and sulphides are the youngest members of the paragenetic sequence. The highest-grade portions of the vein contain as much as 75% CaF_2. The main Josef vein is nearly vertical and shows a decrease of barite and increase of fluorite with depth.

The Hradiště deposit lies near the town of Chomutov in a complex of gneisses and micaschists of the Krušné Hory crystalline mass. The deposit consists of lenses made up of barite, fluorite and quartz, accompanied by strong hematitization or hematite veins. Downwards, the lenses are poorer in fluorite, whereas quartz increases. Fluorite-richer portions (>60–80% CaF_2) are developed only in short segments. A relatively high S content (3–5%) is characteristic of the deposit.

The Jílové deposit near Děčín is the only fluorite vein deposit to be emplaced in Cretaceous sandstones. The veins are up to 8 m thick, but their fluorite content (20–80%) is extremely variable. Regular banding is characteristic of this fluorite.

The Křížany deposit situated near the Lužice Fault in northern Bohemia consists of a system of fluorite–barite veins where carbonates appear in addition to quartz. The veins are up to 7 m thick, but they are mostly very limited in length and their economic value is therefore problematical.

The Javorka deposit (Fig. 19) was recently discovered during a geological survey near an important

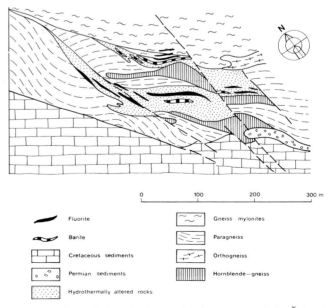

Fig. 19 *Geological map of Javorka fluorite deposit in Železné Hory Mountains. After Jurák*[81]

tectonic line that controls the western margin of the Železné Hory Mountains. It is composed of metasomatic bodies emplaced in crystalline limestones that form intercalations in gneisses. The metasomatism was accompanied by silicification of the limestones and fluorite mineralization. Another deposit—Javorka-Běstvina—is made up of a system of short fluorite veins. The veins originated as a system that accompanied the Železné Hory Fault. They show an irregular content of fluorite and barite.

Kaolin deposits

The kaolin deposits of the Bohemian Massif originated from the weathering of feldspar-rich rocks. Kaolinization mainly affected granites (in the Karlovy Vary area), Carboniferous arkoses and arkosic sandstones (in the region of the Plzeň basin and Podbořany) and feldspar-rich gneisses (in the Kadaň and Znojmo area). With the exception of a small kaolin occurrence near mineral water springs at Kyselka in the Karlovy Vary area, all the deposits formed as a result of hot and humid climates during the Carboniferous, Mesozoic and Tertiary. The distribution of kaolin is thus related to the origin of coal (black coal in the Plzeň basin and lignite in the other areas), but climate is the sole factor to account for this relationship. Climatic conditions favourable for the origin of kaolin in the Bohemian Massif prevailed in the Westphalian and Stephanian, the Jurassic and the Lower Cretaceous, and in the Palaeogene (in places up to the Middle Miocene).[73]

With the exception of some of the Karlovy Vary deposits the kaolinite of all the Bohemian deposits is close to the triclinic type. The quality of the kaolin—in particular, its iron and titanium content—is governed by the composition of the source rock. The bulk of the Czech deposits contain non-plastic kaolin suitable for the production of paper. It is only kaolin from the Karlovy Vary area that is suitable for the production of fine porcelain.

Since the end of the eighteenth century the Karlovy Vary deposits have yielded raw material for the production of porcelain. This kaolin has come from a kaolinized portion of the Karlovy Vary granite, which underlies an area of 80 km². The high-grade upper layer of the kaolinized portion, of a thickness of 20–30 m, is mined in the Sedlec, Bohemia, Podlesí, Božičany, Jimlíkov, Hájek and other deposits. The deposits are in places covered by clays and sands with intercalations of quartzites. The sands are overlain by a brown coal seam of Upper Oligocene age and, locally, by a younger coal-bearing formation of Upper Miocene age. The extraction of kaolinite is increasing, mainly for export.[74]

The *Kadaň deposit* originated through the kaolinization of gneisses composed of 40% potassium feldspar. Kaolinization attains a depth of about 10 m. To a depth of about 4 m, however, the upper part of the deposit is

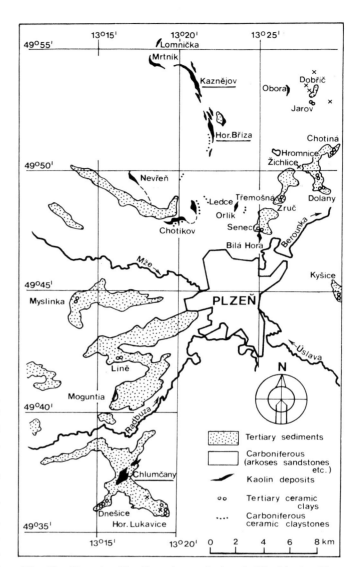

Fig. 20 *Deposits of kaolin and ceramic clays in Plzeň basin. After Konta and Pouba*[74]

usually depreciated by Fe hydroxides that infiltrate into the deposit from the overlying Tertiary tuffs. Kaolinization of Carboniferous and Tertiary age has been proved in the deposit.

The Permo-Carboniferous arkosic sandstones are the parent rock of the *Podbořany deposits*. High-grade kaolin occurs in the upper part (about 30 m thick) of the kaolin profile. Downwards kaolinite decreases, whereas montmorillonite, micas, feldspars and Fe hydroxides increase.

Some twenty deposits of kaolin suitable for the paper and ceramic industries have been known in the *Plzeň basin* (Fig. 20). All the deposits originated from Carboniferous arkoses and the most important—the Chlumčany, the Horní Bříza (Fig. 21) and the Kaznějov—are mined in huge open-pits. The known kaolin reserves are believed to be sufficient for about 70 years of production.[75]

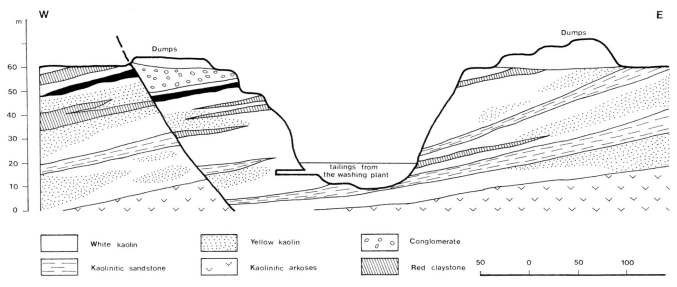

Fig. 21 Section across Horní Bříza kaolin deposit in Plzeň basin. After Kužvart et al.[73]

The kaolin deposits are represented by large lenses of kaolinized arkoses 2–3 km long and 100–300 m wide. Kaolinization reaches a depth of more than 100 m, but the deposits are only minable to a depth of 20–80 m. In the raw material kaolinite completely prevails over illite, often forming pseudomorphs after feldspars. Kaolinite clays in the form of intercalations reveal that the kaolinization is Carboniferous in age, but Tertiary kaolinization is also found to have exerted an influence before the deposition of the Miocene sediments that in places overlie the deposits (e.g. Horní Bříza).

The kaolin of the Plzeň basin is not plastic enough for porcelain production and is mainly used in the production of floor and wall tiles and in the paper industry.

Two types of rocks that gave rise to kaolin occur near *Znojmo* (southern Moravia). These are the granites to granodiorites of the Dyje massif and the orthogneiss of Bíteš type. As a result of post-Miocene denudation the upper kaolin-richer portions of presumably Palaeogene age are not preserved in kaolin profiles. Nevertheless, the kaolin-poorer portions of kaolinized gneisses and granodiorites are mined for ceramic purposes.

All the Bohemian and Moravian kaolins mined show a minimum clay content of 15–20% and are treated in hydrocyclones. The highest-grade Karlovy Vary kaolins have about 1·2% Fe_2O_3 + TiO_2 and show outstanding physical properties for porcelain production. Other types of kaolin are used in various ceramic plants, paper mills and elsewhere.

Deposits of clays and claystones

Among numerous kinds of clays and claystones in the Bohemian Massif, the Carboniferous claystones and the Cretaceous and Tertiary clays are of great importance. They are used in the production of various kinds of earthenware and refractory ware. The Bohemian Massif is very rich in these raw materials, which are intensively mined for domestic use and, in particular, for export.

The refractory claystones of the *Kladno–Rakovník basin*, which accompany the Lubenec coal seam, occur in the upper part of the Carboniferous at the margin of the basin. Their 10-m thickness increases several fold towards the centre of the basin. Commercial deposits are exploited in several mining districts that extend mostly northeast of Rakovník. The claystones often contain coal pigment and an admixture of tuffaceous material. They are mined underground or in large open-pits (the deposits around Hořkovec). In sites where the quality of the claystones is very high the overburden can be several times thicker than the deposit without its economic viability being affected. The raw material is burnt and the resulting fireclay is used in metallurgy, the glass and ceramics industries, etc. The non-refractory claystones are used in the production of red tiles.

Numerous deposits of Cenomanian refractory clays have been known from *Moravia* and also from *eastern Bohemia*. These are fresh-water sediments with three cycles that contain clay deposits. Their overburden mostly consists of glauconite sandstones of marine Cenomanian and of Turonian and Coniacian rocks. The most important deposits are in the Cretaceous beds in the neighbourhood of the Permo-Carboniferous Boskovice Furrow (Březina, Malonín, Hřebeč, Kunštát, etc.). Numerous types of claystones are mined selectively in these deposits and serve for the production of various refractory materials.

The deposits of fresh-water Cretaceous clays (Cenomanian) that occur around *Prague* consist of three layers at the margin of the Cretaceous. The basal layer presumably originated from redeposition of kaolinized Permian clays. The higher layers frequently contain coal pigment. The most important deposits are near Černý Kostelec (Brník) and Vyšehořovice. Claystones with a higher amount of fine-grained quartz are found in a similar geological setting in the *Louny* area. This raw material needs dressing, so mining in other areas is preferred. All the Cretaceous deposits of clays and claystones have been described in detail by Vachtl.[76,77,78]

The clay deposits of *southern Bohemia* lie in Upper Cretaceous and Tertiary sediments that overlie the Moldanubian crystalline mass. Cretaceous beds (Senonian) contain deposits of medium refractory clays. Variable types of raw materials, locally including diatomaceous clays, are found in the Tertiary (Oligocene and Miocene). Clays are mined in several places (Borovany, Ledenice, Mydlovary, etc.) in the Budějovice and Třeboň basins.

Clay deposits are also mined around Písek, Plzeň and elsewhere in small isolated Tertiary basins. (In the surroundings of Plzeň mining has lately been concentrated on the large Kyšice deposit.)

All the clay deposits in western Bohemia are grouped along the Krušné Hory Fault. During the Tertiary this furrow was filled with coal-bearing sediments and clays that constitute deposits of important ceramic raw materials. The best-quality clays lie near Skalná and Nová Ves in the Vildštejn series (Skalná = Vildštejn) in the *Cheb basin*. These are clays of various technological properties that are suitable for the production of different kinds of ceramics. Some of them are very rich in organic components (e.g. the Nero clay). The bulk of the clays form an important export.

The clay deposits in the *Sokolov basin* are older and are associated with the Josef coal seam. A harmful admixture of pyrite is present locally and their content of organic components displays a higher variability. Some of the clays have high Ti content owing to a tuffaceous admixture rich in TiO_2. A further influence of volcanic activity is also perceptible in other types of clays found in the basins in the piedmont of the Krušné Hory Mountains. These clays contain montmorillonite and are mined as bentonites near Braňany, Stránce and elsewhere.

Deposits of glass sands, quartz and dinas quartzites
All the glass sands that are currently mined in the Bohemian Massif are Cretaceous in age (Turonian, Coniacian). The Střeleč, Srní and Provodín deposits fully cover the needs of Bohemia's glass industry and about 50% of Bohemia's foundries. The Cretaceous sandstones of these localities are washed to give glass sands. The Střeleč deposit yields sands of high purity and suitable granulometric properties. These can be used in the production of technical glass and of Bohemian crystal glass. High-quality raw materials for glassmaking, are obtained from other deposits after suitable dressing.

Tertiary sands are used for ceramics purposes. Vein quartz is mined only for the production of quartz glass.

As a result of the secondary silicification of Tertiary and Cretaceous sands and sandstones dinas* quartzites have been formed and these are mined in the basins southeast of the Krušné Hory Mountains.

References

1 **Pošepný F.** Das Goldvorkommen Böhmens und der Nachbarländer. *Arch. prakt. Geol.*, **II**, 1895, 1–480.
2 **Pošepný F.** The genesis of ore-deposits. *Trans. Am. Inst. Min. Engrs*, **23**, 1893, 197–369.
3 **Stille H.** *Grundfragen der vergleichenden Tektonik* (Berlin: Borntraeger, 1924), 443 p.
4 **Svoboda J. et al.** *Regional geology of Czechoslovakia, part I: The Bohemian Massif* (Prague: Czechoslovak Academy of Sciences, 1966), 668 p.
5 **Zoubek V.** Remarques sur le Precambrian des zones mobiles de l'Europe centrale et occidentale. In *Precambrian des zones mobiles de l'Europe* (Prague: Geol. ustav ČSAV, 1973), 33–62.
6 **Chaloupský J.** Precambrian tectogenesis of the Bohemian Massif. *Geol. Rdsch.*, **67**, 1978, 72–90.
7 **Šmejkal V.** Absolutní stáří některých granitoidů a metamorfitů Českého masívu stanovené kalium-argonovou metodou. *Věst. ústřed. Úst. geol.*, **35**, 1960, 441–9.
8 **Šmejkal V.** Absolutní stáří některých metamorfovaných hornin Českého masívu stanovené kalium-argonovou metodou (II.část). *Sb. geol. Věd. G*, **4**, 1964, 121–36.
9 **Šmejkal V.** Anomalous potassium–argon absolute ages of the migmatitic cordierite gneisses from the SW part of the Czech Massif. *Krystalinikum*, **3**, 1965, 157–62.
10 **Dvořák J.** Problem concerning the northeastern closure of the Variscan orogen. *Neues Jb. Geol. Paläont. Mh.*, 1973, 449–54.
11 **Pouba Z.** Polymagmatic zoning of ore deposits on a regional scale. In *Symposium: Problems of postmagmatic ore deposition, Prague, 1963* Kutina J. ed. (Prague: Geological Survey of Czechoslovakia at the Czechoslovak Academy of Sciences, 1963), vol. I, 52–7.
12 **Pouba Z.** On some causes of the repetition of mineralization in ore regions and ore deposits of the Czech Massif. In *Symposium: Problems of postmagmatic ore deposition, Prague, 1965* Štemprok M. ed. (Prague: Geological Survey of Czechoslovakia at the Czechoslovak Academy of Sciences, 1965), vol. II, 82–91.
13 **Losert J. and Chrt J.** Neoidic platform metallogenetic province in the metallogenetic region of the Bohemian Massif. *Věst. ústřed. Úst. geol.*, **37**, 1962, 201–4. (Czech text, English summary)
14 **Legierski J. and Vaněček M.** Lead isotopic composition of some galenas from the Bohemian Massif. *Acta Univ. Carol., Geol.*, **2**, 1967, 153–72.
15 **Sattran V. and Klomínský J.** Petrometallogenic series of igneous rocks and endogenous ore deposits in the Czechoslo-

---
* Ganister-like rock.

vak part of the Bohemian Massif. *Sb. geol. Věd, LG*, **12**, 1970, 65–154.
16 **Pouba Z.** The relationship between the volcanism and the mineragenesis in the Bohemian Massif. In *Paleovolcanites of the Bohemian Massif: collected papers* (Prague: Universita Karlova, 1966), 249–55.
17 **Sattran V. et al.** Problems of metallogeny of the Bohemian Massif. *Sb. geol. Věd, LG*, **8**, 1966, 7–112.
18 **Chrt J. Bolduan H. et al.** Die postmagmatische Mineralisation des Westteils der Böhmischen Masse. *Sb. geol. Věd, LG*, **8**, 1966, 113–92.
19 **Pouba Z.** The history of mineralization in the Czechoslovak part of the Bohemian Massif. *Čas. Miner. Geol.*, **13**, no. 2 1968, 133–40.
20 **Klomínský J. and Bernard J. H.** Segmentation of the Bohemian Massif in the light of Variscan magmatism and metallogeny. *Věst. ústřed. Úst. geol.*, **49**, 1974, 149–57.
21 **Ilavský J. and Sattran V.** Sketch of metallogeny of Czechoslovakia. *Mineralia slov.*, **8**, no. 3 1976, 193–288. (Slovak text, English summary)
22 **Ilavský J. et al.** *Metallogenetic map of Czechoslovakia 1:1 000 000* (Prague: Ústřední ústav geologický, 1965).
23 **Svoboda J. and Fiala F.** The geological and lithological conditions of the Algonkian in the region between Telčice and Týnec nad Labem in the Železné hory Mts. *Sb. ústřed. Úst. geol.*, **23**, 1957, 475–531. (Czech text, English summary)
24 **Pouba Z.** Pre-Cambrian banded magmatite ores of the Desná Dome. *Sb. geol. Věd, LG*, **12**, 1970, 7–64.
25 **Skácel J. and Vosyka S.** Přehled geologie Rychlebských hor. *Rychlebské hory-sborník prací. Krajské nakl.*, Ostrava, 1959, 9–54.
26 **Mísař Z. et al.** *The Ransko gabbro-peridotite massif and its mineralization (Czechoslovakia)* (Prague: Universita Karlova, 1974), 215 p.
27 **Bernard J. H. Klomínský J. and Polanský J.** Relationship between the metallogeny and the gravimetric pattern of the Bohemian Massif. *Věst. ústřed. Úst. geol.*, **51**, 1976, 65–74.
28 **Bernard J. H.** Beitrag zum Vergleich der Entwicklung von Mineralassoziationen auf den Erzgängen von Kutná Hora und Freiberg (Sachsen). *Věst. ústřed. Úst. geol.*, **36**, no. 4 1961, 289–91.
29 **Marek F.** Estimated age of the Ransko basic massif based on palaeomagnetic data. *Věst. ústřed. Úst. geol.*, **45**, 1970, 99–102. (Czech text, English summary)
30 **Žák L.** Sphalerite and apatite from Chvaletice (E. Bohemia). *Bull. int. Acad. tchéque Sci.*, **12**, 1952, 1–12.
31 **Žák L.** Metamorphic paragenesis of the manganese–pyrite horizon in the Železné hory Mts (Bohemia). *Čas. Miner. Geol.*, **17**, 1972, 345–56.
32 **Hoffman V.** Geochemical characteristics of Algonkian rocks and manganese–pyritic ore deposits in the NW branch of the Železné hory Mts (Central Bohemia). *Sb. Úst. nerost. Sur. v Kutné Hoře*, 1962, 121–57. (Czech text, English summary)
33 **Šmejkal V. et al.** Isotopic composition of sulphur of some sedimentary and endogenous sulphides in the Bohemian Massif. *Čas. Miner. Geol.*, **19**, no. 3 1974, 225–38.
34 **Svoboda J. and Prantl F.** Die sedimentären Eisenerze des Barrandiens. I. Das Erzrevier von Zdice. *Geotechnica*, Prague no. 19, 1955, I–X (107 p.) (Czech text, German summary)
35 **Petránek J.** Sedimentary iron ore deposit near Mníšek and Komárov. *Studie ČSAV*, **6**, 1975, 1–82. (Czech text, English summary)
36 **Petránek J.** Sedimentary iron ores of the Lahn–Dill type: a new concept of their origin. *Věst. ústřed. Úst. geol.*, **51**, 1976, 203–7.
37 **Skácel J.** Die Eisenerzlagerstätten des mährisch-schlesichen Devons. *Čs. Akad. Věd, Ř. mat. přír. Věd*, **76**, no. 11 1966.
38 **Škvor V.** Lagerstätte Tisová. *Sb. ústřed. Úst. geol.*, **24**, 1957, 389–447. (Czech text, German summary)
39 **Burdová P. Kříbek B. and Pertold Z.** Organic carbon in the Cu-deposit of Tisová (Krušné hory Mts). *Čas. Miner. Geol.*, **24**, no. 1 1979, 71–6.
40 **Pertold Z. and Constantinides D.** Mineralization of the Zlaté Hory-South deposit in structural-metamorphic development of host rocks. *Acta Univ. Carol.-Geol.*, no. 2 1974, 155–63.
41 **Hoffman V. Pertold Z. and Trdlička Z.** Geochemistry of sulphides from Zlaté Hory deposit. *Sbor. Geol. Věd, TG*, **14**, 1977, 7–65. (Czech text, English summary)
42 **Janečka J. and Skácel J.** Impregnační ložiska barevných kovů v Jeseníkách. *Sb. vlastivěd. úst.*, **A IV**, Olomouc, 1956–58, 1959, 89–100.
43 **Havelka J.** Über die Erscheinungen der regionalen Metamorphose auf Grund des Studiums von Makrotexturen in sulfidischer Vererzung von Kieslagerstätten im Gebiet von Zlaté Hory-West. *Sb. věd. Prací Vys. Šk. báň. v Ostravě*, **9**, no. 4 1963, 531–48.
44 **Barth V.** The Devonian volcanism of the zone Šternberk–Horní Benešov in the Low Jeseník Mountains. *Acta Univ. palackianae Olomoucensis*, Prague, **1**, 1960, 1–131. (Czech text, English summary)
45 **Fojt B.** Keratophyre rocks of the kies deposits in the Jeseníky area. In *Paleovolcanites of the Bohemian Massif* (Prague: Universita Karlova, 1960), 107–14.
46 **Scharm B. and Kühn P.** Křemičité horniny z kyzového polymetalického ložiska Horní Benešov II. *Korelace proteroz. a paleoz. stratiform. lož.* 3, Praha, 1975, 91–6.
47 **Tomšík J.** Die Erzlagerstätte bei Horní Benešov. *Acta Mus. Silesiae*, A, **8**, 1959, 73–94. (Czech text, German summary)
48 **Havelka J. Palas M. and Scharm B.** Zur Entstehung Kieslagerstätten im Devon des Jeseníky-Gebirges. *Ber. geol. Ges. DDR, geol. Wiss.*, **9**, 1964, 507–13.
49 **Scharm B.** Ke genezi kyzových polymetalických ložisek s ohledem na zrudnění u Horního Benešova. Doctoral thesis, Mining Academy VŠB, Ostrava, 1967.
50 **Palas M.** Zur Frage der komagmatischen Beziehung zwischen den Eisen- und Kieslagerstätten im Jeseník Gebirge. *Freiberger ForschHft.* C230, 1968, 259–64.
51 **Morávek P.** Ore-deposits structure and mineralization of the Jílové gold mining district. *Sb. geol. Věd, LG*, **13**, 1971, 7–170. (Czech text, English summary)
52 **Mirovský J. Pluskal O. and Kolář M.** Stručný přehled o geologii čs. ložisek uranu a výskytu uranové mineralizace. *Symposium Hornická Příbram ve vědě a technice, sekce geol.*, Příbram, 1969, 1–33.
53 **Petroš R.** Hloubkový vývoj hlavních strukturních prvků Příbramského uranového ložiska. *Symposium Hornická Příbram ve vědě a technice*, G 2, Příbram, 1970, 1–14.
54 **Kutina J.** The distinguishing of the monoascendent and polyascendent origin of associated minerals in the study of the zoning of the Příbram ore veins. Reference 11, 200–6.
55 **Píša M.** Minerogenesis of the Pb–Zn deposit at Bohutín near Příbram. *Sb. geol. Věd, LG*, **7**, 1966.
56 **Kutina J. and Tělupil A.** The vertical extent of ore

deposition in Příbram, Czechoslovakia. In *Problems of hydrothermal ore deposition* **Pouba Z. and Štemprok M.** eds (Stuttgart: Schweizerbart'sche, 1970), 187–93. (*Int. Union geol. Sci. Series A* no. 2)

57 **Bernard J. H.** Parallelisation der Evolution von Mineralassoziationen an den Erzgängen in Kutná Hora (Böhmen) und Freiberg (Sachsen). *Tschermaks miner. petrogr. Mitt.*, 3rd series, **8**, 1963, 406–16.

58 **Koutek J. and Kutina J.** Rudní žíly a jejich minerály ve štole Sv. Ant. Paduánského u Kutné Hory. *Sb. Stát. geol. Úst. ČSR*, **16**, no. 2 1944, 783–97.

59 **Mrňa E. and Pavlů D.** Lagerstätten der Ag–Bi–Co–Ni–As Formation im Böhmischen Massiv. *Sb. geol. Věd, Ř. LG*, **9**, 1967, 7–104.

60 **Legierski J.** Model ages and isotopic composition of ore leads of the Bohemian Massif. *Čas. Miner. Geol.*, **18**, no. 1 1973, 1–24.

61 **Štemprok M.** Petrografie a vertikální rozsah mineralizace v cínovecké žulové klenbě. (Petrology and the vertical extent of mineralization in the Cínovec (Zinnwald) granite cupola.) *Sb. geol. Věd, LG*, **5**, 1965, 1–106.

62 **Štemprok M.** On the transition of pegmatites into tin, tungsten and molybdenum-bearing veins. *Sbor. geol. Věd, LG*, **2**, 1964, 7–38.

63 **Chrt J. and Reichmann F.** Ložiska fluoritu v ČSSR. *Geol. Průzk.*, **10**, no. 7/8 1968, 278–82.

64 **Reichmann F.** Situace na těžených ložiskách fluoritu v Českém masívu a jejich geologická problematika. *Symposium Hornická Příbram ve vědě a technice*, G 2, Příbram, 1970, 1–58.

65 **Chaloupský J.** Geologisch-petrographische Verhältnisse im Isertal zwischen Harrachov und Dolní Rokytnice (Isergebirge). *Sb. ústřed. Úst. geol.*, **24**, no. 1 1957, 189–236.

66 **Deb S. K.** Nature of rock-alteration in the Harrachov deposit, Riesengebirge, Czechoslovakia. *J. geochem. Soc. India, Patna*, **1**, 1966, 1–6.

67 **Benešová Z. and Čadek J.** Temperature of homogenization of inclusions in fluorite deposits of Czechoslovakia. *Abstracts, third Int. COFFI Symposium on Fluid Inclusions, Montreal*, 1972.

68 **Slánský E.** A contribution to the knowledge of the Ni-hydrosilicates from Křemže in southern Bohemia. *Acta Univ. Carol., Geol.*, **1**, no. 1, 1955, 1–28. (Czech text, English summary)

69 **Čech V. and Koutek J.** La géologie et la génèse des gisements de minerais de fer et de nickel près de Křemže dans le Sud de la Bohême. *Sb. Stát. geol. Úst., Prague*, **13**, 1946, 1–22. (Czech text, French summary)

70 **Tichý L.** Jihočeská grafitová oblast—průzkumné a těžebné perspektivy. *Konference: Nerostné surovinové zdroje, VŠB Ostrava*, 1975.

71 **Harazim S.** Průzkum grafitu ve velkovrbenské oblasti. *Geol. Průzk.*, **18**, no. 10 1976, 296–9.

72 **Reichmann F. and Sattran V.** Les gîtes filoniens à F, Ba (+Pb, Zn, Ag, Cu) de Moldava et de Harrachov (Tchecoslovaquie). *Bull. BRGM II*, no. 3 1982, 309–15.

73 **Kužvart M.** comp. Kaolin deposits of Czechoslovakia. *Rep. 23rd Int. geol. Congr., Prague 1968*, vol. 15, 1969, 47–73.

74 **Konta J. and Pouba Z.** *Second conference on clay mineralogy and petrography, Prague: Excursion guide* (Prague: Charles University, 1961), 1–48.

75 **Kužvart M. Neužil J. Pešek J. and Šindelář J.** Origin and age of kaolin deposits in the Plzeň basin. *Sb. geol. Věd, Prague*, **17**, 1972, 125–94.

76 **Vachtl J.** The deposits of Cenomanian claystones in Bohemia and Moravia I. *Geotechnica, Prague* no. 10, 1950, 1–72. (Czech text, English summary)

77 **Vachtl J.** Lagerstätten der cenomanischen Tonsteine in Böhmen und Mähren. III. Teil. *Geotechnica, Prague* no. 31, 1962, 1–103. (Czech text, German summary)

78 **Vachtl J.** Lagerstätten der cenomanischen Tonsteine in Böhmen und Mähren. IV. Teil. *Geotechnica, Prague* no. 32, 1968, 1–162. (Czech text, German summary)

79 **Aubouin J.** Propos sur les géosynclinaux. *Bull. Soc. géol. Fr.*, **7**, 1961, 629–728.

80 **Baumann L. Štemprok M. Tischendorf G. and Zoubek V.** Metallogeny of tin and tungsten in the Krušné Hory Erzgebirge. In *Symposium: MAWAM Pre-symposium excursion guide* (Prague: Geological Survey and Czechoslovak Academy of Sciences, 1974), 1–66.

81 **Jurák L.** Ložiska fluoritu Javorka. *Symposium Hornická Příbram ve vědě a technice*, G 5, Příbram, 1979, 1–13.

Mineral deposits of the Czechoslovak Carpathians

From the point of view of structure and geology the Western Carpathians can be included in the Alpine–Himalayan fold system. In Europe the system has been divided into super-provinces, provinces and belts.[7] Ilavský distinguished fold belts and non-folded areas with the character of median masses.[7] The Western Carpathians are in the Carpathian–Balkan fold belt and represent a separate metallogenic region. Recent work[3] shows that Eastern Slovakia at the end of the fault line of the Hornád River is a part of the Eastern Carpathians or even of the Ukrainian Carpathians.[7]

History of mining and geological research

In the first century B.C. the Celts founded the mining industry in the Western Carpathians, as was noted by Tacitus and documented by archaeological finds of metal products in Slovakia. Among the materials mined and utilized were iron ores in the form of gossans and iron deposits of various other types, cupriferous ores, salt and gold.[16]

Celtic mining traditions continued in Slavonic mining in the time of Great Moravia (seventh to ninth centuries A.D.). There are numerous archaeological finds of iron, bronze, copper and gold artifacts from that time in the more important ore districts of Slovakia—the Malé Karpaty Mountains, Inovec and Tribeč Mountains, the Nízke Tatry and the Vysoké Tatry Mountains, in the Vepor Mountains, the Spišsko-gemerské rudohorie Ore Mountains, the Štiavnické and the Kremnické pohorie Mountains. Kremnica was founded in 745 and Banská Štiavnica in 770.[16]

The Tartar invasion of Slovakia (1240–42) was followed by the colonization of all Slovakian mining districts by German immigrants supported by the Hungarian kings. The Germans gradually took over the mining industry, including its financing and the marketing of its products. To encourage the development of mining the mining centres were awarded various privileges: they were proclaimed free royal mining towns with their own mining rights, law courts, market rights, the right to develop trade and the sale of their products. They developed deposits of iron, copper, sulphur, silver, lead, gold, antimony and also, since ancient times, salt.

As early as the fourteenth century underground mining was practised at many deposits (e.g. Smolník, Banská Štiavnica, and in the vicinity of Banská Bystrica). The technology of mining was markedly improved by the introduction of gunpowder in 1627, which was used for the first time in Banská Štiavnica. In 1763 the first mining academy in Central Europe was established in Banská Štiavnica and secondary mining schools were founded in Dobšiná and Smolník. By the end of the eighteenth century the mining of Ni–Co ores at Dobšiná had commenced.

In the mid-eighteenth century Maria Therese forbade the use of wood for building, since it was necessary for the production of charcoal for metallurgical purposes. Since then the mining of building materials has developed—stone, sand, limestone, clays for brick production, etc.

In 1860–65 the production of Cu, Pb, Zn, Ni, Co and precious metals decreased in Slovakia because of the competition from overseas ores. On the other hand, the mining of iron ores (siderites, limonites), pyrite and coal increased as the iron industry developed. At the end of the nineteenth and the beginning of the twentieth centuries the mining of non-metalliferous resources (magnesite, talc, asbestos, barite, oil, gypsum) and of metals typical of the Western Carpathians (antimony, mercury) was well developed.

After 1945 there was a boom in mining, geological research and investigations of all types of ore and non-metalliferous resources, such as petrurgical basalt, perlite, bentonite, halloysite, kaolinite, diatomite, expandable shale, glass quartz, limnoquartzite, marble, travertine and, among fuels, lignite and natural gas. Among building materials (besides granitoid rocks), andesites, basalts, quartzites, dolomites, melaphyres, gravels, sands, loess, conglomerates, marls and limestones of high quality for the production of cement are used.

All mineral resources are the property of the State. The planning and building of specialized mining plants, metallurgical plants, geological research institutions, geophysical and prospecting organizations are supervised by the State.

From 1850 geological research in Slovakia was carried out by the Austrian–Hungarian Institute of Geology in Vienna and from 1868 by the Hungarian Institute of Geology in Budapest. After 1918, in the newly formed Czechoslovakia, geological research in Slovakia has been carried out by the State Institute of Geology in Prague. The Dionýz Štúr Institute of Geology was established in Bratislava in 1940. In 1952 the Department of Mineral Resources at the Faculty of Natural History of Comenius University in Bratislava and the Mining Technical University in Košice were founded in Slovakia. In addition, in the 1950s the Institute of Geology in the Slovak Academy of Sciences was established in Bratislava.

A wide variety of geological journals is published.

Some economic data on Slovak ore deposits

At present iron, copper, antimony, mercury, lead and zinc ores are mined in Slovakia. Among those non-metalliferous resources which are exploited are pyrite, magnesite, barite, talc, asbestos, gypsum, anhydrite, halite, halloysite, bentonite, glass quartz, perlite, petrurgical basalt, ceramic clays (kaolinitic), limestones and dolomites, decorative stones (travertines, limestones), building stones, gravel, sand, raw material for bricks, oil, natural gas, lignites and peat.

Table 1 surveys the output of the most important raw materials since the second world war and includes the contents of the recoverable components in the ores.

The Slovak contribution to the total State production of mineral raw materials is: iron ore, about 10%; Cu ore, 8%; Pb–Zn ore, 15%; antimony ore, 80–90%; and mercury, 100%. As regards non-metalliferous resources, Slovakia is responsible for the total national production of magnesite, barite, talc, gypsum–anhydrite, limestone, dolomite, building stone and raw materials for brickmaking. Pyrite, sulphur, asbestos, halite, glass quartz, ceramic clays, decorative stones, gravel and sands are imported from Bohemia or from abroad. Industrial plants to process other raw materials are under development (halloysite, bentonite, perlite, petrurgical basalt).

Geology and structural history

The Western Carpathians can be divided into seven structural-metallogenic zones of particular lithological-stratigraphical character. The individual zones differ in their tectonic history and in their types of ore deposit. The structural-metallogenic zones are aligned along the Carpathian Arc and from north to south are as indicated below (Figs. 1 and 2).

A—The zone of the Carpathian Foredeep, which is composed of Neogene sediments. Typical of the zone are deposits of oil, gas and, to some extent, of gypsum and anhydrite. The zone was affected by intensive Neoalpine–Savian and Villafranchian–Moldavian folding.

B—The Flysch zone, which is mostly composed of Palaeogene sediments, and partly of Cretaceous sediments. In places such volcanic rocks as teschenite and

Table 1 Annual production of ores, 1945–74, $t \times 10^3$. After Ilavský and co-workers[10]

Deposit	1945	1950	1955	1960	1965	1970	1974
Ferruginous ores							
Markušovce–Grétla	2·1	26·2	66·2	30·4	37·8	—	—
Hnilčík–Roztoky	—	—	—	—	8·0	26·2	—
Nálepkovo	—	—	—	23·9	26·3	—	—
Gelnica–Mária huta	3·7	67·0	96·0	45·2	—	—	—
Mlynky	1·7	66·9	113·5	49·4	—	—	—
Dobšiná	—	—	—	62·5	70·4	—	—
Vlachovo	—	—	—	37·2	30·6	61·2	25·9
Nižná Slaná	1·5	165·6	247·4	175·1	235·2	225·1	290·0
Smolník–Mária Snežná	—	—	—	9·4	15·2	14·8	—
Baňa Lucia–Poproč	29·4	81·4	83·5	113·8	74·0	—	—
Železník	12·5	176·4	221·9	112·2	17·8	—	—
Baňa Rákoš	—	—	—	118·3	—	—	—
Štítnik–Hrádok	—	—	—	0·9	2·3	1·1	—
Rožňavské–Bystré	—	—	—	49·0	31·9	40·7	20·1
Rožňava–Mních	—	—	—	43·0	55·5	38·2	51·5
Rožňava–Rudník	16·8	264·3	221·7	58·0	56·0	49·4	58·4
Rožňava–Bernardy	—	—	—	48·0	16·3	11·9	—
Rožňava–Sadlovská	—	—	—	28·0	60·2	59·5	97·1
Rožňava–Štefan	—	—	—	37·0	26·1	47·7	38·3
Drnava–Ignác	—	—	—	13·0	22·1	—	—
Drnava–Anton	—	—	—	59·0	29·5	54·5	—
Drnava–Štefan	—	120·0	142·0	11·5	—	—	—
Drnava–Dionýz	—	—	—	26·3	—	—	—
Drnava–Haraszt	—	—	—	12·0	3·2	—	—
Drnava–Stredná	—	—	—	14·0	2·0	—	—
Total	67·7	967·8	1192·2	1177·1	820·4	630·3	581·3
Complex ores—							
Fe–Cu–Ba–Hg–pyrite							
Rudňany Fe–Cu–Ba–Hg	31·3	246·0	561·4	559·7	680·0	861·0	872·2
Cu, %	—	—	—	—	0·856	0·136	0·121
BaSO$_4$, %	—	—	—	14·7	8·16	13·80	15·70
Hg, %	—	—	—	0·025	0·025	0·019	0·022
Markušovce–Gezwäng	—	—	—	—	8·0	26·2	—
Cu, %	—	—	—	—	0·90	0·92	—
Slovinky–Helcmanovce	—	—	90·0	152·6	197·5	227·1	249·5
Cu, %	—	0·92	0·97	0·87	0·73	0·82	0·80
Gelnica–Krížová	—	—	—	—	—	19·66	8·30
Cu, %	—	—	—	—	—	1·19	0·72
Smolník	0·5	1·06	72·0	162·1	157·5	153·8	145·1
Cu, %	—	—	—	—	0·30	0·38	0·34
S, %	36·0	34·0	8·0	7·0	6·3	5·5	4·8
Baňa Mária–Rožňava	—	—	18·0	87·8	75·8	78·2	48·7
Cu, %	—	—	0·68	0·57	0·53	0·58	0·80
Špania dolina	—	—	—	—	31·6	54·8	41·4
Cu, %	—	—	—	—	0·42	0·43	0·45
Banská Hodruša	—	—	20·0	29·8	41·6	48·3	54·0
Cu, %	—	—	0·52	0·62	0·86	0·79	0·86
Total	31·80	247·06	761·40	992·00	1192·00	1469·06	1419·20
Manganese ores							
Kišovce	}10·7	160·0	150·4	104·7	45·1	} 85·4	—
Švábovce			100·0	49·7	35·1		—
Mn, %	17	17	16·4	15·8	15·8	14·5	
Fe, %	3	3	3	3·4	3·1	3·8	
Total	10·7	160·0	250·40	154·40	80·20	85·4	

picrite occur. Fe mineralization (pelosiderites) in horizons of the Lower, Middle and Upper Cretaceous and up to the Eocene are characteristic of the zone.

C—The Klippen Belt is an extremely narrow but long and conspicuous zone. It consists of Mesozoic and Palaeogene complexes of variable composition with

Czechoslovakia

Table 1—*continued*

Deposit	1945	1950	1955	1960	1965	1970	1974
Gold–silver ores							
Banská Hodruša	—	9·0	—	—	—	—	—
Au, g t^{-1}	—	1·57	—	—	—	—	—
Ag, g t^{-1}	—	170·4	—	—	—	—	—
Kremnica	—	33·9	44·7	37·7	36·0	23·5	—
Au, g t^{-1}	—	2·51	2·74	2·59	2·84	3·46	—
Ag, g t^{-1}	—	4·33	6·41	11·92	9·07	10·11	—
Banská Štiavnica	8·0						
Au, g t^{-1}	2·75	—	—	—	—	—	—
Ag, g t^{-1}	21·95	—	—	—	—	—	—
Total	8·00	42·90	44·70	37·70	36·00	23·50	
Lead–zinc ores							
Banská Štiavnica	—	28·81	48·82	50·35	47·85	62·50	67·08
Pb, %	—	2·04	1·90	1·78	1·55	1·29	1·48
Zn, %	—	2·29	2·17	1·94	2·54	2·18	2·42
Total	—	28·81	48·82	50·35	47·85	62·50	67·08
Antimony ores							
Liptovská Dúbrava	1·00	11·30	19·50	28·70	34·30	30·80	26·50
Sb, %	2·55	4·93	3·35	2·34	1·98	2·06	1·71
Pezinok	5·8	—	14·70	16·60	17·10	28·60	26·90
Sb, %	?	—	2·15	2·36	2·15	1·91	1·85
Poproč	0·96	13·99	9·58	7·99	4·94	—	—
Sb, %	8·2	5·60	3·79	4·23	3·85	—	—
Čučma	0·70	9·89	—	—	—	—	—
Sb, %	3·20	2·86	—	—	—	—	—
Helcmanovce	—	—	—	1·35			
Total	8·46	35·18	43·78	54·64	56·34	59·40	53·40
Magnesites							
Hnúšťa	—	—	—	2·50	16·00	2·90	18·60
Ružiná	7·80	16·00	8·70	—	—	—	—
Podrečany	—	—	—	135·60	177·60	175·80	206·10
Burda–Poproč	—	17·40	31·60	57·50	92·90	95·00	66·50
Ratkovská Suchá	1·10	—	12·10	—	—	—	—
Ploské	—	14·90	23·20	8·20	—	—	—
Latinák	—	—	—	—	—	—	—
Lubeník	3·90	66·70	88·80	162·30	262·10	290·90	402·70
Amag–Sirk	—	—	13·00	34·90	64·80	142·30	7·50
Jelšava	—	67·40	80·30	212·60	332·60	1540·90	1619·20
Ochtiná	—	59·40	76·30	87·80	—	—	—
Košice	4·30	35·40	94·70	408·10	823·90	672·90	491·70
Total	17·10	277·20	428·70	1109·50	1769·90	2920·70	2812·30
Talc							
Hnúšťa	—	20·80	28·50	28·20	32·50	26·00	26·00
Asbestos							
Dobšiná—ore	80·00	85·60	77·90	113·70	95·00	82·10	74·40
Fibrous asbestos, %	2·00	1·40	1·30	2·30	1·10	0·30	0·50
Micro-asbestos, %	3·00	1·20	3·30	8·50	10·00	28·10	39·60
Anhydrite–gypsum							
Novoveská Huta	?	?	?	149·90	123·90	89·50	110·60
Halite							
Prešov–Solivar	?	17·50	18·30	31·50	37·70	41·80	41·20

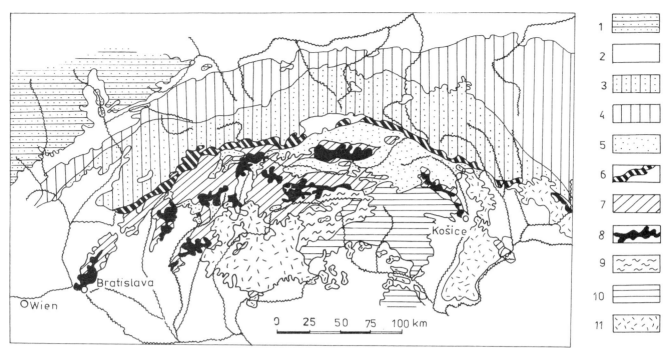

Fig. 1 *Geological sketch map of Western Carpathians: 1, Bohemian Massif; 2, sedimentary Neogene formations; 3, Magura Flysch zone; 4, Dukla Flysch zone; 5, Central Carpathian Palaeogene; 6, Klippen Belt; 7, Mesozoic of Inner Carpathians; 8, crystalline massifs (Tatrotatrides zone); 9, crystalline massifs of the Veporide zone; 10, Palaeozoic–Mesozoic of the Gemeride zone; 11, zone of Neovolcanic rocks. After Ilavský et al.*[10]

carbonates; flysch beds are predominant. In many areas the Liassic and Dogger sediments carry manganese mineralization typical of the Klippen Belt.

D—The Tatroveporide zone is one of the central zones, lying south of the Klippen Belt. The development of the zone was polyorogenic: it comprises crystalline Palaeozoic, Permian, Triassic, Jurassic, Cretaceous, Palaeogene and Neogene formations. The Tatroveporide zone is rich in metallic deposits of various genetic types and metallogenic epochs—Fe, Mn, Cu, Pb, Zn, Mo, Sb, Ba, Au, Ag, Hg, Mg, U, talc and bauxite (Fig. 2).

E—The Gemeride zone is farther south and its development was also polyorogenic. The zone includes epizonally metamorphosed Cambro-Silurian, Devonian, Upper Carboniferous and Permian; and non-metamorphosed Triassic, Jurassic, Palaeogene and Miocene formations. This zone (particularly the Palaeozoic and to some extent the Mesozoic) was affected by metamorphism and folding of the Caledonian, Variscan and Alpine cycles. Tertiary formations are not metamorphosed. Metallogenic processes in the zone were polycyclic and they produced many polymetallic deposits—predominantly of Fe, Mn, Cu, Sb, Hg, Ba, Au, Ag, Ni, Co, U, Mo, Sn, Mg, talc and asbestos.

F—The zone of Miocene volcanic rocks lies along the concave side of the Western Carpathian Arc. Its position and history were controlled by the contact of the folded Western Carpathians with the Pannonian Median Mass. There are petrometallogenic, spatial and time relationships between ore mineralization and volcanism with many types of ores—Pb, Zn, Au, Ag, Hg, Cu, Sb, Bi, Mn, Fe, Mo, Sn, F and U and many specific non-metalliferous raw materials.

G—The zone of the Inner Carpathian Miocene belongs among the Paratethyd Miocene areas that cover the Pannonian massif. The zone comprises Burdigalian to Plio-Pleistocene sediments. Occasionally, the marine clastic sedimentation alternates with, or is laterally replaced by, marine Tortonian or by an evaporitic facies (Helvetian, Pontian). Among the clastic formations, coal-bearing units with lignite occur in the Aquitanian, Tortonian and Pontian.

In areas close to volcanic activity certain mineral raw materials were formed—diatomites (triplites), bentonites, halloysites, limnoquartzites, pelosiderites, marcasite, pyrite, etc.

Metallogenic epochs

In the Czechoslovak Carpathians there were three principal metallogenic epochs—the Caledonian, the Variscan and the Alpine. Although all authors agree on this, there are differences of opinion about the significance of the separate epochs [4,5,12,13,14,17,18]

The deposits that are described below are assigned to their relevant metallogenic epoch and to stages within these by use of stratigraphical-lithological, structural, plutogenic or volcanogenic criteria, together with mineralogical-paragenetic and geochemical aspects and isotopic data.

Caledonian metallogenic epoch

Research in the Western Carpathian crystalline complexes shows that the Caledonian epoch affects the Pezinok–Pernek crystalline groups in the Malé Karpaty Mountains (Little Carpathians) in the Tatride zone, the Hron group and the Hladomorná dolina group in the Veporide zone and the Gelnica group of the Gemeride zone. The degree of metamorphism in the groups is variable—epizonal in the Gemerides, mesozonal-katazonal in the Tatrides and Veporides.

Geosynclinal stage The crystalline groups of the central mountain ranges have geosynclinal characters with some ophiolitic and other volcanism. The volcanism is either acid (Gemerides) or basic (Veporides and Tatrides). Volcanosedimentary, stratiform ore mineralization is associated with the volcanism. These deposits were metamorphosed during the Variscan and the Alpine epochs. The following types of deposit are present, being assigned to this epoch on the basis of geological and, when available, isotopic data.

(1) Pyrite and pyrite–pyrrhotite volcanosedimentary deposits associated with the basic volcanism (Pezinok, Hel'pa, Smolník): they are referred to this epoch on the basis of structural, geological and isotopic data.

According to Kantor and Rybár,[13,15] the common lead isotopes in accessory galenas from the Pezinok, Pernek and Kuchyňa pyrite–pyrrhotite deposits in the Malé Karpaty Mountains yield values that indicate an early Palaeozoic age. Sulphur isotopic work[1,15] on pyrites (38 analyses) gave $\delta^{34}S$ values from 7·6 to 18·88‰. The values of $\delta^{34}S$ in pyrrhotites from these deposits range from 16·1 to 16·9‰. In sphalerite the value is 6·3‰ (one sample).

(2) Polymetallic stratiform volcanogenic ore mineralization with Pb, Zn, Cu and pyrite is known at Mníšek, Alžbeta near Švedlár (Spišsko-gemerské rudohorie Mountains) and in the vicinity of Pernek (Malé Karpaty Mountains). The model lead age of galenas (Holmes–Houterman model) is 630 m.y.[12] A modified model yields 580 m.y. Sulphur isotopes in pyrites of these deposits show $\delta^{34}S$ ranging from 8·8 to 12·8‰.

(3) Stratiform cupriferous pyrite deposits in Smolník (Gemeride zone), in Žiar (Vysoké Tatry Mountains) and others: galenas from Smolník give an age of 480 to 610 m.y.[12] Pyrites from this deposit give $\delta^{34}S$ values of 9·0 to 16·3‰ (15 samples). The $\delta^{34}S$ values of chalcopyrite are 8·6 to 11·2‰ (4 samples), tetrahedrite 11·9‰ (one sample), galena from 8·00 to 13·00‰ (three samples) and sphalerite 9·1‰ (one sample).

(4) Stratiform magnesite deposits overlain in the Veporides by a younger talc-bearing formation (Mútnik–Hnúšťa).

(5) Stratiform siderite deposits such as Nižná Slaná, Žel eznik, Hrádok near Štítnik (Gemeride zone) and Jedl'ové Kostol'any in Tribeč Mountain (Tatride zone) have given Palaeozoic model ages. In the Nižná Slaná siderite deposit metamorphic segregation veins with geocronite occur. These have yielded a Silurian lead isotope age.[16] On the other hand, the siderite horizons at Nižná Slaná alternate with stratiform arsenopyrite mineralization, the isotopic ages of which are very variable. The phosphorus contents in the stratiform siderite deposits have values of 0·5–1% in accordance with a syngenetic origin.[8]

(6) Stratiform magnetite ores of metamorphic origin occur in micaschists in the Veporides at Bacúch and Kokava on the Rimavica River.[5]

(7) Antimony and antimony–tungsten stratiform volcanogenic mineralization is well known from Pezinok, Pernek and Kuchyňa in the Malé Karpaty Mountains and from Malé Železné in the Nízke Tatry Mountains and may occur at Čučma and Bystrý Potok in the Gemeride zone.[1] These deposits suffered both Variscan and Alpine metamorphism.

Antimonites from the Kolársky vrch mine at Pezinok gave values of $\delta^{34}S$ from 2·25 to 8·4‰ (21 samples). Arsenopyrite gave 1·0 to 6·04‰. Pyrites and pyrrhotite in this deposit gave similar values.

(8) Metamorphosed stratiform manganese ores of volcanosedimentary origin are well known from the villages of Čučma, Betliar and Bystrý potok in the Gemeride zone.[16]

Variscan metallogenic epoch

In the Western Carpathians all three of the classic stages are developed: geosynclinal, orogenic and post-orogenic. In the last stage two sub-stages may be distinguished—early and late post-orogenic.

Geosynclinal stage In the Gemeride zone this stage is represented by the Rakovec Group (a phyllite–diabase sequence) of Devonian age. Clastic rocks occur at the base, volcanic in the middle and volcanosedimentary at the top.

Mineralization is mostly associated with the first two, particularly with the middle volcanic part. The following deposits are present.[6,8]

(1) Stratiform hematite–magnetite–quartzites in basal clastic beds (Smolník, Švedlár, Rakovec): these are often referred to as Lahn–Dill types, though detrital Fe minerals appear to be present.

(2) Stratiform siderite ores associated with spilite-diabase horizons are also developed in this stage (Dobšiná): formerly, these ores were referred to as 'metasomatic' types of Alpine age.

(3) Stratiform magnesite occurs in the upper volcanosedimentary section of the Rakovec Group (Kavečany, Košické Hámre, Jelšava–Vel'ká Štet). It too was formerly attributed to 'hydrothermal-metasomatic' Alpine mineralization.

(4) Ni–Co arsenides of intramagmatic type occur in gabbroic rocks of the Rakovec Group near Dobšiná: they form schlieren and veins. For a long time they were regarded as hydrothermal veins associated with the Alpine Gemeride granites.

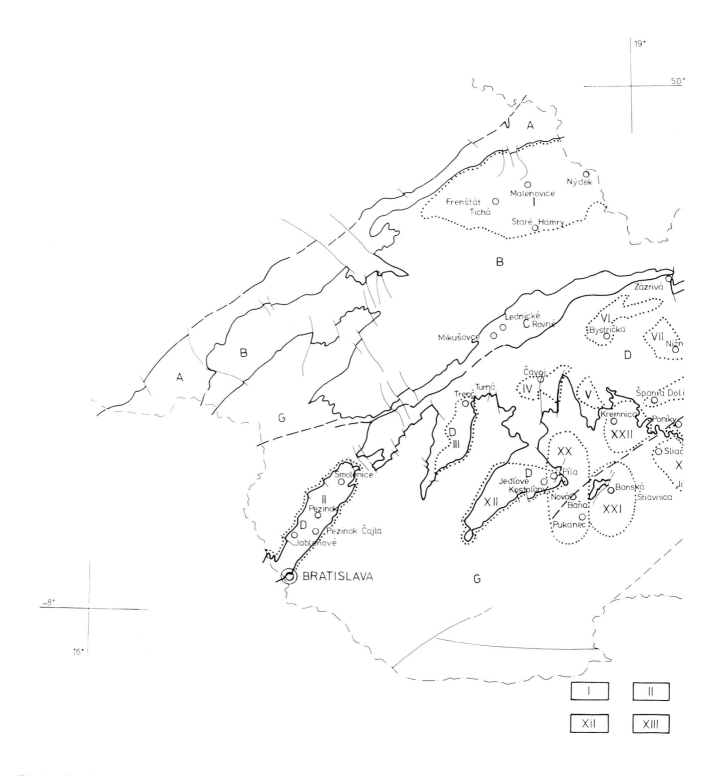

Fig. 2 *Sketch map of structural-metallogenic zones and ore districts in Western Carpathians:* A, *Zone of the pre-Carpathian foredeep* (*Neogene*); B, *Flysch zone* (*Palaeogene*); C, *Klippen Belt* (*Mesozoic–Palaeogene*); D, *Tatrotatrides zone;* E, *Veporides zone;* F, *Gemerides zone* (*Palaeozoic to Neogene*); G, *Neovolcanics and Neogene zone; I–XXV ore districts—I, Moravsko–Sliezské Bezkydy; II, Malé Karpaty; III, Povážsky Inovec; IV, Malá Magura–Suchý; V, Žiar; VI, Malá Fatra; VII, Veľká Fatra; VIII, Vysoké Tatry; IX, Levočské pohorie; X, Branisko and Čierna Hora; XI, Zemplínský ostrov; XII, Tribeč; XIII, Nízke Tatry; XIV, Northern Veporides; XV, Middle Veporides; XVI, Southern Veporides; XVII, Západný Gemer–Rimava; XVIII, Spišsko-gemerské rudohorie; XIX, Slovenský kras; XX, Nová Baňa–Kľak; XXI, Banská Štiavnica and Hodruša; XXII, Kremnica; XXIII, Poľana and Javorie; XXIV, Slánske vrchy–Milič; XXV, Vihorlat; 1, important ore or mineral deposits and their names; 2, boundaries of structural-metallogenic zones; 3, boundaries of ore districts. After Ilavský et al.*[10]

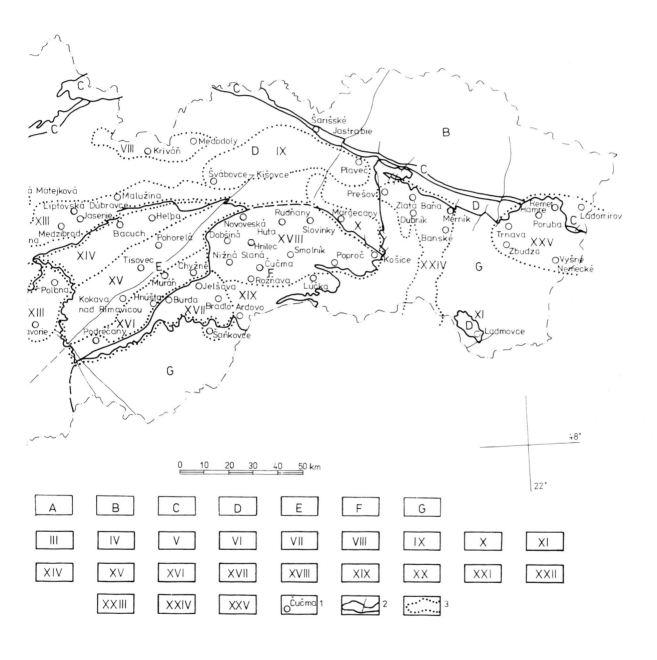

Orogenic stage In the Tatroveporides the culmination of the Variscan epoch was in the Middle Carboniferous when intermediate to acid plutonic rocks were formed. Synkinematic Variscan granites and granodiorites with their pegmatites give ages of 360 to 320 m.y. Pegmatites and aplites of this plutonism have been dated at 320–250 m.y.[11] K–Ar dating of micas from the metamorphic country rocks gives ages of 300–250 m.y. In the Tatroveporides mineralization associated with this igneous activity is as indicated below.

(1) Pyrometasomatic magnetite ores at the contact of

Variscan granites with older gneisses (Kokava on the Rimavica River).

(2) The formation of high-temperature and pegmatitic veins with molybdenite, antimonite and gold (Magurka in the Nízke Tatry Mountains, Ťahanovce in the Čierna Hora Mountains, the Malá Fatra and Vepor Mountains, etc.): the veins are in granites and gneisses. In the Nízke Tatry Mountains at Malé Železné Mo–Sb veins, associated with the pegmatites, give an age of 320 m.y. Lead isotopes from galenas of these deposits give Variscan ages.[13]

(3) Hydrothermal cupriferous quartz veins in the Vysoké Tatry, Nízke Tatry, Malá Fatra and Inovec Mountains: these veins cut granitic rocks and crystalline schists, the age of which has been demonstrated by the K–Ar method as Variscan.[11]

(4) Lead–zinc veins with Cu and Fe in the Nízke Tatry, Malá Fatra, Tribeč, Inovec and Malé Karpaty Mountains: lead isotopic dates of 320 to 220 m.y. indicate a Variscan age.[12,13]

(5) Siderite veins with cupriferous minerals associated with granitic rocks, gneisses and migmatites in the Vysoké Tatry and Nízke Tatry Mountains of the Veporides, the Čierna Hora Mountains and in the Gemerides in phyllites of the Gelnica and Rakovec Groups are also of Variscan age.

(6) Siderite veins in granitic rocks, without sulphides, sometimes associated with gneisses, micaschists, etc., in Nízke Tatry, the Veporides and the Gemerides: both types of siderite veins are associated with lead–zinc mineralization, the model lead age of which was determined as Variscan.

(7) Barite–sulphide and barite–polymetallic hydrothermal veins in the Nízke Tatry and Veľká Fatra Mountains and in the Gemeride zone have also been dated as Variscan by the model lead age method.

(8) Quartz–antimonite veins with or without gold in the granitic rocks or in crystalline schists of the Vysoké Tatry and Nízke Tatry Mountains: again, the lead method gave a Variscan age.[13]

(9) Mercury mineralization with barite, siderite and Cu minerals in granite rocks and in crystalline rocks of the Veporides and Gemerides: sulphide minerals from the above veins give values of $\delta^{34}S$ that range from 1·2 to 7·5‰, the most frequent being values around 3–5‰. In the same samples the ratio $^{32}S/^{34}S$ varies between 22·05 and 22·32 being most frequently around 22·1–22·2.

Early post-orogenic stage The Upper Carboniferous is most extensive in the Gemeride zone. In this zone there was little Variscan plutonism and only minor uplift. The Variscan granite plutonites remained at depth. In the Tatroveporides with extensive Variscan granites the Upper Carboniferous is less extensive and disappears westwards. Mineral deposits in the Upper Carboniferous are associated with both sedimentary and volcanic processes. The following types are present.

(1) Stratiform deposits of crystalline magnesite in carbonate host rocks, particularly in the Gemerides (Podrečany, Burda–Poproč, Jelšava, Košice): these used to be considered hydrothermal-metasomatic in origin. They were slightly affected by the Alpine metamorphism.

(2) Stratiform lead–zinc mineralization in carbonates: these suffered Alpine metamorphism and remobilization (Ratkovská Suchá, Jelšava, Rochovce, Ochtiná).

(3) Stratiform siderite deposits in carbonate horizons (Dobšiná, Mlynky): these deposits also suffered Alpine metamorphism.

Late post-orogenic stage Uplift of the Carpathian region during the Saalian phase produced a mountain system (the Palaeo-Carpathians) the central parts of which during the Permian underwent erosion under hot arid conditions that produced the Verrucano molasse facies. Weathering, erosion, resedimentation and volcanogenic processes produced the following ores during the Permian.

(1) Stratiform U–Mo–Cu mineralization of volcano-sedimentary genesis associated with porphyry volcanism in the Gemerides and Veporides is known near Novoveská Huta, Vikartovce, Čierny Váh and Špania Dolina. A model lead age on galena from Novoveská Huta gives about 200 m.y.[16]

(2) Stratiform cupriferous ore of volcanosedimentary type is well known at Špania Dolina, Ľubietová, Mýto pod Ďumbierom and Šankovce. Galena from veins at Špania Dolina gives an age of 200 m.y.[16]

(3) Hematitic sedimentary breccias, conglomerates and shales controlled by palaeogeographical conditions and developed by lateritic weathering, together with gossans developed on pre-Permian siderite deposits, are very well known at Licince, Folkmár, Dobšiná and Rudňany in the Gemeride zone.[16]

(4) Barite veins and veinlets in peripheral parts of lava flows of the Permian melaphyres are present near Malužiná in the Nízke Tatry Mountains.

(5) Cupriferous impregnations and veinlets in melaphyric lava flows and porphyrites are known from Kvetnica and Malužiná, again in the Nízke Tatry Mountains.

(6) Gypsum–anhydrite deposits of Permian to Lower Triassic age are widespread in the Gemerides and Tatroveporides. Isotopic studies indicate the biogenic origin of the sulphur.[14]

By the end of the Permian the Palaeo-Carpathians had been reduced to an area of low relief which then subsided beneath sea-level to produce the Alpine geosynclinal stage.

Alpine metallogenic epoch

The Alpine metallogenic epoch also included in the Carpathians geosynclinal, orogenic and post-orogenic stages. In each stage certain geological formations and mineral deposits are characteristically developed.

Geosynclinal stage The following types of deposits

were developed in the Western Carpathians during this stage.

(1) Stratiform hematite and hematite–copper ores of volcanosedimentary nature related to basic and intermediate volcanism (Šankovce and Držkovce in the Gemerides) or to palaeogeographical and lithological conditions (Bradlo, Folkmár and Rudňany in the Gemerides).

(2) Deposits of asbestos in Lower Triassic ultrabasic rocks near Dobšiná, Jaklovce and Jasov-Rudník in the Gemerides.

(3) Stratiform Pb–Zn–Cu ore mineralization in the Middle Triassic associated with ultrabasic and basic volcanism, glaucophane schists, diabases, etc. (Drienok–Poniky, Pohorelská Maša and Ardovo near Plešivec, etc.). Model lead ages from these localities give for Poniky–Drienok 240 m.y. and for Ardovo 260 m.y.[13] These ages coincide with those of the hydrothermal veins in the crystalline massifs of the Nízke Tatry Mountains and the lead has been interpreted by Kantor as B-type, remobilized from Variscan deposits at greater depths.

(4) Intramagmatic chromite in dunitic rocks in the Middle Triassic of the South Slovakian karst is known from Tiba near Plešivec.

Early orogenic stage The period that covered the Upper Triassic and the Lower Jurassic in the Carpathians may be referred to as the early orogenic stage of the Alpine epoch.[16] This period is characterized by the following mineral deposits.

(1) Upper Triassic gypsum–anhydrite beds (the so-called Carpathian Keuper facies), which occur mostly in the Krížna unit of the Tatride zone at Záblatie near Trenčín in the Veľká Fatra Mountains, etc. Sulphur isotopes indicate a biogenic origin.[14] These beds contain evaporitic magnesite.

(2) Oolitic hematite beds in the Tatride Rhaetic of the Vysoké Tatry and Veľká Fatra Mountains, etc. These have no economic importance.

(3) Lower Jurassic manganese oxide–carbonate rocks of the Klippen Belt (Lednické Rovné, Zázrivá and Šarišské Jastrabie) and the Tatrides (Vysoké Tatry and Malé Karpaty Mountains). These have no economic importance.

(4) The phosphorite-bearing series in the Lotharingian of the Krížna nappe, formed by a break in marine sedimentation. The series consists of marly limestones (Fleckenmergel type).

Following this stage the entire Carpathian region became once more a deep-water geosynclinal environment for a period lasting until as late as the Albian.

Late orogenic stage The duration of this stage varied in the different zones. In the central zones (Tatroveporides and Gemerides) it lasted from the Albian to the Lutetian and regional metamorphism took place during this stage. This produced diaphthoretic effects in the Variscan crystalline massifs and progressive recrystallization in the Mesozoic formations.

In deeper parts of the inner zones of the Carpathians the intrusion of granitoid masses (Gemeride zone) resulted in small massifs of Jurassic and Cretaceous granites with indications of various types of mineralization. The pre-Variscan and Palaeoalpine deposits underwent metamorphism, recrystallization and remobilization.

The Cretaceous age of the Gemeride granites was shown by Kantor by the K–Ar method and later confirmed by other scientists. Ages of 180 to 85 m.y. were obtained.

In the Klippen Belt and in external zones of the Carpathian Flysch deep-seated crustal faults led to the intrusion of alkaline basic igneous rocks, such as teschenite, picrite, limburgite, etc.

During this stage the following mineral deposits were formed.[10]

(1) Cassiterite-bearing greisens in marginal parts of the Gemeride granites. These carry Mo and W ores and are now being explored near Hnilec, Betliar, Čučma and Poproč.

(2) Quartz–uranium veins and veinlets in the Gemeride granites and in their surrounding rocks are known in the Hnilec and Čučma regions.

(3) Quartz–ankerite–chalcopyrite veins and veinlets in the vicinity of apophyses of the Gemeride granites are known in many localities. They were partly formed by regeneration of Variscan deposits.

(4) Quartz–ankerite–specularite veins, mobilized from older siderite veins of the Variscan age, are widespread in the northern and southern parts of the Gemeride zone.

(5) Quartz–antimonite veins, frequently with gold values, are numerous in the central part of the Gemerides. Most of them may have arisen by remobilization of older Palaeozoic antimony deposits. In the past many were mined (Betliar, Čučma, Spišská Baňa, Poproč, Zlatá Idka, etc.).

(6) Quartz–mercury mineralization with schwatzite (mercurian tetrahedrite) is widespread in the Gemeride zone.

(7) Lead–zinc–copper mineralization in the Triassic–Jurassic of the Tatroveporide zone is either apomagmatic or remobilized from older deposits during the Alpine metamorphism (Bacúch, Malužiná, Brezno, Mýto, Pusté Pole, etc.). These include deposits mentioned above that contain B-type leads of apparent Variscan age (Jasenie, Trangoška, etc.). On the other hand, galenas from Píla in the Tribeč Mountains yield younger ages of 100 to 80 m.y.[10]

(8) Stratiform pelosiderites in the Moravian–Silesian Beskydes overlying teschenite lava flows in flysch sediments have no economic importance (Janovice, Malenovice, Staré Hamry, etc.).

(9) Bauxites in the central zones of the Tatroveporides and Gemerides are widespread, but their economic importance is very minor.

Some authors (e.g. Varček[18]) relate large economically significant deposits of siderite and magnesite, mentioned above in sections on the Variscan and Caledonian metallogenic epochs, to the Alpine orogenic stage.

Early post-orogenic stage The following deposits belong to this stage.[10]

(1) Sedimentary manganese oxide–carbonate ores in the external and central zones. The most important deposits were at Švábovce–Kišovce in the Levočské hory Mountains. The deposits are in the Eocene Flysch. They were exploited for more than 70 years.

(2) Sedimentary pelosiderite seams in the Upper Eocene of the inner Carpathians occur in the Liptovská kotlina, Oravská kotlina and Spišská kotlina depressions. These are only small occurrences.

(3) Sedimentary palaeo placers of gold in the Upper Eocene Flysch occur in the Strihov beds of the Kochanovská unit of the Magura zone in Eastern Slovakia. They were formed by erosion and redeposition of primary deposits that are now covered by younger rocks.

(4) Minor syngenetic pyrite concentrations in pelitic sediments of the Central Carpathian Flysch.

(5) Redeposited marine bauxites in the Palaeogene of the South Slovakian Pannonian facies have only been recognized near the Hungarian frontier around Štúrovo.

(6) Coal-bearing and oil- and gas-bearing formations mostly occur in the Eocene of the periklippen Central Carpathian Flysch areas.

By the end of the Oligocene the Savian folding phase had resulted in uplift and emergence of the whole Central and external Carpathian Flysch above sea-level.

Late post-orogenic stage The uplift of the Central Carpathians forming a mountain range (Neo-Carpathians) took place during the Savian phase of the Alpine folding. The movements gave rise to large regional faults, both parallel and perpendicular to the contact of the Carpathians with the Pannonian massif. Along these dislocations subsequent polycyclic volcanism developed. In the Miocene basins sedimentation of marine, brackish and terrestrial natures was synchronous with the volcanism. The following mineralization belongs to this stage.[10]

(1) The formation of polymetallic veins of Pb–Zn–Cu–Au–Ag ores in andesites: typical deposits are Banská Štiavnica, Nová Baňa, Brehy, Rudno, etc. Model lead ages range from 20–8 m.y.

(2) Stockworks and impregnations with copper mineralization and some Pb, Zn and Au in hypabyssal andesites near the above localities.

(3) Gold–silver–quartz veins in andesites and dacites near Kremnica, which have been mined from the Middle Ages to the present day.

(4) The formation of hydrothermal molybdenite-pyrite ores in andesites at Vtáčnik Mountain.

(5) Mercury mineralization is widespread in the form of impregnations and stockworks in andesitic tuffs near Merník and Dubník in Eastern Slovakia and near Malachov and Tajov in Middle Slovakia.

(6) Antimony–quartz veins in Miocene andesites and dacites are less important (Kremnica mine and Zlatá Baňa in the Slánske vrchy Mountains of Eastern Slovakia).

(7) The formation of volcanogenic stratiform sulphur in Miocene andesitic tuffs is known from Detvianska Huta (formerly Kalinka) in Middle Slovakia.

(8) Interstitial manganese oxides are found in andesitic tuffs at Hriňová and Čelovce in the Middle Slovakian Neovolcanics.

(9) Fluorite is known in the form of impregnations and veinlets in andesitic rocks at Vihorlat Mountain.

(10) The formation of stratiform volcanosedimentary pelosiderite seams in a Miocene coal-bearing series near volcanic rocks of andesitic type (Vyšné Nemecké in the Vihorlat Mountains and Banské in the Slánske vrchy Mountains).

(11) Skarn magnetite ores at the contacts of Miocene diorites or hypabyssal andesites and dacites with Mesozoic carbonate rocks at Vyhne and Tisovec in the Middle Slovakian Neovolcanics.

(12) The formation of skarn magnetite–polymetallic ores at the contact of Miocene andesites with Mesozoic carbonates (Tisovec).

Besides the above, non-metalliferous raw materials of economic significance occur in Miocene, Pliocene and Quaternary formations. These include diatomite (triplite), limnoquartzites, perlite, bentonitic clays and bentonite, halloysite, petrurgical basalt, andesite, halite, lignite, oil and gas, kaolinic clays, nickel-bearing palaeolaterites, clays, loess loams, sands and gravels, travertines, etc.[16]

Geological description of main types of mineral deposits

In this section brief geological descriptions of representatives of the more important mineral deposits in the Western Carpathians are given. The deposits are arranged in order of types of ore. Beginning with ores of ferrous and ferroalloy metals, base-metal ores and then non-metalliferous raw materials are described in turn. Each group is represented by a typical deposit, which is described in detail, followed by a list of localities of the same type. Further details can be found elsewhere.[16]

Iron ores

Among many genetic types of iron ores in the Western Carpathians, the most important ones are stratiform siderite deposits in the Gemeride Palaeozoics, hydrothermal vein deposits of siderite ores in the Gemerides and magnetite skarns in the Miocene of the Neovolcanic zone. Other genetic types are of no economic importance or have already been exploited.[16]

Stratiform siderite deposits in Gemeride zone The

Cambro-Silurian, i.e. the oldest part of the Gemeride Palaeozoics, is the most significant area of stratiform siderite deposits and occurrences. It is a complex of volcanics and sediments of geosynclinal nature, called the Gelnica Group. This group was repeatedly folded and metamorphosed under greenschist facies conditions during the Variscan and Alpine orogenies. The stratiform siderite deposits are in horizons of dark graphitic phyllites with layers of other carbonates, such as limestones, dolomites, ankerites, ferrodolomites, magnesites, etc.[8] The deposit at Nižná Slaná (still in production) is typical of the stratiform siderite ores (Fig. 3). Here the ore reserves occupy an area approximately 3 km long and 1·5 km wide. The thickness of the siderite layers varies from several metres up to (exceptionally) 50 m. The siderite passes into ankerite and limestone both vertically and horizontally.

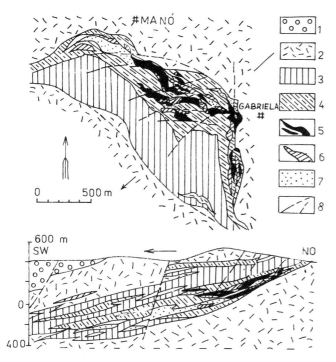

Fig. 3 *Geological sketch map and cross-section of siderite ore deposit of Nižná Slaná, Spišsko-gemerské rudohorie ore district: 1, Upper Carboniferous (conglomerates, sandstones); 2–7 Gelnica Group—2, layers of porphyritic volcanics; 3, graphitic sericitic schists; 4, sericitic and sericitic graphitic schists; 5, lenses of siderite ore; 6, lenses and layers of ankerite ore; 7, limestone layers; 8, faults. After Slávik et al.*[16]

In the deposit and immediately around it the following minerals have been found: siderite (three generations), ankerite, pyrite (three generations), gersdorffite, ullmanite, pentlandite, millerite, chalcopyrite, tetrahedrite, sphalerite, geocronite, bournonite, boulangerite, galena, cinnabar, arsenopyrite, pyrrhotite and many secondary minerals (Varček[18]). Run of mine ore has 30–35% Fe, 2% Mn and 1–8% SiO$_2$. Detailed analyses have been published in the past.

For a long time the deposit had been regarded as hydrothermal-metasomatic and associated with Alpine granitoid plutonism (Varček[18] and other workers). Recent work suggests, however, that it is a syngenetic sedimentary or sedimentary-volcanogenic deposit. That the deposit has been metamorphosed and recrystallized was shown by studies of the fabric and the ratios of lead and sulphur isotopes in some of the sulphides.[16]

The deposit is mined in two pits (Maňo and Gabriela) to a depth of about 500 m from the surface. The mining operations began in pre-historic times on limonitic gossans. This was the basis of the iron industry in the basin of the River Slaná. Siderite has been mined here since 1860. It is one of the largest deposits in Slovakia. Siderite is dressed by roasting to give a concentrate with 65–70% Fe.

Analogous deposits, now worked out, occur in the Gemerides and in the Tatroveporides.[10]

Hydrothermal veins with siderite and sulphides In the Western Carpathians siderite and siderite–sulphide veins occur in the crystalline massifs of granitoid rocks of Variscan age and in crystalline complexes with gneisses, micaschists, migmatites and phyllites. The ore veins mostly follow easterly structures or Variscan cleavages and show a close spatial relationship to Variscan plutonics. During the alpine orogeny the deposits underwent metamorphism, recrystallization, partial mobilization and migration into higher parts of the crust.[5] Such veins are most frequent in the Gemerides, and less often found in the Veporides and Tatrides.

Rudňany (formerly Kotterbach in German, or Ötösbánya in Hungarian) is the largest and most important hydrothermal vein deposit in Slovakia. The deposit consists of three principal veins—Droždiak in the south, Hrubá in the centre and Zlatník in the northern part of the field, mining operations stretching along 6 km. There are also smaller veins. The vertical extent of the mineralization is about 1 km. Vein thicknesses vary between 1 and 30 m, commonly being 4–8 m. In places the veins are regular in shape and slightly lenticular; elsewhere their shape is more complex with branching and the development of systems of veinlets. The morphology of the veins is controlled by the mechanical properties of the wallrocks, which consist of three rock groups (Fig. 4).[16] The veins are cut by much post-mineralization faulting.

The mineralogical composition of the veins is siderite, barite, chalcopyrite, tetrahedrite and cinnabar; accessories include fuchsite, pyrite, gersdorffite, chloanthite, ankerite, dolomite, tourmaline, specularite, arsenopyrite, sphalerite, bornite, chalcocite, covelline, calcite, native mercury, antimonite, magnetite, rutile, albite, illite, dickite and quartz. Monoascendent

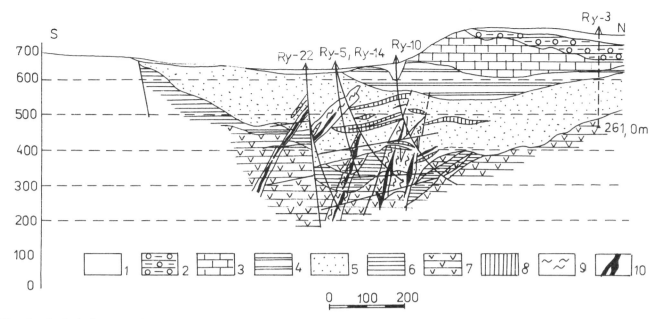

Fig. 4 *Geological cross-section through Droždiak veins in siderite–barite–sulphide ore deposit of Rudňany, Spišsko-gemerské rudohorie ore district: 1, Quaternary (soils); 2, Upper Eocene (conglomerates, sandstones, shales); 3, Middle to Upper Triassic (limestones); 4, Lower Triassic (shales); 5, Permian (conglomerates, sandstones and shales); 6, Upper Carboniferous (black shales and sandstones); 7, Upper Carboniferous (diabases, tuffs and tuffites); 8, Permian (gypsum–anhydrite); 9, hydrothermally altered rocks in vicinity of ore veins; 10, ore veins with siderite-barite and Cu and Hg sulphides. After Slávik et al.*[16]

and polyascendent mineral zoning is present. There are four principal types of ore: siderite, siderite-sulphide (with Cu, Hg, Sb, etc.), barite and ferrobarite. The average composition of all ore reserves in 1965 was: Fe, ~31%; Mn, 1·75%; Cu, 0·19%; Hg, 0·025%; $BaSO_4$, 15%; and SiO_2, 6·8%. Fe, Cu, Sb, Hg and barite are recovered. The ore dressing includes magnetic separation, flotation, roasting, pelletization and agglomeration. The deposit is exploited from four mines along its 6-km length.

There are analogous veins along the northern margin of the Spišsko-gemerské rudohorie (ore mountains) around Gelnica, Žakarovce, Koyšov, Košická Belá and along the southern margin of the Spiš-Gemer Palaeozoics around Rožňava and Drnava. The simpler types are infillings of siderite and copper sulphides (Slovinky, Gelnica, Rožňava, etc.[16]). The same applies to the veins in the North Veporide ore district, the Nízke Tatry Mountains and the Tribeč Mountains.

Skarn magnetite ores in Central Slovakian Neovolcanic zone In the Western Carpathians pyrometasomatic magnetite ores have a limited extent. They are most frequent in the innermost zone of the Neovolcanics associated with intrusions of diorite and granodiorite.[16] The Miocene granodiorite intrusions penetrate the Palaeozoic complexes of crystalline schists and late Palaeozoic and Triassic sediments. At their contacts with Lower and Middle Triassic carbonates skarns were formed with garnets, amphiboles, pyroxenes, vesuvianite, chlorite, calcite, etc. There are two types of skarn—magnesian and calcareous.

The orebodies are near the villages of Klokoč, Hodruša and Vyhne. They are 150–200 to 500 m in length, extend downdip to 250 m and their thickness ranges from 2 to 35 m. Iron runs from 19·6 to 40%, SiO_2 17·15–35·25%, CaO 1·5–20%, MgO 2·4–9·7% and S up to 17%.

The deposits were thoroughly investigated in 1950–65. Because of the poor reserves they are of no economic interest.

Manganese ores
In the Western Carpathians the manganese ores are mostly in the early Palaeozoic, the Jurassic, the Cretaceous and the Eocene.[16] Deposits of sedimentary oxide–carbonate ores in the Upper Eocene of the Intra-Carpathian Palaeogene of the Tatroveporide zone are economically the most important concentrations. Such is the orefield of Švábovce–Kišovce in the ore district of the Levočské pohorie Mountains exploited from about 1850 to 1970. After a century of mining more than 5 000 000 tonne of ore had been mined. In 1970 the mining operations ceased for economic reasons (Fig. 5).

Thin layers of Mn ores in the Eocene occur in the other inner depressions of Palaeogene age.

Cupriferous ores
Besides Fe, copper is also an important metal in the Western Carpathians. Copper deposits of various origins occur in the Silurian, Carboniferous, Permian, Lower Triassic and Miocene. They have been mined since ancient times and through the Middle Ages up to

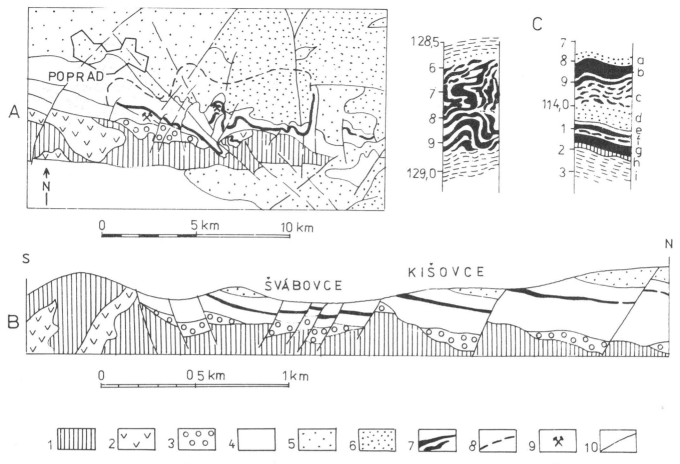

Fig. 5 *Manganese ore deposits of Švábovce–Kišovce, Levočské pohorie ore district:* A, geological sketch map of Švábovce–Kišovce area; B, geological cross-section through deposits; 1, Permian (sandstones, quartzites and variegated shales); 2, Permian (melaphyres and porphyrites); 3, Eocene (conglomerates, sandstones); 4, lower part of Eocene flysch complex with manganese ores (predominantly shales); 5, Flysch Complex (Upper Eocene); 6, Upper Eocene (greywacke flysch); 7, Outcrops of principal manganese horizon; 8, limits of ore field; 9, principal mines; 10, faults; C, detailed cross-sections through manganese horizons in mines and boreholes—a, sandstone on top of Mn horizon; b, oxide–carbonate Mn ore; c, manganiferous shales with Mn oxide ore; d, non-mineralized sandstone; e, finely stratified oxide–carbonate Mn ore; f, manganiferous shale; g, finely stratified oxide–carbonate Mn ore; h, black coal lens at base of mineralized horizon; i, underlying shales. After Slávik et al.[16]

the present day; only the economically more important ones are described here

Stratiform cupriferous pyrite deposits in early Palaeozoic The deposit of Smolník in the Spišsko-gemerské rudohorie (Gemeride zone) is representative of this type of deposit. It is a stratiform volcanogenic-sedimentary deposit in the Silurian of the Gelnica Group.[9,10,16] All the rocks (including the kies deposits) were intensively folded and metamorphosed under greenschist facies conditions during the Variscan and Alpine orogenies. They include graphitic and other phyllites, quartzites, porphyroids, etc. The isoclinal folds have easterly trending axes and their limbs dip southwards at 70°.

The cupriferous pyrite deposits are in a zone of metabasalt lava flows with thick layers of chloritic phyllites, which represent metamorphosed basic tuffs and tuffites. The ore layers are concentrated in a zone about 80–150 m thick. The mean thickness of the layers is about 8 m. The total length of the ore zone is about 3 km. It is divided into blocks by low-dipping and steep faults (Figs. 6 and 7).

As regards the structures and the textures of the ores, they are layered, impregnation-disseminated or massive. Pyrite layers alternate with layers of copper ore or cupriferous pyrite ore or ore of other sulphides, such as Pb and Zn. Among beds of kies ores are frequent metamorphic-secretion veins of quartz with nests of sulphides.

Pyrite (three generations), pyrrhotite, marcasite, chalcopyrite (three generations) and tetrahedrite are the primary minerals of the deposit. Minor minerals include galena, sphalerite, arsenopyrite, calcite, quartz, chlorite, hematite, antimonite, ankerite, dolomite, siderite, tourmaline and rutile. Numerous secondary minerals were present in the gossan.

The chemical composition of the ores varies: Fe, 7–45%; S, 8–47%; As, 0·55%; Sb, to 0·06%; Cu, 0·2–

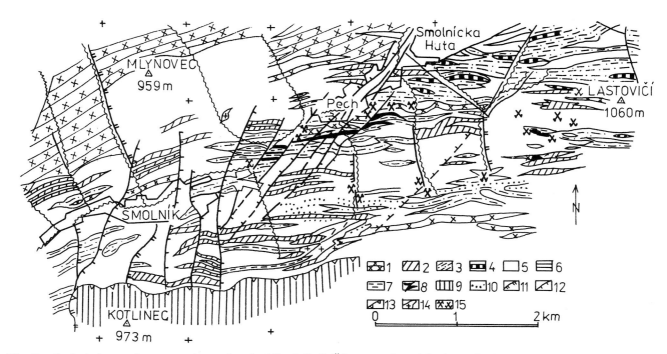

Fig. 6 Geological map of copper–pyrite ore deposit of Smolník, Spišsko-gemerské rudohorie ore district: 1, porphyritic volcanics and their tuffs; 2, quartzites and tuffs; 3, sericitic to graphitic schists; 4, black cherts (lydites); 5, sericitic and siliceous schists; 6, basic volcanic rocks (dolerites and porphyrites); 7, chloritic schists (metamorphosed basic tuffs); 8, lenses of cupriferous pyrite ore (1–8 Gelnica Group of Cambro-Silurian age); 9, Devonian (Rakovec Group) phyllites and diabases; 10, hydrothermal epigenetic veins with siderite ore; 11, older faults; 12, perpendicular younger faults; 13, discordant contact between two formations; 14, Gemeride granites of Cretaceous age; 15—shafts and adits a, accessible; b, inaccessible. After Ilavský[9,10,16]

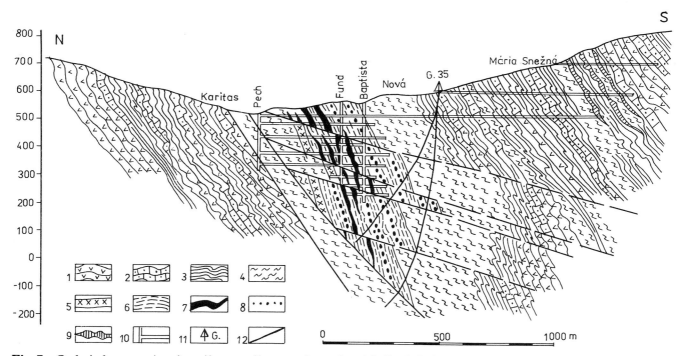

Fig. 7 Geological cross-section of stratiform cupriferous pyrite ore deposit in Smolník, Spišsko-gemerské rudohorie ore district: 1, volcanic acid rocks (porphyroids); 2, quartzites and tuffs; 3, sericitic schists; 4, graphitic schists; 5, basic volcanic rocks (dolerites); 6, chloritic schists; 7, lenses and layers of cupriferous pyrite ore; 8, disseminated ore; 9, hydrothermal epigenetic veins of siderite ore; 10, principal levels; 11, drill-holes; 12, overthrusts. After Ilavský[9,10,16]

4% (exceptionally to 10%); Pb, up to 0·3%; Zn, up to 0·37%; Bi, up to 0·03%; Ag, up to 8 g t^{-1}; and Se, 40 g t^{-1} in pyrite and 80–360 g t^{-1} in chalcopyrite.

For many years mine water has been used to precipitate Cu on iron scrap. Cu contents in this water vary around 122–150 g m^{-3}. During rainfall the Cu content rises to 360 g m^{-3} and higher. At the deposit 140 000 tonne of copper metal has been mined, more than 1 000 000 tonne of pyrite and 120 tonne of silver. At present the deposit is exploited for pyrite, copper, silver and selenium.

Other similar but smaller deposits in the Gemerides occur at Mníšek near Hnilec and at Bystrý Potok near Švedlár.

Hydrothermal vein deposits of cupriferous siderite ores in pre-Permian formations   These veins are mostly in the Spišsko-gemerské rudohorie (ore mountains). The deposits are either polymetallic, such as Rudňany, or they are just cupriferous siderite veins. Slovinky is a typical deposit. It is in the northern part of the Spišsko-gemerské rudohorie on the so-called Spiš 'veins system'.[16] The veins are in the Gelnica Group and partially in the phyllite–diabase series (Rakovec Group) of Devonian age. The Hrubá, Gelnická, Zlatá and Es veins are still being exploited. They have an easterly trend and strike lengths of 3–4·5 km. The veins are slightly lenticular, more or less continuous, yet not exploitable all along their lengths. The veins dip southward at 50–90°. Their vertical extent is 750–800 m. Their thickness varies from 0·5 to 3 m and exceptionally is up to 9 m. The morphology of the veins and their thickness were controlled by the mechanical properties of the wallrocks. The veins have been considerably displaced by faulting.

The main vein filling is siderite, chalcopyrite, tetrahedrite, quartz and other copper sulphides, which form clusters, balls, nests, veinlets and disseminations in the siderite. Pyrite, ankerite, sericite, tourmaline, marcasite, arsenopyrite, sphalerite, galena, bornite, jamesonite, native gold, calcite, antimonite and barite occur in subsidiary to accessory quantities. The minerals can be divided into four or five generations: quartz-ankerite, siderite, sulphide and remobilized phases. Both monoascendent and polyascendent zoning are present. Barite and tetrahedrite decrease with depth, whereas chalcopyrite, arsenopyrite, galena, sphalerite and pyrite increase.

The chemical composition of the ore presently being mined is: Fe, 19–23%; Cu, 0·6–1%; Mn, up to 1·26%; As, up to 0·53%; S, up to 2·29%; and SiO$_2$, up to 25%. As far as reserves go, Slovinky is a medium-size deposit. It has been operated since the Middle Ages with a break in mining activities from 1880 to 1909.

Analogous deposits occur at Gelnica, Rožňava (Maria mine), Fichtenhübel near Mníšek, Prakovce, Medzev-Hummel, etc. Some of these and many other deposits were completely worked out in the past. Some small veins are present in ore districts in the Tatrides and Veporides.[16]

Stratiform volcanosedimentary copper deposits in Permian   Ore mineralization of this kind has been known and exploited from the Middle Ages to the seventeenth century. These deposits have been considered to be hydrothermal veins of Alpine age. Only recently were they recognized to be volcanosedimentary stratiform deposits.[16]

Špania Dolina (Herrengrund in German) is a typical deposit in the Tatrides, in the ore district of the Nízke Tatry Mountains. The area is north of Banská Bystrica (Fig. 8).

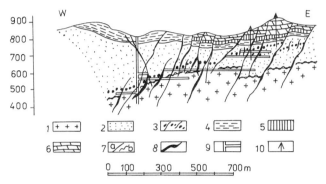

Fig. 8 *Geological cross-section of cupriferous ore deposit of Špania Dolina, near Banská Bystrica, Nízke Tatry ore district:* 1, *crystalline rocks of the Nízke Tatry Massif (granites, gneiss, migmatites);* 2, *Permian (sandstones, conglomerates, variegated shales);* 3, *disseminated copper ores in Permian;* 4, *variegated shales (Lower Triassic–Zeissian);* 5, *marls and shales of Lower Triassic (Campilian);* 6, *limestones and dolomites (Middle Triassic);* 7, *geological boundaries*—a, *normal;* b, *discordant;* 8, *epigenetic hydrothermal cupriferous siderite veins;* 9, *principal workings;* 10, *boreholes. After Čillik*[5,16]

The Permian is represented by polymictic conglomerates, sandstones, variegated shales, arkoses, greywackes and quartz-porphyry tuffs. The Permian is overlain by Lower Triassic and Middle Triassic dolomites and limestones.

The main type of ore mineralization is that of disseminated copper ore in the Permian arkosic sandstones. The mineralization is developed over an area some kilometres in length with a width of 1 km. It is in alternating segments of various grades that have thicknesses of 8–40 m. The main ore minerals are chalcopyrite, tetrahedrite, pyrite and siderite. Barite, galena, sphalerite, antimonite, ankerite, sericite and chlorite occur in small or accessory quantities. Secondary minerals, such as chalcocite, covelline, malachite, azurite, devilline, cuprite, tenorite, langite, olivenite, native copper, bornite, etc., are present.[16]

The deposits were affected by intense deformation and metamorphism during the Alpine orogeny, resulting in many veins and veinlets of remobilized material that were exploited in the past. These gave rise to the earlier hypotheses of epigenetic mineralization.

The contents of recoverable components in the ores are 0·1–1·9% Cu, 5–15% Fe, up to 2% Sb and up to 80 g t^{-1} Ag in Cu ores of tetrahedrite composition or 20 g t^{-1} Ag in chalcopyrite. The deposit was exploited from the Middle Ages to 1800 and yielded 66 890 tonne of metallic copper. Mining activities were at their height in 1494–1545. At that time only rich veins with coarse inclusions and clusters of copper ores were exploited; now the possibility of mining the entire ore zone of disseminated copper is being investigated.

To the east of Banská Bystrica the Ľubietová deposit in the Veporide Permian was intensively exploited in the past. In the Gemeride zone a similar deposit occurs at Novoveská Huta near Spišská Nová Ves.[16]

Cupriferous and polymetallic deposits in Neovolcanics In recent years disseminated copper ores of volcanogenic, hydrothermal and skarn types have been recognized in the Central Slovakian Neovolcanic rocks at Banská Hodruša and Zlatno. Longer known deposits include hydrothermal subvolcanic veins like Rozália with cupriferous and Pb–Zn ores.[10]

The Rozália vein at Banská Hodruša is considered in the sense of the theory of monoascendent zoning of hydrothermal ores to belong to a copper zone situated below a zone of Pb–Zn ores. The vein strikes NNE and is about 1 km long. Its vertical extent is about 700 m and its thickness 1–2 m. It dips southward at 40–50°. The wallrocks are andesites and tuffs, which are cut by dacite dykes. At depth there is a granodiorite intrusion. The Rozália vein cuts this granodiorite.

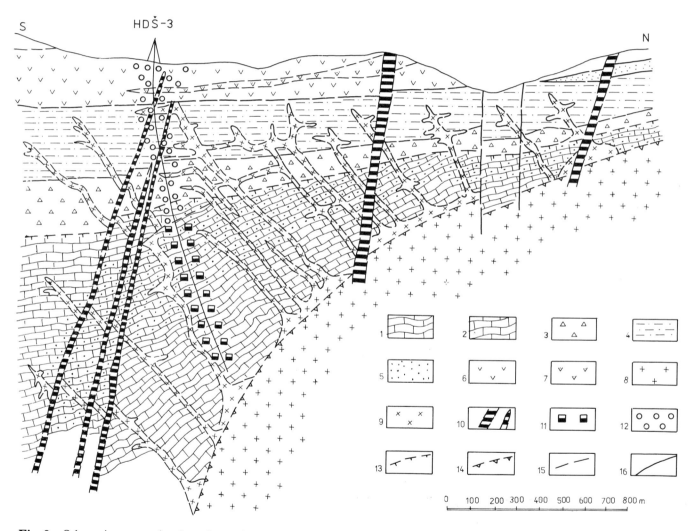

Fig. 9 *Schematic cross-section throughout polymetallic Cu–Pb–Zn ore deposit in Zlatno near Hodruša, Banská Štiavnica ore district: 1, dark limestones and dolomites (Middle Triassic of the Krížna unit); 2, skarns in dark limestones and dolomites of Krížna unit; 3, Permian (conglomerates with arkosic matrices, sandstones, black shales); 4, Permian of Choč unit (conglomerates, sandstones, shales and diabases); 5, variegated shales and sandstones (Zeissian of Choč unit); 6, Middle Miocene (pyroxene–amphibole–andesite—second phase); 7, pyroclastic rocks of pyroxene–amphibole–andesite composition; 8, amphibole–biotite–granodiorite (Miocene); 9, diorites and quartz-diorites (Miocene); 10, amphibole–biotite–dacite—third volcanic phase (Upper Miocene); 11, disseminations and skarns with Pb, Zn and Cu ores in skarnitized carbonate rocks; 12, disseminations of pyrite–pyrrhotite–chalcopyrite ores in Miocene andesites and in Permian; 13, overthrusts (Choč unit overlying Krížna unit); 14, contacts between granodiorites and Krížna unit; 15, contact between Miocene overlying Choč unit; 16, post-Miocene faults. After Ilavský et al.*[10]

The minerals of the Rozália vein are chalcopyrite, quartz, minor galena, sphalerite, pyrite, pyrrhotite, barite, carbonates, etc. Several pulses of mineralization occurred, giving a spatial distribution of minerals that indicates both monoascendent and polyascendent zoning. Detailed geochemical investigations showed increasing amounts of Bi, Ca, Ag, Sn and Mo with depth.

Metal grades in the Rozália vein are: Cu, 0·4–1·5%; Pb, 1·4–2·6%; and Zn, 1·1–2·8%; gold and silver values are widespread. Rozália is a small vein deposit in terms of reserves. Its history is similar to that of the veins of Banská Štiavnica, which will be described in the section on Pb–Zn ores.

Disseminated copper mineralization of ore grade in Miocene granodiorites and in andesites and dacites of the Neovolcanics was discovered in deep drill-holes (Fig. 9) at Zlatno near Hodruša.[10] Detailed prospecting near Zlatno outlined thick zones of disseminated chalcopyrite, pyrite, pyrrhotite and quartz in granodiorite and porphyritic hypabyssal andesites. These rocks are penetrated by dykes of dacite and diorite, which produced skarns and hornfelses at their contacts. The contact aureoles are comparatively richly impregnated with sulphides of Cu, Pb, Zn and Fe and therefore the mineralization appears to be connected with the dacites and/or the diorites.

Exploratory drilling is in progress and appears to confirm the presence of three different types of mineralization: one in Miocene andesites, another in Permian rocks (both copper ores) and a third type consisting of Pb–Zn ores in the Triassic.

Lead–zinc ores
In the Western Carpathians the lead–zinc ores were formed during several epochs. According to Slávik,[10] in the early Palaeozoic stratiform Pb–Zn ores were formed in the Upper Carboniferous veins and stratiform ores were formed in carbonate rocks and further Pb–Zn mineralization occurs in Middle Triassic carbonates, in the contact zones of Neogene diorites and volcanic rocks and in Caenozoic andesites. The most important deposits are veins in the crystalline massifs of the Tatroveporides and hydrothermal, volcanogenic and skarn ores in Neovolcanic areas.

Hydrothermal veins of plutogenic type in crystalline massifs These are found in the ore districts of the Malé Karpaty, the Nízke Tatry, the Malá Magura–Suchý, the Malá Fatra and the Považský Inovec Mountains in the Veporides. The deposit at Soviansko near Jasenie on the southern slopes of the Nízke Tatry Mountains is well known. It is a small deposit situated in gneisses and arteritic migmatites with aplites and pegmatites. The veins strike eastwards for 1 km and dip steeply southward at 60–80°, making various angles with the Variscan cleavage in the wallrocks. The veins are irregular, lenticular in shape and their thickness ranges from 0·5 to 2 m.

The mineral composition of the veins is galena, sphalerite and pyrite. There are small or accessory quantities of gersdorffite, arsenopyrite, ankerite, semseyite, bournonite, jamesonite, chalcopyrite, barite and tetrahedrite. Among non-metallic minerals are quartz, albite, chlorite, epidote, sericite and calcite.[10] Several stages of mineralization took place.

Metal grades in the ores are: Pb, 1·1–7·6%; Zn, up to 0·11%; Cu, up to 0·03%; BaO, up to 5·7%; and Sb, up to 1·7%. In hand sorted ores Pb ran 22%, gold 0·6 g t^{-1} and silver up to 818 g t^{-1}.

Model lead ages of galenas gave 240–250 m.y., which indicates a Variscan age.[10]

Hydrothermal veins, skarns and metasomatic Pb–Zn ores in Neovolcanics This is the most important and largest group of deposits. These deposits are widespread in the Kremnicko-štiavnické vrchy Mountains, including the well-known deposits of Banská Štiavnica (Schemnitz in German). At Banská Štiavnica besides the main metals mined, i.e. Pb and Zn, there are copper, gold and silver values and, at depth, tungsten and molybdenum minerals occur. The geological structure of the area is very complex. The old, pre-Neogene basement consists of crystalline rocks and Mesozoic carbonate rocks. The Miocene volcanic rocks form a large strato-volcano with abundant lava flows and pyroclastic material of pyroxene–andesites (Tortonian) penetrated by dykes and stocks of dacite and rhyolites (Sarmatian). Further andesitic activity followed and the entire volcanic episode terminated with basalt effusions (Pontian). Diorites and granodiorites, dated as Miocene, are plutonic equivalents of the volcanic rocks.

The caldera structure at Banská Štiavnica was tectonically distorted by a system of collapse and graben structures generally following north, northeast and northwest directions.[10] There are three types of mineralization: hydrothermal subvolcanic veins in Neovolcanic rocks, metasomatic ores in Mesozoic carbonates of the basement and skarn ores in the exo-contacts of intrusive granodiorites and diorites.

Hydrothermal subvolcanic veins These are distributed inside the Banská Štiavnica caldera (Fig. 10). They form a system of northeast-striking veins, which dip southeastward at 60–80°. The length of the veins ranges up to 3 km and thicknesses are 0·5–5 m and more. Their vertical extent is about 600 m.

The vein fillings are brecciated, forming vertical ore columns separated from one another by barren quartz areas. As shown by macrostructures, five periods of mineralization were involved.[16] The main minerals in the veins are pyrite, galena, sphalerite, chalcopyrite, quartz and carbonates of Ca, Mn, Mg, Fe (rhodochrosite, dolomite, ankerite, calcite). Barite, chlorite, gypsum, cinnabar, antimonite, tetrahedrite, jamesonite, pyrargyrite, scheelite, etc., are present in small to accessory quantities. In the upper parts of the veins

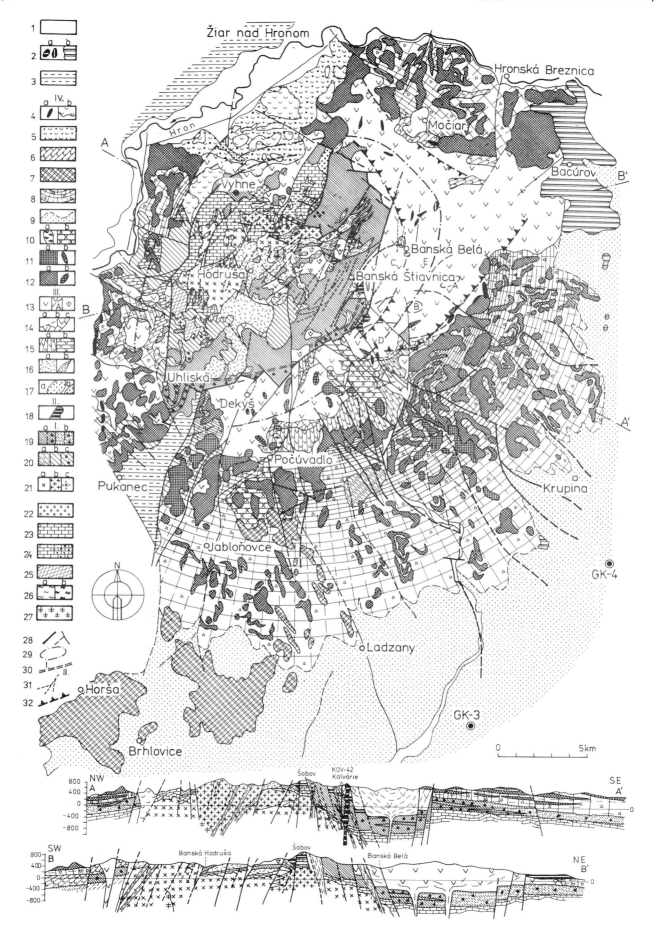

proustite, pyrargirite, argentite, stephanite and other minerals are present.

The tenor of economic metals is extremely variable, both vertically and horizontally. Grades published in 1965 are as follows: Pb, 1·5%; Zn, 2%; Cu, 0·23%; Au, 0·3 g t^{-1}; Ag, 25 g t^{-1}; and S, 2·6%. In higher levels ores that contain Pb–Zn around 5–10% were mined in the past. The size and significance of the Pb–Zn and Au–Ag veins at Banská Štiavnica are evidenced by continuous mining activity from the year 770 to the present with but short breaks as a result of floods, wars, etc.

Metasomatic lead–zinc ores These ores have been known at Banská Štiavnica since the 1960s when they were discovered during mining operations. They are emplaced in Triassic limestones and dolomites. The lead–zinc mineralization is here of high grade with metal tenors above 20% at intersections with the hydrothermal subvolcanic veins and with dacite dykes. The spatial extent of the mineralization is small. The ores contain galena, sphalerite, chalcopyrite, pyrite, dolomite, calcite, chlorite and other minerals. Several periods of mineralization were involved.

Skarn lead–zinc ores This type of mineralization was discovered in the Central Slovakian Neovolcanic areas by drilling at Zlatno near Hodruša (it is described in the section on copper ores). The mineralization is at considerable depth (600–1000 m). Whether mining will be economically possible will depend on total reserves and their grade. A similar Pb–Zn–Cu ore deposit is known at Zlatá Baňa in the Slánske vrchy Mountains of Eastern Slovakia.

Antimony ores
Antimony is another common metal in the Western Carpathians. Deposits of many genetic types were developed in the Caledonian, Variscan and Alpine epochs.

Volcanogenic-sedimentary deposits of Sb ores in Palaeozoic rocks Volcanogenic-sedimentary stratiform Sb ores are widespread in the Malé Karpaty (Little Carpathian) Mountains. The Pod Kolársky deposit at Pezinok–Cajla is typical of these. The country rocks consist of a series of metamorphic rocks. The host rocks of the orebodies are dark graphitic schists of the so-called Malé Karpaty Group. In the Variscan epoch the ore-bearing series was intruded by granitoids in the form of dykes and small intrusions. Intensive folding and faulting of the ore-bearing series also occurred.

The principal minerals in the deposit include pyrite, arsenopyrite, chalcopyrite, löllingite, quartz, gudmundite, berthierite, jamesonite, boulangerite, sphalerite, galena and carbonates of Fe, Mn, Mg, etc. Among the secondary minerals are kermesite, antimonite, native antimony, Sb ochres (sénarmontite, valentinite), limonite, goethite, etc. The mineralization process occurred in three stages: pyrite–arsenopyrite, quartz–carbonate–antimony and antimonite–kermesite. Metal grades are: Sb, 1·77%; and Au, 1·44 g t^{-1}. Flotation results in a concentrate with about 17% Sb and 9 g t^{-1} Au.[1,14,15]

The ore-bearing layer of graphitic phyllites, micaschists and paragneiss is 60–70 m thick. The antimony-bearing lenses are 10–40 m thick with layers of Sb ores that range from centimetres to metres in thickness. They are separated from one another by graphitic phyllite or biotitic micaschists or paragneisses only slightly impregnated with Sb sulphides. The total length of the deposit is 1 km with several ore zones around 300–550 m long. The vertical extent of the mineralization, which dips steeply (70–90°) is about 100 m. The antimony ore deposit at Pezinok has been mined for almost 100 years. More than 1 000 000 tonne of Sb ores was mined there.

In the Malé Karpaty Mountains are some smaller Sb deposits, such as Pernek and Kuchyňa (Fig. 11).

Hydrothermal veins of Sb and Au Hydrothermal veins with Sb sulphides occur in some granitoid massifs of the Western Carpathians, e.g. Malá Fatra, Nízke Tatry, Vysoké Tatry and the Veporides.

Fig. 10 (*Facing page*) Strato-volcanic structure of Banská Štiavnica ore field, Middle Slovakian Neovolcanics, Banská Štiavnica ore district: *1*, Quaternary formations (alluvial beds); *2a*, volcanic necks (basanites); *2b*, lava flows of basaltic rocks; *3*, intravolcanic basins of Neogene age; *4–12*, the fourth volcanic phase—*4*, rhyolites: *a*, dykes; *b*, extrusions; *5*, rhyolitic tuffs and tuffites; *6*, felsitic dacites; *7*, lava flows of pyroxene-andesites with glassy matrix; *8*, volcaniclastic rocks (agglomerates, breccias, etc.) in central part of volcano; *9*, volcaniclastic and volcanosedimentary rocks of peripheral parts of volcano (tuffs, tuffites, breccias, agglomerates, etc.); *10*, porous tuffs of pyroxene-andesite: *a*, ignimbrites; *b*, water-laid; *11*, pyroxene- and biotite-andesites: *a*, lava flows; *b*, dykes; *12*, pyroxene- and amphibole-andesites: *a*, lava flows; *b*, dykes; *13—17*, third volcanic phase—*13*, biotite-andesites: *a*, undetermined; *b*, necks; *c*, lava flows; *14*, volcaniclastic breccias; *15*, volcaniclastic rocks: *a*, pyroclastic andesites; *b*, porous tuffs; *16*, quartz-diorite porphyry: *a*, irregular or concordant intrusions; *b*, dykes; *17*, hydroquartzites; *18*, second volcanic phase—*18*, intravolcanic sedimentary basin (tuffites, coals, conglomerates, andesitic pyroclastics); *19 and 20*, first volcanic phase—*19a*, propylitized pyroxene-andesites (lava flows and volcaniclastics); *b*, pyroxene-andesites (lava flow and volcaniclastics); *20*, propylitized pyroxene-amphibole-andesites: *a*, extrusive with garnets; *b*, lava flow of porphyritic texture; *c*, volcaniclastics; *21*, plutonic bodies: *a*, granodiorites; *b*, diorites and quartz-diorites; *c*, granitic aplites; *22–27*, Neovolcanic basement of pre-Miocene age—*22*, Palaeogene (conglomerates); *23*, Mesozoic rocks (Triassic to Albian); *24*, contact metamorphic rocks (skarns, marbles, etc.); *25*, Palaeozoic rocks (Carboniferous–Permian); *26a*, metamorphosed granites of Variscan age; *b*, migmatites; *27*, crystalline rocks; *28*, tectonic lines: *a*, of primary importance, *b*, of secondary order; *29*, ring structures and concentric structures responsible for andesitic lava flows; *30*, limits between I, central volcanic structure (massive andesites) and II, peripheral zone (predominantly volcaniclastics); *31*, ore veins; *32*, graben structures. After Ilavský et al.[10]

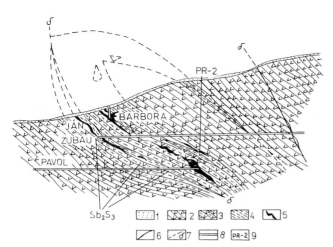

Fig. 11 *Geological cross-section through stratiform pyrite-antimony ore deposit of Pernek, Malé Karpaty ore district: 1, Quaternary (soils); 2, amphibolites; 3, actinolitic graphitic schists; 4, dark graphitic schists—host rocks of orebodies; 5, lenses of pyrite-antimony ore; 6, faults detected during mining; 7, inferred faults; 8, mine workings; 9, boreholes. After Slávik et al.*[16]

granitoids. The vein system extends over a length of 4 km and is 700–800 m wide. The vertical extent of the mineralization is about 500 m. The veins dip at 70–90° and their thicknesses are small, ranging from 0·20 cm to 0·5 m. Mineralization is frequently dispersed in the surrounding granites in the form of impregnations extending over considerable distances from the veins.

Antimonite, berthierite, pyrite and ankerite are the main vein minerals. Accessories are native gold, jamesonite, tetrahedrite, sphalerite, chalcopyrite, hematite and barite. The veins possess massive, banded, inclusion-like, brecciated, impregnation-like structures and textures.

The mineralization took place in three stages: quartz–pyrite, carbonates and sulphides with antimony minerals. Distinct primary vertical monoascendent and polyascendent zoning in the veins is well developed. Antimony, pyrite and gold decrease in quantity with depth—in contrast to increasing quartz, Pb, Zn and Cu sulphides. The quality of the ore is variable and the Sb content varies from 2 to 3% (impregnation type), and from 10 to 15% (massive type). The tenor of gold is $0·1–0·2$ g t^{-1}. Since the beginning of exploitation in the second half of the nineteenth century the Liptovská Dúbrava deposit has yielded more than 1 000 000 tonne of Sb ore.

In the Nízke Tatry Mountains the Magurka Sb deposit was exploited from the Middle Ages to the first world war and the Medzibrod deposit until the second

The largest veins are widespread in the Liptovská Dúbrava deposit on the northern slopes of Nízke Tatry (Fig. 12). The host rocks are granites of two types (Ďumbier type and Prašivá type) with occasional xenoliths of gneiss and of migmatites.[16] The deposit consists of a system of north-trending veins in

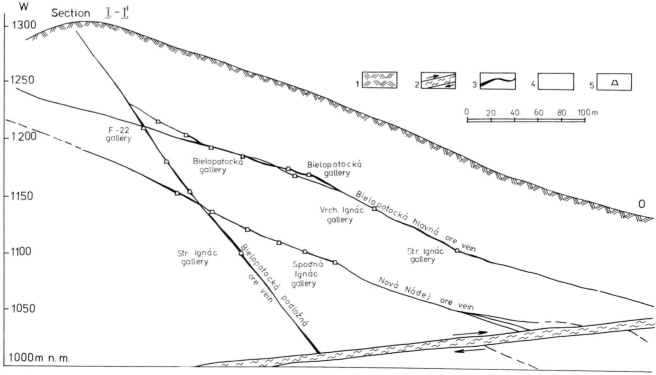

Fig. 12 *Geological cross-section through quartz–antimonite ore veins at Liptovská Dúbrava, Nízke Tatry ore district: 1, Quaternary (altered granites, soils); 2, faults with mylonitic filling; 3, ore veins with antimonite filling; 4, granitic rocks; 5, mine levels. After Ilavský et al.*[10]

world war. There are other smaller veins at Pohronský Bukovec, Jasenie, Horná Lehota, Dolná Lehota, Bystrá, Mýto pod Ďumbierom, etc.[16] In other central massifs (Malé Karpaty, Malá Fatra) smaller Sb veins were exploited in the past.

Subvolcanic hydrothermal veins in Miocene Neovolcanics This is a group of small deposits of ores of good quality. The deposit of Šturec near the town of Kremnica is a typical example. The minerals are antimonite and pyrite with admixtures of arsenopyrite, native gold, pyrite, chalcopyrite, carbonates, etc. The grade is variable—Sb, 0·1–25% (average 4%); As, 0·01–0·4%; Au, up to 3 g t^{-1}; Ag, 2–15 g t^{-1}; and Cu, 0·01–0·08%. The Šturec deposit is small. It was explored after the second world war and mined in 1970 after the mining of gold at Kremnica had ceased. There is similar insignificant Sb mineralization in the Eastern Slovakian Neovolcanics in the Slánske pohorie Mountains.

Tetrahedrite type of antimony ores In the Western Carpathians by-product antimony is present in tetrahedrites of cupriferous deposits in considerable quantities; Sb contents in tetrahedrites range between 3 and 13%, according to the type of deposit. The highest antimony contents (9–19%) are in tetrahedrites of the siderite–sulphide deposits of Rudňany in contrast to the low Sb contents (3–9%) in tetrahedrites at other deposits, such as Rožňava and Gelnica.[9,10]

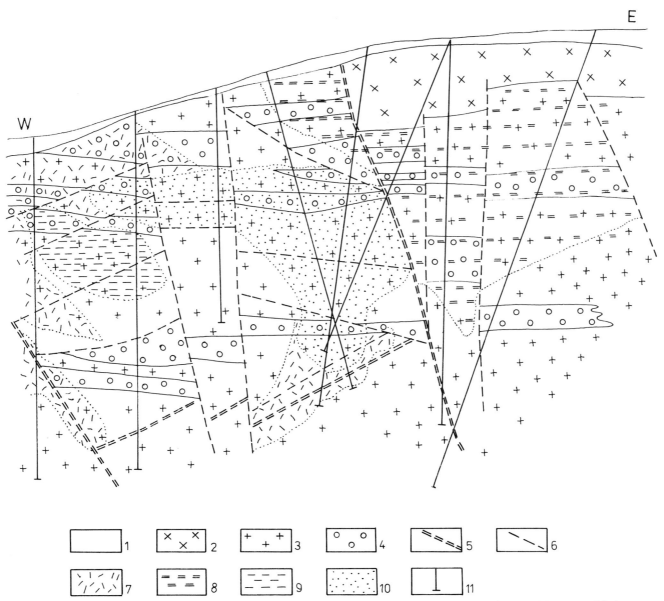

Fig. 13 *Mercury ore deposit at Dubník, Slánske vrchy ore district: 1, Quaternary (soils, breccias); 2, biotite–amphibole–pyroxene andesites; 3, pyroxene andesites; 4, tuffitic and brecciated pyroxene andesites; 5, principal faults; 6, minor faults; 7, zone of chloritization; 8, zone of pyritization; 9, zone with antimony mineralization; 10, mercury mineralization (cinnabar, mercury, metacinnabar); 11, boreholes. After Ilavský et al.*[10]

Mercury ores
Mercury mineralization is present in the Western Carpathians in various formations. The following types have been noted as the most important:[16] hydrothermal siderite–sulphide veins with cinnabar in the Palaeozoic and the Lower Triassic of the Spišsko-gemerské rudohorie Mountains and veins, stockworks and impregnations in the Central Slovakian and East Slovakian Neovolcanic rocks. The first type is regarded as plutogenic, with tetrahedrite as the main mercury mineral and with small quantities of cinnabar in or around the deposits; in the second type cinnabar and metacinnabar are the main Hg minerals.

Hydrothermal siderite–sulphide veins In the Spišsko-gemerské rudohorie siderite–sulphide veins tetrahedrite is the main Hg mineral. Its variety rich in Hg (schwatzite) contains up to 19% Hg. The veins are most frequent on the northern and southern margins of the Spišsko-gemerské rudohorie.

Rudňany is a typical deposit (described in the sections on iron and copper ores). Cinnabar occurs in the upper Permian parts of the deposit. Impregnations of cinnabar extend over a considerable distance from the veins. Native Hg is also more frequent in the upper parts of the veins, mainly in the vein quartz. In the Fe–Cu ores of Rudňany the Hg contents range between 0·01% and 0·03% and, occasionally, up to 1%.

Metallic Hg is obtained from a concentrate of sulphides by roasting. The production of Cu–Fe ore is sufficiently high to yield enough mercury to cover all Czechoslovakian needs and leave some for export.

Mercury deposits in Miocene Neovolcanic rocks Mercury mineralization in the Neovolcanic areas of Central and Eastern Slovakia is in the low-temperature outer zones on the peripheries of volcanic centres with high-temperature Pb–Zn–Cu and occasional gold–silver mineralization in the inner zones.[10,16] The Merník deposit in Eastern Slovakia was exploited from 1830 to 1939. Another example is the Dubník deposit east of Zlatá Baňa in Slánske vrchy Mountain. It is in an external low-temperature zone around the Pb–Zn–Cu zone of the Zlatá Baňa ore field (Fig. 13).

Recent exploration has shown that the volcanic complex contains earlier Sarmatian pyroclastics of amphibole–andesite lava flows and minor intrusions overlain by Pliocene andesitic pyroclastics.

The orebodies are impregnation stockworks of irregular form, sometimes spherical or pear-formed or otherwise completely irregular. The ores contain cinnabar, metacinnabar, rare pyrite and opal chalcedony. The minerals are dispersed in propylitized and kaolinized andesitic Pliocene tuffs. Mercury in the mineralized zones ranges from hundredths of a per cent to 0·2%; richer mineralization runs at >1%.

In the Central Slovakian Neovolcanic rocks, mainly in the Kremnica ore district, similar mercury deposits near Malachov, Tajov and Králiky were exploited in the past. Today these areas are subject to detailed prospecting.

Gold and silver ores
These metals are recovered from a number of the polymetallic deposits described above. They were mined in prehistoric times and in the Middle Ages in the oxidation zones above many of these polymetallic deposits.

Deposits in which gold was the principal metal and which have been exploited from prehistoric times until recently are gold-bearing quartz veins in the Neovolcanic rocks of Central Slovakia (Kremnica) (here the Au contents ranged from bonanzas down to 3 g t^{-1}) and gold-bearing placers in gravels and sands of the Danube and some streams in the Nízke Tatry and Spišsko-gemerské rudohorie Mountains, etc. The gold contents varied between hundredths of a gramme and several grammes per tonne: these were exploited from the Middle Ages to the second world war.

Nickel–cobalt ores
In the Western Carpathians Dobšiná in the Spišsko-gemerské rudohorie Mountains is the best-known locality for Ni–Co ores. The last investigations here were carried out in 1952–60.[10] These ores were exploited from the seventeenth century up to 1880 at two localities that appear to represent two genetically different types of Ni ore—magmatic and hydrothermal veins. Their economic importance is small.

Pyrite ores
Pyrite deposits in the Western Carpathians are of two types: stratiform volcanogenic-sedimentary ores of Palaeozoic age (e.g. Smolník and Pezinok) and veins. At present pyrite is only exploited on a very small scale. One such locality is Smolník, which was described above in the section on cupriferous ores.

Barites
Barite is frequent in deposits of various types in the Western Carpathians, but the only economically significant deposits are the hydrothermal siderite–barite–sulphide veins of plutogenic origin in the Spišsko-gemerské rudohorie Mountains, e.g. the locality of Rudňany, described in the sections on Fe, Cu and Hg ores.

The contents of barite in these ores are variable. Siderite–sulphide ores in Permian rocks near the surface had the highest barite contents, i.e. 50–80% of the total vein filling, in places the vein consisting of almost pure barite. At depth the barite decreased to 30–50%. Polymineralic ores at present mined contain about 15% barite.

At Rudňany gravity treatment of the ores results in a barite concentrate of the following composition: $BaSO_4$, 95%; $SrSO_4$, 2%; and FeO, 2%. The annual production of the concentrate (100 000 tonne) meets the demand for this raw material in Czechoslovakia.

In the Spišsko-gemerské rudohorie Mountains more vein deposits of barite occur at Bindt, Jaklovce, Koyšov and Drnava, etc. Among these only Drnava was mined for barite. In the Tatroveporides barite veins are present in Permian melaphyres (e.g. Malužiná in the Nízke Tatry Mountains and in the Malé Karpaty Mountains).

Magnesite
In the Western Carpathians magnesite deposits of the Veitsch type are most common in the Spišskogemerské rudohorie Mountains. The deposits of Slovakia as a whole may be divided into the following groups.[10]

Deposits of crystalline magnesite in early Palaeozoic of the Gemerides These magnesites were discovered at Vlachovo in the Gemerides by deep drilling.[19] They are in the oldest sequence of the Gelnica Group—the so-called Vlachovo Beds, which probably belong to the Cambrian.[10] The sequence of carbonate rocks with magnesite is very deep and does not crop out. The Cambrian is 2000 m thick and the carbonate horizons are at depths of 800–1200 m in a complex of dark phyllites, sandstones and quartzites. There are also isolated layers of porphyroids.

The mineralogical composition is as follows: dolomite, magnesite, calcite and ankerite with lesser contents of pyrite, talc, sericite, etc. Some minerals appear in more than one generation, which may be due to several stages of mineralization or to several phases of metamorphism. Chemical analyses of the magnesite reveal the following variation in composition: MgO, 38–45%; MnO, 0·03–0·2%; CaO, 1·5–7·6%; Fe_2O_3, 2·1–2·9%; SiO_2, 0·1–0·2%; Al_2O_3, 0·1–2·5%; loss on ignition, 48–51%.

Various hypotheses have been put forward concerning the origin of these deposits.

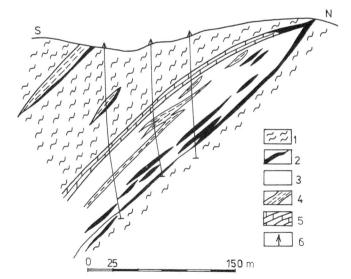

Fig. 14 *Geological cross-section through talc–magnesite deposit of Mútnik near Hnúšťa, Southern Veporides ore district: 1, schists and paragneisses; 2, lenses and layers of talc; 3, crystalline magnesite with many lenses of talc; 4, silicified dolomites and limestones in magnesite beds; 5, dolomites and dolomitic magnesites; 6, boreholes. After Slávik et al.*[16]

Deposits of crystalline magnesite and talc in Veporide crystalline complex Magnesites of this type are well known and are mined mainly for talc.[16] In the last decade, however, magnesite has been produced from these deposits, particularly that of Mútnik near Hnúšťa (Fig. 14), which lies in the so-called Hron Group of early Palaeozoic meso- to katazonally metamorphosed rocks.[10]

The deposit is surrounded by micaschists and paragneisses. In the Hron Group layers of basic volcanic rocks have been metamorphosed into orthoamphibolites. These, in turn, are overlain by dolomites, limestones and magnesites of variable thickness. Magnesite layers range up to 50 m in thickness in a belt more than 150 m thick. The beds strike eastwards and dip south at 45–50°. The deposit is about 1 km long and 800 m deep.

The minerals present are dolomite, magnesite, calcite, talc, quartz, chlorite, sericite, pyrite and chalcopyrite with some tetrahedrite, sphalerite, galena, arsenopyrite, pyrrhotite, bornite, chalcosite, magnetite, cobaltite, native bismuth, covelline and native gold. The minerals can be divided into several paragenetic groups.

The chemical composition of the magnesite is 35–42% MgO, up to 1·7% CaO, up to 2·9% Fe_2O_3, up to 3% SiO_2 and up to 5% Al_2O_3. Sometimes the magnesite contains talc in variable quantities. This magnesite is used in the metallurgical industry.

Similar deposits are found around Hnúšťa and Kokava on the Rimavica River, near Klenovec.[16]

Deposits of crystalline magnesite in Upper Carboniferous of the Gemerides[10,16] The Upper Carboniferous of the Gemerides is the most important geological formation for crystalline magnesite deposits of the Veitsch type. Magnesite has been mined there since the 1890s. Many deposits are already being exploited (Ružiná, Ploské, Sirk, Ochtiná, Ratkovská Suchá) and investigations of others have proved large reserves (Podrečany, Burda-Poproč, Jelšava, Košice).

Typical of these deposits is Dúbrava near Jelšava.[10,16] Here the Upper Carboniferous is overthrust along the Lubeník–Margecany line on to the crystalline complexes of the Veporides and the Gemerides.

The Upper Carboniferous beds strike ENE and dip southeastwards at 30–50°. The mineralized zone with magnesite is 4·5 km long and consists of three divisions—lower, middle and upper.

The middle division of carbonates carries most of the magnesite and is more than 600 m thick. The magnesite forms conformable bodies and beds that are massive and coarse-grained. Their thicknesses generally range up to 70 m and in the central part up to 400 m. The average thickness of the main layer is about 200 m. Smaller layers also alternate with dolomite beds (Fig. 15). The main mass of the deposit consists of magnesite and dolomite of several generations. Among other minerals present are goethite, talc, pyrite,

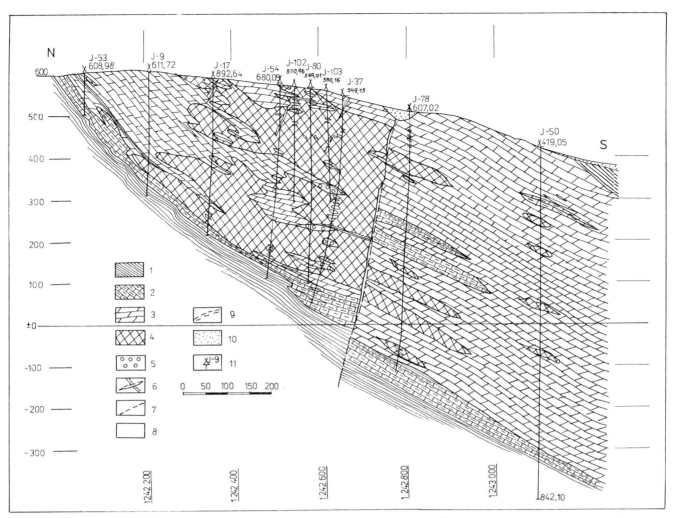

Fig. 15 *Geological cross-section through stratiform deposit of crystalline magnesite in Jelšava-Dúbrava, Western Gemerides–Revúca ore district: 1–5, Upper Carboniferous—1, graphitic schists; 2, stratified crystalline dolomite I; 3, crystalline dolomite II (non-stratified); 4, crystalline magnesite I–II with beds of dolomite I–II; 5, brecciated magnesite with dolomitic matrix; 6, epigenetic veins with magnesite III and dolomite III filling; 7, perpendicular faults; 8, faults with a palygoskite filling; 9, faults with talc filling; 10, Quaternary (soils, detritus, karstic fillings); 11, boreholes. After Ilavský et al.*[10]

hematite, calcite, palygorskite, galena, chalcopyrite, clinochlore, muscovite, rutile and zircon. Longitudinal northwest faults that cut the deposit are filled with ochre, loamy material, aragonite, palygorskite, goethite, hematite and pyrite.

The chemical composition of the Jelšava deposit is 40–42% MgO, 1·5–4·8% CaO, up to 6·1% SiO_2, 0·2–2·5% Al_2O_3, 1·3–4·5% Fe_2O_3 and 0·2–0·4% MnO.

The trace-element content in the magnesites and dolomites has been studied in detail. It is the same as that in Upper Carboniferous diabases. There is a difference of opinion about the genesis of these deposits.

Talc

In the Western Carpathians three genetic types of talc deposits are common: talc in magnesite deposits in the Veporides, e.g. Mútnik near Hnúšťa, which was described above; talc–magnesite deposits in the Upper Carboniferous of the Gemerides, e.g. Kohútik near Jelšava; and talc in ultrabasic igneous rocks in the Gemerides and Veporides (Muránska Dlhá Lúka).

The first type is the most important. In the Mútnik deposit (Fig. 14) the talc is in the main magnesite layers. There are many varieties—from pure talc to chloritic talc and talcose phyllites, etc. Talc concentrations around tectonic dislocations in the magnesite and along the margins of magnesite beds show that the talc is associated with areas of intensive movement and compression.

The chemical composition of the talc deposits is: MgO, 35·48%; SiO_2, 42·4%; Al_2O_3, 16%; Fe_2O_3, 2·92%; and CaO, 1·69%. A part of the talc produced is hand sorted and the purer varieties are utilized in the electrical industry. Talc with magnesite is treated by flotation to give concentrates of pure talc and pure magnesite for pharmaceutical purposes, the chemical industry, etc.

As regards the genesis of the talc, there are two views: the first suggests a hydrothermal origin for the talc and magnesite during the Alpine epoch; the other is that the deposits have resulted from the metamorphism of pre-existing magnesite deposits.[10]

Asbestos

Among many mineralogical varieties of asbestos in the Western Carpathians the most common is chrysotile. It is found in serpentinized ultrabasic rocks mostly of Lower Triassic or Jurassic(?) age.[10] The best-known deposit of this type is at Dobšiná, where asbestos has been mined since 1918.

The serpentinite body at Dobšiná is oval, strikes easterly, is 700 m long, has a width of about 500 m and extends 45 to 60 m in depth. Most of it has already been exploited.

Among the most frequent minerals in the serpentinite are antigorite and amorphous sepiolite. Fibrous chrysotile forms veinlets that range up to 2 cm in thickness. The chrysotile content in the rock is 1–1·2%. Its fibres are 2–8 mm long. Microasbestos is predominant. The total annual production is 2500 tonne of fibre asbestos and 7000 tonne of microasbestos.

Small occurrences of asbestos are known at Danková near Dobšiná, at Breznička near Lučenec and elsewhere.

Gypsum–anhydrite

In the Western Carpathians evaporite formations with anhydrite and gypsum are widespread in the Carboniferous, Permian, Lower Triassic, Upper Triassic and Neogene sediments of the internal zones. At the present time only Permian and Lower Triassic gypsum–anhydrite from the Gemeride zone is mined.

These minerals are exploited in Novoveská Huta, where anhydrites form a layer 70 m thick in the upper part of the Permian.[16] The Permian is folded into asymmetrical folds about east–west axes. Alteration of anhydrite to gypsum extends for considerable distances from dislocation zones. The thickness of the layer of evaporites in the Lower Triassic is 50–70 m.

The anhydrite horizons are several tens of metres long. The parts that are exploited for gypsum and alabaster extend over some hundreds of metres. The composition of the anhydrite zones is 93% anhydrite and 4·3% gypsum. In the gypsum zones it is 91% gypsum and 8% anhydrite. Occasionally, halite and potassium salts are present.

The gypsum is mostly utilized in the pharmaceutical, chemical and building industries, and as an additive in cement manufacture. The quantities mined are comparatively small.

In the Gemerides gypsum–anhydrite deposits are widespread (Dedinky and Mlynky, Silica, Čoltovo, Šankovce, Strelnica). Gypsum and anhydrite are present also in the Upper Triassic and in the Miocene of East Slovakia.[16]

Halite

Deposits of halite occur in the Miocene of the Western Carpathians in two stratigraphic horizons—the Upper Helvetian (Prešov–Sol'ná Baňa) and in the Tortonian (East Slovakia; Zbudza near Michalovce).

The deposit of Sol'ná Baňa near Prešov has been exploited since Roman times (in Latin, *Castrum Salis*). Halite was mined there over the years 1572–1725 until the mines were flooded. Since then salt has been won by evaporation from brines (about 12 000 tonne per annum). The salt-bearing clays are 100–200 m thick and extend over an area of approximately 15 km². Occasionally, they are 600–800 m thick. Besides halite, the clays also contain gypsum and anhydrite. The average content of NaCl in the clays is 15%.

The deposit at Zbudza (Fig. 16) is in the Tortonian clays at depths that range from 160 to 320 m. It was discovered in 1959. There are further deposits at greater depths. The thickness of halite is up to 300 m and NaCl contents are 50–80%.[16]

There are more halite occurrences in the Miocene.

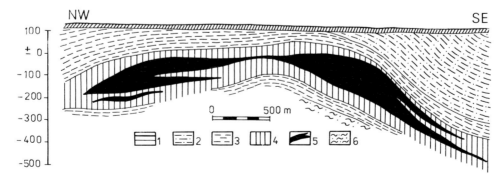

Fig. 16 *Geological cross-section through Zbudza salt deposit, near Michalovce, Vihorlat ore district: 1, Quaternary beds; 2, marls of Rotalina zone; 3, marls of Bullimina–Bolivina zone; 4, marls and clays of Globigerina–Globorotalina zone; 5, salt and salt breccias; 6, sandstones and claystones of Spiroplectamina zone (2 and 3, Upper Tortonian). After Slávik*[16]

Kaolinitic clays
Kaolinitic clays occur in the Miocene and the Pliocene of South Slovakia in the Ipel'ská kotlina depression at Kalinovo, Poltár, Pondelok, Breznička and Pukanec.[16] The beds are 8–10 m thick (Poltár), in places 3–4 m (Breznička) and, occasionally, 3–11 m (Kalinovo). The areal extent of the deposits is considerable. A local ceramic industry is based on these deposits.

Bentonites
These are montmorillonite clays in various horizons of the Miocene (Tortonian–Sarmatian). They are used in the chemical, pharmaceutical and building industries. They were formed by the decomposition of rhyolitic tuffs. The deposits occur at Fintice–Kapušany (2 m thick over a length of 2 km), Nižný Hrabovec (1 m thick over several hundred metres). Other deposits occur at Kuzmice and Lastovce in East Slovakia.

Halloysite
Special clays in the Tortonian to Pliocene of Eastern Slovakia are associated with volcanic rocks of rhyolite type. From these rocks halloysite arose by weathering. The deposit at Biela Hora near Michalovce, which is the most important, is loaf-shaped (300 m × 400 m and 36 m thick). It consists of halloysite and kaolinite and other minerals. Some smaller deposits occur nearby. The products are utilized in the gum industry, in the production of porcelain, pavement tiles and slabstones, and in the chemical and cement industries.[16]

Vein quartz
In the glass industry in Central Slovakia vein quartz has long been exploited. The veins are in the crystalline massifs of the Veporide zone. The deposit of Budina is the most important. Here the veins in granites are up to 30 m thick and several hundred metres long. The filling consists of milky quartz with a SiO_2 content of up to 99·5%. The veins dip steeply. Similar quartz veins occur in the Gemerides near Švedlár.

Dinas quartzites are exploited at Šobov near Banská Štiavnica and at Banská Belá. They are of hydrothermal origin.[16]

Limnoquartzites
These are hot-spring deposits of geyserite type associated with Miocene rhyolite volcanism. They are very hard, with a high SiO_2 (95–98%) content. Such deposits are found in Central Slovakia around Žiar (Hron River) at Bartošova Lehota and Stará Kremnička. They form deposits up to 20 m in thickness and extend over several hectares. Formerly exploited for the production of millstones, they are at present utilized for the production of silex cubes, filtration materials, ferrosilicon, etc.[16]

Quartzites
The Lower Triassic quartzites from the Tribeč Mountains in Central Slovakia (Jelenec–Žírany) are used for the production of silica. They form a horizon up to 20 m in thickness. They are exploited by opencast operations. Their SiO_2 contents are 94·8–98% (plus 1–2·5% Al_2O_3 and 0·8% $CaO + MgO$). There are similar beds at Vyhne, Sklené Teplice and in the Strážovská hornatina Mountains. In the past some of the deposits supplied raw material for the glass industry.[16]

Foundry and glass sands
These occur in the Upper Oligocene near Lučenec, in the Lower Miocene around Modrý Kameň in South Slovakia and in the Záhorská nížina lowlands. The areal extent of the beds is 1 km or more and their thicknesses range from 1 to 20 m. The sands consist of quartz (74%), feldspars (3%), muscovite (3·2%), biotite, garnet, magnetite, tourmaline, staurolite, zircon, rutile, and leucoxene (2·59%) and glauconite (2·52%).

Localities with glass sands, of aeolian origin, are found in the Záhorská nížina lowlands in Western Slovakia and in Eastern Slovakia, where they are of Neogene age. Owing to their mineralogical and chemical composition and the ease with which they can be treated, they are suitable as glass and foundry sands.[16]

Diatomites
Diatomites are found in Neovolcanic lacustrine deposits. The well-known locality of Močiar near Banská Štiavnica is Sarmatian in age. The beds range from 6 to 30 m in thickness, their areal extent being several hectares. Another deposit, Dúbravica near Banská Bystrica, has a thickness of 20 m.[16]

Perlites
Perlites are utilized in the chemical, paper, gum and fertilizer industries. Deposits exploited for perlite are at Lehôtka pod Brehy near Žiar on Hron (Central Slovakia) and at Byšta (Eastern Slovakia).[16]

Petrurgical basalt
Basalts of the Miocene Neovolcanics in Central Slovakia are melted and used for the production of acid-resistant pipes and tiles for various industrial and laboratory purposes. Such deposits are worked near Nová Baňa in Central Slovakia. The production covers home consumption and the surplus is exported.[16]

Volcanic tuffs and tuffites
In the Neovolcanic regions of Central Slovakia volcanic tuffs and tuffites are exploited and utilized for light building materials, hydraulic cement, ceramic materials, etc. The Miocene tuffs and tuffites are of rhyolitic, rhyodacitic and basaltic composition in

Eastern Slovakia and occur at Oreské, Číčava, Nižný Hrabovec and Veľká Tŕňa. In Southern Slovakia they occur at Čajkov, Hodejov and Kostolná Bašta, etc.

Limestones, marls and dolomites

In the Western Carpathians these are most frequent in the Mesozoic formations. They are extremely thick and extensive and have good chemical and technological properties suitable for many industrial uses. Among the most important are the Triassic and Jurassic limestones and dolomites at Krivošťany (Eastern Slovakia); Polom (northeast Slovakia); Margecany (northwest Slovakia); Tisovec (central Slovakia); Gombasek, Včeláre, Drieňovec (southeast Slovakia) and Mojtín, Zongor, Vajarská (western Slovakia).

Marly limestones for the production of cement are mined at many deposits (Horné Srnie, Skrabské, Lietavská Lúčka and Kostiviarska). They are, for the most part, of Lower Cretaceous age.

Middle Triassic dolomites are quarried in central Slovakia at Malé Krštenňany, Lúka on Váh, Mníchova Lehota, Rajec, Kraľovany and Trebejov.[16]

Decorative stones

Decorative stones include Quaternary travertines (Bešeňová, Ludrová, Lúčky and Biely Potok in northern Slovakia, Dreveník in eastern Slovakia and Levice in Southern Slovakia). They are now almost worked out.

Marbles in the crystalline rocks of the Carboniferous and the Middle Triassic have been exploited at Ochtiná, Tuhár, Ružiná in Southern Slovakia and at Silická Brezová.[16]

References

1 **Cambel B. and Kantor J.** Sravnenie isotopnogo i geochimičeskogo issledovanija sulfidov singenetičeskych kolčedannych mestoroždenij Zapadnich Karpat. *Očerki sovremennoj geochimii i analitičeskoj chimii*, 1972, 377–89.

2 **Van Eysinga F. W.** *Geological time table*, 3rd edn (Amsterdam: Elsevier, 1976).

3 **Fusán O. Plančár J. and Slávik J.** Geologická stavba v južnej časti vnútorných Západných Karpát. *Západné Karpaty*, **15**, 1971.

4 **Ilavský J.** Geológia rudných ložísk Spišsko-gemerského rudohoria. *Geol. Pr., Bratisl.* no. 46, 1957, 51–96.

5 **Ilavský J. and Čillík I.** Náčrt metalogenézy Západných Karpát. (Overview of metallogenesis of the Western Carpathians) *Geol. Pr., Bratisl.* no. 55, 1959, 109–35. (Slovak text)

6 **Ilavský J.** Zur metallogenetischen Karte der Westkarpaten 1:1000000. *Geol. Pr., Bratisl., Spravy* 44–45, 1968, 51–72.

7 **Ilavský J.** Conclusions concernant la metallogénie de système plissé Alpin de l'Europe Centrale et Sud-Orientale en 2 500 000. *Proc. 10th Congr. Carpato-Balk. geol. Ass.*, 1973, 45–108.

8 **Ilavský J.** Príspevok ku paleogeografii gelnickej série na základe stratiformných zrudnení. *Geol. Pr., Bratisl. Zborn. geol. vied, ZK, séria Min. petr. geochem.* no. 1, 1974, 54–98.

9 **Ilavský J.** Stratiform copper deposits of the Western Carpathians, Czechoslovakia. *Econ. Geol.*, **71**, 1976, 423–32.

10 **Ilavský J. et al.** Explanation to the metallogenic map of the Western Carpathians, scale 1:500 000. Manuscript, D. Štúr. Geological Institute, Bratislava, 1977, 870 p., 230 figs. (Slovak text)

11 **Kantor J.** Beitrag zur Geochronologie der Migmatite und Metamorphie des westkarpatischen Kristallins. *Geol. Pr., Bratisl.* no. 60, 1961, 303–17.

12 **Kantor J.** Izotopy 'obyčajného' olova na niektorých západokarpatských ložiskách. *Geol. Pr., Bratisl.* no. 61, 1962, 175–94.

13 **Kantor J. and Rybár M.** Isotopes of ore lead from several deposits of west-carpathian crystalline. *Geol. Zb. Bratisl.*, **15**, no. 2 1964, 285–98.

14 **Kantor J.** Sulphur isotopes of the stratiform pyrite deposit Turecký vrch and stibnite deposit Pezinok in the Malé Karpaty Mountains crystalline. *Geol. Zb., Bratisl., Geologica Carpathica*, **25**, no. 2 1974, 311–34.

15 **Kantor J. and Rybár M.** Izotopy síry na Sb ložiskách jadrových pohorí Západných Karpát. (Sulphur isotopes on antimony ore deposits of the Core Mountains in the Western Carpathians). Manuscript. GÚDŠ, Bratislava, 1975, 130 p.

16 **Slávik J. et al.** Nerastné suroviny Slovenska. (Nutzbare Mineralien der Slowakei). *Aktuality Geol. průzkumu, Geofond—in SNT1*, Bratislava, 1967, 510 p.

17 **Varček C.** Metalogenéza Spišsko-gemerského rudohoria. (Metallogenese des Zips-Gömörer Erzgebirges). *Acta geol. geogr. Universitatis Comeniae, Bratisl.*, 2, 1959.

18 **Varček C.** Überblick der Metallogenese der Westkarpaten. *Geol. Zb., Bratisl.*, **18**, no. 1 1967, 3–10.

19 **Beňka J. and Snopko L.** Nový nález magnezitu v gelnickej sérii Spišsko-gemerského rudohoria. (A new find of magnesite in the Gelnica Group of the Spišsko-gemerské rudohorie Mts.). *Záp. Karpaty, séria Min. petr. geochem.*, no. 1, 1974, 99–118.

H. W. Walther

With contributions by K.-H. Emmermann, W. Fenchel, W. Fuchs, H. Gudden, G. Gunzert, R. Gussone, J. Hesemann, E. Hofrichter, H. Lehmann, H.-J. Lippert, M. Lusznat, H. Maus, A. Pilger, P. Podufal, C. Rée, Doris Schachner, R. Schaeffer, H.-J. Schneider, P. Simon, H. Sperling, G. Stadler, F. Stolze, E. O. Teuscher, W. Weinelt, W. Wimmenauer and J. H. Ziegler.

Federal Republic of Germany

Introduction

Geological and metallogenic summary

The following structural-geological units are found in the Federal Republic of Germany (Fig. 1), each with a characteristic sequence of sediments, igneous rocks and mineral deposits (Fig. 2, Table 1).

Variscan basement

A major event in the geological history of Central Europe was the Variscan folding during the Late Palaeozoic. The following zones can be distinguished in the Variscan orogenic belt (Fig. 3).[1,2,3]

The *Moldanubian Zone* in the south includes the Bavarian and Upper Palatinate (Oberpfalz) Forests, the Ries area, and the southern and central Black Forest with gneiss and crystalline schist of late Precambrian and early Palaeozoic age, intruded by mostly acidic igneous rocks. Assyntian (Cadomian) ages of granitic intrusion have been demonstrated by U–Pb zircon ages.[4,5] A very widespread magmatic phase with metamorphism and anatexis is dated as Caledonian (400–500 m.y.) by Rb–Sr whole rock and U–Pb determinations on zircon.[6] Many K–Ar and Rb–Sr determinations on various minerals yield Variscan ages. Ages of 363–328 m.y. have been determined for pre-orogenic Variscan granites in the Black Forest and of 325–261 m.y. for the post-orogenic granites.[7] To the south the Moldanubian basement plunges to about 5000 m below the Alpine Molasse Foredeep.

Mineral deposits, developed during the Assyntian geosynclinal stage of the Late Precambrian, are the massive sulphide layers (Kieslager) in the Bodenmais area and the graphite schists of Kropfmühl, both in the Bavarian Forest. Of proven Variscan age are large pegmatite bodies near Hagendorf in eastern Bavaria, tin–tungsten mineralization near Zell and Triberg and the Co–Ni–Bi–Ag–U veins of Wittichen in the central Black Forest, as well as the Menzenschwand uranium deposits in the southern Black Forest. The numerous lead–zinc veins in both the southern and central Black Forest are probably also of Variscan age.[8,9] This is based mainly on the fact that the Pb–Zn veins of the Untermünstertal, south of Freiburg, are cut by Permian ignimbrites.[10]

The *Saxothuringian Zone*, with the Central German Rise (Mitteldeutsche Schwelle) in its northern part, covers the area between the Moldanubian Zone and the southern part of the Rheinische Schiefergebirge. This sequence of sediments consists of folded and metamorphosed Precambrian rocks outcropping in a few dome-shaped horsts, thick Lower Palaeozoic and very thin Silurian and Devonian sediments, followed by locally thick Lower Carboniferous beds. Diabases, keratophyres and their tuffs were often formed, and gabbro and norite intruded in the Münchberg Gneiss Massif during the Early Ordovician. The main folding phase took place near the end of the Early Carboniferous. Epimetamorphic 'orthogneisses' were formed by granitoid mobilization stemming from planar shear tectonics—for example, the Hirschberg 'granite', north of Hof. These rocks were named 'frictionites' by Stettner.[11] As in the Moldanubian Zone, granitic magmas were intruded in two phases during the Late Carboniferous, followed by lamprophyres, and later, during the Permian, by rhyolites.

The Central German Rise[12] functioned several times as a facies divide between the Thuringian and the Rhenish Troughs of the Variscan geosyncline—most recently during the Early Carboniferous. The Rise sank during folding, forming the Saar–Nahe–Werra depression with its Upper Carboniferous Coal Measures in the Saar Basin.

The oldest mineral deposits in the Saxothuringian Zone are the late Cambrian massive sulphide layers of the Bayerland mine and similar layers of Ordovician age in the Kupferberg-Wirsberg area, as well as marine thuringite iron ores in northeast Bavaria. The

---

This chapter is provided by members of the Section on the Research of Ore Deposits of the GDMB Gesellschaft Deutscher Metallhütten- und Bergleute and with the support of the Federal Institute for Geoscience and Natural Resources as well as the mining companies and the Geological Surveys of the Federal States concerned.

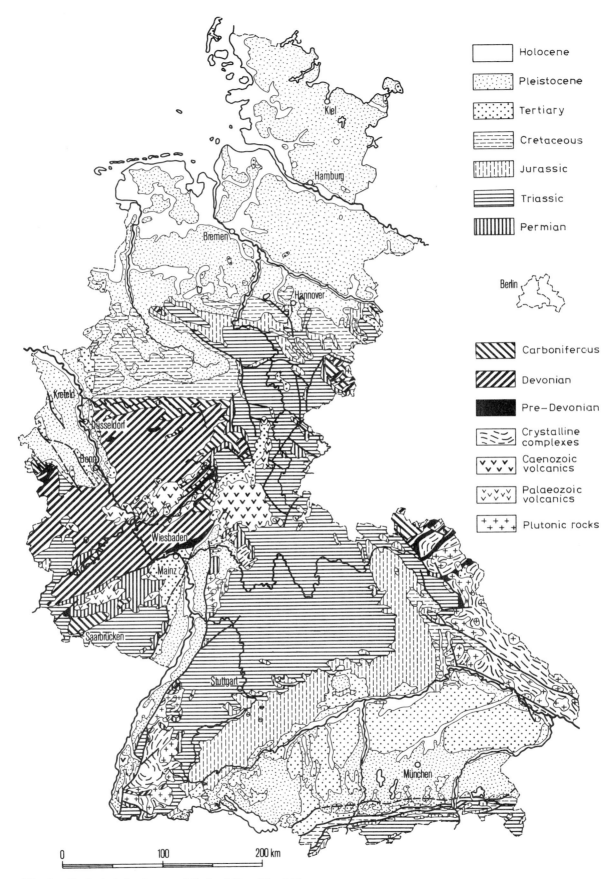

Fig. 1 *Geological sketch map of Federal Republic of Germany*

Variscan metallogenic epoch started in the early Late Devonian with red iron ore layers of the Lahn–Dill type. Tin–tungsten veins and greisen zones near the Fichtelgebirge granite contact zone belong to the Erzgebirge tin province as its westernmost spur. Uraninite was precipitated from later hydrothermal solutions. The gold–quartz veins at Brandholz belong to the same cycle. Talc deposits of different origin occur in some places. Of late Variscan age are the quartz–hematite veins, such as those near Fichtelberg and probably also the metasomatic siderite bodies near Wunsiedel in the Fichtelgebirge, and the Cu–Co–Hg–Ag–U mineralization with Fe, Mn, barite and fluorite in the Nahe depression.

The *Rhenohercynian Zone* is the deepest part of the Variscan geosyncline. It is filled with Devonian and Carboniferous sediments up to 8000 m thick. Thin, older Palaeozoic sediments outcrop only in the cores of a few anticlines. Intercalations of keratophyres and their tuffs are found in the Lower Devonian and intercalations of thick basaltic rocks are found at the boundary of the Middle to Upper Devonian Hauptgrünstein (main greenstone) and in the second volcanic phase of the Lower Carboniferous *Deckdiabas* (cover diabase). Weak Caledonian movements are known in the Hohe Venn mountains southeast of Aachen. Intensive folding and in places foliation took place during the early part of the Late Carboniferous. This was connected with widespread very low-grade metamorphism.[13,14] Granitic magma was intruded during the late part of the Late Carboniferous. These intrusions have been eroded only in the Harz Mountains.

For numerous minerals, especially the Ag–Pb–Zn group, the Rhenohercynian Zone is by far the most important metallogenic belt in the Federal Republic. Mining of stratiform deposits, ore veins and preeminently their supergene enriched parts during the Middle Ages and before the discovery of America made Germany the most important mining country of the then known world.

The volcanosedimentary, polymetallic, barite-bearing ore layers of Middle Devonian age in the Rammelsberg mountain and at Meggen are the largest metal concentrations in the country. The iron ore layers of the Lahn–Dill and some other districts are also of the volcanosedimentary type and are found at the boundary of the Middle to Upper Devonian. Hydrothermal deposits include the siderite veins of the Siegerland district as well as the Pb–Zn veins of the Aachen, Bergische Land, Iserlohn and Ramsbeck districts in the northern part of the Rheinische Schiefergebirge, and those of the Lahn–Hunsrück region with Ems and Holzappel ore districts in the southern part, as well as the Upper Harz vein district. The copper ore stockwork deposit of Marsberg is of Late Variscan age and probably originated after folding and before the transgression of the Zechstein sea. Marine oolitic hematite ores occur in the Lower and Middle Devonian of the Eifel.

The *sub-Variscan Foredeep* contains more than 3500 m of Upper Carboniferous clastic sediments with coal seams in the Ruhr and Aachen districts as well as in small horsts near Osnabrück. These sediments were folded during the late part of the Late Carboniferous. The folding becomes gradually less intense towards the north and the rock sequence becomes part of the epi-Caledonian or epi-Assyntian Platform Cover.

Fracturing took place after the folding, resulting in large transverse faults and secondary strike-slip faults. In the Ruhr district both are mineralized with Pb–Zn barite ores. Similar but less important veins occur in the Velbert anticline northeast of Düsseldorf, and without barite in the Aachen coal measures. Limnic sedimentary siderite ores also occur in the coal measures.

Post-Variscan cover

Post-Variscan sedimentation in northern Germany and in parts of Hesse begins with the Zechstein, the Kupferschiefer being the oldest sedimentary formation that covers the whole region. In southern Germany it begins with littoral or terrestrial sediments of Zechstein age or with the Triassic; in this area an epicontinental platform has developed. Such a platform is also found in the Münsterland Bight, where Aptian and thick Upper Cretaceous overlie folded Upper Carboniferous sediments. In northern Germany subsiding blocks with differential movements came into existence on the southern border of the North Sea Basin.

The Lower Saxonian Block, a graben-like basin between Bentheim and Hannover, began its development at the end of the Middle Jurassic and received 3000–4000 m of Upper Jurassic and Lower Cretaceous sediments. The Bramsche Massif was intruded during the early part of the Late Cretaceous. This laccolith, situated 15 km north of Osnabrück at a depth of about 5000 m, is manifested by a strong magnetic anomaly and high-grade diagenesis with the formation of pyrophyllite and anthracite in rocks up to Santonian age.[15] A tectonic inversion took place during the Turonian.

The Pompeckj Block, in contrast, contains thick Permian beds with locally more than 2000 m of volcanic rock in the lower part and up to 1400 m of terrigenous sediment and evaporite in the upper part. After a rather normal development during the early Mesozoic, subsidence of the block took place again after the Lower Cretaceous.

The oldest mineral deposit in the platform cover is the Kupferschiefer deposit, which was mined in the Richelsdorf Mountains until 1954. The Triassic lead deposits in the Oberpfalz, especially at Freihung, are also of sedimentary origin. The genesis of the Wiesloch Pb–Zn deposit is still an open question. Several

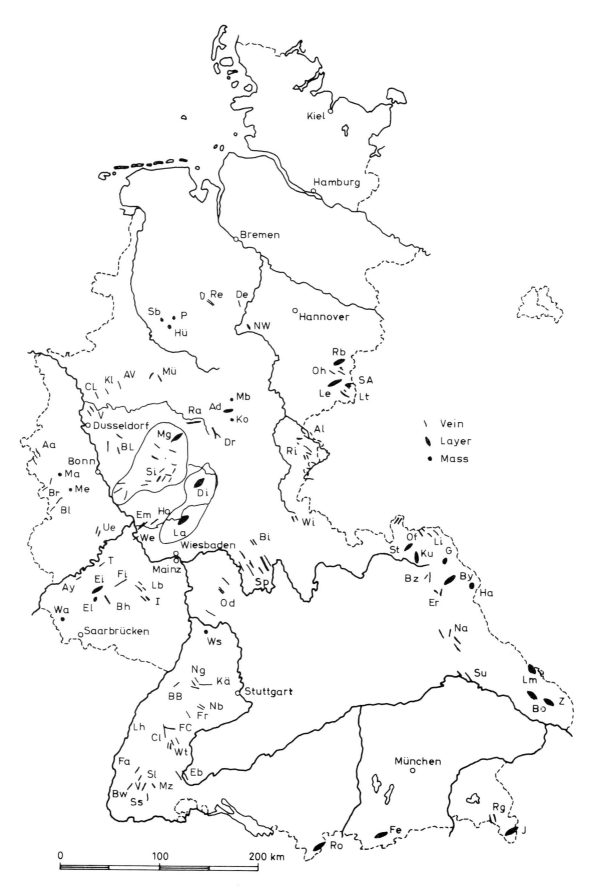

Fig. 2 *Sketch map of hypogene mineral deposits in Federal Republic of Germany* (*see also Table 1*)

Table 1 *List of hypogene mineral deposits in Federal Republic of Germany (see Fig. 2)*

Aa	Aachen	G	Göpfersgrün	Of	Oberfranken
Ad	Adorf			Oh	Oberharz
Al	Albungen	Ha	Hagendorf	Od	Odenwald
Ay	Altlay	Ho	Holzappel		
AV	Auguste Viktoria	Hü	Hüggel	P	Piesberg
BB	Baden-Baden	I	Imsbach	Rb	Rammelsberg
Bw	Badenweiler			Ra	Ramsbeck
Bh	Baumholder	J	Jenner	Rg	Rauschberg
By	Bayerland			Re	Rehden
BL	Bergisches Land	Kä	Käfersteige	Ri	Richelsdorf
Bi	Bieber	Kl	Klara	Ro	Roßkopf
Bl	Bleialf	Ko	Korbach		
Bo	Bodenmais	Ku	Kupferberg	SA	St. Andreasberg
Br	Brandenberg			Sb	Schafberg
Bz	Brandholz	La	Lahn	Sl	Schauinsland
		Lh	Lahr	Si	Siegerland
CL	Christian Levin	Lm	Lam	Sp	Spessart
Cl	Clara	Lt	Lauterberg	St	Stadtsteinach
		Lb	Lemberg	Ss	Südschwarzwald
De	Deblinghausen	Le	Lerbach	Su	Sulzbach
Di	Dill	Li	Lichtenberg		
Dr	Dreislar			T	Tellig
Ei	Eisen	Mb	Marsberg	Ue	Uersfeld
Eb	Eisenbach	Ma	Maubach		
El	Ellweiler	Me	Mechernich	V	Velbert
Em	Ems	Mg	Meggen		
Er	Erbendorf	Mz	Menzenschwand	Wa	Wallerfangen
		Mü	Münsterland	We	Werlau
Fe	Ferchenseewand			Ws	Wiesloch
Fi	Fischbach	Na	Nabburg	Wi	Wildflecken
Fa	Freiamt	NW	Nammen-Wohlverwart	Wt	Wittichen
Fr	Freudenstadt	Nb	Neubulach		
FC	Friedrich-Christian	Ng	Neuenbürg	Z	Zwiesel

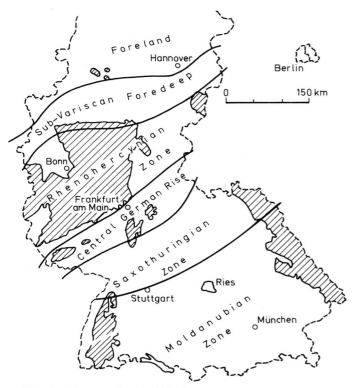

Fig. 3 *Structural units of Variscan orogenic belt*

evaporite layers other than the most important of Permian age developed during the Triassic and Jurassic. They are also found with potash in the Oligocene of the Upper Rhine Graben. Marine iron ores of oolitic and detrital to conglomeratic types originated during the Jurassic and Cretaceous in many parts of the country, the Gifhorn and Salzgitter deposits being the most important. Of limnic sedimentary origin are the Upper Cretaceous iron ores in the Oberpfalz. *In-situ* kaolinized arkosic sandstone of Lower Triassic age is mined near Hirschau in the Oberpfalz.

Alps and Foreland

In the narrow strip of the Eastern Alps in the Federal Republic volcanosedimentary Pb–Zn deposits of the Bleiberg type are present in the Triassic and there are manganese deposits in the Liassic. Oolitic iron ore deposits near the northern margin of the Alps are of Eocene age. Bentonite deposits occur in the Miocene sediments of the Molasse Foreland: these are connected genetically with the impact of the Ries meteorite.

Mesozoic to Tertiary rift system

During the Mesozoic, Central Europe underwent

extensive, multi-phase faulting, which Stille classified as 'germanotype'. The development began in the North Sea with the opening out of the central graben and associated structures in the eastern North Sea, in Schleswig–Holstein and in eastern Lower Saxony during the Permian and Trias (G. Best and F. Kockel, personal communication). It reached its high point in the eastern Moray Firth Basin at the intersection with the Viking and Central Grabens during the Jurassic with the extrusion of basalts 3000–4000 m thick.[16] From the western North Sea the Graben formation extended into the West Netherlands Basin over the Continent at the time of the Triassic–Jurassic boundary. Magmatic activity was known in the Lower Cretaceous (Waddensee–Subvolcano in the northern Netherlands[16a]).

In northern Germany tectonic differentiation began with the subsidence of the Lower Saxony Basin at the boundary of the Dogger and Malm. During the Middle Upper Cretaceous there was formed through inversion in the southern part of the basin the Nordwestfälische–Lippische Rise. The inversion was associated with the intrusion of several massifs in the region of Bramsche–Vlotho on the Weser, accompanied by very weak metamorphism and mineralization.[16b,16c]

Southern Germany was first affected by these developments around the Jurassic–Cretaceous boundary.[16d] Fault tectonics is for the first time observable in the Oberpfalz at the northeast boundary of the South German Block during the higher Lower Cretaceous on the dislocation zone of Amberg–Sulzbach-Rosenberg and Auerbach in association with the formation of the Amberg iron ore formation trough. The dislocations lie in the northwesterly extension of the important Pfahl dislocation zone. Active at approximately the same time, even though following older fault lines, were the Franconian Line (= Thuringian–East Bavarian lineament) and the Danube Boundary Fracture.[16e]

In the west, by contrast, the fault-tectonic phenomena were first initiated in association with the formation of the Rhine Graben in the early Tertiary. The Rhine Graben, 300 km long and 35 km wide, and its strike extension in the Hessian Basin form the western boundary of the South German Block. The graben follows an older structure. Its formation began in the Middle Eocene, and the movements continue to the present day. It contains up to 3350 m of sediment and compensates a distortion of 4·8 km.[16f] Beneath the graben there lies, with its axis parallel to the graben, a pillow-shaped body with P-wave velocities between 7·6 and 7·7 km/s at a depth of between 24 and 28 km between crust and mantle. Illies[16f] traced the emplacement of the graben to the formation and growth of this laccolith, which probably represents ascending mantle material. In the north the graben zone widens in the region of the young Variscan Saar–Werra Basin to form the Mainz Basin in the west and the Hanau Basin in the east before ending at the southern boundary of the Taunus. A greatly reduced extension was formed already in the Jurassic and renewed since the Lower Tertiary in the form of the active fault system of the Hessian Depression with its many small Tertiary basins. They follow the Hessian Strait—important since at least the Zechstein. The Lower Rhine Bight, which cuts deeply into the Rheinische Schiefergebirge, subsided in the Upper Tertiary as the southeasterly extension of the West Netherlands Basin.

Manifestations of Mesozoic volcanism have come to light in recent decades in north Germany for the first time in the form of tuffite layers in the Turonian of eastern Lower Saxony. Brockamp[16g] attributed the high montmorillonite content in the Cretaceous clays of north Germany since the Albian, on the basis of remarkable Cr–Ti contents as well as fragments of volcanic glass, to the supply of volcanic materials. Because of the wide distribution of montmorillonite clays in western Europe he sees an association with the more or less simultaneous formation of the Mid-Atlantic Ridge. Gaida and co-workers[16a] investigated the tuffs of the Upper Aptian of Sarstedt near Hannover and attributed their origin to a trachyte pipe, which had been drilled through the north Netherlands Waddensee.

In the north central European volcanic belt, which stretches from the Eifel through Westerwald, Vogelsberg and northern Bohemia as far as Lower Silesia, volcanic activity began in the Lower Tertiary, reaching its height in the Upper Tertiary and ending in the Eifel and the Westerwald in the Pleistocene. At the intersection of the belt with the Hessian Depression lies the shield volcano of Vogelsberg. Following the strike of the Hessian Depression and the Rhine Graben the volcanic activity reached during the Miocene towards the north as far as northwest of Göttingen and in the south, where volcanic activity was already established in the Upper Cretaceous and was declining markedly, towards the southeast of Heidelberg.[16h]

Further in the south, volcanogenic heavy minerals in the Malm at Urach, 25 km east of Tübingen, represent the oldest signs of Mesozoic volcanism. They originate, according to Knoblauch,[16i] from the Alpine geosyncline.

On both sides of the southern Rhine Graben the volcanism began at the boundary of the Lower and Upper Cretaceous and developed as far as the Upper Tertiary in a 220-km belt from the Hegau as far as eastern Lorraine. In the Rhine Graben and in the Hegau in the Bonndorf Graben the activity began before the Graben formation. At the crossing of both grabens the Miocene volcano group of the Kaiserstuhl is situated. Baranyi and co-workers[16j] postulated, on the grounds of K–Ar dating, an association between the development of this volcanic belt and the formation and widening of the mantle pillow under the

Rhine Graben, the highest point of which lies under the Kaiserstuhl. The Upper Miocene 'Swabian volcano' in the Swabian Jura Hills near Urach, southeast of Stuttgart, consists of some 300 volcanite and tuff pipes. The region shows a markedly high temperature gradient and, moreover, recent earthquake activity.

Numerous epigenetic mineral deposits originated in the course of this tectonomagmatic development, the most important being (a) the siderite–fluorite–barite mineralization around the Bramsche Massif,[16b] (b) the widespread barite and/or fluorite veins, principally in the central and northern Black Forest and in the Middle Harz as well as in some places in the Hessian Depression and in the eastern and southern parts of the Rheinische Schiefergebirge, (c) the Co–Ni–Bi paragenesis, in most cases with barite, which is to be found in many of the Variscan Pb–Zn vein districts in different young faults and the so-called 'Kobaltrücken' at the level of the Kupferschiefer in the Hessian Depression and (d) the Pb–Zn impregnations in the Bunter of Mechernich and Maubach, and, at least partly, the mineralization of Wiesloch.

Weathering deposits
The supergene zones of sulphide ore deposits were important in early mining history. Superficial concentrations of iron and manganese, e.g. bean ore, basalt ironstone, bog iron and Mn–Fe ore in karstic holes of the Lindener Mark type, were still being mined after the last war. Weathering deposits of industrial minerals are phosphorites in the Lahn syncline, kaolin, especially in eastern Bavaria, and bentonite in southeast Bavaria.

History of mining
Mineral production in Central Europe goes back to the younger Stone Age when, for example, flint was mined in several areas north of Basle. Placer gold mining in the Hohe Venn and copper mining near Braunlage in the Harz Mountains probably began during the early Bronze Age. During the early La Tène time iron ore mining started in the Siegerland, the Lahn–Dill area, the Upper Palatinate and other parts of southern Germany, and salt mining near Reichenhall in southeast Bavaria. In Roman times mining was actively pursued behind the Limes Wall in west and southwest Germany, lead and silver being extracted at Mechernich and Maubach, at Ems on the River Lahn as well as at Wiesloch near Heidelberg and Sulzburg and Badenweiler in the southern Black Forest, and copper was mined near Göllheim, northeast of Kaiserslautern, and at Wallerfangen on the River Saar. Galmei (mixed zinc carbonates and sulphates, used as a raw material for brass) was mined near Aachen.

During the Middle Ages, and even before 1200, highly developed mining laws and mining techniques made the Holy Roman Empire the leading mining area and the greatest silver and copper producer of the then known world (Table 2). Although the discovery of America led to a decline in the importance of the Central European mining industry, it was not until the Thirty Years' War that it was destroyed in large areas of the country. In the second half of the seventeenth century the beginnings of industrialization brought a resurgence of mining activity that was in part the result of greatly expanding demand. By the beginning of the twentieth century the industrial use and hence the mining of a range of new metals—principally Sb, Co, Ni, Bi, Zn, Cd, Ra and, later, U—had begun, in addition to that of coal, iron, manganese, barite and fluorite. Cobalt and, subsequently, radium enjoyed a short-lived boom. Small—even very small—mines started production, and in all upland areas numerous stamping mills and ironworks were at work. But when during the last century railways made cheap mass transportation possible, only large or particularly rich mines were able to survive.

Table 2 *Silver production, 1493–1560 (estimates from Strieder[17])*

	Germany	Rest of Europe	America
1493–1520	35 100 kg	10 000 kg	—
1521–1544	50 500 kg	10 500 kg	13 300 kg
1545–1560	53 200 kg	11 500 kg	199 200 kg

Most of these mines, too, have had to be abandoned in recent decades, either because of changing demand or exhaustion. Of the 65 iron ore mines, 26 lead and zinc mines and 44 fluorite and barite mines that were operating in the Federal Republic of Germany in 1952, only two, three and eight, respectively, were still doing so in 1984.

Information on mine production before 1800 and especially during the Middle Ages is rather limited, and for some areas and periods lacking almost completely. In a few cases all that is possible is to make more or less reliably based estimates. What is clear is that mine production was substantial in some areas in former centuries. Kraume et al.[18] have assessed the output of the Rammelsberg mine from the time mining started in about 968 up to 1500 at 4 000 000 tonne of ore, followed by another 4 500 000 tonne between 1500 and 1924. The mine yielded 8 000 000 tonne of ore from 1925 to 1980.

The neighbouring Upper Harz mining district, which was rather inaccessible in early times, had a quite different development. During what was probably its oldest period of activity—from about 1200 to 1350—it was of only limited importance. Actual production data are lacking. Mining restarted after a lapse of nearly 200 years. Then, from 1550 until 1800, some 280 000 tonne Pb and 1900 tonne Ag was produced—approximately one-sixth of the entire lead output and two-fifths of the entire silver production of the district.

Schlageter (personal communication) estimated the silver and lead production of several mining areas in the southern Black Forest between Todtnau and Sulzburg during the thirteenth and fourteenth centuries on the basis of various silver smelters, their capacity and the number of yearly smeltings for which documentary evidence exists. On the basis of available data they arrived at a production figure of 200 tonne Ag and 20 000 tonne Pb, allowing a margin of error of 50%. No data for the period exist for the Schauinsland district, the most important in that area, so it is impossible to give production figures of any reliability for the southern Black Forest.

put at almost 100%.

Some data on mine production

Aggregate production of iron ore for the Federal Republic of Germany up to 1975 has been calculated[20] as 792 000 000 tonne with an average Fe content of 27% or 215 000 000 tonne Fe. No such data are available for other minerals.

Table 3 gives output figures for various minerals between 1950 and 1982 based on mining statistics.[21] Because of regulations relating to certain non-metallic minerals, however, only part of the production of quarries is recorded by the state bureaus of mines. As a

Table 3 *Production[1] of selected ores and minerals, 1950–82 (t). From reference 21*

	1950	1960	1970	1975	1980	1981	1982
Lead[2]	46 895	50 038	40 952	32 383	23 067	21 552	23 509
Zinc[2]	98 363	114 494	128 617	116 072	99 720	91 827	86 920
Copper[2]	1 741	2 227	1 477	1 961	1 274	1 431	1 303
Silver[2]	41·6	57·2	56·4	33·6	32·9	35·0	39·8
Gold[2]	0·05	0·04	0·06	0·07	0·09	0·09	0·06
Niobium[2]	0·06	—	—	—	—	—	—
Uranium ore	—	3 969[3]	1 322[3]	7 487[4]	11 349[4]	6 473[4]	8 243[4]
Iron[5]	2 940 000[6]	5 000 000[6]	1 976 374	1 248 395	784 279	658 150	574 882
Manganese ore	82 125	117 442	30 888	10 702	—	—	—
Bauxite	4 161	3 812	3 038	755	264	79	494
Iron sulphides, S content	233 226	233 901	289 118	270 467	222 178	213 329	228 946
Sulphur	—	—	103 393	384 098	813 732	834 122	871 513
Phosphorite concentrate	533	—	69 467	81 278	—	—	—
Potash (K$_2$O)	1 095 800	2 316 189	2 644 849	2 607 113	2 738 217	2 593 203	2 056 374
Rock salt[7]	3 167 816	5 175 763	10 466 968	9 315 942	12 269 191	13 298 030	11 749 014
Graphite	7 238	11 567	16 406[8]	13 557[8]	11 255[8]	10 445[8]	10 606[8]
Quartzite (for refractories)	320 290	350 061	250 798	383 564	397 805	337 507	193 054
Quartz sand[9]	474 210	543 029	7 775 912	9 405 903	11 593 544	11 167 874	13 903 077
Adhesive and moulding sand[9]	318 196	469 845	382 389	558 873	288 632	241 916	205 751
Calcite	23 494	33 369	15 086	7 390	4 565	3 456	2 744
Feldspar	76 702	268 443	408 809	395 833	380 880	342 148	331 430
Soapstone and talc	27 969	29 281	33 806	21 092	15 499	15 441	15 231
Barite concentrate	285 226	498 167	416 016	254 902	186 435	177 308	179 891
Fluorite concentrate	92 539	130 158	75 114	74 642	78 152	71 808	78 639
Gypsum[9]	355 783	1 045 794	1 977 740	1 726 835	1 625 366	1 317 080	1 102 536
Anhydrite[9]	991	18 568	83 362	357 158	624 398	608 212	618 567
Diatomite	33 003	46 392	38 255	18 768	4 933	4 879	4 769
Silica earth	12 585	49 438	38 137	35 862	47 891	37 494	37 926
Kaolin	250 567	344 203	525 959	419 491	501 701	474 640	454 009
Bleaching clay and bentonite	74 230	326 244	612 123	599 021	638 285	624 776	608 166
Special clays	1 977 145	4 109 062	4 485 072	4 524 865	5 791 263	5 370 127	5 535 834

1, Realizable production (useful ore output). 2, Recoverable metal content. 3, 1961 + 1970 from Feldmann.[22] 4, From OECD.[23] 5, Analytical metal content of ores, including roasted iron sulphides. 6, From Neumann-Redlin and co-workers.[20] 7, Including brine salt and salt in brine. 8, Including production from imported crude graphite. 9, See text.

The high average figures for silver output as compared with lead are explainable by the fact that mining was in cementation zones and especially by the considerable amounts of lead lost during smelting, which calculations by Wilke[19] for St. Andreasberg in the Middle Harz Mountains in the sixteenth century

result, to calculate output for the country as a whole the figures given for these minerals in Table 3 must be multiplied by the following factors: quartz sand by 1·15, adhesive and moulding sand by 17, and the sum total for gypsum and anhydrite, because they are produced by the same quarries, by 2·2.

Federal Republic of Germany

Mineral deposits in the Variscan orogenic belt

Moldanubian and Saxothuringian zones

Pre-orogenic endogenic deposits
Northeast Bavaria The northeast Bavarian basement constitutes the western border area of the Bohemian Massif (Fig. 4). The Upper Proterozoic of the Moldanubian zone to the south of the Erbendorf fault has, in the Upper Palatinate Forest as in the Prague Basin, markedly Assyntic features with slight to medium metamorphism. Further south it has in large areas undergone a metamorphic transformation to cordierite–sillimanite gneisses as a result of the socalled Moldanubian event, which is probably a late Assyntic feature. The edge of the Bavarian Forest near and to the northwest of Passau experienced additional tectonic movements during the Caledonian and Variscan periods.

In the Saxothuringian zone to the north of the Erbendorf fault, Assyntic-folded Upper Proterozoic is discordantly overlain by the Variscan-overprinted Lower Palaeozoic. In the northern Franconian Forest widespread Lower Carboniferous overlies thin Silurian and Devonian. The metagranulitic migmatite gneisses of the Münchberg Massif belong, with the Sächsisches Granulitgebirge, to a major shear zone or what Behr[3] referred to as a subfluence zone on the northern periphery of the Bohemian Massif. The Erbendorf fault is of pre-Variscan or Early Variscan date; granite bodies of middle Variscan age, which intersect the fault zone, show no sign of its influence.[24]

The polymetamorphic 'Kieslager' (massive sulphide layers) near Bodenmais in the Bavarian Forest are intercalated in the Late Precambrian anatexites, which pass into garnet–cordierite–sillimanite gneisses. A group of ore layers stretches for more than 30 km from northwest of Bodenmais to Zwiesel in the southeast. Another ore layer occurs in less strongly metamorphic micaschists in the neighbourhood of Lam. The largest deposit occurs in the Silberberg (silver mountain) near Bodenmais, where two seams approximately 0·5–2 m in thickness are to be found some 30 m apart for a distance of a kilometre and were being mined until 1962. They contain pyrrhotite and pyrite alongside small quantities of sphalerite, chalcopyrite, magnetite and galena rich in silver and have average contents of 40% Fe, 25% S, 2·5% Zn, 0·2% Cu and 0·06% Pb together with 200 ppm Ag and 1–2 ppm Au. The deposits were mined in the Middle Ages for the production of vitriol. Occasional attempts to extract silver-bearing galena were unsuccessful. Jeweller's rouge became the main product in the eighteenth century, until it was ousted by synthetic substances. Some 220 000 tonne of ore was extracted between 1869 and closure in 1962. Geological reserves are just on 1 000 000 tonne of ore. The ore layer in the Johannes mine near Lam is mainly pyrite-bearing and was last investigated between 1951 and 1952.[25,26]

The 'Kieslager' of the Bayerland mine near Waldsassen in the northern part of the Upper Palatinate Forest are located in phyllitic schists of the Late Cambrian and are linked to the Lower Palaeozoic precursors of the Variscan geosyncline.[27] Two layers 200 m apart attain a thickness of 1–6 m and are more than 1 km in length, although marked folding reduces their width to a mere 80 m. The upper '*P* layer' contains 85% pyrite, whereas the '*M* layer', discovered in 1936 as a result of magnetic anomalies, contains both pyrite and fairly substantial proportions of pyrrhotite. Initially, pyrite from the '*P* layer' had 44% S and 42% Fe, but, subsequently, the crude ore proved to have a content of only about 30% S together with 2–3% Zn, 0·5% Cu and 0·4% Pb, partly in typical Pb–Sb and Cu–Bi minerals. Between 1799 and 1875 limonite ores were extracted from the zone of weathering and approximately 1 750 000 tonne of sulphur ore was mined between 1925 and 1971. The mine was shut down in 1971 when extraction of the residual 800 000 tonne of reserves, located at considerable depth, was found not to be economic.[25,26]

The western edge of the Münchberger Gneismassif is the location of the more than 4 km long Kupferberg–Wirsberg group of ore layers interbedded with Ordovician sediments and tuffs of what is known as the 'Randschiefer-Serie' and its metamorphic equivalents. According to Urban and Vaché,[28] this is made up of eight stratiform, elliptical volcanosedimentary deposits of chalcopyrite and pyrite between 100 and 450 m in diameter and averaging 1–3 m (maximum 12 m) in thickness. The primary ores contain pyrite, chalcopyrite, sphalerite and galena with about 35% Fe, 32% S, 0·4% Cu and 0·2% Zn. In the southern area of the orelayer group considerable metamorphism has given rise to the formation of magnetite and pyrrhotite in addition to pyrite. Predominantly Tertiary weathering has led to the formation of rich ores with 10–15% Cu and 1–8% Zn, which were mined during the Middle Ages and, with interruptions, to as late as 1925, occasionally in conjunction with pyrite. In all, some 250 000 tonne of pyritic copper ore, yielding 11 000 tonne of copper metal, was extracted. Reserves of various types of ore total 700 000 tonne, representing approximately 20 000 tonne Cu and rather large quantities of sulphur ores. Similar, though smaller, 'Kieslager' were formerly mined near Bad Berneck in the southwest and near Sparneck on the southern border of the Münchberger Gneismassif.[25,26]

In the early Upper Devonian, numerous bodies of red iron ore were deposited in the Variscan geosyncline in the Franconian Forest between Stadtsteinach and Hof; these are of the Lahn–Dill type and are associated with diabase and diabase tuffs. Over several centuries they were extracted in small mines, the last of which was the Langenbach mine near Bad Steben,[29] which operated from 1913 to 1922.

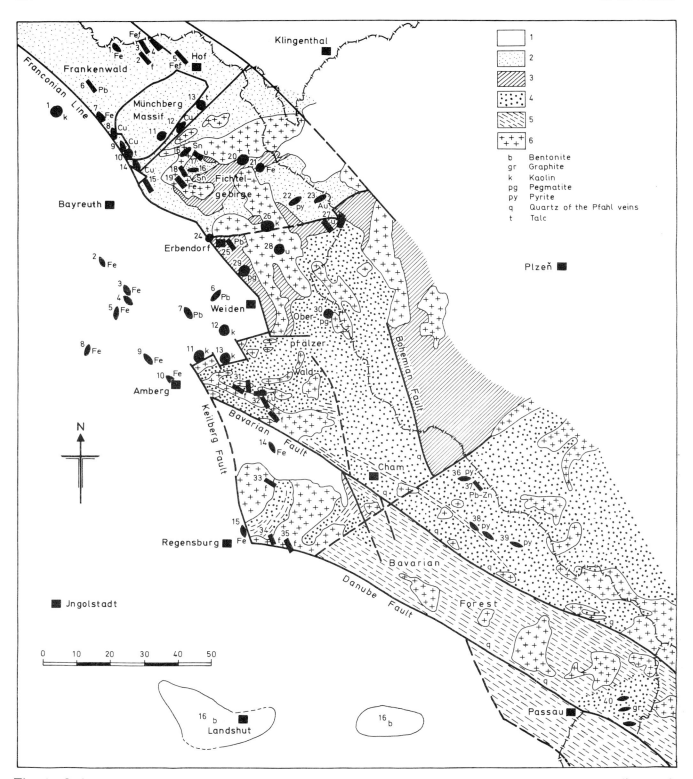

Fig. 4 *Geology and mineral deposits in northeast Bavaria (geology after Stettner[24]): 1, Permian and younger sediments; 2, Palaeozoic, mostly Cambrian and Ordovician; 3, Upper Proterozoic; 4, as 3, reworked during Moldanubian time; 5, as 4, reworked during Caledonian and Variscan time; 6, Variscan granites and related intrusive rocks*

Basement deposits

1. Langenbach, Fe, Upper Devonian
2. Issigau-Kemlas, Pb, fluorite, Late Variscan
3. Lichtenberg, fluorite-Fe, Late Variscan
4. Bescheert Glück, fluorite-Fe, Late Variscan
5. Hof, fluorite-Fe, Late Variscan
6. Wallenfels, Pb, Late Variscan

Black Forest Low-grade nickel and cobalt ores occur in a few small ultramafic rock bodies swimming in anatectic gneiss of probable Late Precambrian age near Todtmoos and Horbach in the southern Black Forest. The ore consists of pyrrhotite, pentlandite, bravoite and chalcopyrite, and has Ni and Cu contents of 0·1–0·3% and 0·1–0·2%, respectively.

Pre-orogenic sedimentary deposits
The Kropfmühl graphite deposits in the Bavarian Forest, 20 km northeast of Passau, are intercalated in high-grade metamorphic and often metablastic Moldanubian gneisses of supposed Late Precambrian age. The whole series is intruded by Variscan granite sills and Permian porphyrite dykes. The gneisses are metamorphosed bituminous euxinic sediments within the 'Varied Series' of pelites and psammites with abundant carbonatic and volcanic intercalations. Graphite lenses occur repeatedly in the so-called 'Varied Series' of the Moldanubian zone along the Danube River between Vilshofen and Passau, where banded biotite-plagioclase-gneisses normally predominate. But in the only important mining district—that of Kropfmühl near Hauzenberg—about half the 150-m thick minable sequence is carbonatic (Fig. 5).

The gneisses show folding textures in decametre and metre dimensions, the axes plunging around 10° to the west. The mobile graphite is enriched in saddles of minor folds and in shear zones. Sometimes it envelops boudins of marble and amphibolite. There are several seams, normally between several decimetres and 1 m thick, with an average content of 20–25% C. In the weathering zone, which extends down to 50 m, it was found to be as high as 50% C. A rather large part of the graphite consists of flakes with an average diameter of 1–2 mm. Associated minerals in the seams are predominantly feldspar and calcite, with some pyrrhotite and pyrite.[25,26]

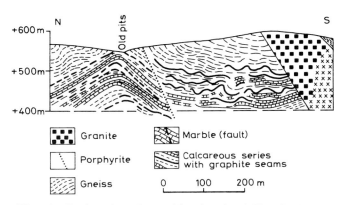

Fig. 5 *Section through graphite deposit of Kropfmühl near Passau. After Teuscher*[29a]

Graphite mining on a small scale went on even in prehistoric times. Modern mining began shortly after 1900 (Table 4). The cumulative production of crude ore amounts to 2 500 000 tonne and the total reserves to 2 000 000 tonne of ore.

Volcanosedimentary rock series of the Upper Proterozoic occasionally have high contents of heavy metals. Strata-bound, probably synsedimentary, scheelite occurs in metamorphic siliceous carbonate rocks to the west of Hagendorf, and near Mähring similar rocks have substantial uranium contents coupled with 200 ppm tin.[30a] It may be assumed that these metals were regenerated during the Variscan folding and deposited in the ore veins of the Fichtelgebirge district (Sn and U) and near Mähring (U).

---

7. Stadtsteinach, Fe, Upper Devonian
8. Kupferberg, Cu–pyrite, Ordovician
9. Wirsberg, Cu–pyrite, Ordovician
10. Wirsberg, talc, Variscan
11. Münchberg, pegmatite, Variscan
12. Sparneck, Cu–pyrite, Ordovician
13. Schwarzenbach a.d.Saale, talc, Variscan
14. Bad Berneck, Cu–pyrite, Ordovician
15. Brandholz–Goldkronach, Au, Variscan
16. Weißenstadt–Wunsiedel, Sn placer, Tertiary
17. Weißenstadt, U, palaeo-weathering
18. Seehaus, Sn, Variscan
19. Gleisinger Fels, Fe, Variscan
20. Göpfersgrün, soapstone, Variscan
21. Arzberg, Fe, Upper Proterozoic and/or Variscan
22. Bayerland, Cu–pyrite, Upper Cambrian
23. Neualbenreuth, Au, Upper Cambrian
24. Erbendorf, soapstone, Variscan
25. Erbendorf, Pb, Upper Proterozoic and/or Permian
26. Tirschenreuth, kaolin, palaeo-weathering
27. Mähring, U, Variscan
28. Falkenberg, U, Variscan
29. Püllersreuth, pegmatite, Variscan
30. Hagendorf, pegmatite, Variscan
31. + 32. Nabburg–Wölsendorf–Altfalter, fluorite, Late Variscan
33. Nittenau, barite–fluorite, Late Variscan
34. Sulzbach, fluorite, Late Variscan
35. Kittenrain, fluorite, Late Variscan
36. Lam-Johanneszeche, pyrite, Upper Proterozoic
37. Lam Fürstenzeche, Pb–Zn, Variscan
38. Bodenmais, pyrite, Upper Proterozoic
39. Zwiesel, pyrite, Upper Proterozoic
40. Kropfmühl, graphite, Upper Proterozoic

Platform cover deposits

1. Kronach, kaolin, Lower Triassic
2. Langenreuth, Fe, Middle Jurassic
3. Leonie, Fe, Upper Cretaceous
4. Maffei, Fe, Upper Cretaceous
5. Katharina, Fe, Upper Cretaceous
6. Manteler Wald, Pb, Middle Triassic
7. Freihung, Pb, Middle Triassic
8. Vorra, Fe, Middle Jurassic
9. Sulzbach–Rosenberg, Fe, Upper Cretaceous
10. Amberg, Fe, Upper Cretaceous
11. Hirschau, kaolin, Lower Triassic
12. Kaltenbrunn, kaolin, Lower Triassic
13. Schnaittenbach, kaolin, Lower Triassic
14. Bodenwöhr, Fe, Lower Jurassic
15. Keilberg, Fe, Lower Jurassic
16. Landshut and Malgersdorf regions, bentonite, Miocene

Baumann[31] described similar relations from the Erzgebirge.

In the Oberpfalz nodules of arsenopyrite and pyrite that contain gold and silver occur with quartz in Late Cambrian phyllites near Neualbenreuth and were mined in mediaeval times. They probably derive, with zircon and monazite, from placer deposits of heavy minerals. The last investigations were terminated in 1936 on grounds of excessive cost.[25,26]

The marine sedimentary chamosite–thuringite ores of the Ordovician in the Franconian Forest and the Fichtelgebirge form part of the periphery of the Thuringian iron ore district. Two oolitic ore horizons show evidence of relatively high phosphorus contents. In the south these are only locally developed, in part metamorphically as magnetite–quartzite ores. Although investigated several times with a view to exploitation, they have never achieved any economic significance.[29]

Table 4 *Production (tonne) of graphite from Kropfmühl, 1908–82*[21,30]

Year	Crude ore	Concentrates
1908	5 000	
1918	41 000	
1936	24 290	6 611
1950	23 090	7 238
1960	42 272	11 576
1970	18 346	16 406*
1975	23 564	13 557*
1980	11 375	11 255*
1981	16 372	10 445*
1982	23 305	10 606*

* Including production from imported graphite.

Variscan epigenetic deposits
Northeast Bavaria Several types of pegmatite are widespread in the basement of eastern Bavaria.[25,26] A special group of about 100 albite pegmatoids that are derived from metamorphic mobilization exists in the Münchberger Gneismassif and are sparsely scattered in the Moldanubian Zone. In the Münchberger Gneismassif these veins, lenses or stocks, the biggest of which contain up to 100 000 tonne of ore, were mined for sodium feldspar between 1940 and 1978. The ore contains 75–80% albite with 9% anorthite, 15–20% quartz and 5% muscovite; production amounted to 5000 tonne per year.

Gneissic metapegmatites of pre-Variscan age have no economic importance in East Bavaria, but similar meta-aplite bodies, found by geophysical prospecting near Hagendorf in recent years, represent a significant reserve of feldspar ore.[30] The large number of pegmatites, crystallized from residual melts of Variscan granites, are rich in volatile constituents and rare elements. Most of them are rather thin dykes or elongated lenses with some tourmaline and muscovite. Deposits of significant economic importance occur in and around the Falkenberg–Flossenbürg granite east of Weiden in the Oberpfalz.[25,26] This pegmatite district is characterized by the presence of beryl and columbite. Moreover, the Hagendorf pegmatites are famous for a great number of phosphate minerals.[32] Most of the pegmatites consist of eutectoid coarse-grained intergrowths of quartz, potash feldspar and mica. The pegmatite stock of Hagendorf-Süd shows a distinct zoning (Fig. 6). In the outer zone we find the rock described with a thin rim of fine-grained aplitic rock combined with the formation of greisen in the granitic wallrock. In the centre there is a differentiation into very coarse-grained, nearly pure potash feldspar in an intermediate zone and pure quartz in the core. Between these two zones exists a sub-zone of albite (clevelandite) and schlieren of phosphates, including 1600 tonne of triphyline with 8·6% Li_2O, which was mined for several years after 1955. The stock of Hagendorf-Süd contains around 8 000 000 tonne of ore with 1 800 000 tonne of pure potash feldspar and 2 000 000 tonne of pure quartz. From the two stocks at Hagendorf more than 1 000 000 tonne of feldspar has been produced. The mine was exhausted in July, 1983. A hundred years ago only the quartz cores of the pegmatite stocks were mined for use in the glass industry. Since then it has only been possible to mine these quartz cores in conjunction with feldspar, which is mostly used in the ceramic industry. Bavaria produces about 75% of the FRG's total output of feldspar and feldspar sands (Table 5).

In the central stock of the Fichtelgebirge granite the most recent intrusion phase gave rise to a pneumatolytic-hydrothermal tin–tungsten paragenesis constituting the weak western offshoot of the Erzgebirge tin-mining district. A more recent hydrothermal phase has yielded uraninite. The principal mass of tin has most probably been eroded. In the Weissenstadt area tin placers have been mined at least since the thirteenth century, and from the fourteenth century onwards until the Thirty Years War the primary deposits were worked as well. In 1940 the residue remaining from this mining activity was assessed as some 30 000 tonne of placer deposits with a content of 0·4% Sn + W and a Sn:W ratio of 2:1.[25,26] Near Mähring, to the east of Tirschenreuth, veins of quartz and pitchblende containing coffinite, brannerite and sulphides with 0·4% U_3O_8 are under investigation.[33]

The 'old' gold–quartz veins at Brandholz–Goldkronach are linked with the intrusion of the Fichtelgebirge granite. They occur in Ordovician schists, are 0·5 m thick and contain gold-bearing pyrite, arsenopyrite, antimonite, a little free gold and quartz. Finds of wolframite, apatite and tin-bearing fahlerz (tetrahedrite) are evidence of the transition to the Sn–W formation. The gold content is 4·5 ppm. Mining was

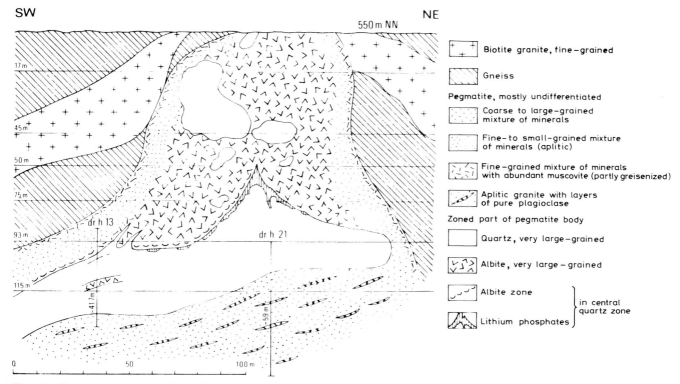

Fig. 6 *Section through pegmatite stock of Hagendorf-Süd*

Table 5 *Production (tonne) of feldspar and feldspar sands from East Bavaria 1936–82[30]*

Year	Feldspar from		Feldspar sands from		Total
	Feldspar mines	Kaolin mines	Arkose mines	Kaolin mines	
1936	9 524	—	14 669	—	24 194
1950	18 263	44 949	11 843	19 201	94 256
1960	49 546	103 672	50 587	9 935	213 740
1970	47 875	132 104	145 840	27 733	353 552
1975	38 125	139 719	73 925	27 247	279 016
1980	42 983	152 358	57 825	31 195	284 361
1981	40 866	146 059	61 344	34 986	283 255
1982	38 188	140 473	78 697	34 527	291 885

carried out during the Middle Ages. More recent studies, such as those carried out between 1923 and 1925,[34] have had little success.[25,26]

Given the extent of erosion, lodes in the Moldanubian zone may be expected to be no more than quartz roots. Only in the case of the Fürstenzeche vein near Lam did Teuscher and Weinelt[25] propose a partial Variscan paragenesis on the basis of the substantial Sn and Ag contents. Also classified as Variscan are the older of the at least three quartz generations of the Pfahl lode. This is a fault zone more than 100 km long and 2–3 km thick penetrated by veins of very pure quartz that in parts are as much as 50 m thick and contain 95–98% SiO_2 with varying Fe and Al contents. Non-ferrous metal sulphides, and in the Bavarian Pfahl (Fig. 4) locally uranium ores, occur only as traces. Quartz is extracted from a number of opencast workings between Regen and Viechtach and in the Altrandsberg district at the rate of 100 000 tonne per year, most being used for the production of ferrosilicon.[30]

By analogy with the quartz–hematite–manganese oxide–carbonate spar sequence in the Thuringian Forest investigated by Schröder,[35] the middle hematite-bearing quartz generation of the Pfahl mineralization is considered to be of Late Variscan age. Moreover, it is compared with the many quartz and quartz–hematite veins in the Fichtelgebirge and the northern part of the Upper Palatinate Forest. The best-known representative of these is the Gleisinger

Fels lode,[29] which, because of its finely flaked hematite, was worked as a coloured ore from the seventeenth until well into the nineteenth century.

In the southern Fichtelgebirge siderite ore deposits 2–12 m thick are widespread in the Wunsiedel marble of the Precambrian Arzberg series and are explained as being sedimentary in the broader sense or as metasomatic. Limonitic weathering products and, ultimately, siderite were mined from the sixteenth century until 1905 and a total of 5 000 000 tonne of iron ore was extracted. The most recent investigations, carried out between 1939 and 1942, revealed reserves of 4 300 000 tonne of ore with an Fe content of 33%.[29]

To the east of Wunsiedel and in a zone 5 km long between Göpfersgrün and Thiersheim lenses and pockets of hydrothermal metasomatic steatite occur irregularly in the marble at its contact with the Lower Permian quartz porphyry.[26] The deposit is up to 35 m thick and has been mined since the last century, annual production being 10 000 tonne and reserves in the region of 200 000 tonne.[30] Talc, too, was formed at the contact between serpentine bodies and greenschist in the peripheral zone of the Münchberger Gneismassif, especially in the area of Wirsberg in the west and Schwarzenbach an der Saale in the southeast. The talc formation took place under the action of circulating water following the formation of chlorite in the greenschist and of tremolite in the serpentine in the declining stages of the metamorphism.[36] In the greenschist zone near Erbendorf, to the NNW of Weiden, talc schist and 'Topfstein' (soapstone) have been extracted since the end of the eighteenth century. Annual talc production fell between 1970 and 1977 from almost 20 000 tonne to approximately 6500 tonne because of increasing competition from other raw materials (see Table 3).[30]

Black Forest The Precambrian and Palaeozoic massif of the Black Forest can be divided, from north to south, into six main geological units of differing extent (Fig. 7): (*a*) the metamorphic Palaeozoic of Baden-Baden; (*b*) the granite area of the northern Black Forest (Variscan granites with subordinate gneiss enclaves); (*c*) the gneiss massif of the Middle and High Black Forest, occupying nearly half the area of the basement (paragneisses and orthogneisses, widely transformed by anatexis of Lower Palaeozoic age); (*d*) the granite of Triberg and its branches; (*e*) the Palaeozoic zone between Badenweiler and Lenzkirch; and (*f*) the area of Variscan granites and pre-Variscan gneisses of the southern Black Forest.

Ignimbrites and quartz porphyries of Permian age rest on the eroded surface of the basement. Towards the east and southeast the Palaeozoic and older rocks disappear under the Permian, Triassic and younger sedimentary cover. In the west and southwest the Black Forest block is cut by the eastern faults of the Rhine Graben, which are of Tertiary age.

There are only a few mineral deposits of undoubted Variscan age in the Black Forest, such as, for example, the tungsten-bearing veins at Rossgrabeneck, the uranium-bearing parageneses of Menzenschwand and Wittichen and the Late Variscan main phase of the iron- and manganese-bearing quartz and quartz-barite veins of Eisenbach. The majority of the Pb–Zn veins, often with barite and/or fluorite, were also considered to be of Variscan age,[8,9] but arguments for a post-Variscan age have been put forward for some of these.[37,38] Because in many cases no definite assertion can yet be made and discussion is still proceeding, the distribution and classification of all hydrothermal veins in the Black Forest are here treated together, regardless of their age.

One particular concentration of veins is found in the High Black Forest, in the Schauinsland–Feldberg–Schönau–Badenweiler area, and another in the valleys of the Kinzig and its tributaries in the Middle Black Forest (Fig. 7). Most of the veins, especially those of the Pb–Zn type, occur in the gneisses and anatexites of units (*c*) and (*f*). Conversely, the veins of the Co–Ni–Bi–Ag–U formation of the Middle Black Forest and the quartz–pitchblende veins of Menzenschwand in the High Black Forest are restricted to granitic country rocks. In the Triassic cover northeast of the Black Forest proper there appear numerous barite veins, poor in ore minerals, which are of post-Variscan age.

The predominant directions of the veins are N–NNE in the south and NW–NNW in the northern part of the basement and in the Triassic cover. For the High Black Forest Schürenberg[8] has demonstrated the relations that exist between the directions of the veins and their parageneses. The Pb–Zn veins proper prefer the directions N–NNE, more or less parallel to the faults of the Rhine Graben border. Other veins of the same area, but with different parageneses, are orientated northwest or northeast. The presence of arsenopyrite is restricted to the veins of the northwest–southeast system. Numerous quartz veins with barite and fluorite, but poor in ore minerals, and also the quartz–pitchblende veins of Menzenschwand have a WNW direction. The region with predominant NNE direction extends towards the north up to the Kinzig valley, where the regime of the NNW–NW directions commences. To this district belong the Pb–Zn, Cu and Co–Ni–Bi–Ag–U veins in the basement and nearly all of the barite veins in the Triassic cover. Some veins, however, such as the Friedrich-Christian, with fluorite, quartz, galena and chalcopyrite, and the Käfersteige, with fluorite, run east–west. The analogies that exist between many veins in the basement and in the sediment cover have often been emphasized in the discussion on the age of the hydrothermal mineralization.[39]

Schürenberg[8] has drawn up a detailed classification of the veins in the High and southern Black Forest. Eight groups can be distinguished (Fig. 7):

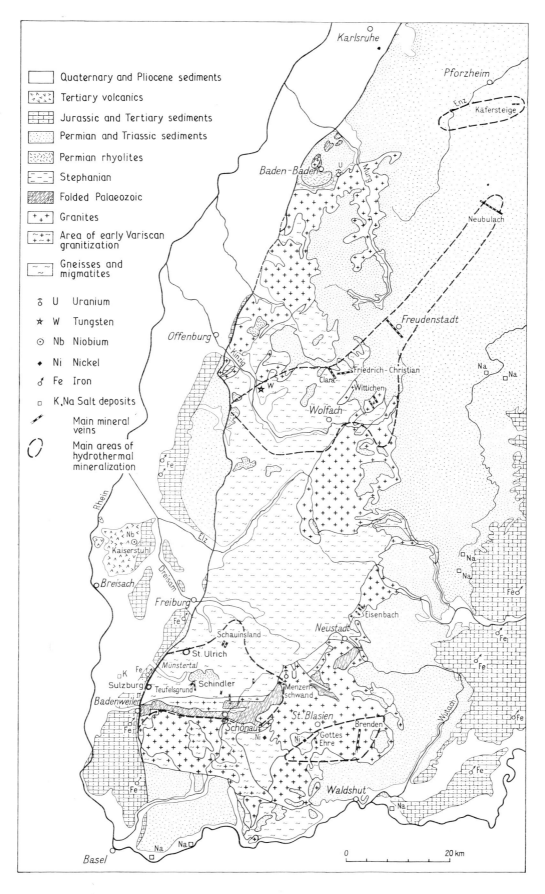

Fig. 7 *Geology and mineral deposits of Black Forest*

(A) Quartz–fluorite veins with galena and sphalerite (Münstertal–Wiesental): the type vein is the Schindler vein (Table 6). Veins of this group exhibit the most complete succession of ores and non-metallic minerals. Mineralization took place in three main phases, the second and third being simplified repetitions of the first. Towards the east the parageneses are impoverished, the quartz–arsenopyrite–pyrite assemblage of the first phase being, for instance, omitted in group (B).

same directions, from which it may be concluded that the formation of the veins extended over a rather long time span, during which the different hydrothermal phases coincided with different stages of the tectonic fracturing.

The exposures that are available at present do not permit the establishment of a chronology for the different vein groups. Faisi and von Gehlen[42] considered the silicification zones of group (H) as the oldest and deepest sections of the system.

Table 6 *Typical parageneses of hydrothermal Pb–Zn veins in southern Black Forest. After Schürenberg[8] and Otto[40]*

Generation	Schindler vein	Schauinsland vein II	Gottesehre vein
I	*Quartz* Ia with pyrrhotite, pyrite, arsenopyrite	Quartz with pyrite	*Quartz* and/or *calcite*
	Quartz Ib		**Fluorite** with galena, chalcopyrite, tetrahedrite, pyrite/marcasite
	Sphalerite	**Sphalerite**	
	Galena	*Galena*	Locally, Co–Ni–Ag minerals
	Fluorite		
	Chalcopyrite		
	Tetrahedrite		
	Ankerite/dolomite	*Calcite*, partly dissolved	Ankerite/siderite
	Barite, partly silicified		*Barite*, sphalerite
II	Quartz	Quartz IIa	Quartz
	Pyrite/marcasite, sphalerite, galena	Sphalerite IIa	
	Fluorite with chalcopyrite and tetrahedrite	Quartz IIb, galena IIb	
		Sphalerite IIb	
		Quartz IIc	
		Sphalerite IIc	
	Ankerite/dolomite		Calcite, dolomite/ankerite, barite
	Barite	*Barite*	
III	Quartz		Quartz
	Galena		
	Ankerite/dolomite	Dolomite/ankerite	Ankerite/siderite
	Pyrite/marcasite	Galena	Calcite
	Calcite	Marcasite	Pyrite/marcasite
		Dolomite/ankerite	Barite
		Calcite	

(B) Quartz–fluorite veins with galena (St. Blasien and surroundings), e.g. Gottesehre vein[40] (Table 6).
(C) Quartz veins with pyrite, arsenopyrite and tetrahedrite (St. Ulrich).
(D) Quartz veins with pyrite, arsenopyrite and antimony ores (not frequent; St. Ulrich, Sulzburg).
(E) Quartz–calcite–barite veins with sphalerite and galena: the important Schauinsland deposit belongs to this group, Schauinsland vein II having the most complete mineral sequence (Table 6).
(F) Veins with a simplified succession of quartz, barite, sphalerite and galena (Münstertal district).
(G) Quartz–siderite–barite veins with chalcopyrite and sphalerite (Münstertal district).
(H) Quartz veins with barite, hematite, pyrite (and sometimes fluorite); the pitchblende-bearing veins of Menzenschwand are in some respects similar to this type.[41] There are many gradations into wide silicification zones.

Veins of identical paragenesis mostly follow the

Some of the veins have been formed immediately on fissures of the main fault of the Rhine Graben: they show much the same mineralization as do many veins in the interior of the basement, which has some bearing on the problem of the age of the hydrothermal veins of the Black Forest in general (see below).

The veins of the central and northern part of the Black Forest can tentatively be classified as follows.
(I) Quartz–tourmaline veins with wolframite, scheelite and bismuth (Rossgrabeneck near Zell am Harmersbach[43]).
(K) Co–Ni–Bi–Ag–U veins with barite, fluorite, calcite and quartz (type locality, Wittichen[44–47]).
(L) Barite veins, mostly devoid of or poor in ore minerals: the most important example is the Clara vein in Oberwolfach, which is up to 8 m wide, and which cuts the gneiss as well as the Triassic sandstone and therefore is at least partly of post-Variscan age. Two principal veins, the barite vein and the fluorite vein, running northwest–southeast, and a number of satelli-

tic veins have recently been studied by several authors.[48,48a,245] Huck[246] distinguished five main phases of mineralization:
(1) Wallrock alteration by a network of veinlets (quartz, pyrite, hematite and others).
(2) Main fluorite phase (fluorite vein, locally with sellaite[48]).
(3) Main barite phase (barite vein).
(4) Later barite phase (affecting the fluorite and the barite veins).
(5) Main quartz phase.

The conditions of formation of the main minerals were investigated by means of fluid inclusion studies by Gerler and Horn (see Huck[246]). The temperatures indicated vary between 160 and 60°C (max. 110–120°C) for fluorite and quartz and are problematic ($\pm 50°C$) only for barite. The solutions in the barite are highly saline; geochemically, they are comparable with evaporitic brines from the earth's surface. Strontium isotopic studies by von Gehlen et al.[242] speak very much in favour of an origin of the barite mineralization by leaching of the country rocks (mostly gneisses) by percolating water ('lateral secretion').

Some of the veins of this group contain tetrahedrite and/or Cu and Bi sulphides (Clara, Daniel near Wittichen, Neubulach).[48a] The large vein of the Käfersteige near Pforzheim[49] with fluorite $\gg$ barite and quartz belongs to the same system.

(M) The Friedrich-Christian vein in Wildschapbach: fluorite, quartz (mostly pseudomorphous after barite), galena, chalcopyrite.[8]

(N) Veins of the Pb–Zn and related types in the middle and lower Kinzig Valley:[8] some of the deposits resemble the 'Edle Quarzformation' (silver-rich quartz formation) of Freiberg (Saxony).

(O) Quartz veins with antimony ores, similar to group (D) of the southern Black Forest district.[50]

(P) Quartz and quartz–barite veins, partly with iron and manganese oxides (e.g. Eisenbach, U-bearing[44,51]).

Hofmann and Schürenberg[51a] studied the geochemistry of many barite occurrences in western and southern Germany. They found a maximum of $SrSO_4$ values around 1·5% in the barites of the High and southern Black Forest; in the Middle and northern Black Forest values between 2 and 5% prevail. A wealth of geochemical data on galena, fluorite, barite, carbonates, and hematite from numerous hydrothermal deposits of Central Europe, including the Black Forest, has been presented by Hofmann.[51b] From his results he deduced a common source and mineralization system for most of the barite occurrences, which was active, although discontinuously, from the upper Carboniferous through the Mesozoic until the Tertiary.

Isotopic age determinations on pitchblende from Menzenschwand gave late Palaeozoic ages of ca 310 m.y.[41] U–Pb model ages of about 237 m.y. from Wittichen are problematic as the Co–Ni–Bi–Ag–U veins do not continue into the Triassic cover. Some Pb–Zn veins of the Münstertal (High Black Forest) are cut by a Permian ignimbrite. On the other hand, Tertiary ages are most likely for the mineralization on the Rhine Graben faults. Von Gehlen et al.[37] and Sperling[38] favoured the post-Variscan age of most of the veins in the High and southern Black Forest, postulating hydrothermal leaching of the strongly sheared and altered country rocks as the source of the most characteristic elements of those veins.[52] As for the time of formation of the Clara veins (see above), a Mesozoic age has been envisaged by von Gehlen[52a] and Bonhomme et al.[224] dated illites from the contact of the barite vein at 188 $\pm$ 5 m.y.

The most prosperous mining activity in the Black Forest took place between the eleventh and fourteenth centuries with the production of silver from galena—an activity that was brought finally to an end by the Thirty Years War.[8] From 1700 until 1845 the Wittichen district was one of the most important cobalt producers in Europe. From 1833 onwards barite, and later also fluorite, were mined in addition to the Pb–Zn ores. From 1901 until it was closed down in 1954 the largest Pb–Zn mine on the Schauinsland produced 80 000 tonne of metal with a Zn:Pb ratio of 5·6:1.

The following mines are currently operating in the Black Forest (Fig. 7 and Table 7): Käfersteige near Pforzheim and Gottesehre at Urberg, south of St. Blasien (fluorite), Clara at Oberwolfach (barite and, since 1978, fluorite), and Menzenschwand for uranium. Another uranium deposit of sedimentary origin is under exploration near Baden-Baden (see below).

Odenwald The crystalline Odenwald constitutes a part of the Central German Rise. Its larger western portion is characterized by basic and acid magmatites, which have penetrated regionally metamorphosed rocks of Palaeozoic or older age, whereas the smaller eastern portion is composed of micaschists and granitoid gneisses.

The Odenwald is very poor in Variscan deposits. The Auerbach marble, famous for the variety of its minerals and a product of contact metamorphism probably of Devonian reef limestone, is extracted by underground mining. Small quantities of feldspar pegmatites have occasionally been mined and in the Schriesheim area, to the north of Heidelberg, small pockets of scheelite occur.

Spessart The crystalline western Spessart is another portion of the Central German Rise. It is made up of Precambrian and Lower Palaeozoic quartzites, micaschists and paragneisses and pre-Variscan orthogneisses and Late Variscan metablastic diorite and granodiorite and is transgressively overlain by the Permo-Triassic cover of the eastern Hochspessart.

The ortho- and paragneisses to the north of

Table 7 *Mineral production (tonne) of Black Forest mines, 1950–82[21] ((2), etc., indicates number of producing mines)*

Year	Pb–Zn concentrates*	U metal in concentrates†	Fluorite concentrates	Barite concentrates
1950	10 467 (2)	—	20 760 (3)	49 924 (5)
1960	—	—	34 755 (5)	21 919 (1)
1970	715 (2)	—	40 422 (5)	36 927 (2)
1975	84 (1)	57 (1)	34 760 (3)	48 562 (1)
1980	— (1)	34 (1)	48 030 (5)	46 074 (1)
1981	—	36 (1)	51 066 (3)	43 030 (1)
1982	93 (1)	34 (1)	68 554 (5)	46 899 (1)

* Since 1970 a by-product of fluorite mining.
† From OECD and IAEA data.

Aschaffenburg contain veins of granite–pegmatite produced, during a late or post-kinematic phase in the area of a 'heat dome' with strong signs of mobilization. They were exploited in feldspar mines. The quartz porphyry of Ober-Sailauf, to the northeast of Aschaffenburg, is associated with a feeble mineralization of uranium with autunite and coffinite. Veins of quartz–hematite that strike southeast–northwest in the Hain diorite and in marble-bearing paragneisses near Haibach–Klingerhof (15 km ENE and 6 km ESE of Aschaffenburg, respectively) probably belong to the Late Variscan mineralization.

Saar–Nahe Depression The Saar–Nahe Depression constitutes the southwest portion of the Central German Rise, which sank in the course of the Late Palaeozoic and is defined to the southwest by the Eifel–Lorraine north–south zone and to the northeast by the Mainz Basin. Following the basaltic to rhyolitic, chiefly volcanic, magmatism during the lower Upper Rotliegende, there came into being an area of hydrothermal deposition characterized by the metals Cu, Hg, Co, Ag and U with calcite and barite. The formations arose at the contact of basic and intermediate intrusions in the pneumatolytic range with local developments of greisenings, tourmalinization and silicification. Veins of higher-temperature calcite are followed by copper ores and hematite and, finally, by low-temperature veins of barite and mercury. The most important copper district was that of Imsbach, 18 km northeast of Kaiserslautern in the southwestern part of the Donnersberg rhyolite stock. Veins between 1 and 10 m thick, alternating with impregnation zones up to 12 m thick, contain chiefly chalcopyrite, chalcocite, tennantite, bornite, linnaeite, pyrite and galena alongside calcite and quartz and numerous secondary minerals. At lesser depths the copper content is 2–3%, but this declines rapidly with depth. Mineralization is in part associated with basic dykes. The beginnings of mining activity date from Roman times, the first mineral extracted being iron. The fifteenth century saw the heyday of copper and silver mining, and in the eighteenth and nineteenth centuries copper was mined together, in particular, with cobalt. Mining ceased after the first world war when reserves were exhausted.

In the Hosenberg copper-mining district near Fischbach, between Idar–Oberstein and Kirn, shear zones with associated stockwork mineralization and impregnation are found in lava flows at the base of the Upper Rotliegende. Primary chalcocite and, occasionally, cinnabar are found here, in addition to chalcopyrite and bornite. Again, mining activity goes at least as far back as the Middle Ages and experienced a revival in the first half of the eighteenth century after the Thirty Years War. Exploration between 1934 and 1937 showed residual reserves of 72 000 tonne of ore with a 1·7% copper content.[53] Today the Fischbach mine is a tourist attraction. Similar though smaller deposits are to be found to the southwest of Idar–Oberstein, especially near Frauenberg–Sonnenberg. The basalts and dacites of the 'Grenzlager' (boundary layer) have, since medieval times, yielded the almond-shaped agates that formed the basis of Idar–Oberstein's agate polishing industry, which has subsequently flourished for diamonds and other gemstones.

Far more important were the mercury mines of the Oberpfalz, which in the second half of the eighteenth century were among the most important in Europe after Idria in Yugoslavia and Almadén in Spain. Impregnations of magmatites and sandstones of the Lower Rotliegende, associated with shear zones, contain cinnabar as the most frequent ore mineral and with it mercury, tetrahedrite, pyrite, antimonite, galena, sphalerite, chalcopyrite, arsenopyrite, chalcocite, hematite, manganese oxide and barite, and also numerous secondary minerals.[53] In fissured zones near the surface mercury contents were in some cases in excess of 10%, but in the impregnation zones below they were generally below 1%. The final 'gleaning' operations, carried out around 1940, yielded ores for processing with a mercury content of a mere 0·05%. Mercury was mined at 60 places at least in an area of 60 km × 25 km between Alzey in the northeast and Birkenfeld in the southwest, but after a boom period in the years around 1770 production dropped sharply and mining activity died out in 1861. Renewed attempts at mining between 1936 and 1941 on the Lemberg, southwest of Bad Kreuznach, on the Landsberg near Obermoschel and on the Stahlberg, 8 km to the south of Obermoschel, yielded 250 tonne of mercury.

Veins of quartz and hematite near Imsbach were last mined in 1938. Such veins are widely found in the Rotliegende of the Saar–Nahe Depression and in the Hunsrück to the north. The Louise mine near Saarburg, 18 km to the south of Trier, has worked several veins of hematite and manganese oxides striking NNE in the Ems quartzite of the Lower Devonian. The last period of operation, from 1938 to 1943, produced 50 000 tonne of ore.[54]

Uranium ores are to be found as hydrothermal impregnations in acid magmatites of the Permian, and especially in the rhyolites of Nohfelden, the Donnersberg and the Königsberg, as also in the form of syngenetic and epigenetic concentrations in the sediments of the Rotliegende. Between 1961 and 1970 55 626 tonne of ore was extracted from the small deposit discovered in 1957 at Ellweiler, on the northern edge of the Nohfeld massif. Apart from pitchblende, pyrite and numerous other sulphides, the ore contained mainly kasolite and zeunerite, and 240 ppm uranium.[22]

In the western part of the Saar–Nahe Depression barite veins occur mostly within Permian rhyolite stocks on the Königsberg near Aschbach, to the west of Wolfstein, and in Permian tholeiites in the Erzweiler and Baumholder areas. These veins pass through hematite, reddish barite I and a white barite II, which is accompanied by iron–manganese oxides, quartz and cinnabar. The Clarashall mine near Baumholder, shut down in 1974, extracted an annual 50 000–60 000 tonne of barite concentrate from a vein 400 m long and 15 m thick (Table 8).

The Permian rhyolites of the Nohfelden massif to the west of Baumholder were converted to a material used in the ceramic industry under the name of Birkenfeld feldspar, probably by water containing carbon dioxide, kaolinite and illite being formed at the same time. Production is in the region of 150 000 tonne in the Saarland and 50 000 tonne in the Rhineland Palatinate part of the massif (Table 8).

Late Palaeozoic strata-bound deposits
Uranium deposit near Baden-Baden A strata-bound uranium deposit has recently been discovered in the arkoses of the Stephanian (Upper Carboniferous) near Baden-Baden (Fig.7). Pitchblende and subordinate coffinite are found in particular coal-bearing fine-grained micaceous arkose layers and diffusely impregnated in massif arkoses. The actual pattern indicates redistribution by circulating groundwater of an earlier mineralization resulting in a 'roll front'-type deposit.[55] A considerable portion of the uranium present is bound by adsorption on the argillaceous and ferruginous matter of the arkoses.

A quite different interpretation of the deposit has recently been given by Brockamp and Zuther.[55a,b] Very strong sericitization of the feldspars and a number of sulphide and arsenide minerals in addition to pitchblende are considered as hydrothermal and epigenetic formations. A temperature of *ca* 260°C is estimated from the degree of carbonization of vitrinite. K–Ar determinations on authigenic micas gave ages of about 150 m.y.

Small quantities of uranium are also found in the coal and coal shales of the Rotliegende near Stockheim in the Franconian Forest, and also in the Rotliegende sediments of the Saar–Nahe Depression. Near Stockheim the uranium has been concentrated by diagenetic and/or epigenetic processes. Beds and concretions of clay ironstone in the coal-bearing Upper Carboniferous and in the Lower Rotliegende of the Saarland were exploited in numerous underground and opencast mines between the sixteenth and nineteenth centuries, the orebody of the Lebach group of the Middle Rotliegende being especially important. From 1850 these ores were rapidly replaced by the minette ores of Lorraine and Luxembourg.[56]

Near Imsbach and Göllheim, to the northeast of Kaiserslautern, mudstones of the Upper Rotliegende contain beds of syngenetic chalcocite. The copper probably derives from the subvolcanic mineralization of the neighbouring Donnersberg.

Rhenohercynian Zone and sub-Variscan Foredeep

The Rhenohercynian Zone includes most of the Rheinische Schiefergebirge, the Harz and small uplifts in the Hessian depression between these two mountainous areas (Figs. 1 and 19). On the left bank of the Rhine the Hunsrück and Eifel are mainly built up of Lower Devonian rocks. A north–south zone with Middle and Upper Devonian rocks and transgressive early Triassic sandstones, which is also metallogenetically significant, separates the Eastern from the

Table 8 *Mineral production (tonne) in Saar–Nahe Depression, 1950–82*[21] *((3), etc., indicates number of producing mines)*

Year	Uranium ore*	Barite concentrates	Feldspar
1950†	—	39 266 (3)	13 490 (1)
1960	3 386‡	83 790 (3)	115 225 (3)
1970	1 159	61 875 (2)	180 955 (5)
1975	—	7 675 (1)	217 989 (4)
1980	—	8 968 (1)§	134 112 (3)§
1981	—	8 052 (1)§	105 905 (3)§
1982	—	9 172 (1)§	109 235 (3)§

* After Feldmann.[22]
† Rhineland Palatinate only.
‡ 1961.
§ Saarland only.

Western Eifel with its strongly Caledonian-folded pre-Devonian rocks of the Hohe Venn, southeast of Aachen. The eastern Rheinische Schiefergebirge includes the Taunus (predominantly Lower Devonian), the Lahn and Dill synclines (Middle and Upper Devonian), the Siegerland anticlinorium (Lower Devonian), the Bergische Land in the northwest and the Sauerland in the northeast (Ordovician to Upper Devonian) and the Kellerwald in the east, composed of Silurian to Upper Devonian rocks. In the north and east is Lower Carboniferous with, in the north, low Upper Carboniferous in a widespread Variscan flysch facies. The western Harz displays a generally similar structure. The Brocken granite, emplaced in the latest Carboniferous at the border with the Middle Harz, is the only pluton exposed to erosion in the Rhenohercynian zone, aside from the Ramberg intrusion in the eastern Harz. The southern portion of the sub-Variscan Foredeep in the Ruhr and near Aachen, with its coal-bearing Upper Carboniferous sequence constituting the molasse of the Variscan orogen, was folded in the latest Carboniferous.

Volcanosedimentary deposits of early Variscan age
In addition to the large orebodies of the Rammelsberg in the Harz and of Meggen in the Sauerland, there are in the Rheinische Schiefergebirge a series of other sulphide–barite deposits. Apart from the Lahn–Dill district, which boasts by far the most important deposit of this type, red hematite deposits were mined in the eastern Sauerland near Adorf and in the Upper Harz. The deposits of red hematite in the Franconian Forest are located to the south of the Central German Rise in the Saxothuringian Zone (see earlier).

Rammelsberg deposit The Rammelsberg deposit lies on the outskirts of the former imperial town of Goslar, on the northern border of the Harz Mountains—an area of renowned geological interest. The ore extends along the foot of the Rammelsberg, which is 600 m high and has lent its name to the deposit. The mine is owned by Preussag Aktiengesellschaft, which also operate the mine in Bad Grund in the Upper Harz Mountains.

The Rammelsberg sulphide deposit is well known to miners, mineral dressers and geologists alike the world over. For some, the history of more than 1000 years of mining is the most interesting aspect,[57,58] whereas others will recall that it was at Rammelsberg that very intimately intergrown ores were for the first time successfully separated by flotation. Mines in other parts of the world that treat similar ores have—consciously or unconsciously—based their operations on methods that were developed at Rammelsberg. To geologists, Rammelsberg is best known as a classical example of a submarine hydrothermal deposit. Generally the Rammelsberg formation is widely recognized as being typical of syngenetic, submarine hydrothermal origin.

The *genesis* of the deposit dates back to the Devonian. Geosynclinal conditions prevailed in the area up to the Lower Carboniferous (Table 9). The development of the geosyncline was accompanied by an initial magmatism recognizable by diabases as well as keratophyric and basic tuffs. The strata sequence in the vicinity of the deposit lay palaeogeographically on the northwestern flank of an intrageosynclinal high, the so-called West Harz Rise, which emerged during the Middle and Upper Devonian and is characterized by a decreasing thickness of sediments, significant distribution of heavy minerals and shallow water carbonate deposition.[18]

The Rammelsberg ores are of Middle Devonian age and form a conformable interlayer in the lower part of the Wissenbach slates. Magmatic activity at that time was very distinct, as is shown by the occurrence of numerous keratophyric tuffs.[59] In connexion with that activity, metalliferous hydrothermal currents arose, leading to the formation of the large deposit that is now seen at Rammelsberg. Hot solutions, rich in hydrogen sulphide, emerged at the sea-bottom, collected in a simple hollow and were there precipitated as submarine, colloidal, rhythmically layered and rapidly crystallizing formations. Thermal activity and precipitation were maintained for a long period, the formation of ore occurring during the period of sedimentation of the Wissenbach slates. Accordingly, the Rammelsberg deposit forms a submarine and, at the same time, synsedimentary concentration of ore, owing its metal supply to ascending hydrothermal solutions at temperatures between 80 and 120°C.[18,60]

Not long ago there were very different opinions on the sequence of ores at Rammelsberg.[18,59,61,62] The assumption that the occurrence of ores in different lenses is mostly due to tectonic developments and that the Grey orebody—the source of many wrong interpretations—represents the youngest member of the mineralization led to a relatively simple sequence of ores.[63,64] Table 10 identifies pre-, main and postphases.

The *pre-phase* is characterized by the concentration of silica, which led to the rock called 'Kniest'—a grey, compact and hard material without foliation. It is brecciated and pervaded by veins of quartz with certain quantities of sulphide minerals. A very early forerunner of the mineralization is represented by a thin sulphidic ore layer in sandstones in the uppermost part of the Lower Devonian Kahleberg sandstone[65] (Table 10).

The *main phase* is represented by the Rammelsberg deposit proper, extending far beyond the Kniest. The sequence of ores starts with a mainly pyritic ore, situated especially in the western part of the lens (Old orebody). In succession follow, first, an ore rich in sphalerite, with some chalcopyrite, then a baritic lead–zinc ore, leading to a baritic lead ore and on to barite.

Table 9 Sequence of strata and magmatism in vicinity of Rammelsberg deposit

Period	Stage	Lithology	Magmatism
Permian		Zechstein (Zechstein Transgression) / Rotliegende (conglomerates, sandstone, shales)	
Upper Carboniferous		Variscan folding (Asturian)	(Synorogenic magmatism)
Upper Carboniferous	Namurian	Greywackes and clay slates 200 m	
Lower Carboniferous	Dinantian	Culm greywacke / Culm clay slate } > 2000 m / Culm siliceous slate } 50 m	Diabase and tuffs
Upper Devonian		Grey and variegated slates–grey limestone –400m –50 m	
Middle Devonian	Givetian	Grey clay slate–limestone intercalations–limestones –300 m –50 m	Diabase and tuffs
Middle Devonian	Eifelian	Wissenbach slate –700 m / Clay slate / Rammelsberg ore deposit / Clay slate / Slate with sandy layers / *Calceola* slates 60–150 m / Upper *Speciosus* beds 10 m	Diabase / Layers of keratophyric tuffs / initial magmatism (Exposed in the mine)
Lower Devonian	Emsian	Lower *Speciosus* beds 20 m / Kahleberg sandstone > 1000 m	

Table 10 Ore succession (*considerably simplified*) in Rammelsberg deposit

Post-phase (footwall ore and grey ore body) to 10 m	Grey ore		Barite, grey, fine-grained, sometimes intercalated with clay and sometimes with sulphides			
ca 30 m	Slates					
			Banded ore			
Main phase Old and New Layer *ca* 10–20 m	Rich ore	Barite ore	Barite with sulphides	Banded ore	Pyrite slate	Layer horizon (*ca* 10 m)
		Lead–zinc ore	Baritic lead–zinc and lead ore / Mottled ore			
		Brown ore	Zinc ore, pyritic and baritic with copper ore			
		Pyritiferous ore	Pyrite ore with sphalerite and chalcopyrite			
		Sulphur ore	Pyrite ore			
Pre-phase (keel-shaped)	Kniest		Silica-rich fine-bedded rocks, breccias			

At the top are predominantly alternations of slate and ore.

Investigation of the sulphur isotopes has led to the conclusion that all of the galena, sphalerite and chalcopyrite are of magmatic hydrothermal origin.[66,67] Within the main ore phase the $\delta^{34}S$ value of these sulphides indicates an increase from the bottom to the top from +7‰ to about +20‰. The pyrite, however, is thought to be derived from both hydrothermal and biogenic sulphur.

At the margins the high-grade ore gives way to banded ore with increasing interbedding of slate and ore layers. Then follows pyritic-banded ore, which finally passes into Wissenbach slates. The so-called horizon of the deposit—a slate series stratigraphically equivalent to the ore deposit—can be traced for several kilometres, its finely layered parts showing abundant pyrite and slightly increased lead–zinc concentrations within the ppm range.

After a short interruption of the thermal activity further deposition of barite occurred in the *post-phase*. It has become known mainly from two isolated deposits; that at the surface in the so-called 'Schiefermühle' and, underground, the 'Grey orebody'. This is a layered, fine-grained barite, which in the surface deposits forms thin and thick layers in the slate, whereas in the Grey orebody the barite is voluminously developed and also carries higher sulphide concentrations.[18] The barium in the barite is a product of hydrothermal solutions, but the sulphate ions are mainly derived from the normal sea water.[66]

The most important minerals in the main-phase sulphide ore are sphalerite, pyrite, marcasite, galena and chalcopyrite. Some 40 other minerals have been described in detail by Ramdohr.[60] Foremost among the gangue minerals is barite, at 20–30% forming an essential accompaniment to the sulphides (Table 11). Although relative proportions of the minerals in the banded ore are fairly constant, the contents of pyrite and marcasite as well as that of silica become gradually higher in direct proportion to the distance from the rich ore. Chemical analyses (Table 11) that show the average of the ore mined (rich and banded ore of the New orebody) indicate the great number of supplementary and trace elements, some of which are of commercial importance. Not all of the mineral species that contain these elements have been identified but, on the whole, the assemblage is well known. Generally, the pyritic ore has the highest content of Co, Ni, As and Te; the mottled ore has the highest content of Au and Bi; the ore rich in sphalerite the highest content of Cd, In, Ge and Hg; and the lead ore the highest content of Ag and Sb.[18]

The baritic mineralization of the Grey orebody of the post-phase includes, besides argillaceous and carbonatic impurities, an average of about 65–75% $BaSO_4$. The content of Sr, though very low, shows a certain increase towards the stratigraphically higher levels. Moreover, the barite contains sulphides with contents of about 4% Pb + Zn or even more in one particular zone in the upper part of the orebody.

The *pre-orogenic structure of the sulphide lens* is similar to a pancake (Fig. 8). Below the ore lens, the wedge-shaped Kniest body dips down like the keel of a ship.

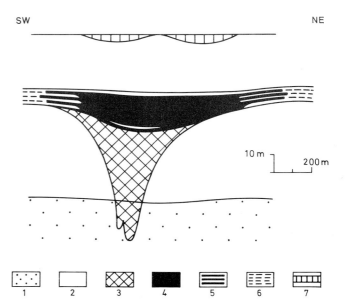

Fig. 8 *Pre-orogenic structure of Rammelsberg deposit: 1–7, Wissenbach slate; 1, slate with sand bands; 2, slate; 3, Kniest; 4, massive ore; 5, banded ore; 6, ore horizon; 7, grey ore (barite)*

Owing to the extremely high concentration of the ore (the hydrothermal minerals in the high-grade ore amount to 90%), there is no doubt that the precipita-

Table 11 *Minerals and chemical composition of crude ore at Rammelsberg mine, %*

Sphalerite	20·8	Zn	13·5	CaO	3·0	Trace elements		
Pyrite/marcasite	16·0	Pb	5·6	MgO	1·5	Sb	Ni	Ga
Galena	6·5	Cu	1·0	Al_2O_3	4·0	As	In	Se
Chalcopyrite	2·9	Ag	100·0 g/t	SiO_2	12·0	Cd	Tl	Te
Barite	18·0	Au	0·8 g/t			Co	Ge	Re
(Slate	35·0)	Fe	9·0			Bi	Pt	Ru
and some 50 minerals		Mn	0·8			Sn	Pd	Rh
and organic substances		S	20·0			Hg	Mo	V
		Ba	12·0					

tion happened directly in the area where the ascending solutions emerged—in other words, the deposit developed at the place where the solutions flowed out. Thus, the Kniest was the route of the ascending hydrothermal fluids.

Conservative assessments reveal that the thermal activity caused a concentration in the range of 35 000 000–40 000 000 tonne of ore with a metal content of 7 000 000–8 000 000 tonne Pb + Zn + Cu, including the parts of the deposit lost to erosion.

In regard to *orogenic development*, the deposit was covered by younger sediments of Devonian and Carboniferous age and sank to even greater depths. During Late Carboniferous time the sediments of the geosyncline, having accumulated to some thousands of metres, were gripped in the vigorous Variscan orogenesis (Table 9).

The whole sequence of the Palaeozoic sediments was intensively folded and cleaved, then cut by faults and overthrusts and, finally, transformed into a consolidated part of the great Variscan mountain range.

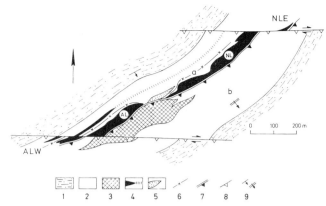

Fig. 10 *Tectonic map of Rammelsberg deposit (showing third level, simplified): 1, Wissenbach sand-banded slate; 2, Wissenbach slate; 3, Kniest; 4, massive ore and ore horizon; 5, Grey orebody; 6, axis of syncline; 7, thrust fault; 8, normal fault; 9, dip (normal and overturned) (AL, Old orebody; ALW, Old orebody–west; NL, New orebody; NLE, New orebody–east; a, axis of syncline of deposit; b, 'hanging-wall')*

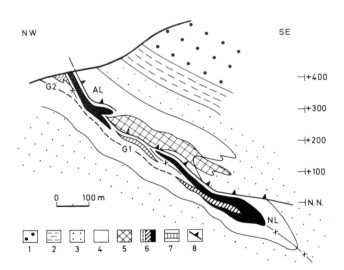

Fig. 9 *Section through Rammelsberg deposit: 1, Kahleberg sandstone and Lower Speciosus beds; 2, Upper Speciosus beds and Calceola slate; 3, Wissenbach sand-banded slate; 4, Wissenbach slate; 5, Kniest; 6, ore bed (ore horizon, banded ore, massive ore); 7, grey ore (barite); 8, thrust fault (AL, Old orebody; NL, New orebody; G1, Grey orebody (barite); G2, Footwall orebody (barite))*

The orogenic movement also resulted in the complete transformation of the outer form of the deposit and its interior texture and structure. Fig. 9 gives a good idea of the *tectonic structure* and Fig. 10 shows the situation of the orebodies at approximately the third level of the mine.

The ore lens was tipped up and transformed to an isoclinal syncline the axial plane of which strikes southwest–northeast and dips about 45°SE.

The major part of the deposit finished up in the inverted limb and the lowest portion of the syncline, whereas the banded ore—initially formed peripherally—and its slate equivalent were relocated on the normal footwall limb. In the core of the syncline, and confined to the upper part of the normal limb, the barite horizon of the post-phase occurs as the youngest member of the sequence.

The Kniest, once situated under the main phase deposit, is now found on the inverted limb of the syncline.

The inverted limb is accompanied by a major shear zone, where the 'hanging' block has been pushed over the ore of the main phase. This overthrust is a dominant feature of the structure of the deposit.

Owing to the driving of the hanging block over the syncline, the formerly connected ore lens of the main phase, now situated below the shear zone, was separated diagonally into two parts. From the sequence of their discovery they are called the Old orebody, which lies at a higher elevation in the southwest, and the New orebody, which occurs at depth in the northeast.

The Kniest involved in the movement has strongly influenced the deformation and disruption of the main ore lens. The hard silicified rock has invaded the ore mass situated below like a wedge, forming a curious chip on the inverted underside of the Old orebody (Fig. 9). At the same time the Kniest has filled the gap between the two parts of the former single orebody, making locally direct contact with the Grey orebody in the normal limb (Figs. 9 and 10).

As a result of this kind of tectonic development the interior structure of the ore shows particularly intense folding of every order, accompanied by many fissures, shear zones and local overthrusts. Of great importance are laminations and relative thickenings, which indicate a disharmonic relation between the ore and the host rock.

The thickness of the ore is impressive at the bottom of the syncline (New orebody), where, owing to tectonic doubling and accumulation, an ore mass has been formed with a horizontal width of as much as 100 m.

The depression of the deposit to considerable depths and the intense tectonic movements are responsible for a new *metamorphic microstructure and fine texture* of the ore.[60] Typical of this is the parallel fabric pattern formed by reorientation of tabular minerals and the squeezing out of the ore fabric together with the crystallization processes connected with it. Some relict primary textures do remain, however, such as colloform textures, rhythmic precipitation layering, framboids and other features. The essentially isochemical metamorphic events occurred at temperatures in the range 225–250°C, as indicated by the mineral assemblage marcasite, cubanite ($CuFe_2S_3$), valleriite ($Cu_3Fe_4S_7$).

Following the Variscan orogenesis and during the Upper Permian the Harz region sank below sea-level. Only during the Upper Cretaceous did uplift (sub-Hercynian movements) cause the Variscan basement to emerge and be subjected to erosion. This process resulted in the loss of a considerable part of the Rammelsberg deposit and it was this erosion that first caused the Old orebody to be exposed. Its gossan led ultimately to the discovery of the deposit. Because of the rather strong erosion and also because of the fine crystalline to dense structure of the ore, superficial alteration has been only slight.

In *commercial terms* the quantity of ore mined since the beginning of operations approached in 1982 25 000 000 tonne (Table 12); of that total about 12 000 000 tonne has been extracted since flotation treatment was introduced in 1936. In recent years ore production has stabilized at about 280 000 tonne per annum. The output, composed of high-grade and banded ore, contains about 5·5% Pb, 13·5% Zn, 1·0% Cu and 100 g Ag and 0·6 g Au per tonne. Remaining reserves in 1982 amounted to 2 000 000 tonne of ore.

The mine currently produces five concentrates from which 90–96% of the mineral values in the ore are recovered. Copper, lead and zinc concentrates are produced with, additionally, pyrite and barite concentrates. The metal content of the annual production is about 50 000 tonne of lead and zinc, 3000 tonne of copper and more than 20 tonne of silver, some gold and other commercial by-products being contained in the concentrates.

The Rammelsberg and Grund mines, the latter operating on the Upper Harz vein system, are the last remaining active mines of the once prosperous Harz ore region. Present annual output of these two mines is, however, many times greater than that in the past, when many small mines were in production. Thus, even today the Harz is an important primary source of lead, zinc and silver, in addition to which Rammelsberg is the only mine in West Germany where gold and minor quantities of copper are recovered.

Rammelsberg supplies *ca* 30% of the lead and zinc output of the Federal Republic of Germany, after due allowance for smelting deductions. Including the Grund mine, the share of national output is about 58%, and for silver nearly 100%. Thus, even now, after a history of more than 1000 years, Rammelsberg mine still makes a significant contribution to the feedstock requirements of the national base-metal smelting industry.

Meggen deposit The Meggen zinc–lead–barite mine is situated in the western Sauerland, 60 km southeast of Dortmund and some 15 km to the east of the district town of Olpe. The deposit has been mined since 1853 and is currently being exploited by Sachtleben Bergbau GmbH—a subsidiary of Metallgesellschaft AG, Frankfurt; Meggen is the company's principal mine in the Federal Republic. Output in 1983 was in the region of 1 000 000 tonne of ore. A flotation plant attached to the mine produces zinc, lead and pyrite concentrates. In 1974 the mine was Europe's largest single producer of zinc concentrate with an annual output of 120 000 tonne and accounted for half of West Germany's zinc production. In 1977 mining of barite ceased because the exploitable reserves on the edge of the deposit had been exhausted (Fig. 11). After deduction of the eroded parts of the deposit, total reserves were 10 000 000 tonne barite and 50 000 000 tonne of closely intergrown pyrite ore with average contents of 15% ZnS and 2% PbS. Some 40 000 000 tonne of sulphide ore and 9 000 000 tonne of barite had been extracted to 1983 (Table 13).

Mining is currently being carried out between the eighth and eleventh levels (Fig. 12). Geological and

Table 12 *Ore production at Rammelsberg mine*

Period	Average production per year, t	Output during each period, t × 10³	Cumulative output, t × 10³
968–1235	8 000	2 140	2 140
1236–1360	5 000	625	2 765
1361–1460	—	—	2 765
1461–1525	20 000	1 300	4 065
1526–1552	15 000	405	4 470
1553–1648	18 000	1 720	6 190
1649–1763	12 000	1 380	7 570
1764–1810	13 000	610	8 180
1811–1866	12 000	612	8 792
1867–1935	58 000	4 000	12 792
1936–1953	188 000	3 385	16 177
1954–1975	304 600	6 700	22 877
1976	278 000	278	23 155
1977	279 000	279	23 434
1978	214 000	214	23 648
1979	282 000	282	23 930
1980	283 000	283	24 213
1981	281 000	281	24 494
1982	286 000	286	24 780

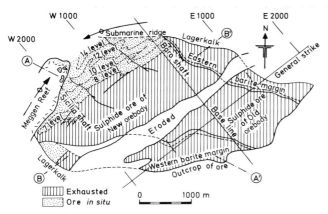

Fig. 11 *Palaeogeographic sketch map of Meggen ore layer*

Table 13 *Cumulative ore production of Meggen mine*

	Sulphide ore, t × 10³	Barite ore, t × 10³*
1853–1900	3 493	—
1901–1945	15 420	4 226
1946–1963	7 719	2 720
1964–1983	13 133	2 033
	39 765	8 979

* 'Sachtleben' Bergbau GmbH, 1901–77, 7 232 000 tonne; Kali-Chemie A.G., 1908–66, 1 747 000 tonne.

mining exploration by drilling, ramp and horizontal drift has now reached the fourteenth level. The drifts are now accessible over a horizontal distance of some 3 km via two shafts and a ramp from above ground. With a distance between levels of 50 m, some 2 000 000 tonne of exploitable ore reserves per level are being developed. Above the tenth level the ore was extracted by rail haulage, diesel loaders and an occasional scraper loader being used at the face. LHD technology has consistently been introduced below the tenth level with rail-less haulage over ramps with an incline of approximately 1 in 7. Since 1978 ore has been tracked to a central ore and waste pass system with associated jaw crusher, from which it is taken by belt conveyor to the skip shaft. Drilling jumbos and diesel loaders are used at the face. Combined chamber and sub-level open stoping at rates of 100 tonne per man-shift is used to extract the ore in areas of the deposit steeper than 60°. Where the seam runs level or slopes only slightly the ore is extracted by room and pillar caving at a rate of up to 50 tonne per man-shift. Back filling is not generally carried out; only in areas of rich ore is a method of packing with lean concrete being developed to minimize losses during mining.

The crude sulphide ore undergoes heavy media separation during which country rock removed with the ore is separated at a pulp density of $\gamma \sim 3 \cdot 0$. The resulting beneficiated ore is then crushed to < 12 mm before being passed to the concentrator, which came on stream in 1963. Here it is processed to yield concentrates of ZnS, PbS and FeS_2. The input material at the flotation stage is currently 85% sulphide ores and 15% host rock and similar material. Recovery from this plant is 92% for zinc, 50% for lead and 75% for pyrite; 54% Zn is achieved in the sphalerite concentrate, 50% Pb in galena and 47% S in pyrite (Tables 14 and 15). Barite has been enriched by jigging to give a concentrate of approximately 96% $BaSO_4$ for further processing in the chemical industry.

Geologically, the Meggen deposit was precipitated in a morphological depression as a submarine, stratiform, hydrothermal deposit of sulphides and barite at the boundary between the Middle and Upper Devonian. Sandy clay sediments of the late Middle Devonian— referred to as the 'Lenneschiefer' or Meggen Beds— occur in the footwall, and calcareous argillaceous slates, limestones and sandstones with facies interfingering over short distances constitute the immediate hanging-wall (Fig. 13).[68,69]

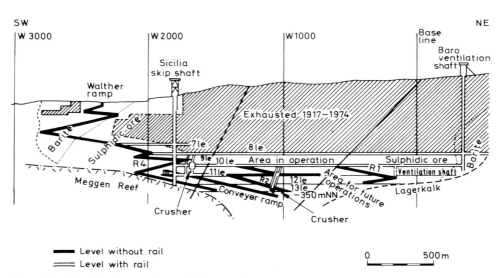

Fig. 12 *Simplified section through Meggen mine*

Table 14 *Meggen mine production*

Year	Concentrator feed* Quantity, t	Content, % Zn	Pb	S	Fe	Concentrate production — Zinc concentrate Quantity, t	Content, % Zn	Lead concentrate Quantity, t	Content, % Pb	Flotation pyrite concentration Quantity, t	Content, % S	Yield, % Zn	Pb	S	Fe	Barite, t*
1958	90 950	9·62		40·41		14 057	49·63			72 861	41·73	79·71		82·75		138 428
1959	70 300	9·84		41·41		11 889	46·22			47 031	43·89	79·42		74·14		148 735
1960	112 876	10·76		41·58		21 151	47·68			72 078	47·60	83·05		73·09		170 545
1961	113 956	10·90		41·35		23 589	46·68			76 620	47·50	88·65		77·21		157 526
1962	122 656	10·89		41·40	31·66	23 831	48·75			81 551	47·87	87·00		76·88		173 586
1963	261 329	10·87	1·35	40·69	31·10	49 504	45·01			146 963	48·14	78·40		66·90		168 542
1964	376 487	10·86	1·28	40·67	31·13	73 636	46·62			226 397	47·69	84·00		72·70	79·30	173 325
1965	420 122	10·98	1·42	39·94	30·52	87 119	47·04	253	39·89	259 755	48·20	88·90		74·60	81·80	176 128
1966 RGJ (9 months)	386 241	10·37	1·35	38·98	29·87	70 145	51·07	3 151	47·94	242 167	47·47	89·40	29·00	76·50	84·80	127 114
1966–67	549 422	10·61	1·32	40·57	31·07	98 452	52·82	5 866	42·64	400 301	43·47	89·29	34·48	78·13	87·75	169 315
1967–68	601 509	10·14	1·21	39·00	30·06	103 411	53·34	7 236	36·35	471 199	41·19	90·39	36·30	83·79	93·65	173 868
1968–69	617 775	9·79	1·21	39·06	30·26	99 759	55·17	7 352	32·30	499 550	40·74	91·00	31·66	84·33	93·84	171 960
1969–70	639 098	9·62	1·30	39·26	30·45	99 579	55·61	7 253	33·95	471 315	43·42	91·66	29·71	81·56	92·18	182 229
1970–71	685 676	9·55	1·33	38·79	30·09	108 703	55·91	8 634	34·06	430 885	47·53	92·81	32·15	76·99	80·91	183 213
1971–72	678 705	9·17	1·30	38·83	30·29	103 965	55·43	7 926	33·11	408 883	47·23	92·63	29·76	73·23	81·68	170 994
1972–73	656 749	9·72	1·49	39·61	31·01	107 980	55·11	9 386	32·57	417 546	47·20	93·23	31·31	75·75	83·66	133 991
1973–74	722 298	9·69	1·47	39·31	30·33	120 255	53·85	8 018	39·74	459 841	46·99	92·50	30·03	76·11	85·30	105 070
1974–75	775 355	8·75	1·29	39·10	30·66	117 796	53·18	8 706	49·64	484 726	46·65	92·31	43·32	74·58	82·40	81 381
1975–76	794 027	8·16	1·13	39·72	31·28	109 650	53·96	8 927	50·72	494 486	46·74	91·33	50·56	73·30	80·60	59 187
1976–77	778 124	8·31	1·14	39·34	30·93	109 501	54·20	9 676	50·07	488 336	46·47	91·77	54·79	74·13	81·79	70 464
1977–78	738 915	8·54	1·17	38·58	30·25	107 828	53·94	9 873	46·73	465 415	46·52	92·17	53·53	75·96	84·06	—
1978–79	677 726	9·46	1·33	37·77	29·16	109 261	54·73	10 758	46·07	417 018	46·09	93·27	55·05	75·08	84·42	—
1979–80	714 788	8·86	1·25	39·06	30·53	109 270	54·48	11 326	41·19	459 764	46·33	93·98	52·16	76·28	84·63	—
1980–81	714 278	8·37	1·14	39·00	30·64	102 870	53·90	10 111	37·75	431 250	46·75	92·78	47·01	72·56	79·88	—
1981–82	743 066	7·77	1·06	39·69	31·52	99 169	53·80	10 038	35·93	459 328	45·79	92·44	45·65	71·51	78·32	—
1982–83	861 384	6·62	0·82	40·31	32·71	97 399	53·51	6 151	46·04	532 371	45·20	91·40	40·11	69·29	74·11	—
1983–84	833 963	6·45	0·85	39·40	31·89	91 871	53·45	5 694	41·96	505 802	45·00	91·31	33·66	69·27	74·34	—

* Run-of-mine ore having passed the heavy media separation plant (crude ore minus 20% waste).

Table 15 *Average chemical composition of concentrator feed, concentrates and barite, Meggen mine (April–June, 1977; dried at 105°C)*

Content	Crude ore input, %	Concentrates — Flotation pyrite, %	Sphalerite, %	Galena, %	Spar, %	
S suitable for roasting	40·48	46·63	34·32	26·46	$BaSO_4(+SrSO_4)$	96·40
S not suitable for roasting	0·30	0·22	0·21	0·57	$SrSO_4$	0·58
Fe	32·00	40·41	6·85	14·78	SiO_2	1·33
Zn	8·46	0·81	54·17	5·48	Fe_2O_3	0·25
Pb	1·15	0·57	0·86	49·33	Al_2O_3	0·40
Cu	0·006	0·033	0·055	0·11	CaO	0·70
Cd	0·0094	0·0014	0·057	0·008	MgO	0·30
Tl	0·024	0·025	0·009	0·094	Mn_3O_4	0·001
Co	0·020	0·026	0·005	0·011	S-sulphide	0·20
Cr	0·005	0·004	0·001	0·005	Loss on ignition	0·50
Ni	0·038	0·042	0·013	0·019	sp. gr.	4·40
TiO_2	0·21	0·12	0·09	0·08		
As	0·069	0·081	0·029	0·047		
Sb	0·042	0·045	0·021	0·061		
Sn	<0·005	<0·005	<0·005	<0·005		
Se	Trace	Trace	Trace	Trace		
F	0·006	0·007	0·005	0·003		
Al_2O_3	2·01	1·38	0·30	0·14		
Mn_3O_4	0·21	0·19	0·21	0·07		
CaO	1·43	0·88	0·11	0·89		
MgO	0·35	0·22	0·06	0·04		
$BaSO_4$	0·24	0·18	0·02	0·01		
K_2O	0·46	0·31	0·064	0·015		
Na_2O	0·067	0·037	0·012	0·0024		
SiO_2	10·13	6·22	1·91	0·41		
CO_2	1·72	1·07	0·20	0·66		
Unaccounted for	0·56	0·48	0·40	0·73		
	100·00	100·00	100·00	100·00		

Federal Republic of Germany

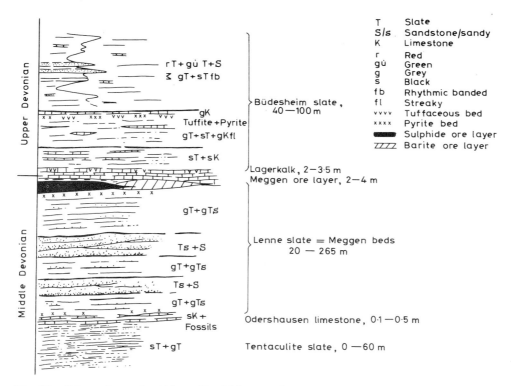

Fig. 13 *Schematic stratigraphic profile of Meggen mine area*

Signs of magmatic activity exist in the Meggen stratigraphic sequence only as a number of acid to intermediate tuffs less than 20 cm thick in the hanging-wall of the deposit. On the other hand, the Meggen deposit lies only 5 km north of a main centre of keratophyric volcanism that was active several times during the Lower to early Middle Devonian period.[69,70]

Although sulphide ores and barite were precipitated simultaneously, their spatial occurrences are very clearly separated within the orebody, the metal sulphides being nearer the centre and the barite on the edge of the deposit. The two overlap in a transitional zone that, generally, is only 20–40 m wide, where the beginnings of the barite lie both above and below the thinning out sulphide ore (Figs. 11 and 14).

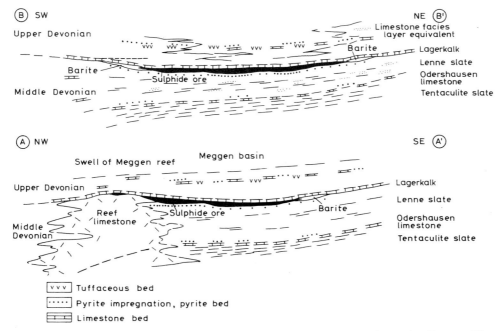

Fig. 14 *Schematic sections through pre-orogenic Meggen ore horizon (for section lines see Fig. 11)*

Pyrite, sphalerite, galena and gangue material have specific relative proportions. Less on the basis of textural and structural features than of chemical composition (Fe–Zn–As–Sb distribution) the sulphide orebody may be subdivided into a peripheral, intermediate and central area. A rough vertical subdivision is possible on the basis of textural features.[71]

The ores richest in Pb and Zn are found in the central part of the deposit, where they are coupled with areas of greater thickness. Both thickness and metal content gradually decline towards the edge of the ore basin. Similarly, in the barite margin the barite content decreases inwards to the sulphide orebody as well as outwards to the Lagerkalk (Fig. 11), whereas the SiO_2, Al_2O_3, $CaCO_3$ and FeS_2 impurities increase.

The Meggen deposit is tectonically connected with the overturned southeast flank of the Attendorn–Elspe double syncline. A comparably overturned eroded anticline (aerial fold) divides the deposit into a flat southern depression, known as the 'Altes Lager' (Old orebody) and the 'Neues Lager' (New orebody), which lies to the north and follows the main structure downward. In the course of the Variscan orogenesis the deposit was considerably folded and imbricated, but the primary ore structures were only slightly affected, with the result that structures that testify to the original gel-like nature of the sulphides and their precipitation and sedimentation in the marine area are well preserved.

In the northwest the barite and sulphide ores border on a reef that, when the ore was being precipitated, acted as a barrier to protect the basin from an influx of erosion material from the nearby land. Concomitantly with the ore sedimentation the toxic environment caused the reef fauna to die out. In the west limestones and argillaceous slates of the Upper Devonian overlie the dead reef in a thin sill facies, whereas recent drilling seems to indicate that in the eastern part of the reef complex, which has been shown to stretch for a distance of 1·5 km, the ore sedimentation overlies the reef and the Meggen ore basin is linked via a barrier with an adjacent basin to the north. The orebody crops out at its southern, eastern and western edges, where it is eroded or passes into its peripheral facies equivalent, which is a fine detrital pelagic limestone horizon, the Lagerkalk.

The exposed orebody extends horizontally for a distance of about 4 km and has, to date, been shown to reach a depth of 750 m, which corresponds to 450 m below mean sea-level (15th level). The pre-orogenic deposit took the form of an ellipse, extending WNW–ESE, with diameters of about 5 km × 3 km.

The limits of the orebody at bottom and top are sharp and tectonically activated bedding planes. A few metres below the ore layer and in the hanging-wall limestone characteristic layers and lenses of pyrite between a few millimetres and up to several centimetres thick occur, as they do in the vicinity of the Upper Devonian tuff zones and the Middle Devonian Odershausen limestone (Figs. 13 and 14). These pyrite sedimentations, which have been described as pre- and post-phases of the Meggen deposit, contain only traces of ZnS and PbS.

The average thickness of the *Kieslager* is 3·5–4 m, and of the barite layers 2·5–3 m. As an exception, in the northwest of the orebody, where it is in contact with the reef, thicknesses of 8–11 m occur, partly owing to a marked dilution of the sulphides by about 25% sedimentary material.

In terms of *ore petrography* the sulphide deposit is composed of iron sulphides (pyrite, marcasite and melnikovite pyrite), sphalerite, galena and gangue (clay minerals, calcite and quartz). The fine grain structure typical of non-metamorphic, synsedimentary sulphide deposits, the close intergrowth of the ore minerals as well as the fluctuation of the melnikovite pyrite content between 10 and 15% initially caused beneficiation problems (Table 14).

Spherical, pancake-shaped or bulbous aggregates of coarse-grained pyrite as much as several centimetres in diameter and in a mainly clay matrix constitute the lowermost part of the orebody. Shrinkage cracks are filled with sphalerite or gangue. This type of ore occurs in a zone that is mostly less than 50 cm thick and in contact with the Middle Devonian Lenneschiefer. It plays only a subsidiary role in the structure of the orebody as a whole.

The characteristic pyrite types show every stage of transition from gel aggregates to recrystallized idiomorphic pyrites.

The gel forms tend to be composed mainly of pyrite spheroids of radiating structure with a diameter rarely in excess of 40 μm. Clay is often the principal substance at the core of the spheroids and forms a matrix between the radially extending columns of pyrite crystal. Other photomicrographs, however, show rounded to oval individuals with a more concentric structure and a core composed apparently of a single pyrite spheroid or an agglomerate of several spheroids surrounded by a halo of radiating crystallites of pyrite or marcasite. Predominant in this mixture of minerals is usually melnikovite pyrite with numerous fine inclusions of shale and quartz, though columnar pyrite crystallites, galena and sphalerite in minute aggregates of less than 5 μm are also represented. A second external ring, which separates the sulphide formation from the surrounding matrix, though including a number of foreign minerals, is mainly composed of pyrite, which has a columnar structure towards the core but usually shows idiomorphic grain shapes outwards.

Under strong magnification the cores of the spheroids prove to be made up of a number of minute pyrite crystals between 2 and 5 μm in size and usually with a marked idiomorphic shape, which are embedded in a matrix of melnikovite pyrite.

Other formations that are worthy of mention because of their quantity are rounded aggregates of minute idiomorphic pyrite crystals with a matrix either of sphalerite, quartz or pyrite, or—frequently—of melnikovite pyrite. The size of these agglomerates varies between 20 and 200 μm and those of the individual crystals between 1 and 5 μm.

In the course of diagenesis additionally an intensive general crystallization took place that involved the formation of largish, idioblastic pyrite individuals with, simultaneously, a process of purification and ejection of foreign matter—particularly clayey material, which subsequently formed an intergranular film or interstitial filling between the pyrite crystals. Depending on the degree of recrystallization of the pyrite, structures emerged the hypidiomorphic individual crystals of which seldom have a grain size of more than 1 mm and generally are less than 0·1 mm.

Spheroids with a generous interbedding of shale, quartz and sphalerite have been preserved with striking frequency in coarser idiomorphic areas of pyrite. The guest minerals are partly concentrically and partly radially orientated. Frequently, these are large spheroids of melnikovite pyrite some 0·2 mm in size with substantial more or less orientated clay inclusions.

As well as in the form already described, melnikovite pyrite also occurs in irregularly defined crust-like areas, often with a radiating texture and always well interspersed with clay material—a fact that probably explains its poor polishing qualities.

The occurrence of marcasite, again frequently in the form of radiating spheroids, is a restricted, local phenomenon and the overall proportion of the mineral in the composition of the ore is minimal and may be disregarded.

Sphalerite is the mineral that is encountered most frequently after pyrite. It occurs in a rather pale variety and measurements of Fe content are a fairly constant 1%. Often in the form of irregular narrow bands between layers of pyrite ore, it is frequently intercalated with numerous pyrite spheroids or individual small pyrite crystals.

Together with galena, which almost always occurs in association with substantial proportions of sphalerite in the ore, it usually forms a complex, fine-grained mixture. Pure sphalerite—that is, sphalerite that displays very little intergrowth in large aggregates—is found almost exclusively as mobilized and recrystallized fillings of cracks in the ore a few millimetres wide. In the pyrite spheroids it is found, like galena, often as inclusions of only a few microns in concentric or radial orientation. In the coarser pyrite ore, on the other hand, it occurs usually as an interstitial filling. Besides, sphalerite also occurs in the form of coarser aggregates between broken areas of pyrite, where it must probably be regarded as a product of mobilization. Locally, it is abundantly interspersed with phyllosilicates—probably sericite. Relatively coarse-grained sphalerite aggregates may reach grain sizes of 100 μm and more, but average only 40–100 μm. This mineral is much finer when—as often—it occurs as an interstitial filling between neighbouring pyrite individuals or even as insets in the groundmass. In this case grain sizes may be well below 30 μm. The sphalerite is always irregularly defined in relation to pyrite or the groundmass and is often closely intercalated with it, and locally even penetrated by it.

In the orebody *galena* is considerably subordinate to sphalerite and is generally much finer-grained. The mineral tends to be found in the interstices of neighbouring pyrite aggregates and, more seldom, in cataclastic cracks and fissures in pyrite. In such cases grain sizes rarely exceed 20 μm. Galena is often also found at the centre or even inside small atoll-like spheroids of pyrite. Occasionally, very fine galena acts almost as a binder for loosely packed pyrite framboids, thus replacing the normally predominant melnikovite pyrite. Sphalerite, however, occurs alongside it in a similar formation.

With Cu and Sb contents of 30 and 400 ppm, respectively, the proportions of *chalcopyrite* and *fahlore* (tetrahedrite) can only be seen very infrequently under the microscope. Since they are also of no importance from the beneficiation point of view they may be disregarded here.

Among the gangue minerals *barite* plays a subordinate role in the sulphide orebody, whereas *quartz* is widespread both in an irregular stratified arrangement with slate and in strings and bands and as fissure filling. Often, it constitutes the groundmass for pyrite spheroids or idiomorphic pyrite crystals, thereby resulting in a noticeable hardness of the ore; it also occurs in more concentrated pyrite accumulations as an interstitial filling between crystals. It often manifests an idiomorphic formation compared with sphalerite and galena.

Calcite is distributed fairly evenly throughout the deposit. Idioblastic development tends to predominate in sphalerite-rich areas, the sulphides often being included in the form of minute aggregates.

Worthy of note is the fact that clayey material occurs throughout the deposit. This was generally only imperfectly eliminated during the process of crystallization of the gel mass and has consequently been retained as a very fine dispersion, especially in the typical gel forms of the pyrite and in the melnikovite pyrite. In denser crystalline formations it tends to be precipitated in a very fine fringe at the grain boundaries and in interstices between crystals.

Clayey material, moreover, also forms stratiform intercalations in the ore in the form of strings of greater or lesser thickness and slaty bands of varying thickness up to a maximum of 2 cm impregnated with pyrite. These clayey layers are mainly composed of quartz and sericite. They contain carbonate and organogenic pigment in varying quantities.

The barite margin of the sulphide orebody is generally free of sulphides. Lenses and bands of pyrite occur only locally, in the New orebody, beyond the transition zone proper as a continuation of the sulphide precipitation.

The barite is dark blackish-grey in colour owing to organogenic pigment. Sedimentary fabrics are barely perceptible in the predominantly fine-grained crystalline barite (grain size 50 μm). A coarse-grained variety occasionally occurs as a layer a decimetre thick and is composed of millimetre-size spheroids. The main mass of barite is very pure with $BaSO_4$ contents of 96–98%; $SrSO_4$ contents are less than 1% and CaO_3, SiO_2 and Al_2O_3 contents are less than 3%.

The sulphide orebody can macroscopically be subdivided from bottom to top into three structural units (Fig. 15). A basal zone is composed of coarse layers of nodular pyrite with slaty interbeds up to a centimetre thick. Towards the hanging-wall the clay layers tend to diminish and the ore takes on a more massive aspect plentifully intercalated with sphalerite, galena and lenses of quartz.

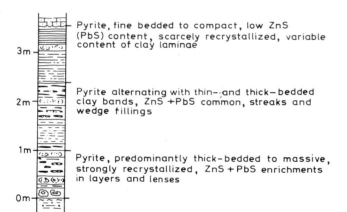

Fig. 15 *Standard section through Meggen ore horizon*

The next zone is composed of a more finely layered, banded ore type. Here again, marked recrystallization is found alongside cataclasis. The zone nearest the hanging-wall is composed of very finely layered pyrite that results from an alternation of pyrite and bands of clay of less than one millimetre in thickness. There is a subordinate presence of sphalerite and galena. This zone best displays the sedimentary nature and gel-like origin of the Meggen deposit. No metamorphic overprinting of the ore has occurred.

ZnS, PbS, FeS and gangue demonstrate a specific relationship to one another. The ratio of Zn to Pb is approximately 8:1. As the contents of these elements decrease, those of iron, sulphur and gangue increase.

Some areas rich in sphalerite and galena are concentrated in the central section of the sulphide orebody and correspond more or less with areas of greater thickness while striking southwest–northeast. The external configuration of the pre-orogenic deposit, however, extends WNW–ESE. Average chemical analyses of ore, barite and concentrates are given in Table 15.

In summary it may be said that the Meggen deposit has arisen syngenetically as a volcanosedimentary formation. It was suggested that the material of the deposit has largely been concentrated at depth in the course of magmatic differentiation and precipitated on the sea-bed in a chemical trap.[68] Alternative origins have been suggested in the case of certain elements. Buschendorf and Puchelt[72] presented arguments to support the thesis that the barite sulphur originated from the sea water, which is also supported by the composition of the sulphur isotopes.[67] Scherp[73] considered the barium to have been derived from barium-rich Ordovician slates from which it was extracted by magmatically heated formation water. The lead isotopes were studied by Wedepohl and co-workers,[124] who postulated the origin of the lead in the detrital sediments of the Precambrian.

The following major *tectonic features* of the Variscan orogeny are exposed in the mine. The folds have a northwest vergence and their steep limbs are overturned. Their hinge-like bends are frequently disrupted and replaced by over- and underthrusts (Fig. 16). The fold axes strike at 55–60° and locally, to the east of the Silicia shaft, plunge 15° towards the northeast. Some 300 m to the west of the shaft and via an area of axial culmination developed in 1977 at the 8th level, the axis begins to dip towards the southwest, thus repeating the fold sequence and the striking tectonic elements familiar from the eastern part of the mine. Cleavage planes and strike faults dip moderately steeply towards the southeast.

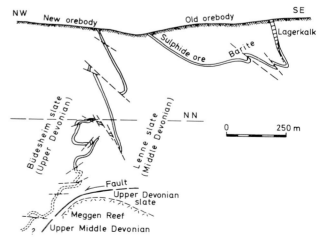

Fig. 16 *Cross-section through Meggen ore deposit, along ca W 1350*

Cross faults of larger displacement are rare. Of those previously known, only two major tension faults—the Markhahn and the Halberbracht faults, with vertical shifts of up to 45 m—have been opened up. Because of their dip to the southwest and the resulting relative pitch of the southwestern blocks they counteract the dip of the axes.

With approach to the reef complex, which is several hundred metres thick, isoclinally folded and imbricated, and underlies the western part of the deposit for at least 1500 m, the tectonic structure of the latter changes. The rather smooth, cascade-like plunging crestal surface, as encountered in the eastern section of the deposit, where it in part shows normal folds, changes in the vicinity of the reef to a complex imbricate structure with major fold units, some of them horizontal. Extremely overturned fold limbs with marked imbrication and doubling of beds are typical.

The southeast dip of the strike faults gradually levels out and may then bend towards the northwest.

The dip and strike of the orebody, together with its hanging- and footwalls, adjust themselves in the neighbourhood of the reef to the surface shape of the latter. The shape of the reef results in such a severe structural change that in parts of the western mine workings the fold axes strike north–south.

Other sulphide barite deposits At the boundary between the Lower and Middle Devonian there occur in the Rheinische Schiefergebirge small stratiform ore deposits, which are also regarded as being volcano-sedimentary, such as the Günterod barite deposit in the Dill syncline,[74] the pyrite deposit in the Auerhahn Field ESE of Meggen in the southern Sauerland, and the pyrite–barite deposit of Lohrheim in the Lahn syncline (Fig. 17). In the late Middle Devonian the barite lens (12–15 m thick) near Eisen[75] developed on the southeast edge of the Hunsrück in the transitional zone of the Variscan geosyncline towards the Central German Rise. This deposit, which is being exploited, contains 250 000 tonne of ore with some 80% $BaSO_4$. In the basal zone there are layers of pyrite, sphalerite, galena and a little fluorite. Until 1976 annual production was running at some 7500 tonne of ore and by 1978 up to 1982 this had been increased to an average of 10 000 tonne of crude barite per year.

Lead–zinc ore deposits bound to Middle to Late Devonian reef limestone in the northern Rheinische Schiefergebirge and to the Early Carboniferous limestone (Kohlenkalk) in the Aachen–Stolberg district are discussed later.

Red iron ore deposits in the Lahn–Dill district In the Variscan eugeosyncline the facies differentiation increased considerably during the Middle Devonian. At the boundary with the Upper Devonian there developed a lively submarine, in part explosive, spilite volcanism with which the red iron ore deposits of the Lahn–Dill type are directly linked. In the southeastern Rheinische Schiefergebirge there appear between the Lower Devonian anticlines of the Taunus in the south and the Siegerland in the north two large synclines striking northeast–southwest—those of the Lahn and

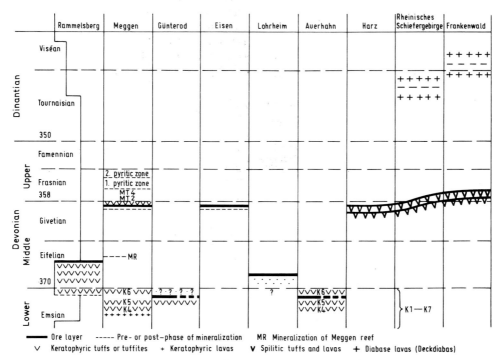

Fig. 17 *Stratigraphic position of stratiform sulphide–barite and red iron ore deposits in the Rheinische Schiefergebirge, Upper Harz and Frankenwald (sulphide–barite deposits after Krebs[76])*

the Dill (Fig. 19), which are built up of marine sediments of the Middle Devonian to Lower Carboniferous with substantial intercalations of volcanic rocks. The southern Lahn syncline is separated from the Dill syncline in the north by the Hörre zone with narrow wedges of Early Devonian rocks and with Late Devonian to Early Carboniferous strata of sandy to quartzitic flysch facies foreign to the synclines, known as the Hörre facies. The many larger and smaller saddles and downfolds and the occasional elongated zones of imbrication of both major structures are interrupted frequently and shifted relative to each other by transverse faults. Characteristic of the two synclines, apart from their limited area and varied tectonic structure, is the fact that rocks of similar age, but differing in thickness and facies, are found side by side. Magmatites, especially keratophyres, spilites and diabases with their appropriate pyroclastics, tuffs, schalsteins (former palagonite tuffs) and a multiplicity of sediments, particularly reef, cephalopod and flaggy limestones, shales, sandstones and detrital accumulations are found in rapidly changing distribution, thickness and composition. This bears witness to a division of the large component troughs of the geosynclinal area into numerous basins and ridges, which began in the Middle Devonian and rapidly gained pace, sometimes with different patterns of sedimentation. This took place as the result of epeirogenetic to early orogenic and/or volcano-tectonic processes in conjunction and alternating with substantial volcanic activity from the Middle Devonian to the early Upper Devonian during what is known as the Givetian–Adorfian phase (main greenstone) of the magmatism. The resulting relief of the sea-bed remained in part effective until Early Carboniferous time. Linked with this magmatic phase are the synsedimentary hydrothermal red iron ores of the Lahn–Dill type. These are 0·5–18 m (average 2 m) thick and constant in horizon though incompletely formed in places. The so-called 'Grenzlager', red iron ore beds at the boundary of the Middle and Late Devonian above the schalsteins or magmatites of the Givetian and below and between the occasional volcanogenic rocks of the deep Adorfian, are widespread. A slightly older deposit, referred to as the 'Schalsteinlager', in the midst of the Givetian schalsteins or magmatites is confined to certain areas. Locally, too, other orebodies may have developed.

The red iron ore is in part massive to (in rare cases) well bedded with a more or less high Fe content and a varying SiO_2 content and in part well bedded and platey, poorer in Fe, rich in carbonate, and with a small content of SiO_2. Its origin is explainable in terms of the hydration of basaltic magma, the development of gas-rich spilitic magma and their pyroclastic extrusion. Where hydrothermal processes took place in the subvolcanic to submarine volcanic range the components of the red iron ore—FeO or Fe_2O_3, SiO_2 and CaO—were able to concentrate in residual solutions. Having emerged and spread on the sea-bed, Fe_2O_3 and SiO_2 were colloidally precipitated. In the area of solution emergence at the conductive joints in the top of the sill markedly flinty and generally thick, massive, dense red iron ores were formed, followed, in the direction of the basin, by high-grade, thinner, bedded ironstone, gradually merging into banks of carbonate iron ore with a steadily decreasing Fe content and a steadily increasing content of simultaneously deposited foreign material. At the perimeter of the basin the ore interfingers increasingly with layers and beds of ore-free country rock and in the basin area there are then only traces of ore representing the ore horizon. In some places there are also detrital ores, rich in carbonate, which have undergone resedimentation as a result of relief-conditioned migration. The occurrence of magnetite, siderite and pyrite, restricted to certain areas, is a function of the varying composition of solutions, environmental conditions in the various areas of deposition (e.g. black shale facies) and, in some cases, early diagenetic processes. In some places magnetite developed metamorphically from hematite at the contact with intrusive diabase of the Lower Carboniferous during the second major magmatic period—the 'Deckdiabas' volcanism.

In line with the small areas of rapidly alternating, varied ore facies, a distinction may be made between the following main ore types from rise to basin[77,78] (Fig. 18): very flinty hematite ore to ferruginous chert; slightly flinty, purer hematite ore; slightly flinty carbonate to carbonate-rich hematite ore; and resedimented carbonate-rich detrital ore.

The individual orebodies are usually small and rarely amount to more than 5 000 000 tonne of ore, the maximum being 10 000 000 tonne of ore or 3 500 000 tonne Fe. A single orefield, corresponding approxi-

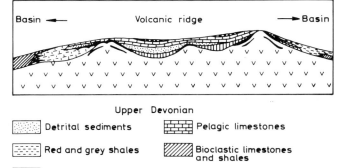

Fig. 18 *Schematic section through complex reef-bearing volcanic ridge with three eruption centres showing different types of sedimentary facies and vertical and lateral distribution of main types of volcanosedimentary ores. After Quade*[78]

mately to a volcanic arc, may add up to a total of 100 000 000 tonne of ore.

The 'Grenzlager' deposit of red iron ore shows widely varying composition, lens-like swelling and reduction in thickness and variations in strike. In the course of the Variscan orogeny it, together with the country rock, underwent marked folding, flattening, overthrusting and imbrication, with the result that the individual orebodies take the form of larger or smaller groups of ore layers or locally defined ore lenses, according to the trend of the individual folding and imbrication zones, and are, in addition, considerably deformed by special tectonic influences. Examples are to be found in the Lahn syncline between Diez, Limburg, Weilburg and Gießen and in the Dill syncline near Dillenburg and Oberscheld.

The ores were mined in the early Middle Ages, the main period of mining activity beginning in the mid-nineteenth century and lasting until about 1960. The very difficult geological conditions often considerably impeded the work of the mainly small mining companies. Only after 1935 was ownership of the mining areas—until then in a variety of hands—concentrated in those of a few large firms, and only when this process had been completed, in 1938, was it possible to begin exploratory work, particularly drilling, on any scale. Only then could be confirmed the synsedimentary origin for the deposits that had been discussed over a hundred years previously and evidence for which had been gained by preliminary microscopic investigation and debated in the 1920s.[77] Recognition of the fact of submarine hydrothermal, volcanosedimentary genesis made possible appropriate exploration for additional deposits, and this view is still accepted today.

The result was a shift away from numerous small mines, the reserves of many of which had already been exhausted, to larger mines able to work at greater depth. This was responsible, in particular, for commencing the exploitation of the larger orebodies that had already been discovered (Table 16). As a consequence of the development of iron ore mining activity on a world scale from 1960 onwards, production declined until the closure of the last mine, the Fortuna mine near Solms (Oberbiel) in the Wetzlar district, on 30 June, 1983.

The ores extracted from the various mines were previously classified for blast-furnace purposes as 'Roteisenstein' (red ironstone), more or less rich and more or less flinty hematite ores with 40–45% Fe, 14–16% SiO_2, 4–15% CaO, and 'Flusseisenstein' (flux ironstone), carbonate-rich hematite and detrital ore with 27–35% Fe, 16–18% SiO_2, 17–28% CaO. Others are subject to local variation—for example, 0·1–0·9% P, 0·1–0·2% Mn and 0·15–0·6% S.

In recent years only flinty hematite ores with a content of 40–42% Fe, 25% SiO_2 and 6–8% CaO have been mined for use as a slag-former in the furnace, together with small quantities of malleabilizing ore, a carbonate and sulphur-free flinty hematite ore for special technical purposes.

The largest output of red iron ore was achieved by the integrated Königszug mine in the Dill syncline near Oberscheld with some 8 300 000 tonne between 1884 and 1967 and by the Fortuna mine in the Lahn syncline with some 4 400 000 tonne since 1849.

Overall, the by world standards small Lahn–Dill mining district has produced some 97 000 000 tonne of ore. Reserves still available are estimated at 10 000 000–20 000 000 tonne.[20]

Other red iron and manganese ore deposits In the eastern Sauerland the 'Hauptgrünstein' of the Upper Givetian attains thicknesses of 150–200 m. Here again, one or more red iron ore beds occur on the flanks of volcanic sills. Individual deposits contain between 100 000 and 1 500 000 tonne of ore. Fine stratigraphic surveys showed that the ore formation had not been simultaneous on the various sills but, instead, had occurred in some cases in the late Middle Devonian and locally not until the earliest Upper Devonian.[79]

Mining dates back as far as Celtic times and between 1840 and 1900 was carried on in up to 20 pits, ceasing temporarily in 1917. Between 1938 and 1963 the Christiane mine near Adorf produced as much as 1 700 000 tonne.

In earlier centuries the red iron ore deposits of the Kellerwald were worked. This small district represents the strike continuation to the northeast of the Dill trough. The last mine to be shut down at the beginning of the twentieth century was the Haingrube near Bergfreiheit.

Further to the northeast is the district of the 'Oberharzer Diabaszug', showing the same structure. Near Lerbach, to the northeast of Osterode and on the Spitzenberg to the SSW of Bad Harzburg—here converted into magnetite in the contact zone of the Brocken granite—2 000 000 tonne of iron ore was extracted from the Middle Ages to 1887.[80] Surveys in 1902 and 1936 confirmed about 3 000 000 tonne of iron ore reserves, without leading to a re-establishment of mining; 25 km to the southeast there is another small district near Wieda and Zorge, representing in its

Table 16 *Iron ore production in Lahn–Dill district, 1830–1982* ($t \times 10^3$)

1830	40	1951	717 (25 mines)
1850	90	1961	756 (15 mines)
1870	627*	1970	256 (3 mines)
1890	974*	1975	112 (1 mine)
1910	1301*	1980	93 (1 mine)
1930	710* (38 mines)	1981	67 (1 mine)
1940	1458*	1982	58 (1 mine)

* Including between 10 and 15% of limonitic iron ore from Lahn–Dill district and basalt iron ore from Vogelsberg area, east of Gießen.

geological position the strike continuation of the Lahn trough. The district has yielded about 1 000 000 tonne of ore.

In the middle of the Lower Carboniferous ferruginous chert layers were formed repeatedly in a similar way as in the Devonian, when the individual extrusions of the diabases had come to an end. They reach a thickness of up to 6 m and sometimes are associated with red iron ores (Fig. 17). Attempts to work them have nowhere led to lasting success.

In the northern Dill trough and in the Kellerwald highly siliceous manganese ore deposits of about the same age occur in siliceous schists of the Lower Carboniferous. The emplacements of rhodochrosite and rhodonite, reaching a thickness of 1–2 m, obviously represent deposits from volcanic solutions, which were transported over long distances. The manganese district of Laisa near Battenberg in the northeastern part of the Dill trough was mined until 1921.[80a]

Stratiform copper and gold mineralization In the northeastern and eastern part of the Rheinische Schiefergebirge, for example, at the Eisenberg near Korbach, near Marsberg and near Dexbach in the Dill trough, stratiform copper mineralization was discovered recently in black shales of the Lower Carboniferous. The dominant mineral of the bedded protores is chalcopyrite with, in addition, bornite and covellite as replacement minerals. At the Eisenberg the content of copper in the black shales (which contain large amounts of bitumen and no carbonate) reaches, on average, 700 ppm. The copper-bearing portion can reach a thickness of several decimetres or, depending on the rock facies, may be restricted to thin sulphide layers in carbonatic black shales.[80b] The stratiform mineralization is found along with the well-known stockwork and impregnation deposits (see later), which were extracted near Marsberg up to 1945. Today research is in progress to determine whether these protores could have been the source of the copper in deposits of the Marsberg type.

In addition, native gold occurs at the Eisenberg near Korbach in concordant tectonic breccias, stratabound in joints as well as in shear zones in Lower Carboniferous alum and siliceous shales separate from the secondary copper enrichments that were formerly worked for short periods. Associated minerals are minor clausthalite (PbSe), traces of copper sulphides and pyrite. The gold mineralization is restricted to small areas and strongly bedding-controlled. Outside the shear zones, reaching a thickness of 5–120 cm, it is restricted to six layers 5–15 cm thick or to parts of them. The contents of gold vary between wide limits from traces to about 1000 ppm of Au; the gangue is calcite.[80b]

Lead–zinc deposits in Palaeozoic carbonate rocks
In reef limestones of the Middle to Upper Devonian along the northern rim of the Rheinische Schiefergebirge from Aachen to Brilon, occur several mineralizations with sphalerite, often as schalenblende, and calamine, with varying amounts of pyrite/marcasite and lead ore. In the Aachen–Stolberg district the majority of the ore is restricted to the Lower Carboniferous 'Kohlenkalk', which is represented by the clastic facies of the culm to the east of the River Rhine. Orebodies are also developed in the Devonian limestones. The deposits were the object of active working from the Middle Ages—near Aachen from Roman times to around 1900—calamine having been the basis for a flourishing brass industry. Along with ore veins with a weakly developed wallrock metasomatism are stockworks, karst mineralization and concordant orebodies. Metasomatic processes play only a minor role.

Aachen–Stolberg district In the Aachen–Stolberg district, with its continuation near Bleiberg and Moresnet in Belgium, ore mineralization is linked to cross- and oblique faults, where the southwest–northeast-trending Palaeozoic beds on the northwest flank of the 'Hohe Venn' (Massif of Stavelot) are displaced up to several hundred metres. Minable deposits are developed only at places where the faults intersect the 'Kohlenkalk' of the Strunian (highest Devonian) and Dinantian or the Devonian 'Eifelkalk'.

Besides fissure veins and stockworks, concordant orebodies are described that occur in fracture zones, on bedding or longitudinal faults where they are intersected by cross-faults. Mineralized karst-sinks were described as 'ore-pipes' or 'ore-caves'.[80c] The mineralization consisted in the upper levels down to around 60 m, maximum 100 m, predominantly of calamine, limonite and minor cerussite with an increasing number of relics of primary sulphide ore further down. In the primary sulphide paragenesis, schalenblende with a variable content of galena and marcasite is predominant. In the pale layers of the schalenblende only sphalerite can be detected, but in the dark layers there is also wurtzite. Single veins carry as the dominant ore silver-rich galena. Between the compact schalenblende and the intact wallrock there is often an impregnation developed, where idiomorphic crystals of sphalerite, pyrite crystals, tetrahedrite, chalcopyrite and quartz are predominant.

Marcasite generally comes at the end of the ore mineralization, and hence forms outermost layers of the schalenblende. Bravoite is a characteristic mineral of the Aachen paragenesis. Several deposits in the Aachen–Stolberg district carried rich and thick calamine ores close to the surface. Underground only thin, unworkable sulphide mineralization occurred. This marked enrichment was described by Krusch[292] as descendent oxidation–metasomatism.

Near Stolberg calamine was being worked in the first century A.D.; this is established by finds of Roman utensils, datable coins and in a note by Pliny (*Historia naturalis*, lib. XXXIV, cap. 2). Besides lead and iron ores, calamine was the main object of working until the nineteenth century. From about the middle of the nineteenth century mining was started in the deeper parts of the orebody below the groundwater level when smelting of the sphalerite found there became possible. From then to the closure of the last mine in 1919 about 300 000 tonne of Zn and 150 000 tonne of Pb were produced in the Aachen–Stolberg district.

Iserlohn–Schwelm district   The mines in the Iserlohn–Schwelm district have been exhausted since the end of the nineteenth century.[80d] The mineralization, predominantly calamine in the form of stock-like layers, occurred in Givetian massive limestone (Elberfeld limestone) near the boundary with the footwall Lenne slates. The orebodies followed the dip of the beds; the footwall was usually smooth, the hanging-wall rather irregular. In some cases the extension vertically to the bedding reached such a size that vein-like deposits were formed. Production for the year 1894 was quoted as about 8700 tonne of calamine, 4200 tonne of blende and about 80 tonne of sphalerite. According to Wettig,[87] the total production of the district amounts to 340 000 tonne of Zn and 4800 tonne of Pb.

Brilon district   In the Brilon calamine district the mineralization is not restricted to the Devonian limestones but extends into the Cretaceous and Tertiary cover rocks. In the Brilon district sphalerite predominates, occurring often along with barite.

The district had little economic importance. The total production from the fourteenth century to the end of the nineteenth century was estimated by Schriel[80e] at about 2700 tonne of Pb and about 800 tonne of Zn. To the east of Brilon in the Sauerland lead–zinc ores were recently struck at depths of 100–400 m, occurring as strata-bound breccia zones in upper Middle Devonian reef limestones, comparable with the ores of the Mississippi Valley type.[80f]

Problems of age and genesis of mineralization in carbonate rocks   The mineralization near Aachen–Stolberg is post-Westphalian—that is, during or after the Variscan folding and before the middle Upper Cretaceous, Santonian, transgression. The metal content is probably regenerated from former mineralization or geochemical anomalies at depth. Borchert[80g] assumed a secondary-hydatogenic reworking of a synsedimentary protore. The supposition that there might also be a syngenetic stratiform mineralization along with the already known epigenetic deposits is confirmed by geochemical anomalies in the Frasnian black slates[80h] and in the Carboniferous limestones to the south of Liège,[80i] and particularly by the findings of Ba–Fe–Zn–Pb mineralization in the Frasnian beds near Chaudfontaine.[81]

On the right bank of the Rhine the latest ore deposition in these deposits took place in Alpine times with the mineralization in the Tertiary—for example, near Paffrath to the northeast of Cologne, Velberth and Lintorf to the northeast of Düsseldorf as well as near Brilon, where there was mineralization also in the Upper Cretaceous (see later). The Palaeozoic mineralization underwent strong rearrangement by intensive supergene processes, which makes the interpretation of the primary genesis more difficult. Some indications in old mining documents point to a syngenetic origin for at least part of the ores, their formation being about the same age as that of the ore deposits of Meggen and Eisen. In addition, near Balve and Iserlohn there are indications of the occurrence of pyrite deposits of the Meggen type, of a thickness of a few decimetres to several metres (G. Stadler, personal communication).

Nickel and copper mineralization in basic magmatites
In the northeastern part of the Dill syncline and to the south of Weilburg in the Lahn syncline nickel and copper sulphides occur in picrite and diabase dykes of Lower Carboniferous age. These ores came into being during partial serpentinization of the basic rocks under hydrothermal conditions and contain pyrite, millerite and chalcopyrite.

Small bodies of nickel–copper ores are present in the Harzburg gabbro south of Bad Harzburg at the contact of norite with partially anatectic hornfelses. There are disseminated and schlieren ores with pyrrhotite, pentlandite, chalcopyrite and pyrite with contents of 0·7% Ni and 0·3% Cu.

Vein deposits of Variscan age
Apart from the volcanosedimentary deposits of sulphide–barite and red iron ore, until a few decades ago the Variscan Pb–Zn vein deposits of the Rhenohercynian were the economically most important group of ore deposits in the Federal Republic of Germany. Following the work of the Freiberg School on the subject of metallogenesis in Central Europe, the age of some of the Pb–Zn ore districts to be discussed below has become a subject of renewed debate. The chief and, ultimately, the decisive criterion in deciding whether to opt for a Variscan or a younger age is the presence or absence of structural relationships between fissuring and vein filling, on the one hand, and Variscan tectonics, on the other. If a relationship can be established, it must be concluded that the deposits came into being during the Variscan period. If, conversely, it is absent, this would point to their being late or even post-Variscan, and thus Alpine (= Saxonian in the sense used by the Freiberg School). In this case other criteria for dating would have to be adopted. A great many later publications have confirmed a number of conclusions and interpretations already expressed by Bornhardt[82] in his classic monograph on the ore veins of the Rheinische Schiefergebirge in 1912.

Iron ore mines of the Siegerland–Wied district   Until 1960 these were economically among the most important ones in Germany, supplying 175 000 000

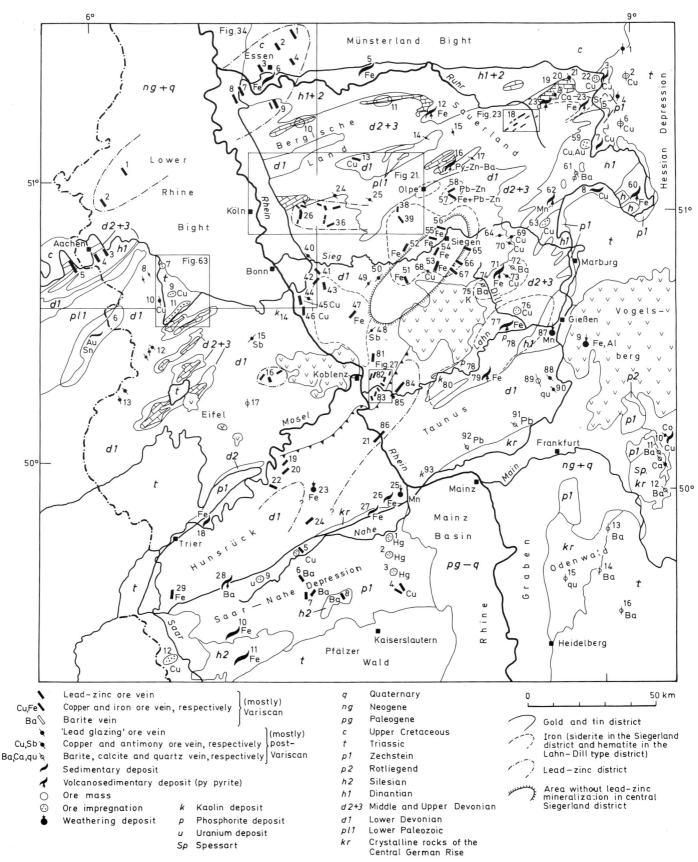

tonne of ore or 22% of the total iron ore production of what is now the Federal Republic of Germany; they enjoyed particular importance because of the high MN content of their siderite.[20] With an area of some 3000 km² the ore district covers a large part of the central and eastern Rheinische Schiefergebirge and

Fig. 19 (*see facing page*) *Mineral deposits of the Rheinische Schiefergebirge and adjacent areas (V, epigenetic deposits of Varsican age; A, epigenetic deposits of post-Variscan (Alpidic) age).* **Left bank of Rhine:** *1, Sophia Jacoba near Erkelenz, Pb–Zn, V; 2, Carolus Magnus near Geilenkirchen, Pb–Zn, V; 3, Diepenlinchen near Stolberg, Pb–Zn, V; 4, Breininger Berg near Stolberg, Pb–Zn, V; 5, Moresnet-Bleyberg-Altenberg (also referred to as Plombières), Belgium, Pb–Zn, V; 6, Hohes Venn, Au–Sn placer, Gedinnian; 7, Maubach, Pb(–Zn), A; 8, Zweifallshammer (Brandenberg range of veins), Pb(–Zn), A; 9, Friedrich Wilhelm ('Knottenerz'), Clara Franziska (vein), Cu, A; 10, Goldkuhle near Hasenfeld, Cu, A(?); 11, Mechernich and Kaller Stollen, Pb(–Zn), A; 12, Wohlfahrt near Rescheid, Pb(–Zn), A; 13, Bleialfer Neue Hoffnung near Bleialf, Pb(–Zn), Cu, A (12 and 13, Bleialf–Rescheid range of veins); 14, Ödingen near Oberwinter on Rhine, kaolin; 15, Ahrbrück near Altenahr, Sb, A; 16, Virneburg, Bendisberg, Silbersand near Mayen, Pb–Zn, V; 17, Bergkrone near Uersfeld, barite, A; 18, Schweicher Morgenstern, northeast Trier, Fe, Emsian; 19, Theodor near Tellig, Pb–Zn, V; 20, Adolf Helene near Altlay, Pb–Zn, V; 21, Gute Hoffnung near Werlau, Pb–Zn, V; 22, Gondenau near Traben-Trarbach, Pb–Zn; 23, Simmern, Hunsrück, Fe; 24, Friedrichsfeld near Bundenbach, Pb–Zn, V; 25, Dr. Geyer at Waldalgesheim near Bingen on Rhine, Mn; 26, Braut near Wald-Erbach, Fe, Emsian; 27, Marienhoffnung near Winterbach, Fe, Emsian (?); 28, Korb near Eisen, barite; Givetian; 29, Louise near Saarburg, Fe.* **Saar–Nahe Depression:** *1, Lemberg near Münster am Stein, Hg, V; 2, Obermoschel, Hg, V; 3, Stahlberg, Hg, V; 4, Imsbach field, Cu, V; 5, Fischbach field near Idar-Oberstein, Cu, V; 6, Clarashall near Baumholder, barite; 7, Erzweiler, southwest Baumholder, barite; 8, Königsberg near Wolfstein, barite; 9, Ellweiler near Birkenfeld, U, V; 10, Lebach, Fe, Rotliegende; 11, Saar district, Fe, Silesian; 12, Wallerfangen near Saarlouis, Cu, A.* **Right bank of Rhine:** *1, Auguste Victoria in Marl-Hüls, Pb–Zn, V; 2, Klara in Gladbeck, Pb–Zn, V; 3, Christian Levin in Essen, Pb–Zn, V; 4, Primus vein near Gelsenkirchen, Cu, V; 5, Dortmund–Hörde, Fe, Silesian; 6, Essen–Werden, Fe, Silesian; 7, Selbeck field near Mülheim on Ruhr, Pb–Zn, V; 8, Lintorf field, NNE Düsseldorf, Pb–Zn, V; 9, Velbert field, NNW Wuppertal, Pb–Zn, V; 10, Schwelm field, east of Wuppertal, Pb–Zn, (?); 11, Iserlohn field, Pb–Zn, (?); 12, Balve, Fe, Givetian; 13, Danielszug near Wipperfürth, Cu, (?); 14, Emilia Theodora near Plettenberg, Pb(–Zn), A; 15, Churfürst Ernst near Sundern-Bönkhausen, Pb(–Zn), A; 16, Meggen, Lennestadt, pyrite, Zn(–Pb), barite, Givetian (Fig. 11); 17, Melusina, Abcoude, east of Altenhundem, Pb(–Zn), A; 18, Ramsbeck district, Pb–Zn, V (Fig. 23); 19, Leo near Brilon-Thülen, Pb, calcite, A; 20, Eichholz near Brilon-Thülen, calcite, A; 21, Gute Hoffnung near Wünnenberg–Bleiwäsche, Pb, barite, A; 22, Marsberg, Cu, V; 23, Christiane near Adorf, East Sauerland district, Fe, Givetian to Adorfian; 23a, Briloner Eisenberg; 24, Neu-Moresnet IV near Bickenbach, Pb(–Zn), A; 25, Alter Bleiberg near Mittelagger, Pb(–Zn), A; 26, Lüderich near Bensberg; 36, Nikolaus-Phönix near Scheid (26–37, Bergisches Land district, Pb–Zn, V (Fig. 21)); 38, Heidberg near Wildbergerhütte, Pb(–Zn), V; 39, Wildberg near Wildbergerhütte, Pb(–Zn), V; 40, Ziethen near Weingartsgasse, Pb(–Zn), A; 41, Silistria near Liesberg, Pb–Zn, V; 42, Altglück near Brennerscheid, Pb–Zn, V; 43, Louise near Krautscheid, Pb–Zn, V; 44, Alter Fritz near Bad Honnef, Pb(–Zn), A; 45, St. Josephsberg near Rheinbreitbach, Cu, (?); 46, St. Marienberg near Rheinbreitbach, Cu, (?); 47, Georg, Wied sub-district, siderite, V; 48, Apollo near Raubach, Sb, A; 49, Hoffnungsthal near Kettenhausen, Pb(–Zn), V, A; 50, Petersbach near Eichelhardt, Pb(–Zn), V, A; 51, Bindweide; 52, Vereinigung; 53, Füsseberg; 54, Eisenzecher Zug; 55, Storch und Schöneberg; 56, Neue Haardt (51–56, Siegen sub-district, siderite, V; 51, 53 and 56 with secondary hematite); 57, Stahlberg near Müsen, siderite, Pb–Zn, V; 58, Viktoria near Silberg, (siderite), Pb–Zn, V (57 and 58, Olpe-Müsen sub-district); 59, Eisenberg near Korbach, Cu, Au, V; 60, Bergfreiheit, Fe, Givetian; 61, Dreislar, barite, A; 62, Laisa, Mn, Dinantian; 63, Dexbach, Cu, Ag, Zn, V; 64, Gonderbach, Pb(–Zn), A; 65, Neue Hoffnung near Wilnsdorf, Pb–Zn, V; 66, Große Burg near Altenseelbach, Pb–Zn, V; 67, Peterszeche near Burbach, Pb–Zn, V; 68, Alte Kupferkaute near Dreisbach, Cu, A; 69, Boxbach near Breidenbach–Klein Gladenbach, Cu, A; 70, Gottesgabe near Roth, Cu, Ag, Hg, A; 71, Königszug near Eibach, Dill sub-district, Fe, d2–d3; 72, Bismarckstollen in Hartenrod, barite, A; 73, Alte and Neue Constanze near Eisemroth, Cu, A; 74, Artzkaute near Herborn-Burg, barite, A; 75, Niederdresselndorf, kaolin; 76, Kölschhausen near Wetzlar, Cu, V; 77, Fortuna near Berghausen, Lahn sub-district, Fe, d2–d3; 78, Lower Lahn, phosphorite; 79, Strichen near Münster, Lahn sub-district, Fe, d2–d3; 80, Diez, kaolin; 81, Hainchen near Höhr-Grenzhausen, Pb–Zn, V; 82, Mühlenbach near Koblenz–Arenberg, Pb–Zn, V (Fig. 27); 83, Ems range of veins, Pb–Zn, V (Fig. 27); 84, Holzappel near Nassau on Lahn, Pb–Zn, V; 85, Pauline near Nassau on Lahn, Pb–Zn, V; 86, Gute Hoffnung near Wellmich (Werlau), Pb–Zn, V; 87, Lindener Mark near Gießen, Mn; 88, Philippseck near Butzbach–Münster, Pb(–Zn), A; 89, Usingen, quartz, A; 90, Kaisergrube near Winterstein, Pb(–Zn), A; 91, Heftrich, E Idstein, Pb–Zn–Cu, A; 92, Naurod near Wiesbaden, barite, A; 93, Geisenheim, kaolin.* **Hessian Depression, Spessart and Odenwald:** *1, Bleikaulen near Blankenrode, Pb(–Zn), A; 2, Wrexen, northeast Marsberg, Cu, U, A; 3, Marsberg, Cu, V, Kupferschiefer (Fig. 42); 4, Matthias near Vasbeck, Pb(–Zn), A; 5, Giershagen, celestine, Zechstein 3; 6, Twiste, northeast Korbach, Cu, U, A; 7, Dorfitter near Korbach, Cu, Kupferschiefer (Fig. 42); 8, Geismar near Frankenberg on Eder, Cu, Zechstein 1 and 2 (Fig. 42); 9, Vogelsberg, Fe (basalt iron stone), bauxite; 10, Bieber, Cu, Kupferschiefer (Fig. 42), Co (Kobaltrücken), A; 11, Groß-Kahl, barite(–fluorite), Co (Kobaltrücken), A; 12, Waldaschaff, barite, A; 13, Klein-Umstadt, barite, A; 14, Ober-Kainsbach, barite, A; 15, Reichenbach, quartz, Cu, A; 16, Beerfelden, barite, A*

boasts a multiplicity of siderite veins, which are, however, irregularly distributed over the region (Fig. 19).

The district is situated at the centre of the Siegen anticline in an area of tectonic uplift within the Rheinische Schiefergebirge. The ores occur exclusively in sandstones, siltstones and argillaceous shales of the Lower Devonian. The entire stratigraphic sequence is 4500–6500 m thick and, in general, plunges towards the northeast, being enclosed by Middle Devonian rocks. In the southeast the Tertiary of the Westerwald unconformably overlies the Palaeozoic strata.

The hydrothermally mineralized fissures of the country rock are an integral part of the complicated tectonic structure of the Siegerland–Wied district. In the course of the Variscan orogeny the Devonian sediments were subjected to folding, foliation, fissuring and relative shifting in the area of faults. These processes overlapped both regionally and in time and may be plotted on a more or less uniform stress plan. Only locally are there deviations in symmetry between older structural elements that are attributable to previous geosynclinal tectonic phenomena and the superimposed Variscan fold structures.

The fold axes and reverse faults generally strike southwest–northeast. The predominant tectonic element of the area is the Siegen upthrust, which continues across the Rhine into the southeastern Eifel Hills. This forms, at the centre of the anticline and together with a number of subsequent upthrusts to the southeast, a zone of imbrication, which also extends from the southwest to the northeast. The folding has produced buckle and buckle-and-shear folds the steeper northwestern flanks of which are locally vertical to overturned. The cleavage, which developed only when the folding was very strong, is generally very clear.

The formation of the vein fissures, mainly in the sense of diagonal shear planes, began at an early tectonic stage. Mineralization took place syntectonically and continued even into the cleavage stage. In the course of the long-lasting process of tectonic deformation the veins themselves were deformed and broken up by later upthrusts and diagonal faulting.

One important indication for the age of the mineralization is the intersection of an ore vein by a diabase dyke, as is observable in several places in the Siegerland and near Burbach. This has resulted in the transformation of the siderite to magnetite by contact metamorphism of greater or lesser intensity over a width of several metres.[82,83,85] This diabase is considered as belonging to the 'Deckdiabas' of early Carboniferous age.

Neither at the surface nor in the iron ore mines is there any indication of a magmatism that might be regarded as the cause of the extensive mineralization. Nor, contrary to earlier belief, have geophysical studies provided any evidence of the existence of magmatic intrusions concealed at not too great a depth. Bosum et al.[83] postulated that a sheet-like expanse of magma, possibly of basic provenance and located at depth (20 km), provided the hydrothermal solutions necessary for the mineralization. Stahl[84] on the basis of isotopic geochemical results ($\delta^{13}C = -8.3$ to $-11.6‰$; $\delta^{18}O = -10.7$ to $-14.0‰$; PDB standard) similarly concluded that the carbon involved is of magmatic origin. From the data so far available, however, a significant involvement of meteoric water heated by sinking to great depths and an increased heat flow cannot definitely be excluded.

In all, several thousand deposits of siderite of varying size are known in the Siegerland district and on the Wied (Fig. 19); they tend to be concentrated in the regions north and south of the main Siegen upthrust. The latter is clearly pre-sideritic, as some ranges of veins terminate against it.

In the Siegen–Betzdorf area the orebodies tend to form linked veins running NNE–SSW. Thus, the Florz–Füsseberg range of veins southeast of Betzdorf is composed of a large number of individual veins and extends over 12 km. In other areas the combination of a series of veins to form larger ranges is more or less a matter of chance. Many deposits occur irregularly and form vein swarms.

The depth of some of the ore veins is considerable: in some mines workings have already reached a depth of more than 1000 m without the end of the vein having been reached. The average thickness of the Siegerland veins is several metres, thicknesses of more than 20 m being rare. The country rock may have influenced the thickness of the veins, given that larger areas of sandstone tend to produce more extensive fractures than slate series. On the other hand, the larger veins particularly have proven to be less sensitive to lithological change.

The veins are mineralized tension faults. The hanging-wall has frequently been displaced obliquely. The veins dip steeply at about 65° to 90° and strike mainly NNE–SSW or WNW–ESE and thus follow the course of the diagonal faults. Generally, owing to the trend of the strata, north–south veins tend to dip westward and east–west veins dip to the south. Not infrequently a vein switches from one principal direction of strike to the other, forming a so-called 'Ganghaken' (hooked vein). In such cases the bend generally coincides with the axis of a saddle or syncline. The dip of the 'hooked vein' follows the direction of the fold axis, which steepens here in the manner of a flexure. Hence, the 'hooked veins' are not folded veins.

Although the vein utilizes one direction of the diagonal faults, it is often sheared by faults in the other direction. At the same time, further tectonic constriction leads to a secondary echelon arrangement of the vein portions, leading in the case of east–west veins to sinistral displacement and in that of north–south veins to dextral displacement. Transverse veins that strike northwest–southeast are less common, as are southwest–northeast veins parallel to the strike of fold axes and cleavage.

The orebodies resemble irregularly elongated lenses, the longitudinal axes of which dip steeply; in horizontal section the vein ends are not superimposed at the various levels.

The chief ore mineral of the Siegerland–Wied district is siderite in a groundmass composed of varying amounts of vein quartz and fragments of country rock. Although sulphide ores are widespread, they are only of limited importance in the peripheral areas of the district.

In chemical terms the siderite is an iron–manganese spar with an isomorphic admixture of small quantities of calcium and magnesium. Its approximate average composition is fairly constant with 38% Fe, 7% Mn, 0.5% CaO and 2% MgO. The Siegerland ore only contains traces ($\leqslant 0.03\%$) of phosphorus. In the last

Table 17 *Average contents (%) of Siegerland crude ore, 1950–1955*[20,83]

Fe	29–31
Mn	5–6
SiO$_2$	16–20
CaO	0·8–1
MgO	2–3
Al$_2$O$_3$	0·4–2·2
Cu	0·1–0·3
P	0·001–0·03
S	0·2–0·5

years of operation the composition of the crude ore extracted was, on average, as indicated in Table 17.

The siderite has a non-orientated grain structure and is subordinately layered to banded. Recrystallizations are widespread and caused by the post-siderite tectonic stress. Of other iron minerals of economic significance only the porous masses of specularite in a few mines—for example, the Neue Haardt NNE of Siegen and Bindweide southeast of Altenkirchen—are deserving of mention. As high-temperature products of siderite transformation they are also manganese-bearing (2–4% Mn with 40–60% Fe). Magnetite is unknown in the Siegerland ore deposits except for sporadic occurrences in the contact zones of diabase and basalt dykes. Weathering ores, such as iron and manganese hydroxides or oxides, were extracted near the surface in the early mining period.

Although sulphides are never entirely absent from the Siegerland siderite level, they are insignificant in quantity. The more frequent are pyrite and chalcopyrite. Lead and zinc sulphides occur, in particular, in the peripheral areas of the district, where they tend to be concentrated in the upper parts of the veins. They have been mined in a few places, as have local enrichments of cobalt and nickel ore in the central parts of the district. The most common gangue mineral is quartz; locally, ankerite–dolomite was formed by metasomatic replacement of the older siderite.

The mineralization continued at intervals over a considerable part of the tectogenetic period: consequently, it is possible to distinguish a number of phases of mineralization of the Variscan paragenesis. These differ from one another and may overlap, but are frequently quite distinct[85] (Fig. 20).
(1) Katathermal to high mesothermal pre-phase over the whole district with emphasis on the Siegen-Betzdorf area.
(2) Mesothermal main siderite phase with subordinate chalcopyrite.
(3) Mesothermal sulphide phase in peripheral zones and in the area surrounding the Siegerland district.
(4) Katathermal rejuvenation phase with specularite in parts of the central district.

Post-Variscan, Mesozoic to Tertiary, parageneses are also found in several phases, partly in the siderite

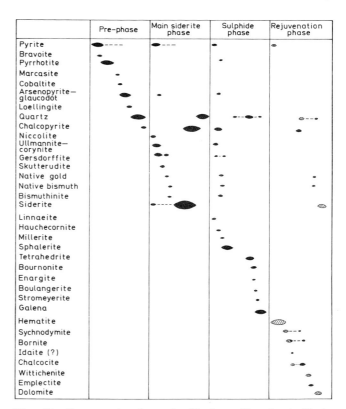

Fig. 20 *Paragenetic scheme for Variscan Siegerland siderite vein district. After Hüttenhain and Gies*[85]

veins and partly in independent veins of tectonically simple structure. Deposits are small in volume and have only locally been worth exploiting.[85]
(1) A katathermal quartz–chalcopyrite phase in parts of the Siegerland district in the narrower sense (Daade valley) and in the Dill syncline, and also scattered about the neighbourhood, with pyrite, bravoite, marcasite, quartz, sphalerite, chalcopyrite, cubanite, tetrahedrite, galena and calcite.
(2) A mesothermal quartz–ankerite phase, especially near Wissen in the western part of the Siegerland, with siderite, calcite and a small quantity of sulphides.
(3) 'Glazing lead ore'* as the most recent phase in siderite veins and on its own, as, for example, near Altenkirchen, Müsen and Burbach, as well as in the Bergische Land and the Eifel, with quartz, coarsely crystalline galena poor in silver, chalcopyrite, pyrite, ankerite and calcite.
(4) An epithermal antimonite phase, mainly in the Wied district, which begins with higher-temperature 20–50 ppm Au-bearing pyrite and leads after chlorite and quartz to the formation of jamesonite and antimonite.

The barite deposits, some of which are cinnabar-bearing and occur especially in the upper parts of the veins near Olpe and Müsen, as well as isolated Co–Ni

---
* 'Glasurbleierz': paperweight-like lumps of galena used by ceramic workers who rubbed them over ceramic articles to improve the quality of the glaze.

ores, should also be attributed to the post-Variscan mineralization.

The Variscan mineralization of the Siegerland district clearly shows zoning of primary mineralization in the form of three mineralization levels that follow one another vertically and laterally. In the highest or outermost part is a sulphide level with, in some cases, rich lead–zinc ores, followed downwards by the siderite level, which is poor in sulphides and more than 1000 m thick. The evidence appears to indicate that at greater than mining depths the siderite veins merge into sterile vein roots with quartz I (Fig. 20).

The beginnings of ore mining in the Siegerland–Wied district date from pre-Christian times, as is witnessed by the discovery of smelting furnaces from the La Tène period. From the Middle Ages into modern times iron ore mining and smelting were decisive in the economic structure of the region. From the middle of the last century onwards ore mining advanced rapidly under the influence of technical innovation and at the turn of the century almost 2 000 000 tonne of ore a year was being obtained from 169 mines. Iron ore production reached its zenith in 1913 with 2 600 000 tonne. Developments in the sphere of beneficiation, such as the introduction of modern sink-and-float separation, efficient roasting furnaces and electromagnetic roasting techniques, enabled the ore to be enriched to concentrates with more than 50% Fe, 10% Mn and 7·5% SiO_2. Because of its high Mn content the ore was much in demand by industry, particularly for the production of spiegeleisen and steel. Five mines were in excess of 1000 m deep, the deepest being the Eisenzecher Zug mine south of Siegen (1320 m) and the largest producer the Storch und Schöneberg mine southwest of Siegen (12 000 000 tonne of ore).

As the economic structure changed, and with the introduction of new metallurgical techniques that meant that the previously much valued high Mn content was no longer desirable and, especially, because of the strong competition from foreign ores, the importance of the siderite deposits declined rapidly from 1960 onwards, although in that year six mines still produced 1 300 000 tonne of crude ore. As early as 1965, however, the shutdown of the two last mines—Füsseberg southeast of Betzdorf and Georg in the subdistrict of Wied—brought iron ore mining to an end throughout the district.[86]

Total output in this area was in the region of 175 000 000 tonne of ore with 52 000 000 tonne of iron in ore, some 150 000 000 tonne of ore being mined in the 1880–1965 period alone (Table 18). Residual reserves of ore are estimated at 40 000 000 tonne.[20,86]

About 500 000 tonne of lead–zinc and copper ores was extracted in the more narrowly defined Siegerland–Wied district from 1825 onwards, the metal content of which may be estimated as at least 40 000 tonne Cu, 120 000 tonne Pb and 10 000 tonne Zn.[87]

Table 18 *Iron ore production in Siegerland–Wied district*

	Tonne $\times 10^3$	Tonne $\times 10^3$ per annum, average	Number of mines at end of period
Until 1839	3 000*	—	383
1840–1869	8 213	274	310*
1870–1899	44 513	1484	169
1900–1929	72 233	2408	19
1930–1945	25 650	1603	39*
1946–1964	21 010	1106	2
	174 619		

* Approximate figure.

Two hundred years ago many of the mines that were later worked for the extraction of siderite were exploiting the copper ores in the cementation zone. From 1900 the mines in the northern part of the Siegerland produced between 13 000 and 17 000 tonne of ore per year and thus, on occasion, more than 10% of the lead–zinc output of the Rheinische Schiefergebirge.[82] In addition, cobalt ores were mined in the Siegen–Betzdorf area between 1767 and 1858 (some 30 000 tonne), nickel ores in the central part of the Siegerland between 1840 and 1910 (some 500 tonne) and mercury ores near Olpe for a short time around 1865.

Lead–zinc ore veins in the northern and central Rheinische Schiefergebirge Bornhardt[82] distinguished several types on the basis of form and content (Fig. 19): diagonal and transverse veins in the Siegerland and Ems districts with a rich siderite content, transverse and longitudinal veins in the Bergische Land with sparse gangue, veins running parallel to the cleavage in Holzappel, Werlau and in the Hunsrück (referred to as cleavage veins), longitudinal veins with a very flat dip in the Ramsbeck district, a widespread group of simply structured veins with poor and often interrupted mineralization, which Bornhardt, by analogy with the 'joint vein' of the Mercur mine at Bad Ems, one of the so-called 'Besteg veins' (see page 227) in the Ems district, grouped together as 'joint veins', and younger veins with 'glazing lead ore' in association with coarse galena with a low silver content and a little light sphalerite as 'rosin jack' (cf. the post-Variscan galena ore phase in the Siegerland).

Later studies have essentially confirmed this classification and in some cases reinforced it with geochemical results. Thus, Hannak[88] was able to demonstrate that the north–south veins of Ems and Mühlenbach belong by paragenesis and especially by the Fe:Mn ratio of the siderite of the pre-phase of 5 to 6 to the Siegerland–Wied district (Fe:Mn = 5) and are clearly distinguishable from the manganosiderites and ferro-rhodochrosites of the Holzappel (1·2) and Werlau (0·6) mines, respectively. In the same way Lehmann and Pietzner[89] showed that both in terms of actual

Fe:Mn ratio (6·56) and of the latter's correlation with depth the siderites of the Nikolaus Phönix mine in the east of the Bergische Land correspond with those of the Siegerland. On the other hand, the siderite of the Lüderich mine in the western part of this same district has a far higher mean Fe:Mn ratio of 9·5 with values that increase from 9·4 to 10·3 at depths down to 165 m.

In addition to the four important orefields with Variscan lead–zinc ores (Bergisches Land, Ramsbeck, Bad Ems and Holzappel), which have produced ores with, respectively, 2 000 000, 950 000, 1 200 000 and 600 000 tonne Pb + Zn metal, there are, in the area bordering the Siegerland especially, a large number of small and medium-size lead–zinc vein deposits, some of which merge at greater depths into siderite veins. Wettig[87] recorded a total of 2429 ore veins in the northern part of the Schiefergebirge on the right-hand bank of the Rhine. Not infrequently, Cu, Ni, Sb and Hg ores are also found, sometimes in pockets in siderite and lead–zinc ore veins and sometimes in veins of their own. Some, like the 'glazing lead ores', are of Alpine age and probably came into existence during the Tertiary (see later).

On the northern edge of the Siegerland district a number of mines near Müsen produced—sometimes in association with siderite—almost 525 000 tonne of Pb–Zn concentrates with 300 000 tonne of zinc and lead with a Zn:Pb ratio of 0·7 and 25 000 tonne of Cu ore and 28 000 tonne of tetrahedrite (fahlore). The last mine was shut down in 1935.

Between 1845 and 1945 just on 220 000 tonne of Pb–Zn concentrates containing 120 000 tonne zinc and lead metal with a Zn:Pb ratio of 1·3 was extracted from some twenty mines to the southeast and south of Siegen and near Burbach, 15 km SSE of Siegen.

The mining of lead, zinc, copper and nickel ores in the northern part of the Dill syncline and of tetrahedrite (fahlore)-bearing lead ores to the south of Weilburg in the centre of the Lahn syncline, and also of lead–zinc and copper ores at Usingen in the eastern Taunus, though very active in previous centuries, as a rule did not progress beyond the exploration stage after 1800. Around Dillenburg, where the ores were mostly the by-products of iron ore mining, and also to the south of Biedenkopf, a total of 5000 tonne of copper, 1300 tonne of zinc and lead and 300 tonne of nickel was extracted.[90] A considerable number of these small deposits, particularly the veins of chalcopyrite and quartz and the veins of 'glazing lead ores' that sometimes contain barite—but neither of which contains siderite and sphalerite—may probably be attributed to the Alpine mineralization cycle.

In the south of the Siegerland district Tertiary sediments and volcanics of the Westerwald cover the Variscan basement. In the southwestern part of the Westerwald ore showings between Montabaur and Vallendar on the Rhine provide the transition to the Ems district. The type of ore present has led to comparison of the vein of the Hainchen mine, 6 km northeast of Vallendar, with the veins near Mayen and Virneburg in the eastern Eifel, which were only discovered in the nineteenth century and where a total of 13 500 tonne of zinc and 6800 tonne of lead metal has since been extracted. Further to the northwest, near Adenau and Altenahr, the many indications of lead–zinc mineralization were investigated during the nineteenth century.

A larger group of veins begins to the south of Bonn and extends along the eastern side of the Rhine to the south and east of the Siebengebirge. Here, between 3 and 6 km to the south of Bad Honnef, are to be found the largest copper vein deposits in West Germany, which can be compared with the above-mentioned quartz–chalcopyrite veins in parts of the Siegerland district and thus regarded as of post-Variscan age. They were, with interruptions, the object of substantial mining activity from Roman times to 1882. Production figures for the post-1850 period, by which time mining had already undercut the 150-m zone of cementation, are only sporadically available, but total output from the three principal mines was probably in the region of 10 000 tonne of Cu metal.

Northwards there runs as far as the lower Sieg between Rosbach and Siegburg a mainly zinc-bearing vein area that during the nineteenth century yielded some 35 000 tonne Zn and 13 000 tonne Pb,[87,90a] followed by the ore veins of the Bergische Land district (see below).

Further to the east and as far as the area surrounding Olpe, an ore-free zone is followed by the sideritic veins of the Olpe–Müsen sub-district at the northern end of the Siegerland. These, in the upper regions, mainly contain galena along with a small amount of sphalerite and occasional chalcopyrite. 'Glazing lead ore' veins are found near Altenkirchen.

Bergisches Land district The district, with its long tradition of mining going back to 1123, is geographically part of the Bergische Land—a hilly region bounded by the Ruhr and the Sieg and forming part of the Rheinische Schiefergebirge on the right-hand side of the Rhine. It forms a rectangle that stretches 800 km² from the western edge of the mountains between Bensberg and Rösrath to the watershed between the Wupper and the Bigge, approximately as far as Wipperfürth and Olpe. The series of strata extends from the Upper Siegenian to the *stringocephalus* limestones of the Givetian. The ore veins occur in the Upper Siegenian and in the early Emsian Bensberg beds, the ore presence having shifted *vis-à-vis* the Siegerland–Wied district upwards into the boundary area between the Siegenian and Emsian stages (Figs. 19 and 21).

The stratigraphic sequence of the Lower and early Middle Devonian, which is between 2000 and 3500 m thick, is composed of shales and sandstones with coloured shales and, in the Bensberg strata, occasional

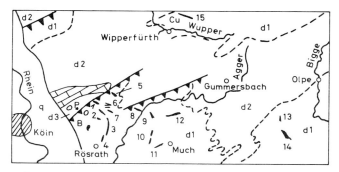

Fig. 21 *Geology and lead–zinc ore veins of Bergisches Land district: 1, Blücher; 2, Weiß; 3, Lüderich; 4, Bergsegen; 5, Washington; 6, Berzelius; 7, Apfel; 8, Castor; 9, Bliesenbach; 10, Nicolaus and Phönix; 11, Nikolaus Phönix; 12, Silberkaule; 13, Heidberg; 14, Wildberg; 15, Danielszug (B, Bensberg; P, Paffrath; q, Quaternary; d3, d2, d1, Upper, Middle, Lower Devonian)*

quartzites. The main keratophyre (K4, Fig. 17) is only incompletely developed, partly in the form of tuff. The late Middle Devonian, the upper parts of which are calcareous, is confined to the Paffrath syncline in the north of the district.[91] The strata, which were folded during the Upper Carboniferous, form a northeast-plunging anticline 25 km wide with numerous minor folds between the Bergische overthrust in the north and the lower Sieg in the south (Fig. 19).[90a]

Apart from sporadic impregnations in the wallrock, the ores tend to be deposited along faults and to be concentrated in the vicinity of host sandstones that tend to form open spaces and below red shales forming clayey vein fillings of very low permeability. The lead–zinc ores in the massive limestones of the Paffrath syncline, which have been interpreted as metasomatic, belong to a different ore type (see earlier).

Tectonically, the area is dominated by two Variscan fault systems of differing age, only the older of which is mineralized. Development begins with the growth of the Bensberg anticline. At the same time, and obviously associated with this, longitudinal and transverse faults developed as distortion and warping cracks, sometimes—as in the case of the vein system of the Lüderich mine—with step faults. These are mineralized, as are the diagonal faults that diverge like fingers from the strike faults that developed at the beginning of the main folding process—for instance, in the Weiß and Berzelius deposits. The orebodies are located in lodes that can be traced over distances of 10–30 km. Under the influence of folding, however, these have been diverted into the direction of the strata and subsequently separated and rotated by block break-up. Hesemann,[92] by reversing the rotation process, was able to identify nine uniform lodes related in terms of both the vein tectonics and the ore infillings.

Only subsequently did the main folding occur, giving rise to the formation of minor upfolds and downfolds and, in a late stage, of new transverse faults, which usually remained unmineralized. The final process involved a further compression with the thrusting of the Bensberg anticline on to the late Middle Devonian of the Paffrath syncline along the Bergische overthrust. It is probable that these individual tectonic phases during the Variscan orogeny were not clearly distinguished from one another because of overlapping and regional overprinting. Dating from the Tertiary are north–south faults with differing mineralization, their origin being linked with the downwarping of the Lower Rhine Valley.

The Variscan ore veins are generally sinuous and deflected at the ends by flexures or step faults. Their character is that of composite veins with a disrupted, mineralized roof and the form is frequently that of a network of ore veinlets. The fault zones are in many cases between 10 and 40 m wide and the thickness of massive ore varies from a few centimetres to 7·5 m. The workable length of the orebodies is usually not greater than 200 m, but occasionally extends to almost 1400 m. The most important single deposit is the 5-km north–south-striking vein system of the Lüderich mine (Fig. 22), which is composed of a number of mineralized faults by which the Lower Devonian strata are step-faulted in an eastward direction.

The ore shoot 'Hangender Sommer', discovered in 1952, demonstrates the way in which mineralization is dependent on the wallrock. At the surface the fault intersects shale with clay banding and is not mineralized. At a depth of 40 m the mineralization begins at the point where the footwall contains host sandstones. The barrier effect of the clayey zone sealing the fault led to the development of massive ore up to 6 m thick. In addition, ore enrichments can be observed, particularly where the uppermost faults change direction from north–south to north–west (Fig. 22(a)). This phenomenon usually occurs along fold axes, urging a comparison with the Siegerland 'vein hooks'.

The *Variscan mineralization* is subdivided into a siderite phase, a later sulphide phase and, following renewed tectonic stress, a weak final phase. Ore is mainly composed of sphalerite and galena with subordinate amounts of pyrite, chalcopyrite and tetrahedrite. At the Idria mine near Bensberg cinnabar and mercury are also found. Quartz and siderite gangue are not depth-related. Galena and sphalerite only alternate where there are substantial amounts of ore at greater depths. In mines more than 200 m deep the silver content exceeded 200 g/tonne lead ore; in less deep mines the content tended to be lower, ranging in general between 70 and 2500 g. Mineralization did not generally continue below the bottom of the valley. Many mines were only up to 200 m deep and only 10 were between 200 and 522 m. In all, output was probably in the region of 20 000 000 tonne of crude ore, half of this stemming from the Lüderich mine. The metal content varied between 8 and 31%, averaging better than 10% as ores with a content lower than this were not mined in former times.

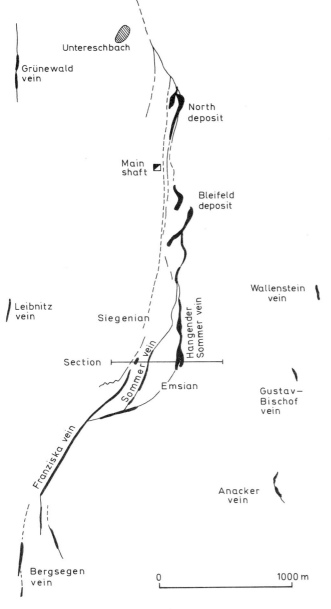

There is some regional variation as regards, among other things, the ratio of non-ferrous metals (Table 19) and the quantity of gangue minerals. The largest individual ore deposits are found in the west, where zinc is markedly predominant. Gangue minerals generally show little enrichment and then only locally. The Mn content of siderite is lower than that in the east (see above). There lead is markedly predominant in several mines. There are substantial occurrences of quartz and siderite, the Mn content of which is comparable with that in the Siegerland.[89]

A divergent, probably post-Variscan paragenesis with quartz and chalcopyrite is found in the east–west-striking lode of the Danielszug mine northeast of Wipperfürth in the north of the district. This mine, which was last in operation in 1944, produced in all some 150 000 tonne of ore yielding 2000 tonne Cu.[87,92]

Tertiary mineralization in the form of north–south veins of usually small dimensions or in older veins mainly consists of siderite along with pyrite and chalcopyrite and minor lead–zinc ores. In contrast to the Variscan mineralization, copper is the chief non-ferrous metal and is accompanied by nickel and cobalt ores (linneite, bravoite, gersdorffite, niccolite, chloanthite and skutterudite), gangue minerals including siderite, dolomite, calcite and barite.

When mining was at its height (between 1830 and 1930) some 150 mines were in operation, to which must be added 180 veins for which a concession was granted but which were not exploited. The takeover of the mines by the Belgian Société Anonyme des Mines et Fonderies de Zinc de la Vieille Montagne in 1852— one of the first companies to successfully smelt zinc ores—marked the beginning of considerably increased activity in the district. The documented output is 1 630 000 tonne Zn and Pb (Table 19). Hesemann[92] estimated the quantities of lead and zinc metal on all veins and dispersed over hair cracks and clefts in the rock at approximately 3 000 000 tonne, considering it

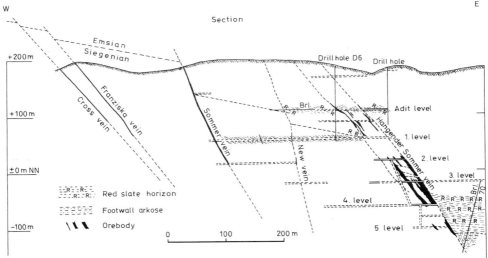

Fig. 22 *Lüderich lead–zinc vein system near Untereschbach, Bergisches Land district: map and section. Simplified after Lehmann and Pietzner*[89]

Table 19 *Concentrate and metal production (t) of most important mines of the Bergische Land Pb–Zn district. From company reports compiled by Stadler*

Mine	Operating period	ZnS conc.	PbS conc.	Zn*	Pb*	Zn + Pb	Zn:Pb
Western part of district (Bensberg sub-district)							
1. Blücher	1854–1893	91 928	9 796	42 930	6 671	49 601	6·4:1
2. Weiß	1847–1929	463 302	16 918	216 362	11 521	227 883	18·7:1
3. Lüderich†	1852–1978	1 288 788	193 484	659 766‡	133 570‡	793 336	4·9:1
4. Bergsegen	1853–1895	27 801	4 177	12 983	2 845	15 828	4·6:1
5. Washington	1853–1892	47 922	12 289	22 380	8 369	30 749	2·7:1
6. Berzelius	1851–1918	281 504	68 995	131 462	46 985	178 447	2·8:1
	1918–1924	29 510	3 645	13 781	2 482	16 263	5·5:1
7. Apfel	1847–1891	43 347	20 552	20 243	13 996	34 239	1·4:1
Eastern part of district							
8. Castor	1853–1906	53 620	50 528	25 040	34 409	59 449	0·7:1
9. Bliesenbach	1882–1909	123 809	56 299	57 819	38 340	96 159	1·5:1
	1919–1926	10 900	6 300	5 090	4 290	9 380	1·2:1
10. Nicolaus and Phönix	1881–1911	14 975	29 142	6 993	19 846	26 839	0·4:1
11. Nikolaus–Phönix§	1841–1966	18 837	13 353	8 797	9 217	18 014	1·0:1
12. Silberkaule	1868–1896	543	30 315	254	20 645	20 899	0·01:1
Eastern extension							
13. Heidberg	1871–1884		13 681		9 317	9 317	
14. Wildberg	1826–1878		50 637		34 484†	34 484	
	1890–1919		17 300		11 781	11 781	
Total		2 496 786	597 411	1 223 900	408 768	1 632 668	

* Calculated on basis of 46·7% Zn and 68·1% Pb in concentrates. After Wernicke[92a].
† Production only from Lüderich mine; foreign material excluded.
‡ As from 1956 calculated on basis of 60% Zn and 70% Pb in concentrates.
§ Includes Gertrudensegen.

to be accompanied by approximately 1 000 000 tonne of iron ore. This makes the Bensberg district an important mining area by world standards. The mining activity carried out by Altenberg AG since 1934 had to cease on 31 October, 1978, because a civil appeal to the courts prevented a shaft being sunk close to the town of Bensberg to enable the newly discovered Olefant deposit to be exploited.

Ramsbeck deposit The Pb–Zn ore deposit is situated in the eastern part of the Rheinische Schiefergebirge to the southwest of the Upper Ruhr Valley (Fig. 19). It takes the form of a multitude of ascendant hydrothermal ore veins dating from the Varsican orogeny, which can be allocated to three vein systems dipping gently southeast and striking ENE. The district extends almost 12 km between the Henne River in the

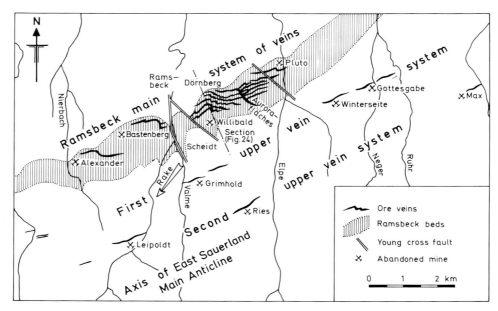

Fig. 23 *Sketch map of Ramsbeck district*

southwest and the Neger and Ruhr in the northeast and is about 4 km in width. The main area of mineralization is at the Dörnberg, near Ramsbeck.[93] An independent mineral-rich but unworkable paragenesis of Tertiary age is located on young NNW-striking faults (Figs. 23 and 57).[98]

The Ramsbeck veins occur in early Middle Devonian strata in the inverted northern limb of the East Sauerland main anticline. The main lode runs through the Ramsbeck beds, which are an alternation of sandy slates and quartzitic sandstones. It extends for a distance of 7 km continuously, being made up of more than 20 veins. A young graben into which the 500-m wide Scheidt fault block has sunk to a depth of 200 m divides the lode into its western Bastenberg and eastern Dörnberg sections.

The two upper vein systems occur in the clayey Fredeburg slates with varying lime content and occasional quartzitic intercalations. The lodes consist of intermittent ore lenses of limited length and width. Only a few of the veins were temporarily of economic importance (Table 23(a)).

Near Silbach, 11 km SSE of Ramsbeck but outside the Ramsbeck district strictly speaking, lead and silver were mined on NNW-striking veins between about 1544 and 1630. The last attempts in the early eighteenth century were unsuccessful. No further information has been handed down. These were clearly 'glazing ores'—very pure galena ores poor in silver and belonging to the Tertiary mineralization.

The principal lode has been mined over its full length from the Alexander mine in the west to the Pluto mine in the east to a depth of 250 m to the valley bottom. Below this level work has been confined to a 2-km section in the Dörnberg where a depth of 360 m was reached before the mine was closed down at the end of January, 1974. Following the shutdown the orefield was investigated by drilling vertical boreholes to a depth of another 300 m, with the result that the mineralization is now proven to a vertical depth of almost a kilometre (Fig. 24).

The Ramsbeck district occupies a special position because of a number of geological features that distinguish it from its surroundings. They determine to some extent the formation of the lead–zinc ore deposits and the geographical distribution of mineralization.

The Ramsbeck district is situated within a zone of uplift extending NNW, transverse to the strike direction and known as the Lippstadt Upfold. This was formed, *inter alia*, by culminations of Variscan fold axes.[94] The Lippstadt Upfold is 90 km long and 20–30 km wide and is bordered near Ramsbeck by the Henne Valley fault in the west and the Altenbüren fault in the east. This southernmost culmination, situated in the area of the East Sauerland main anticline, is known as the Ramsbeck Block.

The Ramsbeck Block is distinguishable from the areas adjacent to it in the east and west by, among other things, the high degree of coalification undergone by the plant remains in the rocks and by the well-developed crystallinity of illite in the shales[94] that identifies them as anchimetamorphic. These facts indicate a more intense heat flow during the Variscan folding[95] and were previously thought to be proof of heating by a magmatic body. Paproth,[96] however, attributed them to the great thickness of the Lower Devonian—a theory that is also favoured by the fact that the heat dome shows a gravity minimum just in the area of the Ramsbeck Block.[94]

The Ramsbeck Block was generally subject to far greater tectonic stress than was the surrounding area.

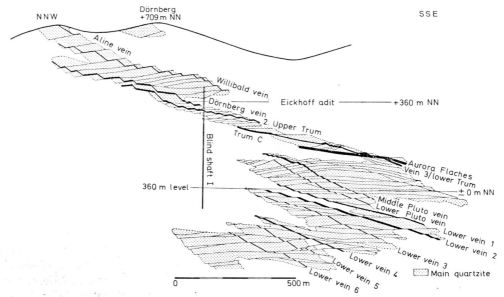

Fig. 24 *Section through Ramsbeck deposit showing distribution of ore veins in Main quartzite (section line in Fig. 23)*

It was deformed between a northern buffer formed by limestone, schalstein and diabasic porphyrite and the counterpressure offered by extensive diabasic intrusions in the south, the result being a complex tectonic formation, characterized by inverted folds and intense cleavage, a large number of different fault and slip planes, block torsion and steeply dipping flexure folds.

The wallrock of the veins, the Ramsbeck Beds, contains a thick series of quartzitic sandstones that favours the opening of cracks. In particular, this complex ultimately underwent a process of imbrication that resulted in flat to moderately steep, southeast-dipping thrust planes, which formed the routes and provided the space for the rise of solutions and ore deposition.

The veins of the main lode are linked with the 300-m thick sandy to quartzitic Ramsbeck Beds. They form in the Ramsbeck Block the most competent part of the Middle Devonian sequence, which is approximately 3000 m thick and mainly composed of slates. They are made up of two similar sedimentary sequences, each with a quartzite, a shaley and an alternating strata horizon (Table 20). Workable veins have developed only in the upper sequence some 200 m thick. Their immediate hanging- and footwalls contain accessory non-ferrous metal sulphides in veins usually only a few centimetres thick.

to be largely workable. In the hanging-wall the veins are only locally workable, whereas in the footwall slates they cannot be worked at all.

Volcanic rocks have played only a subordinate role in the formation of the Ramsbeck Beds. Tuff and tuffite beds exist in the form of centimetre-thick layers of green phyllitic slates and are in some cases important as key horizons. They belong to the keratophyric differentiates of the Variscan initial magmatism. During the late Middle Devonian basic magma ascended and either poured out on the seafloor to form the 'Hauptgrünstein' or solidified subvolcanically as diabase stocks and dykes. To these belong in the Ramsbeck Beds diabase dykes of small thickness, which for some distance are followed by the generally younger ore veins, there usually displaying better mineralization and greater thickness. The diabase dykes, which are as a rule not more than 1 m and never more than 4 m thick, lie parallel to the Variscan-striking cleavage planes dipping gently towards the south. The diabase contains elongated chlorite almonds. They are always well foliated and have sometimes undergone marked hydrothermal alteration, so they resemble the 'dykes of white rock' well known from the Holzappel mine (see later).

Before the veins came into being the wallrock was subjected to intense folding. A first, relatively mild,

Table 20 *Middle Devonian stratigraphy in Ramsbeck district*

Eifelian	Selscheid slate	Partly banded slates with sandstone beds, *ca* 700 m
	Upper Ramsbeck Beds	Quartzite slate horizon, 20–40 m Upper crinoidal slate, 30–70 m Main quartzite, 50–150 m Upper sandy flaser slate, 15–30 m
	Lower	Lower crinoidal slate, 70–120 m Lower sandy flaser slate, 40–70 m Lower quartzite, 0–80 m
	Fredeburg slate	Partly sandy slate with sandstone beds, *ca* 1500 m

The platy main quartzite is a quartzitic sandstone with a few bands of clayey shale and some lenses of crinoidal limestone in the lower part. The petrographically quite similar lower quartzite was only recognized as an independent formation in 1959 as a result of detailed mine mapping by G. Bauer. The crinoidal slate takes the form sometimes of softish slate poor in sand and sometimes as sandy banded slate. The sandy flaser slates represent transitional formations. In the quartzite slate horizon, sand-rich slates with quartzite bands alternate with softish slates containing stromatoporoid reefs.

In the Ramsbeck mine the thick but brittle main quartzite is the optimum wallrock for the veins. Only in such a host are the vein structures mineralized so as

folding took place as early as intra-Devonian and resulted in the first cleavage. This was followed by the diabase dykes, themselves foliated, which were intruded during the latest Middle Devonian period.[97]

The formation of the overturned Eastern Sauerland main anticline with its northwest vergence took place in the course of the main Variscan orogeny during the Upper Carboniferous. The rocks were intensely cleaved. The overturned limb shows, in the Ramsbeck area, marked signs of complex folding. Overturned fold limbs that dip from 30° to 50° SSE alternate with normal, uninverted limbs generally dipping gently southward. From about 120 m above sea-level the overturned position predominates, the normal position doing so as one moves lower. This results in a dip change of the enveloping surface. Above approximately sea-level the enveloping surface of the second-order folds dips towards the south, whereas below it dips gently northwards (Fig. 24).

The formation of the ore veins took place in several tectonic phases. The primary mineralization occurred, as did the anchimetamorphism of the wallrock in the pumpellyite–prehnite–quartz facies, synkinematically with the first cleavage (K/Ar age 305 ± 10 m.y.). The primary mineralized structures are stepped overthrusts that strike, on average, ENE to ESE and intersect the bedding at an acute angle. The vein dip varies between 5° and 60°S with an average of less than 25°S in the upper and more than 30°S in the lower part of the deposit. The direction of movement on the overthrusts took place, judging from the position of slickensides, parallel to the direction of dip. The width is several metres to more than 100 m. These veins generally follow predetermined routes in the rock sequence—first, the cleavage and then locally older diabase dykes, bedding planes or even older faults. The difference between the dip of the veins in the upper and lower parts of the deposit indicates an inverted fan position generally typical of cleavage.

In the course of continued compression the core area of the East Sauerland main anticline was uplifted and the Nuttlar syncline in the northwest subsided. This led in the area of the orefield to a rotation of the overturned anticlinal limb in a northwesterly direction, resulting in a nappe-like tectonic movement with numerous 15°SSE to 10°NNW and, on average, 5°SSE-dipping thrust planes.[93,95] This overthrusting displaced the veins by several decimetres to several tens of metres. The thrust planes themselves are frequently mineralized and constitute the well-known 'Ramsbeck Flachen' (flat-dipping veins) (Fig. 25). All ore in existence was mylonitized and transformed into a grey, fine-grained mixture of ore, gangue and

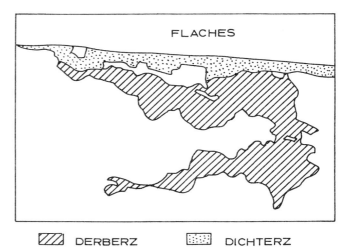

Fig. 26 *Mylonitized ore ('Dichterz') and massive ore ('Derberz') in and below fault plane of a 'Flaches'. From Karl vein, view below Eickhoff adit near crosscut 6*

fragments of wallrock, referred to as *Dichterz* (dense ore) (Fig. 26). In the vicinity of veins these overthrusts tended to develop where they could follow already existing flat sections of a vein. In Ramsbeck the veins are referred to as 'Steile' (steeps) to distinguish them from the 'Flachen' (flats). 'Flache' represent 25–30% of the total vein area.

Numerous veins occur in the Ramsbeck main lode, the uppermost of which in the western part and hence the bottommost in the east (Figs. 23 and 24 and Table 21). The main veins in the upper part of the deposit, that is, the Alexander, Bastenberg and Aurora 'Flache', follow older structures, dipping for some distance gently southwest.

In the Dörnberg area two different groups of veins occur one above the other. Thus, in the upper tectonic level, where the wallrock is mainly overturned, a series of veins runs off the main structure of the Aurora Flache into its hanging- and footwall. The Aurora Flache follows an old normal fault and must be regarded as the path taken by the ascending ore solutions. In the lower level, by contrast, where the

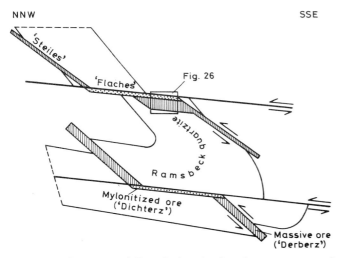

Fig. 25 *Structure of Ramsbeck vein deposit: upper part of deposit in overturned Ramsbeck quartzite, lower part in upward-facing Ramsbeck quartzite*

Table 21 *Mineralized structures of Ramsbeck main vein system*

Bastenberg deposit	Alexander main vein Bastenberg main vein Tigges vein	
Dörnberg deposit, upper stage	Aline—vein Willibald—vein Dörnberg—vein	} Independent veins above Aurora main vein
	II. Upper veinlet Aurora upper veinlet Aurora upper vein Veinlet 'C'	} Upper group of veins connected with the Aurora main vein
	Aurora main vein with vein 3	
	Aurora vein Fastrada vein Karl vein Upper Pluto vein Middle Pluto vein Lower Pluto vein	} Lower group of veins connected with Aurora main vein
Dörnberg deposit, lower stage	Lower vein 1*a* Lower vein 1*b* Lower vein 2*a* Lower vein 2*b* Lower vein 3 Lower vein 4 Lower vein 5 Lower vein 6 Lower vein 7	} Group of independent veins below Aurora main vein

position of the wallrock is mainly original, the 'group of footwall veins' forms structures in their own right, independent of the Aurora Flache.

The thickness of the veins increases with the size of the angle between the vein and the dip of the bedding. Consequently, in the upper level, located in a mainly overturned setting, where the veins and the cleavage dip less markedly than the bedding, the almost horizontal sections of the veins, the 'Flache', are those best mineralized. In the lower level exactly the reverse occurs: here it is generally the steeper sections of the veins that show better mineralization (Fig. 25).

Within both the overturned and the normal locations the veins enter a bed sequence at a higher level from the geological hanging-wall and, after passing through it, leave it again at a lower level to enter the geological footwall (Figs. 24 and 25). The surface of intersection of a vein with a given bed sequence generally dips slightly to the southwest. The surface of intersection of the veins with the Ramsbeck main quartzite, the most favourable wallrock for mineralization,[93] is of importance from the point of view of mining geology. It is referred to as the 'quartzite intersection' of the different veins.

In the upper level a large part of the ore is concentrated in the region of the Aurora Flache and the vein systems connected with it, whereas in the lower level the ore is distributed over the large areas of quartzite intersections of the footwall veins, which cut through the wallrock at a very acute angle. The relatively rich, albeit spatially restricted, ore shoots in the upper level contrast with the extensive, mainly poor and, hence, from a mining point of view, uninteresting mineralization of the lower tectonic level.

The Variscan mineralization is subdivided by tectonic movements into a pre-phase and a main phase, each with several subordinate phases (Table 22). The kata- to high mesothermal pre-phase begins with quartz and is followed by siderite and, finally, pyrite with a little arsenopyrite. It occurs only in older, independent veins (Table 22). Tectonic movements led to a widening of existing cracks and the formation of new cracks and paved the way for the deposition of the workable mineralization. The high mesothermal IIa phase carries dark sphalerite with 2–4% Fe and chalcopyrite and, rarely, pyrrhotite exsolutions and also galena as the principal ore minerals, and a little chalcopyrite and a substantial amount of quartz as the sole gangue mineral. Renewed movement resulted in the formation of 'Dichterz' on the 'Flache'. The ensuing deep mesothermal to epithermal IIb phase bears pale sphalerite without exsolutions, a considerable amount of galena, small quantities of complex sulphides, and quartz. The carbonates of the IIc phase and other minerals to be regarded as lateral secretionary conclude the Variscan paragenesis. Calcite occurs only in the upper vein systems, which are located in the calcareous Fredeburg slates, where it is, along with quartz, the main gangue mineral. This fact points to its probable lateral secretionary origin. Udubasa,[99] finally, demonstrated the presence of cubanite and

Table 22 Paragenetic schemes of Variscan and Alpine cycles of mineralization in Ramsbeck deposit. After Bauer et al.[93] and Müller and Scherp[98]

Phase of mineralization			
Tertiary cycle of mineralization on cross veins		*Carbonatitic phase* Galena, schalenblende, sphalerite, chalcopyrite, pyrite, marcasite, Ni sulphides and arsenides, silver ore minerals, Pb–complex sulphides, quartz, calcite, ankerite	Essentially the mobilization of Variscan ore minerals
		Baritic phase Barite, pyrite, chalcopyrite, galena, gersdorffite	
Main phase of Variscan cycle of mineralization	II*c*	Calcite, ankerite, pyrite, chlorite, kaolinite, dickite	Essentially by lateral secretion
	II*b*	Quartz, galena, sphalerite, chalcopyrite, radial arsenopyrite, tetrahedrite, bournonite, boulangerite, chalcostibnite	Partly mobilized by thrust tectonics
		Formation of 'Dichterze' (dense ores) by flat thrusting	
	II*a*	Quartz, sphalerite, chalcopyrite, galena (pyrrhotite, stannite)	Sphalerite with frequent exsolutions of chalcopyrite and very rare pyrrhotite and stannite
Pre-phase of Variscan cycle of mineralization	I*b*	Siderite, pyrite, arsenopyrite, quartz	At end locally a little sphalerite and chalcopyrite
	I*a*	Quartz	

mackinawite exsolutions in chalcopyrite. Both minerals are important as geological thermometers and furnish evidence of a temperature of formation of approximately 250°C.

The paragenesis described remains unchanged over the entire vertical extent (~1 km) of the ore deposit. The proportions of sphalerite and galena and the distribution of certain trace elements, however, point to zoning of the primary mineralization. The Zn:Pb ratio increases with depth, both within individual veins and in the complete deposit from the hanging-wall to the footwall. According to Wettig,[87] the Zn:Pb

Table 23 Production data for Ramsbeck district

(*a*) Production of concentrates in more important mines[87]

	Date of production	Zn conc., tonne	Pb conc., tonne	Zn:Pb
Ramsbeck vein system				
Alexander mine	1857–1894	2 081	18 518	0·1:1
Bastenberg mine	1855–1910	52 330	35 119	1·0:1
Dörnberg mine[87,93]	1855–1974	1 160 698	353 218	2·1:1
First upper vein system				
Gottesgabe mine	1863–1908	~72 300	~16 300	3·0:1
Second upper vein system				
Ries mine	1857–1884	11 214	2 343	3·3:1
		1 298 623	425 498	

(*b*) Development of metal production of Bastenberg and Dörnberg mines, 1855–1974[93]

Date	Metal, tonne	Average annual production, tonne
1855–1879	49 247	1 970
1880–1913	166 849	4 907
1914–1924	24 894	2 263
1925–1944	180 524	9 026
1945–1974	441 450	14 715
	862 964	

ratio in the uppermost Alexander vein is 0·1:1, whereas in the other veins on the Bastenberg it is 1:1; in the upper stockwork on the Dörnberg about 1·8:1; and in the upper part of the lower stockwork 3·5:1. Drilling has shown that at greater depth within the lower stockwork the zinc content continues to increase.

In the hanging-wall lodes zinc is markedly predominant:[87] the Gottesgabe main mine extracted from the first hanging-wall lode ores with a Zn:Pb ratio of 3·0:1; the Ries main mine, working the second hanging-wall lode, exploited ores with a ratio of 3·3:1 (Table 23(a)).

The occurrence of two different groups of veins established by tectonic analysis is confirmed by the mineral content and the trace elements contained in the main sulphides. The veins of Group I carry the minerals deposited in the pre-phase and the main phases. In the Dörnberg area these are the independent veins of the upper stage, the Aurora Flache and the group of footwall veins. The veins of Group II contain only minerals deposited during the main phase. These are the veins of the upper and lower groups running off the Aurora Flache (Table 21), which, consequently, were only opened up after the formation of the pre-phase veins. The immediate wallrock of the veins has only a very low metal content, if any. Lead and zinc contents are low and vary according to the nature of the rock. Primary dispersion haloes have only formed around upward-closing, feather-like veinlets. The veins of group I frequently reveal an arsenic dispersion halo, which is lacking for those of group II.

H. Pietzner's study[93] of the trace-element contents of 298 samples of sphalerite and 103 of galena taken from six veins may be summarized thus. It was not possible to prove vertical zoning of primary mineralization within the individual veins. This may be explained by the fact that even where a vein is more than 1000 m in length the ends of the vein are only separated vertically by a distance of 200 m. In the veins that were studied it was possible to confirm the existence of the two groups, even as regards the depositions of the main phase. Sphalerites from group I veins show markedly higher contents of Cd and Co and, in some cases, of Ni than do those of group II. For Hg the reverse is true. Galenas in group I veins have a lower Ag content than do those of group II. Limit values for the various metals are

Cd   Group I > 0·3% > Group II
Co:Ni   Group I ≫ 10 > Group II
Ag   Group I < 900 ppm < Group II

A comparison of the trace elements in various veins within one and the same group again gives evidence of zoning. Thus, in both groups Ag and Hg decrease, whereas Cd increases with depth. The concentrations that were found to exist cannot be explained by a gradually decreasing solution temperature as the orebody formation progressed. Pietzner proposed that most of the ores deposited in the first group of veins are older formations. The mineralization of the group II veins is younger and the result of a rejuvenation of the hydrothermal solutions. These also affected the veins of group I. Both phases of mineralization show comparable depth sequences, but the composition of the solutions differed only slightly from one phase to another.

The very much simplified account of the Ramsbeck mineralization presented here indicates the complex interrelation of tectonic developments and ore deposition in the area of the deposit. There is, especially, a very close causal connexion between the main process of mineralization and the flat overthrusts both in terms of time and as regards the principal plane of stress during vein formation. The relationships were described and explained in detail recently.[93]

The epigenetic formation of the orefield is confirmed, in particular, by the following facts: the different vein types, with comparatively rich ores on more or less horizontal sections of the vein (the Flache) in the overturned limb in the upper level, contrasting with even better mineralization on steep vein sections in the normal limb in the lower level; in conjunction with this fact, the discordance of the veins, which dip more gently than the beds in the overturned portion and more steeply than the beds in the normal portion; the occurrence of veins bearing minerals deposited during the pre-phase (group I veins) and later (group II) veins, which do not bear such minerals; and the systematic variation in the Zn:Pb ratio and in the content of a number of trace elements in the deposit, indicating a zoning of primary mineralization.

A recent attempt[99] to demonstrate that the Ramsbeck deposit was the result of volcanosedimentary processes and to compare it with those of Rammelsberg and Meggen must therefore be rejected.

In more recent geological times the northeastern part of the Rheinische Schiefergebirge was affected by rift tectonics, which probably began during the late Jurassic or early Cretaceous and enjoyed several revivals until the late Tertiary. In the case of Ramsbeck this led, *inter alia*, to the marginal faults of the Scheidt block (Fig. 23), which has sunk 200–300 m. The faults, which strike north–south to northwest–southeast, and which in the Dörnberg area mostly dip to the southwest, are accompanied by numerous, in some cases mineralized, parallel faults with dislocations from a few decimetres to 20 m. This 'cross-vein mineralization' differs considerably from that of the Variscan veins[98] (Table 22): it forms part of the post-Variscan metallogenesis that was widespread in Central Europe and is dealt with later. It has no economic significance for the Ramsbeck area, although in the more remote surroundings 'glazing lead ore' was mined in previous centuries—for example, at Silbach,

11 km SSE of Ramsbeck, and near Kallenhardt in the Warstein anticline, 17 km to the north.[87]

The following are the parameters that determine the quality and quantity of the Ramsbeck deposit: (1) the volume of the main quartzite, being the most favourable wallrock, (2) the average distance of the veins from one another and (3) the thickness of the sphalerite–galena mineralization of the veins.

The workable volume of ore depends on the thickness of the quartzite, which, on average, is 120 m, and the vein density. The distance between worked veins normal to the bedding is between 30 and 100 m and averages 60 m. On the basis of these data and the strike length of the deposit the amount of quartzite is calculated as an average 10 000 m^2 per metre depth. On average, half of the structural planes were mineralized.

One million tonne of crude ore with a Pb + Zn content of about 5% was extracted for each 40-m depth above the 360-m level in the worked section of the Dörnberg deposit, which is about 1·5 km long. Two sufficiently workable vein structures were found in the quartzite at each level. Workable mineralization means that the average thickness of massive ore averages ≥ 15 cm ZnS equivalent (Fig. 26).

To determine the characteristics of mineralization in the lower level of the deposit a programme of exploration was put in hand in 1970 and expanded in 1974–75 by the addition of a vertical borehole programme. The intention behind this was to establish definitely the existence of minimum reserves of 8 000 000 tonne of workable ore containing at least 5% Zn + Pb below the 360-m level and down to an assumed 700-m level to provide a basis for a new Ramsbeck mining operation.

To estimate the exploitable reserves in a section of the orebody the thickness of the massive ore was visually measured at 2-m intervals. The results were converted into metal content on the basis of 6 tonne of crude ore per square metre of vein surface and contents of 62% Zn in ZnS and 81% Pb in PbS. This yields 0·4% Zn for 1 cm ZnS and 1% Pb for 1 cm PbS. Because of the optical overestimate for galena it has proved advisable in practice to work on the basis of 1 cm PbS = 0·8% Pb $\approx$ 2 cm ZnS. Measurements for the upper level resulted in figures of 11 cm ZnS and 2 cm PbS, corresponding to 15 cm ZnS equivalent or 6% Pb + Zn, and those for the lower level 7 cm ZnS and 1 cm PbS, corresponding to 9 cm ZnS equivalent or 3·6% Zn + Pb in the crude ore. Underground working is not economic with such contents. Accordingly, the richer veins in the upper level having already been mined, work had to be confined to the better mineralized parts of the lower level.

By use of mining geological and geostatistical techniques it proved possible to optimize development work and selective mining and to increase the contents of the crude ore.[93,100] One necessary condition for the identification of larger areas of inadequate mineralization and avoiding them during subsequent working is a dense system of exposures. When these are driven the crude ore encountered with no possibility of selection is one with a content of approximately 3% Zn + Pb—more or less the average. For the purposes of selective mining an optimum cutoff grade of 2·5% Zn + Pb was determined. This meant that some 45% of the vein planes were to be classed as workable and that 90% of the 'Flaches' and 35% of the 'Steiles' were eliminated; 50% of the crude ore is obtained during development work with an average content of 3% Zn + Pb, and the other 50% by selective mining with 6·5% Zn + Pb (= 16·5 cm ZnS equivalent).

Mining is rendered more difficult by the fact that mineralization is very irregular. Even so, it has been possible to identify zones where the mineralization is either better or worse than average. They run transversely to the strike of the fold axes and more or less in the direction of the vein dip. Generally, the upper half of a quartzite section is better mineralized than the lower half and the thickness of mineralization increases with the angle between the vein and bed strikes.

The evaluation of the borehole programme showed that of the seven footwall veins and a number of associated veinlets, only five could be used to establish the size of reserves. Total probable and possible reserves were calculated as 2 760 000 tonne of ore. Hence, the volume of reserves in the next 300 m below the lowest level was well below the minimum necessary for economic working.[100]

The oldest traces of mining activity[93] in the Ramsbeck area probably date from the early Middle Ages (the first documentary evidence is from the year 1518). Until 1815 only small-scale mining was carried out, but thereafter a number of mining operations combined to form the 'Ramsbecker Gewerkschaft', 1840 witnessing the real beginning of mining on an industrial scale in the Ramsbeck district. In 1854 the 'Aktiengesellschaft für Bergbau and Zinkfabrikation zu Stolberg und in Westfalen' acquired ownership of the orefield, since when it has been mined almost continuously. In 1968 the mining company passed into the hands of Metallgesellschaft AG and in 1970 to Sachtleben Bergbau GmbH—a company in which Metallgesellschaft has a majority holding. For reasons that have already been explained, mining activity had to cease on 31 January, 1974, despite the fact that in the previous year Sachtleben Bergbau GmbH had changed to a modern and efficient method of working that involved a trackless stoping procedure with short rooms and the use of diesel-powered wagon drills and scooptrams and auxiliary vehicles.

Between 1840 and 1974 mining in the Ramsbeck district produced 16 700 000 tonne of crude ore with an average metal content of 4·4% zinc and 2·1% lead (equivalent to 735 000 tonne Zn and 351 000 tonne Pb; Table 23). The 1 700 000 tonne of concentrate that was produced from the crude ore yielded 752 000 tonne of salable metal. The average metal content of the ore extracted during the last years of operation was 3·8% Zn, 1·0% Pb and 7 g/tonne Ag; 3 000 000 m² of vein area was mined between 1840 and 1974 and a roadway system of about 300 km was driven.

Although the Ramsbeck district probably still holds substantial potential reserves, the low metal content of the ore means that for financial reasons any further mining activity is impossible for the foreseeable future. In due course extensive studies—which, given the size of the deposit, will be very costly—will be needed to demonstrate whether workable ores are still present in a quantity to make a revival of mining in the Ramsbeck area a viable proposition.

Pb–Zn ore veins in the Southern Rheinische Schiefergebirge In the Southern Rheinische Schiefergebirge an ore belt up to 20 km in width extends in a northeast–southwest direction for just on 120 km on the lower Lahn and in the Hunsrück and includes a series of lead–zinc ore veins, some of which are substantial. Bornhardt[82] has already differentiated between a number of vein types and Hannak[88] classified them as is indicated below.

(1) The north–south veins from Mühlenbach and Ems–Braubach, which, like those of the eastern part of the Bergische Land district, are to be regarded as part of the Siegerland district *sensu lato*. In the pre-phase these too contain siderite.
(2) The northeast-striking cleavage veins of Holzappel, Werlau and in the Hunsrück sub-district may be compared with the Ramsbeck veins; manganosiderite and rhodochrosite occur in the pre-phase.
(3) The northwest veins of the Pauline type, with calcite in the pre-phase, occur in the same area as the cleavage veins.
(4) Ehrendreich[101] also referred to quartz–chalcopyrite veins with Co–Ni arsenides and Sb minerals on recent north–south and east–west faults probably dating from the Tertiary (see later).
(5) In the Werlau district northwest-striking drusy quartz veins with idiomorphic apatites cross the lead–zinc veins: known as 'cross quartzes', they are similarly of later date.

Table 24 *Lower Devonian stratigraphy in Ems and Lahn-Hunsrück districts*[96,101]

Middle Devonian	Wissenbach slate	
Upper Emsian	Kieselgallen slate	up to 300 m (?)
	Flaser slate	100 m
	Laubach beds	200 m
	Hohenrhein beds	200–250 m
	Ems quartzite	120–140 m
Lower Emsian	Tonschiefer beds	100 m
	Singhofen beds	2000–3000 m
Upper Siegenian	Hunsrück slate	up to 6000 m

The wallrock throughout the area is the clastic Lower Devonian of the Nassau Trough[96] (Table 24). The monotonous pelitic Hunsrück slate, the wallrock of the Altlay and Tellig deposits to the south and southeast of Zell an der Mosel (Fig. 19) is followed by the slaty to sandy Singhofen beds with up to five porphyroid tuffites that extend in synclinal zones from the Lower Lahn into the Hunsrück and in which the Mühlenbach vein, as well as those of Holzappel and Werlau, occur. The Ems quartzite forms anticlinal cores near Bad Ems and the sandy to clayey Hohenrhein and Laubach beds constitute the wallrock for the Ems veins. By increase in the clay fraction the rocks of the upper part of the Upper Emsian provide a transition without a facies break into the Middle Devonian Wissenbach slates, which commence at the eastern edge of the ore belt in the Lahn syncline.

The strata sequence was folded and cleaved before the Givetian.[96] Hannak[102] gave a summarized account of the work done by a group of authors that included the following regional tectonic classification of the area between the Siegerland Block in the northwest and the Taunus in the southeast (Table 25). The continuation of the structures into the Hunsrück is not definitely established owing to changes in the sedimentary facies and the tectonic style.

In a zone that strikes NNE from the Loreley via Nassau an der Lahn towards Siegen the directions of strike change from 35 to 40° with more or less horizontal axes in the west to about 60° with a general axial dip to the northeast. This Nassau–Siegen–Soest lineament plays an important role in the occurrence and spread of magmatism and hydrothermal deposits in the Schiefergebirge on the right-hand side of the Rhine.[102,103]

In this area of complex structure there occur the three groups of Pb–Zn ore veins already mentioned and which differ clearly in terms of tectonic structure and the chemistry of the pre-phase carbonates. Otherwise, the mineralization throughout the area is highly uniform and monotonous. It is divided into three phases:
(1) Pre-phase with quartz I, pyrite I and carbonate
(2a) Main phase, kata- to high mesothermal with quartz II, chalcopyrite I, which for Holzappel shows occasional exsolutions of sphalerite and valleriite,[104] sphalerite I, sometimes with exsolutions of chalcopyrite II, and chalcopyrite III
(2b) Main phase, mesothermal with quartz III, galena I, a little tetrahedrite and sphalerite II
(3) Post-phase, epithermal, with quartz IV and little carbonate

Sperling[104] also described from the Holzappel mine traces of pyrrhotite and bismuthinite in the 2a phase and traces of calcite, dickite, bournonite, ullmanite, gersdorffite, niccolite, linnaeite, millerite, native gold and prochlorite in the 2b phase and traces of the main sulphides in the post-phase.

Table 25 *Fold structures in Lower Lahn area*[88]

Structures	Dip of axial surfaces	Ore veins
Siegerland block	SE	Siderite veins
Mosel syncline, *sensu stricto**	NW	Mühlenbach veins
Lahnstein anticline	NW	
Boppard–Montabaur syncline with Erz and Quellen anticlines	90°	Ems veins
Thrust zone of Boppard–Dausenau	—	
Kirchähr syncline	SE	Quartz roots of schistosity veins
Salzig–Nassau anticline	SE	
Lahn syncline with Balduin syncline and Werlau fold zone	SE	Schistosity veins
Katzenellenbogen Upthrust	—	
Taunus anticline	SE	—

* The Mosel syncline, *sensu lato*, as used elsewhere in the literature, is inclusive of the Boppard–Montabaur syncline.

The *Ems district* is separated from the area of the cleavage veins to the southeast by the Boppard–Dausenau overthrust and to the east by the Nassau–Siegen lineament. Hence the position of the Ems district relative to this major structure is the same as that of the Siegerland district. The north–south veins are regarded as diagonal wrench faults that gape as a result of external rotation and, hence, have been made accessible to mineralization.[102]

The Mühlenbach mine[105] is situated near Arenberg, 3 km to the east of the Rhine at Koblenz. It used to work two north–south veins dipping steeply or fairly steeply eastwards to a depth of 500 m. The orebodies reach lengths of 250–600 m and average 1·50–1·80 m in thickness. The mineralization shows a markedly stockwork structure with a predominance of quartz above the workable sulphide mineralization, which begins at a depth of about 100 m. These sulphide ores, in turn, are gradually replaced by quartz and siderite from 450-m depth.

The mine was in operation as early as the eighteenth century, as is testified by the old shafts and drifts. Between 1847 and the time of closure because of exhaustion of reserves in 1960 the mine yielded 2 130 000 tonne of crude ore with a content of 9·5% Pb + Zn (Table 27).

The Ems lode, which stretches for 15 km, striking northeast and dipping at about 40° from Arzbach, 6 km ENE of Koblenz, via Bad Ems to Braubach am Rhein (Fig. 27), was mined for lead as far back as Roman times. In all, 35 veins were exposed, running mainly north–south to NNW and to a subordinate degree east–west or, occasionally, northwest.[106] The veins are linked to a closely folded, cleaved and imbricated zone on the flanks of the so-called 'Erzsattel' (ore anticline)[101] and lie on or between the axial planar surfaces of oblique overthrust (known as 'Bestege') on either side of the anticline. These *Bestege* served as guides to the ascending solutions and to some small extent themselves carry workable ore (known as Besteg veins).

The individual ore veins are continuously mineralized for lengths of 150–400 m and in individual cases for as much as 1000 m, their thickness varying from 1 or 2 m to more than 10 m. Rapid changes in thickness and vein splitting are frequent, as are parallel veins

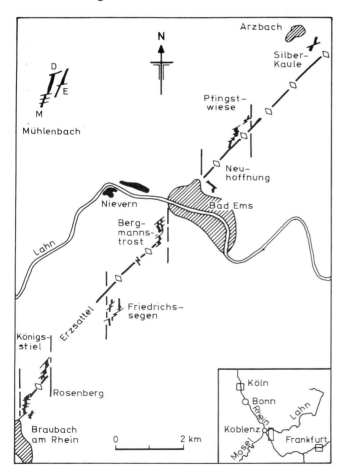

Fig. 27 *Ems lead–zinc vein system with ore anticline and individual veins and veins of Mühlenbach mine (upper left). After Herbst and Müller*[106] *(D, diagonal veinlet; E, Eichelberg vein; M, Mühlenbach vein)*

Table 26 *Mine production (tonne) of Ems vein system*[106]

Mercur	1875–1948	6 600 000
Friedrichsegen mine (estimated)	1853–1912	1 800 000
Rosenberg mine (estimated)	1854–1927	1 250 000
	1952–1963	132 000
Former production (estimated)		700 000
		10 482 000

between 1 and 10 m apart. The northeast-striking 'Besteg veins', however, are generally only 100 to 180 m long and 0·2–0·4 m thick. Generally, the workable mineralization in the southwest extends for a depth of about 400 m and in the northeast for about 800 m. Below this depth the sulphides give way to quartz and siderite. The Ems lode has been opened up to an overall depth of more than 1000 m.

Modern mining began in the Bad Ems district around 1850. The northern pits were grouped together under the Mercur mine in 1872. This mine then produced about two-thirds of the total production of 10 500 000 tonne of crude ore with a content of 9% Pb + Zn (Tables 26 and 27). The Silberkaule mine near Arzbach was only operated for a few years prior to 1880 (Fig. 27).

In the *Lahn–Hunsrück district* the deposits of Holzappel and Werlau, as well as those in the Hunsrück sub-district to the southeast of the Boppard–Dausenau overthrust, belong to a quite different vein type. The mineralization is located in cleavage joints both in the normal or, as in Werlau, in the overturned fold limbs. The workable length of mineralization, which in the case of the Holzappel vein is as much as 3 km, drops to less than 50 m in the case of the Altlay mine in the southwest (Fig. 19).

The origin of the spaces for mineral deposition, that is, the opening up of cleavage surfaces, is in mechanical terms comparable with the vein tectonics of the Ramsbeck district, although there are differences due to the quite different nature of the wallrock— Ramsbeck quartzite as against clayey to sandy Singhofen beds and the clayey Hunsrück slates. Probably because the length of the fold is here much shorter, there is not—as at Ramsbeck—any relationship between vein structure and the normal or inverted bedding of the wallrock.

In the Lahn–Hunsrück district the northeast-striking cleavage veins and more or less horizontal overthrusts form so-called 'Verflachungen' ('flattenings') or 'banks'—a system of cleavage planes with a differing structure in each direction (Fig. 28). This is illustrated by the characteristics of the mineralization on the flattenings. Thus, below the flattening the vein is thicker and usually well mineralized. In the zone of overthrust the vein becomes poorer and often carries only quartz. Small dip-shifts at the vein clefts contrast

Table 27 *Ore and metal production of most important mines in the southern Rheinische Schiefergebirge*

	Crude ore, t × 10⁶	Zn metal, t	Pb metal, t	Zn:Pb	Ag, t	Cu metal, t	Galleries and tunnels, m
N–S veins (Ems district)							
Mühlenbach,[105] 1847–1960	2·133	140 351*	62 284*	2·3:1	64*	5 759*	32 155
Ems vein system[106] 100–1963	10·5	609 000*	336 000*	1·8:1	290*	31 500*	213 150
NE veins (Lahn–Hunsrück district)							
Holzappel[107] 1740–1953	4·964	374 009†	199 121†	1·9:1	141*	11 334*	112 830
Tellig[108] 1911–1959	0·302	21 744*	7 852*	2·8:1	5*	302*	10 935
Werlau,[108] 100–1961	1·68	88 000‡	52 000‡	1·7:1	50‡	2 430‡	48 826
Altlay,[108] 1876–1959	0·48	21 600‡	15 000‡	1·4:1	7‡	550‡	6 119
Bundenbach[90] 1937–1953		1 014‡	760‡	1·3:1	0·3‡		
Weiden[109] 1884–1900		—	11 500	?			
NW veins (Lahn–Hunsrück district)							
Gondenau,[108] 1926–1949	0·039	4 667*	4 590*	1·0:1	2*		

* Contents of crude ore.
† Contents of crude ore and of 111 000 tonne ore in place with 5·1% Zn and 1·3% Pb and 30 000 tonne ore in place with *ca* 6% Zn and *ca* 3% Pb.
‡ Recovered metal contents.

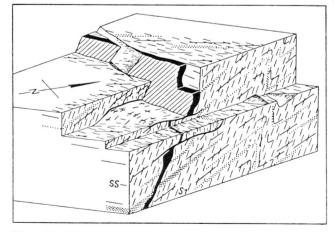

Fig. 28 *Schematic block diagram of schistosity vein. After Hannak*[102]

with greater overthrusting at the flattenings. Moreover, the wallrock is tilted by an angle of about 30° relative to the flattenings. Hannak[102] attributed the tectonic origins of the cleavage veins to a shear stress against the direction of vergence (facing direction) at the end of the folding, the cause of which is probably to be sought in the zone of southwest vergence in the Mosel syncline.

The Holzappel mine is situated near the village of the same name 12 km to the ENE of Bad Ems and 4 km to the north of the Lahn at Laurenburg. The mine, closed because reserves were exhausted in 1952, used to work eight cleavage veins contained in a rock sequence 500 m thick with a maximum strike length of 5·6 km (main vein, three footwall and four hanging-wall veins). The cross-vein, which strikes 150°, had only been opened up nearer the surface and was no longer accessible after the second world war. The veins are grouped together under the name Holzappel lode. The whole vein system strikes northeast and dips 50° southeast. Those of greatest importance were the main vein, which averaged 1·2 m in thickness, and the mineralized 1·25-m hanging-wall 'white rock dyke' (see below), which accompanied it at a distance of 12–25 m, as well as the Weihnähr vein and the footwall vein, 0·15 and 0·35 m thick and located, respectively, 120 and 10–18 m within the footwall of the main vein. Holzappel, with a depth of 1090 m, was the deepest lead–zinc mine in West Germany.[107]

The Pauline mine, with a cleavage vein and a number of northwest veins (vein type no. 3, see above) on the Winden lode 2·5 km in the footwall of the Holzappel lode, was only of minor economic significance. The Morgenröthe lode, 2 km in its hanging-wall, near the Lahn River, contains only quartz and a small amount of sphalerite.

A particular feature of the Holzappel and Werlau deposits is the occurrence of what are known as 'white rock dykes'—hydrothermally altered basic igneous dykes made up of sericite, quartz, ferromagnesite (breunerite), calcite, titanite and accessories. These, like the ores, occur on cleavage joints and sometimes themselves show peripheral cleavage. Five dykes of white rock are known in the Holzappel mine. These may be mineralized and have been worked over a considerable distance in the vicinity of the main vein. The rising magma thus used the same migratory paths as did the hydrothermal solutions a little later. The fact that the white rock itself is foliated shows that the folding process and the opening of the cleavage joints sometimes overlapped.

Only the Holzappel lode shows hints of zoning of primary mineralization. In the deepest parts of the mine the Zn:Pb ratio was 7:1, whereas in the upper parts of the vein it shifted markedly to the advantage of lead. The manganese content of the siderite decreases with greater depth from about 47% to 35% $MnCO_3$.[104] The whole mining depth of more than 1000 m, therefore, is contained within the lead–zinc stockwork. Below this there occurs a chalcopyrite-bearing quartz root that rises towards the southwest at an angle of 30° and reaches the surface in the Lahn valley.

The deposition of the sulphide phase was followed by the formation of diagonal and transverse faults, on which some of the post-phase minerals were deposited. There are no clear indications of a post-Variscan mineral paragenesis at Holzappel.

Mining in the Holzappel district probably dates back to the sixteenth century. Between 1740 and 1952 the mine was, with a few minor interruptions, operated continuously. Up to about 1840 mainly gossan ores were extracted by numerous adit mines. From 1837 onwards sphalerite was also mined. In the following years underground mining and mechanization began and the primary sulphide ores were increasingly extracted. Mining on the Holzappel lode produced, overall, 4 964 000 tonne of crude ore with a content of 11·7% combined lead and zinc (Table 27).

Just on 10 km in the hanging-wall of the Holzappel lode and about 5 km east of the Rhine the mineralization of the Werlau lode begins.[102,108] This can be followed for some 30 km in a southwesterly direction, but only on either side of the Rhine at Werlau, a few kilometres to the northwest of St. Goar, did the mineralization assume economic significance. The Werlau mine, in the vicinity of which there are traces of mining activity in Roman times, until 1961 worked five orebodies that follow one another in the line of strike like a string of beads. Of a total length of 3·6 km, 1·4 km contained workable orebodies, in some cases together with hanging-wall and footwall veinlets. The individual orebodies were between 200 and 600 m long and averaged 1 m in thickness, being worked to depths of from 120 to >800 m. They are linked to fold and imbrication zones and are generally to be found in the form of cleavage veins in the vicinity of fold bends, mainly in the overturned limbs. The orebodies are independent veins that are set off against one another by 5–10 m transversely to the strike. At their ends the lead-zinc ore declines and is replaced by ferrorhodochorosite with quartz and chalcopyrite. A particular feature is the local occurrence of dense tetrahedrite. Flattenings, veins of white rock and younger faults are all comparable with those of Holzappel. The Werlau mine yielded, in all, 1 680 000 tonne of ore with a content of 173 000 tonne (10·3%) of Pb + Zn (Table 27). Accompanying veins in the hanging- and footwalls, such as that of the Camilla mine 7 km WSW of Werlau, were only worked for a short time, as were the minor deposits that extend into the area to the south and southwest of Kastellaun.

Of the very many ore veins in the Hunsrück as far as Saarburg to the south of Trier, more than fifty of which have in the past been investigated and in some cases exploited for a short time, only those of the Tellig and Altlay mines, 5 km ESE and 8 km southeast of Zell an der Mosel, respectively, have been of any economic significance.

In Tellig, which with other mines lies approximately in the extended line of strike of the Winden lode, five lens-shaped vein zones up to 30 m thick strike northeast–southwest transversely to the direction of strike in a rock succession 500 m in thickness. The orebodies, which are only 50–70 m long, are linked to a fold-like warp of bedding and cleavage to the SSW that resulted in rock exfoliation. They dip with the cleavage 25° to the southeast. Flattenings that locally may be horizontal constitute particularly rich ore shoots. At a depth of only 230 m the mine had an inclined depth of 500 m.

Apart from initial investigations carried out around 1912, Tellig was in operation from 1935 to 1959 and yielded 300 000 tonne of ore with 29 596 tonne (9·8%) of Pb + Zn (Table 27).

In Altlay, 4 km SSE of Tellig and more or less on the line of strike of the Holzappel lode, there occurs a 180-m long fracture zone that strikes northeast–southwest and dips 55°SE. Ore lenses several metres thick in flattenings are linked by millimetre-thick ore stringers in the steeper parts. In the hanging-wall of this fracture zone and within the zone of a transverse upswell numerous orebodies 20–40 m long are continued to the southeast in a northwest–southeast-striking vein. Mining, which was carried on as early as the Middle Ages, came to an end in 1959 at a depth of 210 m close to the root zone. Overall, the mine yielded 480 000 tonne of ore containing 36 600 tonne (7·6%) of Pb + Zn (Table 27).

Furthest to the southeast are the cleavage veins of Bundenbach and Weiden, about 10 km northwest of Kirn an der Nahe. These have only seen brief periods of mining activity in recent times (Table 27).

The calcite-bearing northwest veins, chiefly represented by the Pauline mine near Nassau and the Gondenau mine near Traben-Trarbach, were of limited economic significance, being regarded by Hannak[102] as deposits of a late Variscan process of mineralization in the area of the root zone of the cleavage veins. This root zone, with its outcrops of thick quartz veins, stretches from Nassau via Salzig am Rhein to the northeast of Zell, dips 200–300 m below the surface near the Tellig and Altlay mines and re-emerges soon afterwards near Zell. This zone is narrow close to the Rhine and dips steeply northwest of Werlau.

Lead–zinc ore veins in the Western Harz Mountains The Western Harz Mountains enclose, in the shape of the Oberharz district and the orefield of St. Andreasberg, two important ore vein regions, in which, since the Middle Ages or earlier, argentiferous lead ore and later zinc ore and barite have been mined (Fig. 29).

The Oberharz district is considered, as far as metal

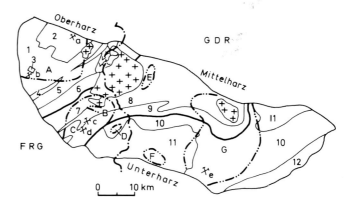

Fig. 29 *Structural units (1–12) and vein orefields and districts (A–G) in Harz Mountains. After Möbus,[111] Mohr[112] and others). 1–12, see text; A, Upper Harz Pb–(Ag–)Zn ore district; B, St. Andreasberg Pb–(Ag–)Zn orefield; C, Southwest Harz barite district; D, Wieda iron ore veins; E, Hasserode Pb–Zn + Co–Ni orefield; F, Ilfeld Mn–Fe–barite orefield; G, Lower Harz Pb–(Ag–)Zn–Fe–CaF$_2$ ore district. Producing mines: a, Erzbergwerk Rammelsberg; b, Erzbergwerk Grund; c, Schwerspatgrube Wolkenhügel; d, Schwerspatgrube Hoher Trost; e, Grube Fluorit*

production is concerned, to be one of the most important lead–zinc mining regions of Europe. In the first half of the sixteenth century it became one of the first entirely industrialized regions of Europe. Among the technical achievements of that region are the invention of the depth indicator, the water column machine (Wassersäulenmaschine), a winding construction that allowed comfortable descent and ascent for miners (Fahrkunst), wire rope, track railway with flanged wheels and dynamite.[110]★

The St. Andreasberg orefield has yielded only a fraction of the metal output of the Oberharz district. Because of its remarkable wealth of crystals and minerals, it has become well known to the scientific world.

The Harz Mountains, the western part of which belongs to the FRG, display an intricate geological structure. The following structural units can be distinguished (Fig. 29). [111,112,113]

In the *Oberharz* (1) the Clausthal zone, in which all the principal ore veins are to be found; (2) the Oberharz Devonian anticline, including the ore layers of the Rammelsberg in the lower Middle Devonian at Goslar and the sporadically mineralized veins in the northern part of the district; (3) the reef limestone block of the Iberg, with young Fe–Mn ores and barite; (4) the Oberharz Diabase zone with volcanosedimentary red iron ore of the Lahn–Dill type; (5) the Söse syncline, in which the most easterly lodes of the Oberharz district were emplaced; and (6) the Acker-

---

★ In 1866 Alfred Nobel and Hermann Koch, government official at the Clausthal Bureau of Mines, experimented with nitroglycerine; this led Nobel to the further development and commercial use of his invention. In 1905 Koch's son, Robert Koch, won the fifth Nobel Prize for medicine.

Bruchberg range, forming the morphological divide to the Mittelharz.

In the *Mittelharz* (7) the Lonau anticline and the Sieber syncline, in which occur the most northerly veins of the barite districts of the Southwest Harz and the iron ore veins at Eisensteinsberg, west of St. Andreasberg; (8) the Herzberg–Andreasberg anticline (Blankenburg zone) with the triangle of veins of St. Andreasberg, together with the young veins of the Englesberg mine south of St. Andreasberg, and in the GDR the veins of Hasserode at the eastern edge of the Brocken massif, as well as the northern parts of the Unterharz vein district around Treseburg; and (9) the Tanne zone, including the main mass of barite veins of the Southwest Harz district (see later).

In the *Unterharz* (10) the Harzgerode zone, in which occur the hematite veins of Wieda (see later) and in the GDR the lead–zinc and fluorite veins of the Unterharz; (11) the south Harz syncline, including the manganese ore veins of Ilfeld in the GDR, and the Selke syncline in the northeast; and (12) the metamorphic zone of Wippra, belonging to the Mid-German Crystalline Rise.

Between Clausthal-Zellerfeld in the centre of the *Oberharz* and Goslar at the northern edge of the Harz some 19 fault zones, striking on average WNW and dipping steeply to the south, with widths of up to 70 m, extend up to just under 20 km. They locally bear rich lead–zinc ores and thus constitute ore veins. These locally mineralized fault zones are collectively designated 'ore-vein systems'.

The most important mineralization is known to be in the southern vein systems between Seesen, Lautenthal and the Oker Valley (10, 11, Fig. 30)—in particular, between Bad Grund, Clausthal-Zellerfeld and Altenau (2–5, Fig. 30). They account for the predominant part of the mining production of the Oberharz. Outside these zones only small orebodies (9, 14–17, Fig. 30) or for all practical purposes mere traces of mineralization have been found.

In the past few decades only the lodes of the Silbernaal vein system (Fig. 31), exposed in the Grund mine, have been accessible to modern researchers.[114,115,116] The resemblances between the various orebodies of the Oberharz, known from earlier work and verified by more recent individual researches,

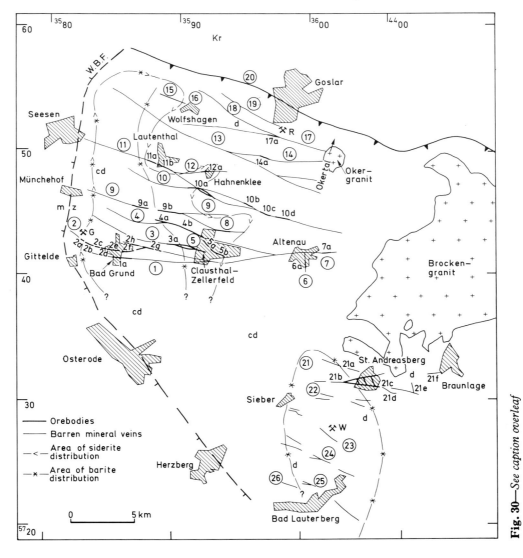

Fig. 30—*See caption overleaf*

might justify a critical generalization of these results.

The wallrocks of the ore veins are greywackes more than 1000 m thick and clay slates of the Lower Carboniferous Culm facies, representing the flysch of the rising Variscan mountains in the southeast. In the northern parts of the district the veins occur in Devonian slates, sandstones and diabases (Table 9).

The stratigraphic sequence was folded in the late Upper Carboniferous. The northeast-striking folds are mainly autochthonous and decrease in intensity to the northwest. Intensive imbrication is restricted to areas with rapidly changing rock types—for example, the Oberharz Diabase zone along with parts of the Söse syncline and the Acker–Bruchberg range.

Although beginning in the late stages of folding, the development of the above-mentioned fault zones came mainly after the folding. They mostly involve inclined faulting with relative movement of the hanging-wall some 100 m to the west. Posthumous movements displaced the discordantly overlying Zechstein on the western borders of the Harz by only a few tens of metres. The main movements along the fault zones must have taken place before the Permian. It is possible that a genetic connexion exists with the post-orogenic intrusion of the Brocken pluton. K–Ar and Rb–Sr biotite dates and Rb–Sr whole-rock isochrons show an average of 290 m.y. for the rocks of the Brocken Massif,[117] which corresponds with the Westphalian–Stephanian boundary. The fault zones, which were formed in a sequence of shearing movements, often show a wavy to strongly curved structure in the area of mineralized vein segments, which made an essential contribution to the formation of cavities. In the progress of mineralization in the late Upper Carboniferous to Lower Permian brecciated, ringed, bedded and banded ore fragments or simply structured debris were formed in empty clefts, some containing rock fragments. The succession of substances as well as repeated shearing movements subdivide the mineralization in different phases (Fig. 32). In the western part of the Grund mine the following strongly simplified sequence has been obtained.[114]

Mineralization phase I started with the formation of small faults, created by shearing forces, from which the wallrock was impregnated with hematite, ankeritized and dolomitized. Small cavities were filled up with siderite I and locally with Fe–Cu sulphides in small quantities. At the end of phase I the wallrocks

Fig. 30 *Ore veins and vein systems of Western Harz Mountains and main orebodies (Kr, Cretaceous; m, Muschelkalk; z, Zechstein; cd, Culm; d, Devonian; G, Grund mine; R, Rammelsberg mine; W, Wolkenhügel mine; WBF, Western Border Fault of the Harz)*

Upper Harz district
- 1 *Laubhütte vein*
  - 1a *Laubhütte orebody*
- 2 *Silbernaal vein system*
  - 2a *Westfeld orebody II*
  - 2b *Westfeld orebody I*
  - 2c *800-West orebody*
  - 2d *Achenbach orebody*
  - 2e *Ostfeld orebody*
  - 2f *Wiemannsbucht orebody*
  - 2g *Silbernaal orebody*
  - 2h *Bergwerksglück orebody*
- 3 *Rosenhof vein system*
  - 3a *Rosenhof orebody*
- 4 *Zellerfeld vein system*
  - 4a *Wildemann orebody*
  - 4b *Zellerfeld orebody*
- 5 *Burgstätte vein system*
  - 5a *Wilhelm orebody*
  - 5b *Dorothea orebody*
- 6 *Schatzkammer ore vein*
  - 6a *Altenau orebody*
- 7 *Schultal ore vein*
  - 7a *Schultal orebody*
- 8 *Haus–Herzberg vein system*
  - 8a *Haus-Herzberg orebody*
- 9 *Spiegeltal vein system*
  - 9a *Hütschental orebody*
  - 9b *Spiegeltal orebody*
- 10 *Bockswiese vein system*
  - 10a *Bockswiese orebody*
  - 10b *Festenburg orebody*
  - 10c *Oberschulenberg orebody*
  - 10d *Mittelschulenberg orebody*
- 11 *Lautenthal vein system*
  - 11a *Bromberg orebody*
  - 11b *Lautenthal orebody*
- 12 *Hahnenklee vein system*
  - 12a *Hahnenklee orebody*
- 13 *Gegental vein system*
- 14 *Schleifsteinstal vein system*
  - 14a *Schleifsteinstal orebody*
- 15 *Burghagen vein system*
- 16 *Heimberg-Dröhneberg vein system*
- 17 *Weißer-Hirsch vein system*
  - 17a *Weißer-Hirsch orebody*
- 18 *Beste-Hoffnung ore vein*
- 19 *Todberg vein system*
- 20 *North Harz overthrust*

Middle Harz district (including barite veins near Bad Lauterberg)
- 21 *St. Andreasberg sub-district*
  - 21a *Eisensteinsberg veins*
  - 21b *Runnermark-Lilienberg vein system*
  - 21c *St. Andreasberg orefield*
  - 21d *Engelsburg ore veins*
  - 21e *Odertal ore veins*
  - 21f *Steinsfeld ore veins*
- 22 *Königsberg barite veins*
- 23 *Wolkenhügel barite vein system*
- 24 *Hoher Trost barite veins*
- 25 *Kupferrose Cu–barite veins*
- 26 *Flußgrube fluorite veins*

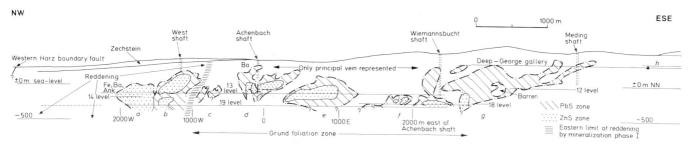

Fig. 31 *Section through Silbernaal vein system of Grund mine. After Sperling et al.*[115] (*a, orebody II in West Field; b, orebody I in West Field; c, orebody '800 W'; d, orebody 'Achenbach shaft'; e, orebody 'East Field'; f, orebody 'Wiemannsbucht shaft'; g, orebody 'Silbernaal'; h, crosscut above 'Tiefer Georg' gallery*)

were highly silicified, leading to hardening and an increased tendency to cleft formation. In several northern ore veins (e.g. 14, Fig. 30) arsenopyrite, gersdorffite and niccolite are found, which should belong to mineralization phase I, along with various selenides in the Burgstätte vein system and in the former quarry in the Trogtal north of Lautenthal. Gaping and quickly extending cavities were opened up by strong block movements within which the formation of the second phase, *the main zinc mineralization*, took place. The great thickness of the ore veins as well as a clear predominance of sphalerite over galena with quartz as the dominant gangue mineral are characteristic features. Phase II can be subdivided into four subphases:

(IIa) Quartz II veinstuff containing small quantities of chalcopyrite and pyrite

(IIb) Main sphalerite, the oldest sphalerite I of which sporadically bears chalcopyrite and pyrrhotite exsolutions. Sphalerite I is younger than galena I. Slightly younger sphalerite I, associated with minor galena I, is almost free of exsolutions

Mineral characteristics	I Quartz	IIa Quartz stringer	IIb Sphalerite stringer	IIc Banded ore stringer	IId Cap quartz stringer	IIIa Calc-spar or cockade stringer	IIIb Siderite stringer	IIIc Barite stringer	IV Druse minerals
Quartz	I	II	II	II	I		III		IX
Hematite									
Dolomite	I								—
Ankerite									
Calcite									—
Siderite	I								—
Celestine									
Barite									—
Strontianite									
Pyrite	—	—				— — —			—
Marcasite									—
Chalcopyrite	—I	—II	—III	IV — — —		V — — —	— — — —	VII	—VIII
Sphalerite			I	— — —	—III	— — — —	V		—VI
Galena			—I	—II — — —	—III			VI	—VII
Fahlore					•	• • •	•	—	
Pyrargyrite						•			
Proustite						•			
Argentite						•			
Native silver						•			
Bournonite						•			
Boulangerite						•			
Antimonite									—
Native antimony									—
Kermesite									
Cinnabar									
Amalgam									
Native mercury									

Frequently >0.5 m thick · Visible under microscope only
A few centimetres thick only or in equal sized single crystals — Tectonic movements

Fig. 32 *Paragenetic scheme of Grund lead–zinc deposit, Upper Harz ore vein district. After Sperling*[114]

(IIc) ZnS II (PbS II) veins, composed of bilaterally symmetric sphalerite, galena, chalcopyrite and calcite, often forming banded ore and less often cockade ores
(IId) Cap quartz veins (quartz VI) with minor sphalerite III

Tectonic movements, recommencing in stronger fashion, created further open spaces, which were filled with deposits of the *main lead mineralization* of phase III. With it came enlargement of the veins, greater gangue thickness and a predominance of galena over sphalerite. Three sub-phases can be defined:
(IIIa) Calcite–quartz veinstuff containing galena, sphalerite and other sulphides
(IIIb) Siderite veinstuff, together with dolomite, galena V, which contains 0·2–0·5% Ag, minor sphalerite V and silver minerals
(IIIc) Barite veinstuff along with minor quartz IX and rare sulphides

Later came only weak tectonic movements, opening passages of migration for a return of hydrothermal solutions. These solutions mobilized in part the deposits of phases I to III and precipitated predominantly in drusy idiomorphic sulphides, sulphates and carbonates of phase IV. Dating of this phase is not possible.

Because of tectonic movements, sphalerite-rich stringers of the second mineralization phase are to be found mainly in the centre of veins, whereas both in plan and profile the peripheral areas of the galena-rich stringers carry the minerals of the later phases.

The subdivision of often similar deposits of mineralization phases II and III may be confirmed by the significantly different $\delta^{34}S$ values of the main sulphides in phases II and III. ZnS ($+2$ to $+5‰$; ZnS I in the Westfeld lode II $+6$ to $+10‰$) contains significantly heavier sulphur than PbS (0 to $+4‰$; in the Westfeld lode II $+4$ to $+7‰$). The δ-differences between PbS and ZnS show on average $1·8‰$ in phase II and ca $3‰$ in phase III.

In the eastern lodes of the Silbernaal vein system, with its weaker tectonic deformation, the paragenesis established in the Westfeld lodes near Grund (Fig. 32) is no longer completely formed. In the more distant veins of the Oberharz district it can be found only locally and sporadically.

Comparing the tectonic character and mineral content of the different veins, zones with approximately similar development of the veins may be established. Sperling et al.[115] differentiated the following four zones.
(A) The *central Oberharz*, between Bad Grund, Clausthal-Zellerfeld, Hahnenklee and Lautenthal: the oldest ore veins (2, 4, 5, 10, 11 and 12, Fig. 30) had opened already at the beginning of the shearing movements, and widened with further movements and lengthened to the west and east, bearing deposits of all mineralization phases. Additionally, further cracks were formed, following the tectonic development, especially during mineralization phase II (e.g. 3, 8 and 10 east, with the orebodies 10b, 10c and 10d, Fig. 30) and III (e.g. 1, 4 west and 9).
(B) The *northern Oberharz*, with the Devonian anticline and adjacent Culm areas to the west and east: the numerous vein systems show, with quartz, siderite, low quantities of sulphides and sporadic Co–Ni minerals, only slight and monotonous mineralization. There are not many exposures and a subdivision by age as in the central zone is not applicable here; a paragenetic classification of the mineralization remains uncertain.
(C) The *eastern zone*, between the line Clausthal, Hahnenklee and Altenau: there occur (1) extensions of vein systems of the central zone (7, Fig. 30), formed during mineralization phases II and III, here trending approximately west–east and (2) single veins in imbricate areas of the Diabase zone and in the western parts of the Söse depression, trending to the NNW and dipping to the east (6, Fig. 30). Both bear deposits of phases IIb and IIIa.
(D) The *western zone*, south of the Lautenthal vein system and west of a line from Lautenthal to the edge of the Harz west of the Iberg hill: the western part of this zone is discordantly overlain by the Zechstein. The western extensions of vein systems of the more central zones (3, 4, 9 and 11) are located in hematitized wallrocks and here carry, besides small quantities of quartz, only dolomite, siderite, barite and anhydrite of phase III, but no sulphides. In the Zechstein horizon there is almost only barite and the Zechstein limestone is locally baritized up to 50 m from the vein (see later).

In the history of German mining the Oberharz district holds a predominant position.[118] The Oberharz district, together with the Erzgebirge, provided in earlier centuries not only the main part of silver required for the German State and neighbouring countries, especially for coinage, but was pre-eminent in the development of mining and smelting technology,[119] mining laws and mining traditions.

Mining started, probably at the Zellerfeld ore veins, in 1200 and lasted for 150 years, when the Black Death brought this first phase to an end. Not for another 150 years was mining re-established in 1500. At the start the silver-rich cementation ores and later the primary lead–silver ores were mined. The production of zinc ores was started in 1850. The 5-km ore veins in the Grund area, the only productive mine today, were first discovered towards the end of the eighteenth century and have been worked continuously since 1831.

Since 1540 mining in the Oberharz ore veins has produced, according to Slotta,[119] a total of 2 000 000 tonne of lead, almost 1 250 000 tonne of zinc and about 5000 tonne of silver (Table 28). The amount mined in the Grund mine can only be estimated as the metal content of the crude ore is not known exactly for the period 1831–99; 15 000 000 tonne of crude ore was extracted with 1 000 000 tonne of lead, 500 000 tonne

Table 28 *Ore and metal production of Upper and Middle Harz districts since sixteenth century*[116]

	Crude ore, t × 10^6	Zn metal, t	Pb metal, t	Ag, t
Upper Harz district				
Silbernaal vein system since 1831	ca 15	500 000	1 000 000	2 000
Rosenhof vein system, 1552–1930	2·06	88 000	110 000	
Zellerfeld vein system, 1526–1930	1·30	—	115 000	
Burgstätte vein system, ca 1548–1930	7·46	325 000	270 000	
Schatzkammer vein / Schultaler vein 1540–1797	?	—	5 000	
Haus-Herzberg vein system, 1595–1768	0·17	—	10 000	
Spiegeltal vein system, 1548–1928	1·39	—	70 000	
Bockswiese vein system, 1561–1931	2·15	30 000	123 000	
Lautenthal vein system, 1524–1945	4·20	280 000	97 000	
Other vein systems	?	—	ca 5 000	
	ca 34	1 223 000	1 805 000	4 700
Middle Harz district				
St. Andreasberg orefield, 1188–1910	?	—	12 500	313

of zinc and 2000 tonne of silver (Fig. 33). The known reserves of the Grund ore mines amount to 3 000 000 tonne of crude ore.

Mining ceased in the northern and eastern veins mainly in the nineteenth century because of depletion. During the economic crisis in 1930 the mines in the central Oberharz, except for the Grund mine, were shut down. The total production of these mines is estimated to be roughly 19 000 000 tonne of crude ore (Table 28). Mining in the Burgstätte vein system in Clausthal has reached a depth of 1000 m.

The vein system of the *St. Andreasberg orefield in the Middle Harz district* is situated on the southern rim of the Brockenmassif. The veins occur in a narrow west-east elongated triangle, 6 km in length and up to 1 km in width (Fig. 30). The ore veins, some 25 in number, very rarely measure more than 1 km in length and up to 1 m in width. They are situated between boundary faults that trend, on average, northwest–NNW and dip southwest. Vein extensions, occasionally found outside the vein triangle, show a quite different mineral paragenesis.

The wallrock of the veins consists mainly of argillaceous schists, quartzites and cherts with flinty limestones of the Devonian along with greywackes of the Lower Carboniferous and Devonian diabases. The paragenesis is fundamentally similar to that of the Oberharz[19] (Table 29). There are, however, significant differences in form and facies. The strike length and thickness of veins are considerably smaller; telescoping, rejuvenations, a drusy vein structure and irregular mineralization with locally rich ore shoots are characteristic and point to subvolcanic conditions during mineral deposition. The temperatures during formation reached 400°C and therefore were significantly higher than those in the Oberharz district (<300°C). Some minerals, especially various silver minerals as well as Co–Ni arsenides and antimonides, are found in much higher quantities than those in the Oberharz district, and others like fluorite are missing (for the distribution of barites see later).

The development of Andreasberg mining paralleled that of the Oberharz district, though activity in the twelfth century cannot be verified.[19,113] In the late fifteenth century the veins were rediscovered and the extraction of Ag–Pb–Cu ores was started in 1480. The first period ended in 1620, when all the rich cementation ores had been extracted. After 1650 mining for primary ores commenced and a gradual consolidation of mining ensued. In 1910 mining operations were shut down because the reserves were exhausted. The Andreasberg orefields yielded a total of 300 tonne of silver, 12 500 tonne of lead and 2500 tonne of copper.

Ideas concerning the *age, origin and causes* of the lead–zinc mineralization in the Harz have changed repeatedly. After the assumption of a connexion between the late Mesozoic–Tertiary uplift of the Harz and the ore veins orientated parallel to the northern rim of the Harz was abandoned, the concept of the Upper Carboniferous Brocken granite and its hypothetical extension to the west as the ore supplier for the ore veins in the Upper and Middle Harz prevailed. In 1950 it was concluded that a deep 'Grund Pluton' was the explanation for the rich mineralization to the south of the Iberg reef.

By the application of geochemical and isotope-geochemical methods it has been possible to show in recent years that a considerable amount of the vein content is derived from underlying sediments or from more or less adjacent wallrocks. Nielsen[122] discovered that the $\delta^{34}S$ values of sulphides in the Oberharz district and near St. Andreasberg correspond to those of the Lower Carboniferous and Devonian–Silurian wallrocks, from which he assumed a contribution of sedimentary sulphur to the mineralization (see also Sperling and Nielsen[123]). Wedepohl and co-workers[124] examined the isotopic composition of lead from various Central European deposits, including the

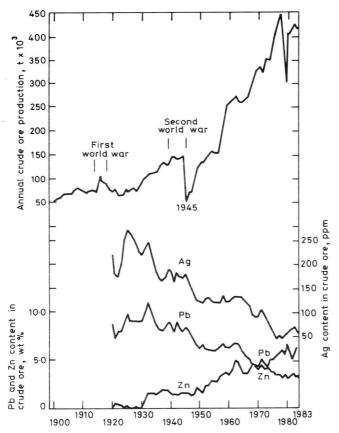

Fig. 33 *Annual ore production of Erzbergwerk Grund since 1900 with corresponding lead, zinc and silver contents (metal contents prior to 1920 not available). After Sperling and co-workers*[114]

Year	Production, t	Pb, %	Zn, %	Ag, ppm
1971	325 000	5.2	4.6	107
1972	355 000	4.8	4.2	92
1973	354 000	4.4	4.3	79
1974	399 000	3.9	5.1	68
1975	434 000	3.8	5.2	52
1976	445 000	3.5	5.4	47
1977	431 000	3.5	5.8	51
1978	309 000	3.2	6.1	48
1979	409 000	3.5	5.7	56
1980	408 000	3.2	6.7	57
1981	421 000	3.4	6.0	65
1982	417 000	3.6	5.4	70
1983	420 000	3.4	6.4	58
1984	430 000	2.7	7.3	40

Grund mine, and came to the conclusion that the lead originated from sedimentary source material containing Precambrian detritus with an age of 1700 m.y.

The distribution of rare-earth elements (REE) and stable isotopes in calcites of the lead–zinc ore veins of the Westharz have been examined by Möller et al.,[125] who were able to differentiate three calcite types and showed that calcite type I was deposited out of magmatic solution, possibly from the Brocken granite; calcite type II originated from heated sediments; and calcite type III crystallized out of cool descendent waters. Calcite type I and sulphides, forming banded ores, are very common in the Grund deposit. This banding proves that the two components originate from different solutions: calcite type I was formed from magmatic waters, whereas calcite type II and the sulphides were deposited from vadose meteoric waters.

Undoubtedly, the intrusions had, as a source of energy, a role to play in the formation of the ore veins. As a supplier of chemical elements or 'ore-bringer' the granite is obviously far less clear than has hitherto been assumed. Most probably the barite of the IIIc phase in the Oberharz district (Fig. 32), as well as IIIb in St. Andreasberg (Table 29) with its accompanying minerals, belongs to the Mesozoic and Tertiary mineralization. The barite and fluorite veins of the southwestern Harz, one of the economically most important barite districts of Europe, are reckoned to be of the same age.

Lead–zinc ore veins in the sub-Variscan Foredeep A number of lead–zinc ore veins, some of them important, occur within a northeast–NNE-trending zone running roughly from Düsseldorf to Recklinghausen in the Ruhr district and its southern border (Fig. 34). They show many similarities of structure and mineralization, but are otherwise significantly different from the ore veins of the Rheinische Schiefergebirge. They were grouped by Schneiderhöhn[126] with the 'Oberharz Quartz–Calcite Type' of lead–zinc vein in contrast to the older 'Rhenish Quartz–Siderite Type'. Not until recent decades were ore veins comparable with those of the Ruhr district also discovered in the Aachen coal district at Erkelenz and near Geilenkirchen, 40 km and 20 km, respectively, to the NNE of Aachen.

Whereas south of the lower Ruhr in the Lintorf–Selbeck sub-district mining was being carried on in the late Middle Ages and again in the second half of the nineteenth century up to 1916, the Ruhr ore veins, cropping out beneath the transgressive Upper Cretaceous at depths of 120 m to more than 200 m, were discovered only in the progress of coal mining, and two veins were brought into production between 1936 and 1962.

The metallogenic district of the *Ruhr area* includes three known PbS–ZnS vein deposits, several smaller occurrences and more than 100 ore showings.[127,128,129] The three important deposits are the ore vein of the Auguste Victoria mine at Marl (PbS, ZnS), that of the Christian Levin mine at Essen (PbS) and the Klara vein of the Graf Moltke mine at Gladbeck (PbS, ZnS). The crude ore at these coal mines averaged 10–12% Zn + Pb metal and sometimes more. All PbS–ZnS occurrences contain quartz, barite and calcite as the main gangue minerals. The

Table 29 *Mineral succession of St. Andreasberg lead–zinc orefield. After Wilke[19,120] and Schnorrer-Köhler[121]*

Phase	Main minerals
I. Pre-phase, kata- to epithermal	(*a*) *Quartz*, hematite (Ca–Fe–Mn carbonates)
	(*b*) *Ca–Fe–Mn carbonates*, siderite, (sulphides)
II. Main phase, mesothermal	(*a*) 'Main sulphides': *galena, sphalerite*, chalcopyrite, tetrahedrite, *quartz*, calcite
High mesothermal (second rejuvenation)	(*b*) 'Noble calcite': *calcite*, native *arsenic*, antimony, silver, *dyscrasite*, As–Sb–Ag-, and Co–Ni minerals
III. Post-phase, kata- to epithermal (third rejuvenation)	(*a*1) 'Redeposited sulphides': iron sulphides, *galena*, sphalerite, chalcopyrite, *quartz*, calcite
	(*a*2) 'Silver-sulpho ore phase' with zeolites, quartz, calcite
	(*b*) Fluorite, barite (only in westernmost part of orefield, but abundant in whole Middle Harz district with barite as main mineral)
	(*c*) Antimonite, realgar, selenides
IV. Oxidation and cementation minerals down to a depth of 100 m, but of only limited economic importance	

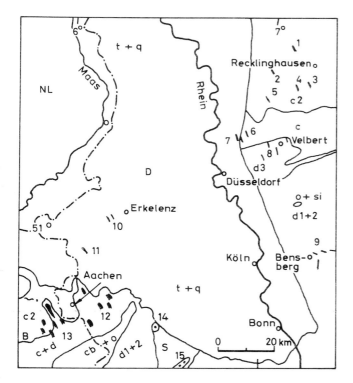

Fig. 34 *Lead–zinc ore deposits around Lower Rhine Bight: 1, Auguste Victoria mine; 2, Klara vein (Graf Moltke mine); 3, Shamrock and Julia mines; 4, Primus fault (Pluto and Hannover–Hannibal mines); 5, Christian Levin mine; (1–5, Ruhr district); 6, Selbeck orefield; 7, Lintorf orefield; 8, Velbert orefield (6–8, Lintorf–Velbert sub-district); 9, Bensberg sub-district (Fig. 21); 10, Sophia Jacoba mine near Erkelenz; 11, Carolus Magnus mine near Geilenkirchen (10–11, Aachen–Erkelenz sub-district); 12, Aachen–Stolberg orefield; 13, Bleiberg–Moresnet orefield; 14, Maubach and 15, Mechernich (Fig. 63); (t + q, Tertiary and Quaternary; c2, Upper Cretaceous; s, Lower Triassic; c, Carboniferous; d3, d2, d1, Upper, Middle, Lower Devonian; si, Silurian; o, Ordovician; cb, Cambrian)*

veins, as well as most of the other occurrences and indications of mineralization, are located along normal faults and strike-slip faults within coal-bearing strata of Upper Carboniferous age. The veins form breccias within the faults and contain ore and gangue minerals that are combined with the coal-bearing sediments, including fragments of coal.

The hitherto known PbS–ZnS occurrences are associated with northwest–southeast, NNW–SSE and WNW–ESE faults and prefer the intersections of the faults with the anticlines of the Ruhr district fold belt. Generally, the PbS–ZnS veins and occurrences are located on pre-Carboniferous lineaments in NNE and WNW directions with which an assemblage of faults, fissures and joints is associated.

The PbS–ZnS mineralization is related to the Variscan orogeny—that is, to young Variscan tectonic movements at the end of the Upper Carboniferous. Therefore, the ore veins and occurrences follow exactly the petrofabric structures of the Variscan *B*-axis (Fig. 35). There was, first, a folding phase during the late Upper Carboniferous when anticlines, synclines and overthrusts developed over a period of about 3 m.y. This folding gave place directly to a block-faulting and tilting phase, when the fold belt was dissected by large normal faults and strike-slip faults. During and as a result of this fracturing the deeper underground was opened by fissures, mainly along the lineaments. Hydrothermal solutions ascended, at the same time as movements along the faults, coming from plutons 4000–5000 m below the Upper Carboniferous denudation surface. Seen as a whole, the mineralization of the Ruhr district shows a uniform sequence from higher to lower thermal crystallization—that is, from mesothermal conditions of about 250°C to epithermal conditions of 100°C and less. Mainly, the

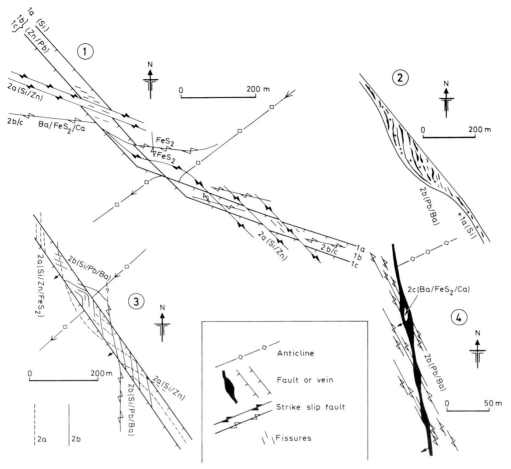

Fig. 35 Sketch maps of PbS–ZnS veins in Ruhr province: 1, Auguste Victoria; 2, Christian Levin; 3, Klara/Graf Moltke; 4, Shamrock (close interrelationship of tectonic structures and mineral generations and sub-generations to B-axes and faults of Young Variscan folding phase)

mineralization of the Ruhr district is part of the paragenesis of sphalerite–galena–barite, but the PbS–ZnS vein of Auguste Victoria also shows an older mineralization containing abundant quartz and the main part of the PbS–ZnS ore (Fig. 36).

Generally, the sequence of all veins starts with quartz I, a few sulphides and ankerite/siderite–sphalerite–chalcopyrite–pyrite–marcasite, especially melnikovite–pyrite and melnikovite–marcasite–calcite. Only in the Primus vein is there another sequence with a local doming of the quartz–chalcopyrite–ankerite paragenesis. It is possible to divide the mineralization into two generations (mineralization phases). The first generation directly followed the opening of the main normal faults. The second generation is linked to strike-slip faults that transect the normal faults and the veins (Fig. 35). Moreover, the two main generations can be subdivided into six sub-generations—$1a$, $1b$, $1c$, $2a$, $2b$ and $2c$ (Fig. 36). As a result of obvious telescoping, all generations and sub-generations occur within the same strata of 300- to 500-m thickness within the middle portion of Westfalian A. In this position they were deposited about 2300 m below the Carboniferous palaeo-surface and the same distance above the plutons.

Between 1936 and 1962 the Auguste Victoria mine produced around 5 000 000 tonne of ore averaging 7·0% Zn, 3·9% Pb and 65 ppm Ag (1300 ppm in PbS). The development of the production is shown in Fig. 37. The Christian Levin mine produced, between 1937 and 1958, 380 000 tonne of ore with 10·7% Pb, 0·5% Zn and 26 ppm Ag (235 ppm Ag in PbS). No ore was exploited from the Klara vein (Table 30). Ore mining in the Ruhr district became uneconomic because of the slump in the metal market around 1960.

Although Christian Levin is practically exhausted, reserves remain at Auguste Victoria of around 3 000 000 tonne of ore with 7% Zn and 3·5% Pb and in the Klara vein more than 2 000 000 tonne of ore with 8·7% Zn and 3·1% Pb.

In the *Lintorf–Velbert sub-district* lead and zinc ore veins occur to the south of the lower Ruhr in northwest-trending cross-faults in Upper Devonian, mainly finely clastic rocks and limestones of the Velbert saddle and about 15 km northwest of Velbert near Selbeck and Lintorf in greywackes of the

Federal Republic of Germany

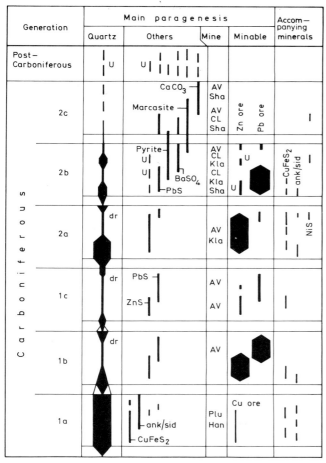

Fig. 36 Generations and sub-generations of PbS–ZnS ore mineralization in Ruhr province: AV, Auguste Victoria; CL, Christian Levin; Kla, Klara/Graf Moltke; Sha, Shamrock; Plu, Pluto; Han, Hannover-Hannibal (ank/sid, ankerite/siderite; dr, drusy minerals; U, due to remobilization)

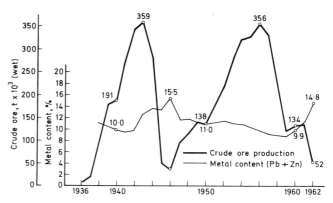

Fig. 37 Crude ore production and Pb–Zn metal content of Auguste Victoria mine at Marl—most important lead–zinc vein deposit of Ruhr district

'Flözleere' of the lower Namurian. In Lintorf they are to be found also in the Lower Carboniferous limestone of the Wattenscheide anticline (Fig. 34). The tectonic structure and the mineral content of veins correspond to those of the Ruhr district, though barite occurs in a similar frequency only in the vein systems near Selbeck. Barite appears in the Lintorf orefield only in minor quantities, and there is none in the vein systems of the Velbert saddle.[80d] Because of the closure of the last mine in 1916 there is no modern research work. A survey of the economic geological circumstances has been made by Kukuk.[80d]

Some attempts at mining had been made before the Thirty Years War, but modern mining began in 1850 (Table 30). Despite occasional success, the mines had to struggle against considerable water incursions, mostly from the Carboniferous limestone. Consequently, mining was in the end halted, considerable reserves being left behind. Water incursions along with the density of population prohibit the future extraction of reserves that still exist mainly in Lintorf and Selbeck.

In the Aachen–Erkelenz sub-district, although mining was carried on in Aachen and Stolberg for around 2000 years, the Upper Carboniferous beds of the Aachen coal-mining district were 20 years ago still considered to be free of epigenetic lead–zinc concentrations—in contrast to the Ruhr district. Only in the 1960s was intensive vein mineralization discovered during research work by the coal-mining industry.[131] In the Carolus Magnus mine near Geilenkirchen massive galena ores were found and in the Sophia Jacoba mine at Erkelenz lead–zinc ores, some of them rich, on northwest-trending fault zones. The ores are brecciated and bear coarse galena, pale sphalerite, pyrite, marcasite and traces of chalcopyrite. According to the sequence of deposition and the trace-element

Table 30 Ore and metal production of Ruhr district and Lintorf–Velbert sub-district. After Pilger,[129] Friedensburg,[90] Stadler[130] and Slotta[119]

Ruhr district	Crude ore, $t \times 10^6$	Zn metal, t	Pb metal, t	Ag metal, t
Auguste Victoria (1936–1962)	4·906	277 000	169 000	250
Christian Levin (1937–1958)	0·377	—	40 000	10
Lintorf–Velbert sub-district	Zn concentrates, t	Zn metal, t	Pb concentrates, t	Pb metal, t
Lintorf orefield (1869–1902)	1 768	849	6 337	5 070
Selbeck orefield (1881–1908)	164 926	85 762	5 271	4 217
Velbert orefield (~1850–1916)	26 306	12 627	32 392	25 914

content, the mineralization corresponds to the second generation of mineralization in the Ruhr district (Fig. 36). Quartz is the only gangue mineral; carbonates and barite are absent.

The relationship of barite to the Variscan vein mineralization is unclear. In ore veins of the Rheinische Schiefergebirge barite is very rare and ought mainly to be ascribed to the Alpine metallogenetic epoch.[82,132] In the Ruhr district barite is the main component of the latest mineralization phase. In the lower Ruhr it occurs only near Selbeck and in very small quantities near Lintorf. There is no barite near Velbert and in the Carboniferous beds to the north of Aachen.[131] Also in the Oberharz, barite is common as the youngest mineral only in certain zones (Fig. 30).[118] Its relationship to the Variscan mineralization cannot be considered as proven.

Venn district
In the Hohe Venn (Stavelot Massif) between Monschau, Malmedy, Vielsalm and Büttgenbach, centred on Belgium, a gold- and cassiterite-bearing district can be found, in the southern part of which occur some unimportant quartz–chalcopyrite veins.[133] Extensive tailings dumps prove that placer ore mining took place in Celtic times, according to excavations made in 1910. In 1895 the leasing of a gold field led to investigations that showed that arkoses of the older Lower Devonian trangressive to the Cambrian should be seen as a primary deposit.[134] In 1911 this area experienced a short-lived gold-rush.

The veins of the vein system of Bleialf–Rescheid and of Brandenberg to the southeast of the Hohe Venn carry galena with low silver content and have been regarded as of Alpine age. The quartz–chalcopyrite veins possibly also belong to this young mineralization (Fig. 19).

Marsberg copper stockwork deposit
Until 1945 the copper stockwork deposit of Marsberg was exploited in the northeast corner of the Rheinische Schiefergebirge, 30 km to the south of Paderborn. In the older literature it was described as the Stadtberge deposit—the old name given to it by the former community of Niedermarsberg. The mineralization is, on the one hand, bound to folded and strongly fractured cherts of the Lower Carboniferous and, on the other, to a fault system that runs northeast acutely angled to the trend of the beds. The mineralization disappears quickly at the boundaries of the cherts, which are polyhedrally brecciated to a thickness of 35 m. The fault system is younger than the major Variscan folding and older than the overlying Zechstein, into which there is only a diminished and stunted extension (G. Stadler, personal communication).

Secondarily enriched massive ores with a copper content of 7–>10% occur in the faults and at the crossing-points reach a thickness of several metres. Beyond them disseminated ores can be found, the copper minerals of which occur in clefts and fault surfaces in the rock, containing, on average, 1·2–2% Cu and, finally, poor impregnation ores in less decomposed wallrock. The minable orebodies reach thicknesses of 20–30 m and lengths of up to several hundred metres.[135]

The primary paragenesis bears pyrite, marcasite and tetrahedrite, followed by orthorhombic chalcocite as the main copper mineral, as well as bornite, chalcopyrite and minor sphalerite and galena. Gangue minerals such as quartz and minor calcite are rather subordinate. The bulk of the calcite is significantly younger (see below). Above the primary zone there is a 30–35 m thick cementation zone developed, bearing descendent chalcocite, minor covelline, native silver and native copper. Among the many oxidation minerals, only malachite and azurite are important. About 70–80% of the ores extracted in Marsberg originated from ore veins and stockworks in the Lower Carboniferous. Additionally, there was some extraction from the copper clays of the Lower Zechstein I and of the socalled 'Rückenerze'* that occur on the extension of veins from the Lower Carboniferous into the Zechstein. These and calcite veins up to 1 m thick, with barite, dolomite and traces of hematite, belong to the youngest paragenesis of the Marsberg district (Table 39).

At the eastern edge of the Rheinische Schiefergebirge a considerable number of small deposits between Marsberg and the lower Dill River at Wetzlar belong to the same type of stockwork mineralization. Among them are the formerly mined deposits at Eisenberg near Korbach and those of the Ludwig mine at Biederkopf–Dexbach (page 208).

The genesis of the Marsberg deposit is controversial. Whereas in the beginning a syngenetic supply of copper[136] in the cherts was assumed, various authors have subsequently interpreted the deposit as being epigenetic-ascendent.[137,138] Paeckelmann,[135] however, considered the deposit to be a descendent formation with the copper coming from the overlying Zechstein beds. Against this theory are the facts that (1) the metal content of the copper marls is too low for the formation of a deposit and (2) similar orebodies have been found that were never covered by the Zechstein sea.

The rediscovery of stratiform copper ores in the Lower Carboniferous at Korbach and Marsberg proves the syngenetic formation of the protores and makes the mobilization and redeposition of copper in faults and clefts in the same area, following the Variscan folding in the Upper Carboniferous, most likely.

* *Rücken* is old miner's term for displacement of the Kupferschiefer bed; cf. *Kobaltrücken*, Co-bearing ore veins displacing the Kupferschiefer.

Mining in Marsberg has been established since 1150, but could be much older. It had its first boom in the Middle Ages and a revival after 1832. In the years between 1840 and 1945 3 230 000 tonne of ore with a copper content of 1·5–1·6% was extracted. The remaining reserves are quoted as 1 000 000 tonne of ore with a copper content of 1·3%. The potential of the deposit amounts to more than 63 000 tonne of copper. Therefore Marsberg is the third largest copper deposit in the FRG after Richelsdorf and Rammelsberg.

Late Palaeozoic sedimentary iron ore deposits
In the Rhenohercynian zone marine-sedimentary iron ores were developed in the late Lower and early Middle Devonian. In connexion with coal formation, limnic-sedimentary iron ores were formed in the Upper Carboniferous of the Ruhr district. The deposits were of some economic importance up to the first decade of the twentieth century (Fig. 19).

The oldest formations are oolitic hematite–iron silicate ores in four deposits at the southern rim of the Bingen Forest in the Hunsrück in sandy schists at the boundary between the lower and upper Emsian. The deposits reach thicknesses between 1 and 3 m and bear 50% Fe at shallow depths and 30% Fe further down, besides high quantities of phosphorus. The ores were extracted from 1839 to 1904 in the Braut mine at Wald-Erbach 6 km west of Bingen.[139]

In a southwest-trending extension of about 15 km at the southern rim of the Soon Forest comparable iron ore deposits of a thickness of 1–2 m occur in phyllites and crossite schists in the metamorphic zone at the southern rim of the Hunsrück. They probably represent the metamorphic equivalents of the ores of the Braut mine. The main ore minerals are magnetite with hematite and/or pyrite. The ores extracted at Gebroth between 1907 and 1924 carried 60% Fe, but were rich in phosphorus and sulphur.[139]

From 1857 to 1891 an oolitic hematite ore deposit 1·5–3 m thick with a content of 50% Fe was worked near Schweich on the Mosel River 12 km northeast of Trier. It occurs in schists of the middle upper Emsian. G. Martin[139] interpreted the deposit in terms of early diagenetic conversion of primary volcanosedimentary siderite from iron-bearing mineral water.

Oolitic iron ore deposits of an average thickness of 2–3 m and a maximum thickness of 17 m occur in the Eifel synclines. They are widespread in the latest Lower Devonian and form local intercalations in Middle Devonian limestones and calcarenites. Dominant minerals are hematite and carbonates along with chamosite and pyrite. They are low-iron carbonate fluxing ores, containing 15–20% Fe, 20–30% CaO and, locally, a high content of MgO and P, and were mined by the Celts and Romans. From the end of the eighteenth century iron ore mining in the Eifel enjoyed a certain prosperity. With the improvement of transportation it lost its competitiveness and was shut down in 1980.[139] In the Ruhr district the lower parts of the productive coal measures of the Upper Carboniferous contain bedded siderite ores with variable coal and clay contents. These are limnic formations, in genetic association with coal formation, laterally and facially replacing the seams. 'Carbonaceous (blackband) ironstone' with an Fe content of 20 to 30% and 10–20% of carbon as well as the rarer siderite with an Fe content of about 43%, were extracted from 1852 to 1912 and again between 1934 and 1942. Altogether about 10 000 000 tonne of iron ore was extracted. In the nineteenth century the coal and iron seams were the basis of the development of iron smelters and steel works in the Ruhr district.[139] In the Aachen coal district the similar iron ore deposits were not minable.

Sedimentary mineral deposits in the epi-Variscan platform cover

Evaporites
Evaporites are chemical sediments deposited in the course of increasing saturation from evaporating sea water in the order of their solubility.

Summary
Rock salt and potassium salt as higher saliferous sediments are developed in the following geological systems in the FRG (inorganic carbonate rocks are not discussed within this context).

Miocene For example, in the northern Rhine Graben
Oligocene For example, in the southern Rhine Graben
Upper Jurassic (Portlandian) In the Lower Saxony basin in northwestern Germany
Triassic (Keuper) In northwestern and in areas of southern Germany at various geological horizons
Triassic (Middle Muschelkalk) In southern and central Germany
Triassic (Upper Bunter) In northern and central Germany
Permo-Triassic In the Calcareous Alps near Berchtesgaden
Permian (Zechstein) In northwest Germany and in the North Sea, in Hesse and Franconia
Permian (Rotliegende) In the northern parts of northwestern Germany and in the North Sea

The Permian and Mesozoic saliferous formations in the northern parts of Central Europe formed in an epicontinental shelf area between the Scandinavian Shield and the Variscan orogenic belt, in which epeirogenic subsidence continued during the Permian and with interruptions during the Mesozoic. The SSW indentations of the saliferous formations during the Zechstein, Bunter and Muschelkalk follow the direction of the Hessian Depression between the Harz and the Rheinische Schiefergebirge (Fig. 38).

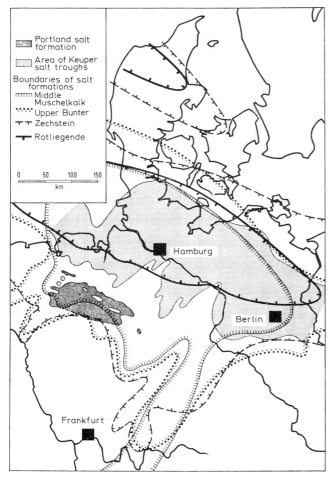

Fig. 38 *Distribution of Late Palaeozoic and Mesozoic salt formations in northwestern Central Europe. After Trusheim[140]*

Chlorides

In the Rotliegende (Lower Permian) a saliferous formation more than 1000 m thick was formed in the southern North Sea and in the adjacent land areas. It is subdivided by sequences with higher clay contamination. Trusheim[140] distinguished three different rock-salt units.

The wide lowland areas that surround the saliferous basin and/or the Devonian salt deposits of the Old Red Continent to the north were considered to be the areas of supply of the salt. On each side of the lower Elbe and in the adjacent southern parts of the North Sea the Rotliegende became mobilized by salt tectonics and forms, interfolded with the Zechstein salt, the salt diapirs of the Rotliegende–Zechstein. In this way the salt–clay breccias, the so-called 'Haselgebirge', were formed.

The most important salt formation in Central Europe is the Zechstein. The salt sequence, reaching a thickness of about 1000 m in the Northwest German Basin, is subdivided into six cycles.[141] The Zechstein Basin was connected with the ocean by a shelf region situated in the northern part of the present-day North Sea.[142] Repeated flooding of the separate interior basins occurred as well as the deposition of clastic sediments at the base of each Zechstein cycle. In the process of increasing concentration of the solutions in the basin, carbonate and sulphate rocks and, finally, thick rock-salt deposits containing potash salt seams were formed (Fig. 39).

In the Zechstein 1 cycle thick saliferous deposits were laid down in the Lower Rhine area, in the Werra–Fulda district and in the Franconian Basin, but the main basin in northwestern Germany remained free of salt deposits. The salt sequence, 250 m in thickness, in the Werra–Fulda basin bears the two potash salt seams 'Thüringen' and 'Hessen', which consist of hard salt or carnallite rock and are worked as very important potash salt deposits.[141]

The thick salt sequences of the Zechstein 2 and 3 bear in the area of the main basin the seams 'Ronnenberg' and 'Riedel' as main potash salt deposits, containing predominantly sylvite, and the 'Staßfurt'* seam, consisting of hard salt and carnallite rock. Potash salt is extracted in the area of Hannover, Celle and Hildesheim. Carnallite rocks are not minable because of their relatively low potassium content.

Rock salt from the Zechstein deposits is also extracted in eastern Lower Saxony and in Nordrhein Westphalia, using mining as well as brine extraction, e.g. near Stade to the west of Hamburg and near Gronau on the German–Dutch border to the west of Rheine. In the marginal regions of the salt basin the Zechstein salt is flat-lying. In the plain of northwest Germany—that is, in an area of extreme salt thickness and stronger tectonic downwarping—salt stocks have formed. These diapirs are raw material reserves of considerable importance for deep brine mining and potentially for storage in caverns.

The structural history of salt stocks has been examined, notably by Trusheim,[144] who introduced in 1957 the expression halokinesis, and by Jaritz.[145] Halokinesis denotes the autonomous salt migration caused by isostatic compensation movements. Provided that there is a sufficient thickness of salt and overlying rock it leads to the formation of flat cupola-shaped salt pillows without apparent orogenic-tectonic action. The salt migration from areas between the salt pillows led to the formation of the so-called primary rim synclines, in which sediments of abnormal thickness were deposited. At a later stage there usually occurred a breakthrough of the salt stock from the salt pillow, penetrating the overlying rocks to the surface or to groundwater level. This is connected with the formation of secondary rim synclines. Jaritz[145] analysed the structural history of the northwest German salt stocks on the basis of dating of the rim synclines assigned to them. He discovered that the first salt movements took place as early as the Triassic, thus

---

* Hard salt in a mixture of halite, sylvite and kieserite.

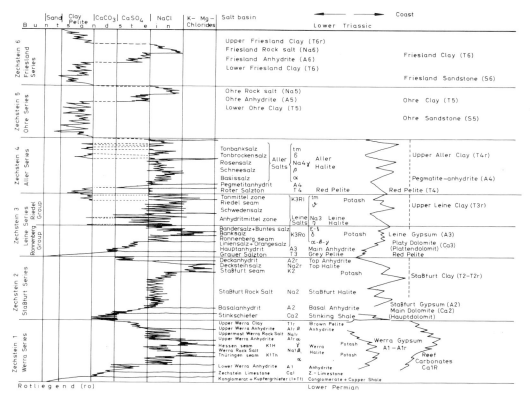

Fig. 39 *Sedimentation and stratigraphy of German Zechstein. After Richter-Bernburg.*[142] *Zechstein 5 and 6 added after Käding*[141,143]

giving rise, especially in areas of great salt thickness on both sides of the Elbe, to the formation of diapirs during the Bunter and the Muschelkalk.

In the area of the northern Calcareous Alps the FRG takes in part of the Alpine salt basins, which contain salt deposits from the Upper Permian to the earliest Triassic. These are tectonized and brecciated mixed salt-clay rocks (Haselgebirge) containing thick series of pure salt. (As the most important deposits are in Austria, they are discussed in greater detail elsewhere in this volume.) In Germany the Berchtesgaden deposit is the only one and is being extracted by underground solution mining.[146]

After the deposition of epicontinental red sediments of the Lower and Middle Bunter there was a marine ingression into the German Basin in north and central Germany. In wide areas in northwestern Germany salt and sulphate rocks of a thickness of almost 200 m were developed in approximately the same area where thick evaporites had already been deposited during the Zechstein (Fig. 38).

After the marine ingression of the Muschelkalk Sea into the Central European area the basin was cut off during the Middle Muschelkalk. The increasing evaporation led to the formation of sulphate rocks and the deposition of a thick rock-salt series. Near Heilbronn the Muschelkalk salt 80–100 m thick is mined and extracted in brines. In the northwest German Basin the salt locally reaches abnormally great thicknesses in the rim synclines of the evolving salt structures.[140]

The locally very thick Keuper salt of the northwest German Basin is restricted to the quickly subsiding rim synclines of the evolving salt structures. According to Trusheim,[140] the origin of the salt can be explained, like that of the Muschelkalk salt of abnormally great thickness, by the dissolution of Zechstein salt, which had flowed out diapirically on the sea-floor. The saliferous sedimentation was interrupted repeatedly by the deposition of pelitic formations. The salt deposits in north Germany belong to different stages of the Keuper. Particularly thick Keuper salt enrichments of locally more than 2000 m in rim synclines of ascending Zechstein salt stocks became mobilized and have formed salt pillows and diapir-like structures.

The northwest German Portlandian Basin was subdivided in several subsidiary basins. The salt sequence (up to 800 m thick) is subdivided by various horizons of a predominantly argillaceous facies. Thick sulphate rocks are developed, especially at the base of the saliferous sequence of the lowest Portlandian.[140] The salt deposits were formed in a small interior basin cut off from the ocean. The high salinity of the basin water can be explained by the supply of dissolved Zechstein salt. In special basins during the Portlandian underlying Zechstein diapirs, which ascended to the surface or to the sea-floor, were dissolved. The celestine deposit, developed in a partial basin, is discussed later together with sulphatic evaporites.

In areas of particularly large salt thickness the Portlandian salt also becomes mobilized, forming salt pillows and salt anticlines.

The depression of the Rhine Graben was temporarily flooded in the Tertiary by the Tethys. In the Upper Eocene and Lower Oligocene thick halites were deposited, partly intercalated with dolomitic clays. During the Lower Oligocene (Pechelbronn beds) two potash salt seams were formed in the south. In the smaller part of the basin on the right bank of the Rhine one of these seams, with a thickness of 4·2 m and a content of 20% K_2O, was worked in the Buggingen potash mine until 1973. Mining is still carried on in various locations in Alsace.

Table 31 *Production ($t \times 10^3$) of rock salt, evaporated salt and industrial brine in Federal Republic of Germany*[21]

	Rock salt	Evaporated salt	Industrial brine, NaCl
1960	4 508	344	477
1965	5 305	447	1 159
1970	8 995	705	1 421
1975	5 878	722	3 151
1980	7 565	873	4 637

In the northern parts of the Rhine Graben between Karlsruhe and Mainz rock-salt deposits were formed during the Miocene.

In Germany salt production had started in the twelfth century. Potash has been extracted since 1840. In 1983 there were in the FRG eight potash and seven rock-salt mines in operation, as well as six common salt

Table 32 *Potash mine production ($t \times 10^3$) in Federal Republic of Germany*[21]

	Lower Saxony	Hesse	Baden
1960			
Crude potash	9 212	8 867	562
K_2O contents	1 313	894	109
1965			
Crude potash	11 119	10 400	684
K_2O contents	1 557	1 058	123
1970			
Crude potash	10 326	10 049	655
K_2O contents	1 420	1 107	118
1975			
Crude potash	10 626	11 379	—
K_2O contents	1 435	1 172	—
1980			
Crude potash	11 985	17 332	—
K_2O contents	1 597	1 710	—

and five industrial brine works. In 1980 29 317 000 tonne of raw potash and 13 075 000 tonne of rock salt, evaporated salt and industrial brine (Tables 31 and 32) was produced.

Sulphates

In a fully developed precipitation cycle gypsum and anhydrite are situated between evaporitic limestones (not dealt with here) and chlorides. Therefore, most salt formations contain more or less thick sulphate rocks. Near to the earth's surface anhydrite is hydrated to gypsum.

The most important deposits belong to the Zechstein and are to be found on the southern border of the Harz and the northeastern border of the Rheinische Schiefergebirge as well as near Stadtoldendorf and the Richelsdorf mountains. To the north the gypsum cap rocks of the Zechstein salt stocks crop out at the surface—for example, at Lüneburg and near Bad Segeberg.[147] The sulphate rocks of the Upper Bunter and the Middle Muschelkalk fall far short of the Zechstein deposits in economic importance. Muschelkalk gypsum is only extracted in an area to the west of the River Weser. In Franconia in southern Germany there are one or two workable deposits of the Middle Keuper.[148]

The saliferous formation of the Upper Jurassic (Portlandian, Münder marls) in northwestern Weserbergland is characterized by thick gypsum deposits. In the area of the Hils syncline workable thicknesses are reached.

Worthy of mention is a celestine deposit in the Upper Malm near Hemmelte in southern Oldenburg where a synsedimentary evaporitic celestine occurrence was drilled in anhydrite rocks.[149] In the area of a submarine rise at the edge of the Lower Saxony main basin heavier evaporation led to a temporary saturation of the sea water with $SrSO_4$, without $CaSO_4$ saturation being reached. The outflow of the heavy lye into the marginal basin constantly brought new volumes of water from the basin to the rise, where they could blend with fresh water from the open ocean. This mechanism of facies differentiation, which must have existed for longer geological periods, led to the formation of a celestine deposit. This deposit was struck at a depth of about 1200 m, the reserves being estimated at several million tonnes of $SrSO_4$.

There is a comparable celestine deposit in the Münder marls of the Upper Malm in the Süntel and Deister hills to the southwest of Hannover. To the north of Springe, in the Deister hills, some rock beds contain more than 50% $SrSO_4$. The mineral occurs mainly in wedge-shaped layers and in lenses, as well as in slate rocks and as druse fillings in limestones and marls. To the northwest of the deposit the celestine layers interfinger with gypsum-bearing horizons, thus concluding the evaporitic–sedimentary formation.[293] Many small celestine beds were encountered in coal drilling in the Upper Cretaceous at the southern boundary of the Münsterland Bight[237] (cf. the strontianite veins in the southeastern Münsterland).

Finally, many celestine occurrences are known in the Zechstein 3 dolomites at the eastern boundary of the Rheinische Schiefergebirge between Marsberg and Korbach (Fig. 19). Celestine was worked at Gembeck until about 1910 and at Giershagen until 1895. Most authors consider these layers and impregnations to be epigenetic (see Scherp and Strübel[237]). Müller[149] interpreted them as sedimentary evaporitic layers in Zechstein 3 Salt, which had been altered by carbon dioxide rich surface waters. The scattered pseudomorphs of strontianite after celestine support that view.

Fluorite

Fluorite concentrations were discovered in 1974 in the main dolomite (Ca 2) and in the platy dolomite (Ca 3) of the Zechstein salt sequence (Fig. 39) at Eschwege and near Sontra in North Hesse.[150] The fluorite is found in dolomite horizons in the form of irregular layers and lenses of a dark colour. The layers reach thicknesses of up to 0·5 m and carry between 10 and 50% CaF_2. Fluorite also occurs in massive beds 18–20 m thick, with CaF_2 concentrations of 10%. Alternations of fluorite and dolomite, the lack of hydrothermal minerals and the contents of REE confirm the sedimentary formation of the fluorite.[151,152] Schulz[152] developed a geochemical-genetic model of marine sedimentary fluorite formation, according to which the fluorine came from the sea water and was diagenetically precipitated in the course of dolomitization of fresh calcareous sediments. The reserves of fluorite are estimated at 5 000 000–7 000 000 tonne of CaF_2.

The Kupferschiefer deposit

The following descriptions are mainly based on the work of Wedepohl[153] and Rentzsch;[154] for the area of the Hessian Depression on the work of Kulick et al.[155] (with detailed bibliographical references); and for the deposits in and to the south of the Richelsdorf Mountains on the work of Messer[156] and Spieth et al.[157] We thank C. Schumacher, Project Manager 'Kupferschiefer' of St. Joe Exploration GmbH, Hannover, for other additional information.

Synopsis

The Kupferschiefer horizon in the Zechstein basin, extending from eastern England to Silesia and to the Baltic, represents the pelitic phase of the salt cycle of the Werra sequence (= Zechstein 1, Upper Permian) (Fig. 39). In the southern marginal region of the basin sapropelic extremely fine-grained slates averaging in thickness 30 to 60 cm and rarely more than 1 m, and in places sandy marlstones, were formed after the Zechstein transgression over assorted underlying Weißliegende or Rotliegende rocks or basement. According to Glennie and Buller,[158] the transgression must have taken place very quickly (~10 years), leaving no appreciable transgression sediments behind.

Fig. 40 *Variscan discordance in Western Harz Mountains. Early Carboniferous folded chert overlain by 15-cm thick Kupferschiefer (dark horizontal layer) and Zechsteinkalk. Old quarry (protected under nature conservancy order) at Fuchshalle, east of Osterode am Harz. From Dahlgrün and co-workers*[159]

The Lower Zechstein with the Kupferschiefer forms the base of the epi-Variscan platform cover (Fig. 40). In an upward direction the Kupferschiefer, with an increasing content of carbonate and mainly through loss of fine lamination along with the onset of bioturbation, passes into Zechstein limestone.[294]

In the southern and western marginal regions of the basin the rock has a higher content of zinc, lead, copper and other metals. In the ore deposit areas the primary ore content of the basal Zechstein averages 1% copper, or 1% of Cu + Pb + Zn, besides a considerable silver content. The total reserves are estimated at Zn,Pb > 10^8 t > Cu. Contents > 0·3% Cu are restricted to about 1% of the area of distribution of the Kupferschiefer of 6 × 10^5 km², and only 0·2% of the total area is or was minable. The synsedimentary distribution of metals in Central Europe is palaeogeographically determined by the subsoil structure and by the facies zonation in the Kupferschiefer. Elevated copper contents occur over the troughs of the Rotliegende and are restricted to sub-littoral areas and zones of rises. Towards the interior of the basin a lead and, finally, a zinc zone follow in order of decreasing electronegativity. A vertical zoning shows elevated copper in the lower layers, followed upwards by zones rich in lead and zinc. Ag, Bi and Cd correlate with Cu, Pb and Zn, respectively. Over a distance of 150 km from the shore the sediment merges into normal black shales with a low content of non-ferrous metals and the usual elevated contents of V, Mo, Ni, Cr, U and Co correlated with organic carbon. According to Rentzsch,[154] there is a link between the highest contents of non-ferrous metals and the Central German Crystalline Rise along the northern rim of the Saxothuringian Zone.

The synsedimentary protores were enriched in the course of a later redeposition, probably during diagenesis.[156,160] Copper contents of economic importance often occur in the neighbourhood of the

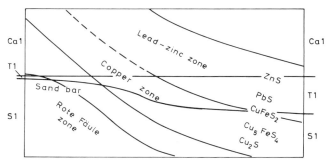

Fig. 41 *Schematic section of epigenetic mineralization of Kupferschiefer in Richelsdorf area. Simplified after Spieth et al.*[157] *(Ca1, Zechsteinkalk; T1, Kupferschiefer bed; S1, Sandstone (Weißliegend) of Rotliegende–Zechstein twilight zone)*

epigenetic hematite facies known by the miners' expression 'Rote Fäule' (red rot). This sometimes has a synsedimentary formation, shown by the existence of shallow water regions with aeration of the surface and abundance of fossils.[161] The 'Rote Fäule' and the ore minerals run discordantly to the bedding, the ore minerals showing a clear secondary fabric (Fig. 41).[157]

The paragenesis of the mineralized Kupferschiefer changes with increasing distance from the 'Rote Fäule' zone. Rentzsch and Knitzschke[162] were able to demonstrate a subdivision into eight types of paragenesis between the hematite type and the pyrite type of the inner parts of the basin characterized by the dominant minerals chalcocite, bornite, galena and sphalerite.

The sulphides occur generally in a grain size <20 to 100 μm, which were diagenetically crystallized. Detrital components are illite, quartz, muscovite and minor chlorite, feldspar and kaolinite. The contents of boron in the mica fraction (from 300 to 400 ppm B) show that the saliferous conditions of the Upper Zechstein did not exist at the time of the Kupferschiefer. The carbonate content, mostly calcite and dolomite, is, like the sulphides, diagenetically crystallized. Marowsky[163] found that, on average, the sulphur in the pyrite of the Kupferschiefer is isotopically lighter than that in the non-ferrous sulphides. The sulphides are not in isotopic balance and for this reason different conditions of precipitation for the two groups of sulphides have to be assumed. Moreover, the elevated contents of lead in the Kupferschiefer mineralization and the high contents of manganese in the associated carbonates prove that the metal contents of the waters out of which the Kupferschiefer ores were precipitated differ significantly from those of normal sea water. Further details and geochemical data were presented by Wedepohl.[153]

The existing facts and findings, especially the restriction of sulphides to the edges of the Rotliegende troughs and to the 'Rote Fäule', can be explained only by syngenetic-synsedimentary deposition and early diagenetic redeposition of ores in the reaction zone between metal-rich waters and the reducing environment of the sapropelite. Thus, the continuation of a supply of metal-rich waters after the sedimentation of the Kupferschiefer, with a simultaneous modification of the syngenetic ores, must be assumed. Groundwaters ascending into the Rotliegende troughs are supposed to be the reason for it, probably caused by compaction of the sediments and/or convection in the area of the Central German Rise. The areas of the 'Rote Fäule', to which the richest mineralizations are bound, presumably form the zones of exit for the ascending waters. Only the post-sedimentary mineral alteration and renewed mineral deposition led to the formation of orebodies of economic importance.

In the FRG ore-bearing Kupferschiefer is common mainly in the Hessian Depression. It is exposed at the eastern rim of the Rheinische Schiefergebirge, at the western rim of the Harz, in the Richelsdorf Mountains and at the northeastern rim of the Spessart. Below surface, it extends to the southwest of Würzburg. It crops out near Osnabrück with only 0.03–0.1% Cu, and was without ore where drilled at Recklinghausen and in the Lower Rhine.

Kupferschiefer ore seam in Hessian Depression
The Hessian Depression, between the Rheinische Schiefergebirge and the Thüringer Wald, runs north-south across the main direction of the Zechstein basin. It was formed in the Lower Permian, during the terminal Variscan folding, and represents, as a shallow depression, a gulf 80–100 km wide in the mass of the eroded Variscan mountains. It is probably the flexure-

Fig. 42 *(see facing page) Palaeogeographic sketch map of Rotliegende and Zechstein 1 in Hessian Depression with abandoned Kupferschiefer mines and prospects. After Kulick et al.*[155] *(northwest German Upper Rotliegende Basin after Hedemann et al.*[166]*). Abandoned copper mines: 1, Richelsdorf; 8, Marsberg; 10, Korbach; 12, Geismar; 14, Bieber; abandoned copper prospects: 2, Baumbach; 3, Albungen; 4, Witzenhausen; 5, Walkenried; 6, Osterode; 7, Hahausen; 9, Leitmar; 11, Stäteberg; 13, Hüttengesäss; 15, Schöllkrippen*

Federal Republic of Germany

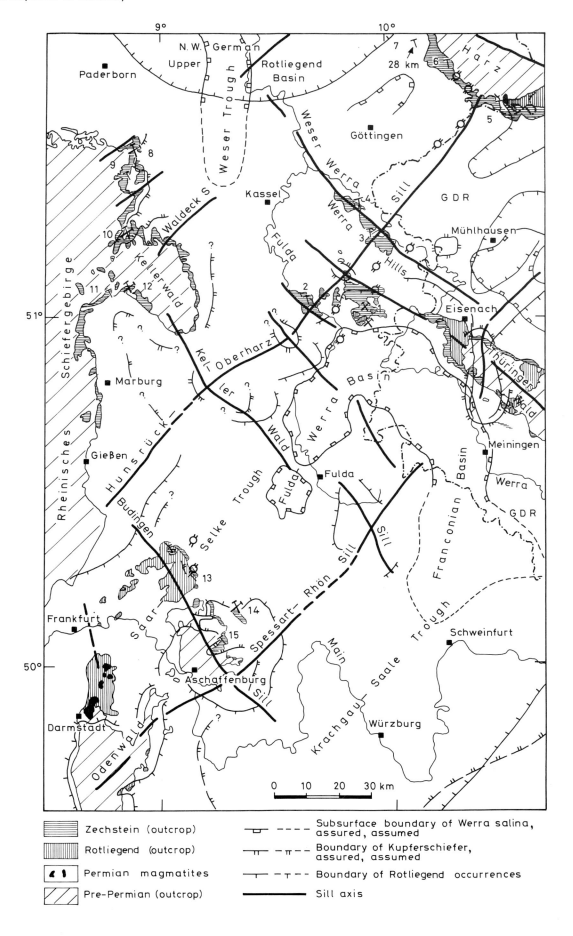

like collapsed end of a Permian graben system running from the Oslo Graben over the Horn Graben to the eastern parts of Lower Saxony (Fig. 42).[164]

Research work from 1979 to 1983 with 24 deep borings in the course of the federal drilling programme and the exploration programme since 1978 of the St. Joe–Preussag consortium has led to important new knowledge about the distribution and development of the Permian in the Hessian Depression and the non-ferrous metal content at the Rotliegende–Zechstein boundary.[155,157]

The following formations can be ore-bearing:
Grau- und Weißliegende—partly bleached clastics of the Rotliegende, on rises also of the pre-Permian, partly primary light sandstones and conglomerates from the boundary Rotliegende–Zechstein
Cornberg sandstone—sandstone, 10–15 m thick, interpreted as a dune formation in the Richelsdorf Mountains
Zechstein conglomerate—locally underlying the Kupferschiefer, to be interpreted partly as gravel in relict troughs, partly as a marine horizon of reworking. Sandstones with pebble layers in the Richelsdorf Mountains are seen as aquatically redeposited Cornberg Sandstone and are considered to be about the same age as the Kupferschiefer (cf. the Weißliegende)[157]
Mutterkalk (Mother seam, Productus limestone, Boundary dolomite)—carbonates rich in fossils, replacing the Kupferschiefer at the rim of the basin or on rises
Kupferschiefer—mainly subdivided by a cyclic and rhythmic repetition of clayey silt and carbonate sediment sequences (Fig. 43). In contrast there are significant facial differences in the lithographic texture, depending on the palaeogeographic situation. The thicker parts between 0·6 and 4 m are not uncommonly secondarily altered by shear slides in the fresh sediments
Zechstein limestone—subdivided in ranges of facies with marly limestones under 10 m thick in the northeast, carbonates 50 m thick, locally up to 100 m, with thick clay and marl intercalations in the south and reef limestones in positive rise areas. Bioturbation in the basal limestones indicates the end of the black shale facies

In this stratigraphic sequence areas with an elevated content of non-ferrous metal are not linked to any special lithofacies. The relation between palaeogeography and the distribution of non-ferrous metals in the northern Fulda–Werra basin to the south of the Richelsdorf Mountains is shown by the appearance of the 'Rote Fäule' in a narrow extended sand bar of the Weißliegende. The bar existed already at the time of sedimentation of the Kupferschiefer. The copper deposit was formed at the interfingering of resorted sands with the clay sedimentation in a weakly reducing environment (Fig. 41).

Palaeogeographically the Hessian Depression is subdivided by northeast- (Variscan) striking rises and troughs and northwest- (Hercynian) striking transverse structures (Fig. 42). In the troughs the Kupferschiefer sinks to a depth of more than 1000 m, and in the Weser Depression to the north to more than 1500 m. As in other ore-bearing districts of the Central European Zechstein, the elevated contents of non-ferrous metals relate here also to a large extent to the northwest structures.

Richelsdorf deposit The Kupferschiefer deposit in the Richelsdorf Mountains is situated 40 km southeast of Kassel (1 in Fig. 42), between Sontra and Bebra, above the Rotliegende basin of Nentershausen (Fig. 44). The deposit is subdivided by denuded anticlines of the Rotliegende in two troughs that strike southwest–northeast. The northern syncline has about 10·5 km² workable orefields, and the southern syncline around 26·5 km².

Ore-bearing layers are the upper 15–30 cm of the (10–12 m thick) Grauliegende, the Kupferschiefer (18–24 cm thick) and, locally, the lower 40–60 cm of the Zechstein limestone. The ores are epigenetic and their occurrence depends on the position of the 'Rote Fäule'. According to their wallrock they are defined as sand ores, slate ores and roof ores. The average content of copper amounts to 0·9–1·2% and of silver several up to a few tens ppm. A detailed list of the mineral content of the Kupferschiefer and the vein deposits of the Richelsdorf Mountains was given by Schnorrer-Köhler.[165]

The 'sand ore' was formed by impregnation of the upper layers of the Grauliegende. Bornite and chalco-

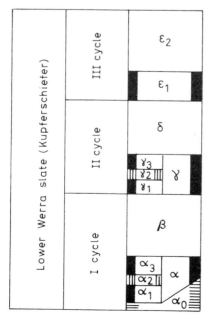

Fig. 43 *Lithostratigraphic subdivision of Kupferschiefer ore seam between Western Harz Mountains and Spessart Hills. After Kulick et al.[155] (black, clayey to silty; horizontally striated, vertically striated, white, increasingly carbonatic)*

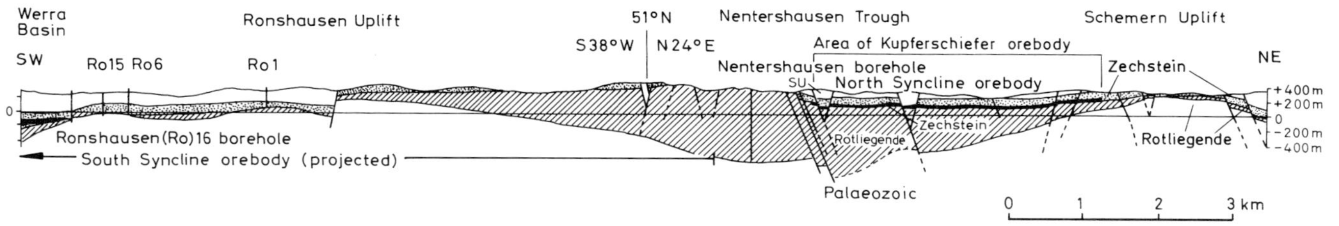

Fig. 44 Section through Nentershausen Rotliegende Trough with Kupferschiefer orebody in North Syncline of Richelsdorf deposit. After Kulick et al.[155] (su, Lower Bunter)

cite are the main copper minerals. They form an enriched zone with a content of 4–10% of copper in the uppermost sand ores known as 'Schwarzkopf' and in the lowermost 2–6 cm of the Kupferschiefer. Depending on the position of the 'Rote Fäule' boundary, the enrichment zone in the northern trough reaches to the Zechstein limestone and is then considered to be of the 'Dachberge' type. The slate ore contains the ore minerals finely disseminated as so-called 'speiss' and occasionally in the form of ore lenses and flasers or thin ore bands, the so-called 'Lineale' (rulers). Above the enriched ore zone—that is, at an increasing distance from the 'Rote Fäule'—the ore mineralization consists mainly of chalcopyrite along with pyrite, galena and sphalerite. The deposit was disrupted into numerous blocks by young Mesozoic–Tertiary fault tectonics, the faults trending northwest and less frequently NNE. Besides the major faults, the ore seam is tectonically heavily disturbed by numerous small dislocations and flexures. The northwest faults often contain barite to a thickness of several metres and with a Co–Ni paragenesis, occurring at the Kupferschiefer horizon, over a vertical extent of several tens of metres and forming the well-known 'Kobaltrücken'.

Along non-mineralized faults, the barren 'Rücken', the ore-bearing rock has been decomposed and made friable by circulating oxidizing solutions. The copper ores are partly disrupted, partly leached and then redeposited on the faults. Besides the 'Kobaltrücken', which are to a large extent filled with barite, the cementation and oxidizing effects on the ore content of the Kupferschiefer are much smaller.[156]

Mining has been documented since 1460 in the Richelsdorf Mountains and went through a first boom in the sixteenth century. In 1708 cobalt production started and in 1870 barite mining. In 1840 falling copper prices caused serious problems. Not until 1934 was there a temporary revival resulting from successful research work. The exploration programme ran until 1942, comprising about 80 deep borings and the sinking of three shafts and extensive mine workings based on them. For the minable area of the two synclines of 37 km^2, a possible total reserve of 40 000 000 tonne of ore without mining loss, with 0·5–3% of copper and a content of 400 000 tonne of copper, was estimated. After the construction of a mill and a copper smelter in Sontra, extraction began in 1939.

During the production periods from 1939 to 1945 and 1948 to 1954 a total of 2 000 000 tonne of ore with a content of 15 300 tonne of copper and 7 tonne of silver was extracted. In 1955 the mine had to be shut down because of technical difficulties—particularly water problems—and poor profitability, without the deposit being exhausted. In 1981 the St. Joe–Preussag consortium started an extensive exploration programme with more than 50 deep borings in the Richelsdorf Mountains and in other parts of the Hessian Depression.

Other copper orefields and prospects in Hessian Depression As in the Richelsdorf Mountains, the numerous other outcrops of the Kupferschiefer at the margin of the depression and Palaeozoic denuded anticlines in its interior gave rise to extensive mining already in the Middle Ages, especially in the fourteenth and fifteenth centuries and probably earlier. The ores consisted mostly of secondary enrichments close to the surface, with copper contents of more than 1% and silver contents of more than 10 ppm.

Palaeogeographically, the areas to the southeast and northwest of the Hunsrück–Oberharz rise are distinguished by the existence of thick Rotliegende sediments in the Saar–Selke trough and their almost complete lack to the northwest of the rise. Here the coarsely clastic rocks of the northwest German Upper Rotliegende basin are first exposed on the margin of the Harz near Seesen and reach under the Weser River up to the latitude of Göttingen.[166]

In higher parts of the rise the Kupferschiefer (5–20 cm thick with a copper content of less than 0·5%) is exposed near Baumbach on Fulda River and in the Unterwerra Mountains. Near Baumbach, Albungen and Witzenhausen (2–4, Fig. 42) it has been mined since the Middle Ages and repeatedly worked for short periods—for the last time in 1849 near Albungen. Old mines near Walkenried–Steina and Bad Lauterberg, as well as to the west of the Eichsfeld rise, the northeast part of the Hunsrück–Oberharz rise near Osterode (5 and 6, Fig. 42), give evidence of similar attempts in the West Harz. On the rise near Scharzfeld there is no Kupferschiefer.

At Neuekrug-Hahausen, 10 km NNE of Seesen, shale 30 cm thick locally carries 1 and 3% of copper. Favourable discoveries apparently led in 1862 to the establishment of the Neu-Mansfeld mine and a smelter. Water inflows into the mine, difficulties in the working of the heavily disturbed seams and in the smelting process forced the operation to shut down after a short period.

The Kupferschiefer is common in an aberrant nearshore facies at the eastern margin of the Rheinische Schiefergebirge from Marsberg up to the Frankenberg Bight. The copper ores, and in the Frankenberg Bight also Cu–Ag and to some extent lead ores, occurring here at the level of the Kupferschiefer and in the upper layers of the Zechstein 1 and 2, were exploited in numerous places. Near Marsberg (8, Fig. 42) alongside the copper stockwork in the Lower Carboniferous the Kupferschiefer in the facies of the copper marl was worked until 1850. The lower bituminous limestone is intercalated with 10 to 30 ore-bearing marl layers between 0·5 and 5 m thick. Eight km to the south of Marsberg a copper clay seam 30–60 cm thick occurs near Leitmar in the Adorf Bay (9, Fig. 42), and is assigned to the lower Zechstein 2 (Table 33). Small-scale mining ended in 1824.

basin Kupferschiefer in normal facies was struck 5 km NNE of Korbach. The mining declined in the early nineteenth century and was halted in 1867. Despite numerous attempts at resumption, the latest between 1940 and 1942, there has been no revival.

Whereas at the eastern margin of the Kellerwald only the higher Zechstein 1 is exposed, it occurs in a local brackish-lagoonal facies in the Frankenberg Bight. The finely clastic carbonate Stäteberg seam 2–10 m thick is restricted to the immediate surroundings of Frankenberg (11, Fig. 42). The mineralization, copper minerals along with pyrite and galena, was workable only in the lowest parts of the seam. Much more important was the younger Geismar copper clay seam 1–2 m thick, which was widely distributed in the eastern part of the Bight (12, Fig. 42; Table 33). It consists of grey calcareous clays with plant remains (Frankenberg 'corn ears' = *Ullmannia bronni*) and contains, in particular, chalcocite along with chalcopyrite, tetrahedrite, pyrargyrite and native silver. The ore, with an average content of 1·0% Cu and 11 ppm

Table 33 Zechstein stratigraphy at western margin of Hessian Depression. After Sauer[167] (stratigraphic position of Stäteberg seam confirmed by Visscher[168])

General lithostratigraphy		Local stratigraphy	
Former	Cyclic[142]	Korbach Bight	Frankenberg Bight
Buntsandstein (Bunter)		Grenzsande (boundary sands)	Bausandstein (structural sands)
Upper Zechstein	Zechstein 4	Red pelite	Younger conglomerates — ? - ? — ? — ? Yellow sandstones
	Zechstein 3	Platy dolomite	
		Platy sandstones and conglomerates	
		Lettenzone (Clay bed)	Geismar beds with Geismar copper seam
	Zechstein 2	Cavernous limestone	
		Lettenzone with gypsum and Leitmar copper seam	
Middle Zechstein	Zechstein 1	Schaumkalk (aphrite)	Stäteberg seam
Lower Zechstein		Stinkkalk (fetid limestone)	
		Productus bed / Kupfermergel	Older conglomerates
Rotliegende			
Silurian to Lower Carboniferous			

Much more important was the working of copper marls at Korbach in the eighteenth century (10, Fig. 42). In the neighbourhood of Thalitter in the narrow Korbach Bight the ores show a quick change in facies. Some 12–15 marl layers, of a total thickness from 30 to 75 cm intercalated between the limestones, make up one-quarter to one-third of the entire thickness and bear up to 4% of copper. In further drilling in the

Ag, was extracted from 1590 to 1818 and again for a short period in the second half of the nineteenth century.[119]

The southernmost Kupferschiefer exposures are in the Saar–Selke trough on the northeast slope of the Büdingen Rise with the old mining districts of Hain-Gründau, at Bieber and at the edge of the crystalline Spessart in the Schöllkrippen area (13–15, Fig. 42).

The Z1 clay occurs here as copper clay and reaches a thickness of some centimetres to 2 m. The mineralization consists of fahlore, galena and chalcopyrite with an average content of 0·4% copper, 0·9% lead and 40 ppm silver.[119] Especially near Bieber there was intensive mining in the eighteenth century. At the beginning of the nineteenth century the works had to be shut down.

Non-ferrous metal mineralization in the Triassic

Elevated contents of non-ferrous metals are common in many Triassic rocks. Only exceptionally do they attain concentrations that have led to mining investigations or to exploitation. Predominantly copper ores are found in the Bunter, whereas mainly galena, chalcopyrite, sphalerite and barite occur in the Muschelkalk and Keuper, which are mainly particularly well established in the galena layer of the lower Gipskeuper in south Germany, strongly linked to the palaeogeography.[169,170]

Copper ores in the Bunter
Hänsel and Schulz[171] reported historic and prehistoric mining of copper ores of the red-bed type and copper smelting in Helgoland in the Bronze Age and in the Middle Ages (around A.D. 1200 from ^{14}C dating). The ore bed, just over 1 m thick, was described by Lorenzen.[172] It occurs in the Middle Bunter and contains irregularly distributed malachite, cuprite and native copper partly in lenses and in nests. There are locally layers 0·5 to more than 5 cm thick with a copper content of about 10%. The main part of the deposit is supposed to have been in the 'copper cliffs' in the former northern part of the island, which is eroded today. Fesser[173] gave a survey of the mineral content and discussed the question of genesis.

Sulphidic ores in the Middle and Upper Triassic
Northern Germany According to Mempel,[174] in northern Germany, the 8–15 m thick Trochitenkalk especially (mo1, Table 34) and subordinately the 100-m thick Wellenkalk (mu), contain strata-bound Pb(Zn), occurring mostly in stringers and veins, which are interpreted as redeposited and recrystallized primary material. Copper in low quantities is found only in the Lower Keuper and zinc and lead in about the same amounts in the Upper Keuper. In addition, Hofmeister and co-workers[175] mentioned bedded intercalations with predominant sphalerite and contents of 10–300 ppm Pb and 100–1000 ppm Zn in the Trochitenkalk. Extensive research work, which included the application of geochemical and isotopic-geochemical methods, led to the conclusion that Pb, Ba and Sr were redistributed together with the calcite by lateral secretion mainly via formation waters. The sulphur of the sulphates originates from the saliferous deposits of the Middle Muschelkalk and the sulphur of the sulphides was formed by bacterial reduction of the sulphates. Zinc, also a syngenetic component of the sediments, behaved differently from lead during the diagenetic and post-diagenetic rearrangement. Also the vein 2–20 cm thick with galena, calcite and barite, occurring in the Külf near Alfeld on the Leine River, which was examined repeatedly for mining purposes, belongs, according to the geochemical data, to the same paragenesis.[176]

Southern Germany In southern Germany, besides

Table 34 *Metal concentrations and ore deposits in the German Triassic*[177]

Region / Stages	South German Basin		North German Basin‡
	Schwarzwald borders*	Oberpfalz†	
Keuper	Cu Schaffhausen Pb (Cu, Ba) Bleiglanzbank	Pb Weissenberg Pb { Creußen, Bodenmühle Hahnbach, Eschenfelden Wollau, Bayreuth Pb { Freihung, Hahnbach, Eschenfelden, Mauleler Wald	Pb–Zn Osnabrück, Mittelweser, Aller
Muschelkalk	mo2 Pb Reiselfingen mo1 Zn–Pb Wiesloch / Pechelbronn mm Pb sporadic mu3 Pb–Zn 2 to 3 mu2 Pb(Zn) to 4 mu1/2 Pb(Zn) PbS–Grenzbank mu1 Pb to 6 Bänke Cu Villingen	Pb Creußen Pb Grafenwöhr	mo1 Pb(Zn, Ba) Weser-Leine-Bergland, Hildesheim, Salzgitter, Helpup, Westphalia mu Pb(Zn) Süd-Niedersachsen
Buntsandstein	Cu Eschbach, Nordschweiz	Pb, Cu, Ba Hirschau Schnaittenbach	Cu Helgoland

* After Hofmann.[178] Galena bed of the Middle Keuper after Weinelt.[169]
† After Gudden,[179] von Schwarzenberg,[180] Klemm and von Schwarzenberg[181] and Schmid.[182]
‡ After Mempel;[174] mo1 after Hofmeister and co-workers;[175] Helgoland after Lorenzen[172] and Hänsel and Schulz.[171]

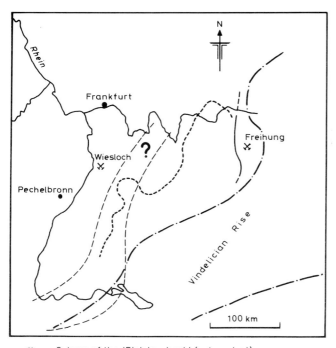

Fig. 45 *Palaeogeographic sketch map of Southern Germany showing border of Vindelician Rise in Late Triassic, lead deposit of Freihung in Upper Palatinate Bight, and zinc–lead deposit of Wiesloch on border of Tertiary Rhine Graben. After Walther*[177]

numerous marl and carbonate banks containing galena, barite and other sulphides, sporadic lead and zinc deposits have come to be formed. They were worked for long periods near Freihung in the Oberpfalz at the Muschelkalk–Keuper boundary, as well as near Wiesloch in the Trochitenkalk (Fig. 45; Table 34). Post-sedimentary processes have contributed in various degrees to the present picture of the deposits. The numerous ore discoveries in the Wellenkalk at the eastern and southern edge of the Black Forest between Rottweil and Basel were first reviewed by Hofmann.[178] Moreover, the distribution of ores is known at least up to Heilbronn. Most common is the boundary bed 5–40 cm thick between the Lower and Middle Wellenkalk, which is called the 'galena bed' (not to be confused with the well-known galena bed of the Middle Keuper).

In its footwall occur up to six and in the hanging-wall three or four 'bedlets', bearing more or less sporadic sulphides. In addition, there are two to three irregularly mineralized 'bedlets' in the deepest parts of the Middle Muschelkalk. Besides one main paragenesis with pyrite, galena, chalcopyrite, minor sphalerite and (so far analysed always As) fahlore as well as rare native As, Hofmann mentioned a similar paragenesis linked to the lowest layers of the Wellenkalk, without galena but with some bornite, which is comparable with chalcopyrite as the dominant mineral in the Bunter. The metals were carried into a neritic zone with increased salinity, showing something of the character of a tidal flat, by continental waters coming from the Vindelician Rise, and deposited by early diagenesis. A late diagenetic dolomitization, widely distributed in the north, is younger than the emplacement of the ores. The heavy metal content of the boundary layer (mu 1/2, Table 34) was given by Hofmann as 0·1–1%.

In the Trochitenkalk of the Kraichgau Depression stratiform sphalerite mineralization occurs.[183] Between 1950 and 1958 similar mineralization of the Middle and Upper Muschelkalk of the Zabern Depression was struck in oil drillings near Pechelbronn at a depth between 1000 and 2000 m. They bear sphalerite, calcite, dolomite and occasionally fluorite.[9] The Zn–Pb deposit of Wiesloch, which is a stratabound occurrence in the Trochitenkalk, underwent its main development in the course of Tertiary fault tectonics (see later).

The galena bed of the lower Middle Keuper, with an average thickness of 20 cm, is exposed in the eastern part of the South German Basin and in the Thuringian Basin in the foreland of the Vindelician–Bohemian rise. Weinelt[169] described the strict palaeogeographic binding of non-ferrous metal sulphides to pelitic sediments rich in organic substances. The ore minerals are galena and chalcopyrite along with rare sphalerite and subordinate pyrite. Barite, however, decreases within the pelitic facies towards the inner parts of the basin, but can be found also in the quartzitic and sandy areas closer to the shore. Weinelt gave as the average content of the ore-bearing layers 0·35% Pb and 0·09% Cu. Schweizer[170] interpreted the galena bed, on the basis of geochemical examinations, as being the result of a regression phase under conditions similar to a 'sabkha'. The metals were carried from the Vindelician continent to the deposition area by a groundwater current in the green marls underlying the galena bed, the marls having been formed during the previous transgression phase. The concentration of metal increased gradually by evaporation in the progression from the continent to the shore. In the green marls metals were deposited by adsorptive binding and in the galena layer as sulphide by H_2S derived from organic substances. The metals were released by the weathering of Triassic arkoses and represent trace metals and barium of the potash feldspar. The mineralization also extends far into the basin in other marlstone beds. Accordingly, the *Acrodus* bed in the lowest Estheria beds to the north of Ansbach contains galena, sphalerite, pyrite and barite.[184] Kühn[185] described similar deposits of a comparable genesis from the Thuringian Basin—for instance, a sphalerite bed from the uppermost Muschelkalk, a galena bed in the lower Middle Keuper and the copper-bearing Lehrberg beds from the upper Middle Keuper. To the north of the

Thuringian Basin only the sphalerite bed of the Harz foreland was found to be ore-bearing.

Mineralization in the Oberpfalz (Upper Palatinate) Bight and Freihung lead deposit In the Oberpfalz (Upper Palatinate) Bight of the South German Triassic Basin there repeatedly occur similar metal concentrations in the strata between the Middle Bunter and the Keuper in the approximate area of Bayreuth, Sulzbach–Rosenberg and Weiden. Gudden[179] described these metal concentrations in their horizontal and vertical distribution. The galena beds are an exception only insofar as they were formed under special palaeogeographical conditions—according to Schweizer,[170] a regression that dried up wide peripheral areas. Near Freihung, possibly secondary enrichment processes in connexion with movements on the younger fracture zone of Freihung have led to economically interesting concentrations. The primary ore minerals are galena, minor sphalerite, rare pyrite as well as some very subordinate minerals. von Schwarzenberg[180] and Klemm and von Schwarzenberg[181] arrived at a similar genetic concept to that of Schweizer[170] for the formation of the galena bed. The ores are restricted to the transition areas from grey clays to sandstone (Fig. 46) and are especially concentrated in areas of rapid facies change. Near Wollau, about 17 km NNE of Freihung, the variable lead-bearing strata extend to a length of 5 km, with contents of lead locally reaching a maximum of 2% over a thickness of several metres. Schmid[182] confirmed this genetic interpretation and showed on the basis of new drilling results that (1) the greatest lead concentrations occur in an area of southwest–northeast strike and are known to extend just 30 km to either side of Freihung; (2) the ores therefore are restricted to the former margin of the basin and (3) the ore facies has evolved regressively towards the margin of the basin from the Lower Muschelkalk to the Middle Keuper. As in the Freihung deposit, the galena is locally replaced to a large extent by cerussite, which not infrequently shows a fine dispersion with covellite.[180] Associated minerals are pyromorphite and coronadite. The cerussitization goes along with kaolinization of the potash feldspars in the wallrock. von Schwarzenberg[180] interpreted Freihung as an epigenetic deposit formed by weathering of a primary sedimentary sulphate mineralization of the Wollau type. Probably movements on the Freihung fracture zone made the galena mineralization accessible to subaerial agents, beginning at the Lower to Upper Cretaceous boundary.

The lead ore occurs in a strata assemblage of an average thickness of 20 m belonging to the Upper Muschelkalk and/or to the Lower Keuper. The lead ore-bearing layers consist of light grey and reddish sandstones, poorly indurated, with intercalated silt and mudstone layers ('Letten'). The sandstones as well as the mudstones contain lead ore in the form of

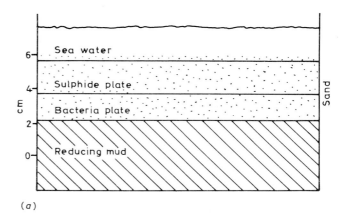

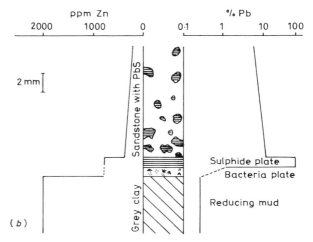

Fig. 46 *Experiment (a) and outcrop (b) with syngenetic precipitation of base metals. After Klemm and von Schwarzenberg.[181] (a) Simplified after Suckow and Schwartz;[295] (b) section from grey clay to sandstone within Estheria beds near Wollau, northeast Weiden (bacteria plate, fine sands(tones) with plant detritus; sulphide plate, millimetre-thick crust of galena)*

cerussite and subordinate galena in a horizontally and vertically irregular distribution and concentration.

The whole complex is more or less steeply upturned along a Saxonian fault zone and strikes northwest-southeast in an outcrop about 8 km long, thus having provided working points for the old miners at numerous places close to the surface.

A document dated 1427 gives the oldest sign of lead ore working already existing at that time near Freihung in the Bavarian Oberpfalz (Upper Palatinate). Exploitation probably dates to the early years of the twelfth century. In 1569 the mining locality, the name of which derives from the mining privileges given to it, received the right to hold markets, to bear a coat of arms and a seal, proof of its importance at that time. Frequently interrupted by wars and devastations, lead ores were extracted for centuries, mining ceasing in 1945.

After the older mining periods, which were mostly restricted to areas close to the surface because of difficulties in dewatering the mines, a 'Bavarian Lead

Mining Company Limited' (registered under English law!) mined between 1877 and 1890 in a more generous way, extracting the last major batch of ore. During the second world war there took place only exploratory mining through 'Bayerische Berg-, Hütten- und Salzwerke AG'. On the basis of this exploration and more in the 1950s the present-day proven, probable and potential reserves to a depth of 350 m and to a lateral extent of 5 km along the hanging-wall of the fault system were estimated at 200 000 tonne Pb with a run-of-mine lead content of 2–3%. In the footwall of the fault zone two deep borings established similar contents of lead, which are not included in the estimate of reserves owing to their location at a depth of 800 m.

The lead content of the deposit is syngenetic-synsedimentary, a later remineralization and migration of material along the fault zone contributing to local changes in concentrations.

Iron ore deposits

Stratiform iron ore deposits are very common in sediments of the epi-Variscan Platform in northwestern and southern Germany (Figs. 47 and 48). The deposits belong to the Jurassic or Cretaceous systems. One deposit near Bremen is of Neogene age (Fig. 49); the Palaeogene iron ores at the borders of the Alps are discussed later.[187,188]

The iron ores form seams and deposits locally more than 100 m thick. The wallrocks are calcareous, marly, arenaceous and argillaceous sediments. Depending on the tectonic stress, the ores occur in flat or steep bedding. Tectonic and to a degree halokinetic processes, as well as palaeogeographic conditions and

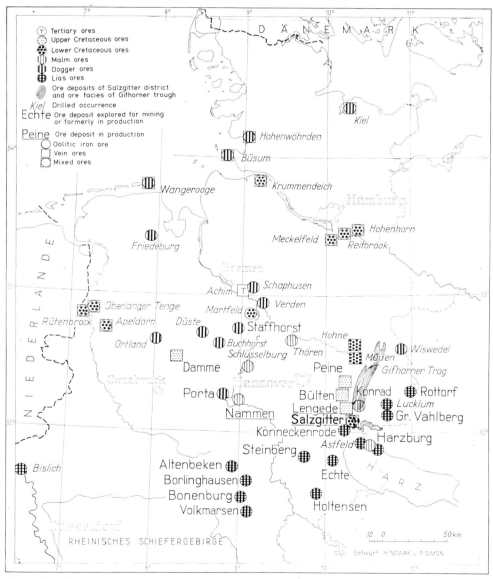

Fig. 47 *More important post-Palaeozoic marine-sedimentary iron ore deposits in northwest Germany. After Simon in Bottke et al.*[187] (*Nammen the last operating mine in 1984*)

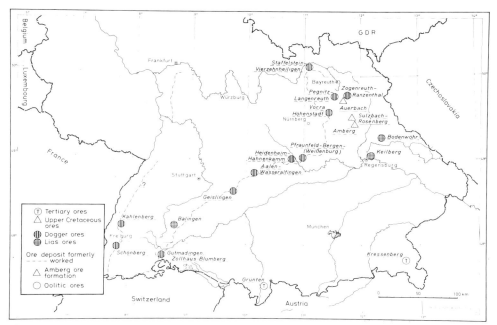

Fig. 48 *More important post-Palaeozoic sedimentary iron ore deposits in south Germany. After Simon in Frank et al.*[188] (*Auerbach the last operating mine in 1984*)

transgressions, were causal factors in the generation of ores, which were frequently synsedimentarily enriched in special ore traps and deeps (so-called 'Kolke').

The deposits that are situated in the mountainous region are usually exposed to the surface and have therefore been known for a long time. In the northwest German lowland the deposits occur down to more than 2000 m and are overlain by younger cover formations. These iron ore deposits were only discovered in the process of oil exploration in the past 50 years. The extraction of iron ores has reached a depth of 1200 m in the Gifhorn trough (Konrad mine) in northwestern Germany and 200 m in southern Germany.

The iron ore deposits in the Jurassic and in the Lower Cretaceous are of marine-sedimentary origin and mainly consist of oolitic ores of the minette type, with varying contents of conglomeratic ore. The iron ores of the Upper Cretaceous and the Neogene are conglomeratic only (Peine–Ilsede type) and of a marine-sedimentary origin. The iron ores of the Upper Cretaceous in the foreland of the Bohemian Massif in southern Germany are earthy to lumpy (Amberg ore formation) and are terrestrial-sedimentary formed in a lacustrine environment. Based on geochemical and mineralogical research results, marine influences on the ore formation are assumed, but this is contested on palaeontological grounds.

The iron in the above-mentioned ores is bound to the minerals chamosite, goethite, hematite, magnetite and siderite. The most important gangue minerals are quartz, clay minerals and mostly organically derived calcite. With a content of Fe of around 25–48%, the

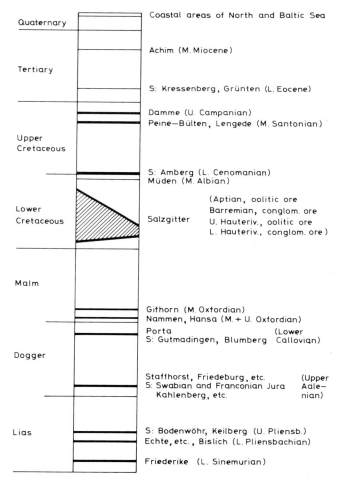

Fig. 49 *Sedimentary iron ore deposits in epi-Variscan platform cover in Federal Republic of Germany (S, deposits in south Germany). After Kolbe*[189]

ores either have a lime or silica surplus or a balanced lime–silica ratio.

The German ores have relatively low contents of iron and high contents of slag constituents and phosphorus in comparison to the rich foreign ores and concentrates that are mainly worked today. Some ores can be used only after processing and/or because of favourable location and transport conditions. Others are important additives used in the smelting of foreign ores. Therefore today only ores from the Upper Cretaceous and Upper Jurassic are exploited, mainly by smelters in Bremen and near Osnabrück as well as in Sulzbach-Rosenberg, east of Nuremberg. The mining of the Lower and Middle Jurassic ores and their smelting in the Ruhr area and in Austria ceased a few years ago for economic reasons. Furthermore, in 1982 the extraction of Lower and Upper Cretaceous iron ores in the Salzgitter–Peine–Ilsede district was also terminated. Especially in the Jurassic and Cretaceous rocks there are still major ore reserves that are not economically minable today.

Ores of the Lower Jurassic
Oolitic iron ores of the Lower Jurassic (Sinemurian and Carixian) are mainly distributed in the foreland of the Harz and the Rheinische Schiefergebirge in northwestern Germany. The basic ores, with a content of 25–28% Fe, 0.4–0.7% P and a thickness of 10 m, were extracted until 1963, especially in the Echte and Friederike mines in the Harz foreland. Half of the reserves of about 70 000 000 tonne of iron ores of the Lower Jurassic that still exist in northwestern Germany is accounted for by the Bislich deposit on the Lower Rhine, which so far has only been drilled. The ore deposits of Echte and Bislich consist of bands of green chamositic and red goethitic–hematitic ore.

In Bavaria the iron ores of the Lower Jurassic (Domerian) were extracted before 1877 along the Pfahl (quartz reef) near Bodenwöhr. At the Keilberg near Regensburg 20 000 000 tonne of iron ore remains.

Ores of the Middle Jurassic (Dogger)
Oolitic iron ores of the Aalenian were extracted in southern Germany from the Middle Ages to the recent past. In the mines near Geislingen, Aalen, Wasseralfingen and Pegnitz in the Swabian–Franconian Alb the siliceous ore rich in quartz was 2 m thick, containing 27–34% Fe and 0.3% P. Near Pegnitz the crude ore with a 29% Fe and 40% SiO_2 content was enriched by magnetic separation, leading to a concentrate with 39% Fe and 19% SiO_2, which was exported from time to time to Austria. In the Kahlenberg mine in the Upper Rhine Depression near Freiburg the basic ore, rich in lime, reached a thickness of up to 11 m, containing 18% Fe and 28% CaO as well as 0.3% P. The fine ore was enriched by magnetic separation leading to a concentrate containing 37% Fe and a $CaO:SiO_2$ ratio of 1.3:1.

In the lowland of northwestern Germany the iron ore deposits of the Aalenian were discovered in the progress of oil exploration at depths of 600–1700 m after the second world war. The deposits of Staffhorst near Nienburg/Weser, Ortland near Quakenbrück, Schaphusen near Bremen and Friedeburg near Wilhelmshaven contain reserves of about 660 000 000 tonne of ore, which are characterized by contents of 35–48% Fe and 0.7–1.5% P and by low contents of lime and silica. In Staffhorst and Ortland the ore is 3–5 m thick, in Schaphusen up to 11 m and in Friedeburg up to 17 m. The bedding is generally shallow trough shaped. The ore consists of chamosite–oolite, which merges into magnetite–oolite (Staffhorst, Schaphusen) or hematite–oolite (Friedeburg) more than 2 m thick. Hitherto, the Staffhorst ore has only been worked in an exploratory operation to a depth of 1030 m. The ores are a resource that cannot be exploited economically today.

The oolitic iron ores of the Callovian were mined in southern Germany near Blumberg and Gutmadingen on the Danube River up to 1942. A concentrate with 38% Fe was produced from crude ore with only 22–23% Fe. The ore seam has a thickness of 3 m. The reserves are considerable, but at the moment not economically minable.

In the Callovian of northwestern Germany the Wittekind seam (1.9 m thick) was worked up to 1962 at the Porta Westfalica near Minden. The ore contains greyish clay-mineral ooids and a siderite groundmass. They contain 25% Fe and 0.6% P with a silica surplus.

Ores of the Upper Jurassic (Malm)
Oolitic iron ores of the Upper Jurassic are very common in northwestern Germany. They belong to the 'coral oolite' (Oxfordian). Near Nammen in the Wesergebirge the 4–6 m thick 'cliff seam' is mined in galleries. The ore contains 13–15% Fe, 9–10% SiO_2 and 33–35% CaO and is used as calcareous fluxing ore in smelters in Bremen and near Osnabrück. Production amounts to a maximum of >400 000 tonne per year. A similar calcareous fluxing ore was extracted up to 1960 near Harlingerode at the northern edge of the Harz.

In the Gifhorn trough between Salzgitter and Vorhop–Wahrenholz, 20 km to the north of Gifhorn, north of Braunschweig, the Upper Jurassic iron ore occurs at a depth of 800–1500 m. The iron reserves amount to some 1 400 000 000 tonne. Extraction started in 1960 in the Konrad mine (1200 m deep) near Salzgitter–Bleckenstedt in the southern part of the trough and reached its climax in 1973 with >700 000 tonne per year. Since then production has gone steadily down and had almost entirely ceased by the end of 1976 for economic reasons. The ore has a thickness of 11–18 m and contains, with a balanced lime–silica ratio, 30–34% Fe and 0.35% P.

Ores of the Lower Cretaceous

The oolitic and conglomeratic iron ores of the Lower Cretaceous (Salzgitter type) are very common in northwestern Germany and have been examined and extracted in many places. Their thickness can reach more than 100 m, with an iron content that ranges from 25 to 48%. These ores mostly show a high silica surplus; consequently, their industrial use did not reach a larger scale until 1937 when the processes of acid smelting and desulphurization with soda were developed. Based on those processes, the smelter in Salzgitter was built, where very large reserves of iron ores of the Lower Cretaceous had been found. After 1950 7 000 000 tonne per year of iron ores was extracted in the Salzgitter district. In very recent years economic reasons forced the closure of operations. The last mine to be shut down (in 1982) was the Haverlahwiese mine. Since 1938 this mine had produced >81 000 000 tonne of ore, of which 14 000 000 tonne was opencast; there are still large ore reserves left. In the Salzgitter district 165 000 000 tonne of Lower Cretaceous iron ores has been extracted to date with 50 000 000 tonne of iron.

The iron ore deposits in the Salzgitter district were formed in narrow bays of the Lower Cretaceous sea located immediately on the coast of the adjacent continent to the south. Typical of this district are the so called 'potholes' (Kolke)[189]—graben-like submarine-synsedimentary basins on the sea-floor, which subsided over flexures or faults, and were filled with ores and minor quantities of adjacent rock. The formation of the 'potholes' is related to tectonic movements and the migration of Permian salt at depth. The ore comes from the siderite concretions in the clay rocks of the Lower and Middle Jurassic, which, as source rocks, were being eroded on the adjacent landmass. According to the intensity of the tectonic movements and the associated relief energy, the siderite concretions reached the potholes and were simply reworked and oxidized as conglomeratic ores (goethite fragments), or the ore dissolved and was available for the formation of oolites. The potholes may be more than 1000 m along strike and contain iron ore deposits more than 100 m thick (Fig. 50).

Ores of the Upper Cretaceous

Large conglomeratic ore deposits of the Upper Cretaceous Peine–Ilsede type occur in northwestern Germany in the area of Peine–Bülten–Ilsede–Lengede, to the west and southwest of Braunschweig and near Damme in south Oldenburg. The ore comes from the siderite concretions in the clay rocks of the Lower Cretaceous, which are reworked, oxidized and enriched as marine placers in front of the shore of the Upper Cretaceous sea.[190,191]

The ores are 2–20 m thick and contain 25–32% Fe as well as 0·6–1·6% P. In Bülten and Peine the ore has a calcareous matrix (basic ores with 23–25% CaO and 6% SiO_2). In Lengede and Damme the ore has a marly matrix and wet-mechanical treatment is easy. For economic reasons all the mines have been closed. The Bülten and Lengede mines are considered to be exhausted. Altogether, 140 000 000 tonne of Upper Cretaceous iron ore with 25% Fe was extracted in northwestern Germany.

In the Oberpfalz (Upper Palatinate) the sedimentary iron ores of the Amberg formation were formed during the Upper Cretaceous in a limnic environment, possibly under temporary marine influences. In pockets and troughs of the Upper Jurassic limestone these ores form stratiform deposits up to 4 km long, 500 m wide and more than 50 m thick shaped like lenses or sills. Goethite ore with 42–49% Fe and siderite ore with 35–39% Fe can be distinguished. Both varieties show an earthy to lumpy appearance. The southwest-verging overthrusting on the fault zone of the Bavarian Pfahl, with free movement of the upper block, preserved the unconsolidated ores from

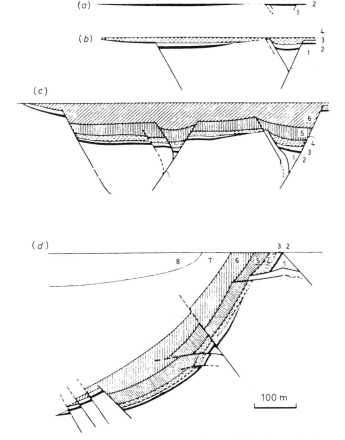

Fig. 50 *Scheme of development of ore-filled depression (so-called 'Kolk') in Early Cretaceous Salzgitter iron ore field. After Kolbe.[189] (a) Beginning of subsidence and ore sedimentation; (b) extension of 'Kolk' during ore sedimentation; (c) end of subsidence after accumulation of around 100 m of iron ore; (d) present situation after post-Cretaceous upturning of 'Kolk' connected with countercurrent fault tectonics; 1, footwall; 2–6, iron ore beds; 7 + 8, hanging-wall*

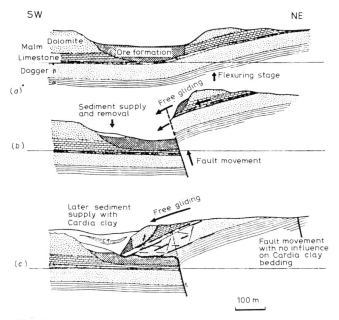

Fig. 51 *Scheme of development of fault zones connected with formation of iron ore deposits of Amberg type during Late Cretaceous in northeast Bavaria. After Gudden.*[179] *(a) Formation of karstic relief and beginning of tectonic strain with formation of flexure zone and of long karstic basins during Lower Cretaceous; later, during early Cenomanian, limnic sedimentation of iron ore; (b) beginning of erosion of ore during Middle Cenomanian; reverse faulting of hanging-wall on to orebody protecting iron ore from further erosion; (c) marine transgression during Late Cenomanian with continuation of synsedimentary tectonics (C. T., Cardium clay, Coniacian)*

erosion (Fig. 51).[179] These ores have been worked since the early Middle Ages in the area Amberg–Sulzbach–Rosenberg–Auerbach (near Nuremberg) for the production of iron and partly for use as coloured earth. Today the Leonie mine near Auerbach produces about 500 000 tonne of ore annually, which is smelted in Sulzbach–Rosenberg. To date, more than 50 000 000 tonne of Upper Cretaceous iron ore with

Table 35 *Mine production from Mesozoic and Caenozoic iron ore deposits in Federal Republic of Germany*[20]

	Crude ore $t \times 10^6$	%	Fe content, $t \times 10^6$	Percentage of country's ore production
Tertiary	1	1	0.3	1
Late Cretaceous				
North Germany	143	31	35	
South Germany	50	11	20	45
Early Cretaceous (Salzgitter)	165	36	50	
Late Jurassic	35	8		
Middle Jurassic	48	11	22	12
Early Jurassic	15	3		

20 000 000 tonne Fe has been worked in northeastern Bavaria (Table 35).

Caenozoic ores
Near Achim on the Weser River to the south of Bremen conglomeratic iron ore in the Lower Tertiary cover rocks was discovered and examined after the second world war. The ores occur at a depth of 6–65 m and reach a thickness of 3–15 m; they contain 25–27% Fe and 0.3–0.45% P with a high silica surplus. Besides the goethite pebbles, there are glauconite and siderite with quartz as the main gangue mineral. The ore is not economically minable.

Recent ilmenite sands, containing zircon and minor rutile, monazite and garnet, occur along the coast of Schleswig Holstein as well as on the East Friesian Islands and their foreshores.[192]

Industrial minerals

Some deposits are discussed below that do not belong to the stratigraphic sequence of the epi-Variscan Platform Cover. In addition, reference is made here to deposits of industrial minerals that are mentioned elsewhere. Not mentioned are graphite, steatite and talc, gypsum and anhydrite and calcite, which are dealt with in other sections. A summary is given of all the important deposits of industrial minerals in the FRG.*

Quartz, quartzite, silica sand and siliceous rocks
The following SiO_2 raw materials with more than 95% (often more than 98%) SiO_2 are extracted in the FRG: vein quartz, rock quartzite, cement quartzite, quartz sand and kieselguhr (diatomite), the inorganic tripoli and the unique siliceous earth of Neuburg on the Danube (Table 36).

Vein quartz and quartzites Vein quartz is extracted in the FRG in the Bavarian Pfahl and in the Taunus Mountains. For the production of optical glasses it should contain more than 99.7% SiO_2, for silicon metal more than 99% and for ferrosilicon and chrome-silicon more than 98% SiO_2. The quartz of the Pfahl contains, on average, more than 2 wt% Al_2O_3; material containing less than 0.5 wt% Al_2O_3 can be extracted by selective working at a few places only. Accompanying quartz veins of smaller thickness are of better quality.

Near Usingen in the eastern Taunus a quartz vein 30–40 m thick that strikes northwest and dips steeply to vertically is extracted in open-pits of some 50-m depth. The exposure of the vein is several kilometres long, but only a stretch of about 1000 m is workable. The quartz is partly pseudomorphous after barite. The vein contains irregularly distributed, in places abundant, wallrock fragments. The selectively extracted material shows an extreme purity and contains 99.5 (–99.9) wt% SiO_2.

---

* Very considerable assistance in the preparation of this section was provided by Professor V. Stein (Hannover) and Professor R. Weiss (Frechen), who kindly made available partly unpublished material (see also Stein[193]).

Table 36 *Stratigraphic position of deposits of quartz, quartzite, siliceous sand and siliceous rocks in Federal Republic of Germany*[194]

System	Vein quartz, quartzites and quartz gravel	Siliceous sand	Siliceous rocks
Quaternary	Hochterassenkiese, Early Quaternary	Many small deposits	Kieselguhr, Lower Saxony, Late Pleistocene
	———Kieseloolith-Schotter———		
Tertiary	Usingen vein Cement quartzite	Duingen, Frechen, Miocene Grasleben, Eocene Eisenberg, kaolinitic sand, Palaeogene	
Cretaceous		Haltern, Santonian Bodenstein, Aptian/Albian	Kieselerde, Neuburg, Early Turonian
Jurassic		Freihung, Dogger	
Triassic		Hirschau-Schnaittenbach, Middle Bunter	Tripoli, Middle Muschelkalk Pforzheim
Permian and Carboniferous	Pfahl, Hagendorf		
Devonian	Ems quartzite, Emsian Taunus quartzite, Siegenian		

Pegmatite quartz, as found near Hagendorf, has no economic importance today and rock crystals, which mostly contain >99.99 wt% SiO_2, have not yet been discovered in deposits in the FRG.

Within quartzites there is a distinction by texture and genesis into (1) *rock quartzite*, which was formed by metamorphic alteration, and shows a mosaic texture because of the recrystallization of SiO_2, and (2) *cement quartzite* with a high content of fine-grained siliceous cement, which was formed by the silicification of kaolinitic sand.

For use in the production of refractory materials the total of impurities should be <4 wt%; the chemical industry needs acid-resistant dense quartzite.

The rock quartzites of the Lower Devonian in the Hunsrück and the Taunus are of a region-wide importance (Taunus quartzite, Ems quartzite). In a southwest–northeast-striking quartzite band in the Taunus, quartzites of a thickness of about 80 m are exposed, dipping moderately steeply to almost vertically southeast. The deposit has a lateral extent of several kilometres. The chemical composition of the material fluctuates. By selective mining, material of a very pure quality with contents of 97.4–99.1 wt% SiO_2 is extracted. Cement quartzites follow the distribution of kaolinitic sands in the Westerwald, the Hessian and southern Lower Saxony hills. Of an especially good quality is the 'Herschbach type' (so called after the village 28 km NNW of Koblenz), with few larger, often corroded quartz individuals suspended within a groundmass cement of micro- to cryptocrystalline quartz. Also in the cement is found the clay component of the former kaolinitic sand. When the basal cement becomes coarser grained it merges into a granulose cement ('Hessen-quartzite type'). Quartzites of this type are of slightly inferior quality to those of the 'Herschbach type'.

The cement quartzites underlie an argillaceous or sandy overburden 4–6 m thick and often form large lenses 1·2–3 m thick near Herschbach and 4–6 m in the Hessian Mountain region. The silification varies locally very much. The reserves near Herschbach are quoted as 1 400 000 tonne of quartzite.

The quartz gravels of the Upper Pliocene Kieseloolith-Schotter in the area of the Neuwied Basin near Koblenz and in the Ville near Cologne consist mainly and locally of up to 99% of vein quartz and very subordinate quartzites and lydites. They reach a thickness of 15–30 m. In the Ville the gravel is separated and reworked to a salable product with a content of 99 wt% SiO_2.

Tertiary high-level terrace gravels are common near Bitburg and in the southern part of the Eifel Mountains, consisting almost entirely of vein quartz. They reach thicknesses of more than 10 m and are partly overlain by several metres of sand. The coarser grain fractions are partially used in the chemical industry.

Unlike the quartz sands, which are to be discussed later, the salable products of the SiO_2 raw material described so far have an average grain size generally less than 20 mm.

Silica sand and silica sandstone About 95% of the production of sand and gravel in the FRG of 300 000 000–400 000 000 tonne goes to the building industry and 15 000 000–20 000 000 tonne with a content of >98 wt% SiO_2 is used as raw material in different industries, mainly in the glass industry,[195] in foundries, the chemical and ceramic industries. They are called industrial sands and predominantly standardized in their physical and chemical characteristics by screening and washing.[196] Natural moulding sands contain kaolin and/or glauconite as binding agent.

Bleached, mostly friable and scarcely consolidated Mesozoic quartz sandstones are extracted mainly in the Oberpfalz and in the southwestern part of Münsterland Bight. Tertiary sands of industrial sand quality are quite common[194] (Table 36). The most important quartz-sand reserves of the FRG are in North Rhine–Westphalia in the shape of the deposits in the basin of the lower Rhine and near Haltern to the north of Recklinghausen. Major deposits in the Miocene reach thicknesses of 20 to some 40 m with a maximum of 8–15 m of overburden, in the area of Herzogenrath to the northeast of Aachen and near Frechen to the west of Cologne. The best quality material has only 0·02 wt% of Fe_2O_3. The reserves are estimated, within the area of Frechen, to be about 400 000 000 tonne. Near Haltern Upper Cretaceous white quartz sands are common. The average thicknesses amount to 100 m with a very low overburden. The best qualities reach 0·024 wt% Fe_2O_3. Reserves exceed 3 000 000 000 tonne.

In Bavaria the quartz sands of the kaolin deposit of Hirschau–Schnaittenbach in the Middle Bunter and the very friable Dogger sandstone to the north of Hischau are of outstanding economic importance. The crude kaolins, with a content of about 80 wt% of quartz sand and gravel, have a thickness of 15–55 m.[202] As there is almost no sand of homogeneous grain size, because of the short distance of transport to the deposition site the desired qualities are achieved by washing, screening and hydrosizing. The best qualities contain about 0·02 wt% Fe_2O_3. Annual production amounts to about 1 000 000 tonne of quartz sand and quartz powder. Reserves are at least 100 000 000 tonne. Between Hirschau and Freihung the Dogger, here 70–75 m thick, contains several sandstone horizons that are bleached and decomposed to a large extent into sand. The usable thicknesses often reach 15–20 m and locally more. The sands show a very narrow grain spectrum with ±80% of the grains between 0·1 and 0·2 mm and reach 0·01 wt% Fe_2O_3 after processing. The reserves exceed 20 000 000 tonne.

In the southeastern parts of Lower Saxony pure Tertiary sands are preserved in tectonic troughs. The best qualities can be found in the Hils trough near Duingen and near Helmstedt, where they form the underlying bed of the brown coal sequence. The thicknesses of the beds here reach more than 40 m and the best sands contain 0·012 wt% Fe_2O_3. Bleached and friable Lower Cretaceous Hils sandstone is extracted near Bodenstein to the northwest of Goslar. The Fe_2O_3 content here amounts to 0·03 wt%. In the northern and northwestern areas of Lower Saxony fine- to medium-grained quartz sands were deposited around the Tertiary–Quaternary transition; they are mined in several places, but are used only in exceptional cases as industrial sand. Other, mostly small, quartz sand deposits are known in the northern parts of Hesse, Rhineland Palatinate, in the Westerwald and in the upper Rhine Valley.

Kaolinitic sand and naturally bonded foundry sand were deposited in Palaeogene times in the Westerwald, in north Hesse, at the southern edge of the Lower Rhine Bight, in the Oberpfalz and in the upper Rhine Valley. The deposits are of local importance. The deposit of Eisenberg in the Pfalz, 25 km NNE of Kaiserslautern, is, however, of greater economic importance; here kaolinitic sands about 40 m thick have been worked for a long time.

Unconsolidated siliceous rocks These consist of >50% of organically or chemically deposited SiO_2 minerals. Such materials used in the FRG are kieselguhr from the Pleistocene, the Upper Cretaceous Neuburg siliceous earth and the Middle Triassic tripoli.

The kieselguhr (*Kieselgur* in German) deposits of northern Germany, which are quite important, occur in a strip 40 km wide in the Lüneburg Heath between Celle and Lüneburg. (*Gur* is a miner's expression for a pulpy, earthy liquid; a synonym for *Kieselgur* is diatomite.) The kieselguhr was discovered in 1836 and, after some futile attempts at utilization, mining was started in 1863. The extremely light and highly porous material with good filtration qualities was used as filling material for the dye industry, as packing material for glass carboys containing nitroglycerine and, later, to meet the demand as an insulating material for steam engines and steam piping. In 1867 Nobel used the absorptive capacity of kieselguhr when he invented dynamite by mixing it with nitroglycerine in the proportion 1:3. Until 1914 it was possible to satisfy world demand almost totally with a kieselguhr production of about 20 000 tonne and an export quota of 30%. In the following decades the production was continuously increased and in 1965 reached about 60 000 tonne, still corresponding to about 3% of world production. After 1950 the greater part was used in the fertilizer industry.

In the early 1970s kieselguhr was replaced in part by cheaper products and production declined (1970, 38 255 tonne; 1975, 18 768 tonne; 1980, 4933 tonne).[21] A research programme promoted by the government of Lower Saxony, starting in 1970, yielded, besides essential hints for technological improvements and usages, the following technical results.[197,198,199] The kieselguhr deposits (10–15 m thick) were deposited during the last interglacial period, in restricted areas even during the penultimate interglacial, in channels of a maximum extent of 4 km and a width of 1 km, which were filled in by fresh water lakes. These channels were formed subglacially during the preceding glaciations. The sides of the deposits are steep. The lamination was found to be a stratification with an annual rate of sedimentation of 1–2 mm. SiO_2 was supplied by inflows or by organic material that was blown into the basins. A volcanic involvement can definitely be excluded. The green, grey to white sediment contains 60–90% SiO_2 in a proportion of detrital material to opal 2–5:1, >20–<5% organic material, 6–<1% Fe as pyrite and clay minerals in low percentages or traces. The very porous material, dried at 105°C, contains, on average, 5% H_2O. The proven reserves amount to approximately 50 000 000 m^3, of which about two-thirds are concentrated in one deposit (Münster–Brehloh). The proportion of overburden to kieselguhr averages 1:1.

Small kieselguhr deposits were formed in the Miocene at the Vogelsberg in Hesse, where they are preserved under layers of basalt. They were mined for a short period in the middle of the nineteenth century.

A SiO_2 raw material unique in the world is the siliceous earth of Neuburg on the Danube River;[26,30,200] it is a light, extremely fine-grained and little cemented rock, containing, on average, 90 wt% SiO_2. It consists predominantly of quartz, opaline substances (organic silica) and kaolinite in a proportion of 4–6:1; 96% of the grains have diameters smaller than 112·5 μm, with 67·6% smaller than 20 μm (BGR analysis 10666). Remnants of siliceous sponges form 90% of the fraction of 20–60 μm and, on average, 50% of the coarser fractions. Scales of kaolinite loosely packed between roundish quartz grains with diameters just below 0·1 μm form a bulky fabric with a large inner surface area. The siliceous earth owes its great technical importance to this characteristic, together with the hardness of quartz and the white colour. The deposits occur in karst funnels in Upper Jurassic limestones and reach a lateral extent of 100 up to a maximum of 250 m and a thickness of about 40 m (in exceptional cases up to 100 m). Their Lower Turonian age is proved by fossils. Cornstones of the same age and a comparable facies and in some parts spongolites near Regensburg and in the northern Frankenalb are not minable because of their lime content. For the formation of the siliceous earths special conditions must be assumed. According to Streit,[200] the sediment must have been permeated by silica solutions while it was still covered by the sea—a process that had already led to the silicification of some parts. In the Tertiary there might have been a further episode of decalcification and silicification.

Siliceous earth was probably worked in Roman times and has been documented since the seventeenth century. Today there is open-pit working, and a few years ago there was also underground mining. The annual production now amounts to 100 000 tonne. The siliceous earth is processed to obtain different products, which find a variety of uses as filler for rubber, latex, plastics, adhesives, paints, as a carrier for chemical substances, in abrasive compounds, polishes and cleaning agents, and so on.

Weakly cemented siliceous rocks of a different, mostly (but not homogeneously) inorganic genesis are defined as tripoli. At the southern edge of the Kraichgau trough and at the southeast edge of the Odenwald a single layer 10–25 cm thick, and locally also two thin layers of a fine-grained siliceous rock, not composed of organisms, occur in the upper parts of the Middle Muschelkalk. It was extracted for centuries as 'tripoli' and constituted a valued polishing material. Metz and Weiner[201] described this material as a synsedimentary inorganic quartz pelite. It consists of 80–85% quartz and contains chemically 92·5% SiO_2. Opal was not observed. By use of electron microscopy grain sizes of <1–3 μm and radiographic particle sizes of 0·2 to 0·8 μm were measured, eluviation analysis giving a flat maximum between 6 and 20 μm. The deposits were discovered around 1745 and extracted in several places until 1925. From 1932 to 1966, with an interruption from 1944 to 1952, a mine near Pforzheim was operated, producing finally about 20 tonne per year. Total production is estimated at 1500–1700 tonne.

Feldspar and feldspar sand
The major part of the feldspar production of the FRG comes from the kaolin deposits of the Weiden Bight, mainly from Hirschau and Schnaittenbach, 70 km to the ENE of Nuremberg. Arkosic grit stones (70–100 m thick) of the Middle Bunter, representing the erosion debris of the Moldanubian crystalline basement, here contain 13–23% kaolinite, 0–7% feldspar and ca 80% quartz.[202] The exogenous kaolinization started during erosion and transport, but took place mainly *in situ*.[203] To the southeast of Schnaittenbach rocks with the highest contents of kaolinite are practically free of feldspar. To the west and, especially, to the north and the northeast of Freihung, 12 km to the north of Schnaittenbach, the content of feldspar increases to more than 20%, kaolinite decreasing to less than 5%. There is an annual production of about 350 000 tonne of kaolinite, 150 000 tonne of feldspar-sand (Table 5) and 1 000 000 tonne of quartz sand and quartz powder, as well as small quantities of heavy mineral concentrate. The reserves exceed 10 000 000 tonne of rock. Similar deposits with a smaller production are worked in north Franconia to the east of Coburg.

The kaolin mines near Tirschenreuth, 30 km to the northeast of Weiden, yield yearly 30 000 tonne of the 'Tirschenreuth pegmatite sand'—a mixture of quartz, feldspar and minor mica. Feldspar production from pegmatites of the Münchberger Gneismassif and of Hagendorf and that of Birkenfeld-Nohfelden have been noted earlier. The silbergite of the Eifel mountains, which belongs to the group of eleolite–syenites, should be mentioned here. The annual production of about 130 000 tonne is used in the glass industry.

Ball clay and mudstone
The old differentiation of clay rocks according to their utilization—for example, into coarse-ceramic, fine-ceramic and fireclay—is now only conditionally applicable because of improved treatment methods—in particular, the production of standardized clay blends. For high-grade coarse-ceramic products, clays must be used that at least come close to fine-ceramic qualities (V. Stein, personal note).

Important sedimentary clay deposits are discussed briefly.[203] Kaolins, owing their formation predominantly to weathering, are described later, as are the Lower Bavarian bentonites.

In the Westerwald, the mountainous region between Lahn, Wied and Siegerland to the east of the Rheinische Schiefergebirge, several small basins or troughs were formed in the Tertiary, in which the weathering material was redeposited after more or less effective sorting. According to environment, depth and extent of the basins, and conditions of transport and sedimentation, all transitions from pure clay to argillaceous and very argillaceous fine sands can be found. The series that contains the valuable clay deposits is 10–15 m thick—locally, 20–25 m. In the lowest parts unctuous, white-firing clays are found, overlain by clays with 25–35 wt% Al_2O_3, which can locally be also red-firing. The uppermost part is often formed by relatively meagre light-firing clays. The clay sequence is often overlain by fragments of basalt cover and basaltic tuffs, and also by fine argillaceous sands to extremely sandy clays, some with a large gravel content. At many places the overburden has an overall thickness of 30–35 m. The majority of the 'Westerwald Clays' today have an Al_2O_3 content of 25–35%; clays with a higher content of Al_2O_3 are rare; the blue clays especially, much sought after in former times, are to a large extent worked out in many deposits. Today many companies offer white-firing, cream-firing, red-firing and yellow-firing clays as standard blends, as well as special blends for structural clay products. Deeply red-firing clays, which are often much sought after, are differentiated sometimes as pure-coloured red firing, almost pure coloured (streaky) red-firing (both >8 wt% Fe_2O_3) and predominantly red-firing clays (5–6 wt% Fe_2O_3). Meagre and pure white-firing clays can show between 10 and 30 wt% Al_2O_3. Purely yellow-firing clays with a high content of TiO_2 are to be found, in particular, in the southeastern part of the Westerwald.

During the Upper Mesozoic and the Lower Tertiary the feldspar-rich rocks of the basement in northern Bavaria underwent an intensive weathering, with formation predominantly of kaolinites. In the Tertiary troughs with a widely branching river system, filled with the eroded material, were formed in the Mitterteich area, along the Naab Valley and at the southern edge of the Bavarian Forest. Kaolinitic clays, often associated with brown coal, were deposited predominantly in the upper parts of the river system and in side valleys. This stratigraphic sequence reaches thicknesses between about 10 and 40–50 m, contents of clay and brown coal being subjected to heavy fluctuations according to either the position of deposits in the channel system or the width of the channels. The clays show a high content of Al_2O_3, some up to 38 wt%, clays with 30–35 wt%, however, being quite frequent. The best qualities are to be found often as argillaceous layers between the brown coal. The individual minable clay horizons often show a thickness of only 1–2 m. A lightweight chamotte as a special product is made from coal-rich clays or from artificially produced clay-brown coal mixtures. The total reserves of fire- and acid-resistant clays in the Naab area are estimated at more than 350 000 000 tonne and in the Hengersberg-Eging area to the southeast of Deggendorf at more than 60 000 000 tonne (Fig. 52).

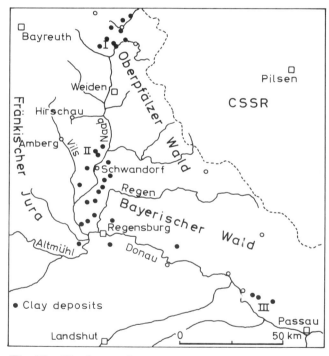

Fig. 52 *Sketch map of geographic location of Tertiary kaolinitic clays in northeast Bavaria. I, Mitterteich basin, northern Oberpfalz; II, Naab valley, central and southern Oberpfalz; III, Hengersberg–Eging area. After Kromer*[203]

It is worth mentioning that in this area also clays of a high quality were deposited in some places in the Upper Cretaceous (e.g. the Ehenfeld clay to the north of Hirschau).

Of supra-regional importance furthermore are the yellow- to white-firing clays several metres thick in the transition beds between the Keuper and the Jurassic under 10–15 m of overburden, which are worked in the region of Coburg, 60 km to the north of Bayreuth.

The high-quality clays and argillaceous rocks of northern Bavaria are used equally for the production of fireclay, stoneware and earthenware, as well as for structural clay products.

In lower Saxony clays and argillaceous rocks are worked exclusively for the production of structural clay products, the production of bricks of all types greatly predominating. Argillaceous rocks and clays of the Bunter, the Keuper, the Lias, the Dogger, the Lower and Upper Cretaceous, the Tertiary and the Quaternary (Pleistocene lake sediments, loess loam, meadow loam, marsh clay) are used as raw material.

From North Rhine–Westphalia we have only an outline of the ceramic raw materials used today. Shales, mudstones and clays of the Devonian, of the Upper Carboniferous, Upper Keuper, Lias, Dogger, the Lower Cretaceous (Valanginian, Hauterivian, Barremian, Aptian), the Upper Cretaceous (argillaceous marlstones of the Campanian and Santonian), the Tertiary (Palaeocene, Eocene, Oligocene, Miocene and Pliocene) and Quaternary (old Pleistocene, Tegelen clay, drift clay, loess loams and meadow loams) are worked. The minable thicknesses often amount to less than 10 m, thus leading to the conclusion that, in particular, the weathered, decalcified and plastic upper parts of the argillaceous stratigraphic sequences have been used.

High-quality fine-ceramic and earthenware clays of the Tertiary are extracted to the west and southwest of Euskirchen to the west of Bonn, in the Ville and to the south of Siegburg. The especially valuable 'blue clays' in an area to the west of Bonn have been already exploited to a large extent. Kaolinitic clays, often of refractories quality, are worked in addition in the Rhineland–Pfalz (Palatinate) in the area of Eisenberg–Grünstadt, 25 km to the northwest of Ludwigshafen, in the Neuwied Basin and in its western marginal regions, as well as in Hesse near Großalmerode, 20 km ESE of Kassel, and in the Spessart near Klingenberg on the Main.

Sulphur and iron sulphides

Approximately 80% of the sulphur that is produced in the FRG is obtained as a by-product of natural gas extraction (Table 37). This sour natural gas, 40% of the natural gas that is produced in the FRG, mainly comes out of the Zechstein layers and has been extracted in increasing quantities since 1970.

The Meggen mine has yielded the greater part of the pyrite. Smaller amounts of pyrite and pyrrhotite were produced in the Bodenmais mine until 1962, and in the Bayerland mine until 1971.

The Eocene brown coal of the sub-Hercynian Basin near Helmstedt contains marcasite concretions in small quantities, along with subordinate pyrite, which are obtained as by-products (Table 37).

Phosphate rocks

Sedimentary phosphate rocks are quite common in the FRG, but at present they are of no economic importance. Small deposits were worked in former times (Fig. 53), but they are now only of historical interest. Phosphorite nodules in the Upper Cretaceous breccia ores of Lengede–Broistedt were at times obtained as by-products from 1875, when production was started, to the closure of the iron ore mine in 1977. Since 1956 1 470 000 tonne of phosphorite with 8–10% pure phosphorus (20–25% P_2O_5) was produced and mostly used in the blast-furnace plants of Ilsede.

During and soon after the two world wars, the following deposits were worked for short periods:[204] autochthonous phosphorites in the Middle Cretaceous glauconite sands at Grünten near Sonthofen in the Allgäu, allochthonous phosphorite nodules in the uppermost Santonian near Bad Harzburg, phosphorite nodules from Palaeogene glauconite sands of the sub-Hercynian Basin near Helmstedt and resorted

Table 37 *Production (t) of sulphur and iron sulphides in Federal Republic of Germany (selected years between 1950 and 1983[21])*

	Sulphur from natural gas	Marcasite and pyrite from lignite	Pyrite and pyrrhotite from massive sulphide deposits		S content (columns 2 to 4)
		Helmstedt	Meggen	East Bavaria	
1950		25 809	469 378	53 774	199 197
1960		20 435	434 970	51 394*	187 360
1970	103 393	29 278	503 840	39 467†	241 041‡
1980	813 732	38 990	463 400	—	222 178
1981	834 122	38 355	444 232	—	213 329
1982	871 513	32 150	475 426	—	228 946
1983	632 243	29 550	524 051	—	ca 245 000

* Bodenmais mine closed down in 1962.
† Bayerland mine closed down in 1971.
‡ Between 1968 and 1973 Rammelsberg mine produced some additional pyrite concentrates—in 1970 16 871 tonne; estimated sulphur content included.

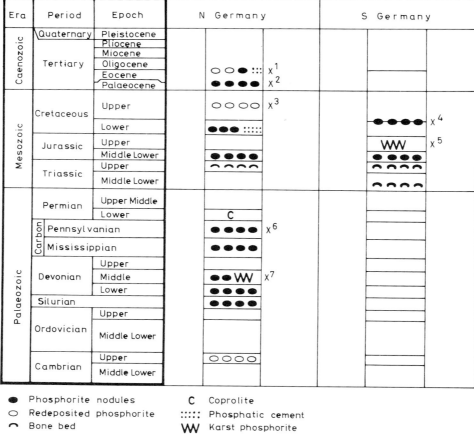

Fig. 53 *Stratigraphic position and types of phosphatic rocks in Federal Republic of Germany. After Paproth and Zimmerle.*[204] (*Former mining localities: 1, Uelsen, Emsland; 2, Helmstedt, east of Braunschweig; 3, Lengede-Broistedt, southwest of Braunschweig; 4, Grünten, Allgäu; 5, Amberg, Oberpfalz; 6, Ruhr district; 7, Middle Lahn River area*)

phosphorites at the base of the Middle Oligocene near Uelsen in the Emsland. Between 1918 and 1922 several thousand tonnes of phosphorite was produced. Phosporite deposits of the region of the middle Lahn River and near Amberg in the Oberpfalz, which were of the greatest importance in the past, are of the karst-phosphorite type.

Finally, attempts were made to work deposits at the beginning of this century near Hattingen on the Ruhr River.

Ore deposits in the Alpine orogenic belt

In the German part of the Alps many small- and medium-size ore deposits occur that were of local importance in the past (Fig. 54). The strata-bound lead–zinc ore and pyrite deposits of Triassic age in the Northern Calcareous Alps belong to the Bleiberg type. During the early mining periods these deposits were worked for the iron ore of the weathering zone. In the stratiform manganese occurrences of late Liassic age in the Northern Calcareous Alps (Nördliche Kalkalpen) sub-economic concentrations occur near Berchtesgaden and in the neighbouring Salzburg Alps in Austria. Sedimentary iron ore deposits of Eocene age occur in the Helvetic Zone.

Lead–zinc ore deposits

The deposits within the area discussed below have not been mined recently. Nevertheless, they have on occasion been of economic importance for local metal production (smelting works and foundries in many places) during the past four centuries and were therefore exploited repeatedly up to the beginning of the 1920s. During the early periods of mining the supergene mineralization (gossan formation) was exploited for limonitic iron ore, secondary zinc ores ('Galmei' for production of yellow brass), and silver-rich secondary lead ores (504, 801–918, 960, Table 38). Around the middle of the last century interest shifted to the exploitation of galena–sphalerite ores (503, 512, 952–53, Table 38) with local attempts at molybdenum–wulfenite production (503, 512, Table 38).

Furthermore, arising from their stratigraphic–palaeogeographic relations, these deposits in the northern zone of the Nördliche Kalkalpen represent a

Federal Republic of Germany

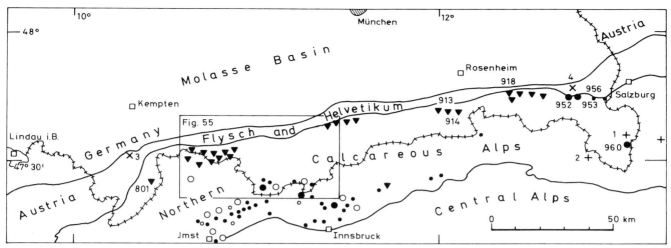

Fig. 54 *Ore deposits in German and neighbouring Austrian Alps. After Maucher and Schneider*[206]

key to the genetic interpretation of the so-called Alpine lead–zinc ores that are generally characterized as of Bleiberg or Mississippi Valley type. Economically important mines have in recent times been developed in the Austrian, Italian and Yugoslav parts of the Eastern Alps.[205,206,207]

On the basis of their stratigraphic and genetic relations the Mid-Triassic iron ore deposits have to be treated in common with the lead–zinc ore deposits, which are all 'strata-bound' and restricted to the Upper Wettersteinkalk (Fig. 55).

Geological setting
The Triassic sequence in the Bavarian part of the Nördliche Kalkalpen represents the geosynclinal development in the northern marginal zone of the Upper Austroalpine nappe unit. Thus, the thickness of the Triassic sediments decreases from about 3000 m in the

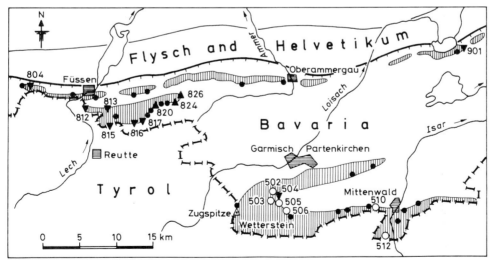

Fig. 55 *Section of Northern Calcareous Alps in southern Bavaria with significant accumulation of Mid-Triassic lead–zinc(–iron) mineralization*

Table 38 *Former mining activity associated with Triassic Pb–Zn(–Fe) ore deposits in Bavarian part of the Northern Calcareous Alps* (outline of more important localities only)

Ref. no.*	Locality (*Name of mine*)	Ore paragenesis — Primary mineralization	Mining production	Genetic type of mineralization†	Range of mining activity‡	Proven time of activity
502	Waxenstein SE	ZnS–PbS	Pb–Zn ores	dcr + vfs + ox	×	1717–95/1916–17
503	Höllental *Johannes-Zeche Zwei-Brüder-Zeche*	PbS–ZnS (FeS$_2$)	Pb–Zn ores wulfenite!	dcr + vfs + ox	× × ×	1826–54/1915–18
504	Hammersbach Alpe	FeS$_2$(PbS)	limonite alums	ls + dcr + ox	× ×	1418/1552–1744
505	Hupfleiten	PbS(CaF$_2$)	Pb ores?	ls + ox	×	(?1780)
506	Gassenalpe	PbS–CaF$_2$	Pb ores?	ls + lbr	○	(?1780)
510	Ferchenseewand *GuteHoffnung-Zeche*	PbS–CaF$_2$	Pb ores?	ls	○	1879–81
512	Riedbodeneck *Franz-Adolf-Zeche*	ZnS–PbS	Pb–Zn ores (wulfenite)	ls/dcr + vfs + ox	× ×	1658/1816–80
801	Rosskopf *Kaisergrube I*	ZnS–FeS$_2$(CaF$_2$)	'Galmei'	l/ls + lbr + vfs + ox	×	1600–1750(?)
804	Pfronten-Meilingen *Meilinger Grube*	FeS$_2$	limonite	dcr + ox	×	? 1605–1708
812	Unterpinswang	FeS$_2$(ZnS)	limonite	l/dcr + ox	×	1120–1250(?)
813	Aelpeleskopf *St. Mang-Grube*	FeS$_2$(barite)	limonite	dcr + ox	× ×	1500–1850
815+)	Saeuling-S *'Bergwerk'*	FeS$_2$ (ZnS + barite)	limonite	l/dcr + ox	× ×	1016/1500–1850
816	Schlagstein	FeS$_2$	limonite	l/dcr + ox	○	?
817	Altenberghuette	FeS$_2$	limonite	dcr + ox	○	?
820	Straußberg *Erzgrube*	ferrodolomite + FeS$_2$	limonite	dcr + ox	○	?
824	Weidental *Weitalpe*	ferrodolomite	limonite	dcr + ox	○	?
826	Hochplatte E *Beinlandl*	ferrodolomite (FeS$_2$ + barite)	limonite	ls + dcr + ox	×	1602–72/1916–17
901	Brandenstein	FeS$_2$	limonite	dcr + ox	×	? 1505/1716–21
913	Wendelstein-Dickelalpe	ferrodolomite	limonite	dcr + ox	×	(1730?)
914	Arzmoosalpe *Karlsgrube*	FeS (PbS, ZnS, CaF$_2$)	limonite	ls/dcr + ox	× ×	1446/1730–60
918	Kampenwand	ferrodolomite (FeS$_2$)	limonite	dcr + ox	× ×	1513–1640
952	Rauschberg W, Centre *Strahlecker Baue, Ewiggang*	ZnS, PbS (FeS$_2$)	Pb–Zn ores	ls/dcr + vfs + ox	× × ×	? 1585/1615–1826
953	Rauschberg-E *Joseph, Maximilian*	ZnS–PbS (FeS$_2$)	Pb–Zn ores	ls/dcr + vfs + ox	× × ×	1847–62 1923–25
956	Hochstaufen	ZnS–PbS (FeS$_2$)	Pb–Zn ores	dcr + vfs + ox	×	1650–1674/1881
960	Königsberg (Jenner) *Anton, Barbara, Georg*	ZnS–PbS (FeS$_2$)	Pb–Zn ores	ls + dcr + ox	× × ×	1568/1710–1819

* Reference numbers refer to Schneider.[296] Most mines are shown in Fig. 55; those with reference numbers 801 and 901 to 960 in Fig. 54.

† Genetic types of mineralization: l, generally layered, stratiform; ls, layered with sedimentary fabrics; lbr, layered, reworked ore sediments (sedimentary breccia); dcr, diagenetic recrystallization predominating; vfs, discordant vein or fissure vein; and ox, (supergene) oxidized ores, gossan formation.

‡ Range of mining activity: ○, diggings, pits, adits, dumps of minor importance; ×, repeated small-scale exploitation; × ×, production of temporary importance only; and × × ×, mining activity during longer periods with important production.

south to approximately 1000 m at the northern margin, which constitutes a northward overthrust nappe front. The thickness of the mid-Triassic ore-bearing formation (Wettersteinkalk) also decreases from about 1000 m in the south to about 200 m in the north (e.g. 503–12/804–901, Fig. 55).

The mid-Triassic palaeogeography reveals a division into extended reef belts of limestones and dolomites (Wettersteinkalk) and widespread basins represented by clayey marls and shales (Partnachschichten) with typical facies transitions. The reef complexes have been shown to be of Ladinian age, locally beginning in the Upper Anisian or extending up to lowermost Carnian.

The carbonate sequences record all facies characteristics of reef origin increasing from the north to the south: in the Wettersteinkalk Mountains an extensive plateau reef reaches its maximum development within the Bavarian Alps, displaying a separation into marginal barrier reefs and central back reef lagoons.[205] The upper part of the sequence—the ore-bearing units—exhibits over the entire area the development of a flat reef surface with cyclic alternation of sub- and supratidal environments.[208,297] During this stage the depositional conditions changed locally into euxinic or weak evaporitic sedimentation or short interruptions by erosion (pockets, channels, cut and fill structures, crosscutting, sedimentary breccias). All these structures and fabrics are significant properties also of the accompanying sedimentary ores.

The ore deposits within the northern strip of the mid-Triassic geosyncline are remarkably clearly restricted to the uppermost part of the reef complexes, whereas the basin sediments are free of ore concentrations, containing base metals in a geochemical distribution only. The ore-bearing units are increasing in thickness corresponding to the regional thickening from north to south. Their continuation into the North Tyrolian Alps reveals a further rise in thickness as well as in ore accumulations leading to larger deposits.

Obviously, the mid-Triassic geosyncline exhibits a palaeogeographic contrast between less fully developed reef chains in the northern strip and larger reef complexes (plateau reefs) in the south separated by extensive basins. In the Wetterstein area well-characterized tuff layers are intercalated with the lowermost part of the Ladinian sequence,[209] thus proving volcanic activity in the geosyncline, which may continue up to the Upper Ladinian, as there are greenish tuffaceous marl beds intercalated with the ore-bearing units. The intensity of the volcanism also increases from north to south.

Although the entire area has undergone a number of strong phases of folding, faulting and thrusting during the Alpine orogeny, the mid-Triassic palaeogeography can be reconstructed from the pattern of the sedimentary facies, and this coincides significantly with the distribution pattern of the mineralization (Fig. 55).

Paragenesis and orebodies
As regards the number of primary ore and gangue minerals, the composition of all deposits is very simple: in the northern zone iron sulphides and carbonates (pyrite, marcasite and an ankerite-like ferrodolomite) predominate, locally accompanied by a little sphalerite and, mainly in microscopic size, galena. The principal gangue mineral is calcite; at a few localities only there is some barite or fluorite (813, 815, 826, 914, Table 38; Figs. 54, 55).

The ore-bearing uppermost 10–15 m of the Wettersteinkalk are bounded at their top by a thin layer of iron sulphides and black shale, which denotes the contact with the transgressive Carnian sandstones and shales over the entire area. The mineralization of the limestones below, however, concentrated only locally, is interrupted by barren areas. The iron sulphides occur disseminated (framboidal or recrystallized grains) in distinct layers, enriched in layered lenses (sedimentary fabrics!) or in cloud-shaped replacement bodies passing into mineralized breccia, local networks and veinlets.[210,211]

The primary sedimentary fabric of the ferrodolomitic ores is preserved locally in various oolites and typical algal pellets, which are accumulated in layers or cut and fill structures a few metres below the transgressive Carnian sandstones (826, Table 38).[211]

The paragenesis with predominating iron sulphides is concentrated along the southern reef segments surrounding the 'bay' of Reutte, whereas the ferrodolomitic ores seem to be scattered over the back reef areas in the northeast (804–17/820–26, Fig. 55).

The stratigraphic and genetic relationship between the iron ore deposits of the north and the lead–zinc ore deposits in the south was discussed by Gümbel,[212] who pointed out the 'Erzkalk' as a stratigraphic unit. In a southerly direction the ores pass into a real sphalerite–galena paragenesis with minor amounts of iron sulphides, forming stratiform lenses and thin layers.

In some occurrences in this area fluorite appears beside calcite in small quantities as a sedimentary constituent,[213] forming a distinct fluorspar–galena paragenesis (506, 510, Fig. 55). The primary ores were, however, never sufficient for mine production.

All ore minerals occur as a primary stage along with abundant significant sedimentary fabrics.[205] The majority of the ore, however, is accumulated in typical diagenetic, coarse-grained replacement bodies, stratabound to the ore-bearing unit or concentrated in fissure veins and geologically 'old' faults (503, 952, 953, Table 38). In these cases the mineralization does not descend deeper than 100–200 m in vertical distance from the overlying source beds.

In most cases the concentration of primary ore has not been sufficient for intensive mining unless a secondary diagenetic process of enrichment or the supergene development of a gossan has occurred. In connexion with the oxidation processes near the outcrops of two Pb–Zn deposits (503, 512, Table 38) some wulfenite has been formed from molybdenum arising from the weathering of the overlying (Triassic–Jurassic) sedimentary sequences that carry bituminous intercalations.

Genetic interpretation
The lead–zinc (iron) ore deposits discussed above are strata-bound within a few levels of the upper part of the mid-Triassic (Ladinian–Carnian) sequence and,

in addition, palaeogeographically bound to the reef complexes (Wettersteinkalk), whereas the basin sediments (Partnachschichten) are barren. Thus, the mineralization must be genetically related to its sedimentary environment.

Sedimentary fabrics and structures of the sulphide ores match the patterns of the host rock and indicate a first stage of synsedimentary to early diagenetic enrichment.[205,206,210,213] After this first stage the ores underwent contemporaneously with their host rock intensive remobilization in the following climactic stages of diagenesis. Prodigious quantities of (thermal) formation water may have migrated under high pressures during the main phases of the Alpine orogeny, causing the formation of real 'replacement bodies' and mineralized fissure veins.

The primary palaeogeographic distribution of the sulphide ores may offer a solution also for the problem of the source of the metals: generally, the size of the deposits as well as the content of lead and zinc increases from north to south, and this is correlated with the occurrence of fluorite and tuffaceous layers. Obviously, the main volcanic activity of the entire geosyncline is concentrated farther to the south.

By means of modern geochemical investigations the sedimentary (early diagenetic) crystallization of the fluorite has been proved, and the volcanic origin of the fluorine has been indicated.[214] Thus, the volcanic activity with its submarine exhalations within the mobile eugeosyncline may be considered to be the source for the ores.

Mining

Within this area mining activity has flourished repeatedly during various historical periods (see introduction), mainly in three centres. Owing to the lack of documentary records, the ancient production can in most cases only be estimated.

Ancient iron ore production, concentrated mainly in the Füssen area (Fig. 55; 804–26, Table 38), might have reached in total about 300 000 tonne of high-grade ore (limonite). As late as the mid-nineteenth century a blast-furnace plant with some small rolling mills was in operation at Halblech near Füssen, supplied by the mines of the area.

Repeated activity since around 1475[119] directed towards Pb–Zn ore production in the Wetterstein area (Fig. 55; 503, Table 38) remained generally without economic results in spite of enormous efforts. The total production may not exceed more than 2500 tonne of lead concentrate. During the first world war remarkable technical efforts were made to produce wulfenite, but without any economic result (some 10 tonne only!).

The third mining centre, which on occasion was the most important, was situated further to the east near Ruhpolding-Inzell (952, 953 'Rauschberg', Table 38; Fig. 54). During intermittent periods of activity from about 1665 to 1826[119] total production might have reached about 50 000 tonne of Pb–Zn concentrates, sometimes with a high Ag content (about 800 ppm). More than half the production has been oxidized zinc ores ('Galmei'), which supplied a local smelter for yellow brass near Inzell up to 1826. Repeated mining attempts to 1925 were unsuccessful in economic terms.

Manganese ore deposits

Sediments rich in manganese, the content of which is generally in excess of 5%, extend over a strike distance of some 250 km in the Northern Calcareous Alps from the Allgäu to Salzburg.[215] Insofar as they can be definitely dated they belong almost exclusively to the Upper Lias—probably mainly to the Toarcian and in part also to the Dogger. They are age- and strata-bound, even though in facies terms very differently developed. In the main they take the form of thin-bedded to foliated, dark-specked marly or dark siliceous limestones (manganese slates) of a thickness that varies considerably between 5 and 200 m. The Mn content of these manganese slates is mainly linked to mixed carbonates of the $CaCO_3$–$MnCO_3$–$FeCO_3$ (rhodochrosite) series, and partly also to braunite. They also contain 15–20% quartz and just under 10% clay minerals. In the oxidation zone a number of manganese oxides, mainly pyrolusite, occur. The substantial overall manganese content in these marine sediments is attributed to entry into the sedimentary basin of ascendent thermal solutions. Known signs of volcanic activity in the immediate neighbourhood, such as celadonite-bearing tuffs interbedded with manganese carbonates, are very few.

Local enrichments of the Mn content, particularly in the area of oxidation near the surface, led in the nineteenth and twentieth centuries to several investigative mining operations, but no output of any substance was achieved.

The only enrichments that, by virtue of volume and content, can today be described as important in terms of economic exploitation are two deposits in the Berchtesgaden and Salzburg Alps (Fig. 54). Of these, only the small deposit on the Jenner actually lies in the territory of the Federal Republic, the other far more significant deposit, only discovered in 1955, being situated on the Hochkranz in Austria.

On the *Jenner* near Königssee village south of Berchtesgaden the manganese slates fill a tectonic syncline some 500 m wide with overturned margins. At the base of the black slates directly above the subjacent light-coloured limestones is the ore bed proper. For tectonic reasons this seam, its manganese content varying between 20 and 30%, fluctuates in thickness between 2 and 12 m. The primary Mn mineral is manganese carbonate, which near the outcrops is partly altered to manganese oxide.

The proven reserves, established by means of a small network of tunnels during the last mining investigations in 1955, are 100 000 tonne ore with 20–30% Mn. The probable and possible reserves, however, are much greater.[216] The deposit is situated at an altitude of 1400 m and is thus unfavourably located for transport purposes. It is, moreover, in a nature reserve. Its economic exploitation cannot be considered for the time being.

Far larger is the neighbouring deposit on the *Hochkranz*, near Lofer in Austria, which should be mentioned here in passing since in terms of content ($\geqslant 22\%$) and volume (20 000 000–30 000 000 tonne possible) it must be considered potentially exploitable.

Iron ore deposits

Early Tertiary iron ores formerly of some local importance are found on the edge of the Alps in the Kressenberg district, 10 km southeast of Traunstein in Upper Bavaria and on the Grünten near Sonthofen in the Allgäu (Fig. 54). They were recently described in detail by Ziegler.[217,218]

The first documenary mention of mining at the Kressenberg dates from 1070. The period of chief activity came in the seventeenth and eighteenth centuries. The last mines at the Kressenberg in the west and in the Achtal in the east of the district were shut down in 1882 and 1924, respectively. Annual output prior to 1914 was in the region of 4000 tonne. Exploratory work in 1937–38 and 1955–58 did not result in mining being resumed.

Although only documented from the end of the fifteenth century, mining on the Grünten is certainly of much earlier date, but it never became as important as that on the Kressenberg and the mine was shut down in 1859.

In the *Achtal–Kressenberg* mine, which is situated on the Munich–Salzburg autobahn near Neukirchen am Teisenberg, three ore horizons strike southwest–northeast and dip about 75° to the south. They were formed in the Palaeocene and Eocene by precipitation from iron-containing solutions in the littoral zone.

A distinction is made between the upper black and the lower red ore. The dark brown, oolitic 'black' ore is composed, in addition to the strikingly uniform öoides (0·5–1·5 mm), of more or less coarse grains of quartz and numerous fossil inclusions that not infrequently contain iron compounds in fine dispersion, as does the carbonate matrix. Apart from layers of ore showing a uniform oolitic structure, öoides are also distributed in nests separated by calcareous beds with only a low Fe content.

The öoides partly consist of pure goethite (FeOOH)—those which show shelly structure—and partly of a mixture of limonite and iron silicates. The black ore horizon developed with different thicknesses between 3 and 6 m throughout the orefield and was the main source of ore. Apart from its colour, the red ore differs from the black in having a generally coarser sandy structure, a lower Fe content and a more clayey cementing material. The öoides are generally rather larger than those in the black ore (up to 2·0 mm), more irregular in shape and sometimes containing fine grains of quartz at the core. The relatively high limestone content of the red ore derives in part from the calcareous, clayey and iron-bearing cementing material and in part from the high fossil content of the seam. The iron-rich layers are not sharply defined, and barren intermediate layers or limestone lenses are by no means rare. The red ore horizon has only developed on the west of the Kressenberg, where it is between 5 and 8 m thick.

The group of thin seams (Schmalflözgruppe) at the base is only present in the Achtal. It splits in a westward direction and is represented on the Kressenberg by calcareous sandstone. The Fe content of the ore varies between 25 and 32% and may reach 35% locally. The average composition is 18–20% SiO_2 with 14–16% CaO.

Proven and probable ore reserves amount to some 32 000 000 tonne. The thickness and bedding of the ore seams would make the use of cheap bulk extraction methods possible but, given the present situation in the mining industry generally, a revival of mining activity in the Achtal–Kressenberg area, where it has a long tradition and in some parts has been extensive, is unlikely in the foreseeable future.

A deposit of the same age and stratigraphy is to be found on the Grünten. The iron ore seams at the surface strike southwest–northeast with an average northwesterly dip of 60°. Because of impoverishments and numerous faults, the seams are not very long. The maximum length of 250 m in the direction of the strike and of 50 m in that of dip explains why mining has been confined to a very small area.

The ore extracted was a fine-grained, red, very dense calcareous ore of oolitic structure with clayey calcareous cementing material that contains ore minerals. In addition to impoverishments and faults, the ore seams are also interrupted, lenticular and nest-like. The extracted material averaged 21% Fe, 20% SiO_2 and 20% CaO.

Because of the unfavourable geographical location of the orefields, the tectonically complex mode of occurrence and the low Fe content, the deposit is not now workable.

Mineral deposits linked to the Mesozoic and Tertiary rift system

The endogene post-Variscan or Alpine, otherwise known as Saxonian, ore deposits in the FRG display in their distribution an association with large young fault zones: Eifel north–south zone, Rhine Graben and Hessian Depression, Western Boundary Fault of the Bohemian Massif and the Lower Saxony Basin; furthermore, many young mineralizations occur in the

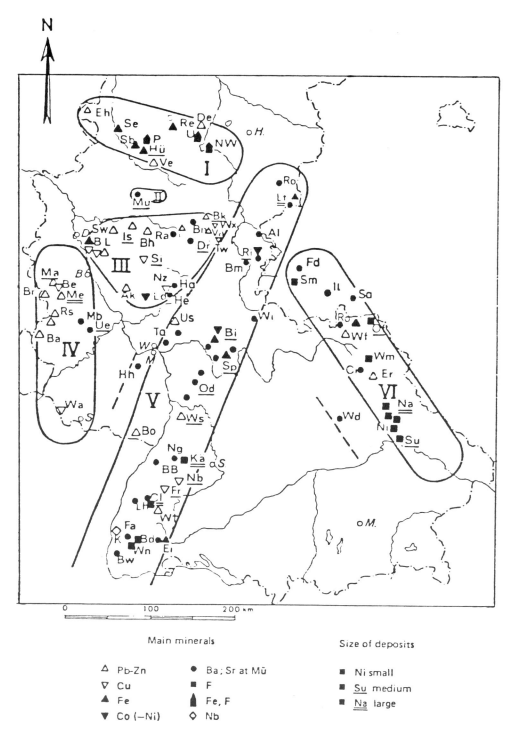

Fig. 56 *See facing page*

young uplift zones of the Rhenish Shield, partly as post-Variscan parageneses in Variscan ore deposits and partly in separate ore deposits (Fig. 56). To this Alpine mineralization belong ore deposits of several types, which in their mineral and element content as well as in the chemistry of fluid inclusions[219] and other properties are clearly distinguished for the most part from those of the Variscan metallogenesis. The geochemical characteristics of the young mineralization have been summarized by von Gehlen.[220] He listed, primarily, the following elements: Fe, Mn; F, Ba, Ca, Mg; Pb, Zn, Cu; Bi, Co, Ni, Ag, (U); Hg, As, Sb; together with O, S and Si. The parageneses are gangue-rich with sulphates, carbonates and fluorite as well as quartz, in comparison with which sulphides are clearly subordinate.

To these ore deposits belong widely distributed barite veins, in some places with predominant fluorite

Fig. 56 *Regional distribution of Alpine mineral deposits and their association with major fault zones in Federal Republic of Germany and adjacent areas. From Walther.*[221] *I, Lower Saxonian Block; II, Münsterland Bight; III, Eastern Rheinisches Schiefergebirge; IV, north–south zone of the Eifel; V, Rhine Graben and Hessian Depression; VI, Thuringian–Franconian fault system (B, Bonn; D, Düsseldorf; H, Hannover; M, Mainz and München; S, Saarbrücken and Stuttgart; W, Wiesbaden)*

List of deposits outside Alps (ore layers and ore masses marked; all others are vein-type deposits)

Ak	Altenkirchen	Pb
Al	Albungen	Ba, Fe
Ba	Bleialf	Pb
BB	Baden-Baden	Ba, Cu, Bi
Bd	Brandenberg, Black Forest	F, Ba, Fe, Pb, Cu
Be	Berg	Cu
Bh	Bönkhausen	Pb
Bi	Bieber	Fe, Mn, Ba, Co, Ni (Pb, Cu)
Bk	Blankerode	Pb–Zn
BL	Bergisches Land	Cu, Fe, Ni, Co, Hg, Ba, Pb
Bm	Baumbach on the Fulda	Ba
Bn	Brilon	Ba, Pb–Zn
Bo	Bobenthal	Pb
Br	Brandenberg, Eifel	Pb
Bw	Badenweiler	Ba, Fe, Pb–Zn, Cu
Cl	Clara mine	Ba, F
Cr	Creußen	Ba, F
De	Deblinghausen	Zn–Pb, Cu
Dr	Dreislar	Ba, Fe, Cu
Eh	Emlichheim	Zn–Pb, Ba
Ei	Eisenbach	Ba, F, Fe, Mn
Er	Erbendorf	Pb–Zn, Cu, Ba
Fa	Freiamt	Ba, Pb–Zn, Cu
Fd	Friedrichroda	Ba, Fe, Mn
Fr	Freudenstadt	Cu, Bi, Ba
Ha	Hartenrod	Ba
He	Herborn-Burg	Ba
Hh	Hackenheim	Ba
Hü	Mt. Hüggel (ore mass)	Fe, Ba, Pb–Zn, Cu
Il	Ilmenau	F, Ba, Fe, Mn
Is	Iserlohn	Zn–Pb
K	Kaiserstuhl (ore mass)	Nb
Kä	Käfersteige mine	F, Ba, Cu, Fe
Ld	Langendernbach (ore layer)	Ni, Co, Cu
Lh	Lahr	Ba, Fe, Pb–Zn
Lt	Bad Lauterberg	Ba, Fe, Cu, Pb
Ma	Maubach (ore mass)	Pb–Zn, Cu
Mb	Müllenbach, Eifel	Ba
Me	Mechernich (ore mass)	Pb–Zn, Cu
Mü	Münsterland	Sr
Na	Nabburg	F, Ba, Cu, Pb–Zn, U, Co, Ni, Bi
Nb	Neubulach	Cu, Bi, Ba
Ng	Neuenbürg	Ba, Fe
Ni	Nittenau	Ba, F
NW	Nammen-Wohlverwahrt	Fe, F
Nz	Nanzenbach	Cu
Of	Oberfranken	F, Ba, Fe, Mn, Cu
Od	Odenwald	Ba, F, Cu, Pb
P	Mt. Piesberg (ore mass)	Fe, Zn–Pb, F, Cu
Ra	Ramsbeck	Ba, Fe, Pb–Zn, Cu, Co, Ni
Re	Rehden	Fe, Ba, Cu, Pb–Zn
Ri	Richelsdorf	Ba, Co, Ni (Zn–Pb, Cu)
Ro	Rothenkirchen	Ba
Rö	Mt. Rösteberg (ore mass)	Ba
Rs	Rescheid	Pb
Sa	Saalfeld	Ba
Sb	Mt. Schafberg (ore mass)	Fe, Pb–Zn, Cu, Ba
Se	Schale	Zn
Si	Siegerland	Cu; Co, Ni
Sm	Schmalkalden	F, Ba
Sp	Spessart	Ba, Fe, Mn, Co (Cu, Pb)
Su	Sulzbach on the Danube	F, Ba
Sw	Schwelm-Langerfeld	Zn
Ta	Taunus	SiO$_2$ (quartz after barite)
Tw	Twiste	Cu
U	Uchte	Fe, F, Cu
Ue	Uersfeld	Ba, Fe, Cu
Us	Usingen	Pb
Va	Vasbeck	Pb–Zn
Ve	Versmold	Pb–Zn
Wa	Wallerfangen (ore mass)	Cu
Wd	Mt. Wendelstein	Ba, F, Cu
Wf	Wallenfels	Pb–Zn
Wi	Wildflecken	Ba
Wm	Warmensteinach	F, Ba, Fe, Cu
Wn	Wieden	F, Ba, Fe, Pb, Cu
Ws	Wiesloch (ore mass)	Zn–Pb, Cu, Co, Ni
Wt	Wittichen	Cu, Bi, Ba, F
Wx	Wrexen (ore mass)	Cu

with quartz, abundant siderite and varying amounts of Fe and Mn oxides and Cu, Co, Ni and Bi sulphides. Pb–Zn ores are concentrated in the major ore deposits of Mechernich and Maubach and are widely distributed in small- and medium-size ore deposits. Strontianite and celestine deposits occur locally.

In what follows, three neighbouring and recently investigated regions in North Germany are first dealt with; linked to that, the important ore deposit types, to which several large ore deposits belong, are indicated in summary form.

Alpine mineralization in the Sauerland district, northeastern Rheinisches Schiefergebirge

In Sauerland, an old mining district, an assessment has been carried out in recent years[222] of the mineralizations with particular reference to the characterization of Variscan and post-Variscan occurrences. Field and laboratory investigations backed up by the interpretation of extensive old mining records provided the criteria for subdivision between young Palaeozoic and Mesozoic–Tertiary mineralization cycles.

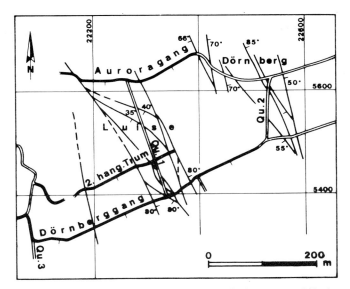

Fig. 57 *Post-Variscan mineralized cross-fault systems of 'Luisenkluft' and 'Dörnberg fault zone' at Ramsbeck mine, Willibald adit III, +473 m NN. After Behrend and Paeckelmann[97] (thick lines show ENE-striking Variscan Pb–Zn veins)*

The 'old' ore veins—for example, in the Ramsbeck district and small occurrences at Plettenberg in the Ebbe anticline—follow the WSW–ENE-trending structure of the folded Palaeozoic basement (Fig. 57) and are strongly deformed syn- and post-mineral as well as being for the most part fine-grained. The multiform, post-Variscan mineralizations, for the most part steeply dipping veins as well as metasomatic orebodies in carbonate rocks, impregnation zones and inter-sedimentary mineral flats in palaeo-karst, are, in contrast, associated with elements that cross the Variscan fault structure; over and above that they also occur in the Permian–Mesozoic and locally in the Tertiary platform cover. These 'young' mineralizations are tectonically relatively slightly strained and have developed a coarsely crystalline texture. They are, as in wide parts of Central Europe, markedly gangue-rich, with barite, carbonates, quartz and in Sauerland and neighbouring regions very minor fluorite and carry only subordinate sulphides and hematite.

Distribution of mineralization

Instances of post-Variscan mineralization are evidenced in the many deposits between the border of the Rheinische Schiefergebirge in the north and east and the Lenne Valley in the south and west (Fig. 19). Beyond this intensively mineralized area the density of mineralization declines and only isolated occurrences are known. This applies also to the Permian–Triassic rocks in the Hessian Depression and the sequence up to the Cretaceous in the Egge Hills and in Münsterland. The oldest instances of the multi-phase 'young' mineralization are developed only locally at the north of Warstein on the northern border of the Rheinische Schiefergebirge as silicification zones of varying intensity in Devonian limestones. Only traces are to be found in the remainder of the region. They have only been observed in Palaeozoic wallrocks. Since the possibilities of comparison are absent, these phases can only be ranked with reservations with the post-Variscan mineralization, and a young Variscan, late Upper Carboniferous to Permian age is not impossible. By contrast, the younger of the six all-told mineralization phases are very regularly distributed over the whole region. Above all, in the regions with intensive tectonic latticing of the major Variscan anticlines with transverse fault structures there came about favourable open-space creation for the rise of hydrothermal fluids leading locally to rich mineralization. Similarly, the crossing and convergence zones of fault systems are notably mineralized.

Supra-regionally, the mineralization up to the uncertainly placed Phase I is causally connected with the uplift and extension of the peneplained Variscan mountains since the Middle Jurassic and especially in the Cretaceous–Tertiary period. This vertical tectonics led to the rejuvenation of old established cross-elements.[223] Thus, some north–south-trending cross structures were also opened: over a relatively short distance these turn into northwest–southeast cross-faults. The WSW–ENE-trending thrust and overthrust surfaces of the Variscan fold belt can, by contrast, have been only very slightly reactivated.

On the basis of geological–stratigraphic discoveries, as well as several palaeomagnetic and radiometric datings, the younger mineralization phases can be more exactly placed in time.[222,224] Parts of the Sauerland paragenesis can be compared with mineralization that was worked in the surrounding areas and, in places, is worked at present (Table 39).

The mineralization ages can be paralleled with known dislocation phases in the Rheinische Schiefergebirge:[222,223] Phase II in the period between the Middle Jurassic and Lower Cretaceous; Phases III and IV between the higher Upper Cretaceous and Eocene; and Phases V and VI, post Upper Oligocene. Published K–Ar dates of ±170 m.y. on clay minerals from the edges of calcite veins of Phase II in the Brilon district[224] lie within the above-mentioned formation periods for this Phase. The barite generations in Sauerland are, nevertheless, on the basis of geological dates clearly younger than the dates of ±190 m.y for Dreislar. The oldest barite generation of Dreislar, however, is absent in Sauerland (see later).

The mineralization structure and the morphology of the orebodies are variable in their interdependence on their respective wallrocks. In the Devonian reef complex the mineral precipitation often ran parallel with karsting initiated by fault tectonics. In the cover rocks the hydrothermal solutions spread laterally, with replacement of reactive wallrocks within the first permeable horizon. In places, and particularly near

Federal Republic of Germany

Table 39 *Paragenetic scheme of the post-Variscan Sauerland mineralization compared with other data*

Phase	'Normal paragenesis'	'Ascendent cementation'	'Other data'
I	Quartz I Calcite I Pyrite–marcasite I Chalcopyrite I Tetrahedrite I		Possibly of late Variscan age
II	Calcite II Chalcopyrite II Quartz II		$CaCO_3$ II: mined at Brilon; 170 m.y.[224] Quartz II: formation at 120–300°C[219]
III	Dolomite I Barite I Chalcopyrite III Hematite I		$BaSO_4$ I: formation at 120–140°C;[219] mined at Dreislar[225]
IV	Barite II	Galena I Cuprobismuthite I	$BaSO_4$ II: post-Cenomanian at Bleiwäsche;[226] mined at Dreislar;[225] known at Ramsbeck[98]
V	Quartz III Chalcedony I Galena II Sphalerite I Chalcopyrite IV Hematite II Apatite I Pyrite-marcasite II Goethite I Mn oxide and hydroxide Dolomite II Siderite I Calcite III Tetrahedrite II Barite III Fluorite I Aragonite I	Ni–Co sulphides and arsenides, Ag sulphide and sulphosalts	Quartz III: formation at 70–100°C;[219] known in Taunus and Odenwald[227] PbS II + ZnS: mined in past at many places (Sauerland, Eifel, Taunus); post-Oligocene near Velbert;[228] Miocene at Brilon and Paffrath[80e, 229] Kobaltrücken: mined in past at Richelsdorf[156] and elsewhere in Hessian Depression; known at Ramsbeck[98]
VI	Barite IV Marcasite III Calcite IV ('Rüdersdorf' and 'Wülfrath III' types) Strontianite I		$SrCO_3$: mined in past in Münsterland Bight

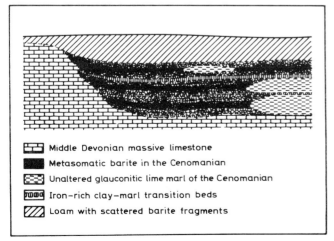

Fig. 58 *Section through ∼2·50-m thick metasomatic barite body of 'Gute Hoffnung' mine near Bleiwäsche, 25 km northeast of Brilon. After Bärtling*[226]

Warstein and Brilon, not only did outflow of thermal waters occur on the surface but also the redeposition of mineral precipitates under the influence of Tertiary lateritic weathering.

In particular, the following types of formation have been observed: simple-structured, steeply dipping veins in clastic and carbonate wallrocks (Fig. 57), poorly mineralized, irregular breccia zones filled with gouge clays in Palaeozoic clay shales and lydites, metasomatic bodies of varying size in Palaeozoic and Permian carbonate rocks, extensive impregnations with replacements in porous Zechstein marls and in marly glauconite-bearing sandstones of the Upper Cretaceous (Fig. 58), irregular and in places richly mineralized Mesozoic–Tertiary sediments in karst pipes and internal sedimentary mineral deposits in karst open spaces and in the open spaces of older mineralization structures.

Mineral succession

The post-Variscan mineralization succession in Sauerland is divided into six phases (Table 39), which may be superimposed in individual occurrences. The subdivision of the complete paragenesis was founded essentially on the systematic development of calcite forms.[230]

The katathermal Phase I is manifested principally as microcrystalline sphaerolitic quartz I, for which Koschinski[231] was able to demonstrate a formation temperature up to 360°C. Silicified breccia zones occur primarily in Devonian reef limestone of the Warstein anticline and to the north of that structure. Somewhat younger sulphides are distributed in traces. The dating is uncertain, and this phase may possibly be of late Variscan age.

During Phase II important quantities of monomineralic calcite of 'Wülfrath' type were separated. Quartz II, known as 'Suttrop quartz' was formed at temperatures up to more than 300°C.[219] Sulphides are very sparse. Quartz and calcite of Phases I and II occur as secondary deposits together with a rich fauna and flora of Aptian age in karst pockets in Devonian massive limestone at Nehden, northeast of Brilon.[232]

Dolomite and hematite of Phase III occur also in larger thicknesses. Hematite ores were worked in small mines up to 1949 at Warstein. The finely crystalline barite I may occur in several sub-phases and constitutes in the veins of the Dreislar mine (Fig. 56) the greater part of the ore.

Phase IV carried principally crystalline barite II, minor galena and only microscopically identifiable copper–bismuth sulphides. Phase V is represented by quartz III pseudomorphous after barite, known as 'Pseudomorphosenquarz', which develops into large crystals, followed by the main mass of sulphides with galena, sphalerite, chalcopyrite and pyrite–marcasite. In karst cavities was formed the widely distributed 'Warsteiner Eisenkiesel' consisting of quartz infillings formed at 100–120°C.[233] Galena is coarsely crystalline and mainly formed as silver-poor *Glasurerz* growing together with iron-poor sphalerite and marcasite.

In the younger parts of Phase V, quartz is replaced by calcite III of the 'Freiberg' and 'Tharandt' types. At the same time there occur nickel–cobalt sulphides and arsenides and sulphosalts.

Phase VI finally brings sulphide, barite and calcite redeposition as supposedly telethermal 'tail-enders'.

Designated as an 'ascendant cementation' was the formation of essentially sulphide- and arsenide-rich parageneses by the penetration of sapropelitic and/or sulphide-rich wallrocks—for example, at intersections with Variscan Ramsbeck ore veins.[98] To this particular paragenesis belong also the well-known *Kobaltrücken* in the Hessian Depression (Fig. 56).

The trace-element content and the isotopic composition of leads of the post-Variscan mineralization[234] indicate that the occurrences belong to an independent mineralization cycle and can incorporate only very subordinately material from Variscan or older ore deposits. The homogenization temperature of fluid inclusions and the Fe–Mn distribution in carbonatic gangue testify to predominantly low formation temperatures between 70 and 250°C and only locally up to 300°C and extensive oxidizing conditions at the time of mineral formation. Moreover, the mineral deposition was probably caused by a mixture of ascendant-hydrothermal solutions with formation waters.[235] In Sauerland one has particularly to consider saline pore waters of the Mesozoic cover rocks.[222]

Economic importance

Since the late Middle Ages lead, zinc, copper and iron ores of the young mineralizations have been worked in Sauerland. The heyday of these mines was the second half of the nineteenth century. In the northwest Iserlohn was the centre of zinc and lead production. The numerous—in places very extensive—mineralization carries sphalerite and calamine ores, galena, iron sulphide, carbonate, barite and quartz in sediment-filled palaeo-karst of the Devonian reef limestones. Between 1870 and 1898 651 000 tonne of zinc ore and 600 000 tonne of lead ore was produced. Numerous other occurrences distributed over the whole region yielded small quantities of lead–zinc ores—in particular, in the 'Briloner Galmeidistrikt',[80e] and in addition the mines 'Emilia-Theodora' at Plettenberg and 'Churfürst Ernst' at Bönkhausen, SSW of Arnsberg.

The widely distributed metasomatic and vein-type iron ores were won primarily in the nineteenth century, e.g. at Arnsberg and Hemer, at Warstein and in the Brilon district. They form the basis for the still active iron-working industry. Manganese ores were worked from a few occurrences at and east of Brilon.

The present mining of post-Variscan mineralization—in particular, of barite and calc-spar—has been established since 1900. The Dreislar mine has worked since 1957 the most important barite vein (see below). Several small barite veins were worked before the second world war west of Arnsberg, which yielded altogether about 50 000 tonne of crude barite. Because of pollution by sulphides or Fe and Mn oxides, the remaining veins and metasomatic barite bodies (e.g. Fig. 58) could for the most part only be worked for short periods in exploratory operations.

Table 40 *Calc-spar production in Sauerland district, 1950–84*[21,222]

	t	Mines		t	Mines
1950	23 494	6	1980	4 565	4
1960	33 369	20	1981	3 456	4
1965	45 660	12	1982	2 744	2
1970	15 086	5	1983	3 500	2
1975	7 390	5	1984	2 854	2

The calc-spar veins of the Sauerland reach thicknesses of a few metres up to 45 m. Primarily at Brilon, and for a time at Arnsberg, calc-spar (primarily calcite II) has been worked up to the present day. The high point for calcite mining was reached after 1960 as from time to time 20 mines yielded an annual production of up to 45 000 tonne. Since then output has declined gradually to around 3000 tonne (Table 40). The product was crushed and used as decorative dressings as well as in the terrazzo industry. Lower-quality material has been put to use as garden or cemetery gravel.

Further possible and potential reserves are to be expected beyond the presently known barite and calcspar reserves. Against that, the sulphide ores of post-Variscan age are already worked out or unworkable. Altogether one can reckon for the post-Variscan mineralization in Sauerland a minimum potential of 10 000 000–20 000 000 tonne, of which 3 000 000–5 000 000 tonne (barite ≫ calcite > hematite > non-ferrous metals) has already been mined.

Strontianite veins of the Münsterland Bight

In the Münsterland Bight between Münster and Hamm, over an area of 1700 km², around 100, mainly northwest- and northeast-striking strontianite veins are known. They traverse lime marls of the Upper Campanian, and are between a few centimetres and 2·5 m thick and up to several kilometres long. The veins extend to depths of 120 m. The vein filling consists of older calcite and younger strontianite and contains, on average, 50–60% (up to 85%) $SrCO_3$ and 5–25% $CaCO_3$. Harder[236] came to the conclusion that the strontium is ascendant and not of lateral-secretion origin. He suggested secondary-hydrothermal deposition from Zechstein salt waters. Scherp and Strübel[237] saw the strontium as carried in deep groundwaters that have risen from the Variscan basement and suggested that the ore deposit is a hydrothermal formation from hybridized thermal waters. They saw a connexion with the post-Variscan barite paragenesis in the sense of the theory that they have developed on Ba–Sr mineralization. The veins were discovered in 1834, and between

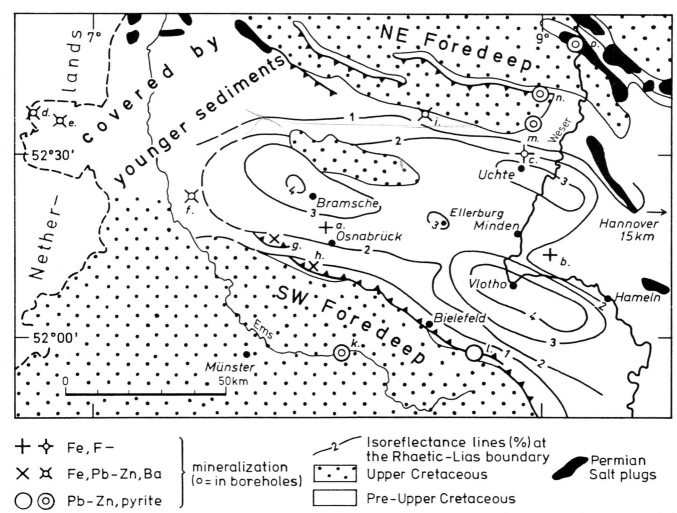

Fig. 59 *Mineralization within Lower Saxony Block and its surroundings*[16b,16c,221] (*a, Mt. Piesberg; b, Nammen-Wohlverwahrt mine; c, boreholes near Uchte; d, e, boreholes near Emlichheim; f, borehole Schale Z1; g, Mt. Schafberg; h, Mt. Hüggel; i, boreholes in Rehden gas field; k, borehole Versmold; l, Helpup; m, borehole Deblinghausen Z1; n, borehole Staffhorst Z1; o, borehole Hoya Z1*)

1870 and 1910 around 100 000 tonne of raw strontianite was won.

Mineralization of the Lower Saxony Block
In the Lower Saxony Block there occurs a zoned, principally mesothermal to epithermal mineralization, which is associated with an Upper Cretaceous intrusion approximately 6 km below the surface. To it belong the massif of Bramsche, Uchte and Vlotho (Fig. 59). Its existence was revealed by magnetic, seismic and gravimetric anomalies, very slight metamorphism and higher coalification of the pre-Upper Campanian beds.[15,16c] The mineralization has produced (1) in the central region higher-temperature siderite veins with fluorite (Piesberg, near Osnabrück; Uchte; Nammen, near Minden), (2) in a middle zone metasomatic siderite as the main mineralization and a post-phase with barite and non-ferrous metals (Hüggel, southwest of Osnabrück; Schafberg, near Ibbenbüren; the Rehden borehole, WNW of Uchte) and (3) in an outer zone, low-temperature lead, zinc, pyrite veins.[16b]

The siderite ores of the main phase occur principally as metasomatic masses in the Zechstein limestone, which at Hüggel and Schafberg were worked, along with limonitic weathering ores, with interruptions over a period of 100 years up to 1963. Total production amounted to around 15 000 000 tonne of ore with around 5 500 000 tonne iron content. From time to time lead–zinc–copper ores were also won. The iron/non-ferrous ratio was estimated by Stadler[16b] as 150 to 1. For some of the veins in the outer zone, which have been proven through oil drilling at more or less great depths, there is a possibility of them belonging to this ore zone, but it is not demonstrable.

The influence of deep intrusions on the mineralization, leading to the concentration of occurrences of unusually large crystals of quartz, siderite, fluorite and pyrite, as well as the occurrence of pyrophyllite, apatite, tourmaline, etc., in Mesozoic rocks in the regions of Bramsche, Vlotho and to some extent also at Uchte, has been pointed out.[238] Carbon and oxygen isotope analyses on carbonate veinlets from the roof of the Bramsche massif, which in part originates from Wealden coal, indicate their hydrothermal origin.[84] The associated carbon dioxide therefore originates to a considerable degree from the thermal decomposition or hydrothermal transformation of marine carbonates. Möller and co-workers[239] came to the same conclusion for calcite and fluorite from the Weserbergland, south of Bückeburg, on the basis of the content of rare earths. The elements Fe, Mn, Si, Mg, F, Ba, Cu and S can be interpreted as differentiations of a juvenile basaltic magma. The remaining elements—in particular, the non-metals—must, by contrast, be explained as lateral secretions.

Possibly the magmatism of the Bramsche massif tallies with the intrusive alkali magmatism postulated by Baumann and Weber[240] (hypothetical simatic plutonism during the Mesozoic).

Barite–fluorite veins
Economically important barite and fluorite–barite veins occur principally in two zones (Fig. 56): in the region of basement uplifts, which accompany the Rhine Graben, and in the Hessian Depression, including the eastern part of the Rheinische Schiefergebirge and the western Harz, as well as in the western (and northern) border regions of the Bohemian Massif; individual veins in the eastern Eifel may be linked with the Eifel north–south zone.

The selective occurrence of barite-fluorite veins was attributed[241] to the sealing of the Mesozoic cover rocks by means of salt beds at depth—in particular, the Zechstein salt—and the absence of large breaks in these regions.

Barite and fluorite show in their deposits markedly separate distribution patterns. In contrast to barite, which is distributed throughout all districts, one finds fluorite veins almost only in areas in which Variscan crystalline rocks are distributed. This makes the origin of fluorine (and, on analogous grounds, barium) from crustal rocks probable.[242,243,244]

The fluorite (barite) veins of Wölsendorf–Nabburg, the stratigraphic dating of which was until very recently controversial, must on the basis of the newest dating (after the completion of the manuscript) be regarded as young Variscan. Barite veins in the Saar–Nahe Basin are by reason of their tectonic position regarded as young Variscan.

Barite–fluorite veins in the Black Forest, Odenwald and Spessart
A Variscan age has been assumed for the majority of the barite–fluorite veins in south and central Schwarzwald.[8,9] In one group of cases, however, a younger age of mineralization is established. Möller and co-workers[245] found in the fractionation of REE in the Schwarzwald fluorite veins an indication of remobilization and inferred a wide-ranging regeneration of older, in part Upper Carboniferous, mineralization in the Tertiary. For the following veins evidence for, or an indication of, a young age is known: the mineralization in the Tertiary boundary faults between the Schwarzwald and the Rhine Graben and the barite–fluorite vein system of the Clara mine (vein group L; see pages 190–1) reaches up into the Bunter Sandstone of the post-Variscan cover rocks. Huck[246] divided the mineralization into four main phases, occurring in spatially and directionally varied fracture systems (Fig. 60; Table 41): (1) main fluorite phase in the fluorspar veins; (2) main barite phase in the barite vein; (3) transition barite phase in WNW–NNW stringers; and (4) main quartz phase in diagonal stringers.

From the development of the tectonics and the

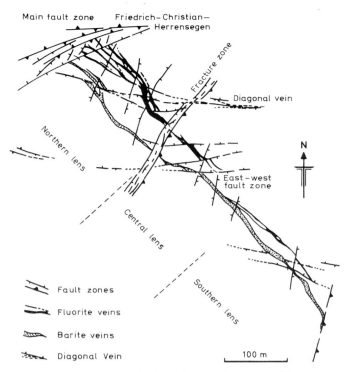

Fig. 60 *Distribution of mineralized fault zones in Clara mine, Oberwolfach, Central Black Forest. After Huck*[246]

geochemistry of hydrothermal solutions Huck concluded that there were longer periods of inactivity between mineralization phases and considered it possible that the beginning of ore deposition came during the Bunter Sandstone period.

Working of barite began in 1850 and has gone on without interruption since 1895; around 2 000 000 tonne of raw barite was produced. Production of fluorite from veins discovered in 1969 began in 1978 and has reached 300 000 tonne. Of the present annual production of 165 000 tonne, about two-thirds is raw fluorspar and one-third raw barite. Reserves amount to 1 300 000 tonne, of which 40% is barite and 60% fluorspar.

The Cu–Bi–barite–fluorite paragenesis with emplectite of the Daniel vein near Wittichen (vein group *L*) also comes to the surface in the Bunter Sandstone. The youngest phase of the Fe–Mn–Ba–F vein of Eisenbach (group *P*) is, according to Faisi,[51] younger than the Middle Bunter Sandstone.

Schürenberg[8] pointed to a post-Variscan age for the tectonically undeformed barite of vein group *C* at St. Ulrich and at Wildsbach in Untermünstertal. Finally, Sperling[38] has, on the basis of tectonic analyses, indicated the likelihood of a young Tertiary age for the fluorite–barite veins of vein group *A* of Wieden and Brandenberg, 8 km south and 10 km southwest of Schauinsland.

The veins in the northern Schwarzwald occur predominantly in the Lower and Middle Triassic cover rocks and strike northwest. They are concentrated in the districts of Freudenstadt–Neubulach and Neuenbürg, south of Pforzheim.[49] At Freudenstadt barite–quartz veins with chalcopyrite, tetrahedrite, emplectite and bornite are located in the boundary faults of a northwest-striking graben 15 km long and 7 km wide depressed to a depth of around 200 m. Fractures in the graben carry an impoverished paragenesis with barite–siderite–limonite. According to Carlé,[247] graben formation occurred in the younger Tertiary. The economic importance of the medieval mines led to the foundation in 1599 of the town of Freudenstadt. Around 1700 the winning of copper–silver ores was gradually replaced by the working of iron ores, which continued to 1860. The barite mining began after 1833 and lasted to 1914.[49]

At Neubulach a 750-m wide northwest-striking horst is intensively mineralized with a similar paragenesis. The production of the medieval copper–silver mines has been estimated from the visible mine dumps to be around 750 000 tonne of ore. The working of dumps for bismuth followed from 1917 to 1924. Similar veins with, in places, impoverished paragenesis occur between both districts in the upper Nagold valley and in the upper Murg valley.

At Neuenburg, south of Pforzheim, 70 larger and many small veins are known,[49] of which about half strike northwest and around one-third east–west. Two parageneses occur: east–west veins carry fluorite, which increases with depth, and quartz with barite and siderite, which decrease with depth in favour of fluorite. Cu–Ag–Bi sulphides increase with depth, but are nevertheless generally sparse. The most important vein of the district, which is presently worked in the Käfersteige ore deposit, belongs to this group.

Barite–hematite–siderite–limonite veins with manganese oxides, but without sulphides, in fractures running in all above-mentioned directions, evidently form a cooler thermal partial paragenesis.

The Käfersteige mine works a vein of raw fluorspar with between 40 and 50% CaF_2 and which is between 2 and 30 m thick and dips more or less vertically. Ncube and co-workers[248] distinguished four mineralization phases, beginning with oligoclase, quartz, the main mass of fluorite and very minor sulphides. After strong deformation with intense brecciation of the vein contents there followed three post-phases with quartz, minor fluorite and barite in several generations as well as goethite and malachite. Fluid inclusion research on fluorite and barite gave temperatures for the main phase of 370 to 300 °C and for the post-phase temperatures that declined from 258 to 65 °C with a salinity of between 27 and 15% NaCl equivalent. The ore deposit has been worked since 1933 and has produced around 1 000 000 tonne of raw fluorspar with 48% CaF_2. Reserves are estimated at around 300 000 tonne of raw fluorspar.

The iron mining in the Neuenburg district goes back to the La Tène period and ceased in 1865. Barite

Table 41 *Paragenetic scheme of mineralization in Clara mine, Oberwolfach, Central Black Forest. After Huck*[246]

1. Alteration and silicification phases	2. Fluorite main phase	3. Barite main phase	4. Baritic transition phase	5. Quartz main phase	
1.1 Quartz–pyrite (a) Quartz–pyrite breccia zones (b) Quartz–pyrite (chalcopyrite) 1.2 Quartz–amethyst 1.3 Quartz–hematite (?) Quartz–sericite (?)	Sub-phase 2.1 Quartz–fluorite Sub-phase 2.2 Quartz–fluorite/sellaite Sub-phase 2.3 Quartz–fluorite/sellaite	Fluorite–barite Barite Barite–tetrahedrite (?) Barite (?)	Barite–(fluorite)–(chalcopyrite–Fe oxides) Barite, pink banded (fluorite) Barite–Fe–Mn oxides	1. Silicification phase barite–fluorite–(pyrite–chalcopyrite) 2. Silicification phase fluorite–barite	Fluorspar veins
		Sub-phase 3.1 Barite–fluorite–marcasite Sub-phase 3.2 Barite–(fluorite) Sub-phase 3.3 Barite–(fluorite)–tetrahedrite Sub-phase 3.4 Barite–(fluorite)	Barite–Fe–Mn oxides Barite, pink banded (marcasite) Barite–Fe–Mn oxides–(fluorite)	Silicification phase with barite–(fluorite)–(pyrite–chalcopyrite) Silicification phase with (barite) (?) Silicification phase barite–fluorite	Barite vein
			Sub-phase 4.1 Barite–siderite–(fluorite–chalcopyrite) Sub-phase 4.2 (a) Barite (fluorite–marcasite) (b) Barite–Fe–Mn oxides (c) Fluorite–Fe–Mn (oxides)	Silicification phase (?) barite–(fluorite)	Barite joints
				Sub-phase 5.1 Quartz–barite–fluorite (pyrite–chalcopyrite) Sub-phase 5.2 Quartz–fluorite–(barite) Sub-phase 5.3 Quartz–barite–(fluorite) (chalcopyrite–galena) Sub-phase 5.4 Quartz–(fluorite–barite) (chalcopyrite–galena)	Diagonal stringers

was worked between 1918 and 1938. Fluorite mining began in 1926.[49] In the Bühler and Lower Murg valleys, southeast of Rastatt, poor hematite veins occur in granite with barite, siderite, quartz, limonite and manganese oxides. On them was based the small-scale mining of iron ores as early as the Middle Ages and at times in the seventeenth and eighteenth centuries.

Also very frequently mineralized with parageneses very similar to those in the Black Forest are the Black Forest boundary fracture and parallel fractures in the Trias opened up in the Tertiary. They are quartz–barite veins most of which also carry sulphides, mainly galena, more rarely sphalerite and in addition chalcopyrite, tetrahedrite and emplectite. These ores were worked in numerous places, especially at Badenweiler, Freiburg, Emmendingen, Lahr and northeast of Bühl.[8]

Northwest-striking barite veins are present in large numbers in the Odenwald and Spessart. They extend from the basement into the Bunter sandstone. In the Zechstein dolomite strata-bound metasomatic orebodies occur. Workable veins are developed in the

Bunter sandstone as a result of reduced thickness of the dolomite, as over the Spessart uplift, and/or as a result of greater displacement of the vein fracture.[25] In the Odenwald only a few veins reach thicknesses of more than 1 m. Particularly in the west, many barite veinlets are intensively impregnated with quartz. In the Spessart 11 northwest-striking vein systems carry abundant barite lenses over a depth of more than 100 m. They are 1–3 m (maximum 6 m) thick. The veins carry quartz and barite (white barite[25]) in two and locally three generations, with subordinate fluorite, siderite, minor chalcopyrite and pyrite and local hematite. In the Zechstein dolomite one finds ankerite and as weathering ores rich iron and manganese oxides. According to Hess,[249] the veins in the Spessart are associated with the intersection of north–south and northwest dislocation zones and the most important ore deposits occur in north–south-trending zones.

The barite mines in the Odenwald ceased operating in 1939 after 100 years of operation. In the Spessart the last mine ceased operating in 1972. The total production of both districts reached around 3 000 000 tonne of barite with 95–98% $BaSO_4$.

Barite veins in Hessian Depression and adjacent areas
Barite veins, in places with manganese oxides, are developed in the extension of the Spessart uplift towards the northeast in the southern Rhön Hills at Wildflecken.

In the Wetterau, north of Frankfurt-am-Main, and in the western margin of the Mainz Basin, fluorite is found as cement in middle Oligocene sands in the form of concretions and rosettes. Gunzert[241] pointed out that they only occur where Tertiary sands overlie the basement without the intervention of reactive rocks. In the Richelsdorf Hills mining operations hundreds of years old shifted from Kupferschiefer between 1720 and 1850 to 'Kobaltrücken' and between 1860 and 1967 to barite. A fair number of predominantly WNW-striking vein systems are known to carry barite and in the Kupferschiefer levels the 'Rücken' paragenesis. Minable barite values are confined to the Rotliegende conglomerate; a vein height of 40 m is scarcely exceeded. The mineralization is similar to that in the southwest Harz.[250] Altogether the area has produced 2 000 000 tonne of raw barite. Similar veins occur in the Fulda Greywacke Hills; there also occur in the Unterwerra Hills veins with an impoverished mineralization consisting practically only of barite and carbonate with minor quartz and pyrite. The Rücken paragenesis is missing. The workable thickness is confined partly to the carbonate rocks of the Zechstein and in other veins to the intrusive Diabase in the Palaeozoic. The Rotliegende is missing and in the Devonian the veins quickly disappear. Barely 3 000 000 tonne of raw barite was produced.[250]

Also in the eastern border region of the Rheinische Schiefergebirge, in the Taunus, in the Lahn and Dill

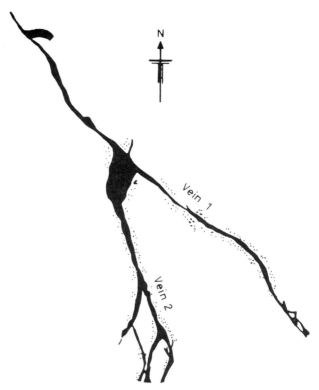

Fig. 61 *Vein map of Dreislar mine, 40-m level. After Gundlach and Weisser[251] (dotted, silicified wallrock)*

syncline, in the Kellerwald and in Sauerland large numbers of barite veins are known. With a few exceptions they only occasionally reach local significance. At Hartenrod, east of Dillenburg, a pinched vein around 1 km long with an average thickness of 5 m was worked from 1884 to 1957, yielding 170 000 tonne of raw barite and locally also some copper ores. The reserves here and in the neighbouring Herborner Hill mine totalled 250 000 tonne. At Dreislar, 30 km southwest of Korbach, on the southeast side of the Sauerland, is the NNW-striking Altenbüren dislocation zone, which already in the Devonian was functioning as a facies boundary; it is mineralized in northeast- to east-dipping and merging veins as well as in numerous wallrock veinlets. The on average 2-m thick vein 1 is worked over a length of 450 m and the 3·5-m thick vein 2 is worked over a distance of 300 m (Fig. 61). According to Tufar and Grassegger,[225] the paragenesis may be divided into a pre-phase with intensive silicification of the wallrock and several barite phases; red barite I, subordinate and only found in vein 1; barite II, which forms 75–80% of the vein filling and occurs in two sub-phases (II*a*, pale reddish with siderite and copper sulphides, and II*b*, as white-pink-red banded spar with layers of quartz 2); barite III, around 15%, pale, coarsely crystalline to drusy; barite IV, less than 5%, white, concretionary, finely crystalline, with iron sulphides.

Various carbonates, strontianite and numerous sulphides comprise less than 2% of the vein filling.

The homogenization temperature in barite lies between 140 and 70°C. According to Schaeffer,[222] the barite I of Dreislar is absent in Sauerland, and he compared the oldest barite generation of Sauerland with barite II of Dreislar. Also K-Ar dates of ±190 m.y. on clay minerals in the selvage of the Dreislar vein, determined by Bonhomme and co-workers,[224] show that the beginning of mineralization in Dreislar is to be placed in the Middle Mesozoic.

The veins have been worked since 1957 and have produced around 1 500 000 tonne of raw barite. The reserves are estimated at 500 000 tonne.

Attached here are the barite veins in the Lower Devonian of the southeast Eifel, which were worked between 1932 and 1967. Several groups of NNE-striking veins, among them the Uersfeld vein, occur in a NNW zone 11 km long and 3 km wide.[252]

The most important barite district of the FRG is located in the southwest Harz between the southern boundary of the Brocken granite, west and southwest of the Ag-Pb-Zn district of St Andreasberg and the southern border of the Harz at Bad Lauterberg (Figs. 29 and 30).[113] Numerous veins group themselves into some eight northwest-NNW-striking vein systems. Against that the richest mineralization lies in a zone 15 km long and 4 km wide that Hess[249] attributed to the intersection of mineralized tension faults with inclined movement of the hanging-walls with a north-south-striking fracture system. The emplacement of the vein fractures was, according to Hess, unassociated with and later than the Variscan folding. The veins reach up into the Lower Permian sediments and volcanics. The fracture system in which they are located dislocates Zechstein and Bunter sandstones. The veins are several hundred metres long, 2-4 m thick and carry barite contents between several tens of thousands and 300 000 tonne. Exceptional is the Wolkenhügel vein system, which is 1000 m long, >400 m wide and 2-3 (up to 25) m thick with an original content of 4 000 000 tonne of barite and, in addition, the Hohe Trost vein system with 2 000 000 tonne of barite.

The paragenesis starts with carbonate, quartz and, in places, abundant hematite, which was worked in the Knollen mine. The main phase carried barite I and II, in each case with quartz, and, in addition, very sporadic fluorite, which only occurred in the south in moderate amounts, and minor sulphides, primarily chalcopyrite. Younger quartz replaces barite; carbonate II replaces both quartz and barite. Gundlach et al.[151] were able to show through research into the rare-earth content that fluorite undoubtedly is of hydrothermal origin. Moreover, they claimed evidence for remobilization of the fluorite.

Veins in the ironstone working district WNW of St Andreasberg carried the first mineralization phase (1) as the main phase and were at one time worked for iron ores. From the Middle Ages to the eighteenth century copper ores were won from several veins in the south of the district. Iron ore mining ended in 1910. Barite has been worked since 1838.

In the Oberharz, west of Bad Grund, Zechstein carbonates have been replaced by barite along northwest fractures. They were worked to around 1900.[226]

The likewise possibly Alpine age of the barite in the Oberharz lead-zinc veins and in the veins in the Ruhr district was hinted at earlier.

Fluorite-barite veins in westernmost Bohemian Massif
As regards the ore and mineral occurrences in northeast Bavaria, the most recent results—in particular, regional metallogenetic, geochemical and isotopic investigations—preclude the classification of at least a part of the fluorite veins of this district as post-Variscan.[253-260] Some of these studies, which are briefly set out below, were available for the first time only on completion of this manuscript.

The fluorite district of Wölsendorf-Nabburg lies 60 km north of Regensburg on the northern border of the Tertiary basin of Bodenwöhr and at the western end of the 140-km long Pfahl dislocation (Fig. 4) in the area of intersection with a NNW-trending dislocation swarm. It is 15 km long and 4 km wide. Around 70 veins are known, of which around two-thirds strike at 135° and dip steeply to the south. North-south- and east-west-striking veins also occur. The wallrocks are Moldanubian gneiss and Variscan granites as well as Permo-Triassic arkoses.[259]

Ziehr[259] divided the mineral assemblage into two in each case multiphase main stages. Phase I carries red hornstone (quartz I), uranium oxides and very minor sulphides. Phase II follows with fluorite II (fetid fluorspar), paradoxite, younger uranium oxides, quartz II, hematite and minor sulphides. Sphalerite carries exsolved chalcopyrite. Assemblages of these older main groupings occur only in the central part of the district, whereas the younger phases are distributed over the whole district. Phase III carries the main bulk of fluorite in alternating violet (II*a*) and green (II*b*) layers, the last with higher contents of REE.[25] In addition, barite I and quartz IV coloured red by hematite flakes occur. After renewed tectonic movements there came phase IV with transparent fluorite III and, after further movements, carbonates in the central part of the district and transparent barite II in the central and western part and, in addition, the ultimate phase (V), which in small quantities is distributed over the whole district as pyrite, marcasite and other base-metal sulphides. At the same time, galena is more important in the east. The post-phase carries, as well as quartz V, mainly redepositions of the vein content. A fuller and wider explanation of the paragenesis was given by Dill.[255]

The ratio of fluorite to barite averages 5 to 1. Barite decreases with depth in favour of carbonate. Only in the outermost northwestern part of the district did barite increase with depth up to a ratio of less than 1 to 1. The content of ore minerals amounts to, on average, <0·1%, though it can in the central regions reach around 1%. In the southeast there occur quartz veins with silver-poor galena, which were worked around 1500 for silver and after 1700 for lead with relatively little success. Fluorite mining began after 1815, first reaching economic importance at the end of the nineteenth century. In total the district produced not quite 3 000 000 tonne of raw fluorite with 80% CaF_2. From veins with a richer content of barite this mineral was occasionally won.

Carl and Dill[256] obtained from pitchblende from the central part of the district a U–Pb age of 295 ± 14 m.y. Rb–Sr dating of paradoxite of phase II[258] gave 264 ± 4 m.y. A similar date came from a K–Ar dating on authigenic feldspar from the same region.[298] Accordingly, for the oldest uranium ore-bearing phases a Variscan age should be confirmed. This was supported by research by Möller,[257] which found in the Oberpfalz fluorites, in contrast to the Schwarzwald and other regions, lanthanide distributions typical of primary crystallization. A younger pitchblende of Altfalter on the transition from the central to the eastern part of the district yielded a U–Pb age of 206 ± 3 m.y. According to Dill,[255] they occur together with younger portions of the total paragenesis, from which he concluded that the greater part of the fluorite-barite mineralization was already formed before 200 m.y. and is therefore pre-Jurassic. Between Wölsendorf and Regensburg lies the small district of Nittenau on the southern boundary fracture of the Bodenwöhr Basin. Two veins are known, of which one was worked for a short time. It strikes northwest and carries breccia ore with barite, quartz and between 10 and 40% fluorite. The district of Donaustauf, east of Regensburg, is situated immediately north of the Danube boundary fractures in the region of their intersection with the Keilberg fault system (Fig. 4). Twelve northwest-striking veins are known, of which one is still worked. Both districts carry younger fluorite and, in Nittenau predominantly and in Donaustauf rarely, barite; uranium ores are absent. The fluorite production in the Donaustauf district has reached nearly 150 000 tonne with 80% CaF_2.

East and north of the three Oberpfalz districts there occur many individual veins with fluorite and barite—for example, at Lam in the Bavarian Forest, east of Weiden, at Warmensteinach in the Fichtelgebirge, north and northeast of Kronach in the Frankenwald. Finally, barite without fluorite occurs as the gangue of the lead–zinc veins of Erbendorf.

Of some economic importance was the Upper Franconian district at Hof–Bad Steben. There occurred in faults of the northwest-striking Frankenwald transverse zone a F–Ba paragenesis with white barite. Of around 20 known veins, seven contained a fluorite mineralization. An older group contained quartz, pyrite and chalcopyrite, pale fluorite I, rich siderite and, finally, calcite and fluorite II, which formed the bulk of the workable fluorite. The younger assemblage is principally associated with the higher levels and begins with barite, followed by ample fluorite III, siderite II and quartz II. The veins were worked since the Middle Ages up to 1923 for iron and at times also for copper ores. The weathering ores were won at first and then later siderite with 2–3% of manganese. After 1930 exploration for fluorite followed, and from 1940 to 1967 two veins were worked and around 200 000 tonne of fluorite with 80% CaF_2 was won.[26,29,255]

Dill[254] has reviewed the small barite veins at Rothenkirchen in the western Fichtelgebirge. Sporadic barite mineralization with quartz, fluorite, minor hematite and very minor sulphides is found on northwest fractures in Middle Keuper sandstones in the area of Bayreuth–Nürnberg. They are considered to be ascendant.[25,254]

Cobalt–nickel–bismuth paragenesis

These parageneses constitute mainly the ore content in barite–(fluorite) veins. The gangue is almost always barite—in southern Germany also fluorite—though, locally, there is much carbonate and for the most part subordinate quartz. The ore minerals are scattered niccolite, rammelsbergite, safflorite, skutterudite-chloanthite and arsenopyrite. In sulphur-rich parageneses gersdorffite and linneite predominate. The sulphides pyrite, sphalerite, silver-poor galena, principally as 'Glasurerz', and chalcopyrite form in the main isolated and then mainly younger partial phases. In some localities silver-rich phases occur. In several regions there occur younger parageneses with copper-bismuth sulphides.

The best known are the central German 'Kobaltrücken', which were of economic importance from the sixteenth to the nineteenth centuries. They are northwest-striking barite veins, which at Sontra in the Richelsdorf Hills and Bieber in the Spessart, 50 km east of Frankfurt-am-Main, contain at the level of the Kupferschiefer Ni–Co arsenides as topomineralic formations. In the conglomerates of the higher Rotliegende 40–50 m under the Kupferschiefer veins are from 1 to several metres thick and contain 90% barite as against quartz, calcite and sporadic ore minerals. In other wallrocks the mineralization is interrupted and the veins pass into fracture zones. Only in the immediate neighbourhood of the Kupferschiefer do they contain rich cobalt–nickel ores over a vertical height of 10–15 m. At Sontra around 25 main and many small veins are known, forming in places vein swarms. Messer[156] distinguished here the following ascendant-epithermal mineralization phases: I, barite–carbonate quartz pre-phase without ore minerals, IIa, main phase with Co–Ni arsenides and minor quartz, IIb, transition phase with barite, arsenopyrite and Co–Ni sulphides and III, main phase, predominantly arsenide-free veins with calcite, marcasite, pyrite, sphalerite, galena and minor chalcopyrite.

It is possible to compare with the Kobaltrücken the barite vein with copper and copper–bismuth sulphides of Freudenstadt and Neubulach (Fig. 7). In addition, the oldest, very mineral-rich paragenesis of Wiesloch with Cu–Ag–Bi–As minerals is to be included. These were compared by Bauer[260] with the mineralization of Nieder-Ramstadt[261] and other localities in the Odenwald. The quantitatively unimportant vein ores here carry galena, skutterudite, safflorite, native silver, argentite, pyrargyrite and sphalerite. A probably older older and unrelated sphalerite–chalcocite–bornite-galena paragenesis occurs in the same vein.

In the fluorite district of Nabburg Co–Ni–Bi minerals are shown to be microscopic accompaniments of uranium oxides. Traces also occur in the siderite veins of the Frankenwald.[25,255]

In the Siegerland Co–Ni–Bi ores are scattered, but only in places are they of younger age. Cobalt ores are concentrated in the Betzdorf–Siegen district and have been worked from time to time. With regard to the dating of the post-Variscan mineralization, a find of sedimentary Ni–Co–Cu minerals in an Oligocene clay basin at Langendernbach in the Westerwald is of interest.[83]

Müller and Scherp[98] described from Ramsbeck a northwesterly fracture oblique to the Variscan lead-zinc ore veins containing a Tertiary paragenesis with a barite phase divisible into two sub-phases that carry iron sulphides, gersdorffite and chalcopyrite and a three-division carbonate phase with (1) galena, sphalerite, pyrite and Co–Ni arsenides, (2) silver sulphides and complex antimonides as well as (3) manganocalcite.

In the lead–zinc district of the Bergische Land there is an individual young fracture system with a Co–Ni–As paragenesis that carries chalcopyrite as the principal ore mineral as well as barite and carbonate as gangue. Monomineralic siderite veins occur in addition.[92] The veins strike north–south and east–west and coincide with Tertiary basalt dykes and boundary steps of the Lower Rhine Bight. They were worked for copper in more than 50 mines, or for siderite. Total production from the Tertiary mineralization of this district can be estimated at close on 20 000 tonne of copper and 1 000 000 tonne of iron. The Variscan ores carry only 0·2–0·4% copper in concentrates.

Lead–zinc ore deposits

Vein and impregnation deposits in northern Eifel Mountains

In the northern Eifel there occur in Devonian sandstones and clay slates between the Hohe Venn in the west and the Schnee-Eifel in the east, lead (–zinc) and copper ore veins that have a spatial, paragenetic

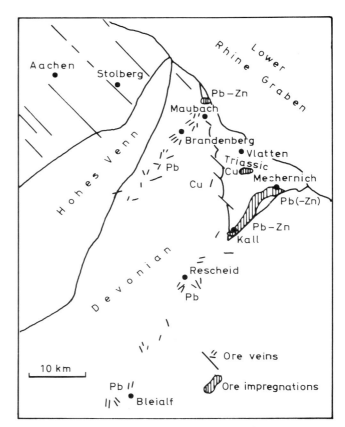

Fig. 62 *Distribution of lead–zinc and copper veins and impregnation deposits in Palaeozoic rocks and Triassic sandstones, respectively, in northern Eifel Mountains. Compiled from Bayer and co-workers*[266]

and thereby also genetic relation to impregnation ore deposits in the Bunter Sandstone of the Trias Triangle.[82,262] In Maubach, as well as in Mechernich, transitions from vein ores in the Lower and Middle Devonian rocks to impregnation ores in the transgressive Trias sandstone are known. Both ore types carry the same paragenesis[263] and were produced together up to 1910 in the Kaller Stollen mine (Kall adit, Fig. 62).

Lead (–zinc) and copper veins in Devonian rocks

From the southwest to SSW direction the Brandenberg and Bleialf–Rescheid vein swarms run towards the northwestern and southern corner of the Trias Triangle, respectively. Where the vein swarms disappear under the Trias the impregnation mineralization of Maubach and Mechernich is located (Fig. 62).

Mining has gone on since the Middle Ages up to the present century on both vein swarms in many mines. The numerous veins carry patchy, at times very rich, ore values, so periods of strong activity alternated with long-extended exploration and stagnation. The last workings were in progress at Bleialf up to 1954 and at Rescheid up to 1940.[119] This change from short blossomings with times of additional payments is presumably the reason that this sub-district of the northern Eifel has not been the subject of systematic studies since the end of the last century. The most recent detailed references are set out in the work cited.

According to Bornhardt,[82] the WNW–north–south-striking veins belong to the type known as *Bleiglasurerzgänge* with stout, coarsely laminated and silver-poor galena (± 10 g of silver per tonne of lead). The mineralization begins with carbonate, bravoite, quartz and chlorite, followed by minor sphalerite, galena and some chalcopyrite. Tetrahedrite, linneite and millerite also occur.[263] Barite was important to a depth of about 100 m and then decreased quickly, being found only sporadically at deep levels to 280 m. According to Bornhardt,[82] sphalerite and siderite are absent at Rescheid. In samples from the Silberberg mine, 10 km south of Kall and a short distance south of

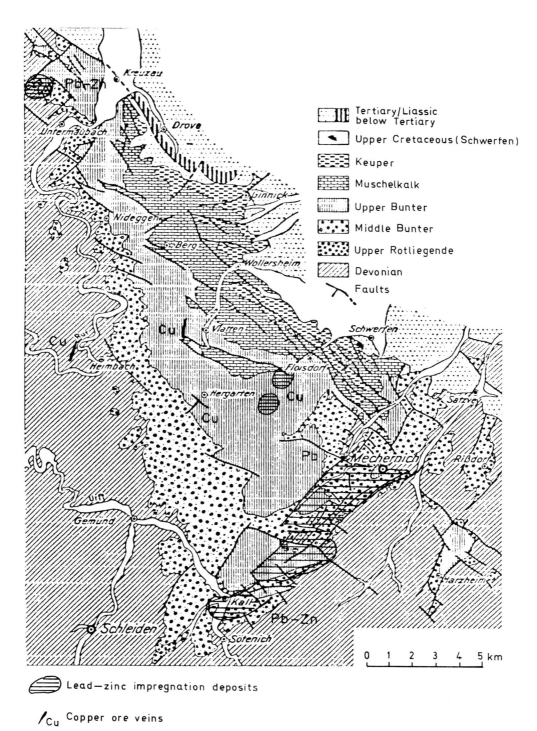

Fig. 63 *Geological map of Triassic syncline of Maubach and Mechernich by E. Schröder from Puffe*[269] *with lead–zinc and copper impregnation deposits and some copper–barite veins*

the Bunter sandstone cover, siderite and, additionally, galena with 400 g of silver per tonne of lead, but no sphalerite, was found.[264]

Between the two vein swarms there lie, 12 km south of Maubach, the veins worked in the old copper mine of Goldkuhle.[263] The zoning Pb–Cu–Pb thereby indicated is found again also in the Trias Triangle, where south and southeast of Vlatten in the Upper Bunter sandstone, alongside copper *Knottenerz* and ore-free barite veins, there occur also copper-bearing veins (Figs. 62 and 63). In particular, the *Knottenerz* were formerly worked locally.[265]

Large and co-workers[234] found that the lead isotope data of the ore deposits in the Devonian and Triassic, and also those of the Aachen–Stolberg districts in the northwest of the Hohe Venn, showed the same characteristics and a linear tendency. They demonstrated thereby a common origin of the ore solutions that led to the formation of these three types of ore deposit. The data are insufficient for an age interpretation. By contrast, the sulphur isotope properties are clearly different.[266] The veins in the Devonian show $\delta^{34}S$ values around 0‰. In the Trias Triangle they lie between -27 and $-12‰$, so the values for Maubach (-21 to $-12‰$) lead one to assume the existence of a very constant isotopic constitution of the sulphur source. In the Aachen–Stolberg district the values are scattered between -18 and $+38‰$ in the series PbS–ZnS (sphalerite–pale to dark schalenblende)–FeS_2, which points to formation at low temperatures. Walther[186] has given a summary review.

Lead–zinc impregnation deposits of Maubach and Mechernich The Trias Triangle with the ore deposits of Maubach and Mechernich lies south of the Lower Rhine Bight in the Eifel north–south zone (Figs. 1 and 56). This zone crosses, following an old zone of weakness, the left Rheinische Schiefergebirge. During the time of the Middle Bunter Sandstone it was reactivated. Northwest of the Kallmuth Rise (Fig. 65) deposition of dune sands occurred locally, which in the higher beds are increasingly supplanted by fluviatile sandstone and conglomerate.[268] The material was for the most part transported from the south. For a part—particularly the conglomerate—one must assume, however, that local accumulation occurred. Already in Upper Bunter Sandstone time, and later during the Muschelkalk, a sea from the north flooded this region. The deposits of this time indicate a coastal marine-dominated zone.

From the geological outline map (Fig. 63) one can see that the lead–zinc occurrences associated with the Bunter Sandstone complex of Maubach lie at the northern point of the Bunter Sandstone triangle and those of Mechernich on the southern flank. The accumulation of the beds of the Middle or Main Bunter Sandstone—the Lower Bunter Sandstone is absent—is not regular. The basement on which the transported material was deposited was unstable and showed local, e.g. northeast-striking, uplifts. Local movements during deposition had, in addition, the effect that thickness and facies in the Middle Bunter Sandstone of the Trias Triangle could vary considerably.

In regard to the *Maubach deposit*, the Middle Bunter Sandstone transgresses over folded and steeply dipping clay slates and sandstones of the Lower Devonian. A

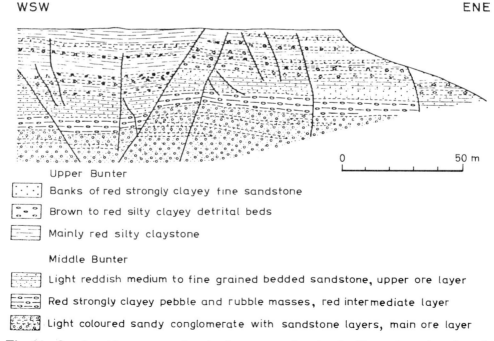

Fig. 64 *Stratigraphic sequence and mode of occurrence of ore-bearing Bunter in northern face of former open-pit mine 'Maubacher Bleiberg' from a sketch by A. Voigt from Knapp and Hager*[267]

layer of clay was formed on the clay slates. The mineralized Middle Bunter Sandstone is between 12 and 14 m thick and may be divided into three units (Fig. 64). The flat-lying sequence, 8–25 m thick, consists of a strongly alternating sequence of sandstone and conglomerates in which the ore occurs as impregnations. Above this ore horizon lies a sequence 4–6 m thick of red sandstone and conglomerates that is unmineralized. Above this 'rote Zwischenschicht' there occurs a facially very homogeneous, up to 8 m thick, pale coloured sandstone horizon. It is locally, and almost always in the vicinity of dislocations, mineralized and has been designated the 'hängendes Lager'. Above this comes the Upper Bunter Sandstone, which is composed of red, clayey and almost unconsolidated sandstones and conglomerates. It constitutes an overburden up to 70 m thick in the process of mining the ores.

Very noticeable and important for the emplacement of the ore deposit are the numerous dislocations that cut the Trias and demonstrably were already active during the deposition of the Bunter Sandstone. In this complicated boundary step-fault system that consists of downthrust, upthrust and overthrust dislocations, there are preferred directions—northwest–southeast and perpendicular to it. The solutions that deposited the ores encountered a very porous rock. They were introduced during the diagenesis of the sandstone and conglomerate. The volume of ore shows a clear, directly proportional dependence on the original porosity of the rocks. The order of crystallization is sulphides, carbonates, chlorite and new quartz. The silicification is related to the act of mineralization or to the diagenesis. Even before the commencement of quartz deposition there took place in some areas—particularly in the lowest part of the ore layers near the Devonian basement—a carbonatic cementing of sandstone and conglomerates. Then an Fe-rich dolomite (ankerite) was separated and, after that, siderite, which could have developed idiomorphically in the remaining open spaces. Simultaneously with the carbonate, and also well before it, bravoite was formed. While homoaxial growth of quartz substance was taking place in the carbonate-free parts pale sphalerite was already forming, which can replace the bravoite parallel to its Ni- and Co-bearing zones. Then galena with reduced silver content and chalcopyrite are deposited in the still free pore spaces. Both can replace the sphalerite, the bravoite and the carbonatic substance. Tetrahedrite, bournonite, gersdorffite and a still unidentified Pb–Bi sulphosalt are subordinate. Dickite reposes in the ore, is cemented by it or fills pore spaces and belongs also to the mineralization cycle.

The ore impregnation described is, of course, to be found everywhere in the lower section of the main Bunter Sandstone, but has locally variable appearance and extent. Parallel to the thrusts there has been in places some enrichment, which may have a vein-like aspect. Here chalcopyrite is mostly dominant. Wider carbonate veins with bravoite and minor chalcopyrite extend in places into the Devonian. Evidence of deformation in galena and chalcopyrite and the knife-sharp cutting of pebbles with later healing by ore indicate tectonic reworking during mineralization. With regard to emplacement of the ores and the origin of the solutions that deposit them, various explanations are possible. A magmatic cycle for primary ore formation cannot be considered because it is missing. One could consider thermal springs, which on their way up dissolved pre-existing sulphides and then redeposited them in the appropriate pore-rich rocks under declining temperatures and specific physico-chemical conditions (thermo-diffusion) ('secondary hydrothermal' in the sense of Schneiderhöhn).

The ore deposit has been known since Roman times and was worked in the Middle Ages and in the sixteenth century.[119] Not till the nineteenth century were there at intervals some further periods of working. In 1950 it was possible to indicate by means of a comprehensive drilling programme and subsequent underground exploration 12 000 000 tonne of ore with an average content of 2·7% Pb, 0·9% Zn, 0·04% Cu and 300 ppm silver. With a metal potential of more than 400 000 tonne of lead and zinc Maubach shows itself to be an important ore deposit in the European realm. Open-pit working began in 1959. The Upper Bunter Sandstone overburden was a severe handicap. Working of the ore deposit stopped in 1969 because of exhaustion.

In the *Mechernich deposit* the regional distribution of ores and their relationship to tectonic fault systems also argues for introduction of the solutions in an early stage of diagenesis. As in Maubach the mineralized beds belong stratigraphically to the Middle Bunter Sandstone. They lie on the southeast flank of the Trias Triangle (Fig. 63).

Unlike Maubach, the mineralization is predominantly to be found in the sandstone and is only subordinate in the conglomerates. 'Sandstone seams' and conglomerate layers alternate with each other (Fig. 65). Whereas in the east of the ore district there is indeed only a 10-m sandstone layer present, further southwest it is accompanied by a hanging-wall and a footwall conglomerate bank. In the western part of the field in the southwestern part of the area there is developed a swollen sequence up to 90 m thick, including four sandstone seams and five conglomerate layers. The diagenetic lithification of the rocks increases with total thickness. The mineralized area extends for 9 km in this direction. Above the ore-bearing beds there reposes, as in Maubach, the higher Middle Bunter Sandstone and, above that, red clayey Upper Bunter Sandstone. In the southeast of the ore deposit there lies the northeast–southwest-striking Kallmuth Rise, which is considered to be an epeirogenetically predetermined structural element, on

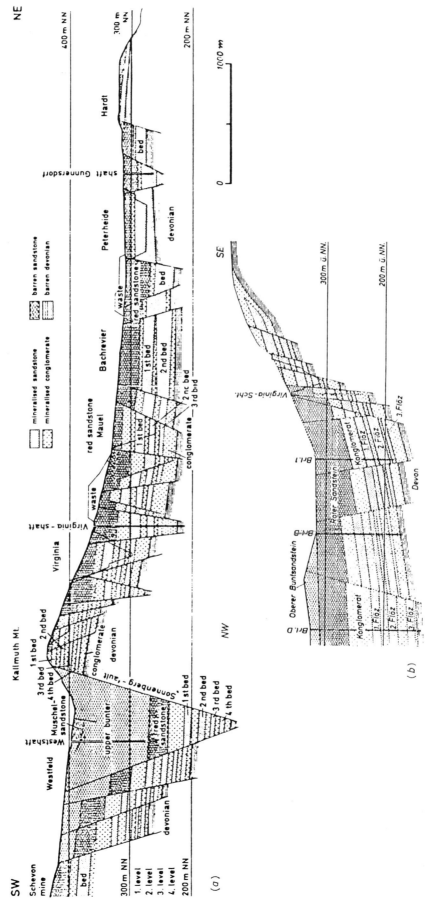

Fig. 65 Longitudinal (a) and transverse (b) profile through Mechernich deposit[269]

which the Middle Bunter Sandstone is absent. From the edge of the Rise the beds subside towards the northwest in a flexure-like manner (Fig. 65(b)). Numerous longitudinal and transverse dislocations exist, of which a few reach displacements of up to 200 m (Sonnenberg fault, Fig. 65(a)). In the down-warped western field sphalerite increases markedly in the ore. Diagonal to these principal tectonic lines occur displacement planes on which movement has occurred before, during and after ore deposition, showing slickensides with polished ore surfaces.

The ore solutions also encountered here a porous rock. First, there was a partial cementing of sandstones by carbonate, principally ankerite and siderite, which in the majority of cases form a very coarsely crystalline cementing material. In this way there arose bank- and mat-shaped bodies, the so-called 'carbonate banks', and also spherical, frequently shell structures, the 'Karbonattutten'. The 'banks' can extend for several metres parallel to the bedding and for some decimetres vertically. They caused damming of the ore solutions, so rich mineralization could take place at its boundaries. The carbonate banks and carbonate 'Tutten' contained no ore inclusions—in contrast to the carbonate veins and veinlets in the underlying Devonian, which from time to time carry bravoite and chalcopyrite.

The deposition of sulphide is locally preceded also by a silicification event. Bravoite is the oldest sulphide, followed by sphalerite, galena and chalcopyrite. In the areas near to the surface more than half of the galena has been altered to cerussite.

All sulphides can occur as the so-called 'Knotten'—that is, they cement, often as single crystals, several quartz grains and constitute three-dimensional nodules, known as 'Knotten'. The 'Knotten' reach a diameter of 1–2 cm, thus giving the almost always pale sandstone a flecked appearance. These typical 'Knottenerze' are also developed in Maubach. Tetrahedrite, boulangerite and other sulphosalts occur rather rarely. One must assume for Mechernich, as for Maubach, a 'secondary-hydrothermal' emplacement in the sense of Schneiderhöhn.

According to Slotta,[119] Celtic mining is probable in Mechernich and Roman mining confirmed. From the end of the Middle Ages until after 1800 low-yield one-man working was carried out. After 1860 mining blossomed. The content of the ores worked at that time lay between 1·5 and 2·5% Pb—in rich parts up to 4% Pb. In 1952 Mechernich produced 41% of the output of the lead–zinc mines in West Germany and nearly 20% of the lead production. On the basis of the raw ore production at that time and the known ore reserves the life-span of the mine was estimated at 55 years. The metal content, however, soon declined to just short of 1% Pb, which led to the cessation of working in 1957.

Henneke[270] estimated the overall production of Mechernich as 2 500 000–3 000 000 tonne of lead metal. He quoted the known reserves in the eastern field of the ore deposit as 40 000 000 tonne of ore with 0·78% Pb and 1·58% Zn, and the established resources in the unworked west field to amount to 60 000 000 tonne of ore with 0·57% Pb and 1·11% Zn. This gives a total metal content of 5 000 000 tonne Pb + Zn, and for the unworked ore deposit the whole metal content (including zinc, which was not looked for in former times) runs to at least 7 000 000 tonne of metal.[186]

Wiesloch deposit

The lead–zinc ore deposit of Wiesloch, which occurs south of Heidelberg in the region of the eastern boundary fracture of the Rhine Valley Graben, is a strata-bound deposit in the Upper Muschelkalk of the Middle Trias. It has originated, as far as the main mass of its ores is concerned, as an epigenetic formation in association with the Tertiary graben tectonics, and it is micritic, bituminous limestone in the Trochitenkalk that is mineralized. Probably a part of the ore and gangue had previously been concentrated syngenetically. Wiesloch was worked for more than a thousand years and from 1853 to its closure in 1953 yielded ores that carried 120 000 tonne of zinc and lead metal.

The most recent workers suggest for this genetically controversial ore deposit, primarily on the basis of mining geological mapping[260] and on ore microscopic research,[271] an epigenetic origin and geologically young ore emplacement. When, however, Seeliger[271] comments that it is really only a question of personal opinion that will ascribe the Wiesloch ore deposit to this or that type—in other words, to interpret it as the redeposition of older ores and merely the integration of a number of bedded occurrences poses certain difficulties, and that they are hardly or not at all to be distinguished from very similar, primarily syngenetic, occurrences—it seems that, according to present-day knowledge, this purely epigenetic interpretation of a very complex formation history is not conclusive.

The oldest mineralization phase is the Cu–Ag–Co–Bi partial paragenesis in northwest veinlets up to 10 cm thick. Younger Pb–Zn partial parageneses occurred after the migration of oil from the Rhine Graben in parts of the neighbourhood of the ore deposit. It consisted principally of sphalerite in the form of schalenblende, galena and jordanite with barite and calcite as the gangue. A possibly primary sedimentary portion of the ore deposit could have been redeposited in the Tertiary through ascendant solutions and after a short transport, in part under the reducing influence of oil, might have been redeposited in joint-controlled karst cavities and in fissures. These cavity-fillings and their oxidation products constitute much more than 90% of the workable ores.

Barite from Wiesloch shows $\delta^{34}S$ values up to $+93‰$—the highest content hitherto known in minerals. von Gehlen[67] interpreted the findings as the result of the reworking of a circumscribed sulphate source, which probably had its origin in the flow of oil into the vicinity of the ore deposit in the Tertiary, with a high fractionating effect through sulphate-reducing bacteria.

Wiesloch shows in numerous characteristics similarities with the strata-bound lead–zinc ores in the Lower Muschelkalk of Upper Silesia. The metal content of the 16 000 000 tonne of zinc and 4 000 000 tonne of lead ore worked here in the first half of the twentieth century,[272] however, exceeds that of Wiesloch by more than 150 times.

Other lead–zinc mineralization
Veins of 'Glasurbleierz' (glazier's lead ore) are also scattered over the right-bank Rheinische Schiefergebirge. They occur predominantly in the environs of the Siegerland district, but also within this siderite district there are clear indications of them. In the northwest they are particularly frequent in a broad band from the lower Sieg above Olpe as far as the northeast Sauerland as well as at Bad Honnef on the Rhine and in the siderite-free zone between the Siegen and Wied districts at Altenkirchen and Wissen.[82,87]

In the eastern Siegerland district a few 'Glasurbleierz' veins lead to an area of greater concentration in the Wittgensteiner Land with the formerly important veins of the Gonderbach mine as Laasphe, 30 km east of Siegen (Fig. 19).[273,274] Isolated 'Glasurbleierz' veins occur in the northern Dill syncline near Wetzlar and in the Kellerwald. Another district is located at Usingen in the eastern Taunus, where mining was carried on in Roman times. Later investigations up to around 1935 had no long-term success.[119]

At the northern edge of the Rheinische Schiefergebirge lead–zinc mineralization is known at several places in Mesozoic and Tertiary wallrocks and has been mined over a long period of time in some places.[229] In the brown coal-bearing, probably Middle Oligocene, clays of the Paffrath syncline, north of Bensberg, there occur laterally impersistent beds, bands and veins with galena. Barite veins with lead ores in Devonian massive limestones at Bleiwäsche, 14 km northeast of Brilon, were interpreted by Schriel[229] as feeder channels for the metasomatic barite layers in the Cenomanian.

The mainly northwest–southeast- to north–south-striking veins are generally between 0.5 and 1 m, and, more rarely, but locally important, 2 m thick. The orebodies reach strike lengths of several hundred metres and up to more than 100-m extension in depth. The ores often show a markedly drusy character. The parageneses contain quartz, mostly in pale crystals, but partly also chalcedonic and massive.

Silver-poor galena (= 'Glasurerz') occurs in large zonal crystals up to several kilogrammes in weight or massive or coarsely laminated, the silver content amounting to, on average, 100 g Ag/t Pb[87] along with mainly subordinate chalcopyrite and pyrite, as well as varying quantities of carbonate ('Bitterspat'[82]).

Sphalerite occurs in the form of honey blende; this was only known in a few occurrences, but would occasionally reach half the amount of the galena and sometimes more.

Similar veins were worked in the Mesozoic borderlands in the northeast of the Rheinische Schiefergebirge. In the southern Egge Hills the north- to NNW-striking Westheim fault, the northerly extension of the eastern border step of the Rheinische Schiefergebirge, is mineralized at Blankenrode, 10 km NNE of Marsberg, for 2 to 3 km in length with galena, calamine, calcite and minor quartz. The wallrocks are Bunter sandstone and Cenomanian limestones as well as subordinate Zechstein limestone. The limestones are partly metasomatized. These ores were mined in the Bleikaulen mine from antiquity up to and after 1870 and supplied lead for the building of St. Peter's in Rome.[229] Some 17 km further south at Vasbeck Zechstein limestones are metasomatically mineralized in a similar manner, emanating from the same fracture zone. These ores were worked up to 1909 in the Mathias mine.

The occurrence of 'Glasurbleierz' veins is quite separate from that of the Variscan lead–zinc ore veins. Also, their parageneses clearly differ from those of older veins in regard to the almost total absence of siderite, the markedly diverse chemistry of galena and sphalerite as well as through the frequent absence of sphalerite.

Lead ore veins with barite and calcite occur locally in southern Lower Saxony and eastern Westphalia in the Trochitenkalk—an, on average, 10-m thick bed in the Upper Muschelkalk. At Kulf, 20 km southwest of Hildesheim, and at Helpup, 15 km southeast of Bielefeld, a number of trial workings were undertaken on the ~1-m thick veins. According to Hofmeister and co-workers,[175] their formation is in the wider sense lateral-secretionary. The lead is not magmatic and originates from clay rocks of the wider surroundings, sulphur and probably also barium and strontium stemming probably from the Middle Muschelkalk salt.[175] Comparable formations were described by Rose and Gödecke[238] from the Teutoburger Wald.

The dating of the majority of lead–zinc ore veins in south Germany is uncertain. The problems of mineralization in the Schwarzwald were referred to earlier.

In the border region of Pfalz–Alsace at Bobenthal, 25 km southeast of Pirmasens, two veins located in Bunter Sandstone were mined from time to time from the sixteenth century up to around the eighteenth.[119] The veins carried mainly galena, with smithsonite and numerous secondary ores. Exploration was stopped around 1900 because of water problems, and in 1971 no more promising mineralization was encountered. Müller[275] considered the lead–zinc ores to be geologically young on the basis of their similarity to the general mineralization in the region Saar–Nahe-Pfalz.

The approximately north–south-striking, steeply dipping and 30- to 60-cm (maximum 2·6-m) thick lead–zinc ore veins at Erbendorf in the Oberpfalz occur in gneiss and in coal-bearing Permian. They carry coarsely laminated galena with 300–800 ppm Ag, subordinate sphalerite, accessory pyrite and up to 10% chalcopyrite in the ores, in addition to quartz, subordinate carbonate and rare barite. From the fourteenth century, and particularly in the sixteenth century, the veins were actively mined. Later investigations up to and beyond 1945 had no lasting success.[119] Dill compared the ores with the veins of Wallenfels in the Frankenwald and ranked them with the youngest part of the Variscan metallogenesis.[254,255] In contrast, he described the occurrence of Dürrenwaid, 10 km further to the northeast, and till now compared with Wallenfels, which carries relatively silver-rich galena (600–1600 ppm Ag), as a stratiform and chemically and mineralogically distinct mineralization, which is lateral-secretionary to diabase.

Copper and uranium impregnations

In the Bunter Sandstone at the eastern edge of the Rheinische Schiefergebirge and in the Eifel north–south zone in the Trias Triangle, the Trier Bight and in the western Saarland there occur, quite often, mainly small-scale copper and uranium impregnations, in places together. They were mined for copper in some places for long periods of time—for example, at Twiste, 10 km northeast of Korbach and 40 km west of Kassel, periodically from the Middle Ages to 1861, and at Wallerfangen, 50 km WNW of Saarbrücken. There Roman mining could be confirmed and possibly Celtic; from the Middle Ages to 1715 azurite was worked as a dyestuff. The ore impregnations extend out from younger fractures and are associated with bleached sandstone beds.[119] The copper impregnations in the Upper Bunter Sandstone in the Trias Triangle of the northern Eifel have already been mentioned.

At Wrexen, 11 km northeast of Marsberg, copper–uranium ores are found with metazeunerite as the principal uranium-bearing mineral in channels with plant remains that recall the roll-front type of mineralization. Meisl[276] compared the parageneses with the vanadium-free Cu–U ore deposits of Colorado. Small-scale to spot-shaped uranium concentrations with up to 1% U were found by Meisl[277] in Tertiary lignites in the Kassel area and in cement quartzites at Dillich, 40 km SSW of Kassel. Wrexen and Dillich uranium occurs together with an epigenetic Cu–Fe paragenesis with bravoite. On the basis of radiometric anomalies, Meisl considered the supply of the uranium in the lignites or the last redepositions, at Wrexen and Dillich, respectively, as Quaternary to Recent. The metals are derived from the Kupferschiefer or from the Variscan basement.

Niobium mineralization in carbonatites of the Kaiserstuhl

The Kaiserstuhl volcano, of Miocene age, lies in the southern part of the Upper Rhine Graben. It has a roughly rhombic outline with a major axis of nearly 16 km in a southwest–northeast direction and a maximum width in a southeast–northwest direction of 12·5 km. Three main geological units can be distinguished: I, the sedimentary platform cover in the east (predominantly Oligocene and some Jurassic); II, the Kaiserstuhl volcano proper (lavas and pyroclastics, mostly leucite–tephrite); III, the centre, composed of sub-volcanic rocks (essexite, ledmorite, alkali syenite, carbonatite, various dyke rocks and sub-volcanic breccias). To the sub-volcanic formations belong also the phonolite stocks and numerous dykes appearing in units I and II outside the centre.

A carbonatite body of about 1 km^2 in surface area and many carbonatite dykes intrude into the sub-volcanic rocks at the centre of the Kaiserstuhl.[278] Most of the rocks are sövites, composed of calcite, apatite, magnetite, mica and forsterite. Pyrochlore and niobian perovskite are sparse accessories. In 1935–36 the carbonatite was explored for possible niobium extraction; the average contents in the most favourable parts of the body were 0·2–0·35% Nb_2O_5. A second period of mining from 1949 to 1952 also failed to achieve economic production. Geochemical studies by van Wambeke et al.[279] demonstrated the very irregular distribution of Nb all over the carbonatite body, ranging from <0·01 to 1·42% Nb, the average of 25 analyses being 0·078%.

Mineral deposits associated with Ries impact

The Nördlingen Ries and the Steinheim Basin 35 km to the southwest have definitely been confirmed from comprehensive multidisciplinary researches in the last 20 years, triggered by the evidence of coesite by Shoemaker and Chao,[280] as an impact crater.[281] Coeval with the Ries are the Bohemian moldavites (K-Ar and fission dating to 14·8 ± 0·7 m.y. and 14·7 ± 0·7 m.y., respectively).[282] The 1206-m deep Ries borehole of 1973 showed a flat crater with a depth/diameter ratio of 1:33.[281] In a zone 16 m deep immediately beneath the crater floor Goresy and Chao found in shock-induced breccias a metal coating 0·1 μm thick and showed this to be a condensate of vaporized meteorite material.[281] On the basis of composition—in particular, the Co–Ni content, which suggests achondrites—they concluded that it was a stony meteorite.

The south German bentonite, thought to stem from microtectite rain following the Ries event, has since

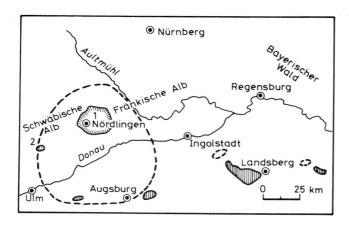

Fig. 66 *Surroundings of Nördlingen Ries Basin with spread of foreign Jurassic blocks and Lower Bavarian bentonite deposits*[283,284]

1900 been worked at Landshut, Meinberg and Moosburg around 50 km northeast of München (Fig. 66). They are weathering products of glass tuffs, which, on the basis of their chemical composition, are similar to suevite tuffs (suevite is an impactite, consisting of a breccia of basement fragments). Age dating has given 14.6 ± 0.8 m.y.[282]

The bentonites were laid down in a sub-basin of the upper Freshwater Molasse (Middle Miocene) and in layers and lenses centimetres to a few metres thick and 20–250 m across. Frequently, the layers contain intercalations of marls and sands. The bentonites contain from 60 to 90% montmorillonite and, additionally, quartz, mica, feldspar and carbonate. Working is by open-pit with overburden up to 30 m thick. The average proportion of bentonite to overburden is 1:11. Average production reached 300 000 tonne around 1960 and since 1970 600 000 tonne. The known reserves are sufficient for barely ten years of mining. Bentonite is principally used as a binder, a bleaching material and a catalyst, among many other uses.[284,285]

On the basis of very recent stratigraphic, petrographic and geochemical data, Unger and Niemeyer[299] derived the acid glass from which the bentonites originated from the Miocene ryolite volcanism in the Carpathian Mountains.

Weathering deposits

Gossans

The development of weathering ores from pre-existing ore deposits has generally been slight in the FRG. The weathering zones of the ore veins in the Oberharz are only a few metres thick because of young uplift and rapid erosion. The same goes for the majority of the lead–zinc districts. Exceptions are, for example, in the Schwarzwald in the outcrops of veins on the plateau. In individual veins in Schauinsland the weathering ores reach down to 150 m and in the Friedrich-Christian vein at Wolfach down to 185 m. Weathering deposits of various depths were encountered on the siderite veins of Siegerland, where in various parts of the district to depths of more than 100 m and in places up to 300 m limonite ores form the principal vein content. In the Ems vein swarm southwest of Bad Ems oxidized ores were still found at 700-m depth next to lead–zinc sulphides.

For the formation of economically important cementation ore-enrichment zones the Alpine lead–zinc ore deposits come first, followed by the copper ore deposits in the Nahe, where they reach a depth of 150 m, and the copper-bearing veins in the Siegerland. Silver-rich cementation ores periodically played a role in St. Andreasberg in the Middle Harz and occurred as rarities at Müsen in the northern Siegerland. The cerussite–galena ore deposit of Freihung in the Oberpfalz is a weathering enrichment on the Freihung Fracture, produced from a galena protore.

Iron and manganese

Weathering enrichments of iron and manganese that came into being during the Mesozoic and Tertiary are widespread and played an important role in early industrial times. Individual deposits were mined until as late as 1950 and after.[20,286] In most of the non-ferrous orefields and in the Siegerland mining began with the iron-bearing gossan. Over the last hundred years, however, only the weathering deposits of iron and manganese have been of any significance.

In the Hunsrück numerous small mines at one time extracted ore from the limonite lens contained in the Devonian rock. The last such mine, near Simmern to the south of Koblenz, was until 1925 producing a concentrate with 42% Fe, 20% SiO_2, 0.25% Mn and 0.5% P. The volume of output was, however, small.

Until 1968 in the Lindener Mark near Giessen and until 1971 near Waldalgesheim to the west of Bingen on the Rhine ferromanganese and pure manganese ores on and in the karstic limestones and dolomites of the Devonian were extracted. These ores contain 20–40% Fe and 15–20% Mn, and the pure manganese ores contain up to 42% Mn. Production (tonne) was as noted below.

	Lindener Mark	Waldalgesheim
1950	28 863	62 232
1960	48 267	85 386
1965	44 456	47 553
1970	16 076	14 812 (from heaps)

Similar ores in carbonate rocks of the Zechstein were earlier mined at a number of places. The last mine closed down in about 1926.

Laterite and basaltic iron ore were obtained on the Vogelsberg, southeast of Giessen from about A.D. 1000 to 1968. The ore contains 18–35% Fe and 16–40% SiO_2. In all some 20 000 000 tonne of crude ore was extracted and yielded about 3 000 000 tonne of concentrate. Output of commercial ore in specific years was, in 1950, 93 984 tonne from four pits; in 1960, 60 500 tonne from one pit; in 1965, 59 365 tonne from one pit; and, in 1968, 15 055 tonne from one pit.

Bean ores (*Bohnerz*) are limonite concretions that have separated out from rising groundwater in mainly semi-arid climates. They are widespread and are found particularly in the Muschelkalk and the Upper Jurassic limestone of southern Germany. Near Königsbronn, southeast of Stuttgart, these ores were mined and smelted as early as the fourteenth century. They contain about 50% Fe, 6–11% SiO_2 and 0·5–2% CaO. Around 1850 annual production was in the region of 12 000 tonne. The last mine at Mardorf, near Kassel, produced 17 481 tonne of commercial ore in 1950 and was shut down because reserves were exhausted in 1953.

The mining of bog iron ores with an average content of 40–45% Fe, which were of local significance even in prehistoric times, enjoyed a brief revival in Lower Saxony and Schleswig-Holstein after the second world war, the mining operations being small or very small. In 1950, ten such mines were operating in Lower Saxony with an average output of 2000 tonne ore per year. The maximum output was achieved in 1953 with 31 315 tonne, after which production dropped sharply and tailed off completely in 1965.

Bauxite
As the relic of Tertiary lateritic weathering cover on basalts and basalt tuffs, bauxite is found often in the vicinity of lateritic and basaltic iron ores at various places. It has, however, only been mined on the Vogelsberg to the southeast of Giessen, where it occurs in the form of nodules in the earthy laterite. It used to be used as a fluxing agent in steelmaking and around 1900 also as a refractory clay. On average, it contains 35–45% Al_2O_3 + TiO_2 with 3–6% TiO_2, 20% Fe_2O_3 and 10–13% SiO_2.[287] Annual output up to 1970 was between 3000 and 4000 tonne, after which it declined to reach 755 tonne by 1975. Operations ceased in 1976.

Phosphorite
Phosphorites were actively mined on the Lower Lahn during the last third of the nineteenth century. In this area massive limestones are overlain by coverings of apatite-bearing tuffs and tuffites of the Middle Devonian (7, Fig. 53). Mesozoic and Tertiary weathering led to the karstic transformation of the limestone, and phosphoric acid, which had passed into solution, was precipitated out again in the form of dense nodular or earthy phosphorite, with a P content in excess of 10%, which replaced the limestone. The volume extracted was between 20 000 and 30 000 tonne per year, maximum annual output being 53 807 tonne in 1884. From about 1890 onwards competition from imported ores and especially the increased use of basic slags, coupled with the fact that reserves were in any case becoming exhausted, led to a decline in mining activity, which by 1900 had practically ceased.

In the area of the Amberg Cretaceous iron ore deposit nodular phosphorite occurs widely in layers and lenticular formations in the ore and its wallrock, as also in pockets in the flat-lying Malm limestone (5, Fig. 53). This phosphorite derives from eroded clays of the Upper Dogger, where it was already present in the form of concretions alongside limonite and hornstone. A chemical migration took place in addition to a predominantly mechanical one, leading to the relatively high phosphorus content in the iron ore (1·3–1·6%). The phosphorites were extracted in their own right in the 1930s.[188] In 1950 annual output was still running at about 1000 tonne and production ceased in 1953.

Kaolin
Lippert et al.[288] have given a summary account of the West German kaolin deposits. More than 95% of the country's production of raw kaolin and 82% of usable production came in 1983 from deposits in northeast Bavaria (Table 42). Raw kaolin is relatively rarely used

Table 42 *Usable production of kaolin in Federal Republic of Germany*[21]

| 1950–83 | | |
Year	Number of mines	Production, t
1950	13	250 567
1955	17	350 294
1960	18	344 203
1965	16	399 581
1970	24	525 959
1975	23	419 491
1980	21	501 701
1981	20	474 640
1982	20	454 009
1983	17	406 571

| 1983 production | | | |
Land	Number of mines	Production, t	%
Bavaria	9	333 672	82·1
Hesse	3	23 525	5·8
Lower Saxony	(1)*	436	0·1
North Rhine–Westfalia	2	22 629	5·6
Rhineland–Palatinate	3	26 309	6·5
Total	17	406 571	100·1

* Silica sand pit.

industrially, whereas applications in the ceramic industry and the refractory industry are dominant. Washed kaolins are products of intensive dressing processes and are used in the paper industry and as filling materials in the colour, rubber and plastics industries. The composition and properties of ceramic kaolin vary more markedly than those of paper kaolin.

Feldspar-rich rocks are frequent in the northeast Bavarian basement and in the sediments of the immediate foreland. These underwent in the Upper Cretaceous and Tertiary—in part also—earlier an intensive weathering with kaolinization. This formerly widely distributed weathering cover is preserved over large surfaces only in tectonically distinct depressions—for example, at Tirschenreuth, Wiesau and Mitterteich, under protective basalt cover—or at the edges of tectonic basins—in particular, at Hirschau and Schnaittenbach (Fig. 4). Many small and very small kaolin occurrences prove the formerly wide distribution of this weathering cover.[203]

In the region of Tirschenreuth are found pocket-like, middle-size kaolin deposits buried in the Falkenberg granite, some of which have been worked for a long time. The kaolinization is irregular. Locally, particularly in the deeper parts of the ore deposit, a considerable proportion of unkaolinized feldspar is to be found. The kaolinization reaches to about 30 m (in places up to 40–60 m) in depth. The proportion of raw kaolin smaller than 63 μm is around 30 wt%. With around 0·3 wt% Fe_2O_3, the raw kaolins are low in iron.

South of Hirschau and Schnaittenbach there stretches in a belt approximately 400 m wide and more than 60 km long the 15–55 m (average 35-m) thick, intensively kaolinized higher Upper Bunter Sandstone under a maximum of 18 m of cover. In part the underlying Kulmbach conglomerate is also kaolinized. Because the rocks overlying the Upper Bunter Sandstone are not kaolinized, one assumes kaolinization during or at the end of the Middle Bunter Sandstone. The kaolinization increases from the west to the east, so the deposits in the western part carry, in addition to 10 wt% kaolinite, 20 wt% feldspar, whereas in the east the feldspar is almost totally missing and correspondingly the raw kaolin contains 25 wt% kaolinite. The portion of the fraction smaller than 63 μm is approximately 30 wt%. The fraction smaller than 2 μm contains noteworthy quantities of quartz and feldspar only in the western part of the ore deposit. In the middle and eastern parts the quartz and feldspar content in this fraction is significantly smaller. The kaolins have a slightly higher iron content than those of Tirschenreuth.

The reserves of kaolin in northeast Bavaria amount to 50 000 000–60 000 000 tonne.

Also in the Rheinische Schiefergebirge feldspar-rich rocks were intensively kaolinized during the Upper Cretaceous and the Lower Tertiary. The kaolinitic weathering products were for the most part eroded; only in tectonically favourable places or under protective covering, e.g. basalt or basalt tuffs, were they preserved.[203]

The feldspars in keratophyres were kaolinized, as in Lohrheim south of Dietz on the Lahn and in Geisenheim in the Rheingau—here kaolinization resulted probably from the participation of Tertiary hot springs—and in greywackes, as in Oedingen west of Oberwinter on the Rhine, as well as chlorites and feldspars in clay-slates—for example in Niederdresselndorf, 20 km SSE of Siegen, as well as in Oedingen. Crystallographically, well-ordered kaolinite is primarily derived from feldspars, whereas crystallographically disordered kaolinite comes from chlorites. The pale mica that occurs abundantly in the primary rock was for the most part unaltered. The mineral content of fractions smaller than 63 μm fluctuated by wide margins as a result of varying primary rocks and differing intensities of kaolinization—kaolinite, 0–35 wt%; pale mica and micaceous clay minerals, 25–75 wt%; feldspar, 5–25 wt%; and quartz, 5·40 wt%. Through selective working and homogenization of the mine output it is possible to produce a salable product with a kaolin content of around 20–30 wt% in spite of the difficulties presented by nature. The kaolinization often reaches a depth of 25–35 m. In cases where the weathering profile is still widely preserved thicknesses of 50 m and possibly even more may be reached.

Additionally, other bleached rock sequences occasionally possess a high kaolin content. For instance, quite a few quartz sands had clay admixtures with often high contents of kaolinite. Also to be included here are the quartz-feldspar sands ('Pegmatitsand') of the Weiden Bight, Bavaria, and the partially kaolinized porphyry at Birkenfeld on the Nahe. These occurrences, however, contain so little kaolinite that one cannot envisage economic working. The same also goes for the kaolinite content in kaolinitic sands.

Placer deposits

Heavy mineral accumulations are rare in the FGR and, to date, have no economic significance. Eluvial and redeposited tin sands were mined until 1827 at Weissenstadt and Wunsiedel in the Fichtelgebirge.[25]

On the High Rhine and the Upper Rhine gold washing was carried on from pre- and early historical times. The stream regulation led in the nineteenth century to a gradually smaller output and mining ceased after 1900.[119] Gold values are also known from other rivers, such as the Danube, the Mosel and, particularly, the Eder, its gold content originating from the Eisenberg deposit near Korbach (59, Fig. 19).

Ilmenite sands with zircon, minor rutile, monazite and garnet are known in Schleswig-Holstein on the islands of Sylt and Amrum, as well as locally on the Baltic coast and, finally, on the East Friesian islands and their foreshores.[192,289]

Near Midlum, 15 km south of Cuxhaven, Lower

Saxony, marine placer deposits were newly discovered in fine-grained sands, of Pliocene age, which are about 10 m thick and covered by around 50 m of Quaternary sands and boulder clay. The proved reserves amount to 110 000 000 tonne of crude sand with 9% heavy minerals, including 4% ilmenite, 0·9% zircon and 0·5% rutile. Further reserves are possible.

Other mineral concentrations by superficial enrichment

At Rudolfstein near Weissenstadt in the Fichtelgebirge descendent solutions led to the concentration of meagre primary uranium contents in granite, mainly as torbernite in joints. Lenz and co-workers[290] assumed, on the basis of U–Pb dating, a Miocene age for the torbernite. Around 50 tonne of uranium was recorded with a content of 600 ppm.[291] The greater part of these small uranium occurrences are also of descendent origin—well known as joint and fissure mineralizations in many places in the northeast Bavarian Basement.

Ochre and coloured earths, as well as iron ores for colour preparation, are mined in the FRG in small amounts. The output has, since 1950, averaged between 15 000 and 20 000 tonne (1983, 19 886 tonne). Considerable parts of the output come from the area of Sulzbach–Rosenberg in the Oberpfalz and from Hesse, where the material is mined partly as a by-product of brown coal mining. About 15–20% of the total production stems from deposits of special clays in the Rhineland–Pfalz.

References

1 **Kossmat F.** Gliederung des varistischen Gebirgsbaues. *Abh. Sächs. geol. Landesamt* no. 1, 1927, 40 p.
2 **Dvorak J. and Paproth E.** Über die Position und die Tektogenese des Rhenoherzynikums und des Sudetikums in den mitteleuropäischen Varisziden. *Neues Jb. Geol. Paläont., Mh.*, 1969, 65–88.
3 **Behr H.** Subfluenz-Prozesse im Grundgebirgs-Stockwerk Mitteleuropas. *Z. dt. geol. Ges.*, 129, 1978, 283–318.
4 **Gebauer D. and Grünenfelder M.** Vergleichende U–Pb- und Rb–Sr-Altersbestimmungen im bayerischen Teil des Moldanubikums. *Fortschr. Miner.*, 50, Beiheft 3, 1973, 4.
5 **Todt W.** U–Pb-Untersuchungen an Zirkonen aus prävaristischen Gesteinen des Schwarzwaldes. *Fortschr. Miner.*, 56, 1978, 136–8.
6 **Jäger E.** The evolution of the Central and West European continent. In *La chaîne varisque d'Europe moyenne et occidentale.* — *Coll. intern. CNRS* 243, 1977, 227–39.
7 **Brewer M. S. and Lippolt H. J.** Petrogenesis of basement rocks of the Upper Rhine region elucidated by rubidium-strontium-systematics. *Contr. Miner. Petrol.*, 45, 1974, 123–41.
8 **Metz R. Richter M. and Schürenberg H.** Die Blei-Zink-Erzgänge des Schwarzwaldes. *Beih. geol. Jb.* no. 29, 1957, 277 p. (*Monographien der Deutschen Blei-Zink-Erzlagerstätten* 14)

9 **Fluck P. Weil R. and Wimmenauer W.** Géologie des gîtes minéraux des Vosges et des régions limitrophes. *Mém. B.R.G.M.* no. 87, 1975, 189 p.
10 **Schürenberg H.** Die Erzgänge Teufelsgrund und Schindler im Untermünstertal und ihr quantitativer Mineralgehalt. *Neues Jb. Miner. Abh.*, 81, 1950, 123–82.
11 **Stettner G.** Orogene Schollentektonik und granitoide Mobilisation im Westteil der Böhmischen Masse. *Geol. Rdsch.*, 60, 1971, 1465–87.
12 **Brinkmann R.** Die mitteldeutsche Schwelle. *Geol. Rdsch.*, 36, 1948, 56–66.
13 **Scherp A. and Stadler G.** Die Pyrophyllit führenden Tonschiefer des Ordoviziums im Ebbesattel und ihre Genese. *Neues Jb. Miner. Abh.*, 108, 1968, 142–65.
14 **Ahrendt H. Hunziker J. C. and Weber K.** K/Ar-Altersbestimmungen an schwach-metamorphen Gesteinen des Rheinischen Schiefergebirges. *Z. dt. geol. Ges.*, 129, 1978, 229–47.
15 **Stadler G. and Teichmüller R.** Zusammenfassender Überblick über die Entwicklung des Bramscher Massivs und des Niedersächsischen Tektogens. *Fortschr. Geol. Rheinld Westf.*, 18, 1971, 547–64.
16 **Woodhall D. and Knox R. W. O'B.** Mesozoic volcanism in the northern North Sea and adjacent areas. *Bull. geol. Surv. Gt Br.* 70, 1979, 34–56.
16a **Gaida K.-H. Kemper E. and Zimmerle W.** Das Oberapt von Sarstedt und seine Tuffe. *Geol. Jb.*, A no. 45, 1978, 43–123.
16b **Stadler G.** Die Vererzung im Bereich des Bramscher Massivs und seiner Umgebung. *Fortschr. Geol. Rheinld Westf.*, 18, 1971, 439–500.
16c **Deutloff O. Teichmüller M. Teichmüller R. and Wolf M.** Inkohlungsuntersuchungen im Mesozoikum des Massivs von Vlotho (Niersächsisches Tektogen). *Neues Jb. Geol., Mh.*, 1980, 321–41.
16d **Schönenberg R.** Südwest-Deutschland zwischen atlantischer Drift und alpiner Orogenese. *Jh. Ges. Naturkunde Württ.*, 130, 1975, 54–67.
16e **Pilger A.** The importance of lineaments in the tectonic evolution of the earth's crust and in the occurrence of ore deposits in Middle Europe. *Publ. Utah geol. Ass.* 5, 1974, 555–64.
16f **Illies J. H.** The Rhein Graben rift system—plate tectonics and transform faulting. *Geophys. Surv.*, 1, 1972, 27–60.
16g **Brockamp O.** Nachweis von Vulkanismus in Sedimenten der Unter- und Oberkreide in Norddeutschland. *Geol. Rdsch.*, 65, 1976, 162–74.
16h **Lippolt H. J.** K/Ar age determinations and the correlation of Tertiary volcanic activity in Central Europe. *Geol. Jb.*, D no. 52, 1982, 113–35.
16i **Knoblauch G.** Sedimentpetrographische und geochemische Untersuchungen an Weißjurakalken der geschichteten Fazies im Gebiet von Urach und Neuffer. Dissertation, Tübingen, 1963, 106 p.
16j **Baranyi L. Lippolt H. J. and Todt W.** Kalium–Argon-Altersbestimmungen an tertiären Vulkaniten des Oberrheingraben-Gebietes: II. Die Altersverse vom Hegau nach Lothringen. *Oberrhein. geol. Abh.*, 25, 1976, 41–62.
17 **Strieder J.** Die deutsche Montan- und Metall-Industrie im Zeitalter der Fugger. *Abh. Ber. Deutsches Museum*, 6, 1931, 188–226.
18 **Kraume E. Dahlgrün F. Ramdohr P. and Wilke A.** Die Erzlager des Rammelsberges bei Goslar. *Beih. geol. Jb.* no.

18, 1955, 394 p. (*Monographien der Deutschen Blei–Zink-Erzlagerstätten* 4)

19 **Wilke A.** Die Erzgänge von St. Andreasberg im Rahmen des Mittelharz-Ganggebietes. *Beih. geol. Jb.* no. 7, 1952, 228 p. (*Monographien der Deutschen Blei-Zink-Erzlagerstätten* 2)

20 **Neumann-Redlin C. Walther H. W. and Zitzmann A.** The iron ore deposits of the Federal Republic of Germany. In *The Iron ore deposits of Europe and adjacent areas, volume 1* **Walther H. W. and Zitzmann A.** eds (Hannover: Bundesanstalt für Geowissenschaften und Rohstoffe, 1977), 165–86.

21 **Bergbehörden der Länder und Bundesministerium für Wirtschaft.** *Der Bergbau in der Bundesrepublik Deutschland* (Clausthal-Zellerfeld: Pieper, 1950–84).

22 **Feldmann F. K.** Zehn Jahre Uranproduktion in Ellweiler. *Atomwirtschaft Atomtechn.*, 17, 1972, 74–7.

23 **OECD/Nuclear Energy Agency and IAEA.** *Uranium; resources, production and demand* (Paris: OECD, 1982), 213 p.

24 **Stettner G.** Der Grenzbereich Saxothuringikum–Moldanubische Region im Raum Tirschenreuth–Mähring (Oberpfalz) und die Situation des Uran-führenden Präkambriums. *Z. dt. geol. Ges.*, 130, 1979, 561–74.

25 **Teuscher E. O. and Weinelt W.** Die Metallogenese im Raume Spessart–Fichtelgebirge–Oberpfälzer Wald–Bayerischer Wald. *Geol. Bavarica*, 65, 1972, 5–73.

26 **Schmid Hubert and Weinelt W.** Lagerstätten in Bayern. *Geol. Bavarica*, 77, 1978, 160 p.

27 **Maucher A.** Über die Kieslagerstätte der Grube 'Bayerland' bei Waldsassen in der Oberpfalz. *Z. angew. Miner.*, 2, 1939, 219–75.

28 **Urban H. and Vaché R.** Die Kupfererzlagerstätten von Kupferberg–Wirsberg (Oberfranken) im Lichte neuer Aufschlüsse. *Geol. Bavarica*, 65, 1972, 74–106.

29 **Horstig G. v. and Teuscher E. O.** Die Eisenerze im alten Gebirge NE-Bayerns. *Geol. Jb.*, D no. 31, 1979, 7–47.

29a **Teuscher E. O.** Die Graphitlagerstätten des Passauer Waldes. *Aufschluß Sonderh.*, 31, 1981, 91–100.

30 **Bayerisches Staatsministerium für Wirtschaft und Verkehr.** *Rohstoffprogramm für Bayern* (München, 1979), 129 p.

30a **Richter P. and Stettner G.** Das Präkambrium am Nordrand der moldanubischen Region im Raum Tirschenreuth—Mähring (NE-Bayern) und dessen metallogenetische Aspekte. *Geol. Jb.*, D no. 61, 1983, 23–91.

31 **Baumann L.** Some aspects of mineral deposits formation and the metallogeny of Central Europe. *Verh. geol. Bundesanst., Wien, 1978*, 1979, 205–20.

32 **Schmid Hans.** Verbandsverhältnisse der Pegmatite des Oberpfälzer und Bayerischen Waldes (Hagendorf–Pleystein–Hühnerkobel). *Neues Jb. Miner. Abh.*, 88, 1955, 309–404.

33 **Bültemann H.** Die Uranvorkommen im ostbayerischen Grundgebirge, Raum Mähring, Krs. Tirschenreuth/Opf. *Z. dt. geol. Ges.*, 130, 1979, 575–95.

34 **Buschendorf F.** Die primären Golderze des Hauptganges bei Brandholz im Fichtelgebirge unter besonderer Berücksichtigung ihrer Paragenesis und Genesis. *Neues Jb. Miner. Geol. Paläont. BeilBd.*, 62A, 1930, 1–50.

35 **Schröder N.** Die magmatogenen Mineralisationen des Thüringer Waldes und ihre Stellung im varistischen und saxonischen Mineralisationszyklus Mitteleuropas. *Freiberger ForschHft.* C261, 1970, 7–52.

36 **Rost F.** Die Talklagerstätten der Münchberger Gneismasse. *Aufschluß Sonderh.*, 8, 1960, 128–43.

37 **Gehlen K. v. Zeino H. Murad E. and Samman A.** Neue Ergebnisse zur Genese der Vererzung im südlichen Schwarzwald. *Z. dtsch. geol. Ges.*, 121, 1970, 75–8.

38 **Sperling H.** Zur Altersstellung der Wiedener und Brandenberger Flußspatgänge (Südschwarzwald). *Mineral. Deposita*, 7, 1972, 351–9.

39 **Schneiderhöhn H.** Fortschritte in der Erkenntnis sekundär-hydrothermaler und regenerierter Lagerstätten. *Neues Jb. Miner. Mh.*, 1953, 223–37.

40 **Otto J.** Der Fluoritgang der Grube 'Gottesehre' bei Urberg, Kr. Säckingen (Südschwarzwald). *Jh. geol. Landesamt Baden–Württ.*, 9, 1967, 25–50.

41 **Wendt I. Lenz H. Höhndorf A. Bültemann H. and Bültemann W.-D.** Das Alter der Pechblende der Lagerstätte Menzenschwand, Schwarzwald. *Z. dt. geol. Ges.*, 130, 1979, 619–26.

42 **Faisi S. and Gehlen K. v.** Verkieselungszonen und ihre Bedeutung für die varistische Vererzung im südwestlichen Schwarzwald. *Neues Jb. Miner. Abh.*, 91, 1957, 351–6.

43 **Walenta K. Sawatzki G. and Dayal R.** Die Wolframerzvorkommen im Gebiet des Nordracher Granitmassivs und seiner Umgebung. *Jh. geol. Landesamt Baden-Württ.*, 12, 1970, 207–26.

44 **Kirchheimer F.** Bericht über das Vorkommen von Uran in Baden-Württemberg. *Abh. geol. Landesamt Baden–Württ.*, 2, 1957, 1–127.

45 **Wimmenauer W.** Mikroskopische Untersuchungen an Uranerzen aus dem mittleren Schwarzwald. *Mitt. bad. geol. Landesanst.*, 1951, 75–83.

46 **Walenta K.** Die Sekundärmineralien der Co–Ni–Ag–Bi–U-Erzgänge im Gebiet von Wittichen im mittleren Schwarzwald. *Aufschluß Sonderh.*, 23, 1972, 279–329.

47 **Kluth G. C.** Die Kupfer–Wismut-Erze des mittleren Schwarzwaldes und ihre Geschichte. Dissertation, Heidelberg, 1965, 200 p.

48 **Maus H. Gundlach H. and Podufal P.** Über den Sellait (MgF_2) der Grube Clara, Oberwolfach, Mittlerer Schwarzwald. *Neues Jb. Miner. Abh.*, 136, 1979, 10–25.

48a **Walenta K.** Sulfidische Erzmineralien aus der Grube Clara im mittleren Schwarzwald und ihre Paragenesen. *Aufschluß*, 35, 1984, 235–46.

49 **Metz R.** *Mineralogisch-landeskundliche Wanderungen im Nordschwarzwald, besonders in dessen alten Bergbaurevieren*, 2. Edn. (Lahr, Schwarzwald: Schauenburg, 1977), 632 p.

50 **Walenta K.** Die antimonerzführenden Gänge des Schwarzwaldes. *Jh. geol. Landesamt Baden-Württ.*, 2, 1957, 13–68.

51 **Faisi S.** Die Eisen- und Manganerzgänge von Eisenbach (südöstl. Schwarzwald) und ihre tektonische Stellung. *Neues Jb. Miner. Abh.*, 83, 1951, 53–150.

51a **Hofmann R. and Schürenberg H.** Geochemische Untersuchungen gangförmiger Barytvorkommen in Deutschland. *Monogr. Ser. Mineral Deposits* no. 17, 1979, 1–80.

51b **Hofmann R.** Die Entwicklung der Abscheidungen in den gangförmigen, hydrothermalen Barytvorkommen Mitteleuropas. *Monogr. Ser. Mineral Deposits* no. 17, 1979, 81–214.

52 **Murad F.** Hydrothermal alteration of granitic rocks and its possible bearing on the mineral deposits in the southern Black Forest, Germany. *Econ. Geol.*, 69, 1974, 532–44.

52a **Gehlen K. v.** Trias–Jura-Gangmineralisation in der Bundesrepublik Deutschland? *Fortschr. Miner.*, 60, Beih. 1, 1982, 82–4.

53 **Schneiderhöhn H.** *Lehrbuch der Erzlagerstättenkunde, I. Die Lagerstätten der magmatischen Abfolge* (Jena: Fischer, 1941), XXIV + 858 p.
54 **Rée C.** Die hydrothermalen Eisenerzgänge der Grube Louise bei Saarburg. *Geol. Jb., D.* no. 31, 1979, 115–7.
55 **Kneuper G. List K.-A. and Maus H.** Geologie und Genese der Uranmineralisation des Oostroges im Nordschwarzwald. *Erzmetall*, **30**, 1977, 522–6.
55a **Zuther M.** Das Uranvorkommen Müllenbach–Baden-Baden, eine epigenetisch-hydrothermale Imprägnationslagerstätte in Sedimenten des Oberkarbon, I. Der Erzmineralbestand. *Neues Jb. Miner., Abh.* **147**, 1983, 191–216.
55b **Brockamp O. and Zuther M.** Das Uranvorkommen Müllenbach–Baden-Baden, eine epigenetisch-hydrothermale Imprägnationslagerstätte in Sedimenten des Oberkarbon, II. Das Nebengestein. *Neues Jb. Miner., Abh.* **148**, 1983, 22–33.
56 **Rée C.** Die Toneisensteine im Saar–Nahe-Gebiet. *Geol. Jb., D* no. 31, 1979, 153–5.
57 **Bornhardt W.** Geschichte des Rammelsberger Bergbaus von seiner Aufnahme bis zur Neuzeit. *Arch. LagerstättForsch.*, **52**, 1931, 366 p.
58 **Kraume E.** *1000 Jahre Rammelsberg* (Goslar: Preussag Aktiengesellschaft, 1968), 76 p.
59 **Abt W.** Ein Beitrag zur Kenntnis der Erzlagerstätte des Rammelsberges auf Grund von Spezialuntersuchungen der Tuffe und der Tektonik. *Z. dt. Geol. Ges.*, **110**, 1958, 152–204.
60 **Ramdohr P.** Mineralbestand, Strukturen und Genesis der Rammelsberger Lagerstätte. *Geol. Jb.*, **67**, 1953, 367–494.
61 **Hannak W.** Die Rammelsberger Erzlager. *Aufschluß Sonderh.*, **28**, 1978, 127–40.
62 **Schot E. H.** The Rammelsberg mine, a synopsis. In *8th Int. Sedimentol. Congr., Heidelberg, 1971: Guidebook to excursions* **Müller G.** ed. (Frankfurt/Main: W. Kramer), 264–72.
63 **Gunzert G.** Altes und Neues Lager am Rammelsberg bei Goslar. *Erzmetall*, **22**, 1969, 1–10.
64 **Gunzert G.** Die Grauerzvorkommen und der tektonische Bau der Erzlagerstätte am Rammelsberg bei Goslar. *Erzmetall*, **32**, 1979, 1–7.
65 **Gundlach H. and Hannak W.** Ein synsedimentäres, submarin-exhalatives Buntmetallerz-Vorkommen im Unterdevon bei Goslar. *Geol. Jb.*, **85**, 1968, 193–226.
66 **Anger G. Nielsen H. Puchelt H. and Ricke E.** Sulfur isotopes in the Rammelsberg ore deposit (Germany). *Econ. Geol.*, **61**, 1966, 511–36.
67 **Gehlen K. v.** Schwefel-Isotope und die Genese von Erzlagerstätten. *Geol. Rdsch.*, **55**, 1966, 178–97.
68 **Ehrenberg H. Pilger A. Schröder F. Goebel E. and Wild K.** Das Schwefelkies–Zinkblende–Schwerspatlager von Meggen (Westfalen). *Beih. geol. Jb.* no. 12, 1954, 352 p. (*Monographien der Deutschen Blei-Zink-Erzlagerstätten* 7)
69 **Krebs W.** The geology of the Meggen ore deposit. In *Handbook of strata-bound and stratiform ore deposits, volume 9* **Wolf K. H.** ed. (Amsterdam: Elsevier, 1981), 509–49.
70 **Rippel G.** Räumliche und zeitliche Gliederung des Keratophyrvulkanismus im Sauerland. *Geol. Jb.*, **68**, 1953, 401–56.
71 **Gasser U. and Thein J.** Das syngenetische Sulfidlager von Meggen im Sauerland. *Forschungsber. Nordrh.-Westf.* 2620, 1977, 171 p.
72 **Buschendorf F. and Puchelt H.** Untersuchungen am Schwerspat des Meggener Lagers. *Geol. Jb.*, **82**, 1965, 499–582.
73 **Scherp A.** Die Herkunft des Baryts in der Pyrit–Zinkblende–Baryt-Lagerstätte Meggen. *Neues Jb. Geol. Paläont. Mh.*, 1974, 38–53.
74 **Stoppel D.** Das Schwerspatlager vom Schönscheid bei Günterod. *Geol. Jb. Hessen*, **107**, 1979, 93–104.
75 **Müller G. and Stoppel D.** Zur Stratigraphie und Tektonik im Bereich der Schwerspatgrube 'Korb' bei Eisen (N-Saarland). *Z. dt. geol. Ges.*, **132**, 1981, 325–52.
76 **Krebs W.** Moderne Suchmethoden auf Buntmetallerze im mitteleuropäischen Grundgebirge. *Erdöl Kohle Erdgas Petrochem.*, **31**, 1978, 128–33.
77 **Lippert H.-J. Hentschel H. and Rabien A.** *Erläuterungen zur Geologischen Karte von Hessen 1:25 000, Blatt Nr. 5215 Dillenburg*, 2. Aufl., 1970, 550 p.
78 **Quade H.** Genetic problems and environmental features of volcano-sedimentary iron-ore deposits of the Lahn–Dill type. In *Handbook of strata-bound and stratiform ore deposits, volume 7* **Wolf K. H.** ed. (Amsterdam, etc.: Elsevier, 1976), 255–94.
79 **Bottke H.** Die exhalativ-sedimentären devonischen Roteisensteinlagerstätten des Ostsauerlandes. *Beih. geol. Jb.* no. 63, 1965, 147 p.
80 **Harder H.** Zur Mineralogie und Genese der Eisenerze des Oberharzer Diabaszuges und ein Vergleich mit denen des Harzvorlandes. *Aufschluß Sonderh.*, **28**, 1978, 110–26.
80a **Schaeffer R.** Vulkanogen-sedimentäre Manganerzlager im Unterkarbon bei Laisa (Dillmulde, Rheinisches Schiefergebirge). *Geol. Jb. Hessen*, **108**, 1980, 151–70.
80b **Kulick J. and Theuerjahr A.-K.** Mineralisationen am Eisenberg bei Goldhausen, 5 km SW Korbach. *Fachsekt. Lagerstättenforsch., GDMB, Excursion guidebook Warstein meeting*, 1983, 71–89.
80c **Gussone R.** Untersuchungen und Betrachtungen zur Paragenesis und Genesis der Blei–Zink-Erzlagerstätten im Raume Aachen–Stolberg. Dissertation, Aachen, 1964, 130 p.
80d **Kukuk P.** *Geologie des niederrheinisch-westfälischen Steinkohlengebietes* (Berlin: Julius Springer, 1938), 706 p.
80e **Schriel W.** Der Briloner Galmei-Distrikt. *Z. dt. geol. Ges.*, **106**, 1954, 308–49.
80f **Brinckmann J. and Siewers U.** Stratabound sulphide-barite deposits in the Rhenohercynian zone. *Erzmetall*, **33**, 1980, 137–44.
80g **Borchert H.** Genetische Unterschiede zwischen varistischen und saxonischen Lagerstätten Westdeutschlands und deren Ursachen. *Freiberger ForschHft.* C209, 1967, 47–63.
80h **Scheps V. and Friedrich G.** Geochemical investigations of Paleozoic shales and carbonates in the Aachen region. *Mineral. Deposita*, **18**, 1983, 411–21.
80i **Oersmael J. v. Viaene W. and Bouckaert J.** Lithogeochemistry of Upper Tournaisian and Lower Visean carbonate rocks in the Dinant Basin, Belgium: a preliminary study. *Meded. Rijks geol. Dienst*, **32-12**, 1980, 96–100.
81 **Dejonghe L.** Discovery of a sedimentary Ba (Fe, Zn, Pb) ore body of Frasnian age at Chaudfontaine, Province of Liège, Belgium. *Mineral. Deposita*, **14**, 1979, 15–20.
82 **Bornhardt W.** Über die Gangverhältnisse des Siegerlandes und seiner Umgebung. *Arch. LagerstättForsch.*, **2**, 1910, 415 p.; **8**, 1912, 515 p.
83 **Bosum W. et al.** Geologisch-lagerstättenkundliche und geophysikalische Untersuchungen im Siegerländer–Wieder-Spateisensteinbezirk. *Beih. geol. Jb.* no. 90, 1971, 139 p.
84 **Stahl W.** Isotopen-Analysen an Carbonaten und Kohlendioxid-Proben aus dem Einflußbereich und der weiteren

Umgebung des Bramscher Intrusivs und an hydrothermalen Carbonaten aus dem Siegerland. *Fortschr. Geol. Rheinld Westf.*, **18**, 1971, 429–38.

85 **Fenchel W. et al.** Die Sideriterzgänge im Siegerland–Wied-Distrikt. *Sammelwerk dt. Eisenerzlagerst., I. Eisenerze im Grundgebirge, vol. 1: Geol. Jb.*, D no. 77, 1985, 517 p.

86 **Reichenbach R.** Geschichtlicher Abriß über den Spateisensteinbergbau im Siegerland. *Markscheidewes.*, **86**, 1979, 2–13.

87 **Wettig E.** Die Erzgänge des nördlichen rechtsrheinischen Schiefergebirges, ihr Inhalt und ihre tektonischen Zusammenhänge. Dissertation, Clausthal, 1974, 363 p.

88 **Hannak W.** Die Eisen–Mangan-Verteilung in der Karbonspat-Generation I der Blei–Zink-Erzgänge des südlichen rheinischen Schiefergebirges. *Max Richter-Festschrift*, 1965, 203–23.

89 **Lehmann H. and Pietzner H.** Der Lüderich-Gangzug und das Gangvorkommen von Nikolaus-Phönix im Bergischen Land. *Fortschr. Geol. Rheinld Westf.*, **17**, 1970, 589–664.

90 **Friedensburg F.** Die Nichteisen-Metallerzlagerstätten in der Bundesrepublik Deutschland und die Möglichkeiten für ihre weitere Nutzung. *Erzmetall*, **24**, 1971, 369–78, 441–5.

90a **Fuchs Y. and Lang-Villemaire C.** Sur quelques concentrations plombo-zincifères du Dévonien inférieur du Massif Schisteux Rhénan. *Mineral. Deposita*, **16**, 1981, 339–55.

91 **Hesemann J. Lehmann H. Pietzner H. and Scherp A.** Die Blei–Zink-Erzgänge des Bergischen Landes. *Monogr. dt. Blei–Zink-Erzlagerst. 5: Geol. Jb.*, D, in preparation.

92 **Hesemann J.** Der Blei–Zink-Erzbezirk des Bergischen Landes (Rheinisches Schiefergebirge) als Prototyp einer frühorogenen und palingenen Vererzung. *Dechenia*, **131**, 1978, 292–9.

92a **Wernicke F. A.** Beitrag zur Kenntnis des Bensberger Zink-Bleierz-Reviers. *Neues Jb. Miner. Abh.*, **93**, 1960, 257–323.

93 **Bauer G. et al.** Die Blei–Zink-Erzlagerstätten von Ramsbeck und Umgebung. *Geol. Jb.*, D no. 33, 1979, 375 p. (*Monographien der Deutschen Blei–Zink-Erzlagerstätten 6*).

94 **Hoyer P. Clausen C.-D. Leuteritz K. Teichmüller R. and Thome K. N.** Ein Inkohlungsprofil zwischen dem Gelsenkirchener Sattel des Ruhrkohlenbeckens und dem Ostsauerländer Hauptsattel des Rheinischen Schiefergebirges. *Fortschr. Geol. Rheinld Westf.*, **24**, 1974, 161–72.

95 **Weber K.** Das Bewegungsbild im Rhenoherzynikum: Abbild einer varistischen Subfluenz. *Z. dt. geol. Ges.*, **129**, 1978, 249–81.

96 **Paproth E.** Zur Folge und Entwicklung der Tröge und Vortiefen im Gebiet des Rheinischen Schiefergebirges und seiner Vorländer, vom Gedinne (Unter-Devon) bis zum Namur (Silesium). *Nova Acta Leopoldina*, N.F., **45/224**, 1976, 45–58.

97 **Behrend F. and Paeckelmann W.** Der geologische Bau und die Lagerstätten des Ramsbecker Erzbezirks. *Arch. LagerstättForsch.*, **64**, 1937, 198 p.

98 **Müller D. and Scherp A.** Die tertiäre Mineralisation auf der Blei–Zink-Erzlagerstätte Ramsbeck (Sauerland) und ihre Genese. *Neues Jb. Miner. Abh.*, **106**, 1967, 131–57.

99 **Udubasa G.** Syngenese und Epigenese in metamorphen und nichtmetamorphen Pb–Zn-Erzlagerstätten, aufgezeigt an den Beispielen Blazna-Tal (Ostkarpaten, Rumänien) und Ramsbeck (Westfalen, BR Deutschland). Dissertation, Heidelberg, 1972, 145 p.

100 **Wellmer F.-W. and Podufal P.** A statistical model for exploration of the Ramsbeck Pb/Zn mine (F. R. of Germany). In *Application of computer methods in the mineral industry: proceedings of the fourteenth symposium, Pennsylvania State University, 1976* **Ramani R. V.** ed. (New York: AIME, 1977), 431–40.

101 **Ehrendreich H.** Stratigraphie, Tektonik und Gangbildung im Gebiet der Emser Blei–Zinkerzgänge. *Z. dt. geol. Ges.*, **110**, 1958, 561–81.

102 **Hannak W.** Ergebnisse von Untersuchungen im Blei–Zink-Erzbezirk des südlichen Rheinischen Schiefergebirges. *Erzmetall*, **17**, 1964, 291–8.

103 **Pilger A.** Über den Untergrund des Rheinischen Schiefergebirges und Ruhrgebietes. *Geol. Rdsch.*, **46**, 1957, 197–212.

104 **Sperling H.** Neue lagerstättenkundliche Untersuchungen am Holzappeler Gangzug im Lichte stratigraphisch-tektonischer Kartierungsergebnisse auf Blatt Schaumburg-Ost. Dissertation, Clausthal, 1955, 121 p.

105 **Herbst F.** Die Blei–Zinkerz-Lagerstätten der Grube Mühlenbach im Bereich Ehrenbreitstein–Arenberg. *Gewerkschaft Mercur*, 1966, 64 p.

106 **Herbst F. and Müller H.-G.** Raum und Bedeutung des Emser Gangzuges. *Gewerkschaft Mercur*, 1964, 72 p.

107 **Herbst F.** Über die im Raum Holzappel–Nassau aufsetzenden Blei–Zinkerzgänge. *Gewerkschaft Mercur*, 1969, 86 p.

108 **Herbst F. and Müller H.-G.** Der Blei–Zinkerzbergbau im Hunsrück-Gebiet. *Gewerkschaft Mercur*, 1966, 68 p.

109 **Keller A.** Die Grube Aurora bei Weiden. *Ver. Heimatkunde Landkr. Birkenfeld*, Sonderh. no. 1, 1958, 59–65.

110 **Dennert H.** Der westliche Oberharz als erstes geschlossenes Industriegebiet im Lande Niedersachsen. *Erzmetall*, **25**, 1972, 640–4.

111 **Möbus G.** *Abriß der Geologie des Harzes* (Leipzig: Teubner, 1966), 219 p.

112 **Mohr K.** *Geologie und Minerallagerstätten des Harzes* (Stuttgart: Schweizerbart, 1978), 387 p.

113 **Stoppel D. Gundlach H. Heberling E. Heinrich G. Hüser M. Kallies H.-B. and Schaeffer R.** Schwer- und Flußspat-Lagerstätten des Südwestharzes. *Geol. Jb.*, D no. 54, 1983, 269 p.

114 **Sperling H. Lange J. and Scotti H.-H. v.** Die Erzgänge des Erzbergwerks Grund. *Monogr. dt. Blei–Zink-Erzlagerst. 3: Die Blei–Zink-Erzgänge des Oberharzes, Lfg. 2: Geol. Jb.*, D no. 2, 1973, 205 p.

115 **Sperling H. Stoppel D. Berthold G. and Dennert H.** Beschreibung der Oberharzer Erzgänge. *Monogr. dt. Blei–Zink-Erzlagerst. 3: Die Blei–Zink-Erzgänge des Oberharzes, Lfg. 3: Geol. Jb.*, D no. 34, 1979, 347 p.

116 **Sperling H. Stoppel D. Dennert H. and Tiemann K.-C.** Gangkarte des Oberharzes mit Erläuterungen. *Monogr. dt. Blei–Zink-Erzlagerst. 3: Die Blei–Zink-Erzgänge des Oberharzes, Lfg. 4: Geol. Jb.*, D no. 46, 1981, 85 p.

117 **Schoell M.** Radiometrische Altersbestimmungen am Brocken-Intrusionskomplex im Harz als Beispiel der Interpretation diskordanter Modellalter. *Clausthaler tekt. H.*, **13**, 1972, 102–25.

118 **Buschendorf F. Dennert H. Hannak W. Hüttenhain H. Mohr K. Sperling H. and Stoppel D.** Geologie des Erzgang-Reviers, Mineralogie des Ganginhalts und Geschichte des Bergbaus im Oberharz. *Monogr. dt. Blei–Zink-Erzlagerst. 3: Die Blei–Zink-Erzlagerst. des Oberharzes, Lfg. 1: Beih. geol. Jb.* no. 118, 1971, 212 p.

119 **Slotta R.** *Technische Denkmäler in der Bundesrepublik Deutschland, 4: Der Metallerzbergbau* (Bochum: Deutsches Bergbau-Museum, 1983), 1520 p.
120 **Wilke A.** Die Erzgänge von St. Andreasberg. *Aufschluß Sonderh.*, **28**, 1978, 94–102.
121 **Schnorrer-Köhler G.** Das Silbererzrevier St. Andreasberg im Harz. *Aufschluß*, **34**, 1983, 153–75; 189–203; 231–51; 317–32.
122 **Nielsen H.** Schwefel-Isotopenverhältnisse aus St. Andreasberg und anderen Erzvorkommen des Harzes. *Neues Jb. Miner. Abh.*, **109**, 1968, 289–321.
123 **Sperling H. and Nielsen H.** Schwefel-Isotopenuntersuchungen an der Blei–Zink-Erzlagerstätte Grund (Westharz, Bundesrepublik Deutschland). *Mineral. Deposita*, **8**, 1973, 64–72.
124 **Wedepohl K. H. Delevaux M. H. and Doe B. R.** The potential source of lead in the Permian Kupferschiefer bed of Europe and some selected Paleozoic mineral deposits in the Federal Republic of Germany. *Contr. Miner. Petrol.*, **65**, 1978, 273–81.
125 **Möller P. Morteani G. Hoefs J. and Parekh P. P.** The origin of the ore-bearing solution in the Pb–Zn veins of the Western Harz, Germany, as deduced from rare-earth element and isotope distributions in calcites. *Chem. Geol.*, **26**, 1979, 197–215.
126 **Schneiderhöhn H.** *Erzlagerstätten, 2. Auflage* (Jena: Fischer, 1949), 371 p.
127 **Hesemann J. and Pilger A.** Der Blei–Zink-Erzgang der Zeche Auguste Victoria in Marl-Hüls (Westfalen). *Monogr. dt. Blei–Zink-Erzlagerst. 1. Die Blei–Zink-Erzvorkommen des Ruhrgebietes und seiner Umrandung, Lfg. 1: Beih. geol. Jb.* no. 3, 1951, 7–184.
128 **Buschendorf F. Richter M. and Walther H. W.** Der Erzgang Christian Levin. *Monogr. dt. Blei–Zink-Erzlagerst. 1. Die Blei–Zink-Erzvorkommen des Ruhrgebietes und seiner Umrandung, Lfg. 2: Beih. geol. Jb.* no. 28, 1957, 163 p.
129 **Hesemann J. et al.; Pilger A.** Die übrigen (kleineren) Gangvorkommen; Übersicht über die Gangvererzung. *Monogr. dt. Blei–Zink-Erzlagerst. 1. Die Blei–Zink-Erzvorkommen des Ruhrgebietes und seiner Umrandung; Lfg. 3: Beih. geol. Jb.* no. 40, 1961, 233–95; 297–350.
130 **Stadler G.** Erze und Industrieminerale. *Dt. Planungsatlas, 1. Nordrhein–Westfalen, Lfg. 6, Erl. Kt. Lagerst. II*, 1973, 5–11.
131 **Herbst G. and Stadler G.** Blei–Zink-Vererzung. In *Die Karbonablagerungen in der Bundesrepublik Deutschland, Oberkarbon, Revier von Aachen–Erkelenz. Fortschr. Geol. Rheinld Westf.*, **19**, 1971, 73.
132 **Bärtling R.** *Die Schwerspatlagerstätten Deutschlands* (Stuttgart: Enke, 1911), 188 p.
133 **Voigt A.** Die Metallerzprovinz um das Hohe Venn. *Erzmetall*, **5**, 1952, 223–33.
134 Goldbergbau in der Eifel. *Z. Prakt. Geol.*, **4**, 1896, 453.
135 **Paeckelmann W.** Das Kupfererzvorkommen von Stadtberge in Westfalen. *Glückauf*, **66**, 1930, 1057–64; 1096–105.
136 **Stelzner A. W. and Bergeat A.** *Die Erzlagerstätten* (Leipzig: Felix, 1904), 1330 p.
137 **Boden K.** Das Kupfererzvorkommen im unteren Glindetal bei Niedermarsberg (Stadtberge) in Westfalen. *Glückauf*, **48**, 1912, 937–46; 981–8.
138 **Schwake F.** Erzmikroskopische Untersuchung des Kupfererzvorkommens von Nieder-Marsberg (Westfalen). *Chemie Erde*, **9**, 1935, 486–528.
139 **Horstig G. v. et al.** Die Eisenerze in NE-Bayern, im Schwarzwald, Harz, linksrheinischen Schiefergebirge, Saar–Nahe- und Ruhrgebiet. *Geol. Jb.*, D no. 31, 1979, 183 p.
140 **Trusheim F.** Zur Bildung der Salzlager im Rotliegenden und Mesozoikum Mitteleuropas. *Beih. geol. Jb.* no. 112, 1971, 51 p.
141 **Käding K.-C.** Stratigraphische Gliederung des Zechsteins im Werra–Fulda-Becken. *Geol. Jb. Hessen*, **106**, 1978, 123–30.
142 **Richter-Bernburg G.** Saline deposits in Germany. In *Geology of saline deposits* **Richter-Bernburg G.** ed. *Earth Sciences, UNESCO*, **7**, 1972, 275–85.
143 **Käding K.-Ch.** Salinarformation des Zechstein. In *Erl. geol. Kt. Niedersachsen 1:25,000, Bl. 4323 Uslar*, 1977, 13–15.
144 **Trusheim F.** Mechanism of salt migration in Northern Germany. *Bull. Am. Ass. Petrol. Geol.*, **44**, 1960, 1519–40.
145 **Jaritz W.** Zur Entstehung der Salzstrukturen Nordwestdeutschlands. *Geol. Jb.*, A no. 10, 1973, 77 p.
146 **Ambatiello P. and Ney P.** The Berchtesgaden salt mine. In *Mineral deposits of the Alps and of the Alpine epoch in Europe: proceedings of the IV. ISMIDA, Berchtesgarden, 1981* **Schneider H.-J.** ed. (Berlin, etc.: Springer, 1983), 146–54. (*Spec. Publ. Soc. Geol. appl. Mineral Dep.* no. 3)
147 **Herrmann A.** Gips- und Anhydritvorkommen in Nordwestdeutschland. *Silikat-J.*, **3**, 1964, 442–66.
148 **Herrmann A.** Lagerstätten, Abbau und Rekultivierung fränkischer Gipslagerstätten. *Erzmetall*, **29**, 1976, 53–8.
149 **Müller G.** Zur Geochemie des Strontiums in ozeanen Evaporiten unter besonderer Berücksichtigung der sedimentären Coelestin-Lagerstätte von Hemmelte–Westerfeld (Süd-Oldenburg). *Beih. geol. Jb.* no. 35, 1962, 90 p.
150 **Ziehr H. Matzke K. Ott G. and Voultsidis V.** Ein stratiformes Fluoritvorkommen im Zechsteindolomit bei Eschwege und Sontra in Hessen. *Geol. Rdsch.*, **69**, 1980, 325–48.
151 **Gundlach H. Möller P. Parekh P. P. and Stoppel D.** Zur Genese des Fluorits auf den Barytgängen des Südwest-Harzes. *Geol. Jb.*, D no. 20, 1976, 3–22.
152 **Schulz S.** Verteilung und Genese von Fluorit im Hauptdolomit Norddeutschlands. *Berliner geowiss. Abh.*, A **23**, 1980, 85 p.
153 **Wedepohl K. H.** The geochemistry of the Kupferschiefer bed in Central Europe. In *European copper deposits* **Janković S. and Sillitoe R. H.** eds (Belgrade: Department of Geology, Belgrade University, 1980), 129–35. (*Spec. Publ. SGA* no. 1)
154 **Rentzsch J.** Mineralogical-geochemical prospection methods in the Central European copper belt. *Erzmetall*, **34**, 1981, 492–5.
155 **Kulick J. Leifeld D. Meisl S. Pöschl W. Stellmacher R. Strecker G. Theuerjahr A.-K. and Wolf M.** Petrofazielle und chemische Erkundung des Kupferschiefers der Hessischen Senke und des Harz-Westrandes. *Geol. Jb.*, D no. 68, 1984, 223 p.
156 **Messer E.** Kupferschiefer, Sanderz und Kobaltrücken im Richelsdorfer Gebirge (Hessen). *Hess. Lagerst. Arch.*, **3**, 1955, 125 p.
157 **Spieth V. Schumacher C. Schmidt F. P. Kaidies E. and Friedrich G.** Results of the recent exploration for a Cu–Ag deposit of Kupferschiefer type in West Germany. In

Geology and metallogeny of copper deposits **Friedrich G. et al.** eds. *Spec. Publ. Soc. Geol. appl. Mineral Dep.* no. 4, in press.

158 **Glennie K. W. and Buller A. T.** The Permian Weissliegend of NW Europe: The partial deformation of aeolian dune sands caused by the Zechstein transgression. *Sedimentary Geol.*, **35**, 1983, 43–81.

159 **Dahlgrün F. Erdmannsdörffer O. H. and Schriel W.** Geologischer Führer durch den Harz, 1. Oberharz und Brockengebiet. *Samml. geol. Führer*, **29**, 1925, 228 p.

160 **Gunzert G.** Über die Bedeutung nachträglicher Erzverschiebungen in der Kupferschieferlagerstätte des Richelsdorfer Gebirges. *Notizbl. hess. Landesamt Bodenforsch.*, **81**, 1953, 258–83.

161 **Autorenkollektiv.** Kupferschiefer und 'Rote Fäule'. *Freiberger ForschHft.* C193, 1965, 259 p.

162 **Rentzsch J. and Knitzschke G.** Die Erzmineralparagenesen des Kupferschiefers und ihre regionale Verbreitung. *Freiberger ForschHft.* C231, 1968, 189–211.

163 **Marowsky G.** Schwefel-, Kohlenstoff- und Sauerstoff-Isotopenuntersuchungen am Kupferschiefer als Beitrag zur genetischen Deutung. *Contr. Miner. Petrol.*, **22**, 1969, 290–334.

164 **Drong H.-J. Plein E. Sannemann D. Schuepbach M. A. and Zimdars J.** Der Schneverdingen-Sandstein des Rotliegenden—eine äolische Sedimentfüllung alter Grabenstrukturen. *Z. dt. geol. Ges.*, **133**, 1982, 699–725.

165 **Schnorrer-Köhler G.** Die Minerale des Richelsdorfer Gebirges. *Aufschluß*, **34**, 1983, 535–40; **35**, 1984, 7–20, 37–62, 93–109, 119–36.

166 **Hedemann H. A. Mascheck W. Paulus B. and Plein E.** Mitteilung zur stratigraphischen Gliederung des Oberrotliegenden im Nordwestdeutschen Becken. *Nachr. dt. geol. Ges.*, **30**, 1984, 100–7.

167 **Sauer E.** Das Perm am Schiefergebirgsrand zwischen Gilserberg und Lollar. Dissertation, Universität Marburg, 1964, 185 p.

168 **Visscher H.** The Permian and Triassic of the Kingscourt outlier, Ireland—a palynological investigation related to regional stratigraphical problems in the Permian and Triassic of Western Europe. *Spec. Pap. geol. Surv. Ireland* no. 1, 1971, 114 p.

169 **Weinelt W.** Beiträge zur Paläogeographie und Lithologie der Bleiglanz-Bank des mittleren Keupers im Raum zwischen Klettgau und Coburg. Dissertation, Würzburg, 1955, 121 p.

170 **Schweizer V.** Geochemische Untersuchungen zur Erzanreicherung in der Bleiglanzbank des süddeutschen Gipskeupers (km 1, Karn). *Oberrhein. geol. Abh.*, **28**, 1979, 55–71.

171 **Hänsel B. and Schulz H. D.** Frühe Kupferverhüttung auf Helgoland. *Spektrum Wiss.*, **2**, 1980, 11–20.

172 **Lorenzen W.** *Helgoland und das früheste Kupfer des Nordens* (Otterndorf: Niederelbe-Vlg., 1965), 102 p.

173 **Fesser H.** Kupfermineralien auf Helgoland. *Aufschluß*, **22**, 1971, 221–5.

174 **Mempel G.** Verbreitung und Genese der Buntmetallerz-Spuren in den paläozoischen und mesozoischen Sedimenten Nordwestdeutschlands. *Erzmetall*, **15**, 1962, 62–72.

175 **Hofmeister E. Simon P. and Stein V.** Blei und Zink im Trochitenkalk (Trias, Oberer Muschelkalk 1) Nordwest-Deutschlands. *Geol. Jb.*, D no. 1, 1972, 103 p.

176 **Hofmeister E. and Simon P.** Bleierz-Vorkommen und Bergbauversuche im Külf bei Alfeld/Leine. *Bergbau*, **22**, 1971, 215–23.

177 **Walther H. W.** Zur Bildung von Erz- und Minerallagerstätten in der Trias von Mitteleuropa. *Geol. Rdsch.*, **71**, 1982, 835–55.

178 **Hofmann B.** Blei-, Zink-, Kupfer- und Arsenvererzungen im Wellengebirge (unterer Muschelkalk, Trias) am südlichen und östlichen Schwarzwaldrand. *Mitt. naturforsch. Ges. Schaffhausen*, **31**, 1980, 157–96.

179 **Gudden H.** Zur Bleierz-Führung in Trias-Sedimenten der nördlichen Oberpfalz. *Geol. Bavarica*, **74**, 1975, 33–55.

180 **Schwarzenberg T. v.** Lagerstättenkundliche Untersuchungen an sedimentären Bleivererzungen der Oberpfalz. Dissertation, Universität München, 1975, 54 p.

181 **Klemm D. D. and Schwarzenberg T. v.** Die Bleierzvorkommen am Rande des Oberpfälzer Waldes. *Erzmetall*, **30**, 1977, 531–6.

182 **Schmid Hubert** Zur Bleierzführung in der Mittleren Trias der Oberpfalz. *Erzmetall*, **34**, 1981, 652–8.

183 **Thürach H.** *Erläuterung geol. Spezialkt. Großherzogtum Baden*, Bl. Sinsheim: no. 42, 1968, 70 p.

184 **Strebel O.** Erläuterungen zur geologischen Kartierung des Blattes Ansbach. Diplom Arbeit, Würzburg, 1953, 34 p.

185 **Kühn W.** Buntmetallführende Karbonatbänke der höheren Trias im Thüringer Becken. *Chemie Erde*, **35**, 1976, 76–94.

186 **Walther H. W.** Criteria on syngenesis and epigenesis of lead-zinc ores in Triassic sandstones in Germany. In *Syngenesis and epigenesis in the formation of mineral deposits* (*Festschrift Amstutz*) **Wauschkuhn A. Kluth C. and Zimmermann R. A.** eds (Berlin, etc.: Springer, 1984), 212–20.

187 **Bottke H. et al.** Die marin-sedimentären Eisenerze des Jura in Nordwestdeutschland. *Sammelwerk dt. Eisenerzlagerst. II. Eisenerze im Deckgebirge* no. 1: *Beih. geol. Jb.* no. 79, 1969, 391 p.

188 **Frank M. et al.** Sedimentäre Eisenerze in Süddeutschland. *Sammelwerk dt. Eisenerzlagerst. II. Eisenerze im Deckgebirge* no. 3: *Geol. Jb.*, D no. 10, 1975, 280 p.

189 **Kolbe H.** Die Eisenerzkolke im Neokom-Eisenerzgebiet Salzgitter. Beispiele zur Bedeutung synsedimentärer Tektonik für die Lagerstättenbildung. *Mitt. geol. Staatsinst. Hamburg*, **31**, 1962, 276–308.

190 **Fehlau K.-P.** Sedimentpetrologie der Trümmereisenerz-Lagerstätte von Bülten–Adenstedt (Oberkreide, NW-Deutschland). *Mitt. geol.-paläont. Inst. Univ. Hamburg*, **42**, 1973, 81–160.

191 **Ferling P.** Mineralogische, petrographische, fazielle und chemische Untersuchung der Brauneisen-Trümmererzlagerstätte von Lengede–Broistedt. *Geol. Jb.*, **75**, 1959, 555–90.

192 **Gotthardt R. and Picard K.** Anreicherungen von Schwermineralien an den Küsten Schleswig-Holsteins. *Geol. Mitt.*, **4**, 1965, 249–72.

193 **Stein V. ed.** Lagerstätten der Steine, Erden und Industrieminerale: Untersuchung und Bewertung (Vademecum 2). *Schriftenr. GDMB* 38, 1981, 248 p.

194 **Weiss R.** Quarzrohstoffe für die Glasindustrie. *Glastechn. Ber.*, **49**, 1976, 12–25.

195 **Becker-Platen J. D. and Stein V.** Abschätzung der vorhandenen Rohstoff-Ressourcen für die Herstellung von Hohlglas. In *Verpackung und Umwelt* **Thomé-Kozmiensky K. J.** ed (Berlin: E. Freitag, 1982), 187–95.

196 **Weiss R.** Zur Gewinnungs- und Verfahrenstechnologie für Industriesande. *Erzmetall*, **31**, 1978, 450–7.

197 **Benda L. and Brandes H.** Die Kieselgur-Lagerstätten Niedersachsens: I. Alter und Genese. *Geol. Jb., A* no. 21, 1974, 3–85.

198 **Benda L. and Mattiat B.** Die Kieselgur-Lagerstätten Niedersachsens: II. Rohstoffanalyse und Qualitätskennzeichnung im Hinblick auf die Verwertbarkeit. *Geol. Jb., D* no. 22, 1977, 107 p.

199 **Benda L. Hofmeister E. Miehlke K. and Müller H.** Die Kieselgur-Lagerstätten Niedersachsens, 3. Neue Prospektionsergebnisse (Lagerstätte Dethlingen). *Geol. Jb., A* no. 75, 1984, 585–609.

200 **Streit R.** Blatt Nr. 7232 Burgheim Nord. *Erl. geol. Kt. Bayern*, 1978, 222 p.

201 **Metz R. and Weiner K. L.** Die Tripellagerstätten im Kraichgau und im Bauland. *Oberrhein. geol. Abh.*, 12, 1963, 95–117.

202 **Tillmann H.** Blatt Nr. 6337 Kaltenbrunn. *Erl. geol. Kt. Bayern*, 1958, 118 p.

203 Clays and clay minerals in the Federal Republic of Germany. *Geol. Jb., D* no. 39, 1980, 136 p.

204 **Paproth E. and Zimmerle W.** Stratigraphic position, petrography, and depositional environment of phosphorites from the Federal Republic of Germany. *Meded. Rijks geol. Dienst*, 32-11, 1980, 81–95.

205 **Schneider H.-J.** Facies differentiation and controlling factors for the depositional lead–zinc concentration in the Ladinian geosyncline of the eastern Alps. In *Developments in sedimentology, volume 2* **Amstutz G. C. ed.** (Amsterdam, etc.: Elsevier, 1964), 29–45.

206 **Maucher A. and Schneider H.-J.** The Alpine lead–zinc ores. In *Genesis of stratiform lead–zinc–barite–fluorite deposits in carbonate rocks (the so-called Mississippi Valley type deposits)* **Brown J. S. ed.** (Lancaster, Pa.: Economic Geology Publishing House, 1967), 71–89. (*Econ. Geol. Monogr.* 3)

207 **Höll R. and Maucher A.** The strata-bound ore deposits in the Eastern Alps. In *Handbook of strata-bound and stratiform ore deposits, volume 5: regional studies* **Wolf K. H. ed.** (Amsterdam: Elsevier, 1976), 1–36.

208 **Germann K.** Reworked dolomite crusts in the Wettersteinkalk (Ladinian, Alpine Triassic) as indicators of early supratidal dolomitization and lithification. *Sedimentol.*, 12, 1969, 257–77.

209 **Vidal H.** Neue Ergebnisse zur Stratigraphie und Tektonik des nordwestlichen Wettersteingebirges und seines nördlichen Vorlandes. *Geol. Bavarica*, 17, 1953, 56–88.

210 **Taupitz K. C.** Die Blei-, Zink- und Schwefelerzlagerstätten der nördlichen Kalkalpen westlich der Loisach. Dissertation, Bergakademie Clausthal, 1954, 120 p.

211 **Schneider H.-J. and Waldvogel F.** Sedimentäre Eisenerze und Faziesdifferenzierung im oberen Wettersteinkalk. *Erl. geol. Kt. Bayern 1:25 000, Nr. 8430 Füssen*, 1964, 101–50.

212 **Gümbel C. W.** *Geognostische Beschreibung des bayerischen Alpengebirges und seines Vorlandes* (Gotha: Perthes, 1861), 950 p.

213 **Schneider H.-J.** Die sedimentäre Bildung von Flußspat im Oberen Wettersteinkalk der nördlichen Kalkalpen. *Abh. bayer. Akad. Wiss., Naturwiss. Kl., N.F.*, 66, 1954, 37 p.

214 **Schneider H.-J. Möller P. and Parekh P. P.** Rare earth elements distribution in fluorites and carbonate sediments of the East-Alpine Mid-Triassic sequences in the Nördliche Kalkalpen. *Mineral. Deposita*, 10, 1975, 330–44.

215 **Germann K.** Verbreitung und Entstehung manganreicher Gesteine im Jura der nördlichen Kalkalpen. *Tschermaks miner. petrogr. Mitt.*, 17, 1972, 123–50.

216 **Gudden H.** Über Manganerzvorkommen in den Berchtesgadener und Salzburger Alpen. *Erzmetall*, 22, 1969, 482–8.

217 **Ziegler J. H.** Alttertiäre Eisenerze am bayerischen Alpenrand. *Geol. Jb., D* no. 10, 1975, 239–53.

218 **Ziegler J. H.** Eocene iron ore deposits at the northern welt of the Bavarian Alps. Reference 146, 136–45.

219 **Behr H. J. Hess H. Oehlschlägel G. and Lindenberg H. G.** Die Quarzmineralisation vom Typ Suttrop am N-Rand des rechtsrheinischen Schiefergebirges. *Aufschluss Sonderbd*, 29, 1979, 205–31.

220 **Gehlen K. v.** Geochemie und stabile Isotope der postvaristischen Mineralisation. In *Postvaristische Gangmineralisation in Mitteleuropa* **Walther H. W. ed.** *Schriftenr. GDMB* 41, 1984, 245–54.

221 **Walther H. W.** The Alpidic metallogenic epoch in Central Europe north of the Alps. Reference 146, 313–28.

222 **Schaeffer R.** Die postvariszische Mineralisation im nordöstlichen Rheinischen Schiefergebirge. *Braunschw. geol.-paläontol. Diss.* 3, 1984, 297 p.

223 **Fuchs K. et al.** Plateau uplift; the Rhenish Shield—a case history. *Int. Lithosp. Progr. Publ.* 0104, 1983, 411 p.

224 **Bonhomme M. G. Bühmann D. and Besnus Y.** Reliability of K–Ar dating of clays and silicifications associated with vein mineralizations in western Europe. *Geol. Rdsch.*, 72, 1983, 105–17.

225 **Tufar W. and Grassegger G.** Zur Mineralparagenese der Baryt-Lagerstätte von Dreislar, Sauerland. Reference 220, 47–64.

226 **Bärtling R.** Über metasomatische Schwerspatlagerstätten in Deutschland. *Z. dt. geol. Ges.*, 78, 1926, 32–43.

227 **Schneiderhöhn H.** Schwerspatgänge und pseudomorphe Quarzgänge in Westdeutschland. *Neues Jb. Miner. Mh., A*, 1949, 191–202.

228 **Stockfleth F.** Die geographischen, geognostischen und mineralogischen Verhältnisse des südlichen Teils des Oberbergamtsbezirks Dortmund. *Verh. naturhist. Ver. Rheinld Westf.*, 52, 1895, 45–129.

229 **Schriel W.** Zusammenhänge alter (varistischer) und junger (tertiärer) Erzparagenesen, geschildert anhand von Blei–Zinklagerstätten am Nord- und Ostrand des Rheinischen Schiefergebirges. *Freiberger ForschHft.* C57, 1959, 125–50.

230 **Kalb G.** Die Kristalltracht des Kalkspats in minerogenetischer Betrachtung. *Centralbl. Miner.*, 1928, 337–9.

231 **Koschinski G.** Mikrostrukturelle und mikrothermometrische Untersuchungen an Quarzmineralisationen aus dem östlichen Rheinischen Schiefergebirge. Dissertation, Göttingen, 1979, 146 p.

232 **Huckriede R. and Schaeffer R.** Die Bedeutung der unterkretazischen Karsthöhlen-Füllung von Nehden für Altersfragen der Mineralisation des Sauerlandes. Reference 220, 399–402.

233 **Kretzschmar M.** Fossile Pilze in Eisen-Stromatolithen von Warstein, Rheinisches Schiefergebirge. *Facies*, 7, 1982, 237–60.

234 **Large D. Schaeffer R. and Höhndorf A.** Lead isotope data from selected galena occurrences in the North Eifel and North Sauerland, Germany. *Mineral. Deposita*, 18, 1983, 235–43.

235 **Behr H. J. and Horn E.-E.** Unterscheidungskriterien für Mineralisationen des varistischen und postvaristischen Zyklus, die aus der Analyse fluider Einschlüsse gewinnbar sind. Reference 220, 255–69.
236 **Harder H.** Geochemische Untersuchungen zur Genese der Strontianit-Lagerstätten des Münsterlandes. *Beitr. Miner. Petrogr.*, **10**, 1964, 198–215.
237 **Scherp A. and Strübel G.** Zur Barium–Strontium-Mineralisation: Experimentelle und geologische Ergebnisse und Überlegungen erläutert am Beispiel des westlichen Deutschlands. *Mineral. Deposita*, **9**, 1974, 155–68.
238 **Rose K.-H. and Gödecke C. P.** Mineral-Neubildungen des Osnabrücker Berglandes im Vergleich mit dem übrigen Nordwestdeutschland. In *Geologie des Osnabrücker Berglandes* **Klassen H. ed.** (Osnabrück: Naturwissenschaftliches Museum, 1984), 567–643.
239 **Möller P. Parekh P. P. and Simon P.** Seltene Erden als geochemische Indikatoren für die Genese von Fluorit und Calcit auf Gang- und Kluftlagerstätten im Weserbergland (Nordwest-Deutschland) und benachbarten Gebieten. *Geol. Jb.*, D no. 20, 1976, 77–112.
240 **Baumann L. and Weber W.** Deep faults, simatic magmatism, and the formation of mineral deposits in Central Europe outside the Alps. In *Metallogeny and plate tectonics in the northeastern Mediterranean* **Janković S. ed.** (Belgrade: Faculty of Mining and Geology, University of Belgrade, 1977), 541–51. (*IGCP–UNESCO Correlation Project* no. 3)
241 **Gunzert G.** Über das selektive Auftreten der saxonischen Schwerspatvorkommen in Deutschland. *Neues Jb. Mineral. Mh.*, 1961, 25–51.
242 **Gehlen K. v. Baumann A. Hoffmann R. Grauert B. and Nielsen H.** Strontium-Isotope in Barytgängen des Schwarzwaldes. *Fortschr. Miner.*, **62**, 1984, Beih. 1, 1984, 70–1.
243 **Walther H. W.** Über mögliche Ursachen der unterschiedlichen Verbreitung der postvaristischen Baryte und Fluorite im westlichen Mitteleuropa. *Z. dt. geol. Ges.*, **134**, 1983, 143–51.
244 **Fürst M. Platen H. v. Leipziger K. and Wartha R.** Das Wölsendorfer Flußspatrevier, tektonische und genetische Aspekte. *Geol. Jb.*, A no. 75, 1984, 553–83.
245 **Möller P. Maus H. and Gundlach H.** Die Entwicklung von Flußspatmineralisationen im Bereich des Schwarzwaldes. *Jb. geol. Landesamt Bad.-Württ.*, **24**, 1982, 35–70.
246 **Huck K.-H.** Die Beziehungen zwischen Tektonik und Paragenese unter Berücksichtigung geochemischer Kriterien in der Fluß- und Schwerspatlagerstätte "Clara" bei Oberwolfach, Schwarzwald. Dissertation, Heidelberg, 1984, 198 p.
247 **Carlé W.** Bau und Entwicklung der Süddeutschen Großscholle. *Beih. geol. Jb.* no. 16, 1955, 272 p.
248 **Ncube A. N. Horn E. E. and Amstutz G. C.** The fluorite deposit Käfersteige in the Buntersandstein near Pforzheim, Black Forest. *Neues Jb. Miner. Mh.*, 1979, 49–61.
249 **Hess G.** Zum geologisch-tektonischen Rahmen der Schwerspatlagerstätten im Südharz und im Spessart. *Geol. Jb.*, D no. 4, 1973, 65 p.
250 **Stoppel D. and Gundlach H.** Zur Geologie und Bergbaugeschichte der Schwerspat- und Kobalterzvorkommen im Unterwerra-Grauwackengebirge und Richelsdorfer Gebirge. *Aufschluß Sonderbd*, **28**, 1978, 261–85.
251 **Gundlach H. and Weisser J.-D.** Zur Geochemie der Barytgänge von Dreislar (östliches Sauerland). *Geol. Rdsch.*, **55**, 1966, 375–85.
252 **Weisser D.** Tektonik und Barytgänge in der SE-Eifel. *Z. dt. geol. Ges.*, **115**, 1965, 33–68.
253 **Dill H.** Zur Erzmineralogie und Nebengesteinsalteration von Flußspatvorkommen im Bereich der "Frankenwälder Querzone" (N-Bayern). *Neues Jb. Miner., Abh.*, **146**, 1983, 66–81.
254 **Dill H.** Zur Geologie und Mineralogie der Schwerspatvorkommen in N-Bayern. *Geol. Jb.*, D no. 61, 1983, 93–148.
255 **Dill H.** Die Vererzung am Westrand der Böhmischen Masse—Metallogenese in einer ensialischen Orogenzone. *Geol. Jb.*, D no. 73, 1985, 461 p.
256 **Carl C. and Dill H.** U/Pb-Datierung an Pechblenden aus dem Nabburg–Wölsendorfer Flußspatrevier. *Geol. Jb.*, D no. 63, 1984, 59–76.
257 **Möller P.** Lanthaniden-Fraktionierung in Fluoriten aus Vorkommen Mitteleuropas. Reference 220, 283–93.
258 **Lippolt H. J. Mertz D. F. and Ziehr H.** The Late Permian Rb–Sr age of a K-feldspar from the Wölsendorf mineralization (Oberpfalz, FR Germany). *Neues Jb. Miner. Mh.*, 1985, 49–57.
259 **Ziehr H.** Das Nabburg–Wölsendorfer Flußspatrevier. *Aufschluß Sonderh.*, **16**, 1967, 215–53.
260 **Bauer G.** Die geologische Stellung der Pb–Zn-Lagerstätte im Raume von Wiesloch in Baden. Dissertation, Heidelberg, 1954, 90 p.
261 **Ramdohr P.** Der Silberkobalterzgang mit Kupfererzen vom Wingertsberg bei Nieder-Ramstadt im Odenwald. *Aufschluß Sonderbd*, **27**, 1975, 237–43.
262 **Voigt A.** Die Bleizinkerzvorkommen im Buntsandstein und Unterdevon der Nordeifel. *Geol. Jb.*, **66**, 1952, 1–13.
263 **Schachner (Schachner-Korn) D.** Bravoitführende Blei–Zinkvererzungen im Devon und Buntsandstein der Nordeifel. *Neues Jb. Miner., Abh.*, **94**, 1960, 469–78.
264 **Ribbert K.-H.** *Erläuterungen zur geologischen Karte von Nordrhein-Westfalen 1:25 000, Blatt 5505 Blankenheim*, 1983, 101 p.
265 **Schröder E. and Pfeffer P.** *Erläuterungen zur geologischen Karte von Nordrhein-Westfalen 1:250 000, Blatt 5305 Zülpich*, 2. Aufl., 1979, 65 p.
266 **Bayer H. Nielsen H. and Schachner D.** Schwefelisotopenverhältnisse in Sulfiden aus Lagerstätten der Nordeifel im Raum Aachen–Stolberg und Maubach-Mechernich. *Neues Jb. Miner. Abh.*, **113**, 1970, 251–73.
267 **Knapp G. and Hager H.** *Erläuterung zur geologischen Karte der nördlichen Eifel, 1:100 000, 2. Auflage* (Krefeld: Geologisches Landesamt Nordrhein-Westfalen, 1978), 152 p.
268 **Mader D.** Aeolische und fluviatile Sedimentation im Mittleren Buntsandstein der Nordeifel. *Neues Jb. Geol. Paläont. Abh.*, **165**, 1983, 254–302.
269 **Puffe E.** Die Blei–Zink-Erzlagerstätte der Gewerkschaft Mechernicher Werke in Mechernich in der Eifel. *Erzmetall*, **5**, 1953, 302–10.
270 **Henneke J.** Die bergwirtschaftliche Bedeutung der Blei-Zink-Erzlagerstätte Mechernich. *Glückauf ForschHft.*, **38**, 1977, 9–18.
271 **Seeliger E.** Die Paragenese der Pb–Zn-Erzlagerstätten am Gänsberg bei Wiesloch (Baden) und ihre genetischen Beziehungen zu den Gängen im Odenwaldkristallin, zu Alt-Wiesloch und der Vererzung der Trias im Kraichgau. *Jb. geol. Landesamt Baden–Württ.*, **6**, 1963, 239–99.
272 **Gruszczyk H. and Pouba Z.** Stratiform ore deposits of the Bohemian Massif and of the Silesia-Cracow area. *23rd Int.*

geol. Congr., Prague, 1968: Excursion guide 23 AC (Prague: Academia, 1968), 48 p.

273 **Kolbe E.** Die Bleierzlagerstätte Gonderbach bei Laasphe und ihre Entstehung. Neues Jb. Miner. Geol. Paläont. BeilBd, **52A,** 1925, 286–333.

274 **Katsch A.** Geochemisch-lagerstättenkundliche Untersuchung im Bereich der ehemaligen Blei–Silber-Lagerstätte Gonderbach, Krs. Wittgenstein. Thesis, Aachen, 1973, 106 p.

275 **Müller G.** Mineralisationen im Raum Saar–Nahe–Pfalz; Paragenesen und Abfolgen. Reference 220, 115–26.

276 **Meisl S.** Meta-Zeunerit in uranführenden vererzten Pflanzenresten im Oberen Buntsandstein bei Wrexen, Waldeck (Nordhessen). Notizbl. hess. Landesamt Bodenforsch., **93,** 1965, 266–80.

277 **Meisl S.** Eine uranführende sulfidische Erzparagenese im tertiären Braunkohlenquarzit von Dillich, Hessische Senke. Notizbl. hess. Landesamt Bodenforsch., **93,** 1965, 281–91.

278 **Wimmenauer W.** The eruptive rocks and carbonatites of the Kaiserstuhl, Germany. In Carbonatites **Tuttle O. F. and Gittins J.** eds (New York, etc.: Wiley, 1966), 183–204.

279 **Wambeke L. van et al.** Les roches alcalines et les carbonatites du Kaiserstuhl. EURATOM Rapp. EUR 1827 d, e, f, 1964, 1–232.

280 **Shoemaker E. M. and Chao E. C. T.** New evidence of the impact origin of the Ries Basin, Bavaria, Germany. J. geophys. Research, **66,** 1961, 3371–8.

281 Ergebnisse der Ries-Forschungsbohrung 1973: Struktur des Kraters und Entwicklung des Kratersees. Geol. Bavarica, **75** (Ries Band), 1977, 470 p.

282 **Gentner W. and Wagner G. A.** Altersbestimmungen an Riesgläsern und Moldaviten. Geol. Bavarica, **61,** 1969, 296–303.

283 **Herold R.** Eine Malmkalk-Trümmermasse in der Oberen Süßwassermolasse Niederbayerns. Geol. Bavarica, **61,** 1969, 413–27.

284 **Fahn R.** Die Gewinnung von Bentoniten in Bayern. Erzmetall, **26,** 1973, 425–8.

285 **Vogt K.** Bentonite deposits in Lower Bavaria. Geol. Jb., D no. 39, 1980, 47–68.

286 **Bottke H. Bartz J. Eichler J. Gudden H. Lippert H.-J. and Simon P.** Verdrängungs- und Verwitterungslagerstätten. Sammelwerk Deutsche Eisenerzlagerstätten, vol. 2, 4: Geol. Jb., D, in preparation.

287 **Cabral C.** Die tertiären Laterite des westlichen Vogelsberges und ihre Eignungen als Steine und Erden-Rohstoffe. Clausthaler geol. Abh., **16,** 1973, 153 p.

288 **Lippert H.-J. Lob F. Meisl S. Rée C. Salger M. Stadler G. and Teuscher E. O.** Die Kaolinlagerstätten der Bundesrepublik Deutschland. Rep. 23rd Int. geol. Congr., Prague, 1968 (Prague: Academia, 1969), vol. 15, 85–105.

289 **Ludwig G. and Figge G.** Schwermineralvorkommen und Sandverteilung in der Deutschen Bucht. Geol. Jb., D no. 32, 1979, 23–68.

290 **Lenz H. Wendt I. and Gudden H.** Altersbestimmungen an sekundären Uranmineralien aus dem Fichtelgebirge und dem nördlichen Oberpfälzer Wald nach der Pb/U-Methode. Geol. Bavarica, **4,** 1962, 124–33.

291 **Gudden H.** Uran in Bayern. Bergbau, **27,** 1976, 361–7.

292 **Krusch P.** Über primäre und sekundäre metasomatische Processe auf Erzlagerstätten. Z. prakt. Geol., **18,** 1910, 165–80.

293 **Schönfeld M.** Stratigraphische, fazielle, paläogeographische und tektonische Untersuchungen im Oberen Malm des Deisters, Osterwaldes und Süntels (NW-Deutschland). Clausthaler geol. Abh., **35,** 1979, 270.

294 **Paul J.** Zur Rand- und Schwellen-Fazies des Kupferschiefers. Z. dt. geol. Ges., **133,** 1982, 571–605.

295 **Suckow R. and Schwartz W.** Geomikrobiologische Untersuchung, 10: Zur Frage der Genese des Mansfelder Kupferschiefers. Z. allg. Mikrobiol., **8,** 1968, 47–64.

296 **Schneider H.-J.** Die Blei–Zink-Erzlagerstätten Bayerns, 2. Die Vorkommen der bayerischen Alpen. Geol. Jb. (Monographien der Deutschen Blei–Zink-Erzlagerstätten 13), in preparation.

297 **Bechstädt T.** Lead–zinc ores dependent on cyclic sedimentation. Mineral. Deposita, **10,** 1975, 234–48.

298 **Brockamp O. and Zuther M.** K/Ar-Datierungen zur Alterseinstufung lagerstättenbildender Prozesse. Naturwiss., **72,** 1985, 141–2.

299 **Unger H. J. and Niemeyer A.** Die Bentonite in Ostbayern—Enstehung, Lagerung, Verbreitung. Geol. Jb., D no. 71, 1985, 3–58.

300 **Simon P.** Fossile Schwermineral-Seifen bei Cuxhaven. Geowiss. in unserer Zeit, **4,** 1986, 55–61.

L. Baumann, B. Kölbel, M. Kraft, S. Lächelt, J. Rentzsch and K. Schmidt

German Democratic Republic

Geotectonic-minerogenetic survey of the German Democratic Republic

Geotectonic-minerogenetic subdivision

The geotectonic-minerogenetic subdivision of the territory of the German Democratic Republic (GDR) is controlled by two structural complexes—the basement complex, which was consolidated in pre-Variscan and Variscan times, including the molasse stage (Riphean–Lower Permian), common especially in the southern parts of the GDR, and the post-Variscan platform cover complex (Upper Permian–Caenozoic), common mainly in the middle and northern parts of the GDR.

The basement complex can be subdivided laterally, following two different criteria (Fig. 1). In terms of a subdivision into two major complexes, one complex corresponds to the mobile Variscan foredeep (sub-Variscan marginal deep, Variscan outer zone), with its basement consolidated partly in the Precambrian and partly in the Caledonian (Ostelbe massif, Caledonide aulacogene), as well as to the European Variscan belt, deformed in the Asturic phase. This region forms the basement of the northern parts of the GDR.

The other major complex to the south is characterized by the more stable Variscan orogen region, folded in the Sudetic phase (Rhenohercynian zone and Saxothuringian zone) with its pre-Variscan-consolidated units, its widespread zones of epithermal and katathermal metamorphism and its magmatic rocks.

In the Variscan subsequent stage of both major units the sedimentary and effusive formations of the molasse have a relatively wide distribution in different tectonic positions.

In terms of a subdivision into the *main zones of the Variscan orogen* that can be differentiated in central Europe, in the territory of the GDR all zones except the Moldanubian are developed in a more or less characteristic form.

The *Saxothuringian* minerogenetic zone occupies a transitional position between the Moldanubian Zone and the typically geosynclinal Rhenohercynian Zone (high content of old crystalline complexes), affecting its geological structure and development. This is expressed in a relatively minor geosynclinal sedimentation, which took place in narrow troughs and with a comparatively weak initial magmatism. In contrast, there is an intensive *synorogenic* to *post-orogenic* and *subsequent* magmatism. A series of mineralizations, some of them forming deposits, preferentially linked to the anticline of the Fichtelgebirge–Erzgebirge, is genetically connected with acid, geochemically specialized, Variscan granitoids. In the area of the Central European Rise there occur syn- to post-kinematic granodiorites and granitoids, partly also of pre-Variscan age. Besides the intrusive forms, the subsequent magmatism led to widespread and in places thick effusive formations of only minor or non-existent minerogenetic specialization (Fig. 2). As a whole, the Saxothuringian Zone shows extensive miogeosynclinal traits.

The Rhenohercynian minerogenetic zone corresponds to the geosynclinal Rhenish trough. In comparison to the Saxothuringian Zone the geosynclinal sedimentation and the initial magmatism and associated volcanogene-sedimentary mineralization become more evident. During the subsequent stage post-kinematic granitoids with polymetallic mineralization were again intruded. Large parts of the zone are overlain by formations of the molasse stage and the platform cover.

The *sub-Variscan* minerogenetic zone borders the Rhenohercynian Zone on the north. The regional transition between the two zones, and also questions regarding their development as a foredeep, as well as their northern boundary, are still unclarified (Fig. 1). Its minerogeny is little understood because of its great depth (overlain by deposits of the molasse and platform stage).

The same applies to the *Variscan* minerogenetic outer zone, overlying the Caledonian- and probably also Precambrian-deformed basement. Accordingly, its geotectonic position should be seen as the pre-Permian part of the platform cover.

The *post-Variscan platform cover complex* achieves in the central and northern parts of the GDR an areally

This chapter is provided by members of the Central Geological Institute, Berlin, and the Bergakademie Freiberg, German Democratic Republic.

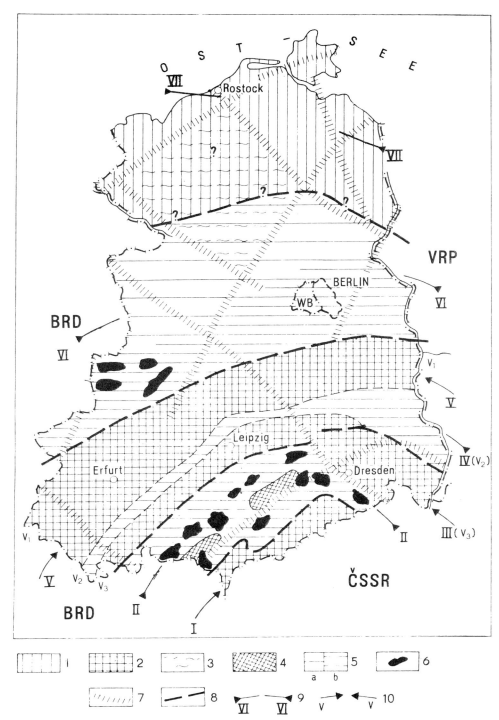

Fig. 1 *Tectonic-minerogenetic regional division of basement complexes (in part after Glusko et al.,[35] Tischendorf et al.,[74] Lächelt and Tischendorf,[44] Baumann and Tischendorf[17] and Baumann et al.[18]). 1, Caledonian-folded Lower Palaeozoic (concealed); 2, Variscan anticlines; 3, East Elbe massif (concealed) with probable Precambrian basement and Caledonian and Variscan reworking; 4, intrageosynclinal uplifts (pre-Variscan complexes); 5, foredeeps and troughs of (a) outer Variscides and (b) synclinal troughs of inner Variscides; 6, distribution area of Variscan geosynclinal magmatic rocks; 7, lineaments and deep fractures; 8, boundary lines of Variscan structural units; 9, direction of Variscan synclinal troughs; 10, direction of Variscan anticlinal uplifts. Structural units: I, Fichtelgebirge–Erzgebirge anticline; II, syncline of Thuringian trough and the Elbtal; III, anticline of Lausitz Block (continuation of southern anticlinal zone of Central European Rise); IV, synclinal zone of Görlitz trough (continuation of synclinal zone of Central European Rise); V, anticline of Central European Rise (V_1, crystalline zone; V_2, synclinal zone; V_3, southern anticlinal zone/Schwarzburg–North Saxony–Lausitz anticlinorium); VI, syncline of Rhenish trough and sub-Variscan marginal deep; VII, Variscan external zone*

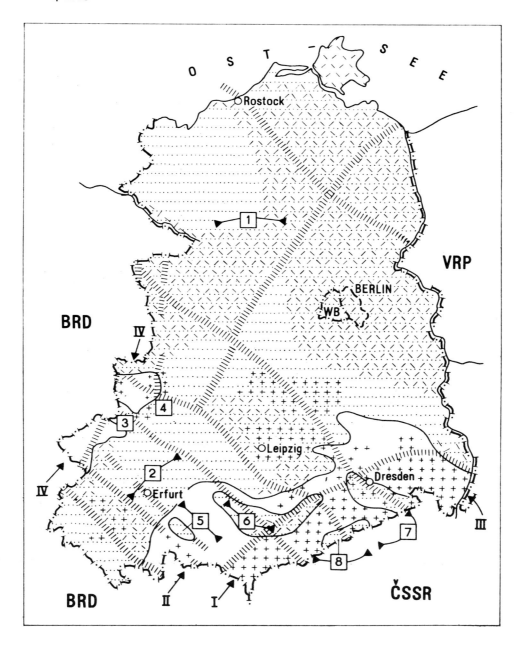

Fig. 2 Tectonic-minerogenetic regional division of Variscan transition structural stage (in part after Tischendorf et al.,[74] Glusko et al.,[35] Lächelt and Tischendorf,[44] Baumann and Tischendorf[17] and Baumann et al.[18]). A, region of denudation; B, post-orogenic granitization and intrusive granitoid rocks; C, sedimentary and sedimentary volcanic formations; D, subsequent volcanic rocks; E, lineaments and deep fractures; F, designation and direction of depressions and troughs. 1, Part of Central European Depression; 2, Oos–Saale Trough; 3, Ilfeld Trough; 4, Meisdorf Trough; 5, Rudolfstadt Trough; 6, Erzgebirge Trough; 7, Döhlen Trough; 8, Olbernhau–Brandov Trough. G, position of regions of denudation; I, Fichtelgebirge–Erzgebirge anticlinorium; II, East Thuringian Rise; III, Lausitz Block; IV, Eichsfeld–Oberharz Rise

uniform distribution. The sediments of the platform cover, transgressing southwards to a varying extent over the Permo-Carboniferous molasse formations and the basement complex, are subdivided by fracture and block tectonics in single units. The following characteristic minerogenetic sub-provinces can be defined: the sub-Hercynian, the Thuringian, the South Thuringian–Franconian Basin and the Elbe Valley Zone (Fig. 3).

Minerogenetically, the platform cover complex is

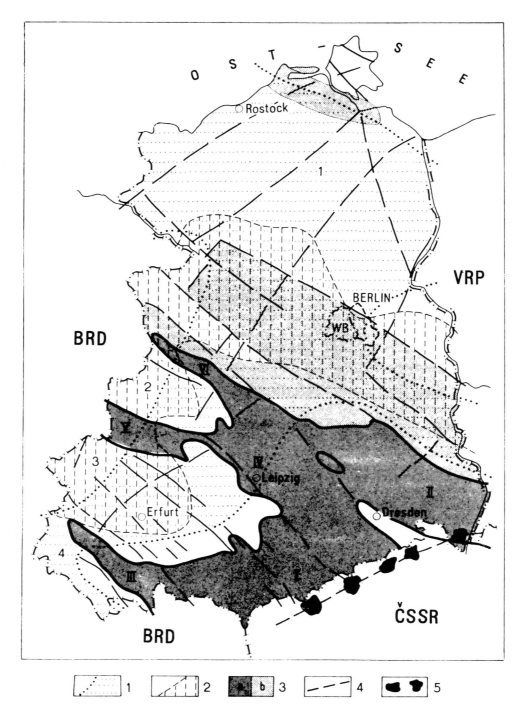

Fig. 3 *Tectonic-minerogenetic regional division of post-Variscan platform superstructure (after Nöldeke and Schwab[51]). 1, Main subsidence stage, Zechstein–Lower/Middle Keuper (Old Cimmerian); 2, stage of differentiation, Upper Keuper–Lower Albian (Young Cimmerian); 3, stage of stabilization, Middle Albian–Quaternary (sub-Hercynian–Laramide): a, highs (upstanding); b, marine cover; 4, important deep fractures and faults; 5, centres of Tertiary basic magmatism. Structural units: I, Erzgebirge; II Lausitz Block; III, Thüringer Wald; IV, Northwestern Saxony and Halle District; V, Harz; VI, Flechtingen–Roßlau Block (1, part of Central European Depression; 2, sub-Hercynian Basin; 3, Thuringian Basin; 4, South Thuringian–Franconian Basin (Werra region))*

characterized by exogene–sedimentogene mineralizations, which predominate in all platform stages. Characteristic also is endogene (magmatogene) mineralization, which should be attributed to an alkaline–basic platform magmatism, with which the Tertiary basaltic volcanism is also connected.

Geotectonic-minerogenetic stages of development

Six major geotectonic-minerogenetic stages or cycles can be deduced from the geological-minerogenetic development of the territory of the GDR and from the chronological succession of the mineralization processes (Fig. 4)—(1) the Moldanubian–Dalslandian; (2) the Assyntic–Cadomian (Brioverian); (3) the Caledonian (Cambro-Ordovician); (4) the Variscan geosynclinal-orogen; (5) the Variscan molasse; and (6) the post-Variscan platform stage.

The appearance and the development of the geotectonic-minerogenetic stages in the GDR are characterized in detail below.

(1) The *Moldanubian–Dalslandian* and *Assyntic–Cadomian* (Brioverian and also Baikalian) *stages* of the Precambrian are assigned to the Riphean (= Upper Proterozoic; ca 1500–570 m.y.). According to Magnusson,[45] Zeman[80] and Hofmann and co-workers,[39] a new development started with the Moldanubian-Dalslandian stage by a Dalslandian tectonomagmatic reactivation of Middle and Lower Proterozoic tectogenes and concluded with the formation of a geosynclinal-orogene tectogene about 1000 m.y. ago. The aligned Granulitgebirge and the older structural units of the Ruhlaer Krystallin in the area of the Central European Rise, where there are more Moldanubian crystalline complexes under cover, are assigned to this early Riphean, Moldanubian age group.

(2) The *Assyntic–Cadomian* (*late Riphean*) *stage* attains a wide distribution in the southern part of the GDR. It forms, like the Moldanubian-Dalslandian stage, an independent geosynclinal-tectogene cycle, the development of which started about 900 m.y. ago and was finished in the latest Precambrian with regional Assyntic (Cadomian) movements.[2] Typical representatives are the greywacke formations of Lausitz and Leipzig, which may be interpreted as flysch or early molasse, as well as the Precambrian of the 'Schwarzburg Saddle', some magmatic rocks and anatexites of the Lausitz Block, the older gneiss series (Freiberg–Fürstenwald and the Annaberg Block) and the Pressnitz Series of the Erzgebirge. Among those formations only the Pressnitz Series with its genetically differently interpreted 'felsite horizon', representing the real geosynclinal type (alternating volcanogenic and sedimentary groups), is of some minerogenetic importance.

(3) The *Caledonian* (Cambro-Ordovician) *stage* occupies a transitional position, for large parts of the GDR, between the Assyntic–Cadomian stage and the Variscan geosynclinal-orogen cycle. Characteristic of this stage is the appearance of folded Ordovician on the Isle of Rügen, and the magmatic intrusions and effusive formations known in the southern part of the GDR. The folding movements in the northern part of the GDR took place in a marginal deep, similar to an aulacogene, situated in front of the East European Platform. They led to the formation of a structurally disconformable complex of Upper Ordovician age as part of the Dobrudsha–North Sea Lineament. The southern boundary of the aulacogene-like depression opposite the Asturic-folded sub-Variscan marginal deep is assumed to be in the northern part of the East Elbe Massif.[30,35,72]

Besides a typical intrusive magmatism and synsedimentary volcanism, there was an intensive deep tectonometamorphism, especially in the older crystalline core zones of the Saxothuringikum in the northern frame of the Bohemian Massif, which led to a far-reaching, intracrustal mobilization of material (the Lausitz anatexites, etc.). In the Erzgebirge volcanogenic-sedimentary formations with local stratiform mineralization of the element combinations Fe–Cu–Pb–Zn and Sn are associated with the Cambro-Ordovician rock sequences.[40,77] In the Thuringian slate mountains chamositic–thuringitic iron ores were formed, the genesis of which (exogene-sedimentary or submarine-effusive) is still not satisfactorily clarified. These iron ores are largely worked out.

(4) Because of the lack of a clear marking of the transition from the Caledonian to the *Variscan geosynclinal-orogen stage*, the boundary between the Silurian and the Ordovician in the Saxothuringian Zone is seen as the beginning of the Variscan geosynclinal development. *The Variscan geosynclinal region* is distinguished by relatively clearly definable tectonic zones (Fig. 1).

In comparison to the Thuringian Trough, the Rhenish Trough shows a higher sedimentation rate as well as a stronger geosynclinal magmatism (diabase–keratophyre-spilite formation), especially in the middle Upper Devonian. Associated with this initial magmatism are submarine-hydrothermal and impregnative Fe–(Mn) mineralizations of the Lahn–Dill type as well as local pyrite mineralization (Elbingerode Complex/Harz). The latter can be assigned in the wider sense to the Rio Tinto type.[64] The geosynclinal stage ends for the area of the Saxothuringian and Rhenohercynian troughs with the Variscan main folding (Sudetic phase) in the late Lower Carboniferous to Namurian; the sub-Variscan foredeep was first involved in folding in the Asturic phase. Therefore the final formation of the Variscan geosynclinal-orogen stage falls roughly into the Middle to Upper Westphalian period.

(5) In synchronism with the progressive south to north formation of the tectogene, the Variscan (Permo-Carboniferous) molasse stage starts at different times. Intramontane troughs with limnic coal deposits were formed in consequence of the Sudetic phase; they are of no economic importance. Following the Erzgebirge phase (Namurian), the real development of the molasse stage took place. The main characteristics are huge molasse troughs as well as a

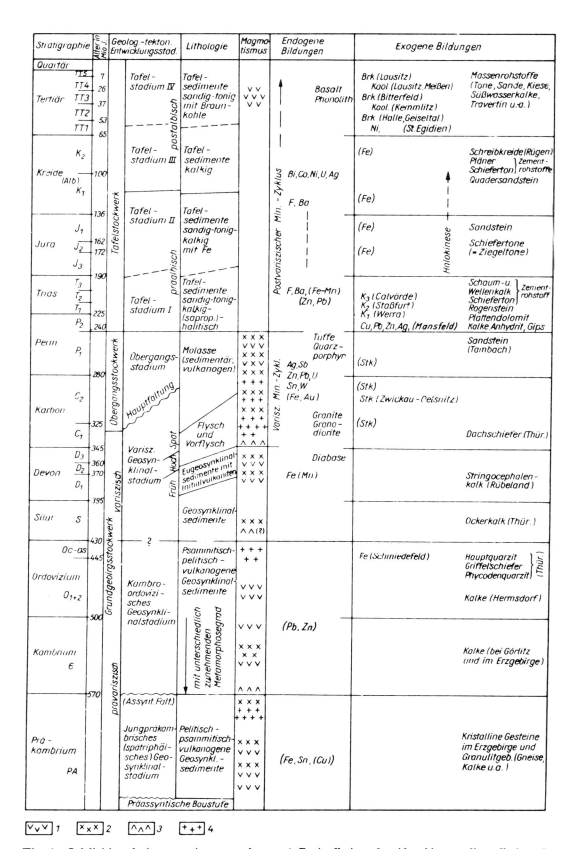

Fig. 4 *Subdivision of minerogenetic structural stages. 1, Basic effusives; 2, acid and intermediate effusives; 3, basic intrusives; 4, acid and intermediate intrusives (Stk, black coal; Brk, brown coal; K_{1-3}, potash salt deposits)*

pronounced effusive and intrusive subsequent magmatism in the course of intensive fault-block tectonics (Fig. 2).

The development of the intramontane troughs generally follows the Variscan zonal structure. The Oos–Saale Trough was formed by inversion of the crystalline core zone of the Central European Rise, the Erzgebirge Trough, along the central Saxony lineament. Hercynian faults are important for the formation of molasse sub-troughs (Ilfeld, Döhlen Basins) as well as for the pattern of units of the adjacent platform superstructure (Lausitz Block, Elbe Valley Zone, Thuringian Forest, Harz, Flechtingen-Roßlau Block). Overlying the outermost parts of the Central European Variscan belt, which were folded in the Asturic phase or deformed in a germanotype pattern, was formed the northern zone of subsidence, starting in Stephanian times as a widespread molasse depression in which the Rotliegende achieves a widespread distribution. The strong effusive volcanism of the Lower Rotliegende is obviously caused and regulated by taphrogenic processes. Areas of intersection of major fault zones of Variscan (southwest–northeast), Hercynian (southeast–northwest) and, in particular, the more distinctly prominent Rhenish directions (north–south) are the preferred areas of activity for the incipient volcanism. The taphrogenesis, which started in the Stephanian and finished in the Saxonian I, is interpreted as an intra-plate tectonic process.

No mineralization is known in the heterogeneous, partly volcanogene-sedimentary, molasse formations of the Permo-Carboniferous. Especially during the Upper Carboniferous and to a lesser degree in the Lower Rotliegende there was locally limnic coal formation in individual troughs (Erzgebirge Basin, Saale Trough), which, however, did not attain any major economic importance. In comparison with the genetically ineffectual effusive magmatism, the Permo-Carboniferous granitoid intrusive magmatism achieved a greater metallogenetic importance. Among others, the granitoids of Meissen, Kirchberg, Bergen, Eibenstock, Henneberg, Königshain, Brocken and Ramberg, as well as those of the Central European Rise, are grouped with the granitoids of Carboniferous and Lower Permian age.

Iron skarns and tungsten mineralization (Erzgebirge) are to some extent connected with the older of these magmatic rocks. The youngest Sn, F and Li specialized Lower Permian granitoids led to widespread tin mineralization—among others, to the formation of the Altenberg and Ehrenfriedersdorf deposits. Also, the polymetallic vein formations of the Erzgebirge and the Harz, which were worked in former mining periods, are attributed to the complex tectonic-magmatic activities in the transitional stage (Variscan polymetallic mineralization cycle).

(6) The *post-Variscan platform stage* is characterized by a discontinuous, sinking process, which is regulated mainly by the heterogeneous basement leading to an increasing stabilization of the crustal movements.

The development of the platform stage took place in four stages (Fig. 4).[51]

(a) In the *taphrogenic stage* (Stephanian–Saxonian I) the structural pattern of the Central European Depression results from an overall modification of the crustal regime (tectonomagmatic activation). With the collapse of the main ridge of a wide zone of updoming a gaping structure is formed, which is controlled by NNE–SSW and northwest–southeast deep fractures and within which the effusion of the thick subsequent volcanic rocks takes place.

(b) The main subsidence stage starts with the Saxonian II and comes to an end in the Middle Keuper (Old Cimmerian movements). With the expansion of the area of sedimentation, a Saxonian basin with thick deposits of a later-formed Variscan molasse was developed in the northern parts of the GDR. The progressive, widely extensive sinking process led towards the south to a transgression of the Zechstein over the Variscan tectogene. The real platform stage starts with the inclusion of the inner Variscan zone in the generally north–south-trending transgression regime. Bunter, Muschelkalk and the lower Middle Keuper cover almost entirely the territory of the GDR, with the exception of the high prominences of the Erzgebirge and the Lausitz.

During the *main subsidence phase* predominantly terrestrial, brackish, neritic and lagoonal sediments were deposited in a sandy, clayey-calcareous, sapropelitic and halite facies. Kupferschiefer was formed with local mineralization of Cu, Pb, Zn, Ag and other elements,[57] as well as anhydrite, gypsum and rock salt, and potash salt deposits,[69,70] in addition to clays and limestones, which are used for various industrial purposes. Because of the palaeotectonic control of the mineralization the Kupferschiefer mineralization belongs genetically to the Variscan molasse stage.[57,58]

(c) With the *differentiation stage*, which was introduced through the Old Cimmerian movements in the Upper Keuper, a structural alteration of the hitherto relatively undifferentiated sedimentation province took place. With the activation of east–west and northwest–southeast fracture zones and the onset of halokinesis, mainly narrow deposition depressions and troughs were formed that are characterized, in contrast to the surrounding uplands, by thick stratigraphic sequences (e.g. the southwest Mecklenburg depression). The orogenic stage of differentiation reaches its climax with the Young Cimmerian movements in the transition period from the Jurassic to the Cretaceous and lasts until the Aptian–lower Albian. Minerogenetically, the differentiation stage is mainly characterized by marine sedimentary iron enrichment of the minette and Salzgitter type.

(*d*) In the succeeding *stabilization stage* (Middle Albian to Recent) the stages of sinking and differentiation of the earlier and middle platform stage are repeated in a diminished form. The first phase of the stabilization stage starts with the Albian–Cenomanian transgression, which is predominantly orientated west–east and controlled by east–west as well as marked northwest–southeast-directed elements.

With the effects of the Austric movements the compression tectonics intensify in the Upper Cretaceous, reaching their climax with the sub-Hercynian–Laramide movements. Significant results are tectonic inversions and the 'stabilization' of the boundary- or fault-block structures in connexion with processes of intensive erosion and halokinesis. These processes mould today's tectonic pattern, which is delineated mainly by fault systems running parallel to the southwestern border of the East European Platform (Fig. 3). The consolidation that was achieved by the sub-Hercynian–Laramide movements determines the further tectonic development and processes of sedimentation during Phase 2 of the stabilization stage (Caenozoic). Predominant is a repeated alternation of transgression and regression taking place under the influence of northwest–southeast/north–south intersecting block structure. Typical manifestations are the marginal deeps filled with thick Tertiary sediments, resulting from salt diapirism, which was especially active in the Lower Tertiary. The stabilization stage is minerogenetically characterized by its Tertiary brown coal content, especially in the southern parts of the GDR. In addition, there occur various kinds of raw materials for the construction, ceramic and glass industries in the Tertiary and Quaternary. Among these are the kaolin deposits, which were formed by erosion processes in the late Upper Cretaceous and Early Tertiary.

Besides the exogene minerogenetic processes, which are typical for platform stages, there were also endogene mineralization processes. They are strongly connected in space and time with the tectonomagmatic activation of the platform stage. Only the fluorite and barite deposits associated with this post-Variscan mineralization cycle are presently of economic importance (Fig. 4). Of temporary economic interest in the past were iron–manganese and lead–zinc mineralizations, as well as Bi–Co–Ni–Ag formations in the Erzgebirge, the Thüringer Wald and the Harz.

Minerogenetic units in the GDR

In the territory of the GDR 12 minerogenetic (metallogenetic) units can be defined (Fig. 5).

The Fichtelgebirge–Erzgebirge Anticline (sub-zone I)
The Fichtelgebirge–Erzgebirge Anticlinal zone was formed in the course of Variscan syn- and post-orogenic development. The oldest Precambrian rocks (probably from the Lower to the Middle Riphean) occur in the form of the so-called 'grey gneiss' in the eastern parts of the Erzgebirge. The Upper Riphean, Cambrian and Lower Ordovician are represented in the central areas of the zone by metamorphic series (gneiss, micaschist, metagreywackes, amphibolites, porphyroids and calc-silicate rocks).

Ordovician of a lower metamorphic grade (phyllite) is widespread mainly in the western parts of the Erzgebirge. Silurian formations are preserved only in intermontane troughs. Devonian rocks occur predominantly in the western parts of the Erzgebirge Anticlinal zone. In the Dinantian the development begins with a calcareous facies, which is followed by thick Culm. In the Upper Carboniferous to Lower Permian small molasse troughs were formed at the edge and in the eastern parts of the Erzgebirge Anticline. In contrast, the post-orogenic to subsequent magmatism, consisting of two major intrusive complexes, achieved a greater importance.

Whereas tungsten mineralization (Pechtelsgrün type) is associated with the granites of the older complex, with the granites of the younger complex is connected a tin mineralization (Altenberg type). The polymetallic mineralizations (Freiberg type, etc.) are probably controlled mainly by the post-orogenic subsequent magmatism. In the eastern parts of the Erzgebirge there are also widespread late Variscan volcanic rocks (quartz porphyry, granite porphyry). Post-Variscan vein mineralizations (F–Ba, Pb–Zn, Bi–Co–Ni–Ag), as well as Tertiary basic volcanism (basalts, phonolites) are associated with Meso–Caenozoic fault tectonics (platform stage).

Central Saxony Lineament (sub-zone II)
This sub-zone forms a syncline between the Fichtelgebirge–Erzgebirge zone and the Eastern Thuringian–Northwest Saxony zone—that is, the Granulitgebirge—reflecting the course of the Central Saxony Lineament. The uplifted Precambrian crystalline complexes comprise the 'Saxony median massif'. They consist of Precambrian orthogneisses and paragneisses as well as ortho-amphibolites.

Lower Palaeozoic rocks can be found in the marginal region of the zone as well as in the basement beneath the Erzgebirge molasse trough developed over the Central Saxony Lineament.

Silurian siliceous and alum schists and limestones, Devonian siliceous schists, flysch sediments and limestones and flyschoidal Lower Carboniferous constitute the Variscan geosynclinal development. During the Variscan transition stage the lineament acted as an axis of sinking, resulting in the deposition of fluviatile-limnic rocks and the effusion of subsequent volcanic rocks that make up the molasse formation of the Erzgebirge trough. Economically important fluorite and barite mineralization is associated with this sub-zone.

German Democratic Republic

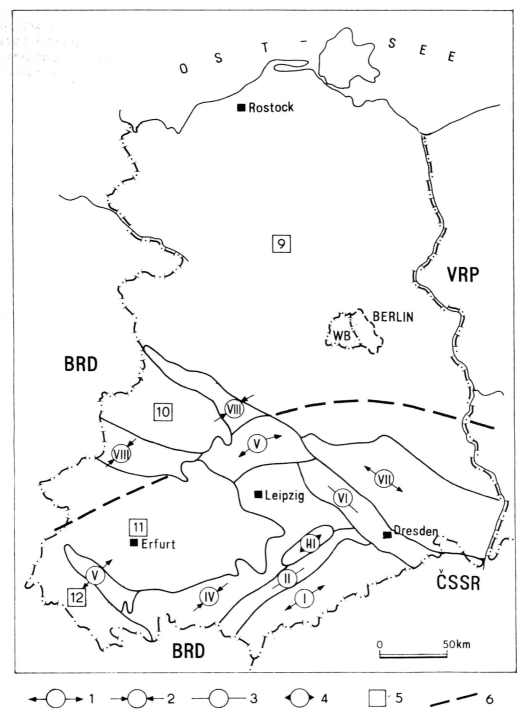

Fig. 5 *Minerogenetic units of GDR territory. 1, Anticlinoria; 2, synclinoria; 3, Lineament zones; 4, positive massifs; 5, units of post-Variscan platform cover; 6, boundary line between Saxothuringian and Rhenohercynian zones. Minerogenetic units: I, Fichtelgebirge–Erzgebirge sub-zone; II, Central Saxony sub-zone; III, Granulitgebirge; IV, Eastern Thuringian–North Saxony sub-zone; V, Central European Rise; VI, zone of Elbtal; VII, Lausitz Block; VIII, Harz–Flechtingen–Roßlau Block; 9, part of Central European Depression; 10, sub-Hercynian Basin; 11, Thuringian Basin; 12, South Thuringian–Franconian Basin*

The Granulitgebirge (sub-zone III)
The tectonic position of this sub-zone is interpreted, among others, as an upwedging structure in connexion with the Central Saxony Lineament. The sub-zone is predominantly built of crystalline pre-Variscan formations. Most common rock types are, along with several granulite varieties, gneisses and gneiss–mica schists with interstratified Precambrian amphibolites.

In the schist mantle the Caledonian and Variscan stages are represented by gneiss–micaschists through to phyllites, initial magmatic rocks (diabases and tuffs) and granitoids (the so-called 'bedded granites'). Bronzite–serpentinites intruded at the junction of the granulite core and the schist mantle form the source rock of the small nickel hydrosilicate deposits of St. Egidien.

East Thuringian–North Saxony Synclinorium (sub-zone IV)
This zone existed as a syncline (Thuringian Trough of the Variscan geosyncline) since the Lower Palaeozoic. The Precambrian rocks are predominantly greywackes. In the Cambrian there occur mica slates and more greywackes, as well as quartzites and conglomeratic arkoses. In the Ordovician geosynclinal sequences were deposited that consisted of schists and quartzites, locally bearing silicate iron ores. The Silurian is represented by typical early geosynclinal formations (siliceous alum shales, ochre limestones). In the Devonian limestones and clay slate sequences predominate. Diabases and diabase tuffs of the Upper Devonian occur mainly in the eastern parts of the sub-zone. In the Dinantian flysch sequences (Culm) were deposited in the whole sub-zone. During the platform stage kaolin deposits were formed over late Variscan effusives in the Northwest Saxony area. In the Tertiary important brown coal formations were deposited.

Central European Rise (sub-zone V)
Pre-Variscan crystalline rocks are exposed in the Ruhlaer Krystallin of the Thüringer Wald and in the Kyffhäuser. Similar formations were found in concealed areas of the Central European Rise. In the Cambrian limestones and sandstones were deposited and, in the Ordovician, schists and quartzites. In the Upper Ordovician an incipient rise became evident, reaching a climax in the Upper Devonian. With the Dinantian the inversion of the rise started with the formation of troughs filled with Carboniferous limestones, greywackes, clay shales and limnic–paralic coal formations. From the Upper Westphalian to the Autunian the troughs widened out to an extended zone of subsidence in the axis of which runs the Oos–Saale trough (Fig. 2). Besides the effusive late Variscan (subsequent) volcanic rocks of the molasse stage, late to post-kinematic granitoids were intruded in the area of the Central European Rise.

As development progressed, the former rise was included in the platform development. During the Zechstein came the copper mineralization associated with sapropelite formation of the Kupferschiefer, mainly on the northern flank of the crystalline zone; the four saliferous cycles are developed over the whole area. After an initial fluvial-limnic phase (Bunter) and marine development (Muschelkalk) in the Triassic, a progressive emergence took place in the Keuper. Jurassic sedimentation penetrated into this area only as spurs. Cretaceous sedimentation is continuous only to the north of the rise; to the south sediments are distributed only sporadically. In the Tertiary mainly sands and clays were accumulated. Of special economic importance are the brown coal deposits.

Elbtal Zone (sub-zone VI)
The Elbtal zone is orientated along a northwest-southeast-striking lineament, the influence of which is traceable from pre-Variscan times to the present. The Elbe lineament separates the Erzgebirge Anticline from the Lausitz Block, causing a change in direction of the structure lines, leading to the formation of narrow troughs, mainly following the direction of the lineament.

The following Precambrian rocks can be found in the Elbtal zone: greywackes, biotite gneiss and andalusite–muscovite micaschists. To the east the pre-Variscan granitoids of Lausitz reach out into the Elbtal zone. The Cambrian development cannot be exactly established.

Clearly distinct is the Ordovician development with schists, spilites and sandstones, as well as effusive diabases with their tuffs. In the Silurian follow schists and limestones. The Devonian consists of limestones, diabases and tuffs, as well as argillaceous slatey rocks, some of them siliceous schists. In the Dinantian occur hornstones as well as conglomerates and Culm greywackes. In the Variscan transition stage (molasse stage) the Döhlen Rotliegend trough was formed.

Variscan intrusives of the Elbtal zone, like the Meissen monzonite–granitoid massif, are connected with the intersection areas of the Elbe lineament with other lineament zones—for example, the Central Saxony Lineament.

After an incomplete or absent sedimentation in the Triassic, in the Jurassic and the Lower Cretaceous, sandstones are predominantly deposited in the Albian–Cenomanian transgression. In the Tertiary there is mainly basic volcanism. No important mineralization is known.

Lausitz Block (sub-zone VII)
Characteristic of the Lausitz Block are mainly Precambrian greywackes, which were anatectically modified in the central part. Precambrian granitoids also occur in this area. Post-orogenic granites and subsequent volcanic rocks are of Variscan age. The lamprophyre and dolerite dykes with traces of Ni–Cu mineralization are considered to be of early Variscan age. For long periods the Lausitz Block formed an area of denudation with which kaolin formations, among others, are associated. In the Tertiary came the effusion of basic volcanic rocks (basalts and phonolites). During the

Tertiary and Quaternary sediments were deposited in superposed local basins, the Tertiary encroaching to the north on the basement rock and with which brown coal deposits, among others, are associated.

Harz and Flechtingen–Roßlau Block (sub-zone VIII)
The Harz and the Flechtingen–Roßlau Block are uplifted basement units of the former Rhenish Trough. Unlike the Thuringian, the Rhenish Trough shows a more geosynclinal character. There are no definite indications of the presence of Cambrian or Precambrian rocks. Some metamorphic formations of the Wippra Zone are classed as Ordovician. In the Silurian the sedimentation started with coarsely clastic rocks, especially quartzites and greywackes. In the Devonian geosynclinal deposits with clay slates, quartzites, limestones and initial magmatic rocks were developed with which iron ore enrichments and pyrite are associated. From the Upper Devonian and Dinantian the flysch facies (Culm) becomes dominant. Characteristic of the Rhenohercynian Zone are olistostromes and slide sheets. In the Upper Carboniferous Lower Permian there follow Variscan molasse together with subsequent volcanic rocks. The post-kinematic magmatism expresses itself in the Harz in the granitoids of Brocken and Ramberg. Unimportant polymetallic vein mineralization is associated with the latter. The development of molasse in the Rhenohercynian Zone culminated in the external molasse. The late Cimmerian and especially the sub-Hercynian–Laramide movements caused uplift of horst-like denuded anticlines of both of the basement units. Of some interest is the post-Variscan fluorite–barite mineralization, which is associated closely with the above-mentioned Variscan polymetallic vein mineralization.

Trough in the northern GDR (sub-zone IX)
As the central part of the Central European Depression, this trough occupies the whole northern part of the GDR (Figs. 3 and 5). The pre-Upper Carboniferous basement is better known only from boreholes on the Isle of Rügen, where Devonian and Lower Carboniferous formations were drilled in an arenaceous–argillaceous–calcareous platform facies. The Rotliegende molasse formations with their subsequent volcanic sequences occur widely in the trough, as well as the Kupferschiefer and saliferous formations of the Zechstein. During the platform stage the trough went through the stages of development mentioned above. The Tertiary is developed in a marine facies—in contrast to the southern part of the GDR. Minerogenetically, the deposits of gravels, sands and clays of the Quaternary as well as the chalk ('writing chalk') of Rügen, small clay deposits and local iron ore enrichments are of special interest.

Sub-Hercynian Basin, Thuringian Basin, South Thuringian–Franconian Basin (sub-zones X, XI, XII)
The development of these units starts with the formation of molasse troughs during the Variscan Transition Stage. The molasse that was formed in the Upper Carboniferous–Lower Permian corresponds to the common terrestrial, limnic-fluvial type with subsequent volcanic rocks and, locally, minor coal formation. From the beginning of the platform stage in the Zechstein to the end of the main subsidence stage in the Middle Keuper the individual basins in their present outline, as components of the Central European Depression, were only weakly delineated. Only the late Cimmerian and sub-Hercynian–Laramide movements brought about their location and delimitation as largely independent units (Figs. 3 and 5). In all three basins the Zechstein formation is almost everywhere completely developed; in the Trias follow clays, saliferous rocks, muschelkalk and clastic sequences. Jurassic and Cretaceous formations occupy large parts of the sub-Hercynian Basin; in the Thuringian and Thuringian–Franconian Basin only residual deposits are left. The basins are partly delimited by major faults, leading to the uplifting of individual blocks (horsts), to the tilting of blocks and a general block disintegration. Most of the faults strike southeast–northwest; post-Variscan mineralization, especially fluorite and barite, is associated with some of them.

Minerogeny (metallogeny) of the GDR territory with regard to typical mineralization

In the individual stages and phases of the structural-geological development various endogenous and exogenous mineralizations and ore depositions came about. Accordingly, the stages of development (geosynclinal, orogenic, molasse and platform stages) show characteristics that are expressed in different minerogenetic productivities. According to their type and temporal position the minerogenetic processes follow the general conformity of minerogenetic epochs, cycles and stages that have been elaborated by Soviet geologists—notably, Yu. A. Bilibin and V. I. Smirnov.

In spite of the relative variety of minerogenetic events in the GDR, the *exploitable* deposits represent only a small part. Because of centuries of mining important deposits—for example, the polymetallic vein formations—are now exhausted. With that in mind, in the following the historically important mineral concentrations as well as those which are being worked at present are separated as types of deposits. Occurrences and mineralization localities are only mentioned for the discussion of minerogenetic questions. At present deposits of brown coal, natural gas, potassium salts, Kupferschiefer, tin, fluorite and barite are extracted in the GDR. Of importance, additionally, are the various raw materials for the glass, ceramic, construction and chemical industries, such as clay, kaolin, gravel, sand, limestone, gypsum and anhydrite.

Pre-Variscan Stages

The predominantly metamorphic pre-Variscan basement complex contains only a few minerogenetically important rock formations. These are formations of eugeosynclinal and geosynclinal character of the Assyntian–Cadomian (series of Pressnitz) and the Caledonian stage. Stratiform mineralization, carrying Fe, Sn, Cu, Zn and Pb enrichments, is associated with some of the strongly metamorphosed rock sequences of volcanosedimentary origin.[16,40,77] The sedimentation conditions point to primary syngenetic ore formation during the deposition of the volcanosedimentary rock sequences (Fig. 6). As regards the tin, a genetically different type of mineralization in contrast to the mineralizations (greisen and vein deposits) associated with granite so far known must be considered.[6,9,16,17,77] A definite genetic attribution has not so far been established. A typical example of this possibly stratigenetic development is the so-called felsite horizon of the Pressnitz series at the northwestern margin of the Freiberg gneiss cupola. It carries in association with metamorphic porphyroid rocks local enrichments of magnetite, pyrite, cassiterite, sphalerite and other ore minerals, which are not economically minable.

The ore deposits of *Schwarzenberg–Pöhla* and *Breitenbrunn* of the Cambro-Ordovician stage in the Erzgebirge belong to this genetic type. Most of the stratiform oxide and sulphide mineralization (magnetite, pyrite, pyrrhotite, arsenopyrite, sphalerite, cassiterite, scheelite, etc.) occurs together with intensely metasomatized horizons of carbonate rock (skarns). In the past these ore deposits were mined on a small scale, but closure was a consequence of the reserve situation and the difficulty of smelting the complex ores.

Outside the Erzgebirge in the Cambro-Ordovician stage only oolitic iron ores of the chamositic-thuringitic type were formed in the Upper Ordovician (Gräfenthal Series).[38,66] These acidic ores had no economic importance except for the southeastern flank of the Schwarzburg Saddle in the Thuringian slate mountains (Fe, 30–38%; SiO_2, 10–30%). The mines, which had been in operation at the Schmiedefeld and Wittmannsgereuth deposits, were shut down at the beginning of the seventies because the reserves were exhausted.

Variscan geosynclinal-orogen and molasse stage

The Variscan Geosynclinal Stage, initiated in the transition from the Ordovician to the Silurian, is characterized by types of mineralization genetically connected with initial magmatism. The Middle to Upper Devonian oxidic iron ore formation of the Lahn–Dill type as well as sulphidic ores are characteristic in this respect.

Oxidic iron ores were formed at several sites in the Variscan geosynclinal areas in the southern part of the GDR. Only the iron ores of the *Elbingerode Complex* in the Harz were of some economic importance, with the formerly mined deposits of Büchenberg and Braunesumpf (Fig. 7). The mineralization occurs in the hanging-wall of the so-called 'Schalstein' series with diabases, spilites and keratophyres. In the 15-m thick ore layers the Fe content is associated with hematite, siderite, magnetite, and partly with iron silicate.[61] The complex conditions of formation led to dense, laminated, banded and brecciated types of fabric. Rösler[60] came to the conclusion that the iron content of the mineralizing solutions derives from the hydrothermal alteration of spilitic–keratophyric tuff bodies. He defined this ore type as 'submarine-hydrothermal-sedimentary'. Recently, hydatogenic leaching of volcanic series has been assumed to be the origin of the solutions.

Sulphidic Middle Devonian ore formation in the Harz is known only from the pyrite enrichments of the

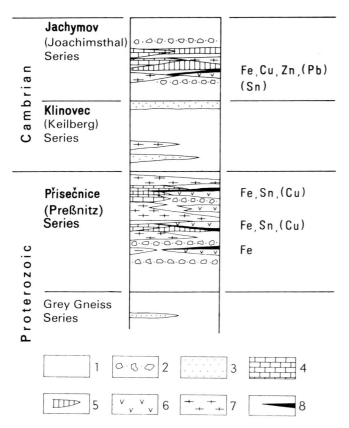

Fig. 6 *Mineralization in pre-Variscan basement complex of eastern Erzgebirge (principal elements and position in lithostratigraphic profile) (in part after Weinhold;[77] from Baumann and Tischendorf[16]). 1, two-mica gneiss, micaschist; 2, metagreywacke, metaconglomerate; 3, quartzite; 4, marble, dolomite; 5, metalydite, meta-sapropelite; 6, metabasites (amphibolite, greenschist); 7, meta-porphyroids ('red gneiss'); 8, stratiform mineralization*

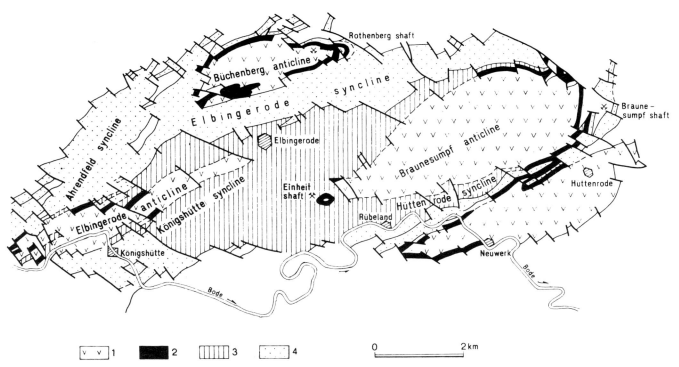

Fig. 7 *Elbingerode Complex with its four 'Schalstein' saddles and associated iron mineralization (from Möbus[46]). 1, Keratophyre, Schalstein (Middle Devonian); 2, iron ore; 3, limestones (Upper Devonian); 4, Lower Carboniferous*

Elbingerode Complex, which have been worked from the sixteenth century to the present (*Einheit mine*, Fig. 7). In contrast to the true Rio Tinto type, the mineralization is practically free of non-ferrous metals; the main ore mineral is pyrite, traces of pyrrhotite, chalcopyrite and sphalerite pointing to a katathermal temperature of formation, according to Lange.[42] These orebodies, consisting of three types, are associated with chloritized quartz keratophyres with high alkali contents (6% K_2O; 3% Na_2O) located beneath beds of the Middle Devonian Massenkalk. Although there is a close spatial connexion between the initial magmatism (keratophyre) and the pyrite mineralization, the enrichment of light sulphur isotopes indicates a predominantly non-magmatic origin of the sulphur.[64]

Already, with the Sudetic folding at the end of the Lower Carboniferous, the minerogeny of the Variscan Molasse Stage is initiated in association with the syn- and post-orogenic magmatism. Preferred areas of the Variscan tectogene were the Fichtelgebirge–Erzgebirge Anticline and the Harz.

Whereas there was no significant mineralization associated with the relatively widespread rhyolitic-andesitic effusive magmatism, the granitoid intrusive magmatism, which was, in the main, synchronous, gained a major importance. The following mineral formations are mainly associated with this intrusive magmatism: tungsten–quartz formation, tin (tungsten) formation and polymetallic vein formation.

Morphogenetically, vein mineralization is predominant, but types in the shape of stocks or layers, with impregnation and skarn types, characterize the minerogenetic manifestations.

The tungsten–quartz formation is preferentially developed in the western Erzgebirge–Vogtland as wolframite–quartz veins. Because of their close relation to granites of the older intrusive complex, they are considered to be the earliest formation of the endogenous mineralization of the Variscan orogen subsequent stage. Among the mostly steeply dipping vein swarms developed as chevron veinlets with minor strike extension, the deposits of *Pechtelsgrün*[22,26] had some importance in the past and *Tirpersdorf*[23,52] for short periods.

The mineralization of these and other deposits is relatively simple. The main gangue mineral is quartz with subordinate orthoclase and carbonates. Besides wolframite, pyrite and molybdenite, subordinate pyrrhotite, marcasite, galena and chalcopyrite are found. The Pechtelsgrün deposit was worked for about 20 years. The reserve situation and the very patchy wolframite content brought tungsten working to an end.

The *tin (tungsten) formation*, on the other hand, is of economic importance. It is mainly associated with the minerogenetic sub-zone of the Fichtelgebirge–Erzgebirge Anticline. From the early Middle Ages tin was extracted from various deposits close to the surface (Ehrenfriedersdorf, 1248; Geyer, 1315; Altenberg, 1440; Zinnwald, *ca* 1500). Presently, mining is carried on in Altenberg and Ehrenfriedersdorf.

The tin mineralization occurs exclusively in the endo–exo contact area of the Sn–F–Li granites of the younger intrusive complex. Their association with high-level granites is paramount, but tin mineralization can also be found at relatively large distances from the original granite contact. The tin (tungsten) formation is controlled by fault-tectonic structures related to high-level granites. Apart from a few exceptions, all tin deposits of the Erzgebirge are younger than the granites of the later intrusive complexes. Based upon K–Ar determinations a period of formation of 260 to 220 m.y. for the mineralization may be assumed.[36]

The granites of the later intrusive complex show petrographical, mineralogical and geochemical peculiarities (reversal of the normal sequence of rock-forming minerals, strong autometasomatism, proto-lithionite, topaz and cassiterite occurrence, and high contents of F, Rb, Li and Sn). This points to a connexion not only spatially but also genetically between the granites of the later intrusive complex and the tin accumulation.[16,43]

From the age relations and the geological position of the tin deposits it must be assumed, however, that the ore-forming solutions are not derived from the granites directly adjacent to the deposit but from a more deeply located magmatic reservoir. The tin (tungsten) formation occurs in different morphogenetic types,[9,75] among which the stock- and layer-shaped types were of greater economic interest.

Correspondingly, several formation types can be distinguished, of which the cassiterite–quartz–topaz type, partly with lithium–mica, partly with muscovite, as well as the stratiform cassiterite–amphibolite type (skarn-type) are of interest for mining.[16,24]

All the tin mineralization is connected with distinct metasomatic processes, begun after the consolidation of the granites (late magmatic) with the formation of muscovite, K-feldspar and albite (autometasomatism). The subsequent, tectonically controlled greisening represents the most widespread stage of metasomatism in which the mineralization also took place. The Altenberg deposit (Fig. 8) is one of the best-known tin deposits of Europe. The great Pinge opening came in 1620, the rubble of which is still worked. The deposit is in the contact zone of the Altenberg granite porphyry and the Teplice quartz porphyry. Both belong as extrusive, more particularly sub-intrusive, phases to the Variscan subsequent magmatism.

The Altenberg granite forms a stock-shaped intrusion in the granite porphyry. Large parts of the granite

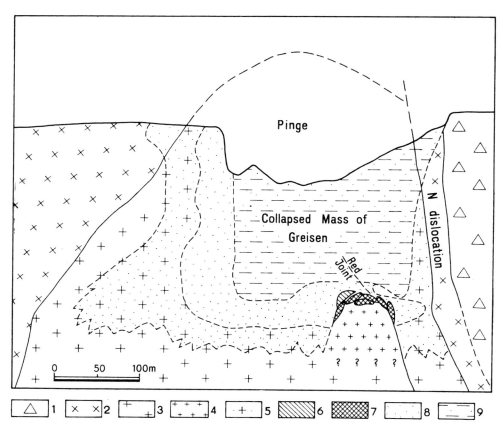

Fig. 8 *Profile through granite–greisen stock of Altenberg. 1, Rhyolite; 2, porphyritic microgranite; 3, outer granite; 4, inner granite; 5, outer granite with greisen veining; 6, feldspar pegmatites; 7, pycnite; 8, completely greisened outer granite; 9, greisen mass*

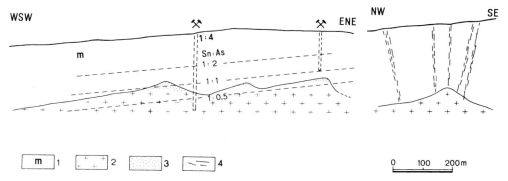

Fig. 9 *Schematic section through Ehrenfriedersdorf tin deposit with indication of Sn–As content of mineralization (after Baumann and Tägl[15]). 1, Gneiss-micaschists; 2, granite; 3, greisen; 4, tin-bearing veins*

are greisened and mineralized. The greisening has a diameter of 300–400 m and a vertical extent of 230 m.[14] Primary pre-existing marginal pegmatite formations (*Stockscheider*) are metasomatically altered to topaz (pycnite), zinnwaldite and quartz. Besides the main ore mineral cassiterite, there occur subordinately numerous other ore minerals (wolframite, molybdenite, etc.). The occurrence of cassiterite is controlled by clefts,[14] thus also proving that the mineralization processes did not take place until after the complete consolidation and jointing of the granite.

In the Ehrenfriedersdorf deposit the mineralization occurs in 'exo-contact' (veins, vein systems) as well as in 'endo-contact' (greisening). Neighbouring rocks are gneisses and micaschists. The vein systems are situated above a granitic high consisting of three smaller archings (Fig. 9). Parts of these granite archings are greisened and mineralized. The main ore mineral of the veins is cassiterite. There occur, in addition, subordinate wolframite, arsenopyrite, löllingite, molybdenite, scheelite and bismuthinite. Other typical minerals are topaz, apatite, triplite and beryl. In the greisening there occur, besides cassiterite, arsenopyrite, quartz, topaz, mica, fluorite, dickite and nacrite.[25]

The ore mineralization in Ehrenfriedersdorf is grouped in zones. The Sn–As content of the veins changes from one set of values close to the surface to others at depth, as indicated in Fig. 9. This tendency can be found also in greisen bodies. In contrast to the other tin mineralization, arsenic can be identified as an important indicator element for the Ehrenfriedersdorf type.

Besides the Altenberg and Ehrenfriedersdorf deposits, where extraction continues, other deposits are known—for example, Geyer, Mühlleithen–Gottesberg and Sadisdorf, which were worked in former times.

The Variscan polymetallic vein formations occur mainly in the Erzgebirge and in the Harz. As early as the Middle Ages there were mining prospects and workings for various non-ferrous metals and silver. Thus the first documents to describe mining in the Erzgebirge near Freiberg date from the year 1168; Schneeberg is mentioned as a mining locality for the first time in 1460; Annaberg in 1470; and Marienberg in 1519. The first mine workings in the Harz (vein districts of Straßberg and Harzgerode) go back to the tenth century. Silver was the focal point of early mining in all those ore districts. This period lasted until the last decades of the nineteenth century. Increasingly, lead and zinc and, locally, nickel and cobalt gained importance. After the second world war the extraction of uranium was started.

Although mining in the Harz was terminated decades ago, without ever reaching any great economic importance, it lasted near Freiberg (Erzgebirge) until 1968. The polymetallic vein formations that occur in the GDR have gained, over and above the mining aspect, a special importance for the present stage of scientific knowledge concerning fundamental questions of paragenesis, age relations, tectonic control and the relationship to different geotectonic–magmatic stages of endogenous ore formation. The starting point therefore was principally the research work carried out in connexion with former vein mining. After Georgius Agricola[1] had given a more detailed geological–mineralogical description of the St. Jachymov (Joachimsthal) deposit of the Erzgebirge, de Charpentier[28] and Werner[78] furnished the first comprehensive description of the mineralization pattern of the vein districts of the Erzgebirge. Werner for the first time used the expression 'vein-ore formation', differentiating eleven of them. Thereafter the knowledge of the science of mineral deposits was extended by the work of Freiesleben,[33] Breithaupt,[27] von Cotta,[29] Müller[47,48,49] and Beck.[20,21] At the turn of the century several monographs had been published.

By the application of new methods research into the paragenesis of ores has been continued systematically, especially in the past 30 years.[3,5,7,8,37,52,54] Besides the deepening of knowledge of the paragenetic and relative age patterns of the vein formations, the research has led to the view that the parageneses of the polymetallic vein formations belong to two different geotectonic-magmatic stages of development as regards age and genesis. Accordingly, two mineralization cycles can be differentiated—an older Variscan (Carboniferous–Lower Permian) and a younger post-Variscan (Upper Triassic–Tertiary).

As well as the Variscan, so also are the post-Variscan mineralizations common in the Erzgebirge and, furthermore, in the Harz and in the Thuringian Forest. The formation maxima of the individual parageneses and their major elements may differ regionally to a large degree. The vein mineralization of both cycles occurs in many cases in close association, i.e. associated with the same tectonic structures.[4,5,8,55,62] Accordingly the following course of mineralization for the Variscan cycle can be established: the quartz–polymetallic association (pyritic-sphaleritic lead ore formation, kiesig-blendige Bleierz-formation; 'kb formation') with the pyritic ('kiesigen') Zn–Sn–Cu and Pb sequence; the uranium–quartz–carbonate association ('uqk formation'); and the carbonate–polymetallic silver–antimony association (precious brown spar formation, edle Braunspat-formation; 'eb formation') with the sulphide (–selenide) and silver–antimony sequence.

This course of mineralization, characteristic of the polymetallic vein districts of the Erzgebirge, can be recognized in its essential aspects also in the Unterharz.[11,12,19,41] It expresses itself there mainly by the appearance of Sb–Pb and Zn–Cu–Pb sequences (e.g. the vein district of Straßberg-Neudorf).

The following mineralizations and mineralization sequences are assigned to the post-Variscan cycle: quartzy iron–barite association ('eba formation'); fluorite–barite association ('fba formation', partly polymetallic) with the barite–quartz, fluorite–barite (main fluorite sequence) and barite–fluorite (lime-barite) sequence; Bi–Co–Ni–As–Ag (–U) association ('BiCoNiAg formation') with the arsenical Co–Ni and silver–sulphide sequence; and the quartz Fe–Mn association ('Fe–Mn formation').

An example of the general occurrence of associations and sequences of both mineralization cycles is the well-known vein ore district of Freiberg ('Freiberger Revier'). More than 1000 ore veins, intersecting the crystalline basement of the Eastern Erzgebirge, were exposed in the course of mining activities up to 1968. They are associated with two fissure systems that run perpendicular to each other, one trending north–south and the other approximately WNW–ESE. Within each of the two fissure systems two tectonic-structural elements are differentiated that are interpreted as shear fissures and feather joints.

The shear fissures are distinguished by a large strike extension, steep dip and thicknesses of up to 6 m, the rock material being in part strongly compressed. The mineralization manifests itself principally in an impregnative form. The feather joints show, in contrast, a smaller extension along the strike and a shallower dip. The predominant structure of the mineralizations is coarse to laminated. Among those structural systems the spatially extensive, steeply dipping shear fissures served predominantly as structures transporting ore solutions, whereas the feather joints, running diagonally to them and less steeply dipping, must be seen as ore-precipitating structures.

In the early days of Freiberg mining it was found that several vein formations could be differentiated, characterized by a specific lode direction. The following ore formations were deposited in the lode directions (Fig. 10):

Variscan cycle
kb formation—predominantly in north–south veins
uqk formation—only sporadically developed
eb formation—predominantly in northwest–southeast veins

Post-Variscan cycle
fba formation—predominantly in vein systems trending WNW–ESE (Halsbrücke vein system)
BiCoNiAg formation—developed only in a lesser intensity and predominantly in the vicinity of vein intersections

The chronological sequence of mineralization corresponds to a spatial distribution of individual formations. The older mineralization occurs almost exclusively on north–south-trending veins, the younger ones increasingly on northwest–southeast veins—more specifically at the end of those which trend west–east (post-Variscan tectonic reactivation of the WNW–ESE systems and separation of the younger fba and BiCoNiAg formations). The close relation of the mineralization to the strike and dip of the veins was used by miners as a means of discovering the mineralized parts of the veins. The sequence of mineralization in the Freiberg ore veins suggests a lateral 'zoning'.[3,5]

Post-Variscan Platform Stage

The minerogenetic regime of the post-Variscan Platform Stage, covering the period from Zechstein to the Quaternary, displays sedimentogenic as well as magmatogenic mineralization processes. In this connexion the sedimentogenic-minerogenetic processes led to a great variety of types and to the formation of deposits (Kupferschiefer, potash salt, brown coal, kaolin, clays, and sands). In contrast, the magmatogenic minerogeny is diminished; only the fluorite and barite deposits of the post-Variscan mineralization cycle are important.

Sedimentogene mineralization and deposits

The *Kupferschiefer* horizon at the base of the marine Zechstein is the oldest sediment of the post-Variscan platform cover in the Central European

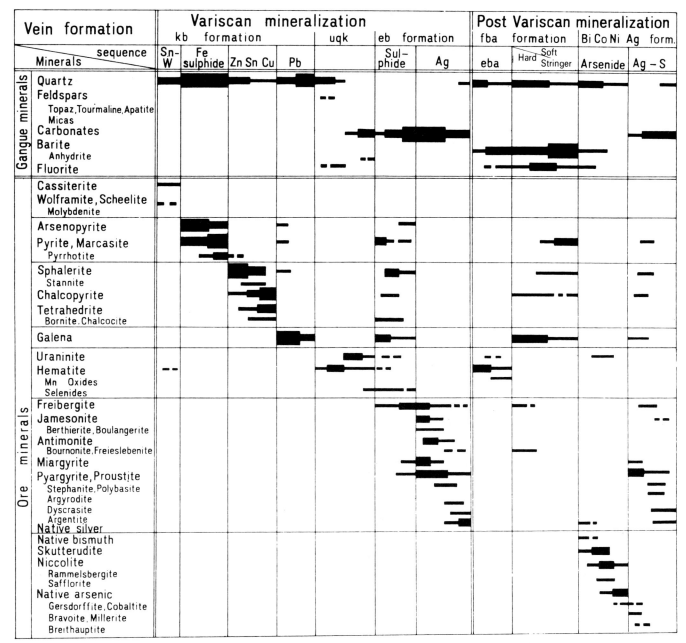

Fig. 10 *Mineral associations ('vein ore formations') of ore veins of Freiberg ore district (after Baumann[7])*

area.* A significantly increased content of non-ferrous metals is to be found, especially over intermontane troughs of the Variscan molasse stage. The Cu mineralization achieves the status of deposits, in particular, in the areas of distribution of the underlying Central European Crystalline Zone (region of the Oos–Saale Trough) of the basement structural storey (the Central European 'Copperbelt').[57]

The Kupferschiefer horizon, which extends from southeast England through the Netherlands, the FRG and the GDR to Poland and the U.S.S.R., represents the largest concentration of non-ferrous metals in Europe. The regional distribution of the metals Cu, Pb, Zn and Ag is controlled palaeotectonically, palaeohydrologically and palaeogeographically (Fig. 11).

In the area of the former and present mining regions of the territory of the GDR there are cross-bedded sand bars in the clastic sediments situated directly under the Kupferschiefer—more specifically, the Zechstein limestone. These sand bars are generally closely connected with the red-coloured Zechstein basal sediments ('Rote Fäule' facies). Copper enrichments occur exclusively at the boundary between

---

*The Rotliegende is here regarded as the Variscan molasse and not therefore the basal formation of the epi-Variscan platform cover.

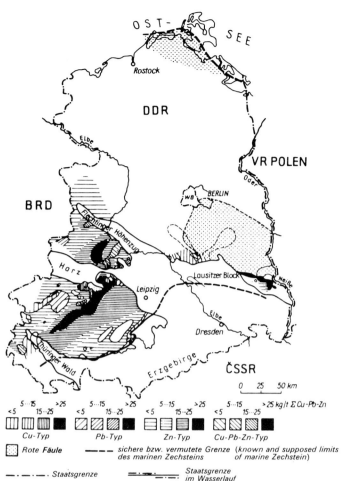

Fig. 11 Regional distribution of Kupferschiefer and its metal types in GDR (after Rentzsch and Knitzschke[59])

grey-black and red-coloured basal sediments (Fig. 12). In the region of the 'Rote Fäule' facies with its extremely low content of non-ferrous metals, areas with sandy accretions in the Kupferschiefer, with sandstone layers as well as with a rich fossil content (corals, ostracods) and submarine slides in the Zechstein limestone could be distinguished, proving their sedimentation in shallow waters. In the areas of the 'Rote Fäule' facies the Kupferschiefer is thinner than in the areas of the Sapropel facies and, in places, it wedges out completely on the sand bars.

Although the conditions of sedimentation and the fixation of metals are generally agreed, the question of the origin of metals is still not entirely settled. It is now assumed that the ore-controlling zonality in regions of ore deposition was caused by a metal supply from Rotliegende sediments in connexion with the transgression of the Zechstein sea and ensuing diagenetic processes of redeposition. According to that, it is apparent that the metal supply from areas showing today a 'Rote Fäule' facies started with the ingression of the Zechstein sea and that there was at least a secondary rearrangement of material by palaeohydro-dynamically regulated waters of compaction, which ascended from underlying sediments of the Lower Permian. These waters underlay a pressure release preferentially in the highly permeable marginal regions of the old molasse troughs of the Saxonian. Passage through the overlying, not yet completely diagenetically consolidated, Zechstein sediments (Kupferschiefer horizon to Zechstein limestone) resulted, according to the physico-chemical conditions (reduction barriers) in the formation of a lateral zoning of the deposit (Rote Fäule, Cu, Pb and Zn facies). This zonality runs transversely to the stratigraphical rock horizons. The 'cementative' ore-enrichment zones are accreted regularly to the 'Rote Fäule' facies.[57]

The zonality of metals corresponds to a zonality of the parageneses hematite type, covelline–idaite type, chalcocite type, bornite–chalcocite type, bornite type, bornite–chalcopyrite type, galena–sphalerite–chalcopyrite type, galena–sphalerite type, pyrite type. A Cu, a Pb, a Zn and a Cu–Pb–Zn mixed type can be found. Over parts of the elevations of the basement that form highs in the Zechstein Sea, a Cu type with a low metal content is developed. In association with the 'Rote Fäule' facies the metal-rich Cu type occurs in front of these highs over the edges of the Permo-Carboniferous sedimentation basins. The, by contrast, widely distributed Zn type predominates mainly in the centre of the marginal basins (Fig. 11). In the area of the Kupferschiefer investigated in the southern part of the GDR the proportion Cu:Pb:Zn in the ore-bearing zone is 1:1·6:3·5.[58]

In the GDR the metal-rich copper type is developed in an especially typical way in the Mansfeld and Sangerhaus syncline in the southeastern Harz foreland. Mine workings in the Mansfeld syncline carried on until a few years ago are considered to be the oldest in the GDR. Presently the mining of the Kupferschiefer is carried on in the Sangerhaus syncline. The ore-bearing zone itself forms a slightly wavy layer, encroaching only to a small extent from the sapropelic Kupferschiefer formation to the footwall and hanging-wall rocks.

The potassium salt that was also deposited during the Zechstein is counted as one of the most important raw materials of the GDR. Mining is concentrated at present on the deposit districts of the Werra area, the Südharz–Unstrut area and the Calvörde Block (Zielitz area).

The exploitation, industrial treatment and utilization of potash salts as fertilizer have taken place in Germany since 1860, when its value as a plant nutrient was recognized by Justus von Liebig. Until then, rock-salt exploitation was predominant and as late as 1852 the potash and magnesium salts, cut through during the sinking of shafts for rock salt in the Staßfurt district, were considered to be useless overburden. Staßfurt developed quickly in the following years to

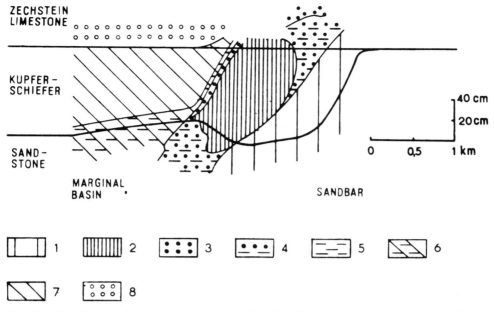

Fig. 12 Distribution of mineral associations of Kupferschiefer at boundary of area with 'Rote Fäule' facies (after Rentzsch and Knitzschke[59] and Rentzsch[57]). *1*, Hematite type; *2*, chalcopyrite type; *3*, bornite–chalcocite type; *4*, bornite–chalcopyrite type; *5*, chalcopyrite–pyrite type; *6*, galena–sphalerite type; *7*, galena–sphalerite–chalcopyrite type; *8*, pyrite type

become the centre of potash mining with the well-known Berlepsch shaft (Fig. 13). Before the turn of the century the Werra and southern Harz–Unstrut areas were also opened, whereas the potash salts of the Calvörde Block were worked only for a relatively short period.

The scientific research of previous decades, proceeding along with the mining operations, has led to a detailed state of knowledge about the genetic processes that affect the present form of the potash seams and has yielded, in addition, new knowledge about regional development of the whole Zechstein formation.

The salt deposits of the GDR belong almost entirely to the Zechstein and are part of the Central European Zechstein Basin, in which five consecutive salinar (evaporation) cycles are developed. In the GDR the potash salt deposits are preserved in three of the cycles. The regional distribution and formation of the cycles is variable; mining is carried out in several districts.

Zechstein Cycle	Potash seam	Mining district
(1) Werra	'Hessen', 'Thüringen'	Werra potash district
(2) Staßfurt	'Staßfurt'	Southern Harz potash district
(3) Leine	'Ronnenberg'	Calvörde district

The potash seams of the Werra Cycle are restricted to the Werra–Fulda sub-basin (GDR/FRG), whereas the Staßfurt potash seam occurs throughout the central part of the main basin. The different facies (hard salt, carnallitite) and the greater depth in the northern parts of the GDR limit the mine workings. Because of the shrinkage of the basin (Fig. 14) the 'Ronnenberg' seam is developed in a small area only and is only accessible at a minable depth over the tectonic block of Calvörde.

In the *Werra potash district* the potash seams 'Thüringen' (2·5–4 m) and 'Hessen' (2·5 m) are intercalated within the 250–300-m thick rock-salt deposits of the Werra Series (Fig. 15). Both show in vertical section kieseritic hard salt in the footwall and carnallitite in the hanging-wall. Facies and thickness of the seams depend on the original structure of the basin. Because of the uplift of the Thuringian Forest Block the stratigraphic sequence today dips gently to the southwest. In the marginal areas, and also in the central part, there occur characteristic solution surfaces.

In the Tertiary the deposition was strongly disrupted by fault tectonic processes (in connexion with basaltic volcanism). Over the tectonic structures that do not show more severe dislocation, valuable zones of sylvinite are developed, often bearing CO_2 (gas eruptions). Their formation is attributed to pre-basaltic ascent of solutions. Important potash plants are Merkers, Unterbreizbach and Springen.

The *Southern Harz potash district* comprises the northern parts of the Thuringian Basin. In the hanging-wall of the second cycle the potash salt seam 'Staßfurt' (5–25 m) is developed, which, in keeping with the stronger subdivision of the sub-basin, shows considerable fluctuations in thickness and facies. Within the extensive area of distribution of carnallite in the centre of the basin there occur island-shaped and

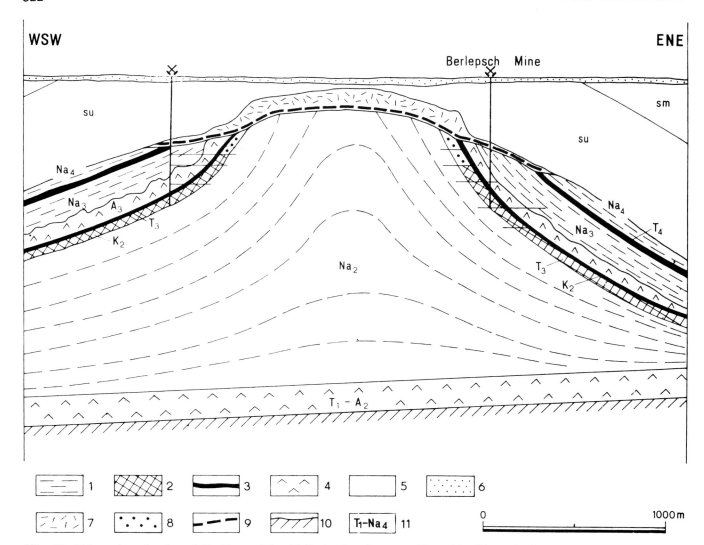

Fig. 13 *Schematic section through Staßfurt saddle with Zechstein cycles z_2–z_4 (from Gimm[34]). 1, Rock salt; 2, potash salt; 3, clay; 4, anhydrite; 5, Lower and Middle Bunter (su–sm); 6, Pleistocene (diluvium); 7, gypsum cap rock; 8, kyanite cap; 9, salt reflector; 10, basement; 11, T_1–Na_4 (T, Zechstein cycles clays; A, anhydrite; Na, rock salt K, potash salts)*

marginal areas of hard salt with transition zones. The salt distribution is often complicated by very extensive barren patches. An increasing appearance of anhydrite within the hard salt is typical, but also kieseritic as well as polysulphatic hard salts can be found.

This factor imposes great demands on the exploration as well as on the control of exploitation and treatment. For the future an increasing exploitation of carnallite is envisaged. This district has had to suffer great tectonic stress. Arching of the basal horizon has led to a shallow directional tectonic flow movement. Extensive solution surfaces were formed in the direction of the Harz, occasioned by uplift at the rim of the basin. Important potash plants are Sondershausen, Roßleben, Bischofferode, Bleicherode, Sollstedt and Volkenroda.

The *Calvörde Block* is part of a residual basin of the Leine Cycle. The potash salts of the third cycle (carnallitite and sylvinite) are, unlike those of the first and second cycles, characterized by a strong diminution of the sulphate content. The 'Ronnenberg' seam (ca 10 m thick) shows a relatively settled salt distribution and is tectonically disturbed. To the north its wider distribution at greater depth is to be expected (2000–3000 m). It is underlain by cycle 2 with the 'Staßfurt' seam in a carnallititic facies. This tectonic block is mined by the Zielitz potash plant.

Besides the Kupferschiefer, and especially the potash salt, the rocks of the Zechstein formation have other economic applications. Among these are the exploitation of rock salt (table salt, soda and hydrochloric acid production), of anhydrite and gypsum (sulphuric acid and cement manufacture; building material) and dolomite (lime extraction, additive in iron smelting).

In the process of development of the platform cover the local formation of sedimentary iron ores came

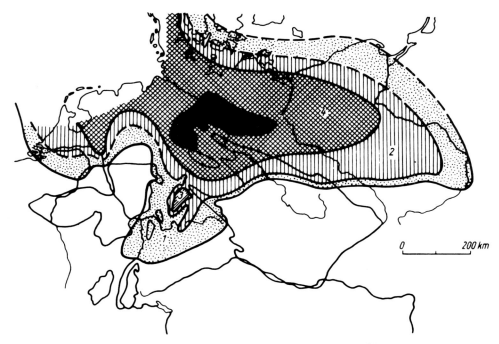

Fig. 14 *Palaeogeography of Zechstein in Central Europe (from Gimm[34]). 1, Salt-free marginal zone; 2, distribution of the potash seams: only NaCl deposited; 3, Werra Series (cycle 1); 4, Staßfurt Series (cycle 2); 5, Leine Series (cycle 3)*

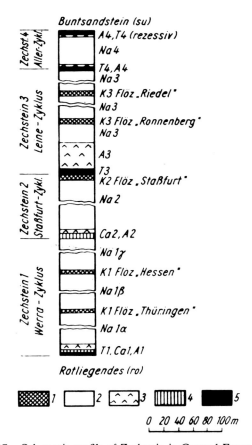

Fig. 15 *Schematic profile of Zechstein in Central Europe (after Stolle[69]). 1, Potash salts (K); 2, halite (Na); 3, anhydrite (A); 4, carbonate (Ca); 5, clay rock (T)*

about. They are to some degree confined to the northern part of the GDR, as well as to the area of the sub-Hercynian Basin. The chronological and genetic formation of iron ores is closely connected with the stage of differentiation (Upper Rhaetic to Lower Cretaceous), when epeirogenic fault-tectonic and halogenic movements led to the formation of special troughs and rises and the extensive subdivision of the sedimentation zone, which up to that time was little structured. The thus created and constantly changing structural-palaeogeographic conditions favoured facies differentiation and predetermined the iron ore mineralization, which mostly occurs in the sandy-argillaceous–calcareous interfingering area between basin and rise.

During the stage of stabilization there was only a little iron mineralization in the Coniacian–Santonian (Upper Cretaceous). Predominant is an oolitic facies with, in places, widely varying oxidic, silicate, and carbonate bonding of the iron. The main stages of formation of the mineralization[50] occurred during the Lias (lower Sinemurian), the Dogger (Bathonian) as well as the Malm (Upper Oxfordian) and during the Lower Cretaceous (Upper Hauterivian to Aptian).

Economic exploitation of the Mesozoic iron ores did not get beyond local efforts because of the limited reserve situation, relatively low contents of iron and their limited suitability for beneficiation and smelting.

Another characteristic of the exogene minerogenetic events during the platform stage is the occurrence of weathering crusts, the formation of which was associated with the kaolinization processes. The formation of weathering crusts is closely correlated with the palaeotectonic–palaeogeographic development, especially with tectonic phases of movement and extensive epeirogenic uplift. Thus, kaolinization took place as a result of the old and young Cimmerian movements, which are preserved only in relicts. Of greater importance are, by contrast, the Upper Cretaceous–Tertiary weathering crusts with their kaolin enrichments, formed in association with and in consequence of the sub-Hercynian–Laramide movements (among them the high-quality white kaolin). The main area of distribution of the kaolins is the southern part of the GDR, where there are several kaolin deposits[71] (Fig. 16). The distribution of the kaolin zone therefore runs to a large extent parallel to the southern boundary of the Tertiary outcrop. The kaolins were formed by extensive weathering of the different primary rocks. By this process almost all types of rock that contained feldspar were kaolinized (acid and alkaline magmatic, metamorphic and sedimentary rocks). An autochthonous bedding is predominant for most of the kaolins (Fig. 17). Studies of the kaolin deposits make it evident that the mineral content of the kaolins is substantially dependent on the primary rock. The quartz-porphyry and Zechstein kaolins are characterized by quartz, kaolinite, minor halloysite and illite–montmorillonite mixed layer minerals, whereas the granodiorite kaolins are characterized by quartz, kaolinite, minor halloysite, muscovite and siderite, as well as various accessory minerals. The chemistry of the kaolins also shows the same dependence as that of the primary rocks; just as evident is the correlation between the grain-size distribution and the mineral content of the source rocks. These correlations were discussed in detail by, among others, Störr and co-workers.[71]

Among the weathering formations of the platform stage also mined is the small nickel hydrosilicate deposit of St. Egidien in the Granulitgebirge. The deposit occurs in the form of relict weathering products of serpentinites. The main process of formation also took place at the end of the Upper Cretaceous and in the Palaeogene, as the host rocks of the serpentinites show the same signs of kaolinization as the above-mentioned weathering crust. Because of the relatively low content of nickel, and its limited range as well as previous working, the deposit has little economic importance.

Magmatogene mineralization and deposits
The magmatogene mineralization and formation of deposits of the platform stage (= post-Variscan mineralization cycle) are connected with the tectonic-magmatic activation. Only the fluorite–barite deposits are of economic importance. Their distribution is shown in Fig. 18. The following are assigned to the post-Variscan endogene mineralization (predominantly veins and metasomatites), which took place in four main associations.

Fe–Mn–Ba association Associated with hematite or siderite, Mn oxides, or carbonates, barite, quartz and calcite ('eba' type of the Erzgebirge; Fig. 10) are veins and metasomatites in the Erzgebirge, the Thüringer

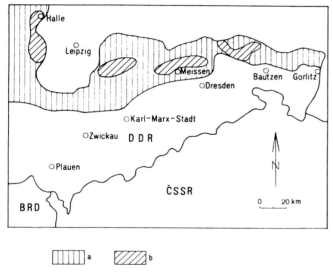

Fig. 16 *Regional distribution of kaolin deposits (after Störr and co-workers[71]): (a) kaolin zone; (b) areas of kaolin deposits*

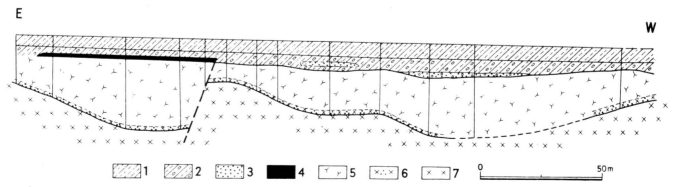

Fig. 17 *Geological section through typical kaolin deposit (after Störr and co-workers[71]). 1, Loess loam; 2, boulder clay; 3, sand; 4, quartzite; 5, kaolin; 6, replaced quartz porphyry; 7, quartz porphyry*

Wald and the Harz. They have their main distribution in the northern and southern marginal fissure systems of the Thüringer Wald in the form of metasomatic siderite–ankerite mineralization, oxidic iron–manganese ore veins as well as barite (–fluorite) veins.

For several centuries the Fe–Mn deposits in the Schmalkalden area were mined, providing the raw material base for the historic iron industry of Schmalkalden.

The ankerite and siderite veins and metasomatic replacement bodies in the area of the southern marginal fracture of the Thüringer Wald, mostly altered by oxidation and hydration, are controlled by important tectonic faults with their shear and feather joints. When the reserves were exhausted mining shifted increasingly to the fluorite–barite veins, which show a close genetic and spatial connexion. The same genetic type is to be found in the metasomatic sideritic Zechstein limestones of Kamsdorf at the northern marginal fracture of the Thüringer Wald at Saalfeld. Besides the metasomatic mineralization there are further siderite–ankerite veins (with Fe–Cu sulphides and Co–Ni arsenide accessories), though of no economic importance, as well as oxidic Fe–Mn mineralization. The latter occurs (in parts also as pure Mn veins) in the Thüringer Wald, the Erzgebirge and the Harz. The mineral content of the northwest-southeast-striking veins was locally mined in the past, but on the whole does not reach minable conditions and is economically of no importance today.

F (–Ba) association Associated with predominant fluorite as well as quartz, carbonates, barite and scarce sulphides (normal 'fba' type) are mostly veins and metasomatites in the Thüringer Wald, the Erzgebirge–Vogtland and the Harz. The economically useful fluorite–barite deposits of the GDR are part of this association.

The best-known deposits are in the Thüringer Wald, the Erzgebirge and Vogtland. The deposits in the Harz are of minor importance (Fig. 18). In the Thüringer Wald the F–Ba mineralization is located on the northern and southern marginal fractures as well as on activated northwest faults within the basement and molasse units. In the Schmalkalden area the

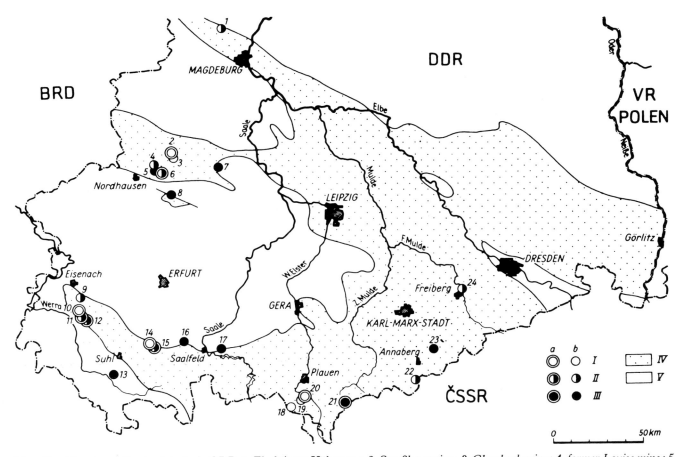

Fig. 18 *Fluorite and barite deposits in GDR. 1, Flechtinger Höhenzug; 2, Straßberg mine; 3, Glasebach mine; 4, former Louise mine; 5, former mine near Stollberg; 6, Rottleberode fluorite mine; 7, Mansfeld 'Rücken'; 8, former mine at Kelbra; 9, former Friedenstein mine at Ruhla; 10, Fortschritt mine near Steinach (Schmalkalden); 11/12, Einheit and Trusetal mine (Hühn, Mommel); 13, Little Thüringer Wald, Gethless; 14/15, Ilmenau, Gehren; 16, former mine near Leutnitz; 17, former mine near Könitz; 18, former Wiedersberg mine; 19, Bösenbrunn mine; 20, Schönbrunn mine 21, Schneckenstein mine (Brunndöbra); 22, former Niederschlag–Bärenstein mine; 23, former Marienberg mine; 24, former Halsbrücke mine. I, fluorite; II, fluorite and barite; III, barite; IV, basement; V, cover rocks: (a) mines and mine departments; (b) deposits or exhausted mines*

mineralization occurs spatially together with the Fe–Mn associations. The vein mineralization consists, principally, of ankerite, quartz and two generations of fluorite.

Also in other regions—for example, in Ilmenau–Gehren—the association of the deposits with the northern marginal fracture of the Thüringer Wald is characteristic. The deposit is controlled by a predominantly northwest–southeast-striking vein zone that extends for several kilometres and is tectonically complicated by a north–south fault. The wallrock consists mainly of sediments and eruptives of the Lower Rotliegende. There were also strong post-mineralization movements (Tertiary) along the main faults, leading to a completely mylonitized mineral content in some parts.[79] The mineralization proceeded in several sequences.[68] As for the regional distribution of the mineralization, fluorite, ankerite, calcite and quartz predominate in the northwestern part; fluorite, barite and quartz in the southeastern part.

In the Vogtland district there are several northwest–southeast-striking fault structures with fluorite mineralization—the fault zones of Schönbrunn, Bösenbrunn and Wiedersberg. The wallrocks of the veins are sediments and basic magmatites of the Upper Devonian and Lower Carboniferous.

The fluorite deposit of Schönbrunn is situated over veins that strike NNW–SSE to northwest–southeast and dip northeast with a lateral extent of up to 10 km. The mineral bodies are mostly arranged in the form of lenses. The first mineralization of the vein fissures was Variscan—the fluorite-bearing 'uqk' formation as well as, locally, a minor sulphide mineralization of the 'kb' formation. The post-Variscan mineralization consists of three sequences—the *star quartz–paradoxite–fluorite sequence*, with rhythmic interbedding of quartz, fluorite and paradoxite (adular), the *main fluorite sequence*, with predominant fluorite and subordinate quartz in a mainly coarse development, and the *quartz–siderite sequence*, with quartz, carbonates, chalcopyrite and minor arsenopyrite as well as minerals of the Bi–Co–Ni formation.[56] Almost analogous conditions exist in the veins of Bösenbrunn and Wiedersberg.

A barite deposit, completely free of fluorite, is Schneckenstein near Brunndöbra. Several barite bodies are developed on a northwest–southeast fault zone. The barite is often hematite-bearing; locally, strong silicification is apparent. There are other fluorite–barite occurrences of this type in the Erzgebirge.

In the Harz, with its numerous vein systems, the fluorite association is especially linked to WNW–ESE-striking vein systems. In the Rottleberode district there occur in an Upper Devonian and Lower Carboniferous series WNW-striking fluorite veins in an important fault system. This fault system and the other WNW–ESE faults in the Lower Harz acted

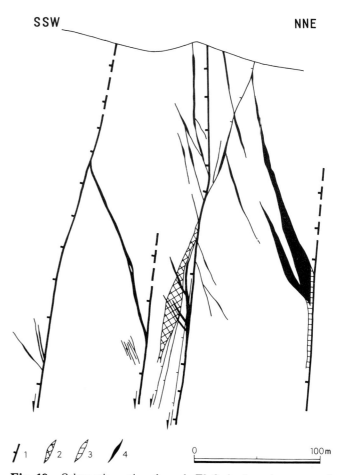

Fig. 19 *Schematic section through Flußschacht vein system of Rottleberode (from Franzke[31]). 1, Shear planes; 2, quartz veins with hematite and sulphides (pyrite, chalcopyrite); 3, carbonates, mainly siderite; 4, fluorite ± barite*

during the mineralization period as systems of shears. From this may be deduced a mechanical connexion between the Mesozoic uplift of the Harz along its northern marginal dislocation and the step-fault like shearing system to the south of this upthrust zone, which led to the formation of space for the vein systems in the Lower Harz (Fig. 19). The post-Variscan main mineralization consists of fluorite, barite and quartz carbonates with economically unimportant chalcopyrite, sphalerite, galena and tetrahedrite ore mineralization.[32] Similarities in many respects to the vein mineralizations of the Erzgebirge and the Thüringer Wald can be detected.[19]

Polymetallic F–Ba association Associated with fluorite, barite, quartz and carbonates as well as galena, sphalerite, chalcopyrite, pyrite and others (type 'fba' formation of Freiberg–Halsbrücke) are veins in the Erzgebirge, Granulitgebirge and the Harz.

The association is locally developed in the area of distribution of the fluorite–barite deposits, but is especially characteristic in the Erzgebirge.

The preferred occurrence of this mineralization type in vein formations with older polymetallic sulphide mineralization ('kb' formation) leads to the conclusion that there was an interaction of the younger post-Variscan F–Ba solutions in the veins with pre-existing sulphide mineralization, thus making the formation of the relatively sulphide-rich 'fba' paragenesis possible.

This type was of no economic importance except for lead and zinc in the Freiberg district.

Co–Ni–Ag–As association Associated with quartz, barite, fluorite, carbonate, Co–Ni–Fe arsenides as well as Ag, Bi, U and polymetallic mineralization (type BiCoNiAg formation of the Erzgebirge) are veins in the Erzgebirge, the Thuringian basin ('Kobaltrücken' of Mansfeld) and in the Harz. This mineralization type reached its characteristic development in the western Erzgebirge. There it formed the basis of the former mining district of Schneeberg (Fig. 20), Annaberg and Johanngeorgenstadt/Jachymov. The vein system, situated between the Eibenstock granite massif in the southwest and the granites of Aue-Oberschlema in the northeast is limited to the northeast by the northwest–southeast main faulting 'Roter Kamm'. The mineralization was concentrated predominantly on WNW- and NW-directed veins. An older Co–Ni arsenide sequence can be differentiated from a younger silver–sulphide sequence restricted to the upper parts of the veins. Mining, carried on for centuries, was terminated some time ago.

References

1 **Agricola G.** *Bermannus* (Basel, 1530).
2 **Bankwitz P.** Probleme des Faltenbaus, besonders in den Katzhütter Schichten (Präkambrium) im Schwarzburger Sattel (Thüringen). *Geologie, Berlin*, **16**, 1967, 1083–102.
3 **Baumann L.** Tektonik und Genesis der Erzlagerstätte von Freiberg (Zentralteil). *Freiberger ForschHft.* C46, 1958, 208 p.
4 **Baumann L.** Neue tektonische und paragenetische Erkundungsergebnisse im Freiberger Lagerstättenbezirk. *Freiberger ForschHft.* C163, 1963, 13–43.
5 **Baumann L.** Die Erzlagerstätten der Freiberger Randgebiete. *Freiberger ForschHft.* C188, 1965, 268 p.
6 **Baumann L.** Zur Erzführung und regionalen Verbreitung des 'Felsithorizontes' von Halsbrücke. *Freiberger ForschHft.* C186, 1965, 63–82.
7 **Baumann L.** Zur Frage der varistischen und postvaristischen Mineralisation im sächsischen Erzgebirge. *Freiberger ForschHft.* C209, 1967, 15–38.
8 **Baumann L.** Die Mineralparagenesen des Erzgebirges—Charakteristik und Genese. *Freiberger ForschHft.* C230, 1968, 217–33.
9 **Baumann L.** Tin deposits of the Erzgebirge. *Trans. Instn Min. Metall.* (*Sect. B: Appl. earth sci.*), **79**, 1970, B68–75.
10 **Baumann L. and Gorny S.** Neue tektonische und petrographische Untersuchungsergebnisse in der Zinnerzlagerstätte Tannenberg-Mühlleithen. *Freiberger ForschHft.* C181, 1964, 89–117.
11 **Baumann L. and Leeder O.** Paragenetische Zusammenhänge der mitteleuropäischen Fluorit–Baryt-Lagerstätten. *Freiberger ForschHft.* C266, 1969, 89–99.
12 **Baumann L. and Leeder O.** Zur Minerogenie der Fluorit–Baryt-Lagerstätten in Mitteleuropa. In *Metallogenetische und geochemische Provinzen, Symposium, Leoben, November 1972* (Vienna, 1974). Schriftenreihe Erdwissenschaftliche Kommission Österr. Akad. Wiss. vol. 1, 142–59.
13 **Baumann L. Nikolskij I. L. and Wolf M.** *Einführung in die Geologie und Erkundung von Lagerstätten* (Leipzig: VEB Deutscher Verlag Grundstoffindustrie, 1979), 503 p.
14 **Baumann L. and Schlegel G.** Zur Geologie und Mineralisation der Zinnerzlagerstätte Altenberg. *Freiberger ForschHft.* C218, 1967, 9–34.
15 **Baumann L. and Tägl F.** Neue Erkundungsergebnisse zur Tektonik und Genesis der Zinnerzlagerstätte von Ehrenfriedersdorf. *Freiberger ForschHft.* C167, 1963, 35–63.
16 **Baumann L. and Tischendorf G.** The metallogeny of tin in the Erzgebirge. In *Metallization associated with acid magmatism* **Štemprok M. Burnol L. and Tischendorf G.** eds (Prague: Geological Survey, 1978), 17–28. (*MAWAM* volume 3)
17 **Baumann L. and Tischendorf G.** *Einführung in die Metallogenie–Minerogenie* (Leipzig: VEB Deutscher Verlag Grundstoffindustrie, 1976), 458 p.
18 **Baumann L. Tischendorf G. Schmidt K. and Jubitz K. B.** Zur minerogenetischen Rayonierung des Territoriums der Deutschen Demokratischen Republik. *Z. geol. Wiss.*, **4**, 1976, 955–73.
19 **Baumann L. and Werner C.-D.** Die Gangmineralisation des Harzes und ihre Analogien zum Erzgebirge und zu Thüringen. *Ber. dt. Ges. geol. Wiss., Reihe B, Berlin*, **13**, 1968, 525–48.

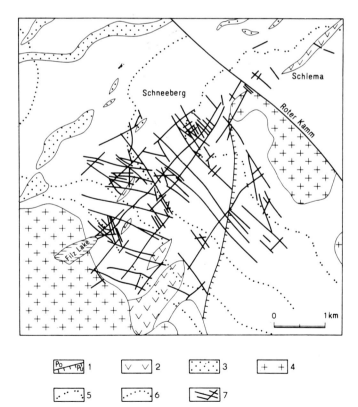

Fig. 20 *Geological–tectonic scheme of former ore district of Schneeberg/Erzgebirge. 1, Boundary line between lower (Pu) and upper phyllite series (Po); 2, augite and hornblende schist; 3, quartzite schist; 4, granite; 5, inner contact zone (andalusite–micaschist); 6, outer contact zone ('Fruchtschiefer'); 7, ore veins*

20 **Beck R.** *Lehre von den Erzlagerstätten* (Berlin: Verlag Gebrüder Borntraeger, 1901).
21 **Beck R.** Die Erzlagerstätten der Umgebung von Marienberg. *Jb. Berg- u. Hüttenw. Sachs.*, 1912, 63–133.
22 **Bolduan H.** Genetische Untersuchung der Wolframitlagerstätte Pechtelsgrün/V. unter besonderer Berücksichtigung der Verteilung des H/F-Koeffizienten und der Spurenelemente Niob und Tantal im Wolframit. *Freiberger ForschHft.* C10, 1954, 46–61.
23 **Bolduan H.** Mineralogisch-lagerstättenkundliche Verhältnisse der Wolframitgänge von Tirpersdorf i.V. *Freiberger ForschHft.* C181, 1964, 57–79.
24 **Bolduan H.** Zinnmineralisation im Erzgebirge—Typen und Verteilung. *Geologie, Berlin*, 21, 1972, 677–92.
25 **Bolduan H. and Hoffmann M.** Geologie und Erkundungsergebnisse der Zinnlagerstätte 'Vierung' bei Ehrenfriedersdorf. *Freiberger ForschHft.* C167, 1963, 65–83.
26 **Bolduan H. and Sippel H.** Die Wolframitvorkommen im Raum Stangengrün-Röthenbach i.V. *Freiberger ForschHft.* C181, 1964, 37–56.
27 **Breithaupt A.** *Paragenesis der Mineralien* (Freiberg, 1849).
28 **Charpentier J. F. W. de** *Mineralogische Geographie der Chursächsischen Länder* (Leipzig, 1778).
29 **Cotta B. v.** *Gangstudien oder Beiträge zur Kenntnis der Erzgänge* (Freiberg, 1847–62), 10 volumes.
30 **Dikenstein G. Ch. Glusko V. V. and Schmidt K.** *Dokl. Akad. Nauk SSSR*, 214, no. 4 1974, 885–7.
31 **Franzke H. J.** Zur Bruchtektonik im Unterharz. *Z. geol. Wiss.*, 4, 1976, 1009–22.
32 **Franzke H. J. Haupt M. and Hofmann J.** Die Tektonik der Fluoritlagerstätte Rottleberode (Harz). *Z. angew. Geol.*, 15, 1969, 389–97.
33 **Freiesleben J. C.** Die sächsischen Erzgänge. *Magazin Oryktographie von Sachsen, Freiberg*, 1. and 2 Extraheft, 1843/1844.
34 **Gimm W. ed.** *Kali- und Steinsalzbergbau, Band 1: Aufschluß und Abbau* (Leipzig: Deutscher Verlag Grundstoffindustrie, 1968), 600 p.
35 **Glusko V. V. Dikenstein G. Ch. Schmidt K. and Goldbecher K.** Zur tektonischen Rayonierung des Nordteils der DDR nach dem Alter des gefalteten Untergrundes. *Jb. Geologie, Berlin*, 7/8 1976, 9–16.
36 **Haake R.** Zur Altersstellung granitoider Gesteine im Erzgebirge. *Geologie, Berlin*, 21, 1972, 641–76.
37 **Harlass E. and Schützel H.** Zur paragenetischen Stellung der Uranpechblende in den hydrothermalen Lagerstätten des westlichen Erzgebirges. *Z. angew. Geol.*, 11, 1965, 569–82.
38 **Hetzer H.** Feinstratigraphie, Sedimentationsverhältnisse und Paläogeographie des höheren Ordoviciums am SE-Rand des Schwarzburger Sattels. *Geologie, Berlin, Beiheft* 23, 1958, 96 p.
39 **Hofmann J. Mathé G. and Wienholz R.** Metamorphose und zeitliche Stellung tektonometamorpher Prozesse im östlichen Teil des Saxothuringikums. *Z. geol. Wiss.*, 9, 1981, 1291–308.
40 **Hoth K. and Lorenz W.** Die skarnhöffigen Horizonte des westlichen Erzgebirges. *Geologie, Berlin*, 15, 1966, 769–99.
41 **Klaus D.** Zur paragenetischen Stellung des Baryts im südlichen Unterharz. *Neue Bergbautechnik*, 2, 1972, 413–6.
42 **Lange H.** Paragenetische und genetische Untersuchungen an der Schwefelkies-Lagerstätte 'Einheit' bei Elbingerode (Harz). *Freiberger ForschHft.* C33, 1957, 93 p.
43 **Lange H. Tischendorf G. Pälchen W. Klemm I. and Ossenkopf W.** Zur Petrographie und Geochemie der Granite des Erzgebirges. *Geologie, Berlin*, 21, 1972, 457–89.
44 **Lächelt S. and Tischendorf G.** On the problem of metallogenic zonation of the territory of the German Democratic Republic. In *The current metallogenic problems of Central Europe* Fedak J. ed. (Warsaw: Geological Institute Poland, 1976), 115–24.
45 **Magnusson N. H.** Age determinations of the Swedish Precambrian rocks. *Geol. För. Stockh. Förh.*, 82, 1960, 407–32.
46 **Möbus G.** *Abriß der Geologie des Harzes* (Leipzig: B. G. Teubner Verlagsgesellschaft, 1966), 219 p.
47 **Müller H.** *Geognostische Verhältnisse und Geschichte des Bergbaues der Gegend von Schmiedeberg, Niederpöbel, Naundorf und Sadisdorf* (Freiberg, 1867).
48 **Müller H.** *Die Erzgänge des Annaberger Bergreviers.* Erläuterung zur Geologischen Spezial-Karte des Königreiches Sachsen, Leipzig, 1894.
49 **Müller H.** *Die Erzgänge des Freiberger Bergreviers.* Erläuterung zur Geologischen Spezial-Karte des Königreiches Sachsen, Leipzig, 1901.
50 **Nöldeke W.** Überblick über die Eisenerzführung in Jura und Kreide des Nordteils der DDR. *Ber. dt. Ges. geol. Wiss., Reihe A, Berlin*, 12, 1967, 315–27.
51 **Nöldeke W. and Schwab G.** Zur tektonischen Entwicklung des Tafelgebirges der Norddeutsch–Polnischen Senke unter besonderer Berücksichtigung des Nordteils der DDR. *Z. angew. Geol.*, 23, 1977, 369–79.
52 **Oelsner O.** Die Abhängigkeit der Paragenesen erzgebirgischer Lagerstättenbezirke vom Intrusionsalter der zugehörigen Granite. *Freiberger ForschHft.* C3, 1952, 24–34.
53 **Oelsner O.** Die pegmatitisch-pneumatolytischen Lagerstätten des Erzgebirges mit Ausnahme der Kontaktlagerstätten. *Freiberger ForschHft.* C4, 1952, 1–80.
54 **Oelsner O.** Die Lagerstätten des Freiberger Bezirks. *Bergbautechnik, Leipzig*, 2, 1952, 555–61.
55 **Oelsner O.** Aussichten und Methodik für die Auffindung verdeckter Lagerstätten im Gebiet der DDR. *Bergakademie, Leipzig*, 14, 1962, 563–6.
56 **Quellmalz W.** Lagerstättengenetische und tektonische Untersuchungen der an die Schönbrunner Spalte geknüpften hydrothermalen Lagerstätten. *Jb. st. Mus. Miner. Geol. Dresden 1959*, 1960, 1–38.
57 **Rentzsch J.** The Kupferschiefer in comparison with the deposits of the Zambian copperbelt. In *Gisements stratiformes et provinces cuprifères* Bartholomé P. ed. (Liège: Société Géologique de Belgique, 1974), 395–418.
58 **Rentzsch J.** Minerogenie von Lagerstätten des Molasse- und Tafelstadiums (Buntmetalllagerstätten vom Kupferschiefertyp). Reference 17, 308–20.
59 **Rentzsch J. and Knitzschke G.** Die Erzmineralparagenesen des Kupferschiefers und ihre regionale Verbreitung. *Freiberger ForschHft.* C231, 1968, 189–211.
60 **Rösler H. J.** Genetische Probleme der Erze des sogenannten erweiterten Lahn–Dill-Typs. *Ber. Geol. Ges. DDR, Berlin*, 9, 1964, 445–54.
61 **Rösler H. J. Baumann L. and Jung W.** Postmagmatic mineral deposits of the northern edge of the Bohemian Massif (Erzgebirge-Harz). *23rd Int. geol. Congr., Prague, 1968: Excursion guide 22* AC(c) (Prague: Academia, 1968), 57 p.

62 **Rösler H. J. and Pilot J.** Die zeitliche Einstufung der sächsisch-thüringischen Ganglagerstätten mit Hilfe der K–Ar-Methode. *Freiberger ForschHft.* C209, 1967, 87–98.

63 **Rösler H. J. and Werner C.-D.** Zur stofflichen Entwicklung und strukturellen Stellung variszischer Initialmagmatite in Mitteleuropa. *Z. geol. Wiss.*, **6**, 1978, 967–83.

64 **Scheffler H.** Die geologischen Verhältnisse der Schwefelkiesgrube 'Einheit' bei Elbingerode/Harz. *Freiberger ForschHft.* C186, 1965, 223–7.

65 **Schmidt K.** Der altpaläozoische Magmatismus. *Z. dt. geol. Ges.*, **178**, pt 1 1977, 121–41.

66 **Schmidt K. Hetzer H.** *et al.* Zu einigen Fragen der faziellen Entwicklung im höheren Ordovicium des thüringisch–vogtländischen Schiefergebirges. *Geologische Gesellschaft in der DDR, Exkursionsführer 10. Jahrestagung, Berlin*, 1963, 93–125.

67 **Schmidt K. and Lächelt S.** Zu Aufgaben und Problemen der Forschungsarbeiten auf feste mineralische Rohstoffe. *Z. angew. Geol.*, **20**, 1974, 444–8.

68 **Schröder N.** Die magmatogenen Mineralisationen des Thüringer Waldes und ihre Stellung im varistischen und saxonischen Mineralisationszyklus Mitteleuropas. *Freiberger ForschHft.* C261, 1970, 7–52.

69 **Stolle E.** Salzlagerstätten und geologische Erkundung. Reference 34, 54–135.

70 **Stolle E. and Döhner Ch.** Die Erforschung der Kalilagerstätten der DDR in den vergangenen 20 Jahren. *Z. geol. Wiss.*, **4**, 1976, 577–90.

71 **Störr M. Schwerdtner G. and Buchwald J.** Kaolinlagerstätten der Deutschen Demokratischen Republik. *Rep. 23rd Int. geol. Congr., Prague, 1968* (Prague: Academia, 1969), vol. 15, 107–40.

72 **Teschke H.-J.** Entwicklung und tektonischer Bau des südwestlichen Randbereichs der Osteuropäischen Tafel. *Schriftenreihe Geologische Wissenschaft, Berlin*, 1975.

73 **Tischendorf G.** Zu Problemen der Metallogenie in der Deutschen Demokratischen Republik. III. Das System metallogenetischer Faktoren und Indikatoren als Grundlage für die Prognose endogen–epigenetischer Zinnlagerstätten im Erzgebirge und der Versuch der Ableitung eines allgemeinen metallogenetischen Wirkprinzips. *Z. angew. Geol.*, **17**, 1971, 81–8.

74 **Tischendorf G. Lächelt S. and Rentzsch J.** Zu Problemen der Metallogenie in der Deutschen Demokratischen Republik. I. Die metallogenetische Rayonierung des Territoriums der DDR. *Z. angew. Geol.*, **15**, 1969, 455–72.

75 **Tischendorf G. Schust F. and Lange H.** On the relation between granites and tin deposits in the Erzgebirge, GDR. Reference 16, 123–7.

76 **Wagenbreth O.** *Naturwissenschaftliches Grundwissen für Ingenieure des Bauwesens. Band 3: Technische Gesteinskunde* (Berlin: VEB Verlag für Bauwesen, 1970).

77 **Weinhold G.** Zur prävaristischen Vererzung im Erzgebirgskristallin aus der Sicht seiner lithofaziellen und geotektonisch–magmatischen Entwicklung während der assyntisch–kaledonischen Ära. *Freiberger ForschHft.* C320, 1977, 53 p.

78 **Werner A. G.** *Neue Theorie von der Entstehung der Gänge* (Freiberg, 1791).

79 **Wolf M.** Der Floßberggangzug bei Ilmenau und Gehren. *Freiberger ForschHft.* C148, 1964.

80 **Zeman J.** Die Krustenentwicklung im präkambrisch und paläozoisch mobilen Europa außerhalb der Osteuropäischen Tafel. *Z. geol. Wiss.*, **8**, 1980, 393–404.

Name index

In the Name and Subject indexes alphabetical order has been 'anglicized' in that such letters as Ł, Ř, Ch and Č, for example, have been treated as if they were L, R, C and C. It is believed that the system adopted, though incorrect, will be more readily followed by the average reader, who will be unfamiliar with Slavonic conventions and orthography.

Abt W. 295
Agricola 117, 317, 327
Ahrendt H. 293
Allemann F. 52
Ambatiello P. 297
Amsler A. 51
Amstutz G. C. 40, 299, 300
Ancion Ch. 110
Andrussov D. 11
Angel F. 37
Anger G. 295
Aubert D. 51
Aubouin J. 119, 146
Ayrton S. N. 51
Azer J. N. 39

Bächtiger K. 52
Badoux H. 51, 52, 54
Balcon J. 102, 110
Banaś M. 97
Bankwitz P. 327
Baranyi L. 180, 293
Barbey O. 52
Barth V. 129, 145
Bartholomé P. 102, 110
Bärtling R. 273, 297, 299
Bartz J. 301
Bastin J. 109, 110
Baudet J. 110
Bauer F. K. 37
Bauer G. 220, 223, 282, 296, 300
Bauer Georgius *see* Agricola
Baumann L. 2, 12, 13, 146, 186, 276, 294, 300, 303, 304, 305, 314, 317, 319, 327, 328, 329
Baumberger E. 52
Bayer H. 282, 300
Bearth P. 52
Bechstädt T. 34, 40, 301
Beck R. 317, 328
Beck-Mannagetta P. 37
Becker-Platen J. D. 298
Becquerel H. A. 117
Behr H. 183, 293
Behr H. J. 299, 300
Behrend F. 272, 296
Belyaevskiy N. A. 12
Benda L. 299
Benešová Z. 138, 146
Beňka J. 173
Beran A. 23, 39
Berg G. 64
Bergeat A. 297

Berger P. 110
Bernard J. H. 12, 123, 145, 146
Bernhard J. 22, 37
Bernstein K. H. 12, 37
Berthold G. 296
Besnus Y. 299
Best G. 180
Bianconi F. 54
Bickle M. J. 38
Bilibin Yu. A. 313
Blaser R. 52
Bless M. J. M. 110
Blondel F. 38
Bocquet J. 52
Boden K. 297
Bodmer Ph. 54
Bohdanowicz K. 55
Bolduan H. 12, 37, 145, 328
Bolesław Chrobry *King* 55
Bolewski A. 55
Bonhomme M. G. 191, 280, 299
Bonnin J. 37
Borchert H. 12, 37, 209, 295
Borisov A. A. 12
Bornhardt W. 209, 214, 226, 283, 295
Bosselini A. 37
Bosum W. 212, 295
Bottke H. 254, 295, 298, 301
Bouckaert J. 112, 295
Bourguignon P. 111, 112
Bouvier M. 35, 36, 40
Brandes H. 299
Breithaupt A. 317, 328
Brewer M. S. 293
Briegleb D. 37
Brigo L. 34, 35, 40, 53
Brinckmann J. 295
Brinkmann R. 12, 293
Brockamp O. 180, 193, 293, 295, 301
Brown J. S. 38, 97, 111, 299
Buchwald J. 329
Budkiewicz M. 97
Bühmann D. 299
Buller A. T. 245, 298
Bültemann H. 294
Bültemann W.-D. 294
Burdová P. 126, 145
Burnol L. 327
Burret C. F. 12
Buschendorf F. 204, 294, 295, 296, 297
Buxtorf A. 52

Cabalzar W. 52
Cabral C. 301
Čadek J. 12, 138, 146
Cadisch J. 52
Caesar Gaius Julius 109
Calembert L. 110
Cambel B. 173
Camerman C. 110
Campbell F. A. 97
Carl C. 281, 300
Carlé W. 277, 300
Cauet S. 103, 110, 111
Cayeux L. 110
Čech V. 138, 146
Chaix A. 52
Chaloupsky J. 144, 146
Chao E. C. T. 289, 301
Charpentier J. F. W. de 317, 328
Chen T. T. 40
Cheneval R.-E. 52
Chilińska H. 97
Chrt J. 12, 37, 134, 141, 144, 145, 146
Čillík I. 161, 173
Clar E. 16, 32, 37, 40
Claude L. 110
Clausen C.-D. 296
Coelewij P. A. J. 116
Coen-Aubert M. 103, 105, 110
Cogné J. 13
Collet L. W. 52
Constantinides D. 127, 145
Coogan A. H. 116
Corin F. 111
Cornelius H.-P. 37
Cotta B. von 317, 328
Cox R. 116
Curie M. 117
Czarnocki J. 65, 70, 91, 97

Dahlgrün F. 245, 293, 298
Dal Piaz G. V. 52
Daniec L. 79
Dayal R. 294
de Charpentier J. F. W. *see* Charpentier J. F. W. de
de Magnee I. 102, 103, 104, 108, 111
de Quervain F. *see* Quervain F. de
de Rauw H. 110, 111
de Walque L. 103, 111
de Wijkerslooth P. 111
Deb S. K. 137, 146

Dejonghe L. 99, 100, 101, 102, 103, 105, 106, 111, 112, 295
Delaloye M. F. 52
Delevaux M. H. 297
Delmer A. 108, 111
Dennert H. 296
Deutloff D. 293
Deutsch S. 111
Déverin L. 52
Dewey J. F. 37
Dewez L. 111
Dietrich V. 52
Dikenstein G. Ch. 328
Dill H. 280, 281, 289, 300
Dimanche F. 107, 111
Doe B. R. 297
Döhner Ch. 329
Dolezel P. 40
Dony J. J. 99
Dosogne Ch. 111
Doyen L. 104, 111
Dreesen R. 106, 111
Drong H.-J. 298
Dumont J. M. 111
Dvořák J. 144, 293
Dziedzic K. 97
Dżułyński S. 77, 97

Ehrenberg H. 295
Ehrendreich H. 226, 296
Eichler J. 301
Ek C. 111
Ekiert F. 75, 77, 97
El Ageed A. 40
Emmanuilidis G. 37
Emmermann K.-H. 175
Epprecht W. 52
Erdmannsdörffer O. H. 298
Erkan E. 31, 40
Escher E. 52
Evans A. M. 16, 37
Evrard P. 111

Fabry J. 111
Fahn R. 301
Faisi S. 190, 277, 294
Fandrich K. 12
Fedak J. 328
Fehlau K.-P. 298
Fehlmann H. 52
Feldmann F. K. 182, 193, 294
Felser K. O. 39
Fenchel W. 175, 296
Ferling P. 298
Fesser H. 251, 298
Fiala F. 145
Figge G. 301
Fijałkowska E. 97
Fijałkowski J. 97
Finlow-Bates T. 16, 40
Flajs G. 40
Fleischer M. 52
Fluck P. 293
Fojt B. 129, 145
Fourmarier P. 103, 111
Frank M. 255, 298
Frank W. 52
Fransolet A. M. 111
Franzke H. J. 326, 328

Frei A. 52
Freiesleben J. C. 317, 328
Frenay J. 111
Frey D. 53
Frey M. 52
Friedenreich O. 52
Friedensburg F. 239, 296
Friedlaender C. 52
Friedrich G. 295, 297, 298
Friedrich O. M. 16, 20, 32, 33, 34, 37, 40
Frisch W. 12
Fritsch W. 37
Fuchs H. W. 32, 40
Fuchs K. 299
Fuchs W. 175
Fuchs Y. 296
Fürst M. 300
Fusan O. 173

Gabl G. 37
Gaida K.-H. 180, 293
Gajewski Z. 97
Gałkiewicz T. 75, 97
Garlicki A. 89, 95, 97
Gasser U. 295
Gassmann F. 52
Gawel A. 94, 97
Gebauer D. 293
Gehlen K. von 190, 191, 270, 287, 294, 295, 299, 300
Geiger Th. 52
Gentner W. 301
Gérard E. 102, 110
Gerler J. 191
Germann K. 20, 37, 299
Gidon M. 54
Gies H. 213
Gil Z. 81, 97
Gillet J. C. 111
Gilliéron F. 52
Gimm W. 322, 323, 328
Gittins J. 301
Glennie K. W. 245, 298
Glusko V. V. 304, 305, 328
Gödecke C. P. 288, 300
Goebel E. 295
Goldbecher K. 328
Goresy A. El 289
Gorny S. 327
Górzyński Z. 81
Gotthardt R. 298
Graeter P. 52
Graniczny A. 80
Grassegger G. 279, 299
Grauert B. 300
Greiner G. 12
Grill R. 38
Groll R. 37
Grumbt E. 4, 12
Grünenfelder M. 52, 293
Gruszczyk H. 55, 77, 90, 91, 97, 300
Gudden H. 37, 175, 251, 253, 258, 298, 299, 301
Guilhaumou N. 111
Gumbel C. W. 267, 299
Gundlach H. 279, 280, 294, 295, 296, 297, 300

Günzert G. 175, 279, 295, 298, 300
Gussone R. 175, 295
Gwinner M. P. 4, 12, 52
Gysin M. 52

Haake R. 328
Haditsch J.-G. 33, 38, 40
Hager H. 284, 300
Hajek H. 23, 38
Haldemann E. G. 54
Halm E. 52
Hannak W. 214, 226, 228, 229, 230, 295, 296
Hänsel B. 251, 298
Hanssen E. 110, 111
Harańczyk C. 97
Harazim S. 140, 146
Harder H. 275, 295, 300
Harlass E. 328
Harsveldt H. M. 113, 116
Hauber L. 52, 116
Haug G. M. W. 116
Haupt M. 328
Havelka J. 128, 145
Hawkesworth C. J. 38
Heberling E. 296
Hedemann H. A. 246, 298
Heflik W. 97
Hegemann F. 33, 38
Heinrich G. 296
Heissel W. 20, 38
Henneke J. 287, 300
Hentschel H. 295
Herbosch A. 110, 112
Herbst F. 227, 296
Herbst G. 297
Herold R. 301
Herrmann A. 297
Hesemann J. 175, 217, 296, 297
Hess G. 279, 280, 300
Hess H. 299
Hetzer H. 328, 329
Hiessleitner G. 38
Hirst D. M. 112
Hoefs J. 297
Hoffman V. 125, 145
Hoffmann M. 328
Hoffmann R. 300
Hofmann B. 251, 252, 298
Hofmann J. 307, 328
Hofmann R. 191, 294
Hofmänner F. 53
Hofmeister E. 251, 288, 298, 299
Hofrichter E. 175
Höhndorf A. 294, 299
Höll R. 12, 16, 23, 25, 26, 27, 30, 32, 38, 40, 299
Holler H. 38
Holzer H. 37, 38, 40
Holzer H. F. 15, 38, 40
Horkel A. 40
Horn E.-E. 191, 300
Horstig G. von 294, 297
Hösel 119
Hoth K. 328
Hoverkamp F. 54
Hoyer P. 296

Name Index

Hsu K. J. 37
Hubacher W. 54
Huck K.-H. 191, 276, 277, 278, 300
Huckriede R. 299
Hugi E. 52
Hügi Th. 53, 54
Hunziker J. C. 52, 293
Huonder N. 52
Hüser M. 296
Huttenhain H. 213, 296
Huttenlocher H. F. 52, 53

Ilavský J. 38, 117, 145, 146, 148, 150, 152, 160, 162, 165, 166, 167, 170, 173
Illies J. H. 12, 180, 293

Jaffé F. C. 41
Jäger E. 52, 293
Janěcka J. 128, 145
Janković S. 12, 297, 300
Jans D. 100, 103, 111
Jaritz W. 242, 297
Jaskólski S. 82, 97
Jeannet A. 53
Jenni J.-P. 53
Jerzmański J. 90, 97
Jubitz K.-B. 12, 328
Jung W. 329
Jurák L. 141, 146

Kaboth D. 111
Käding K.-C. 243, 297
Kaidies E. 297
Kalb G. 299
Kallies H.-B. 296
Kanaki F. 38
Känel F. von 53
Kantor J. 151, 155, 173
Karl F. 38
Katsch A. 301
Keller A. 296
Kellerhals P. 53
Kemper E. 293
Kern A. 38
Kienzle M. V. 111
Kieslinger A. 38
Kirchheimer F. 294
Klar G. 38
Klassen H. 300
Klaus D. 328
Klemm D. D. 40, 251, 253, 298
Klemm I. 328
Klominský J. 121, 123, 144, 145
Kluth C. 298
Kluth G. C. 294
Knapp G. 284, 300
Kneuper G. 295
Knitzschke G. 246, 298, 320, 321, 328
Knoblauch G. 180, 293
Knox R. W. O'B. 293
Koch Hermann 230
Koch K. E. 20, 38
Koch Robert 230
Kockel F. 180
Koehn Ph. 53

Koenigsberger J. 53
Kolář M. 145
Kolbe E. 301
Kolbe H. 255, 257, 298
Kölbel B. 1, 12, 303
Kölbel H. 4, 12
Konstantynowicz E. 79, 97
Konta J. 142, 146
Köppel V. 53
Koschinski G. 274, 299
Kossmat F. 1, 2, 12, 293
Kostelka L. 38, 39, 40
Koutek J. 138, 146
Kozlowski S. 97
Kozydra Z. 96
Kraft M. 303
Krajewski R. 65, 66, 97
Kramers J. D. 53
Kramm V. 108, 109, 111
Kraume E. 181, 293, 295
Kraus E. 4, 12
Krebs W. 205, 295
Kretzschmar M. 299
Kříbek B. 145
Kromer H. 262
Krusch P. 111, 208, 301
Ksiazkiewicz M. 97
Kubicki S. 62, 97
Kühn P. 145
Künn W. 252, 298
Kukuk P. 239, 295
Kulick J. 245, 246, 248, 249, 295, 297
Kündig E. 53
Kutina J. 144, 145, 146
Kužvart M. 143, 146

Labhart T. P. 53
Lächelt S. 303, 304, 305, 328, 329
Lacroix D. 103, 105, 110
Ladame G. 53
Lahusen L. 30, 38
Lang-Villemaire C. 296
Lange H. 12, 315, 328, 329
Lange J. 296
Large D. 284, 299
Laubscher H. P. 12
Lechner K. 38
Ledermann H. 53
Leeder O. 12, 13, 327
Legierski J. 12, 37, 122, 144, 146
Legraye M. 112
Lehmann H. 175, 214, 217, 296
Leifeld D. 297
Leipziger K. 300
Lenz H. 293, 294, 301
Lepersonne J. 110, 111
Lesko I. 23, 25, 38
Lespineux G. 111
Leuteritz K. 296
Liebig Justus von 320
Lindenberg H. G. 299
Lindgren W. 103, 111
Lippert H.-J. 175, 291, 295, 301
Lippolt H. J. 293, 300
List K.-A. 295
Lob F. 301

Lombard A. 52
Lorenz W. 328
Lorenzen W. 251, 298
Losert J. 144
Loup G. 53
Lucius M. 111
Ludwig A. 12
Ludwig G. 301
Lukas W. 20, 38, 39
Lusznat M. 175

Macar P. 110
Mader D. 300
Magnee I. de see de Magnee I.
Magnusson N. H. 12, 307, 328
Majerowicz A. 97
Marek F. 145
Maria Therese *Empress* 147
Marlière R. 111
Marowsky G. 246, 298
Martin G. 241
Martini J. 53
Marvier L. 38
Mascheck W. 298
Máska 119
Mastrangelo F. 54
Mathé G. 328
Mathiass E. P. 33, 38
Mattiat B. 299
Matzke K. 297
Maucher A. 12, 16, 23, 25, 26, 29, 30, 38, 265, 294, 299
Maus H. 175, 294, 295, 300
Medwenitsch W. 21, 39, 40
Meier R. 12
Meisl S. 289, 297, 301
Meixner H. 31, 32, 37, 38, 40
Melon J. 109, 111
Mempel G. 251, 298
Mertz D. F. 300
Messer E. 245, 297
Metz R. 261 293, 294, 299
Miehlke K. 299
Mirovský J. 132, 145
Misař Z. 124, 145
Möbus G. 230, 296, 315, 328
Modjtahedi M. 38
Mohr K. 230, 296
Möller P. 39, 40, 236, 276, 297, 299, 300
Monseur G. 103, 112
Morávek P. 145
Morawiecki A. 81, 91, 97
Moreau P. 40
Morel F. 54
Morteani G. 25, 40, 297
Mostler H. 25, 37, 38, 40
Mrňa E. 135, 146
Mueller St. 12
Muir J. E. 54
Mulder A. J. 116
Müller D. 223, 282, 296
Müller G. 245, 288, 295, 297, 301
Müller H. 317, 328
Müller H.-G. 227, 296, 299
Murad E. 294
Murad F. 294

Nabholz W. 52
Natale P. 54
Ncube A. N. 277, 300
Netels V. 111
Neumann-Redlin C. 182, 294
Neuwirth K. 38
Neužil J. 146
Ney P. 297
Niedermayr G. 40
Nielsen H. 235, 295, 297, 300
Niemeyer A. 290, 301
Niggli E. 52, 53
Niggli P. 53
Nikolskij I. L. 327
Nobel Alfred 230, 260
Nöldeke W. 12, 306, 328

Oberc J. 78, 97
Oberhauser R. 12, 40
Oehlschlägel G. 299
Oelsner O. 328
Oersmael J. v. 295
Olszak G. 12
Omenetto P. 40, 53
Osika R. 55, 56, 57, 59, 61, 67, 68, 78, 93, 94, 97
Ossenkopf W. 328
Ott G. 297
Otto J. 190, 294
Oxburgh E. R. 18, 39

Paar W. H. 40
Paeckelmann W. 240, 272, 296, 297
Pak E. 40
Palas M. 145
Pälchen W. 328
Panayiotou A. 40
Paproth E. 219, 264, 293, 296, 299
Parekh P. P. 39, 297, 299, 300
Parker R. L. 53
Pasteels P. 111
Paul J. 301
Paulus B. 298
Pausweg F. 39
Pavlů D. 135, 146
Pawłowska J. 90, 92, 97
Pawłowski S. 84, 85, 97
Pel J. 103, 112
Pertold Z. 122, 127, 145
Pešek J. 146
Peters Tj. 53
Petránek J. 126, 145
Petrascheck W. 15, 39
Petrascheck W. E. 12, 16, 38, 39, 70, 97
Petroš R. 132, 145
Pfeffer P. 300
Picard K. 298
Pietzner H. 214, 217, 296
Pilger A. 175, 239, 293, 295, 296, 297
Pilot J. 329
Pirkl H. 39
Pirlet H. 102, 112
Piša M. 132, 145
Pittard J.-J. 53
Pittman W. C. 37
Plančár J. 173

Platen H. von 300
Plein E. 298
Plöchinger B. 37
Pluskal O. 145
Poborski C. 65, 66, 97
Poborski J. 85, 86, 87, 88, 97
Podufal P. 175, 294, 296
Polanský J. 145
Polegeg S. 37, 39
Polybius 25
Pöschl W. 297
Pošepný F. 117, 144
Pouba Z. 12, 117, 121, 128, 142, 144, 145, 146, 300
Pożaryski W. 97
Prantl F. 126, 145
Prey S. 29, 37, 39
Przeniosło S. 75
Puchelt H. 204, 295
Puffe E. 283, 300

Quade H. 206, 295
Quellmalz W. 328
Quervain F. de 51, 52, 53, 54

Rabien A. 295
Ramani R. V. 296
Ramdohr P. 53, 196, 293, 295, 300
Ramsay J. G. 51
Rauw H. de see de Rauw H.
Rée C. 175, 295, 301
Reichenbach R. 296
Reichmann F. 141, 146
Reimann C. 30, 40
Reinold P. 39
Rentzsch J. 245, 246, 297, 298, 303, 320, 321, 328, 329
Rey M. 112
Ribbert K.-H. 300
Richter M. 293, 297
Richter P. 294
Richter-Bernburg G. 243, 297
Ricke E. 295
Rickenbach E. 52, 53
Ridge J. D. 77, 97
Rippel G. 295
Rose K.-H. 288, 300
Rösler H. J. 7, 12, 314, 329
Rost F. 294
Routhier P. 107, 112
Rubinowski Z. 74, 91, 97
Rüdlinger G. 52
Ruttner A. 38
Ryan W. B. F. 37
Rybach L. 52, 53
Rybár M. 151, 173
Rye R. O. 111

Saager R. 40
Saheurs J. P. 53
Salger M. 301
Samman A. 294
Sannemann D. 298
Sass-Gustkiewicz M. 77, 97
Sattran V. 12, 121, 123, 141, 144, 145
Sauer E. 250, 298
Sawatzki G. 294
Sawicki L. 97

Schachner (Schachner-Korn) D. 300
Schachner D. 300
Schachner Doris 175
Schaeffer R. 175, 280, 295, 296, 299
Schaer J. P. 54
Schaetti H. 52
Schardt H. 52
Scharm B. 145
Schauberger O. 40
Scheffler H. 12, 329
Schenker M. 54
Scheps V. 295
Scheriau-Niedermayr E. 39
Schermann O. 37
Scherp A. 204, 223, 245, 275, 282, 293, 295, 296, 300
Schlegel G. 327
Schley F. 40
Schmid Hans 294
Schmid Hubert 251, 253, 294, 298
Schmid K. 54
Schmidegg O. 39
Schmidt F. P. 297
Schmidt K. 1, 12, 303, 328, 329
Schmidt Kl. 13
Schneider H.-J. 16, 39, 40, 175, 265, 266, 297, 299, 301
Schneiderhöhn H. 16, 34, 39, 40, 236, 285, 287, 294, 295, 297, 299
Schnorrer-Köhler G. 237, 248, 297, 298
Schoell M. 296
Schönenberg R. 293
Schönfeld M. 301
Schönlaub H. P. 40
Schot E. H. 295
Schriel W. 288, 295, 298, 299
Schröder E. 283, 300
Schröder F. 295
Schröder N. 187, 294, 329
Schroll E. 16, 39, 40
Schuepbach M. A. 298
Schulz H. D. 251, 298
Schulz O. 13, 16, 20, 21, 22, 39, 40
Schulz S. 245, 297
Schumacher C. 245, 297
Schürenberg H. 188, 190, 191, 277, 293, 294
Schust F. 329
Schützel H. 328
Schwab G. 12, 306, 328
Schwake F. 297
Schwartz W. 253, 301
Schwarzenberg T. von 251, 298
Schweizer V. 252, 253, 298
Schwerdtner G. 329
Scotti H.-H. von 296
Seeliger E. 287, 300
Shoemaker E. M. 289, 301
Siegl W. 23, 38, 39
Siewers U. 295
Sigg J. 54
Sillitoe R. H. 297
Simon P. 175, 254, 255, 298, 300, 301

Name Index

Sindelar J. 146
Sippel H. 328
Skácel J. 128, 145
Skoczylas-Ciszewska K. 87, 97
Škvor V. 126, 145
Slánský E. 146
Slánský M. 13
Slávik J. 157, 158, 159, 163, 166, 169, 171, 173
Slotta R. 234, 239, 287, 297
Smejkal V. 125, 144, 145
Smirnov V. I. 313
Smith F. W. 112
Smolarska I. 77, 91, 97
Snopko L. 173
Sobczyński P. 76, 77
Sommerauer J. 54
Souchez-Lemmens M. 112
Spangenberg K. 97
Sperling H. 175, 191, 226, 233, 234, 235, 236, 277, 294, 296, 297
Spieth V. 245, 246, 297
Spross W. 39
Stadler G. 175, 209, 218, 239, 240, 276, 293, 297, 301
Stahl W. 212, 295
Stalder H. 54
Staub T. 54
Steck A. 54
Stein V. 258, 262, 298
Steiner H.-J. 40
Stellmacher R. 297
Stelzner A. W. 297
Štemprok M. 12, 144, 146, 327
Sterk G. 39
Stettner G. 184, 293, 294
Stille H. 1, 11, 13, 119, 144, 180
Stockfleth F. 299
Stolle E. 323, 329
Stolze F. 175
Stoppel D. 295, 296, 297, 300
Störr M. 324, 329
Strebel O. 298
Strecker G. 297
Streit R. 261, 299
Strieder J. 181, 293
Strong D. F. 39
Strübel G. 245, 275, 300
Strucl I. 40
Stucky K. 54
Stumpfl E. F. 26, 30, 32, 40
Suana M. 54
Subieta M. 63, 64
Suckow R. 253, 301
Svoboda J. 119, 124, 126, 144, 145
Swennen R. 112
Swysen L. 112
Szałamacha M. 79, 97
Szuwarzyński M. 76, 77

Tacitus 146
Tägl F. 317, 327
Taupitz K. C. 299
Teichmüller M. 293
Teichmüller R. 293, 296
Tělupil A. 145
Teschke H.-J. 329

Teuscher E. O. 39, 175, 185, 187, 294, 301
Thalmann F. 39, 40
Thein J. 295
Theuerjahr A.-K. 295, 297
Thierbach H. 12, 13
Thome K. N. 296
Thomé-Kozmienski K. J. 298
Thorez J. 112
Thürach H. 298
Tichý L. 146
Tiemann K.-C. 296
Tillmann H. 299
Timmerhans Ch. 112
Tischendorf G. 2, 12, 146, 304, 305, 314, 327, 328, 329
Tischler S. E. 16, 40
Todt W. 293
Tollmann A. 13, 39
Tomšík J. 145
Touray J. C. 111
Toussaint G. 107, 111
Trdlička Z. 145
Tröhler B. 54
Trojer F. 37
Trümpy R. 54
Trusheim F. 242, 243, 297
Tufar W. 13, 16, 39, 40, 279, 299
Turner F. J. 39
Tuttle O. F. 301

Uberna J. 89, 97
Udubasa G. 222, 296
Unger H. J. 39, 290, 301
Urban H. 183, 294

Vaché R. 28, 29, 183, 294
Vachtl J. 144, 146
Van Eysinga F. W. 173
Van Kuijk H. 116
Van Leckwijck W. 110
Van Orsmael J. 112
Van Wambeke L. 103, 109, 112, 289, 301
Vaněček M. 122, 144
Varček C. 155, 157, 173
Verhoogen J. 39
Viaene W. 110, 111, 112, 295
Vidal H. 299
Visscher H. 250, 298
Vogt K. 301
Vohryzka K. 22, 39
Voigt A. 284, 297, 300
von Cotta B. see Cotta B. von
von Gehlen K. see Gehlen K. von
von Horstig G. see Horstig G. von
von Känel F. see Känel F. von
von Liebig Justus see Liebig Justus von
von Platen H. see Platen H. von
von Schwarzenberg T. see Schwarzenberg T. von
von Scotti H.-H. see Scotti H.-H. von
Vosyka S. 145
Voultsidis V. 297

Wagenbreth O. 329
Wagner G. A. 301
Wagner J.-J. 54

Waldvogel F. 299
Walenta K. 294
Walque L. de see de Walque L.
Walther H. W. 175, 252, 271, 284, 294, 297, 298, 299, 300
Wambeke L. van see Van Wambeke L.
Wartha R. 300
Waters D. J. 38
Wauschkuhn A. 298
Weber F. 39
Weber K. 296
Weber L. 22, 33, 39, 40
Weber W. 12, 13, 276, 300
Wedepohl K. H. 204, 245, 246, 297
Weil R. 293
Weinelt W. 39, 175, 187, 251, 252, 294, 298
Weiner K. L. 261, 299
Weinhold G. 13, 314, 329
Weis D. 109, 110, 112
Weiss R. 258, 298
Weisser D. 300
Weisser J.-D. 279, 300
Wellhauser F. 54
Wellmer F.-W. 296
Wendt I. 294, 301
Wenger H. 39
Werneck W. L. 39
Werner A. G. 117, 317, 329
Werner C.-D. 7, 12, 328, 329
Werner Z. 86, 97
Wernicke F. A. 218, 296
Wery A. 112
Westenberger H. 38
Wettig E. 209, 215, 223, 296
Wieden P. 38
Wienholz R. 328
Wieseneder H. 38, 39
Wijkerslooth P. de see de Wijkerslooth P.
Wild K. 295
Wilke A. 182, 237, 293, 294, 297
Wilson H. D. B. 97
Wimmenauer W. 175, 293, 294, 301
Wolf K. H. 12, 295, 299
Wolf M. 297, 327, 329
Woodhall D. 293
Woodtli R. 53
Wyżykowski J. 71, 72, 73, 97

Zak L. 125, 145
Zeino H. 294
Zeman J. 13, 307, 329
Ziegler J. H. 175, 269, 299
Ziegler P. A. 13
Ziehr H. 280, 297, 300
Zimdars J. 298
Zimmerle W. 264, 293, 299
Zimmermann R. A. 298
Zimnoch E. 63, 97
Zitzmann A. 53, 294
Znosko J. 67, 69, 97
Zoubek V. 5, 13, 119, 144, 146
Zucchetti S. 54
Zuther M. 193, 295, 301
Zweifel H. 54

Subject index

Aachen deposits, Federal Republic of Germany (FRG) 177, 181, 194, 236, 241
Aachen–Erkelenz lead–zinc deposits, FRG 239–40
Aachen–Stolberg lead–zinc deposits, FRG 205, 208–9, 284
Aalen iron deposit, FRG 256
Aar Massif, Switzerland 46
Aar–Gotthard Massif, Switzerland 45
Abertamy deposit, Czechoslovakia 121
Abtenau–Werfen deposits, Austria 19
Achim iron deposit, FRG 254, 258
Achtal–Kressenberg mine FRG 269
Acker-Bruchberg range, FRG 230–1, 232
Acrodus 252
Adamello pluton, Austria 33
Adenau lead–zinc mineralization, FRG 215
Adolph van Nassau concession, Winschoten salt dome, Netherlands 114
Adorf hematite deposit, FRG 194
Aelpeleskopf lead–zinc deposits, FRG 266, 267, 268
Aflenz basin, Austria 18
Aiguilles Rouges Massif, Switzerland 45, 46
Aisemont Formation, Belgium 103, 105
Alabaster
  Poland 95
Albungen copper deposit, FRG 249
Alexander mine, Ramsbeck, FRG 219
Alexander vein, Ramsbeck lead–zinc deposit, FRG 221, 224
Alfeld sulphide deposit, FRG 251
Aller cyclothem 85, 113
Allondon placer gold deposits, Switzerland 44
Almadén mercury mine, Spain 192
Alpeiner Scharte molybdenum deposits, Austria 26
Alpine-Carpathian Foredeep 5, 11
Alpine Foreland, Austria 18
Alpine geosynclinal orogen superstructure 1, 5, 9–11
Alpine orogenic belt, FRG 179, 264–9
Alp Nadèls lead–zinc deposit, Switzerland 46

Alp Taspin lead–zinc deposit, Switzerland 49
Alp Ursera copper deposit, Switzerland 47
'Altalpidikum' 10
Altaussee salt mine, Austria 21
Altenahr lead–zinc mineralization, FRG 215
Altenau mineralization, FRG 231, 234
Altenberg lead–zinc deposit, Belgium *see* La Calamine lead–zinc deposit, Belgium
Altenberg tin deposit, Czechoslovakia 117
Altenberg tin deposit, German Democratic Republic (GDR) 309, 310, 315–7
Altenberghuette limonite mine, FRG 266
Altenbüren dislocation zone, FRG 279
Altenbüren fault, FRG 219
Altenkirchen mineralization, FRG 215, 218
'Altes Lager', Meggen, FRG 202
Altfalter mineralization, FRG 281
Altlay lead–zinc deposit, FRG 226, 228, 230
Altrandsberg quartz deposits, FRG 187
Aluminium
  FRG 187
Alžbeta mineralization, Czechoslovakia 151
Amag-Sirk magnesite deposit, Czechoslovakia 149
Amberg ore formation, FRG 180, 255, 257, 258, 264, 291
Amrum ilmenite sand deposits, FRG 292
Andělská Hora Group, Czechoslovakia 127
Andorf illite deposit, Austria 18
Anhydrite
  Austria 20, 31
  Czechoslovakia 149, 171
    Novoveská Huta 149, 171
  GDR 309, 314, 322, 323
  Poland 83, 84, 85, 94
Ankogel-Sonnblick Gruppe, Austria 26
Anna mine, Czechoslovakia 132
Annaberg Block, GDR 307

Annaberg lead–zinc deposit, Austria 19
Annaberg mining district, GDR 317, 327
Annopol-on-the-Vistula phosphorite deposits, Poland 89
Ansbach mineralization, FRG 252
Antigorio nappe, Switzerland 48
Antimony
  Austria 29–30
    Schlaining 29–30
  Czechoslovakia 149, 165–7
    Liptovská Dúbrava 166
    Pod Kolársky 165
    Šturec 167
  FRG 191
Anton, Barbara, Georg mines, FRG 266
Aral basin 11
Arbrefontaine manganese deposit, Belgium 109
Ardenne Massif, Belgium 110
Ardennes 5
Ardennes–Rheinisches Schiefergebirge 2
Ardovo mineralization, Czechoslovakia 155
Arlberg deposits, Austria 20
'Arlberg Dolomit', Switzerland 49
Arnsberg iron deposits, FRG 274, 275
Arsenic
  Poland 59, 78–9
    Czarnów 78–9
    Złoty Stok 78
Arsenopyrite
  Austria 33
Artstetten graphite deposit, Austria 17
Arzbach lead–zinc deposit, FRG 227
Arzberg series, FRG 188
Arzmoosalpe limonite deposit, FRG 266
Aspang leucophyllite deposit, Austria 31
Astano gold deposits, Switzerland 47–8
Astrancia minor L. 46
Attendorn–Elspe double syncline, FRG 202
Aue–Oberschlema granites, GDR 327
Auerbach iron deposits, FRG 258
Auerbach marble, FRG 191
Auerhahn Field, FRG 205

Auguste Victoria mine, Marl, FRG 236, 238
Aurora vein, Ramsbeck lead–zinc deposit, FRG 221–2, 224
Ave-et-Auffe barite deposit, Belgium 104, 105

Bacúch deposit, Czechoslovakia 151, 155
Bad Berneck sulphide deposits, FRG 183
Bad Ems mineralization, FRG 214, 215, 226, 227
Bad Grund mine, FRG 194, 208, 231, 234, 280
Bad Harzburg phosphate rock deposits, FRG 263
Bad Honnef copper deposits, FRG 215, 288
Bad Ischl salt mine, Austria 21
Bad Lauterberg mineralization, FRG 249, 280
Bad Segeberg gypsum deposit, FRG 244
Baden-Baden uranium deposit, FRG 193
Badenweiler mineralization, FRG 181, 278
Baicolliou mine, Switzerland 47
Baltschiedertal molybdenum deposit, Switzerland 46
Balve pyrite deposits, FRG 209
Baňa Lucia–Popročiron deposit, Czechoslovakia 148
Baňa Mária–Rožňava deposit, Czechoslovakia 148
Baňa Rákoš iron deposit, Czechoslovakia 148
Banská Belá quartzite deposit, Czechoslovakia 172
Banská Bystrica deposit, Czechoslovakia 147
Banská Hodruša deposits, Czechoslovakia 148, 149, 162–3
Banská Štiavnica deposits, Czechoslovakia 11, 146, 147, 149, 156, 163–5
Banské mineralization, Czechoslovakia 156
Baranowskie sediments, Poland 83–4
Barbençon lead–zinc deposits, Belgium 103
Barcinek quartz deposits, Poland 91
Bärenbühl lead–zinc deposit, Switzerland 49
Barite
　Austria 25, 31, 32–3
　Belgium 103–4
　　Chaudfontaine 103, 105
　　Fleurus 104
　　Vierves-sur-Viroin 104, 105
　Czechoslovakia 148, 168–9
　　Rudňany 148, 168–9
　FRG 188, 190, 191, 192, 193, 194–205, 209, 230, 236, 249, 251, 252, 270, 272, 274, 275, 276–82
　　Meggen 198–205
　　Rammelsberg 194–8
　GDR 310, 313, 324–7

Barite (continued)
　Poland 58, 59, 90–1
　　Boguszów 90
　　Stanisławow 90
　　Strawczynek 90–1
Barrandian area, Bohemian Massif, Czechoslovakia 120, 121, 122
Bartošova Lehota limnoquartzite deposit, Czechoslovakia 172
Barycz salt deposit, Poland 87
Bastenberg lead–zinc deposit, FRG 219, 221, 224
Baudour phosphate deposits, Belgium 109
Baumbach copper deposit, FRG 249
Baumholder barite deposit, FRG 193
Bauxite
　Austria 20
　　Unterlaussa 20
　FRG 291
　Poland 59, 61, 80–1
　　Nowa Ruda 80–1
Bavaria, FRG 5, 175, 181, 183, 185, 186–8, 262, 263, 265
Bavarian Forest, FRG 183, 185, 262, 281
Bay of Puck salt deposits, Poland 55
Bayerland mine, FRG 175, 183, 263
Bayreuth–Nürnberg barite mineralization, FRG 281
Bean ores 291
Beinlandl mine, Hochplatte E, FRG 266
Bensberg deposits, FRG 215–8
Bentonite
　Austria 18
　Czechoslovakia 172
　FRG 289–90
　Poland 60, 96
　　Chmielnik 96
　　Górki 96
　　Jawor 96
Berchtesgaden deposits, FRG 243, 264
Bergen granite, GDR 309
Bergisches Land deposits, FRG 177, 194, 213, 214, 215–8
Bergla tungsten smelter, Austria 26
Berlepsch mine, GDR 321
Bernstein copper deposit, Austria 29
Berzelius lead–zinc deposit, FRG 216
Bešeňová mineralization, Czechoslovakia 173
Besteg veins, definition of 227
Betliar manganese deposit, Czechoslovakia 151, 155
Betzdorf deposits, FRG 212, 213, 214
Betzdorf–Siegen ore district, FRG 282
Bex deposits, Switzerland 50, 51
Bezau phosphorite beds, Austria 19
Bezmichowa pyrite deposit, Poland 83
Białaczów iron deposit, Poland 67
Bieber copper deposit, FRG 250, 251, 281
Biedenkopf deposits, FRG 215
Biela Hora halloysite deposit, Czechoslovakia 172

Biely Potok mineralization, Czechoslovakia 173
Bierleux manganese deposit, Belgium 108
Bihain manganese mineralization, Belgium 109
Bindt barite deposit, Czechoslovakia 168
Bindweide mine, FRG 213
Bingen Forest, FRG 241
Birkenfeld mineralization, FRG 193, 292
Birkenfeld–Nohfelden feldspar deposits, FRG 261
Bischofferode potash plant, GDR 322
Bislich iron deposit, FRG 256
Bismuth
　Czechoslovakia 134–5
　　Jáchymov 134–5
　FRG 188, 190, 271, 277, 281–2
　GDR 310
Bitburg gravels, FRG 259
Black Forest, FRG 9, 175, 181, 182, 183, 185, 188–91, 252, 276–9, 281, 288
Black Forest–Vosges massif, 1, 5
Blankenburg zone, FRG 231
Blankenrode mineralization, FRG 288
Bleialf–Rescheid vein system, Venn district, FRG 240, 282–4
Bleiberg lead–zinc deposit, Belgium 99, 102
Bleiberg lead–zinc deposit, Switzerland 49
Bleiberg–Kreuth lead–zinc deposit, Austria 33–7
Bleicherode potash plant, GDR 322
Bleikaulen mine, Blankenrode, FRG 288
Bleiwäsche mineralization, FRG 288
Blumberg iron deposit, FRG 256
Bobenthal lead–zinc deposit, Pfalz-Alsace, FRG 288–9
Bochnia salt deposits, Poland 87
Bodenmais sulphide deposits, FRG 175, 183, 263
Bodenstein silica sandstone, FRG 260
Bodenwohr basin, FRG 280, 281
Bodenwohr iron deposit, FRG 256
Boekelo salt concession, Netherlands 115
Boguszów deposits, Poland 74, 90
Bohemia 5, 9, 142
Bohemian Massif 5, 7, 9, 10
　Austria 15, 17–8
　Czechoslovakia 117–46
　FRG 183, 255, 269, 276, 280–1
　GDR 307
Bohnerz see Bean ores
Bohuliby mineralization, Chechoslovakia 130
Bohutín ore field, Czechoslovakia 132
Bolesławice deposits, Poland 55, 95, 96
Bomal lead–zinc deposits, Belgium 101
Bonndorf Graben, FRG 180

Subject index

Boppard–Dausenau overthrust, FRG 227
Borovany clay deposit, Czechoslovakia 144
Bösenbrunn fluorite deposit, GDR 326
Boskovice Furrow, Czechoslovakia 143
Bovigny gold mineralization, Belgium 110
Božičany kaolin deposit, Czechoslovakia 142
Brabant Massif, Belgium 102, 103
Bradlo hematite deposit, Czechoslovakia 155
Bramsche Massif, FRG 177, 181
Bramsche mineralization, FRG 276
Bramsche–Vlotho mineralization, FRG 180
Braňany bentonite deposit, Czechoslovakia 144
Brandenberg vein system, Venn district, FRG 240, 277, 282–4
Brandenstein limonite deposit, FRG 266
Brandholz gold–quartz deposits, FRG 177
Brandholz–Goldkronach gold–quartz deposit, FRG 186–7
Braubach am Rhein lead–zinc deposit, FRG 227
Braunesumpf iron deposit, GDR 314
Braunlage copper mine, FRG 181
Braunschweig rock salt deposits, Netherlands 115
Braut mine, Wald-Erbach, FRG 241
Brehy mineralization, Czechoslovakia 156
Breitenau magnesite deposits, Austria 23
Breitenbrunn deposit, GDR 314
Brenntal–Untersulzbach copper deposit, Austria 29
Březina clay deposits, Czechoslovakia 143
Breznička deposits, Czechoslovakia 171, 172
Brezno mineralization, Czechoslovakia 155
Březové Hory ore field, Czechoslovakia 132
Brilon mineralization, FRG 209, 273, 274, 275
'Briloner Galmeidistrikt', FRG 274
Bristenstock lead–zinc deposit, Switzerland 46
Brno granite, Czechoslovakia 121
Brocken granite
    FRG 194, 207, 235, 280
    GDR 309, 313
Brocken Massif, FRG 231, 232, 235
Bromriesen mine, Austria 32
Brunndöbra barite mineralization, GDR 326
'Brunnia', Czechoslovakia 121
Buchegg–Radmer iron deposit, Austria 23
Büchenberg iron deposit, GDR 314
Bückeburg calcite–fluorite deposit, FRG 276

Budeč deposit, Czechoslovakia 122
Budějovice basin clay deposits, Czechoslovakia 144
Budina vein quartz deposit, Czechoslovakia 172
Büdingen Rise, FRG 250
Buggingen potash mine, FRG 244
Buhl quartz–barite mineralization, FRG 278
Bühler valley hematite deposit, FRG 278
Bülten iron deposit, FRG 257
Bundenbach lead–zinc deposit, FRG 230
Burbach iron deposit, FRG 212, 213, 215
Burda–Poproč magnesite deposit, Czechoslovakia 149, 154, 169
Burgstätte vein system, Clausthal, FRG 233, 235
Burnot Formation, Belgium 109
Burzenin phosphorite deposit, Poland 89, 90
Byšta perlite deposit, Czechoslovakia 172
Bystrá mineralization, Czechoslovakia 167
Bystrý Potok mineralization, Czechoslovakia 151, 161
Bytom lead–zinc deposits, Poland 73, 74

Cadmium
    Poland 82
Čajkov mineralization, Czechoslovakia 173
Calamagrostis villosa (Chaix) 46
C. arundinacea L. 46
Calanda gold deposit, Switzerland 44
Calcareous Alps 5, 10–11
    Austria, 19–21
    Switzerland, 44–5, 47, 50
Calcite
    FRG 192, 274, 275
Calvörde Block, GDR 320, 322
Camilla mine, FRG 229
Campo nappe, Switzerland 48
Caradoc ore horizon, Czechoslovakia 126
'Carbonate banks', Mechernich, FRG 287
Cardita 34, 35
Carinthia, Austria, earthquakes in, 16
Carolus Magnus mine, FRG 239
Carpathian Foredeep
    Czechoslovakia 147
    Poland 60, 83–5, 86–8, 94–5
Carpathian Molasse Foredeep 11
Carpathians
    Czechoslovakia 146–75
    Poland 55, 59–60, 69, 67, 96
Casanna schists, Switzerland 47, 49
Caspian basin 11
Celestine
    FRG 244–5, 271
        Hemmelte area 244
        Springe area 244
Celle salt deposits, FRG 242

Čelovce manganese mineralization, Czechoslovakia 156
Čendova vein, Harrachov fluorite–lead deposit, Czechoslovakia 137
Central Alps–Inner Carpathian zone 10
Central Bohemian Highlands, Czechoslovakia 123
Central European Crystalline Zone 3, 5, 7, 319
Central European Depression 2, 3, 8, 309, 313
Central European Platform 10
Central European Rise 1, 3, 7, 303, 307, 309, 312
Central German Crystalline Rise 246
Central German Ridge 1
'Central Gneiss', Eastern Alps, Austria 25
Central Graben, North Sea 180
Central Saxony Lineament, GDR 309, 310, 311, 312
Central Slovakian Neovolcanic zone 156, 158, 162–3, 165, 167, 168, 172–3
Central Zone, Eastern Alps, Austria 16, 19, 21, 23, 25–37
Černý Kostelec clay deposit, Czechoslovakia 144
České Středohoří Mountains, Czechoslovakia 120
Českomoravská vrchovina, Czechoslovakia 123
Český Krumlov graphite deposit, Czechoslovakia 140
Chamoson iron deposit, Switzerland 44
Chaudfontaine barite deposit, Belgium 103, 105
Chaudfontaine lead–zinc deposit, Belgium 209
Cheb basin clay deposits, Czechoslovakia 144
Chęciny anticline, Poland 74
Chęciny deposits, Poland 70, 74
Chełmiec deposits, Poland 63, 70, 74
Chełmno massif, Poland 90
Chłapowo salt deposits, Poland 86
Chlumčany kaolin deposit, Czechoslovakia 141, 142
Chmielnik bentonite deposits, Poland 96
Christian Levin mine, Essen, FRG 236, 238
Christiane iron mine, FRG 207
Chromite
    Poland 59, 77–8
Chrustenice–Nučice iron deposit, Czechoslovakia 126
Chrzanów copper deposits, Poland 73, 74
Churfürst Ernst mine, Bönkhausen, FRG 274
Chvaletice FeS_2–Mn deposit, Czechoslovakia 118, 121, 122, 124–5
Čičava mineralization, Czechoslovakia 173
Čierny Váh mineralization, Czechoslovakia 154

Cieszyn iron deposit, Poland 69
Cínovec tin–tungsten–lithium deposit, Czechoslovakia 117, 118, 136–7
Ciply chalk, Belgium 109
Clara mine, Oberwolfach, FRG 190, 191, 276–7
Clarashall mine, FRG 193
Clausthal zone, FRG 230, 234, 235
Clausthal–Zellerfeld mineralization, FRG 231, 234
'Clay Fault', Příbram ore district, Czechoslovakia 131, 132
Clays and claystones
　Czechoslovakia 143–4
　GDR 312, 314, 318
Cobalt
　Austria 22
　Czechoslovakia 134–5, 168
　　Jáchymov 117, 121, 134–5
　FRG 185, 188, 191, 192, 213, 214, 249, 271, 281–2
　GDR 310, 317, 327
　Switzerland 49
　　Kaltenberg 49
Coburg feldspar/clay deposits, FRG 261, 263
Čoltovo gypsum–anhydrite deposit, Czechoslovakia 171
Condroz deposits, Belgium 107, 110
Copper
　Austria 21–2, 33
　　Kitzbühel 21–2
　　Mitterberg 22
　　Schwaz–Brixlegg 21
　Belgium 109
　　La Helle river 109
　Czechoslovakia 118, 124, 126–8, 148, 158–63
　　Banská Hodruša 162–3
　　Slovinky 161
　　Smolnik 159–61
　　Špania Dolina 161–2
　　Staré Ransko 118, 124
　　Tisová 126
　　Zlaté Hory 118, 122, 126–8
　FRG 188, 191, 192, 194–8, 208, 209, 214, 215, 217, 235, 240–1, 245–51, 252, 271, 274–5, 277, 279, 282–4, 289, 290
　　Eisenberg 208
　　Hosenberg district 192
　　Marsberg 240–1
　　Rammelsberg 194–8
　　Richelsdorf 248–9
　GDR 309, 312, 314, 319, 320
　Poland 55, 58, 59, 61, 69–73
　　Chełmiec 70
　　Miedziana Góra 70, 71
　　Miedzianka 69, 70
　　Stara Góra 69–70
　Switzerland 44, 45, 47
　　Alp Ursera 47
　　Grimentz 47
　　Leysin 44
　　Mürtschenalp 44
　　Puntaiglas 45
Cornberg sandstone, FRG 248
Cornubian–Rhine Basin 2
Costa mine, Switzerland 48

'Coticule' beds, Belgium 109
Couthuin iron deposits, Belgium 99, 106
Couvin iron mineralization, Belgium 108
Čučma mineralization, Czechoslovakia 149, 151, 155
Czajków sulphur deposits, Poland 83
Czarkowy sulphur deposits, Poland 83
Czarnów silver mineralization, Poland 73, 78–9, 82
Czerna kaolin deposit, Poland 96
Czernica gypsum deposit 95
Czerwona Woda kaolin deposit, Poland 96
Częstochowa–Kłobuck iron deposits, Poland 55

Daade valley mineralization, FRG 213
Dąbrowa iron deposit, Poland 65
Dachstein limestone 10
Damasławek salt diapir, Poland 86
Damme iron deposit, FRG 257
Daniel vein, Wittichen, FRG 191, 277
Danielszug mine, FRG 217
Danish–Polish Furrow 3, 5, 7, 85
Danková asbestos deposit, Czechoslovakia 171
Danube Boundary Fracture 180
Danube gold deposits, Austria 26
'Deckdiabas' volcanism 7, 206
Dedinky gypsum–anhydrite deposit, Czechoslovakia 171
Dědov Fault, Czechoslovakia 132
Delemont iron deposit, Switzerland 41–3
Dent Blanche nappe, Switzerland 47
De re metallica 117
Desná dome, Czechoslovakia 127
Detvianska Huta sulphur deposit, Czechoslovakia 156
Dexbach copper mineralization, FRG 208
Diatomite
　Austria 18
　Czechoslovakia 172
　FRG 260–1
　Poland 60
Diest Formation, Belgium 107, 108
Diez red iron ore deposit, FRG 207
Dill River copper deposit, FRG 240
Dill syncline, FRG 194, 205, 206, 207, 208, 209, 213, 215, 279, 288
Dillenburg deposits, FRG 207, 215
Dillich mineralization, FRG 289
Dinant synclinorium, Belgium 99, 101, 102, 103, 105, 107
Diplopora Dolomites, Poland 74–6
Dobrudsha–North Sea Lineament 307
Dobšiná mineralization, Czechoslovakia 147, 148, 149, 151, 154, 155, 168, 171
Döhlen basin, GDR 309
Dohlen Rotliegend trough 312
Doische fluorite deposit, Belgium 105

Dolembreux copper mineralization, Belgium 109
Dolná Lehota mineralization, Czechoslovakia 167
Dolní Bory feldspar deposit, Czechoslovakia 140
Domaradz pyrite deposit, Poland 83
Domažlice feldspar deposit, Czechoslovakia 140
Domoradice graphite deposit, Czechoslovakia 140
Donaustauf ore district, FRG 281
Donawitz steel works, Austria 17
Donnersberg mineralization, FRG 192, 193
Dony process 99
Dornberg lead–zinc deposit, FRG 219, 221–2, 224, 225
Doupovské Hory Mountains, Czechoslovakia 135
Drau River gold deposit, Austria 26
Drau valley stibnite deposits, Austria 30
Drauzug strata, Austria 33–7
Dreislar mine, FRG 272, 274, 279–80
Dreveník mineralization, Czechoslovakia 173
Drienok–Poniky mineralization, Czechoslovakia 155
Drieňovec mineralization, Czechoslovakia 173
Drnava deposits, Czechoslovakia 158, 168
Drnava–Anton iron deposit, Czechoslovakia 148
Drnava–Dionýz iron deposit, Czechoslovakia 148
Drnava–Haraszt iron deposit, Czechoslovakia 148
Drnava–Ignác iron deposit, Czechoslovakia 148
Drnava–Štefan iron deposit, Czechoslovakia 148
Drnava-Stredná iron deposit, Czechoslovakia 148
Droždiak vein, Rudnany ore district, Czechoslovakia 157
Držkovce hematite deposit, Czechoslovakia 155
Dubenec–Druhlice Fault, Czechoslovakia 132
Dubník mercury deposit, Czechoslovakia 156, 168
Dúbrava magnesite deposit, Czechoslovakia 169–70
Dúbravica diatomite deposit, Czechoslovakia 172
Duingen sand deposits, FRG 260
Dürrenwaid mineralization, FRG 289
'Dürrerz' 132
Dürrnberg salt mine, Austria 21
Dyje massif, Czechoslovakia 143
Dzierzkow kaolin deposit, Poland 96
Dzierzysław gypsum deposit, Poland 95

Earthquakes 16
East Elbe Massif 3, 5, 303, 307
Eastern Alps, Austria 18–37

Subject index

East European Platform 1, 3, 5, 7, 310
East Holland Ridge 1
East Sauerland main anticline, FRG 219, 220, 221
East Sudeten, Czechoslovakia 126, 128
East Thuringian–North Saxony Anticlinorium, GDR 312
Ebbe anticline, FRG 272
Echte mine, FRG 256
Eferding–Prambachkirchen phosphate deposits, Austria 18
Eggenburg diatomite deposits, Austria 18
Ehenfeld clay, FRG 262
Ehrenfriedersdorf tin deposit, GDR 309, 315–7
Eibenstock granite, GDR 135, 309, 327
Eibenstock–Karlovy Vary granite, Czechoslovakia 126
Eifel deposits, FRG 180, 193, 212, 213, 215, 259, 262, 280
Eifel fault zone, FRG 269
Eifel north–south zone, FRG 276
Eifel synclines, FRG 241
Eifel–Lorraine north–south zone 192
Einheit mine, GDR 315
Eisen barite deposit, FRG 205, 209
Eisenbach mineralization, FRG 188, 191, 277
Eisenberg deposits, FRG 208, 240, 260
Eisenberg–Grünstadt clay deposits, FRG 263
Eisenkappel intrusive suite, Austria 33
Eisensteinsberg iron deposit, FRG 231
Eisenzecher Zug mine, FRG 214
Eiskar mine, Austria 32
Ejpovice iron deposit, Czechoslovakia 125, 126
Elberfeld limestone, FRG 209
Elbingerode Complex, GDR 307, 314
Elbingerode pyrite deposits, GDR 7
Elbtal Zone, GDR 312
Ellweiler uranium deposit, FRG 193
Emilia-Theodora mine, Plettenberg, FRG 274
Emmendingen quartz–barite mineralization, FRG 278
Ems–Braubach lead–zinc deposits, FRG 226
Ems ore district, FRG 177, 181, 227–8, 290
Ems quartzite, FRG 193, 226, 259
Engadine Window, Austria 25, 29, 33
Engis lead–zinc deposit, Belgium 99, 102
Englesberg mine, FRG 231
Ennetmoos gypsum deposit, Switzerland 50
Erbendorf deposits, FRG 188, 281, 289
Erbendorf Fault, FRG 183
Erkelenz lead–zinc deposit, FRG 236, 239

'Eruptive Sequence', Mittersill, Austria 26, 27
Erzberg iron deposits, Austria 9, 10, 23
Erzegg iron deposit, Switzerland 44
Erzgebirge 5, 7, 8, 9, 11
 FRG 177, 186
 GDR 317, 325, 326, 327
Erzgebirge Anticline, GDR 310, 312
Erzgebirge Trough, GDR 309, 310
Erzgebirge–Vogtland, GDR 315
Erzweiler barite deposit, FRG 193
Es vein, Slovinky, Czechoslovakia 161
Eschbroich lead–zinc deposit, Belgium 99
Eschwege fluorite deposit, FRG 245
Esneux iron deposit, Belgium 107
Estheria beds, Ansbach, FRG 252
Euskirchen clay deposits, FRG 263

Falkenberg granite, FRG 292
Falkenberg–Flössenbürg granite, FRG 186
Fehring illite deposit, Austria 18
Feldbertal scheelite mine, Austria 10, 26–9
Feldkirch phosphorite beds, Austria 19
Feldspar
 Austria 18
 Czechoslovakia 140–1
 FRG 186, 191, 193, 261–2, 292
 Poland 91–2
  Pogórze Izerskie 91, 92
  Strzeblów 91–2
Felsenau gypsum deposit, Switzerland 50
Fennoscandian Shield 113
Ferchenseewand lead–zinc deposits, FRG 266
Fichtelgebirge deposits, FRG 177, 185, 186, 187, 188, 281
Fichtelgebirge granite, FRG 177
Fichtelgebirge–Erzgebirge Anticline, GDR 303, 310, 315
Fichtenhübel mineralization, Czechoslovakia 161
Fieberbrunn–Hochfilzer uranium mineralization, Austria 20
Finero peridotites, Switzerland 49
Fintice–Kapušany bentonite deposit, Czechoslovakia 172
Fireclay
 Poland 59, 96
Fischbach mine, FRG 192
'Flachen' 221
Flechtingen–Roßlau Block, GDR 2, 309, 313
Fleurus barite orebody, Belgium 99, 104
Florz–Füsseberg deposits, FRG 212
Fluorite
 Austria 30
 Belgium 105
 Czechoslovakia 118, 121, 137–8, 141–2
  Harrachov 118, 121, 137–8, 141
  Hradiště 141

Fluorite (continued)
 Javorka 141–2
 Moldava 141
 FRG 188, 190, 191, 231, 236, 245, 270, 276–82
  Wölsendorf–Nabburg 280–1
 GDR 309, 310, 313, 324–7
 Poland 90
 Switzerland 50
  Les Trappistes 50
Flysch 5, 11
 Carpathian region, Poland 59, 60, 69, 87, 96
 Czechoslovak Carpathians 147–8, 155, 156
 Eastern Alps, Austria 18, 19
Foisches fluorite deposit, France 105
Folkmár mineralization, Czechoslovakia 154, 155
Fore-Sudetic block, Poland 71, 72, 73, 95
Fore-Sudetic monocline, Poland 55, 61, 62, 67, 69, 71, 72, 85, 86
Forstau uranium deposit, Austria 31
Fortuna mine, Wetzlar district, FRG 207
Fossey lead–zinc deposit, Belgium 99, 102
Franconian Basin, FRG 242
Franconian Forest, FRG 183, 186, 194
Franconian Line, FRG 180
Frankenberg Bight 250
Franz-Adolf mine, Riedbodeneck, FRG 266
Frauenberg–Sonnenberg copper deposits, FRG 192
Frechen quartz-sand deposit, FRG 260
Fredeburg slates, FRG 219, 222
Freiberg deposits, Czechoslovakia 117, 132
Freiberg gneiss, GDR 314
Freiberg ore district, GDR 310, 314, 317, 318, 326, 327
Freiberg quartz–barite mineralization, FRG 278
'Freiberger Revier', GDR 310, 314, 317, 318
Freiberg–Fürstenwald series, GDR 307
Freihung deposits, FRG 177, 252, 253, 260, 261, 290
Freudenstadt barite–quartz deposit, FRG 277
Friedberg bentonite deposit, Austria 18
Friedeburg iron deposit, FRG 256
Friederike mine, FRG 256
Friedrich-Christian mineralization, FRG 188, 191, 290
Friuli area, Italy, earthquakes in, 16
Fromelennes Formation, Belgium 105
'Frühalpidikum' 9–10
Fulda Greywacke Hills barite deposits, FRG 279
Fulda–Werra basin, FRG 248
Fürstenzeche mineralization, FRG 187

Fusch gold deposit, Austria 26
Füsseberg mine, FRG 214

Gabriela pit, Nizna Slana, Czechoslovakia 157
'Gailtal Line' Austria 19, 33
'Galena beds', FRG 252
Garantiana garantiana 67
Gassenalpe lead-zinc deposits, FRG 266
Gebroth iron deposits, FRG 241
Gehren mineralization, GDR 326
Geilenkirchen lead-zinc deposit, FRG 236
Geisenheim mineralization, FRG 292
Geislingen iron deposit, FRG 256
Geismar copper clay seam, FRG 250
'Gelnavská' vein, Horní Slavkov-Krásno ore district, Czechoslovakia 136
Gelnica group, Czechoslovakia 151, 154, 157, 159, 161, 169
Gelnica mineralization, Czechoslovakia 158, 161, 167
Gelnica-Krížová deposit, Czechoslovakia 148
Gelnica-Mária huta iron deposit, Czechoslovakia 148
Gelnická vein, Slovinky, Czechoslovakia 161
Gelria concession, Winterswijk salt deposits, Netherlands 115
Gelrode iron deposit, Belgium 107
Gembeck celestine deposit, FRG 245
Gemerides 10, 11
Gemeride zone, Czechoslovak Carpathians 150, 151, 154, 155, 156-7, 159-61, 162, 169, 170, 171, 172
Georg mine, FRG 214
German Basin 243
Geyer tin deposit, GDR 315, 317
Gierałtów gypsum-anhydrite deposit, Poland 94
Gierczyn tin deposit, Poland 79
Giershagen celestine deposit, FRG 245
Giessen mineralization, FRG 290
Giessen red iron ore deposit, FRG 207
Gifhorn iron deposit, FRG 179
Gifhorn trough, FRG 8, 255, 256
Giglerbaue mine, Austria 32
Gimnée fluorite deposit, Belgium 105
Givet lead-zinc deposits, Belgium 101
Glarner nappe, Switzerland 44
Glass sands
  Czechoslovakia 139, 144
'Glasurbleierz' *see* 'Glazing lead ore'
Glatschach cinnabar deposit, Austria 32
'Glazing lead ore' 213
Gleichenberg bentonite deposit, Austria 18
Gleisinger Fels lode, FRG 187-8
Glockner Gruppe, Austria 26
Głogów copper deposits, Poland 72

Gogolin beds, Poland 74, 76
Gogołów magnesite deposits, Poland 92, 93
Gold
  Austria 25-6
  Belgium 109-10
  Czechoslovakia 117, 118, 130, 149, 168
    Jílové 117, 130
  FRG 186, 194-8, 208, 240, 292
    Eisenberg 208
    Rammelsberg 194-8
  Switzerland 44, 45, 47-8
    Allondon 44
    Astano 47-8
    Calanda 44
    Gondo 48
    Napf 44
    Salanfe 45
Goldkuhle mine, FRG 284
Göllheim copper deposit, FRG 181, 192
Gombasek mineralization, Czechoslovakia 173
Gondenau mine, FRG 230
Gonderbach mine, Laasphe, FRG 288
Gondo gold deposit, Switzerland 48
Gonzen manganese deposit, Switzerland 45
Goppenstein lead-zinc deposit, Switzerland 46
Góra salt diapir, Poland 85, 86
Góra Biała arsenic orebody, Poland 78
Góra Hanig arsenic orebody, Poland 78
Góra Krzyżowa arsenic orebody, Poland 78
Góra Łysa arsenic orebody, Poland 78
Goraźdze beds, Poland 74
Górki bentonite deposits, Poland 96
Góry Izerskie tin deposits, Poland 59, 79
Góry Kaczawskie deposits, Poland 5, 59
Góry Świętokrzyskie, Poland 5, 9, 55, 57-9, 70-1, 82, 89-90
Góry Świętokrzyskie-Rudki deposits, Poland 65
Gosau Basin 11
'Gosau Beds', Austria 19
Goslar mineralization, FRG 230
Göstritz gypsum-anhydrite deposits, Austria 31
Gottesehre mine, FRG 190, 191
Gottesgabe mine, FRG 224
Gotthard Massif, Switzerland 45, 46, 50
Götzis phosphorite beds, Austria 19
Gräfenthal Series, GDR 314
Graf Moltke mine, Gladbeck, FRG 236
Granatspitz Dome, Austria 26
Granges gypsum deposit, Switzerland 50
Granulitgebirge, GDR 5, 307, 310, 311-2, 323, 326

Graphite
  Austria 17, 25
    Kaiserberg 25
    Sunk-Hohentauern 25
  Czechoslovakia 139-40
    Domoradice 140
    Koloděje 140
    Velké Vrbo 140
  FRG 185
    Kropfmühel 185
Grauwacken Zone, Eastern Alps, Austria 19, 21-5
Grejf deposit, Kutná Hora ore district, Czechoslovakia 134
'Grenzlager', Lahn-Dill district, FRG 206, 207
Grey orebody, Rammelsberg, FRG 194, 196, 197
'Greywacke Zones' 10, 19, 21-5
Grimentz copper deposit, Switzerland 47
'Gröden Sandstone', Austria 34
Grodziec depression, Poland 71-2
Groenendael iron deposits, Belgium 107
Gronau salt deposit, FRG 242
Gronauer upthrust, Netherlands 114
Großalmerode clay deposits, FRG 263
Grossarl copper deposit, Austria 29
Grossfragant copper deposit, Austria 29
Grosstübing pyrite mine, Austria 33
Grund deposit, FRG 231, 232, 234, 235, 236
'Grund Pluton', FRG 235
Grünten deposits, FRG 263, 269
Grybów bentonite deposits, Poland 96
Günterod barite deposit, FRG 205
Gurktal lead-zinc deposits, Austria 33
Gute Hoffnung lead-zinc mine, Ferchenseewand, FRG 266
Gutmadingen iron deposit, FRG 256
Gypsum
  Austria 20, 31
  Czechoslovakia 149, 171
    Novoveská Huta 149, 171
  FRG 244
  GDR 309, 314, 322
  Netherlands 116
  Poland 83, 84, 85, 94-5
    Nida River 94-5
    Rzeszów 95
  Switzerland 50

'Habach Series', Austria 10, 26
Hageland iron deposits, Belgium 107
Hagendorf deposits, FRG 175, 185, 186, 259, 261
Hahnenklee deposits, FRG 234
Haibach-Klingerhof mineralization, FRG 192
Haidbachgraben gypsum-anhydrite deposits, Austria 31
Haies-Monet lead-zinc deposit, Belgium 99
Hain diorite, FRG 192

Subject index

Hainchen mine, FRG 215
Haingrube, FRG 207
Hain–Gründau mining district, FRG 250
Hájek kaolin deposit, Czechoslovakia 142
Halanzy mine, Belgium 99
Halberbracht fault, FRG 205
Halblech plant, FRG 268
Hall salt mine, Austria 21
Hallberg gypsum–anhydrite mine, Austria 20
Halle–Bitterfeld–Lausitz brown coal deposits, GDR 9
Hallein salt deposit, Austria 21
Hallstatt Limestone, Austria 20
Halobia Beds, Austria 20
Halokinesis, definition of 242
Halsbrücke vein system, GDR 318, 326
Haltern quartz-sand deposits, FRG 260
Hammersbach limonite deposits, FRG 266
Hanau Basin, FRG 180
'Hangender Sommer' oreshoot, FRG 216
'Hangendes Lager', Maubach, FRG 285
Hannover salt deposits, FRG 242
Harlingrode iron deposit, FRG 256
Harrachov fluorite–lead deposit, Czechoslovakia 137–8, 141
Hartenrod barite mineralization, FRG 279
Harz Mountains 2, 9
  FRG 177, 181–2, 193, 194, 198, 230–6, 244, 246, 249, 256, 280
  GDR 310, 313, 315, 317, 318, 320, 325, 326, 327
Harzburg nickel–copper deposit, FRG 209
Harzgerode ore district, GDR 231, 317
'Haselgebirge' 20–1, 242
Hasquempont lead–zinc deposit, Belgium 102
Hasserode mineralization, FRG 231
Hattingen phosphorite deposits, FRG 264
Hauptdolomit 10
Haverlahwiese mine, Salzgitter, FRG 257
Heilbronn salt deposit, FRG 243
Heiligenblut gold deposit, Austria 26
Heiterwand lead–zinc deposits, Austria 19
Helcmanovce antimony deposit, Czechoslovakia 149
Helgoland, copper smelting in 251
Helmstedt deposits, FRG 260, 263
Hel'pa mineralization, Czechoslovakia 151
Helpup mineralization, FRG 288
Helvetic flysch 11
Helvetic molasse trough 10
Helvetic Zone, Eastern Alps
  Austria 19
  FRG 264

Helvetikum, Eastern Alps, Austria 19
Hemer iron deposits, FRG 274
Hemmelte celestine deposit, FRG 244
Hengersberg–Eging clay deposits, FRG 262
Henne Valley fault, FRG 219
Henneberg granite, GDR 309
Herborner Hill mine, Dillenburg, FRG 279
Hercynian Massifs, Switzerland 45–7, 50
Herrenbaumgarten diatomite deposits, Austria 18
Herrengrund deposit see Spania Dolina copper deposit, Czechoslovakia
Herschbach quartzites, FRG 259
Herve–Vesdre–Theux Massifs, Belgium 100, 101, 102
Herzberg–Andreasberg anticline, FRG 231
Herznach–Fricktal iron deposit, Switzerland 43–4
'Herzogenhügel' copper mineralization, Belgium 109
Herzogenrath quartz-sand deposit, FRG 260
Hesbaye phosphate deposits, Belgium 109
Hessen brown coal deposits, FRG 9
'Hessen' potash salt seam, FRG 242, 321
'Hessen-quartzite type' 259
Hessian Basin 180
Hessian Depression, FRG 180, 181, 241, 245, 246–51, 269, 272, 274, 276, 279–80
Hessian Strait 180
Heure lead–zinc deposit, Belgium 102, 103, 108
Hildesheim salt deposits, FRG 242
Hils trough, FRG 244, 260
Hirschau mineralization, FRG 179, 261, 292
Hirschau–Schnaittenbach kaolin deposit, FRG 260
Hirschberg 'granite', FRG 175
Hladomorňa dolina group, Czechoslovakia 151
Hlavní vein, Příbram ore district, Czechoslovakia 132
Hnilčik–Roztoky iron deposit, Czechoslovakia 148
Hnilec mineralization, Czechoslovakia 155
Hnůšt'a deposits, Czechoslovakia 149, 169
Hochfilzen magnesite deposits, Austria 23
Hochobir–Eisenkappel lead–zinc deposit, Austria 37
Hochplatte E limonite deposits, FRG 266, 267, 268
Hochranz river manganese deposit, Austria 268, 269
Hochstaufen lead–zinc deposits, FRG 266
Hodejov mineralization, Czechoslovakia 173

Hodruša magnetite deposit, Czechoslovakia 158
Hof-Bad Steben mineralization, FRG 281
Hohenrhein beds, FRG 226
Hohe Tauern deposits, Austria 10, 25–6
Hohe Trost vein system, FRG 280
Hohe Venn Mountains, FRG 177, 181, 193, 208, 240, 284
Höllental lead–zinc deposits, FRG 266, 267, 268
Hollersbach lead–zinc deposit, Austria 30–1
Holy Cross Mountains, Poland see Góry Świętokrzyskie, Poland
Holy Ghost shaft, Röhrerbühel mine, Austria 15
Holzappel lead–zinc deposit, FRG 177, 214, 215, 220, 226, 228, 229
Horbach nickel–cobalt deposit, FRG 185
Hořkovec claystone deposits, Czechoslovakia 143
Horn Graben, FRG 248
Horná Lehota mineralization, Czechoslovakia 167
Horné Srnie mineralization, Czechoslovakia 173
Horní Benešov lead–zinc deposit, Czechoslovakia 7, 118, 122, 128–30
Horní Bříza kaolin deposit, Czechoslovakia 143
Horní Slavkov–Krásno tin–tungsten deposits, Czechoslovakia 118, 135–6
Hornické Skály copper deposit, Zlaté Hory, Czechoslovakia 128
Horre facies, FRG 206
Horyniec sulphur deposits, Poland 84
Hosenberg copper-mining district, FRG 192
Hradiště fluorite deposit, Czechoslovakia 141
Hrádok siderite deposit, Czechoslovakia 151
Hřebeč clay deposit, Czechoslovakia 143
Hriňová manganese mineralization, Czechoslovakia 156
Hromnice iron deposit, Czechoslovakia 121
Hron group, Czechoslovakia 151, 169
Hrubá vein, Rudnany ore district, Czechoslovakia 157, 161
Hub tin–tungsten deposit, Czechoslovakia 135
Hüggel mineralization, FRG 276
Hunsrück, FRG
  deposits 193, 205, 214, 226, 228–30, 241, 259, 290
  slates 228
  –Oberharz rise 249
Hupfleiten lead–zinc deposits, FRG 266
Hüttenberg siderite mine, Austria 31, 32

Iberg reef, FRG 235

Idar–Oberstein mineralization, FRG 192
Idria mercury mine, Yugoslavia 192
Idria mine, Bensberg, FRG 216
Ilfeld Basin 309
Ilfeld manganese deposit, FRG 231
Illite
  Austria 18
Ilmenau–Gehren ore district, GDR 326
Ilmenite sands
  FRG 292
Ilsede iron deposit, FRG 256, 257
Imsbach mineralization, FRG 192, 193
Inner Carpathian Miocene, Czechoslovakia 150
Inner Sudetes basin, Poland 59
Innsbruck Quartz-Phyllite Unit, Austria 23
Inntal nappe, Austria 19
Inovec Mountains, Czechoslovakia 146, 154
Inowrocław salt diapir, Poland 85–6
Insubric Line, Austria 19
Ipel'ská kotline depression, Czechoslovakia 172
Iron
  Austria 17, 19–20, 23, 31–2
    Buchegg–Radmer 23
    Erzberg 23
    Hüttenberg 31, 32
    Waldenstein 32
  Belgium 105–8
  Czechoslovakia 118, 125–6, 148, 156–8
    Nižna Slaná 148, 157
    Rudňany 148, 157, 161
  FRG 186, 187–8, 191, 192, 193, 205–15, 218, 230, 241, 254–8, 264, 265, 267, 268, 269, 271, 274–5, 277, 278, 280, 290–1, 293
    Achtal–Kressenberg 269
    Lahn–Dill district 205–7
    Siegerland–Wied district 209–15
  GDR 307, 308, 309, 310, 312, 313, 314, 323, 325
    Braunesumpf 314
    Büchenberg 314
    Elbingerode 314
  Poland 55, 58, 59, 61, 62–9
    Białaczów 67
    Kalisz 68
    Kłobuck 67–8
    Końskie–Starachowice 65, 66–7
    Kowary 62–3
    Krzemianka 62
    Kudowa 64–5
    Łęczyca 55, 62, 67, 68–9
    Łobez 65–6
    Męcinka 63, 64
    Przytyk 69
    Stanisławów 63–4
    Żarki-Częstochowa–Kłobuck 65, 66–7
  Switzerland 41–4, 45, 48
    Chamoson 44
    Delemont 41–3

Iron (continued)
    Erzegg 44
    Herznach-Fricktal 43–4
    Mont Chemin 45
    Val Ferrera 48
Isérables uranium deposit, Switzerland 49
Iserlohn lead–zinc deposits, FRG 177
Iserlohn–Schwelm lead–zinc deposits, FRG 209
Ivrea zone, Switzerland 49
Izbica salt diapir, Poland 86

Jáchymov ore district, Czechoslovakia 117, 121, 134–5
Janovice mineralization, Czechoslovakia 155, 168
Jasenie mineralization, Czechoslovakia 155, 167
Jasov–Rudnik asbestos deposit, Czechoslovakia 155
Javorka fluorite deposit, Czechoslovakia 141–2
Javorka–Běstvina fluorite deposit, Czechoslovakia 142
Jawor bentonite deposits, Poland 96
Jedl'ové Kostol'any siderite deposit, Czechoslovakia 151
Jelenec–Zi'rany quartzite deposit, Czechoslovakia 172
Jelšava magnesite deposit, Czechoslovakia 149, 154, 169–70
Jelšava–Vel'ká Štet magnesite deposit, Czechoslovakia 151
Jenner river manganese deposit, FRG 268–9
Jeseniky Mountains, Czechoslovakia 126
Jílové deposits, Czechoslovakia 117, 130, 141
Jílové zone, Czechoslovakia 130
Jimlíkov kaolin deposit, Czechoslovakia 142
Joachimsthal deposit, Erzgebirge 317
Johannes mine, Höllental, FRG 266
Johannes mine, Lam, FRG 183
Johanngeorgenstadt/Jachymov mining district, GDR 327
Jordanów chromite deposits, Poland 77
Josef coal seam, Sokolov basin, Czechoslovakia 144
Josef mine, Moldava, Czechoslovakia 141
Joseph Maximilian mine, Rauschberg, FRG 266
Judicarian Line, Austria 19
Juncus trifidus L. 46
'Jungalpidikum' 10
Jura metallogenic province, Switzerland 41–4, 50

Kaczawski Block, Poland 71
Kadaň kaolin deposit, Czechoslovakia 142
Käfersteige mineralization, FRG 188, 191, 277
Kahleberg sandstone, FRG 194

Kahlenberg mine, near Freiburg, FRG 256
Kaisergrube I, Rosskopf, FRG 266
Kaisersberg graphite mine, Austria 25
Kaiserstuhl volcanic belt, FRG 180–1, 289
Kalinka sulphur deposit, Czechoslovakia 156
Kalinovo kaolinitic clay deposit, Czechoslovakia 172
Kalisz iron deposit, Poland 67, 68
Kallenhardt mineralization, FRG 225
Kaller Stoller mine, FRG 282
Kallmuth Rise, FRG 284, 285–7
Kalno kaolin deposit, Poland 95
Kaltenberg nickel–cobalt deposit, Switzerland 49
Kammerling Alm manganese deposit, Austria 20
Kammern talc deposit, Austria 25
Kampenwand limonite deposits, FRG 266
Kamsdorf mineralization, GDR 325
Kaolin
  Austria 17–8
    Kriechbaum 17
    Mallersbach 17–8
    Niederfladnitz 17–8
    Weinzierl 17
  Belgium 110
  Czechoslovakia 142–3, 172
    Karlovy Vary 142, 143
    Plzeň basin 142–3
  FRG 260, 261, 291–2
    Kirschau–Schnaittenbach 260
  GDR 310, 312, 314, 318, 324
  Poland 59, 95–6
    Czerna 96
    Czerwona Woda 96
    Wyszonowice 95
    Żarów 95
    Zebrzydowa 96
Kapfenberg illite deposit, Austria 18
Karawanken Range, Austria 33, 37
'Karbonattutten', Mechernich, FRG 287
Karchowice beds, Poland 74
Karczówka lead deposit, Poland 74
Karkonosze granite, Poland 62, 63, 69, 70, 83
Karlovy Vary granite, Czechoslovakia 134, 135, 141, 142
Karlovy Vary kaolin deposits, Czechoslovakia 142, 143
Karlsgrube, Arzmoosalpe, FRG 266
Kasnějov kaolin deposit, Czechoslovakia 142
Kašperské Hory gold mineralization, Czechoslovakia 130
Kassel mineralization, FRG 289
Kastellaun lead–zinc deposits, FRG 229
Kavečany magnesite deposit, Czechoslovakia 151
Kazimierz phosphorite deposits, Poland 90
Keilberg fault system, FRG 281
Keilberg iron deposit, FRG 256

Kellerwald, FRG 194, 207, 208, 279, 288
Kielce deposits, Poland 58, 65, 70, 74
Kienberg gypsum deposit, Switzerland 50
Kieselguhr see Diatomite
Kindberg gypsum–anhydrite deposit, Austria 31
Kinzig valley mineralization, FRG 188, 191
Kirchberg granite, GDR 309
Kišovce manganese deposit, Czechoslovakia 148
Kitzbühel copper deposits, Austria 21–2
Klabava ore horizon, Czechoslovakia 126
Kladno–Rakovník basin refractory claystones, Czechoslovakia 143
Klara vein, Graf Moltke mine, Gladbeck, FRG 236, 238
Kleinkogel barite deposit, Austria 31
Klement vein, Příbram ore district, Czechoslovakia 132
Kletno fluorite deposit, Poland 90
Kliening Au–As deposit, Austria 32
Klingenberg clay deposits, FRG 263
Klippen Belt, Czechoslovak Carpathians 148–50, 155
Klobásy ore zone, Czechoslovakia 130
Kłobuck iron deposits, Poland 67
Kłodawa salt diapir, Poland 85
Klokoč magnetite deposit, Czechoslovakia 158
'Kniest', Rammelsberg, FRG 194, 196, 197
Knollen mine, FRG 280
'Knotten', definition of 287
'Kobaltrücken' 249, 274, 279, 281–2, 327
Kochanovská unit, Magura zone, Czechoslovakia 156
Kocour ore vein, Jílové gold deposit, Czechoslovakia 130
Kohútik talc–magnesite deposit, Czechoslovakia 170
Kokava mineralization, Czechoslovakia 151, 154, 169
Kolársky vrch mine, Pezinok, Czechoslovakia 151
'Kolk', Salzgitter ore field, FRG 257
Koloděje graphite deposit, Czechoslovakia 140
Komárov iron mineralization, Czechoslovakia 126
Königsberg (Jenner) lead–zinc deposits, FRG 266
Königsberg uranium deposit, FRG 193
Königsbronn mineralization, FRG 291
Königshain granite, GDR 309
Königszug mine, FRG 207
Konrad mine, FRG 255, 256
Końskie–Starachowice iron deposit, Poland 62, 65, 66
Konstantin graphite deposit, Czechoslovakia 140

Konstanty magnesite deposit, Poland 93
Kopaniec leucogranite deposit, Poland 92
Koralpe lithium deposit, Austria 33
Korbach deposits, FRG 240, 245, 250
Košice magnesite deposit, Czechoslovakia 149, 154, 169
Košická Belá mineralization, Czechoslovakia 158
Košické Hámre magnesite deposit, Czechoslovakia 151
Kostiviarska mineralization, Czechoslovakia 173
Kostolná Bašta mineralization, Czechoslovakia 173
Kottaun iron deposit, Austria 17
Kotterbach ore district see Rudňany ore district, Czechoslovakia
Kowary iron deposit, Poland 62–3
Koyšov mineralization, Czechoslovakia 158, 168
Kraichgau Depression, FRG 252, 261
Krákořice iron deposit, Czechoslovakia 126
Krakow–Dębica salt deposits, Poland 87
Králiky mercury deposit, Czechoslovakia 168
Kral'ovany mineralization, Czechoslovakia 173
Krasków quartz deposit, Poland 91
Kraslice mineralization, Czechoslovakia 126
Krásna Hora gold deposit, Czechoslovakia 118, 130
Krásno tin–tungsten deposits, Czechoslovakia 135–6
Krásno–Vysoký Kámen feldspar deposit, Czechoslovakia 141
Kraubath magnesite deposits, Austria 23, 25
Křemenný val vein, Harrachov fluorite–lead deposit, Czechoslovakia 137
Kremnica ore district, Czechoslovakia 11, 146, 149, 156, 167, 168
Křemže nickel deposit, Czechoslovakia 138
Kressenberg iron deposits, FRG 269
Kreuzeckgruppe, Austria 30, 33
Kriechbaum kaolin deposit, Austria 17
Krivoi Rog iron deposit, U.S.S.R. 118, 126
Krivošt'any mineralization, Czechoslovakia 173
Křížany fluorite deposit, Czechoslovakia 141
Krížna nappe, Czechoslovakia 155
Krkonoše granite, Czechoslovakia 137
Kronach mineralization, FRG 281
Kropfmühl graphite schists, FRG 175
'Krušek' 132
Krušná Hora iron deposit, Czechoslovakia 125, 126
Krušné Hory, Czechoslovakia crystalline mass 141

Krušné Hory (continued)
  Fault 144
  granite 136
  Mountains 136, 141, 144
Krzemianka iron deposit, Poland 62
Kuchyňa mineralization, Czechoslovakia 151, 165
Kudowa iron deposit, Poland 64–5
Kujawy rock salt deposit, Poland 55, 61, 82, 85
Kulf mineralization, FRG 288
Kulmbach conglomerate, FRG 292
Kunštát clay deposit, Czechoslovakia 143
Kupferberg–Wirsberg sulphide deposits, FRG 175, 183
Kupferschiefer 8
  FRG 177, 245–51
  GDR 319–20
Kutná Hora, Czechoslovakia
  crystalline complex 132
  Ag–Pb–Zn deposit 117, 118, 132–4
Kuzmice bentonite deposit, Czechoslovakia 172
Kvetnica copper mineralization, Czechoslovakia 154
Kyanite
  Austria 31
Kyselka kaolin deposit, Czechoslovakia 142
Kyšice clay deposit, Czechoslovakia 144

La Calamine lead–zinc deposit, Belgium 99, 102–3
Lafatsch lead–zinc deposit, Austria 19
Lagerkalk, Meggen, FRG 202
Łagów lead deposits, Poland 74
La Grande-Montagne lead–zinc deposit, Belgium see La Calamine lead–zinc deposit, Belgium
La Helle River copper mineralization, Belgium 109
Lahn deposits, FRG 264, 291, 292
Lahn syncline, FRG 181, 194, 207, 208, 209, 215, 226, 279
Lahn–Dill red iron ore deposits, FRG 177, 181, 194, 205–7
Lahn–Hunsrück lead–zinc deposits, FRG 177, 228–30
Lahr quartz–barite mineralization, FRG 278
Laisa manganese district, FRG 208
Lam mineralization, FRG 183, 281
Lammereck–Strubberg manganese deposit, Austria 20
Landsberg mercury deposit, FRG 192
Landshut bentonite deposit, FRG 290
Langenbach mine, FRG 183
Langendernbach mineralization, FRG 282
Łanięta salt diapir, Poland 86
La Rochette lead–zinc mineralization, Belgium 105
Lassing talc deposit, Austria 25

Lastovce bentonite deposit, Czechoslovakia 172
Latinák magnesite deposit, Czechoslovakia 149
Laubach beds, FRG 226
Läufelfingen gypsum deposit, Switzerland 50
Lausitz Block 307, 309, 312–3
Lausitz Rise 7
Lautenthal mineralization, FRG 231
La Vieille Montagne lead–zinc deposit, Belgium see La Calamine lead–zinc deposit, Belgium
Lead
  Austria 17, 19, 30–1, 32, 33–7
    Bleiberg 33–7
  Belgium 99–104
    Bleiberg 99, 102
    La Calamine 99, 102–3
  Czechoslovakia 118, 121, 126–34, 137–8, 163–5
    Banska Stiavnica 149, 163–5
    Harrachov 118, 121, 137–8
    Horní Beneškov 118, 122, 128–30
    Kutná Hora 117, 118, 132–4
    Příbram 117, 118, 130–2
    Soviansko 163
    Zlaté Hory 126–8
  FRG
    Aachen–Erkelenz sub-district 239–40
    Aachen–Stolberg district 208–9
    Bensberg district 215–8
    Ems district 227–8
    Lahn–Hunsrück district 228–30
    Lintorf–Velbert sub-district 238–9
    Maubach 284–5
    Mechernich 284, 285
    Meggen 198–205
    Rammelsberg 194–8
    Ramsbeck 218–26
    Ruhr area 236–8
    St. Andreasberg orefield 230, 231, 235
    Wiesloch 287–8
  GDR 309, 310, 314, 317
  Poland 55, 58, 59, 61, 73–7
  Switzerland 46, 48–9
    Alp Nadels 46
    Alp Taspin 49
    Bärenbühl 49
    Bleiberg 49
    Bristenstock 46
    Goppenstein 46
    Praz Jean 49
    St. Luc–Bella Tola 49
    S-charl 48–9
    Silberberg 49
    Trachsellauenen 46
Łeba elevation, Poland 61, 82, 85, 86, 89, 90
Lebach group, FRG 193
Le Chatelard and Les Marecottes uranium deposit, Switzerland 46
Lechtaler Alpen manganese deposit, Austria 20
Łęczyca iron deposit, Poland 55, 61, 62, 67, 68

Ledenice clay deposit, Czechoslovakia 144
Lednické Rovné mineralization, Czechoslovakia 155
Legnica gold mineralization, Poland 81
Lehôtka pod Brehy perlite deposit, Czechoslovakia 172
Lehrberg beds, FRG 252
Leine cyclothem 85, 113, 322
Leipzig greywacke formation, GDR 307
Leissigen gypsum deposit, Switzerland 50
Leitmar copper deposit, FRG 250
Lemberg mercury deposit, FRG 192
Lena copper deposit, Poland 72
Lengede iron deposit, FRG 257
Lengede-Broisedt mine, FRG 263
Lenne shales, FRG 209
Lenne Valley mineralization, FRG 272
'Lenneschiefer', Meggen, FRG 199
Leogang Cu–Ni–Co deposits, Austria 22
Leonie mine, Auerbach, FRG 258
Lerbach iron deposit, FRG 207
Les Trappistes fluorite deposit, Switzerland 50
Leucophyllite
  Austria 31
Levice mineralization, Czechoslovakia 173
Levočské pohorie Mountains ore district, Czechoslovakia 158
Leysin copper mineralization, Switzerland 44
Ležatá vein, Příbram ore district, Czechoslovakia 132
Łężkowice–Siedlec salt deposit, Poland 87–8
Libčice gold mineralization, Czechoslovakia 130
Lichtaart iron mineralization, Belgium 107
Licince mineralization, Czechoslovakia 154
Lienne Valley manganese deposit, Belgium 108–9
Lierneux mineralization, Belgium 109
Lietavská Lúčka mineralization, Czechoslovakia 173
Lignica–Głogów mining region, Poland 55
Limburg red iron ore deposit, FRG 207
Limestone Alps see Calcareous Alps
Lintorf mineralization, FRG 209
Lintorf–Selbeck lead–zinc deposits, FRG 236, 238–9, 240
Lippstadt Upfold, FRG 219
Liptovská Dúbrava antimony–gold deposit, Czechoslovakia 149, 166
Liptovská kotlina depression, Czechoslovakia 156
Lithium
  Austria 33

Lithium (continued)
  Czechoslovakia 136–7
    Cínovec 117, 118, 136–7
  FRG 186
  GDR 309
Łobez iron deposit, Poland 65
Łódź basin, Poland 90
Lohrheim mineralization, FRG 205, 292
Lohrheim pyrite–barite deposit, FRG 205
Lonau anticline, FRG 231
London–Brabant Massif 1, 113
Longvilly lead–zinc deposit, Belgium 102
Longwy limestone, Belgium 108
Łopuszka Wielka alabaster deposit, Poland 95
Louise mine, FRG 193
Louny claystone deposits, Czechoslovakia 144
Lower East Alpine Unit, Austria 31
Lower Rhine Bight 9, 180, 260, 282, 284
Lower Rhine Ems Basin 1
Lower Saxony Basin 180, 269
Lower Saxony Block 177, 276
Lower Silesia, Poland 55, 59, 77, 81, 91–4, 95–6
Lubaczów sulphur deposits, Poland 83
Lubenec coal seam, Czechoslovakia 143
Luberík magnesite deposit, Czechoslovakia 149
Luberík–Margecany line, Czechoslovakia 169
Lubichów copper deposits, Poland 71–2
Lubień salt diapir, Poland 86
Ľubietová deposit, Czechoslovakia 154, 162
Lubin copper mine, Poland 72
Lublin phosphorite deposits, Poland 90
Lúčky mineralization, Czechoslovakia 173
Lüderich mine, FRG 216
Ludrová mineralization, Czechoslovakia 173
Ludwig mine, Biederkopf–Dexbach, FRG 240
Lúka/Váh r. mineralization, Czechoslovakia 173
Lüneburg gypsum deposit, FRG 244
Lüneburg Heath kieselguhr deposits, FRG 260–1
Lužice Fault, Czechoslovakia 141
Lužnice Valley feldspar deposits, Czechoslovakia 141
Lwówek depression, Poland 71
Łysogóry dislocation, Poland 58

Magnesite
  Austria 23–5
    Kraubath 25
    Tux 25

Magnesite (continued)
  Czechoslovakia 149, 169–70
    Jelšava 149, 169–70
    Vlachovo 169
  Poland 92–4
    Konstanty 93
    Sobótka 92–3
    Sczęśc Boże 93
    Szklary 93–4
    Wiry 92, 93
Magura zone, Czechoslovakia 156
Magurka mineralization,
  Czechoslovakia 154, 166
Mahring mineralization, FRG 185, 186
Mainz Basin, FRG 180, 192, 279
Malá Fatra ore district, Czechoslovakia 163, 165, 167
Malá Magura–Suchý Mountains ore district, Czechoslovakia 163
Malachovo mercury mineralization, Czechoslovakia 156, 168
Malé Karpaty Group, Czechoslovakia 165
Malé Karpaty Mountains ore district, Czechoslovakia 146, 151, 155, 163, 167, 169
Malé Krštenňany mineralization, Czechoslovakia 173
Malé Vrbno graphite deposit, Czechoslovakia 140
Malé Železné mineralization, Czechoslovakia 151, 154
Malempré manganese mineralization, Belgium 109
Malenco serpentinites, Switzerland 49, 50
Malenovice mineralization, Czechoslovakia 155
Mallersbach kaolin deposit, Austria 17–8
Malonín clay deposit, Czechoslovakia 143
Małopolska Massif, Poland 57
Malužiná mineralization, Czechoslovakia 154, 155, 169
Malvoisin kaolin deposit, Belgium 110
Manganese
  Austria 20, 23
  Belgium 108–9
    Lienne valley 108–9
  Czechoslovakia 118, 124–5, 148, 158
    Chvaletice 121, 122, 124–5
    Švábovce–Kišovce 158
  FRG 188, 193, 207–8, 209–15, 217, 230, 231, 268–9, 271, 290–1
    Jenner river 268–9
    Siegerland–Wied district 209–15
  GDR 310, 325
  Poland 60
  Switzerland 45, 49
    Gonzen 45
    Oberhalbstein 49
Mano pit, Nizna Slana, Czechoslovakia 157
Mansfeld mineralization, GDR 73, 327

Mansfeld syncline, GDR 320
Marcasite
  Poland 83
Mardorf mine, FRG 291
Margua nappe, Switzerland 49, 50
Maria mine, Rožňava, Czechoslovakia 161
'Marie' vein, Horní Slavkov-Krásno ore district, Czechoslovakia 136
Marienberg ore district, GDR 317
Markhahn fault, FRG 205
Markušovce–Geswäng deposit, Czechoslovakia 148
Markušovce–Grétla iron deposit, Czechoslovakia 148
Marsberg copper deposit, FRG 177, 208, 240–1, 245, 250
Massif Central, France 1
Mathias mine, Vasbeck, FRG 288
Matka Boží vein, Příbram ore district, Czechoslovakia 132
Maubach lead–zinc deposits, FRG 8, 181, 271
Mautern talc deposit, Austria 25
Mayen lead–zinc deposit, FRG 215
Mazury elevation, Poland 62
Mazury–Suwałki uplift, Poland 61
Mechernich lead–zinc deposits, FRG 8, 181, 271
Męcinka iron deposit, Poland 63, 64
Mecklenburg depression, GDR 309
Mediterranean–Mjösen zone 1, 3
Medlov iron deposit, Czechoslovakia 126
Medzev–Hummel mineralization, Czechoslovakia 161
Medzibrod antimony deposit, Czechoslovakia 166
Meggen Beds, FRG 199
Meggen zinc–lead–barite deposit, FRG 7, 130, 198–205, 209, 224, 263
Meilinger mine, Pfronten-Meilingen, FRG 266
Meinberg bentonite deposit, FRG 290
Meiselding mine, Austria 33
Meissen granite, GDR 309
Membach lead–zinc deposit, Belgium 103
Menzenschwand uranium deposits, FRG 175, 188, 190, 191
Mercur mine, Bad Ems, FRG 214, 228
Mercury
  Austria 32, 37
    Vellacher Kotschna 37
  Czechoslovakia 148, 168
    Rudňany 148, 168
  FRG 192, 193, 214, 216
Merkers potash plant, GDR 321
Merník mercury deposit, Czechoslovakia 156, 168
Meuville manganese deposit, Belgium 108
Miasteczko iron deposit, Poland 69
'Mica-kaolin' see Leucophyllite
Mid-Atlantic Ridge 180
Mid-German Crystalline Rise 231
Midi-Eifel thrust, Belgium 99

Midlum mineralization, FRG 292–3
Miedziana Góra copper deposit, Poland 58, 70, 71
Miedzianka deposits, Poland 58, 69, 70, 71, 73
Mielnik phosphorite deposits, Poland 90
Mieroszyno salt deposits, Poland 86
Mierzęcice iron deposit, Poland 69
Miess–Mezica lead–zinc deposit, Yugoslavia 33, 34
Miglieglia zone, Astano region, Switzerland 48
'Minette' iron deposit, Belgium 99
Mitterberg copper deposits, Austria 22
Mitterberg–Kreuzen lead–zinc deposit, Austria 37
Mittersill scheelite deposit, Austria 9, 26–9
Mitterteich mineralization, FRG 292
Mlynky deposits, Czechoslovakia 148, 154, 171
Mníchova Lehota mineralization, Czechoslovakia 173
Mníšek mineralization, Czechoslovakia 125, 151, 161
Močiar diatomite deposit, Czechoslovakia 172
Modrý Kameň mineralization, Czechoslovakia 172
Mogilno salt diapir, Poland 86
Mojtin mineralization, Czechoslovakia 173
Molasse Basin, Switzerland 44
Molasse Foreland, FRG 179
Molasse Zone 5, 11, 18
Moldanubian–Dalslandian Supergroup 5, 7
Moldanubian Zone 1, 3, 175, 183–93, 303
Moldanubikum 11, 17, 120, 121, 122, 132, 138, 139, 144
Moldava fluorite deposit, Czechoslovakia 141
Möll River gold deposit, Austria 26
Molybdenum
  Austria 26
  Poland 61
  Switzerland 46
    Baltschiedertal 46
Mons Basin, Belgium 109
Mont Blanc Massif, Switzerland 45, 50
Mont Chemin iron deposit, Switzerland 45
Monte Rosa gold province, Italy 48
Moosburg bentonite deposit, FRG 290
Moosegg gypsum–anhydrite mine, Austria 20
Moravia, Czechoslovakia 118, 121, 122, 138, 139, 140, 143
Moravikum, Bohemian Massif 17
Moray Firth Basin, North Sea 180
Morcles nappe, Switzerland 44
Moresnet lead–zinc deposit, Belgium see La Calamine lead–zinc deposit, Belgium

Morgenröthe lode, Lahn–Hunsrück district, FRG 229
Mosel syncline 229
Moszczenica–Łapczyca salt deposits, Poland 87
Mount Isa base-metal deposit, Queensland, Australia 34, 36
Mühldorf graphite deposits, Austria 17
Mühlenbach lead–zinc deposit, FRG 214, 226, 227
Mühlleithen–Gottesberg tin deposit, GDR 317
Münchberg Gneiss Massif, FRG 5, 175, 183, 186, 188, 261
Münder marls, FRG 244
Münster–Brehloh kieselguhr deposit, FRG 261
Münsterland Bight, FRG 177, 244, 260, 275–6
Munstertal–Wiesental lead–zinc deposits, FRG 190, 191
Mur River gold deposit, Austria 26
Murg valley mineralization, FRG 277, 278
Mürtenschalp deposits, Switzerland 44, 45
Müsen iron deposit, FRG 213, 215, 290
Musson mine, Belgium 99
Mútnik–Hnúšťa magnesite–talc deposit, Czechoslovakia 151, 169, 170
Mydlovary clay deposit, Czechoslovakia 144
Mýto mineralization, Czechoslovakia 155
Mýto pod Ďumbierom mineralization, Czechoslovakia 154, 167

Naab Valley clay deposits, FRG 262
Nabburg fluorite district, FRG 282
Nadbużańskie depression, Poland 61
'Nagelfluh' 11
Nagold valley mineralization, FRG 277
Nahe copper deposits, FRG 290
Nahe Depression, FRG 177
Nálepkovo iron deposit, Czechoslovakia 148
Nammen mineralization, FRG 256, 276
Namur synclinorium, Belgium 2, 99, 101, 102, 108
Napf placer gold deposits, Switzerland 44
Nassau mineralization, FRG 230
Nassau–Siegen–Soest lineament 226
Nassau Trough 226
Naters uranium deposit, Switzerland 46
Nehden Limestone, FRG 274
Nentershausen Basin, FRG 248
Nephrite
  Switzerland 50
    Scortaseo 50
Nero clay, Czechoslovakia 144
Netherlands Platform 3, 5

Neualbenreuth mineralization, FRG 186
Neubalach mineralization, FRG 277, 282
Neuburg siliceous earth, FRG 258, 260, 261
Neue Haardt mine, FRG 213
Neuekrug–Hahausen copper deposit, FRG 249
Neuenbürg mineralization, FRG 277–8
'Neues Lager', Meggen, FRG 202, 204
Neu-Mansfeld mine, Neuekrug-Hahausen, FRG 249–50
Neuwied Basin, FRG 259, 263
New barite vein, Moldava, Czechoslovakia 141
New orebody
  Meggen, FRG 202, 204
  Rammelsberg, FRG 197
Nickel
  Austria 22
  Czechoslovakia 118, 121, 124, 134–5, 138, 168
    Jáchymov 117, 121, 134–5
    Křemže 118, 138
    Staré Ransko 118, 124
  FRG 186, 188, 190, 209, 213, 214, 215, 271, 281–2
  GDR 310, 312, 324, 327
    St. Egidien 312, 324
  Poland 59, 79–80
    Szklary 79–80
  Switzerland 49
    Kaltenberg 49
    Palagnedra 49
    Poschiavo 49
    Totalp 49
Nida River gypsum deposits, Poland 94–5
Niederdresselndorf mineralization, FRG 292
Niederfladnitz kaolin deposit, Austria 17–8
Nieder-Ramstadt mineralization, FRG 282
Nikolaus Phönix mine, FRG 215
Niobium
  FRG 289
Nismes iron mineralization, Belgium 108
Nittenau mineralization, FRG 281
Niwice gypsum–anhydrite deposit, Poland 94
Nízke Tatry Mountains, Czechoslovakia 146, 151, 154, 155, 158, 161, 165, 166, 168, 169
Nízke Tatry Mountains ore district, Czechoslovakia 161, 163
Nízký Jeseník Mountains, Czechoslovakia 128
Nižná Slaná iron deposit, Czechoslovakia 148, 149, 151, 157
Nižný Hrabovec bentonite deposit, Czechoslovakia 172
Nižný Kralovec mineralization, Czechoslovakia 173

Nohfelden uranium deposit, FRG 193
Nördlingen Ries, FRG 289
Nordwestfälische-Lippische Rise, FRG 180
Northern Zone, Eastern Alps, Austria 19–25
North German–Polish Depression 3, 8
North Sea Basin 1
North Sea–Dobruja Lineament 1
North Sudetic Depression 69, 71, 72, 94
North Veporide ore district, Czechoslovakia 158
Nová Baňa mineralization, Czechoslovakia 156, 172
Nová vein, Harrachov fluorite–lead deposit, Czechoslovakia 137
Nová Ves clay deposit, Czechoslovakia 144
Nové Těchanovive Culm slates, Czechoslovakia 129
Novoveská Huta mineralization, Czechoslovakia 149, 154, 162, 171
Nowa Ruda mineralization, Poland 71, 80–1
Nowa Sól salt deposit, Poland 86
Nowy Kościół copper deposit, Poland 72
Nowy Ląd mine, Poland 94
Nučice iron deposit, Czechoslovakia 125, 126
Nuttlar syncline, FRG 221

Oberdorf magnesite deposit, Austria 25
Oberhalbstein manganese deposit, Switzerland 49
'Oberharzer Diabaszug', FRG 207
Oberpfalz 181, 187, 253–4, 260, 281
Ober-Sailauf quartz porphyry, FRG 192
Oberscheld red iron ore deposit, FRG 207
Obertal mine, Austria 32
Oberzeiring Pb-Ag deposit, Austria 32
Obrázek sphalerite deposit, Czechoslovakia 122, 124
Ochre
  FRG 293
Ochtiná mineralization, Czechoslovakia 149, 154, 169, 173
Odenwald deposits, FRG 1, 191, 261, 276–9
Oder lineament 2
Odershausen Limestone, FRG 202
Oedingen mineralization, FRG 292
Oker Valley mineralization, FRG 231
Okrzeszyn copper mineralization, Poland 71
Old orebody
  Meggen, FRG 202
  Rammelsberg, FRG 194, 197, 198
Oldřich vein, Harrachov fluorite–lead deposit, Czechoslovakia 137
Olefant deposit, FRG 218

Subject index

Olkusz lead–zinc deposits, Poland 73, 74
Olpe iron deposit, FRG 213, 215
Oos–Saale Trough, GDR 2, 8, 309, 312, 319
Oravská kotlina depression, Czechoslovakia 156
Oreské mineralization, Czechoslovakia 173
Oret kaolin deposit, Belgium 110
Ortland iron deposit, FRG 256
Osel deposit, Kutná Hora ore district, Czechoslovakia 117, 134
Oslo Graben/Oslo Rift 8, 248
Osnabrück mineralization, FRG 246
Ostalpen see Eastern Alps
Ostalpin 9, 10, 11
Ostelbe Massif see East Elbe Massif
Otänmäki iron deposit, Finland 62
Ötösbánya ore district see Rudňany ore district, Czechoslovakia

Paffrath mineralization, FRG 209
Paffrath syncline, FRG 216, 288
Palaeozoic platform, Poland 61–2
'Palaeozoics of Graz', Austria 33
Palagnedra nickel deposit, Switzerland 49
Pannonian Basin 18
Panzendorf mine, Austria 33
Papoušek fluorite veins, Moldava, Czechoslovakia 141
Parczów iron deposit, Poland 67, 69
Parkinsonia compressa 67, 68
P. ferruginea 68
Pasel adit, Rashausberg gold mine, Austria 26
Pauline mine, FRG 229
Pechelbronn mineralization, FRG 244, 252
Pechtelsgrün mineralization, GDR 310, 315
Pecten beds, Poland 84
Pegnitz iron deposit, FRG 256
Peine iron deposit, FRG 256, 257
Pennine Zone, Eastern Alps 25–31
Penninic, Austroalpine and southern Alps, Switzerland 47–9
Penninikum 9, 11
 Eastern Alps 25–31
Periadriatic Lineament 1
'Periadriatic suture', Austria 34
Pernek mineralization, Czechoslovakia 151, 165
Pezinok deposits, Czechoslovakia 149, 151, 168
Pezinok–Pernek groups, Czechoslovakia 151
Pfahl
 dislocation 180, 280
 lode 187
Pforzheim 'tripoli' deposit, FRG 261
Pfronten–Meilingen limonite deposits, FRG 266, 268
Phosphates/phosphate rocks
 Austria 18, 19
 Belgium 109
 FRG 186, 263–4, 291

Phosphates (continued)
 Poland 62, 88–90
  Burzenin 90
  Łeba 90
  Radom-Gościeradów 89–90
 Switzerland 50
  Pizzo Corandoni 50
Piesberg mineralization, FRG 276
Píla lead deposit, Czechoslovakia 155
Pinczów sulphur deposits, Poland 84
Pinge opening, Altenberg, GDR 316
Písek clay deposits, Czechoslovakia 144
Pizzo Corandoni phosphate deposit, Switzerland 50
Platta nappe, Switzerland 49
Plesching phosphate deposits, Austria 18
Plettenberg mineralization, FRG 272
Ploské magnesite deposit, Czechoslovakia 149, 169
Pluto mine, FRG 219
Plzeň basin kaolin/clay deposits, Czechoslovakia 142–3, 144
Poběžovice feldspar deposit, Czechoslovakia 140
Podbořany kaolin deposits, Czechoslovakia 142
Pod Kolársky antimony deposit, Czechoslovakia 165
Podlasie depression, Poland 61
Podlesí kaolin deposit, Czechoslovakia 142
Podrečany magnesite deposit, Czechoslovakia 149, 154, 169
Poederlee iron mineralization, Belgium 107
Pogórze Izerskiw feldspar deposits, Poland 91
Pohronský Bukovec mineralization, Czechoslovakia 167
Polish Furrow 2
Polkowice copper mine, Poland 72
Polom mineralization, Czechoslovakia 173
Poltár kaolinite clay deposit, Czechoslovakia 172
Pompeckj Block 177
Pondelok kaolinitic clay deposit, Czechoslovakia 172
Poproč mineralization, Czechoslovakia 149, 155
Porchelská Maša mineralization, Czechoslovakia 155
Porta Westfalica 256
Posądza sulphur deposits, Poland 83
Poschiavo nickel deposit, Switzerland 49
Post-Variscan cover, FRG 177–9
Post-Variscan Platform cover complex, GDR 303–6
Post-Variscan Platform Stage, GDR 318–27
Potash
 FRG/GDR 241–4, 320–3
  Calvörde block 322
  Southern Harz district 321–3
  Werra district 321
 Poland 55, 61

'Potholes' 257
Považský Inovec Mountains ore district, Czechoslovakia 163
Prague Basin 7, 183
Prakovce mineralization, Czechoslovakia 161
Praz Jean lead–zinc deposit, Switzerland 49
Préalpes Médianes nappe, Switzerland 44
Precambrian platform, Poland 60–1
Prešov–Solivar halite deposit, Czechoslovakia 149
Preßnitz series, GDR 307, 314
Pre-Variscan
 basement complex 1–3
 stages, GDR 314
Příbram Ag–Pb–Zn deposit, Czechoslovakia 117, 118, 130–2
Přílezy feldspar deposit, Czechoslovakia 140
Primus vein, Ruhr district, FRG 238
Prokop mine, Czechoslovakia 130, 132
Provodín glass sand deposit, Czechoslovakia 144
Przysucha iron deposits, Poland 66
Przytyk iron deposit, Poland 69
Pszów sulphur deposits, Poland 83
Puchberg gypsum–anhydrite mine, Austria 20
Puck Bay salt deposits, Poland 82, 86
Pukanec kaolinitic clay deposit, Czechoslovakia 172
Puntaiglas copper deposit, Switzerland 45
Pusté Pole mineralization, Czechoslovakia 155
Pyrite
 Austria 22–3, 33
 Czechoslovakia 118, 124–5, 168
  Chvaletice 124–5
 FRG 194–8
  Rammelsberg 194–8
 GDR 307, 313, 314, 315
  Einheit 315
 Poland 55, 82–3
  Rudki 55, 62, 65, 69, 82
  Wieściszowice 83
Pyrrhotite
 Austria 33
 GDR 314

Quartz/quartzites
 Austria 18
 Czechoslovakia 144, 172
 FRG 186, 187, 188, 190, 191, 192, 193, 217, 258–9, 274
  Bavarian Pfahl 258
  Usingen 258
 Poland 59, 91
  Krasków 91
  Rozdoże Izerskie 91
  Sady 91
 Switzerland 50–1

Rabenwald talc deposits, Austria 31
Radenthein magnesite deposits, Austria 23

Radhausberg gold mine, Austria 25–6
Radom–Gościeradów phosphorite deposits, Poland 89–90
Radzionków mine, Poland 96
Raibl–Cave del Predil lead–zinc deposit, Italy 33, 34
Rajec mineralization, Czechoslovakia 173
Rakovec Group, Czechoslovakia 151, 154, 155, 161
Ramberg Granite 309, 313
Ramberg intrusion 194
Rammelsberg sulphide deposit, FRG 7, 177, 181, 194–8, 224, 230, 241
Ramsbeck Beds, FRG 219, 220
Ramsbeck Block, FRG 219–20
'Ramsbeck Flachen' 221
Ramsbeck lead–zinc deposit, FRG 177, 214, 215, 218–26, 228, 272, 274
'Randschiefer-Serie', FRG 183
Rätikon Range, Austria 25
Ratkovská magnesite deposit, Czechoslovakia 169
Ratkovská Suchá deposits, Czechoslovakia 149, 154
Rauschberg lead–zinc deposits, FRG 266, 267, 268
Regensburg iron deposit, FRG 256
Rehden borehole, Uchte, FRG 276
Reichenhall salt deposits, FRG 181
Rejská vein, Kutná Hora ore district, Czechoslovakia 134
Rescheid mineralization, FRG 282–4
Resteigne fluorite deposit, Belgium 105
Rettenegg uranium mineralization, Austria 31
Reutte lead–zinc mineralization, FRG 267
Rheinfelden salt deposit, Switzerland 51
Rheinisches Schiefergebirge, FRG 5, 9, 175, 177, 180, 193, 194, 205, 208, 210, 211, 214, 215, 218–30, 240, 244, 246, 271–5, 279, 288, 292
Rhenish Massif 106, 113
Rhenish Shield 270
Rhenish Trough 1, 7, 303, 307, 313
Rhenohercynian zone 1, 2, 7
  FRG 177, 193–241
  GDR 303, 307
Rhine–Danube flysch zone 10
Rhine Graben 102, 180, 181, 188, 190, 244, 269, 276, 287
Richelsdorf deposits, FRG 177, 241, 248–9
Richelsdorf Mountains, FRG 246, 248, 279, 281
Riedbodeneck lead–zinc deposits, FRG 266, 267
'Riedel' potash salt seam, FRG 242
Ries main mine, Ramsbeck, FRG 224
Ries meteorite 179, 289
Riesenferner Tonalite, Austria 33
Řimbaba vein, Příbram ore district, Czechoslovakia 132
Ringkøbing-Fyn High 3, 5
Rocheux-Oneux sulphide deposit, Belgium 100, 108

Rochovce lead–zinc mineralization, Czechoslovakia 154
Rock salt see Salt/Rock salt
Rocroi Massif, Belgium 109
Rogoźno salt diapir, Poland 86
Röhrerbühel mine, Austria 15, 21
'Ronnenberg' potash seam 242, 321, 322
Rossgrabeneck tungsten deposit, FRG 188, 190
Rosskopf lead–zinc deposits, FRG 266
Roßleben potash plant, GDR 322
'Rote Fäule' 246, 319, 320
Rothenkirchen mineralization, FRG 281
Rotselaar iron deposit, Belgium 107
Rottleberode fluorite deposits, GDR 326
Roudný gold mineralization, Czechoslovakia 130
Rouveroy copper deposit, Belgium 109
Rozália vein, Banska Hodrusa, Czechoslovakia 162–3
Rozdroże Izerskie quartz deposits, Poland 91
Rožňava deposits, Czechoslovakia 158, 161, 167
Rožňava–Bernardy iron deposit, Czechoslovakia 148
Rožňava–Bystré iron deposit, Czechoslovakia 148
Rožňava–Mních iron deposit, Czechoslovakia 148
Rožňava–Rudník iron deposit, Czechoslovakia 148
Rožňava–Sadlovská iron deposit, Czechoslovakia 148
Rožňava–Štefan iron deposit, Czechoslovakia 148
'Rückenerze', definition of 240
Rudki deposits, Poland 55, 58, 62, 65, 69, 82
Rudna copper mine, Poland 72
Rudňany ore district, Czechoslovakia 148, 154, 155, 157–8, 161, 167, 168
Rudno mineralization, Czechoslovakia 156
Rudolfstein mineralization, FRG 293
Rügen chalk deposits, GDR 313
Ruhla crystalline/Ruhlaer Krystallin 1, 307, 312
Ruhpolding–Inzell lead–zinc deposits, FRG 268
Ruhr deposits, FRG 177, 194, 236–8, 239, 240, 241
Ružiná mineralization, Czechoslovakia 149, 169, 173
Rybnik deposits, Poland 88, 95
Rzeszów deposits, Poland 87, 94, 95

Saale Trough, GDR 309
Saar Basin, FRG 175
Saar–Nahe
  Basin 276
  Depression 192–3

Saar–Nahe–Pfalz region, FRG 289
Saar–Nahe–Werra Depression, FRG 175
Saar–Selke Trough, FRG 8, 249
Saar–Werra Basin, FRG 180
Saarburg lead deposit, FRG 229
Sächsisches Granulitgebirge 183
Sadisdorf tin deposit, GDR 317
Sady quartz deposit, Poland 91
Saeuling-S limonite (ZnS + barite) deposits, FRG 266, 267, 268
St. Andreasberg orefield, FRG 182, 230, 231, 235–6, 280, 290
St. Bernard–Monte Rosa nappe, Switzerland 47, 49
St. Blasien deposits, FRG 190
St. Egidien nickel deposits, GDR 312, 324
St. Leonhard manganese deposit, Austria 20
St. Luc–Bella Tola lead–zinc deposit, Switzerland 49
St. Mang iron mine, Aelpeleskopf, FRG 266
St. Ulrich deposits, FRG 190, 277
Salanfe gold deposit, Switzerland 45
Salmchâteau deposits, Belgium 109
Salt/Rock salt
  Austria 20–1
    Hallein 21
  Czechoslovakia 149, 171–2
    Sol'ná Baňa 149, 171
    Zbudza 171
  FRG 241–4
    Zechstein 242–4
  GDR 309, 320, 321, 322
  Netherlands 113–5
    Boekelo 115
    Hengelo 115
    Weerselo 114
    Winschoten 113, 114
    Zuidwending 113, 114
  Poland 55, 59, 61, 82, 85–8
    Inorocław 85–6
    Kłodawa 85
    Puck Bay 86
    Wapno 85, 86
    Wieliczka 55, 87
  Switzerland 51
    Bex 51
    Rhinefelden 51
    Schweizerhalle 51
Salzach River gold deposit, Austria 26
Salzgitter iron deposit, FRG 8, 179, 256, 257
Salzgitter–Peine–Ilsede iron deposits, FRG 256
Salzig am Rhein mineralization, FRG 230
Sangerhaus syncline, GDR 320
Šankovce mineralization, Czechoslovakia 154, 155, 171
Sapropel facies, GDR 320
Šarišské Jastrabie mineralization, Czechoslovakia 155
Sarstedt mineralization, FRG 180
Sauerland, FRG 194, 198, 205, 207, 271–5, 279, 280

Subject index

Sautour lead–zinc deposits, Belgium 103
'Sb–W–Hg Formation', Austria 25, 26, 29, 30
'Saxony median massif', GDR 310
Saxothuringian zone 1–2, 3, 7, 119, 136, 175–7, 183–93, 303, 307
Schafberg mineralization, FRG 276
'Schalsteinlager', Lahn–Dill district, FRG 206
'Schalstein' series, GDR 314
Schamser nappe, Switzerland 48, 50
Schaphusen iron deposit, FRG 256
Schärding graphite deposit, Austria 17
S-charl lead–zinc deposit, Switzerland 48
Schauinsland deposits, FRG 182, 190, 191, 290
Schauinsland–Feldberg–Schönau–Badenweiler deposits, FRG 188
Scheelite
  Austria 25, 26–9
    Mittersill 26–9
    Tux 25, 26
  FRG 191
  GDR 314
Scheidt fault block, FRG 219, 224
Schellgaden–Rotgülden gold mineralization, Austria 26
'Schiefermühle', Rammelsberg, FRG 196
Schindler vein, FRG 190
Schladming scheelite deposit, Austria 29
Schladminger Tauern, Austria 32
Schlagstein limonite deposits, FRG 266, 268
Schlaining antimony deposit, Austria 29–30
Schmalgraf lead–zinc deposit, Belgium 99
Schmalkalden ore district, GDR 325, 326
Schmiedefeld iron deposit, GDR 314
Schnaittenbach mineralization, FRG 261, 292
Schneckenstein barite deposit, GDR 326
Schneeberg ore district, GDR 317, 327
Schnöd tin–tungsten deposit, Czechoslovakia 135
Schöllkrippen copper deposits, FRG 250
Schönbrunn fluorite deposit, GDR 326
Schoonlo salt dome, Netherlands 116
Schriesheim scheelite deposits, FRG 191
Schwarzburg Saddle 307, 314
Schwarzenbach an der Saale talc deposit, FRG 188
Schwarzenberg–Pöhla deposit, GDR 314
Schwarzwald see Black Forest
Schwaz–Brixlegg copper deposits, Austria 21
Schweich iron deposit, FRG 241

Schweizerhalle salt deposit, Switzerland 51
Scortaseo nephrite deposit, Switzerland 50
Sedlec kaolin deposit, Czechoslovakia 142
Seekar mine, Austria 32
'Seengebirge', Switzerland 47–8
Seesen mineralization, FRG 231, 249
Selbeck lead–zinc deposit, FRG 238, 239, 240
Selke syncline, FRG 231
Semmering magnesite deposits, Austria 23
Semmering Pass–St. Michael graphite district, Austria 25
Semmering Window, Austria 31
Serpont Massif, Belgium 109, 110
Ševčín vein, Příbram ore district, Czechoslovakia 132
Sieber syncline, FRG 231
Siegburg clay deposits, FRG 263
Siegen anticline, FRG 211, 212, 288
Siegen–Betzdorf deposits, FRG 212, 213, 214
Siegerland anticlinorium, FRG 194
Siegerland deposits, FRG 64, 177, 181, 226, 227, 282, 288, 290
Siegerland–Wied iron deposits, FRG 209–15
Sieroszowice copper mine, Poland 72
Silbach deposit, FRG 219
Silberberg lead–zinc deposit, Switzerland 49
Silberberg mine, FRG 183, 283
Silberkaule mine, FRG 228
Silbernaal mineralization, FRG 231, 234
Silesia, Poland see Lower Silesia, Poland; Upper Silesia, Poland
Silesia–Krakow deposits, Poland 67, 73, 74–7, 82, 83, 94
Silesicum, Czechoslovakia 121, 122
Silica gypsum–anhydrite deposit, Czechoslovakia 171
Silica sand
  FRG 260, 261, 292
Silica shaft, Meggen, FRG 204
Siliceous rocks
  FRG 258, 260–1
    Neuburg, 258, 261
Silická Brezová mineralization, Czechoslovakia 173
Silver
  Austria 32–3
    Oberzeiring 32–2
  Czechoslovakia 117, 130–5, 149, 168
    Jáchymov 117, 121, 134–5
    Kutná Hora 117, 118, 132–4
    Příbram 117, 118, 130–2
  FRG 186, 187, 188, 190, 191, 192, 194–8, 216, 226, 234, 235, 238, 245, 250, 251, 264, 277, 280, 282, 290
    Rammelsberg 194–8
  GDR 309, 310, 317, 327
  Poland 55, 82
Simmern mine, FRG 290

Singhofen beds, FRG 226, 228
Sirk magnesite deposit, Czechoslovakia 169
Sivretta nappe, Switzerland 49
Skalná clay deposit, Czechoslovakia 144
Sklené Teplice quartzite deposit, Czechoslovakia 172
Skrabské mineralization, Czechoslovakia 173
Slánske pohorie Mountains, Czechoslovakia 167
Slánske vrchy Mountains, Czechoslovakia 156
Śląsk–Kraków monocline, Poland 61
Slojíř ore vein, Jílové gold deposit, Czechoslovakia 130
Slovinky mineralization, Czechoslovakia 158, 161
Slovinky–Helcmanovce deposit, Czechoslovakia 148
Słowatycze uplift, Poland 61
Smiałowice kaolin deposit, Poland 95
Smolník copper deposit, Czechoslovakia 148, 159, 168
Smolník–Mária Snežná iron deposit, Czechoslovakia 148
Sobótka deposits, Poland 77, 92–3
Šobov quartzite deposit, Czechoslovakia 172
Sokolov basin clay deposits, Czechoslovakia 144
Sollstedt potash plant, GDR 322
Sol'ná Baňa salt deposit, Czechoslovakia 171
Solre-Saint-Géry lead–zinc deposits, Belgium 103
Sondershausen potash plant, GDR 322
Sonnenberg fault, FRG 287
Sontra mineralization, FRG 245, 281–2
Sontra plant, FRG 249
Soon Forest iron deposits, FRG 241
Sophia Jacoba mine, Erkelenz, FRG 239
Söse syncline, FRG 230, 232, 234
South German Basin 252, 253
South German Block 180
South Harz
  Syncline 231
  Unstrut ore district 320, 321
'Southern deposit', Cínovec, Czechoslovakia 136, 137
South Vincent sector, Schlaining antimony deposit, Austria 29–30
Southwest Harz barite district, FRG 280
Soviansko deposit, Czechoslovakia 163
Sowie Góry block, Poland 59, 92
Špania Dolina copper deposit, Czechoslovakia 148, 154, 161–2
Sparneck sulphide deposits, FRG 183
Spessart, FRG
  deposits 191–2, 276–9, 281
  uplift 1, 279
'Spielberg Dolomite', Austria 25

Spiennes flint workings, Belgium 99
Spiš 'veins system',
 Czechoslovakia 161
Spišská Baňa mineralization,
 Czechoslovakia 155
Spišská kotlina depression,
 Czechoslovakia 156
Spišsko-gemerské rudohorie,
 Czechoslovakia 146, 151, 158, 159,
 161, 168, 169
Spisz iron deposits, Czechoslovakia
 64
Spitzenberg iron deposits, FRG 207
Springe celestine deposit, FRG 244
Springen potash plant, GDR 321
Srebrna Góra deposits, Poland 74, 90
Srní glass sand deposit, Czechoslovakia
 144
Stade salt deposit, FRG 242
Stadtberge copper deposit see
 Marsberg copper deposit, FRG
Stadtoldendorf salt deposit, FRG 244
Staffhorst iron deposit, FRG 256
Stahlberg mercury deposit, FRG 193
Stalowa Wola sulphur deposits,
 Poland 84
Stanisławów barite deposit, Poland 90
Stanisławów iron deposit, Poland 63,
 64
Stanisławów zinc–lead ores, Poland
 74
Stará Góra deposits, Poland 69–70,
 73, 82
Stará Kremnička limnoquartzite
 deposit, Czechoslovakia 172
Starachowice iron deposit, Poland 65,
 66
Staré Hamry mineralization,
 Czechoslovakia 155
Staré Město mica-schist series,
 Czechoslovakia 140
Staré Ransko sulphide deposits,
 Czechoslovakia 118, 124
Staročeská deposit, Kutná Hora ore
 district, Czechoslovakia 134
Staßfurt cyclothem 85, 94, 113, 114
Staßfurt potash seam, GDR 320, 321,
 322
'Staßfurt' salt seam, FRG 242
Staszów sulphur deposits, Poland 83
Stäteberg seam, FRG 250
Stavelot Massif 108, 109, 110, 208,
 240
Steinheim Basin, FRG 289
Šternberk–Benešov zone,
 Czechoslovakia 122
Šternberk–Horní Benešov zone,
 Czechoslovakia 129
Štítnik–Hrádok iron deposit,
 Czechoslovakia 148
Stockenboi–Buchholzgraben mercury
 deposit, Austria 32
Stockheim uranium deposit, FRG
 193
Stolberg deposits, FRG 208–9, 239
Storch und Schöneberg mine, FRG
 214
Strahlecker Baue Ewiggang lead–zinc
 mine, Rauschberg, FRG 266

Strahlers 50–1
Stránce bentonite deposit,
 Czechoslovakia 144
Straßberg ore district, GDR 317
Straßberg–Neudorf ore district, GDR
 318
Straußberg limonite deposits, FRG
 266, 268
Strawczynek barite deposit, Poland
 90–1
Strážovská Mountains,
 Czechoslovakia 172
Střeleč glass sand deposit,
 Czechoslovakia 144
Strelnica gypsum–anhydrite deposit,
 Czechoslovakia 171
Stříbro deposit, Czechoslovakia 118
Strihov beds, Czechoslovakia 156
Strontianite
 FRG 271, 275–6
Strzeblów feldspar deposits, Poland
 91–2
Strzegom–Sobótka massif, Poland 91,
 92, 95
Strzelin massif, Poland 95
Šturec deposit, Czechoslovakia 167
Štúrovo bauxite deposits,
 Czechoslovakia 156
Sub-Hercynian Basin, GDR 323
Subsudeten Block 1, 2
Sub-Variscan foredeep 177, 193–241
Sub-Variscan zone 2
Suchá magnesite deposit,
 Czechoslovakia 169
Sudeten 5, 7, 9, 121
Sudetes zinc–lead deposits, Poland
 73–4
Südharz see South Harz
Sullivan base-metal deposit, British
 Columbia, Canada 34
Sulphur
 FRG 263
 Poland 55, 60, 82, 83–5
Sulzbach salt mine, Austria 21
Sulzbach–Rosenberg deposits, FRG
 253, 256, 258, 293
Sulzburg mineralization, FRG 181,
 182, 190
Sunk–Hohentauern graphite mine,
 Austria 25
Suretta nappe, Switzerland 47, 48
'Suttrop quartz', FRG 274
Suwałki Alkaline Massif, Poland 62
Suwałki deposits, Poland 55
Švábovce manganese deposit,
 Czechoslovakia 148
Švábovce–Kišovce orefield,
 Czechoslovakia 156, 158
Švedlár mineralization, Czechoslovakia
 151, 172
'Swabian volcano' 181
Swarzewo salt deposits, Poland 86
Swoszowice sulphur mine, Poland 83
Sylt ilmenite sand deposits, FRG
 292
Szczecin–Łódz–Miechow downfolds,
 Poland 61
Szczęść Boże magnesite deposit,
 Poland 93

Szklary magnesite deposit, Poland
 93–4
Szklary nickel deposit, Poland 79
Szwoszowice sulphur deposit, Poland
 55

Ťahanovce mineralization,
 Czechoslovakia 154
Tajov mercury deposit, Czechoslovakia
 156, 168
Talc
 Austria 31
  Rabenwald 31
 Czechoslovakia 149, 170–1
  Mútnik 170
 FRG 188
 Switzerland 50
Taminser crystalline series,
 Switzerland 44
Tanne zone, FRG 231
Tąpadła chromite deposit, Poland 77–
 8
Tarnobrzeg sulphur deposits, Poland
 55, 83, 84, 118
Tarnów salt deposits, Poland 87, 88
Tarnowskie Góry deposits, Poland
 55, 69, 73, 74
Tatra 10
 subregion, Carpathian region 59–
 60
Tatride zone, Czechoslovakia 155,
 161
Tatroveporide zone, Czechoslovak
 Carpathians 150, 153, 154, 155,
 157, 158, 169
Taunus Mountains, FRG 194, 205,
 258, 259, 279
Taunus quartzite, FRG 259
Tavetscher Zwischenmassif,
 Switzerland 46
Teisseyre–Tornquist line, Poland 55
Tellig lead–zinc deposit, FRG 226,
 229, 230
Teplice quartz porphyry,
 Czechoslovakia 137, 141
Teplice quartz porphyry, GDR 316
Teplice Spa, Czechoslovakia 124
Terebratula beds, Poland 74
Tessenberg mine, Austria 33
Tête des Econduits fluorite deposits,
 Switzerland 50
Teuchen pyrite mine, Austria 33
Thalitter copper deposit, FRG 250
Thallium
 Poland 82
Thomas dephosphoration process 105
'Thüringen' potash seam 242, 321
Thüringer Wald, GDR 9, 310, 321,
 325–6
Thuringian Basin 252
Thuringian Forest see Thüringer Wald
Thuringian Trough 2, 7, 307, 312
Tiba chromite deposit, Czechoslovakia
 155
Tin
 Czechoslovakia 117, 135–7
  Cínovec 117, 118, 136–7
  Horní Slavkov–Krásno 118, 135–
  6

Subject index

Tin (continued)
  FRG 185–6, 187, 240, 292
  GDR 309, 310, 313, 314, 315–7
    Altenberg 309, 315–7
    Ehrenfriedersdorf 309, 315, 317
  Poland 79
    Gierczyn 79
Tirpersdorf tungsten deposit, GDR 315
Tirschenreuth mineralization, FRG 292
Tisová copper deposit, Czechoslovakia 126
Tisovec mineralization, Czechoslovakia 156, 173
Tobola ore vein, Jílové gold deposit, Czechoslovakia 130
Todtmoos nickel–cobalt deposit, FRG 185
Todtnau mineralization, FRG 182
Tornquist–Teisseyre zone 1
Totalp nickel deposit, Switzerland 49
Tournai sulphide deposits, Belgium 108
Trachsellauenen lead–zinc deposit, Switzerland 46
Trangoška lead deposit, Czechoslovakia 155
Trass
  Austria 18
Trebejov mineralization, Czechoslovakia 173
Třeboň basin clay deposits, Czechoslovakia 144
Trias Triangle, FRG 284, 285, 289
Tribeč Mountains, Czechoslovakia 146, 151, 154, 155, 158
Triberg granite, FRG 188
Triberg tin–tungsten mineralization, FRG 175
Trier Bight 289
Tripoli
  FRG 258, 260, 261
Trun uranium deposit, Switzerland 46
Trzebionka zinc–lead deposit, Poland 76–7
Tuhár mineralization, Czechoslovakia 173
Tungsten
  Czechoslovakia 135–7
    Cínovec 117, 118, 136–7
    Horní Slavkov-Krásno 118, 135–6
  FRG 186, 188
  GDR 309, 310, 315–6
    Pechtelsgrün 315
    Tirpersdorf 315
Turkaňk deposit, Kutná Hora ore district, Czechoslovakia 134
Türnitz lead–zinc deposit, Austria 19
Turrach mercury deposits, Austria 32
Tux deposits, Austria 25, 26
Tweng uranium mineralization, Austria 31
Twenthe–Rijn concession, Braunschweig salt deposits, Netherlands 115
Twiste copper deposit, FRG 289

Tychowski Range, Poland 69
Tynagh base-metal deposit, county Galway, Ireland 34, 36

Uchte mineralization, FRG 276
Uelsen phosphorite deposits, FRG 264
Uersfeld barite vein, southeast Eifel, FRG 280
Ullmannia bronni 250
Unstrut mineralization, GDR 320, 321
Unterbreizbach potash plant, GDR 321
Untermünstertal lead–zinc deposits, FRG 175
Unterpinswang limonite deposits, FRG 266, 268
Untersulzbach valley kyanite deposits, Austria 31
Unterwerra Hills barite mineralization, FRG 279
Upper Bunter rock salt deposits, Netherlands 115
Upper Harz mining district 177, 181–2 (*see also* Oberharz)
Upper Palatinate *see* Oberpfalz
Upper Rhine
  Depression 256
  Graben 179, 289
Upper Silesia, Poland 55, 59
Urach mineralization, FRG 180
Uranium
  Austria 20, 31
    Forstau 31
  Czechoslovakia 117, 134–5
    Jáchymov 117, 121, 134–5
  FRG 185–6, 187, 190, 191, 192, 193, 289, 293
    Baden-Baden area 193
  GDR 317
  Switzerland 45, 46–7, 49
    Isérables 49
    Le Chatelard and Les Marecottes 46
    Mürtschenalp 45
Usingen deposits, FRG 215, 258, 288
Uskoku vein, Harrachov fluorite–lead deposit, Czechoslovakia 137
Uzbornia fold, Poland 87

Václav vein, Příbram ore district, Czechoslovakia 132
Vajarská mineralization, Czechoslovakia 173
Val d'Anniviers copper deposits, Switzerland 47
Val Ferrera iron deposit, Switzerland 48
Vanadium
  Poland 61
Variscan
  Basement, FRG 175–7
  Foreland 2
  Geosynclinal stage, GDR 314–8
  Molasse stage 8
Vasbeck mineralization, FRG 288
Včeláre mineralization, Czechoslovakia 173

Vedrin sulphide mine, Belgium 99, 100, 108
Veendam salt pillows, Netherlands 116
Veitsch Mountains manganese deposits, Austria 23
Velbert
  anticline, FRG 177
  mineralization, FRG 209
  saddle, FRG 238, 239
Vel'ká Tŕňa mineralization, Czechoslovakia 173
Velké Vrbo graphite deposit, Czechoslovakia 140
Vellacher Kotschna cinnabar deposit, Austria 37
Venn gold–cassiterite district, FRG 240
Vepor Mountains, Czechoslovakia 10, 146, 154
Veporide zone, Czechoslovak Carpathians 151, 154, 162, 165, 169, 170, 172
'Verflachungen', definition of 228
Vermiculite
  Austria 18
Verrucano molasse facies, Czechoslovakia 154
Vezin iron deposits, Belgium 105
Vielsalm, *see under* Salmchâteau
Vienna Basin, Austria 11, 18
Vierves-sur-Viroin barite deposit, Belgium 104, 105
Vihorlat Mountain, Czechoslovakia 156
Vikartovce mineralization, Czechoslovakia 154
Viking Graben, North Sea 180
Vildštejn series, Czechoslovakia 144
'Ville' deposits, FRG 259, 263
Villers-en-Fagne deposits, Belgium 104, 105
Villgraten mine, Austria 33
Villgraten Range, Austria 33
Vindelician Rise, FRG 1, 252
Virneburg lead–zinc deposit, FRG 215
Vlachovo
  Beds, Czechoslovakia 169
  iron deposit, Czechoslovakia 148, 169
Vlastějovice deposit, Czechoslovakia 122
Vlatten mineralization, FRG 284
Vlotho mineralization, FRG 276
Vodecée lead–zinc deposits, Belgium 103
Vogelsberg mineralization, FRG 180, 261, 291
Vogtland ore district, GDR 326
Vojtěch mine, Czechoslovakia 130, 132
Volkenroda potash plant, GDR 322
Vorhop–Wahrenholz iron deposit, FRG 256
Vosges 9
Vrančice deposits, Czechoslovakia 118, 130
Vrbno Group, Czechoslovakia 122, 124

Vrchoslav fluorite deposit, Czechoslovakia 141
Vtáčnik Mountain, Czechoslovakia 156
Vyhne mineralization, Czechoslovakia 156, 158, 172
Vyšehořovice clay deposit, Czechoslovakia 144
Vyšné Nemecké mineralization, Czechoslovakia 156
Vysoké Tatry Mountains, Czechoslovakia 146, 151, 154, 155, 165
Vysoký Kámen tin–tungsten deposit, Czechoslovakia 136

Waddensee–Sub-Volcano, Netherlands 180
Wader Alm manganese deposit, Austria 20
Wagrein scheelite deposit, Austria 29
Wałbrzych barite deposits, Poland 90
Walchen pyrite mine, Austria 33
Waldalgesheim mineralization, FRG 290
Waldenstein iron mine, Austria 32
Walkenried–Steina copper deposit, FRG 249
Wallenfels mineralization, FRG 289
Wallerfangen copper deposit, FRG 181, 289
Wapno salt diapir, Poland 85, 86
Warmensteinach mineralization, FRG 281
Warstein
  anticline, FRG 225, 274
  mineralization, FRG 272, 273, 274
'Warsteiner Eisenkiesel' 274
Waschgang gold deposit, Austria 26
Wasseralfingen iron deposit, FRG 256
Wattenscheide anticline, FRG 239
Waxenstein lead–zinc deposits, FRG 266
Weerselo salt pillar, Netherlands 114
Weiden Bight, FRG 261, 292
Weiden deposits, FRG 230, 253
Weidental limonite deposits, FRG 266, 268
Weihnähr vein, Holzappel deposit, FRG 229
Weilburg deposits, FRG 207, 215
Weinzierl kaolin deposit, Austria 17
Weiss lead–zinc deposit, FRG 216
Weissenstadt tin deposits, FRG 186, 292
Weisskirchen leucophyllite deposit, Austria 31
Weitalpe mine, Weidental, FRG 266
Wendelstein–Dickelalpe limonite deposits, FRG 266
Werbomont manganese deposit, Belgium 109
Werfen beds see Werfener Schichten
Werfener Schichten 10, 19, 20
Werlau lead–zinc deposit, FRG 214, 226, 228, 229, 230
Werra cyclothem 72, 73, 85, 113, 114, 115, 245

Werra potash district, GDR 320, 321
Werra–Fulda saliferous deposits 242
Werra–Fulda sub-basin 321
Wesemaal iron deposit, Belgium 107
Weser Depression, FRG 248
Weserbergland calcite–fluorite deposits, FRG 276
West European Platform 3
West Harz Rise, FRG 194
West Netherlands Basin 180
West Sudeten Mountains, Czechoslovakia 141
Western Boundary Fault, Bohemian Massif 269
Western Carpathian Arc 10, 150
Westerwald, FRG 180, 211, 215, 260, 262, 282
'Westerwald Clays', FRG 262
Westfeld lodes, Grund, FRG 234
Westheim fault, Egge Hills, FRG 288
Wetterau fluorite mineralization, FRG 279
Wetterstein lead–zinc mineralization, FRG 267, 268
Wetterstein sequence, Austria 10, 19, 34, 35
Wettersteinkalk 267
Wetzlar mineralization, FRG 207, 288
White Pine copper deposit, Michigan, U.S.A. 44
Wied deposits, FRG 213, 214, 288 (see also Siegerland–Wied iron deposits, FRG)
Wieda iron deposit, FRG 231
Wieda–Zorge iron deposit, FRG 207–8
Wieden fluorite–barite deposit, FRG 277
Wiedersberg fluorite deposit, GDR 326
Wieliczka salt mine, Poland 55, 87
Wielkopolski Block 3
Wiesau mineralization, FRG 292
Wieściszowice pyrite deposit, Poland 83
Wiesloch lead–zinc deposit, FRG 177, 181, 252
Wildflecken barite deposit, FRG 279
'Wildflysch' 11
Wildsbach mineralization, FRG 277
Winden lode, Lahn–Hunsrück district, FRG 229
Windisch-Bleiberg lead–zinc deposit, Austria 37
Winschoten salt dome, Netherlands 113, 114
Winterswijk salt deposits, Netherlands 114–5
Wippra zone 231, 313
Wirsberg talc deposit, FRG 188
Wiry magnesite deposit, Poland 92, 93
Wiśniowa iron deposit, Poland 69
Wissen mineralization, FRG 213, 288
Wissenbach slates, FRG 194, 196, 226
Wittekind seam, Porta Westfalica, FRG 256

Wittgensteiner Land mineralization, FRG 288
Wittichen mineralization, FRG 175, 188, 190, 191
Wittmannsgereuth iron deposit, GDR 314
Witzenhausen copper deposit, FRG 249
Wolfach mineralization, FRG 290
Wolfendorn kyanite deposits, Austria 31
Wolkenhügel vein system, FRG 280
Wollau lead deposit, FRG 253
Wölsendorf–Nabburg fluorite deposit, FRG 276
Wrexen mineralization, FRG 289
Wunsiedel deposits, FRG 177, 292
Wunsiedel marble, FRG 188
Wurzburg mineralization, FRG 246
Wyszonowice kaolin deposit, Poland 95

Zaben Depression, FRG 252
Ząbkowice Śląskie deposits, Poland 77, 79, 92, 93
Záblatie gypsum–anhydrite deposit, Czechoslovakia 155
Zagórze bentonite deposits, Poland 96
Záhorská nížina lowlands, Czechoslovakia 172
Žakarovce mineralization, Czechoslovakia 158
Żar pericline, Poland 71
Żarki–Częstochowa–Kłobuck iron deposits, Poland 62, 67
Żarów kaolin deposit, Poland 95
Żarska Wieś gypsum–anhydrite deposit Poland 94
Zawiercie deposits, Poland 55, 73, 74
Zázrivá mineralization, Czechoslovakia 155
Zbudza salt deposit, Czechoslovakia 171
Zdice iron deposit, Czechoslovakia 125
Zdrada salt deposits, Poland 86
Zebrzydowa kaolin deposit, Poland 96
Zechstein Basin salt deposits, GDR 321
Zechstein Formation, Poland 61, 72–3, 82, 85–6
Zechstein rock salt deposits, Netherlands 113–5
Zechstein salt formation, FRG 242–5
Železné Hory Fault, Czechoslovakia 142
Železné Hory Mountains, Czechoslovakia 121, 122, 141
Železník deposit, Czechoslovakia 148, 151
Železný Brod deposits, Czechoslovakia 122
Zell mineralization, FRG 175, 230
Zellerfeld ore veins, FRG 234
'Zentral Gneissen', Hohe Tauern 10
Zettlitz graphite mine, Austria 17

Subject index 355

Žiar mineralization, Czechoslovakia 151, 172
Zielitz potash plant 320, 322
Ziller Valley gold mineralization, Austria 26
Zinc
  Austria 19, 30–1, 33–7
    Bleiberg 33–7
  Belgium 99–104
  Czechoslovakia 118, 124, 126–34, 163–5
    Banská Štiavnica 149, 163–5
    Horní Benešov 118, 122, 128–30
    Kutná Hora 117, 118, 132–4
    Příbram 117, 118, 130–2
    Soviansko 163
    Staré Ransko 118, 124
    Zlaté Hory 126–8
  FRG
    Aachen–Erkelenz sub-district 239–40
    Aachen–Stolberg district 208–9
    Bensberg district 215–8
    Ems district 227–8
    Lahn–Hunsrück district 228–30
    Lintorf–Velbert sub-district 238–9
    Maubach 284–5

Zinc (continued)
    Mechernich 284, 285
    Meggen 198–205
    Rammelsberg 194–8
    Ramsbeck 218–26
    Ruhr area 236–8
    St. Andreasberg orefield 230, 231, 235
    Wiesloch 287–8
  GDR 309, 310, 314, 317
  Poland 55, 59, 61, 73–7
  Switzerland 46, 48–9
    Alp Nadels 46
    Alp Taspin 49
    Bärenbühl 49
    Bleiberg 49
    Bristenstock 46
    Goppenstein 46
    Praz Jean 49
    St. Luc–Bella Tola 49
    S-charl 48–9
    Silberberg 49
    Trachsellauenen 46
Zinkwand–Vöttern mine, Austria 32
Zinnwald tin deposit, GDR 315
Zlambach Marls, Austria 20
Zlatá Baňa orefield, Czechoslovakia 156, 165, 168

Zlatá Idka mineralization, Czechoslovakia 155
Zlatá vein, Slovinky, Czechoslovakia 161
Zlaté Hory Cu–Pb–Zn deposit, Czechoslovakia 7, 118, 122, 126–8
Zlatník vein, Rudnany ore district, Czechoslovakia 157
Zlato mineralization, Czechoslovakia 162, 163, 165
Złotoryja Depression, Poland 71, 72
Złotoryja gold deposit, Poland 55, 81
Złoty Stok deposits, Poland 59, 78, 81
Znojmo kaolin deposits, Czechoslovakia 143
Zongor mineralization, Czechoslovakia 173
Zuidwending salt dome, Netherlands 113, 114
Županovice deposit, Czechoslovakia 122
Zurzach salt deposit, Switzerland 51
Zwei-Brüder mine, Höllental, FRG 266
Zweinitz mine, Austria 33
Zwiesel sulphide deposits, FRG 183